A Companion to the Cantos of Ezra Pound

A Companion to the Cantos of Ezra Pound

by

Carroll F. Terrell

Published in Cooperation with
The National Poetry Foundation
University of Maine at Orono
Orono, Maine

UNIVERSITY OF CALIFORNIA PRESS
Berkeley · Los Angeles · London

Published in Cooperation with
The University of Maine at Orono
Orono, Maine

University of California Press
Berkeley and Los Angeles, California

University of California Press, Ltd.
London, England

ISBN: 0-520-03687-5
Library of Congress Catalog Card Number: 78-054802
Copyright © 1980 by
The Regents of the University of California

Printed in the United States of America

Contents

Preface

Early in life Ezra Pound dedicated himself to the art of poetry, for him the most exalted vocation possible to man. His approach was programmatic: he would take twenty-five years to learn and practice all that was known about the craft of poetry; he would use as models only the best work of the greatest masters [Homer, Dante, Chaucer, Shakespeare, Browning] or of minor poets whose discoveries had advanced the art [Sappho, Ovid, Catullus, Propertius, the Provençal poets, Waller, Laforgue, et al.]. He also realized early on that if he was to be numbered among the greatest himself, his masterwork would have to be of epic proportions. For more than a dozen years (1908-1921) Pound contemplated possible forms and structures for his "poem of some length." After making several false starts he had moments of despair. One such moment occurred in Venice in 1908, when he was tempted to throw the page proofs of *A Lume Spento* into the San Vio Canal and take up a different vocation. He did not yield to the temptation. Other moments of doubt occurred during the period 1915-1920 while he was reading the manuscripts of *Ulysses*: he had fears that the age of poetry was over and that the verbal arts of the future would have to be in prose. The wide variation in tone of the cantos written and published during these years shows these fears. Some passages reflect a Cavalcanti-Dante attitude; others show that Pound had adopted Browning's tone, diction, and toughness of texture as most appropriate to the twentieth century.

Then, around 1922, something happened to Pound: he started *The Cantos* anew, adapting some passages from earlier versions but discarding much more, and from that moment on he never wavered. There is no uncertainty as to form, content, or direction; an ambience of confident control informs each canto and the way each canto articulates with the whole. Whether 100 or 120 cantos would be needed fully to realize the design was a decision left for the future, but all the themes to be developed were known to him in July 1922, when he wrote to Felix Schelling:

> Perhaps as the poem goes on I shall be able to make various things clear. Having the crust to attempt a poem in 100 or 120 cantos long after all mankind has been commanded never again to attempt a poem of any length, I have to stagger as I can.
>
> The first 11 cantos are preparation of the palette. I *have to* get down all the colours or elements I want for the poem. Some perhaps too enigmatically and abbreviatedly. I hope, heaven help me, to bring them into some sort of design and architecture later [*L*, 180].

Over the years Pound made a number of other statements about the form and content of *The Cantos*. Among the most important is this excerpt from a letter: "Afraid the whole damn poem is rather obscure, especially in fragments. Have I ever given you outline of main scheme . . . or whatever it is? 1. Rather like, or unlike subject and response and counter subject in fugue. A.A. Live man goes down into world of Dead. C.B. the 'repeat in history.' B.C. the 'magic moment' or moment of metamorphosis, bust thru from quotidien into 'divine or permanent world.' Gods, etc." [*L*, 210]. He also called *The Cantos* "the tale of the tribe" and "a poem containing history." Pound and others have drawn some parallels with *The Divine Comedy*, but not to suggest the neat categories of Hell, Purgatory, and Paradise perceived in Dante's time. In 1928 Yeats tried to convey his understanding of Pound's explanations of the poem's form: "He has scribbled on the back of an envelop certain sets of letters that represent emotions or archetypal events—I cannot find any adequate definition—ABCD and then JKLM, and then each set of letters repeated, and then ABCD inverted and this repeated, and then a new element XYZ . . . and all set whirling together" [Yeats, *A Packet for Ezra Pound*, 1928, 4-5]. Pound is on record as saying that Yeats's explanation did more harm than good because he had no more idea of a fugue than a frog did. The significance of the quotation is less in its accurate description than in Yeats's conviction that Pound knew exactly what he was doing and why, whether anyone else did or not. Yeats added: "He has shown me upon the wall a photograph of a Cosimo Tura decoration in three compartments, in the upper the Triumph of Love and the Triumph of Chastity, in the middle Zodiacal signs, and in the lower certain events in Cosimo Tura's day." The parallels between the panels and Dante's structure are clear: the upper panel suggests Paradise, the middle one Purgatory, and the lower one Hell.

Although it is not possible now—nor will it ever be—to make a complete statement about all the themes in *The Cantos*, it is possible to posit a hypothesis that can help the reader, a hypothesis he can alter to his own bent as his experience dictates. To me, *The Cantos* is a great religious poem. The tale of the tribe is an account of man's progress from the darkness of hell to the light of paradise. Thus it is a revelation of how divinity is manifested in the universe: the process of the stars and planets, the dynamic energy of the seed in motion (*semina motuum*), and the kind of intelligence that makes the cherrystone become a cherry tree. Hell is darkness ["there is only the darkness of ignorance"]; thus the highest manifestation of divinity flows from the mind and the spirit of man. Whatever gods there be act through man's mind and perceptions and are revealed in (1) his intelligence, (2) his ethical sense and his thirst for perfectibility, (3) his power to love (*amo ergo sum*), (4) his perception of beauty (*tò kalón*), (5) his sense of mystery, (6) his power and urge to be a maker (in music, painting, sculpture, poetry, prose), and (7) his aspiration to create a paradise on earth. These are the major ways divinity is manifested in the mind, spirit, and heart of man. But there are obverse cues: (1) hatred of injustice and tyranny over people, (2) disgust with moneymongers and those who lust for possessions ("hoggers of harvest are the curse of the people"), and (3) revulsion from the ooze of the material hell many men create and happily wallow in.

The hundreds of people who inhabit *The Cantos* were all born into the darkness of hell. From then on they fall into three groups: (1) those who enjoy their hellish state and remain the same; (2) those who experience a metamorphosis and, desiring to get out of darkness, are drawn to follow a vision of fire and light; and (3) the highly endowed few who become leaders of the mass moving toward the land of light (*paradiso terrestre*). Toward the end of the poem Pound says that it was his dream to create this special group, but by the end of the poem he had lost his love ("what do I love and / where are you?"), and he had lost his "center / fighting the world. The dreams clash / and are shattered— / and that I tried to make a paradiso/ terrestre" [802]. The last line of this fragment is an appeal to mankind: "To be men not destroyers." Men, we assume, are those who dedicate themselves to the betterment of the human condition; the destroyers do not. Thus, the central conflicts and tensions of the poem are the same as those of all other great epics, prose or poetry, of the past: the eternal struggle of the forces of good against the forces of evil.

If the major import of the poem can be stated so simply, why then has the text bewildered so many? The reasons are many, but they are also simple: although traditional moral values of the West—say the seven deadly sins of the Christians and the lists of primary virtues—are all to be found in the poem, their order of importance is quite different. Also, that Pound opted for a musical thematic structure rather than the more traditional historical or narrative structure has made even so basic a statement less than clear to most readers. Finally, the extreme concentration of his gists and piths, which comes from an impulse to present a great deal in a small space, makes the text difficult to adjust to.

In spite of the difficulties few critics these days would dissent from the view that Ezra Pound is one of the most significant men of letters of the twentieth century and that his influence on poets of all nations has been pervasive and formative. His own place as an individual poet in the tradition is, however, quite another question. In the end, whether Pound will be assigned a place in the hierarchy as a major poet will depend on a fuller if not a final critical evaluation of *The Cantos*. Before that can be accomplished the text must be made more broadly accessible.

Although hundreds of books, articles, and reviews have been written about Pound and his work and continue to be written with increasing frequency, there has been no tradition of literary criticism, for three quite understandable reasons. First, Pound has been identified as a partisan on the wrong side in the most violent upheavals of a violent century. In the mind of the public he is a man who endorsed and promoted the Fascist cause; who sponsored and propagandized for bizarre theories of economics, money, and banking; who was identified as a rabid anti-Semite of the Henry Ford—Father Coughlin kind; who made pejorative statements about organized religions, including Christianity (both Catholic and Protestant) and Buddhism; and who became a henchman of Mussolini and used all the means at his disposal in seeking the defeat of the Allies in World War II and was therefore guilty of treason. A decade of war propaganda, which still lingers in the minds of those who lived through it, has made it almost impossible to get past the public image of the poet formed in those years so as to consider what he really believed in and thought he was doing or to get past the mythical man to consider the work—especially *The Cantos*—as an object of art. Indeed, since many critics insist that one cannot and should not consider the work apart from the poet, most published criticism about *The Cantos* has been less than evenhanded; articles have been either defenses written by the poet's fans or castigations written by his detractors. The result is a series of apologetics or animadversions rather than temperate evaluation.

Second, no final literary criticism about *The Cantos* could begin until after 1970 when the complete text was published in one volume. Although serious critical inquiry about the work of other major writers of the twentieth century, such as T. S. Eliot and James Joyce, began in the 1920s, thoughtful examination of Pound's ideas and methods did not begin until 1951 with the publication of Hugh Kenner's *The Poetry of Ezra Pound*. This book opened up new worlds and set the reader high on a peak in Darien. But even such astute critics and interpreters as Kenner, Eva Hesse, Clark Emery, Forrest Read, Guy Davenport, and Walter Baumann (to list but a few) could deal only with parts of the poem or special themes until the whole was available in one volume.

Third, serious literary evaluation of *The Cantos* has been impossible for most critics because of the difficulty of the text. Before a genuine dialogue is possible, the text of *The Cantos* must be made more easily comprehensible to a sizable audience of students and professors as well as critics. Although some progress has been made, it becomes clearer, as time goes on, that the problems are not so much in the abstruse levels of thinking as in the extraordinary and wide-ranging fields of reference. The "luminous details" or "gists and piths" or "ideas in action" which Pound gives us in his epic are drawn from sources quite outside the humanist tradition in which literary scholars have been trained; hence the need for *A Companion to the Cantos*.

By far the most important work published to date to help readers has been *The Annotated Index to the Cantos of Ezra Pound* by John Hamilton Edwards and William W. Vasse, with the assistance of John J. Espey and Frederic Peachy (University of California Press, 1957). The *Index* lists alphabetically and annotates all proper names and foreign phrases of the cantos (1-84) then in print. At that time little exegesis and even fewer source studies had been done. In the more than twenty years since the appearance of the *Index*, a great deal of basic work has been published, though much remains to be done. Furthermore, after the poem was completed through the fragments to Canto 120, the *Index* became dated, and requests to update it with an alphabetical supplement or to replace it by redoing the whole, canto by canto, became clamorous. I started an alphabetical supplement in 1972, but at the Pound conference held in Orono, Maine, in 1975, the decision to redo the whole in two volumes was finally made. In philosophy and design, the *Companion* was conceived to be the logical step between the *Index* of 1957 and the definitive variorum edition of *The Cantos* which would be the function of the future.

The most time-consuming if not the most difficult part of the work has been the constant readjustments of design. To bring the final text to publishable form, original manuscripts were pruned of several kinds of information which I had hoped it would be possible to include; the following guiding statement was finally adopted:

> Practical considerations dictate what the *Companion* must be and what it must not be. It is not being prepared for Pound scholars who do not need it. It is being prepared as a handbook for new students of *The Cantos* who need it badly. Therefore it is not designed as a complete compendium of present knowledge about *The Cantos*, with exegeses and analyses of the text; such a 10-volume work must be left to the future. The projected 2-3 volume work (I:1-71; II:74-120) must be budgeted to not more than 800 pages.
>
> The book is designed for the beginner so as to (1) answer his first and most immediate questions; (2) tell him where to go next for exegesis and comment; and (3) tell him where to go to find the sources EP used. The text will be based on the edition of 1975 published by New Directions and Faber.
>
> Certain kinds of information were finally pruned from the glosses: (1) textual variants from one edition to another, (2) citations from sources which did not contribute to the meaning; (3) cross-references except for the most important; (4) dates of composition which have not been precisely established.

Procedures for preparing the manuscript have been systematic. First, the information contained in the *Index* was converted to glosses for each canto. Although the data from the *Index* were supplemented with additional information from Pound's sources, and although the number of glosses was doubled to cover materials other than those to which this work was limited, my most important debt for the *Companion* is to the *Index*. Although I have rewritten and expanded most entries, a few translations or parts of sentences have been used verbatim. Efforts to indicate all such exact quotations had to be abandoned as confusing and space-consuming; I make this general acknowledgment instead.

The *Companion* is indebted, too, to the dozens of Pound scholars who since 1957 have done basic exegetical studies on the text. The list of abbreviations of books on Pound stresses the importance of such works as Kenner's *The Pound Era*, Davie's *Poet as Sculptor*, and Hesse's *New Approaches* for numerous glosses. The unpublished doctoral dissertation of Achilles Fang, "Materials for the Study of Pound's Cantos" (Harvard University, 1958) has been extremely valuable in locating numerous sources. A very special debt is owed to a few scholars who have made direct contributions to the text: Eva Hesse (Cantos I-XI); Ben Kimpel and T. Duncan Eaves (Cantos XLII-XLIV, L); John Nolde (Cantos LII-LXI); Frederick Sanders (Cantos LXIII-LXVIII); James Wilhelm (Italian and Provençal, passim); John Espey, (passim).

Eva Hesse not only corrected a number of errors in the drafts I sent her for Cantos I-XI, but she also made additions that literally doubled the length of the text. During the years she spent in translating *The Cantos* into German, she gathered one of the most complete files available of Pound's original sources; she thus possesses information known only to her and the scholars with whom she has shared it. She was in fact so generous with both her time and her knowledge that, as early plans had to be modified because of the exigencies of time, money, and space, some of her materials, especially of the interpretive kind, had to be deleted. Nevertheless, the final glosses for these cantos carry Eva Hesse's very substantial authority, although all infelicities of expression must be attributed to me. Since she worked with an earlier version of the Faber text, some instances may be found in places where adjustments to the 1975 common text were made.

The text for the three Leopoldine cantos [XLII-XLIV] is almost exactly in the form submitted by Ben Kempel and T. Duncan Eaves. My additions were mostly of the cross-referencing and apparatus-dictated kind. I am indebted to them also for checking all the glosses for Cantos XXV-XXX against the original (mostly Italian) sources; I followed their advice in a number of places and quite often used their phrasing as a more accurate reflection of Pound's idea about the significance of some "luminous detail" in the source than my own. The glosses for Canto L are based in large part on their source article (*Paideuma*, VII, 2-3).

John Nolde, who is in process of completing detailed studies of the Mailla sources for Cantos LIII-LXI, has given careful scrutiny to the glosses for these cantos and in particular has standardized the transliteration of all Chinese characters and names according to the Wade-Giles Tables. When the historical data used by Pound are inaccurate, Nolde has so indicated. Frederick Sanders, author of *John Adams Speaking: Pound's Sources for the Adams Cantos*, started with the drafts based on the *Index* and made substantial contributions to the glosses for the six central Adams cantos, LXIII-LXVIII. Thereafter, in a reverse role, I added glosses not covered by proper names. James Wilhelm, who had already provided coded glosses for all Italian and Provençal materials in Cantos LXXXV-CXX, also gave me annotated translations for such materials in the earlier cantos. Wilhelm must not, however, be held responsible for any deficiencies in the final text. Although Pound expressed satisfaction with most of the work in the *Index* he had no enthusiasm for idiomatic translations of Italian. Because of that the method of translating Italian, especially medieval and Renaissance, has been a controversial issue. It is not a question of scholarly knowledge as opposed to dilettante knowledge; those who know most about the documents and locutions involved disagree. In this dilemma I have chosen the translation that seemed closest to the Poundian spirit, and a few times, in a spirit of complete abandon, I rejected them all and used my own. In such decisions I have been guided by Pound's rendition of *Tan mare fustes* ("You came at a bad moment") or of *J'en ai marre* ("I'm fed up") [*L*, 210]. I say "rendition" because "translation," in any literal sense, is hardly involved. Pound preferred to use colloquial expressions in English which would satisfy the emotional attitudes found in the original. Over the years his attitude changed; in expressing his idea of *Tan mare fustes* to his father in 1927, he would more likely have said: "This is a hell of a time to show up." Thus neither Wilhelm, nor the other experts who have advised me in Italian and Provençal, such as Eva Hesse, John Espey, and Ben Kimpel, can be held responsible. Although their interpretations have varied they have all been quite correct.

We all owe a particular debt to John Espey, who made major contributions to the *Index* and has kept current with all problems of sources and glosses. If the present text is relatively free from error, it is because of a final check he gave to the entire manuscript against the original sources and a final accuracy test of almost all numbers. Other scholars who should be mentioned include Stephen Fender, University College, London, with whom I exchanged material for Canto XXXVIII, and who Xeroxed and forwarded all of Pound's contributions to the *New English Weekly*; Hugh Witemeyer who read many of the early manuscript for errors and made many suggestions for alterations and additional glosses, which I meticulously followed; Forrest Read and Herbert Schneidau who read the early drafts for Cantos XII-XX; Hugh Kenner who convinced me I should do this job and who has been ready with valuable advice on editorial procedures; Mary de Rachewiltz, Donald Gallup, Donald Davie, and David Gordon who have helped resolve some especially difficult problems. The list could go on but I must end with a general acknowledgment to the dozens of scholars who during the last thirty years have contributed to my knowledge of the cantos. Otherwise, credits are given under the heading "Exegeses," a standard unit in the prefatory matter for each canto. It is here that the value of the contributions made by the *Analyst* and the authors of exegetical work in *Paideuma*, as well as in a number of books and journals, is acknowledged.

Particular acknowledgment must be given to the Research Grants Office of the University of Maine at Orono which has provided annual financial support to the project since 1972. The work could not have been done without this support. A summer stipend granted by the National Endowment for the Humanities made it possible for me to continue the work during the summer of 1977. The entire staff of the Folger Library of the University of Maine at Orono assisted me by generously responding to dozens of calls to obtain materials worldwide through interlibrary loan as well as by searching for material in our own archives.

On a personal level, I am deeply grateful to my colleagues in the English Department at Orono—particularly Burton Hatlen, Robert Hunting, and Richard Sprague—for hours of assistance in proofreading and help in making my writing, if not more palatable, at least endurable. Most of all I am indebted to my office staff: Nancy Nolde, my research assistant, who has devoted hundreds of hours trying to keep errors of every kind, especially those of cross-referencing and numbering, out of the text; and Sharon Stover, Marilyn Emerick, and Diane Kopek who typed and retyped the manuscript a number of times as the design and limits of the contents were developed by experience.

Abbreviations

WORKS BY POUND

WORKS ABOUT POUND
(For complete citations see bibliography.)

R. Bush, *Genesis* . . . . Bush, Ronald, *The Genesis of Ezra Pound's Cantos*
Davis, *Vision* . . . . Davis, Earle, *Vision Fugitive*
DD, *Ezra* . . . . Davie, Donald, *Ezra Pound*
DD, *Sculptor* . . . . Davie, Donald, *Ezra Pound: Poet as Sculptor*
Dekker, *Cantos* . . . . Dekker, George, *Sailing after Knowledge: The Cantos of Ezra Pound*
CE, *Ideas* . . . . Emery, Clark, *Ideas into Action: A Study of Pound's Cantos*
JE, *Mauberley* . . . . Espey, John, *Ezra Pound's Mauberley: A Study in Composition*
EH, *Approaches* . . . . Hesse, Eva, ed., *New Approaches to Ezra Pound*
EH, *B.E.P.* . . . . Hesse, Eva, *Beckett. Eliot. Pound. Drei Textanalysen*
HK, *Poetry* . . . . Kenner, Hugh, *The Poetry of Ezra Pound*
HK, *Era* . . . . Kenner, Hugh, *The Pound Era*
LL, *Motive* . . . . Leary, Lewis, ed., *Motive and Method in the Cantos of Ezra Pound*
DP, *Barb* . . . . Pearlman, Daniel S., *The Barb of Time*
M de R . . . . Rachewiltz, Mary de, *Discretions*
NS, *Exile* . . . . Stock, Noel, *Poet in Exile: Ezra Pound*
NS, *Life* . . . . Stock, Noel, *The Life of Ezra Pound*
NS, *Reading* . . . . Stock, Noel, *Reading the Cantos*
JW, *Later* . . . . Wilhelm, James, *The Later Cantos of Ezra Pound*
JW, *Epic* . . . . Wilhelm, James, *Dante and Pound: The Epic of Judgement*

Authors Frequently Cited

GD . . . . Guy Davenport
JE . . . . John Espey
DG . . . . David Gordon
EH . . . . Eva Hesse
HK . . . . Hugh Kenner
BK . . . . Ben Kimpel
JN . . . . John Nolde
RO . . . . Reno Odlin
FR . . . . Forrest Read
NS . . . . Noel Stock
CFT . . . . Carroll F. Terrell
JW . . . . James Wilhelm

Standard Reference Works

EB . . . . *Encyclopaedia Britannica*, 1911
Loeb . . . . . . Loeb Classical Library
OBGV . . . . . *Oxford Book of Greek Verse*
OCD . . . . . . Oxford Classical Dictionary

Languages

<pre>
AS . . . . Anglo-Saxon
C . . . . Chinese
D . . . . Dutch
F . . . . French
G . . . . German
H . . . . Greek
I . . . . Italian
J . . . . Japanese
L . . . . Latin
LSc . . . . . . Lowland Scottish
ME . . . . . Middle English
MF . . . . . Middle French
ML . . . . . Medieval Latin
NK . . . . . Na-Khi
OE . . . . . . Old English
OF . . . . . . Old French
P . . . . Provençal
R . . . . Russian
S . . . . Spanish
Scot . . . . . Scottish
SGae . . . . . So. Gaelic
</pre>

Other abbreviations follow MLA style conventions.

OTHER EDITORIAL CONVENTIONS

Cross-references to other glosses are given in brackets with number of the canto followed by a colon and the number of the gloss. Thus [12:16] means gloss 16 of Canto 12. But [81/517] refers not to a numbered gloss but to Canto 81, page 517, of the text of *The Cantos*. A cross-reference to a gloss in the same canto is given as either [cf. 12 above] or [see 75 below]. To save space, proper names have not been repeated in the glosses unless the name in the text is (1) incomplete, (2) misspelled, or (3) a variant from standard usage: for example, the gloss for *Robert Browning* [2:1] repeats neither name; the gloss for *Divus* [1:21] is given as "Andreas D."; *Cabestan* [4:10] is followed by "Guillems de Cabestanh or Cabestaing" to give the more usual designation; and *So-shu* [2:4] is followed by "Corruption of Shiba Shōjo . . ." to give needed explanation. As with *So-shu*, a few glosses have been expanded to review scholarship, if confusion of names is possible.

In the headnotes, under the heading "Sources," all titles have been spelled out, but in the text itself standard abbreviations are often used: *Od.* for *Odyssey* and *Meta.* for Ovid's *Metamorphoses*. Also in the glosses *Inf., Pur.*, and *Par.*, followed by Roman numerals for canto and Arabic numbers for lines, are used for the *Commedia* (e.g., *Inf.* V, 28). The names of some historical characters who appear often in certain cantos are sometimes abbreviated, as SM for Sigismundo Malatesta, JA for John Adams, and TJ for Thomas Jefferson.

CANTO I

Sources

Homer, *Odyssey* XI: the Nekyia passage in which the ghosts of the dead are called up and consulted about the future, in the ML translation of Andreas Divus of Justinopolis (Capodistria) and the First and Second Homeric Hymns to Aphrodite and the First Hymn to Hermes in the ML interpretation of Georgius Dartona of Crete, all published in the volume entitled *Homeri Odyssea ad verbum translata*, Andrea Divo Justinopolitano interprete, *Eiusdem Hymni Deorum XXXII*, Georgio Dartona Cretense interprete, Parisiis, In officina Christiani Wecheli, 1538.

Background

EP, Discarded Cantos: "Three Cantos" (1), *Poetry*, X, 5, 1917, "The Fourth Canto," *Dial*, LXVIII, 1920, "Three Cantos" (2), *Dial*, LXXI, 1921; *P*, "Mauberley I," "The Seafarer"; Cantos 23, 39, 47, 82, 90; *L*, 210 (to Homer Pound) and 274 (to W. H. D. Rouse); *LE* "Early Translators of Homer," "Notes on Elizabethan Classicists"; J. G. Frazer, *The Golden Bough*.

Exegeses

E. Glenn, *Analyst* I and VIII; Dekker, "Myth and Metamorphosis," JE, "The Inheritance of Tò Kalón," CB-R, "Lay me by Aurelie," GD, "Persephone's Ezra," Rachewiltz, "Pagan and Magic Elements in Ezra Pound's Works," HK, "Blood for the Ghosts," FR, "Pound, Joyce, and Flaubert: The Odysseans," all in EH, *Approaches*; CE, *Ideas*; HK, *Era*, 361.

Glossary

1. **Circe**: Goddess living on fabulous island of Aeaea who is powerful in magic; sister of Acoetes; daughter of Helios and Perse [*Od.* X, 210 ff.]. Witch-goddess, particularly associated with sexual regeneration and degeneration. Circe, Aphrodite, and Persephone form the archetypal triad of feminine deity: sorceress, lover, girl—identities "compenetrans." Also Circe Titania, Kirké, Kirkh.

2. **Kimmerian lands**: Territory of the Cimmerians, a people whose city and land were perpetually shrouded in mist and cloud [*Od.* XI, 14-19].

3. **Perimedes**: One of Odysseus's crew.

4. **Eurylochus**: "Great-hearted and godlike Eurylochus" was Odysseus's second-in-command. He was the leader of the first band of men who sought out Circe.

5. **pitkin**: Word invented by Pound: "little pit."

6. Ithaca: Island kingdom of Odysseus near coast of Hellas in Ionian Sea. Countertheme to Troy, the archetypal city that Odysseus helped to destroy. The epic "nostos" [return journey] of *The Cantos* is thus polarized between the destruction and the rediscovery of civilization and sovereignty.

7. Tiresias: Given the power of prophecy by Zeus, Tiresias was the Theban seer "Who even dead, yet hath his mind entire!" [cf. 47/236]. Associated with house of Cadmus and the founding of Thebes [cf. Sophocles, *Oedipus*; *Od*. X, XI; Ovid, *Meta*. III].

8. Erebus: Dark place through which souls must pass on way to Hades.

9. dreory: AS, "blood-dripping."

10. Pluto: God of Hades, the underworld or hell. Also called Hades or Dis. Consort of Persephone for the winter months. Also the god of wealth, particularly of gold and all precious metals and stones below the earth's surface [cf. 16, 31 below].

11. Proserpine: Daughter of Zeus and Demeter. She was condemned to live half the year in the underworld, but the Eleusinian rites brought her and all nature back to life in the spring. Also known as Persephone, Flora, Kore. She divides her time between Dis and Demeter, between the realm of death and the realm of vegetation. As the chthonic Persephone she is a goddess of death. The rising [*anodos*] of Persephone from the underworld was associated with the rising of Aphrodite from the sea in the Greater Eleusinian Mysteries. Persephone and Aphrodite were also closely linked in the myth of Adonis, who was the consort of chthonic Persephone for one-third of the year and of Aphrodite for the other two-thirds.

12. Elpenor: Youngest of Odysseus's men; drunk when Odysseus left Aeaea, he fell down a ladder, broke his neck, and "his spirit went down to the house of Hades" [Loeb]. Stands for luckless incidental companion of the hero (or poet) whose only fame after death rests in the fact that the hero has placed his name on record.

13. ingle: Inglenook. LSc, "chimney corner," ingle being derived from SGae *aingeal*, "fire." Pound is using the vocabulary of Gavin Douglas's translation of *Aeneid* where, however, "ingle" by itself always means "fire."

14. Avernus: Pound's Ovidian translation of Andreas Divus's *infernus*. Homer's Hades, "A deep lake near Puteoli.... its reputed immense depth, and its situation amid gloomy-looking woods and mephitic exhalations inspired the belief that it led to the underworld" [*OCD*].

15. Anticlea: Mother of Odysseus. She died during his absence.

16. golden wand: A double of the golden bough, key to the underworld, and of the caduceus with which Hermes summoned the souls of the dying to the underworld. The golden bough belongs to the artificial vegetation of Persephone's underground garden [cf. 10 above and 31 below; *Aeneid* VI, 141 ff.].

17. "A second time?": Pound's translation of Andreas Divus's Latin translation of the Greek word δίγονοϛ which was apparently printed in place of the now accepted διωγενὲϛ in line 92 of Book XI of the *Odyssey*. Divus was probably using a corrupt Renaissance edition of the Greek text. Scholarly regularized editions still place this line in square brackets to indicate restoration of a corrupt text. Whereas δίγονοϛ means twice-born or double, διωγενὲϛ means "sprung from Zeus" or, in a general sense, "noble," as used in the above line with reference to Laertes [cf. *LE*, 262; 48/241, 74/425, 449, 77/472; also Virgil, *Aeneid* VI, 134 ff.] [EH].

18. fosse: ME, "ditch."

19. bever: LSc, "drink" [cf. beverage].

20. Neptune: Roman god of water identified with the Greek Poseidon, whose son, Polyphemus, held Odysseus and his men captive in a cave. Odysseus blinded Polyphemus while he was in a drunken sleep in order to escape [*Od*. IX, 106 ff.]. Neptune, for vengeance, sought to oppose Odysseus's home-coming in every way.

21. Divus: Andreas D. of Justinopolis (originally Aegida, renamed J after Justinian I; now Capodistria) [cf. *LE*, 259].

22. In officina Wecheli: ML "In the workshop of Wechelus," Paris publisher of Divus.

23. Homer: Greek epic poet regarded by Pound as the originator of the epic tradition he sought to continue with *The Cantos*.

24. Sirens: Inhabitants of island near Scylla and Charybdis. Sailors lured by their song land and perish. In ancient times they were depicted as harpies or bird-women waiting to carry off the souls of men. Pound, however, sees them as mermaids. The specific lure of their song becomes clear in 79/488 ("as the fish-tails said to Odysseus"): it is praise for his past achievements. Pound is thinking of the line [*Od*. XII, 189] which he has also quoted in *Mauberley* ("we shall tell you of all that happened at Troy") [cf. *Od*. XII, 39 ff., 142-200].

25. Venerandam: ML, "worthy of veneration." Beginning of Georgius Dartona's ML interpretation of the Second Homeric Hymn to Aphrodite [*LE*, 266].

26. Aphrodite: Goddess of love, beauty, and fertility. Born of blood and seafoam. She supported the Trojans against the Greeks until the end of the war, opposing Athena, defender of the Greeks. Also called Kypris after her island of Cyprus, Cytherea after her island of Cythera, as well as Venus, Venere, and Dione/Diona (i.e., the daughter of Dione and Zeus invoked in the *Pervigilium Veneris* as the spring goddess of vegetation) [cf. *SR*, 19-20, 39/195]. Her birth [*anados*] from the sea rhymes with Persephone-Kore's ascent from the earth's nether regions celebrated at Eleusis and the original of the late canto motif of "Reina" rising from the deeps [91/610]. She was also the mother of Aeneas who, after Troy's fall, set out like Odysseus to found the archetypal city anew under her protection. Her voyage in *The Cantos* is a double of that of Odys-

seus, but unlike his it is undertaken in a spirit of serene confidence.

27. Cypri munimenta sortita est: ML, [who] "held sway over [all] the Cyprian heights." Continuation of Georgius Dartona's ML interpretation [*LE*, 266]. The reference is still to Aphrodite, later referred to in *The Cantos* as the Cyprian goddess.

28. mirthful: Pound's translation of Georgius Dartona's *hilariter*.

29. orichalchi: ML, "of copper." The Latin word for copper is *Cyprium*, the "Cyprian metal," which takes its name from the island of Cyprus, center of the Aphrodite cult. In his ML interpretation of the Second Homeric Hymn to Aphrodite, Georgius Dartona uses the word *orichalchi* with reference to Aphrodite's earrings. Pound later uses it to describe the color of her eyes as being of "copper and wine" [cf. 25, 26 above and 102/730 ff., 93/631, 97/675].

30. with golden / Girdles and breast bands, thou with dark eyelids: Pound's translation of Georgius Dartona's "Collum autem molle, acpectora argentea / Monilibus aureis ornabant"; the "dark eyelids" come from Dartona's interpretation *nigras . . . palpebras* for the Greek *elikoblephare*, a word of uncertain meaning which is generally taken to mean "flashing eyes."

31. Bearing the golden bough of Argicida: Pound's mistranslation of Georgius Dartona's *habens auream virgam Argicida* in his interpretation of the First Hymn to Aphrodite (v. 117), where Aphrodite relates that she has been abducted by *chrusórrapis* 'Argeîphóntes, i.e., 'Argeiphóntes (Slayer of Argos, the epithet for Hermes) with the golden bough or wand. Dartona translates 'Argeîphóntes as "Argicida," the epithet for Mercury which likewise has the literal meaning "Slayer of Argos." The golden bough later came to be associated with Aeneas, who was required to find one as an offering for Proserpine before he could descend to Hades (*Aeneid* VI); still later it reappeared as the Golden Bough of Aricia, a region in the Alban Hills south of Rome consisting of a grove and a lake (now known as Nemi) associated with Diana Nemorensis (Diana of the Wood) [4:16].

32. Argicida: L, "Slayer of Greeks" as in Greek term *'Argeiphóntes*. A reference to

Aphrodite's championship of the Trojans and especially of Aeneas against Greeks and against Odysseus. The epithet indicates that Aphrodite is associated with Persephone as the goddess of death.

CANTO II

Sources

Ovid, *Meta*. III, 511-733; X, 560-707; Euripides, *Bacchae*; Homeric Hymn to Dionysos; R. Browning, *Sordello*; Homer, *Od*. XI, 235-259; *Iliad* III, 139-160; *Mabinogion*; Aeschylus, *Agamemnon*; Arthur Golding, *P. Ovidius Naso: The XV Books, entytuled Metamorphosis*; Camille Chabaneau, *Les Biographies des Troubadours en Langue Provençale*, Toulouse, 1885; Fenollosa Notebooks (inedit.), University of Virginia Library.

Background

EP, *SR*, 16, 132; *Quia Pauper Amavi*; "Three Cantos, II," *Poetry*, 1917 [Discarded Cantos]; "Famam Librosque Cano," "Mesmerism" in *P*; Dante, *Pur*. 6, 7; Mary de Rachewiltz, *Discretions*, Boston and Toronto, 1971; La Chronique de Rains, in *Three Old French Chronicles of the Crusades*, trans. E. Noble Stone, Seattle, 1939.

Exegeses

E. Glenn, *Analyst* XVIII; N. C. de Nagy, "Pound and Browning," and Dekker, "Myth and Metamorphosis," both in EH, *Approaches*; CE, *Ideas*; EH, *Pai*, 7, 1 & 2, 179-180.

Glossary

1. Robert Browning: 1812-1889, author of the epic poem, *Sordello*, based on the life of the Italian troubadour of that name who wrote in Provençal. Browning gives an unconventional image of the troubadour as a lyrical persona or mask of himself (a "dramatic monologue"), just as Pound later uses him and other historical characters. The point is that there is no way of seeing the personality of Sordello objectively but only of seeing subjective perspectives of the facts. Browning's *Sordello* is, for Pound, the last instance of the epic tradition in the English language, which he intends to take up from there on. Pound traces his personal literary lineage back to Browning in *L* [letter to R. Taupin of May 1928 ("Und überhaupt ich stamm aus Browning. Pourquoi nier son père?")], but he intends to include the mythological dimension as well. In introducing the persona "Sordello" and the epic of Browning, he is recycling material from the discarded cantos which is now subsumed into the persona of Odysseus and the epic of Homer [cf. *SR*, 132; *LE*, 33; *ABCR*, 78, 188-191; and letter to W. C. Williams, *L*, 7].

2. Sordello: ?1180-?1255, Italian troubadour, son of a poor cavalier, who came to the court of Count Ricciardo de San Bonifazzio, fell in love with the count's wife, Cunizza da Romano, and abducted her at the behest of her brothers. He then lived with Cunizza and was forced to flee to Provence. Later on he performed military service for Charles I of Anjou, Naples, and Sicily, who rewarded him with five castles which, however, he returned, considering himself far richer through his poetry [cf. *LE*, 97-98; Browning's *Sordello*; *Pur.* 6, 7].

3. Lo Sordels ...: P, "Sordello is from Mantua." Direct translation from a *vida* (P, "life") of Sordello in Chabaneau, which begins "Lo Sordels si fo de Mantoana, de Sirier, fils d'un paubre cavallier que avia nom sier el Cort. E deletava se en cansos aprendre & en trobar, e briguet com los bons homes de cort, & apres tot so qu'el poc; e fetz coblas e sirventes. E venc s'en a la cort del comte de San Bonifaci; el coms l'onret molt; & enamoret se de la moiller del comte a forma de solatz, & ella de lui. Et avenc si quel coms estet mal com los fraires d'ella, e si s'estranjet d'ella. E sier Icellis e sier Albrics, li fraire d'ella, si la feiren envolar al comte a sier Sordel; e s'en venc estar com lor en gran benanansa. E pois s'en anet en Proensa, on el receup grans honors de totz los bos homes, e del comte e de la comtessa, que li deron un bon castel e moiller gentil." For Pound's translation, see *LE* 97 ff. [EH].

4. So-shu: Corruption of Shiba Shōjo, Japa-

nese name for Chinese Han dynasty poet, Ssu-ma Hsiang-ju (179-117), a representative of the rhyme-prose school criticized by Li Po in an allegory from which the line quoted is derived via a translation by Fenollosa in the Fenollosa Notebooks (inedit.). Li Po scouts Ssu-ma Hsiang-ju, an imitator of Ch'u Yüan, for creating foam instead of waves. Pound quotes from Fenollosa's notes: "Yoyu and Shojo stirred up decayed (enervated) waves. Open current flows about in bubbles, does not move in wave lengths" [*Affirmations*, Jan. 28, 1916]. Not to be confused with "So-shu" in "Ancient Wisdom, Rather Cosmic" (*P*), which is a Japanese transliteration of the name of the Chinese philosopher Chuang Chou (more commonly known as Chuang Tzu), or with "So Shu, king of Soku," in *J/M* (p. 100), where "So Shu" is an incorrect Japanese transliteration of the Chinese name Ts'an Ts'ung, the first king of Shu (now Szechwan) in W China, earlier referred to as "Sanso, King of Shoku," in the motto to Li Po's poem "Leave-taking near Shoku" in *Cathay* [*P*, 138] [EH].

5. Lir: Old Celtic sea-god. Pound regards seals as being Lir's daughters [cf. chapter "Branwen the Daughter of Llyr" in *Mabinogion*, where Branwen means "White Crow"].

6. Picasso: The reference to Picasso's seal's eyes evokes the artist's faculty for changing the shape of the things he sees. In ancient mythology the seal is the animal most closely linked with Proteus, who among other things used to assume the shape of a seal [cf. 30 below].

7. Eleanor: Helen of Troy, also Elena, Tellus-Helena, Helen of Tyre, Tyndarida. Also Eleanor of Aquitaine [cf. 9 below].

8. ἐλέναυς and ἐλέπτολις!: H, *helenaus* and *heleptolis*, "ship-destroying and city-destroying." Aeschylus's puns on the name of Helen in *Agamemnon*, 689.

9. Eleanor: E. of Aquitaine, 1122-1204. Like Helen of Troy, Eleanor was the archetype of the femme fatale, inspiring both strife and poetry. She was the granddaughter of Guillaume of Poitiers, 1071-1127, 9th Duke of Aquitaine, who, according to Pound, superimposed the music of Moresco Spain upon the poetry of S France, an important cultural synthesis of different ethnic elements such as Eleanor was also destined to bring about and which Pound too had hoped to achieve for America. Eleanor married Louis VII of France and accompanied him on a crusade to the Holy Land, where she allegedly had an affair with Saladin, the great Kurdish Moslem warrior, a tale invented by her enemies and spread, for instance, in the Chronique de Rains. Louis divorced her and a few months later she married Henry II of England, bringing him all Aquitaine as dowry. When Henry II proved untrue and even held Eleanor captive, she turned her sons, notably the "young king" Henry and Richard (later the Lion-Heart), against their father. Her political activities and the legal tangles resulting from her two marriages were the cause of the Hundred Years War between England and France. Thus, she was truly a "Helen," agent of both love and death.

10. Let her go . . . : [*Iliad* III, 139-160]. The fear that the elders of Troy, the old men (the husks of life), experienced when confronted with Helen's living but death-bringing beauty [7:3, 5, 32, 35, 37].

11. Schoeney . . . : Schoeneus, father of Atalanta who, like Helen, through her beauty caused the death of many men. Pound is misremembering Arthur Golding's spelling, Schoenyes, in his translation of Ovid [*Meta*. X, 566-707]. For Pound an instance of the metamorphosis and transmission of beauty by translation. Refractions of ephemeral beauty through time [cf. *LE*, 235-236; 7:29; 102/730].

12. Tyro: Daughter of Salmoneus. She became enamored of the divine river, Enipeus. Poseidon, at the mouth of the river, took on Enipeus's form, shed sleep upon her, and, while a dark wave rose like a mountain to screen him, raped her [*Od*. XI, 235-259].

13. Scios: Ancient Chios, modern Scio, Aegian island about 70 miles north and slightly east of Naxos.

14. Naxos: Largest island of the Cyclades, famous for its wine. The island was a center of the Dionysus cult [cf. *Meta*. III, 636-637, and Homeric Hymn to Dionysos].

15. young boy: The young god, Bacchus, Dionysus, Zagreus, Iacchus, Lyaeus, originally Cretan, god of wine, fertility, and ecstasy whose cult arose to challenge that of Apollo. He is on his way to Naxos.

16. vine-must: New wine.

17. King Pentheus: Grandson of Cadmus. Refusing to worship Dionysus he was torn to pieces by Dionysus's followers, the Maenads, led by Pentheus's mother, who wrenched off his head and carried it home in triumph. Acoetes is telling the story of his crew's attempt to kidnap the god as a warning to Pentheus.

18. Acoetes: A Lydian of humble parents, skilled in navigation, captain of the ship.

19. Lyaeus: Refers to Dionysus in his function as the god of wine and ecstasy.

20. Olibanum: L, "frankincense." The Romans believed Bacchus responsible for the use of incense in ritual [cf. Ovid, *Fasti* III, 727].

21. Lycabs and Medon: Other members of Odysseus's crew. Ovid lists more names.

22. dory: The *Zeus faber*, a kind of fish.

23. Tiresias: Theban seer. In Euripides' *Bacchae*, he appears with Cadmus on the way up the mountain to join the women in *orgia* and worship of the god. Given the power of prophecy, he advises Pentheus to worship the god also. Pentheus pays no heed [1:7].

24. Cadmus: Son of Phoenician King Agenor. Europa, sister of Cadmus, was carried off by Zeus, who took the form of a bull. Sent by his father to find her, Cadmus wandered as far as the oracle at Delphi, where he was given directions which led to the founding of Thebes. According to the myth the stones of the walls of Thebes rose to the rhythm of the music Amphion played on his lyre. The walls are conceived as the magical protective walls around the archetypal city which were traced in the air by ritual dance, music, and incantation, as were also the walls of the Knossian labyrinth, the walls of Troy, and the walls of Alba Longa [*Aeneid* V, 583-602]. Grandfather of Pentheus and father of Ino ["Ino Kadmaia" at 98/685, 102/728, 109/774; 4:4].

25. Ileuthyeria: Apparently an inadvertent conflation of Eileithyia, the goddess of childbirth, with *Eleutheria*, H, "freedom," a marine organism of the genus of bisexual jellyfishes. On Greek amphoras, where the goddess is sometimes depicted in company with Hermes, Apollo, and Ares attending Zeus as he is about to give birth to Dionysus, she is variously identified in Greek letters as Ileíthya [ΗΙΛΕΙΘΥΑ] (cf. Eduard Gerhard, *Auserlesene griechische Vasenbilder*, Vol. I, Pl. IV, Berlin, 1840) and Ilíthyia, as she also appears in Horace, *Carm. Sec.* 14, and Ovid, *Meta.* IX, 283 [EH].

26. Dafne: Daphne, daughter of Peneus, a river-god. In headlong flight from the amorous Apollo, she invoked the aid of Peneus who transformed her into a laurel tree [*Meta.* I, 546-552]. Pound said: "a theme of Ovid—Dafne, my own myth, not changed into a laurel but into coral" [cf. Mary de Rachewiltz, *Discretions*, 159].

27. So-shu: [cf. 4 above].

28. Poseidon: Greek god of the sea. The reference is to the rape of Tyro [cf. 12 above].

29. Hesperus: Evening star sacred to Aphrodite. Always associated in Pound's mind with the nuptial hymns of Sappho and Catullus [cf. 79/488, 492].

30. Proteus: Sea-god who had power of metamorphosis and knowledge of past and future. In Aristophanes' *The Frogs* Dionysus and his servant Xanthias, descending into Hades in search of a "good poet," are greeted by the thunderous chorus of infernal frogs, which they try to drown out. Dionysus, first dressed up as Heracles, goes through a series of quick disguises. Speciality of Aristophanes' comedies: the hemichant, setting one part of the chorus against the other. That Pound was aware of the function of the hemichant in Aristophanes' plays, as well as in the Eleusinian Mysteries, is documented by an early poem: "Salve O Pontifex—for Swinburne; an hemi chaunt." In *LE*, 293-294, he praises S. for his "surging and leaping dactyllics" and "rhythm-building faculty," the very faculty that represents the horse or goat hindquarters of poetry, the centaur [cf. *LE*, 52].

CANTO III

Sources

R. Browning, *Sordello* III; *Cantar de mio Cid* (anon.); Luiz de Camoëns, *Os Lusíadas* III; G. D'Annunzio, *Notturno*, Milan, 1921; Catullus LXIV, 17-18; LXI, 13.

Background

EP, *SR*, 67-68, 218; "Cavalcanti" in *LE*, 149-160; "Terra Italica" in *SP*, 54-60; "Three Cantos" (2), in *Poetry*, X, 5, 1917, and in *Quia Pauper Amavi*; "Burgos: A Dream City of Old Castile" in *Book News Monthly*, Oct. 1906; "Lettere E 9 Cartoline Inedite" in *Nuova Corrente*, 5/6, 1956.

Exegeses

E. Glenn, *Analyst* XXV; CE, *Ideas*, 86-91 and passim; HK, *Era*, passim; GD, "Persephone's Ezra," and FR, "Pound, Joyce, and Flaubert: The Odysseans," both in EH, *Approaches*.

Glossary

1. Dogana: Customhouse in Venice. Gives striking view across the Grand Canal to buildings surrounding St. Mark's [see photograph, HK, *Era*, 418]. In earlier version, Pound responds to Browning's "I muse this on a ruined palace-step / At Venice" [*Sordello* III, 675] by "Your palace steps? / My stone seat was the Dogana's vulgarest curb."

2. that year: Prób. 1908, the year Pound went into exile. His lack of funds introduces the economic problem as a theme for the first time.

3. "those girls": Echo of Browning's "Let stay those girls" [*Sordello* III, 698].

4. one face: Unidentified. Earlier version reads: "there was one flare, one face. / 'Twas all I ever saw, but it was real . . . . / And I can no more say what shape it was . . . / But she was young, too young."

5. Buccentoro: Bucentoro or Bucintoro, meaning "Golden Bark," a rowing club situated around the corner from the Dogana; originally, for some eight centuries, the name of the barge used by the Doges of Venice for the ceremony in which they "married" Venice to the sea by the act of dropping a ring into the Adriatic. In 1908 Pound heard the club members singing traditional Venetian songs [cf. 27/129].

6. Stretti: I, "in close embrace." From "La spagnuola" [I, "The Spanish Girl"], a Neapolitan song by Vicenzo de Chiara which was popular in the first half of the 20th century: "Stretti, stretti / nell'estasi d'amor / La spagnuola sa amar cosi / bocca a bocca la notte e il di" ["In close embrace, in close embrace / in love's ecstasy / the Spanish girl is that way when in love / mouth to mouth, night and day"] [cf. 26/121; 27/130].

7. Morosini: Aristocratic Venetian family. Name of a square and a palace. Earlier version reads: "And at Florian's under the North arcade / I have seen other faces, and had my rolls for breakfast. / Drifted at night and seen the lit, gilt crossbeams. / Glare from the Morosini."

8. Koré's house: In 1922 (*Dial*, Nov.) Pound translated a D'Annunzio line "La casa di Corè è abitata dai pavoni bianchi" in *Notturno* as: "In Koré's house there are now only white peacocks." D'Annunzio appears to refer thus to the neglected grounds of the Palazzo dei Leoni on the Grand Canal, which had become a rookery. (See *Notturno*, 105, 410, 443, 449, 480) Kore(H) daughter, i.e. Persephone, daughter of Demeter.

9. Gods float in the azure air: One of the "three sorts of blue" to which Pound attached special significance, the azure stands for the continuum in which the gods exist, i.e., collective memory; sapphire, for personal memory; and cobalt, for oblivion [cf. 5:8; "Blandula, Tenella, Vagula"; and *Mauberley* in *P*].

10. Panisks: H, Paniskos. Little woodland Pans, half human and half goat [cf. "goatfoot" at 4/13].

11. dryas: L, ME, tree nymph that lives only during the life of its tree. Also dryad [cf. 76/452; 83/530].

12. maelid: H, *maliades* or *meliades*, nymphs of fruit trees and flocks [cf. 4/13; 79/489, 491].

13. The silvery . . . nipple: Not Poggio's exact words but an image easily evoked by a scene he witnessed at the baths in Baden, Switzerland, in the spring of 1416 and recorded in the well-known letter to his friend Niccolò de'Niccoli. Pound's imitation of this letter appeared under the title "Aux étuves de Weisbaden, A.D. 1451" [sic] in the *Little Review*, July 1917 [rpt. in *PD*, 98-103], indicating perhaps that he had read the French translation of the original. The ML text runs [*Opera Omnia*, Basle, 1538], with the ligatures omitted: "Quotidie ter aut quater balnea intrant, maiorem in his diei partem agentes, partim cantando, partim potando, partim choreas exercendo. Psallunt & iam in aquis paululum subsidendo. In quo iocundissimum est videre puellas iam maturas viro, iam plenis nubilas annis, facie splendida ac liberali, in Dearum habitum ac formam psallentes, modicas vestes retrorsum trahunt desuper aquam fluitantes, ut alteram Venerem extimares." ["They (members of both sexes who are privileged by family connections or high favor) go to the pools three or four times daily, dividing their time among singing, drinking, dancing. Even in the water they play an instrument. There is nothing more delightful than to watch the young ladies, some just turning nubile and others in full bloom, with their beautiful faces, frank looks, shaped and draped like

the goddess, playing an instrument while leaning back in the water with their shift, which they have pulled back slightly, floating behind them so that they look like a winged Venus." Like all ML, the text contains various ambiguities. In particular, *habitus* can alternatively mean "status" or "bearing." Since Pound's figures, however, are not reclining in the water, he may have conflated Poggio's young ladies with the nude Nereids rising up out of the spindrift in Catullus LXIV, 18 [HK, *Era*, 143]: "viderunt . . . mortales oculis nudato corpore Nymphas / nutricum tenus extantes e gurgite cano" [EH].

14. Poggio: Gian Francesco P. Bracciolini, 1380-1459, Renaissance Italian humanist who rediscovered many of the lost Latin classics.

15. gray steps: From Discarded Canto I (June 1917): "gray gradual steps / Lead up beneath flat sprays of heavy cedars, / Temple of teak wood, and the gilt-brown arches / Triple in tier, banners woven by wall, / Fine screens depicted, sea waves curled high, / Small boats with gods upon them, / Bright flame above the river!" The steps lead to the ancestral temple, dedicated to the Duke of Chou, which Confucius entered for the first time at the beginning of his service with the Chi family, which ruled the principality of Lu, his native state [cf. *Lun-yü* III, 15; 13/58] [EH].

16. My Cid . . . Burgos: S, my "commander" or "Lord," a title given by the Moors to Ruy Díaz (Rodrigo Díaz de Bivar, 1040?-1099), hero of the Spanish epic, *Cantar de mío Cid*, ca. 1140. Díaz was exiled by Alfonso VI for bearing false witness against him. Pound quotes from Part I ("The Exile") of the epic. Like Odysseus and Sigismundo Malatesta, Ruy Díaz was resourceful, adventurous, and cunning: "a live man among duds," a "glorious bandit," the factive personality. He lived and was buried in Burgos, capital of Burgos Province in Old Castile.

17. Una niña . . . : S, "a little girl nine years old." An incident from the biography of El Cid conflated with personal memory of Pound's 1906 visit to Spain [cf. "Burgos: A Dream City of Old Castile," *Book News Monthly*, Oct. 1906; 80/493, 95/645].

18. voce tinnula: L, "with ringing voice." From Catullus LXI, 13 [cf. 4/15; 28/137].

19. Bivar: Or Vivar, variant of name of the Cid.

20. Raquel and Vidas: Two Jewish money-lenders. The Cid, in order to pay his knights and followers, tricked the moneylenders into believing that two trunks, loaded with sand, really contained gold. They lent him 600 marks, accepting the trunks, which they promised not to open, for security.

21. menie: ME, "retinue," but here referring to a private army.

22. Valencia: A region of E Spain occupied by the Moors from 714 to 1094, when they were expelled by the Cid.

23. Ignez da Castro: Inés de Castro, d. 1355. Pedro, son and heir of Alphonso IV of Portugal, secretly married Inés after his wife Constance died. Pound writes: "Her position was the cause of jealousy, and of conspiracy; she was stabbed in the act of begging clemency from the then reigning Alphonso IV. When Pedro succeeded to the throne, he had her body exhumed, and the court did homage, the grandees of Portugal passing before the double throne of the dead queen and her king, and kissing that hand which had been hers. A picture of the scene hangs in the new gallery at Madrid, in the series of canvasses which commemorate the splendid horrors of the Spanish past" [*SR*, 218]. Inés is a Kore figure untimely forced into Hades, representing the overlapping of the past into the present, a discrepancy between the fine image held in the mind and the actual fact of the rotting corpse from the past, as may occur when time, for a mind like Pedro's, has stood still. [cf. 30/148; Camoëns, *Os Lusíadas* III].

24. Drear waste: Decay of the splendors of the Renaissance during 400 or more years of an increasingly usurious civilization.

25. Mantegna: Andrea M., 1431-1506, Renaissance painter who spent his last years in Mantua under the patronage of the Gonzagas, painting the frescoes in the ducal palace and in the countryside at Goito, whence the Sordello family came. Mantegna also painted the fresco of "Gonzaga and his heirs and concubines" mentioned in the Usura Canto [45/229] as a prime example of the quality of art in a nonusurious era.

26. Nec Spe Nec Metu: L, "neither by hope nor by fear"— to achieve anything, you must act. Motto in the rooms of Isabella d'Este Gonzaga, 1474-1539, in the ducal palace at Mantua.

CANTO IV

Sources

Euripides, *Troades*, opening scene; Virgil, *Aeneid* II, III; Pindar, *Olympian* II; Catullus LXI; Sappho 93D, 117D; Ovid, *Meta.* II, III, IV, V, VI, XII; Horace, *Odes* IV, xii, 5; Camille Chabaneau, *Les Biographies des Troubadours en Langue Provençale*, Toulouse, 1885; Arnaut Daniel, "Lancan son passat li giure"; R.

Browning, *Sordello* V, 163; Fenollosa Notebooks (inedit.), University of Virginia Library, "Takasago" and "Sō Gyoku" (= Sung Yü); Herodotus, *Historiae* I, 8-14 and 98; Guido Cavalcanti, Sonnet 35.

Background

EP, *ABCR*, 47-48, 56; *PM*, 56; *P*, "The Coming of War: Actaeon," "Provincia Deserta," "The Unmoving Cloud"; *LE*, 49, 52; *SR*, 44, 87-100; *T*, 95, 221-222, 246-247, 269 ff.; *L*, 178 (to F. E. Schelling); J. G. Frazer, *The Golden Bough*; Virgil, *Eclogues*; Philip Grover, *Ezra Pound: The London Years*, Sheffield University Library, 1976.

Exegeses

E. Glenn, *Analyst* I and addenda in II, III, IV; WB, *Rose*; CB-R, GD, Dekker, and B. de Rachewiltz, all in EH, *Approaches*; HK, *Era*, 6-7, 215, 375, 417; R. Bush, *Genesis*, 145; EH, *Pai*, 7.

Glossary

1. **Palace . . .** : Scene at the opening of Euripides' *The Trojan Women* recalling the burning of the archetypal city [cf. also *Aeneid* II, 309-310, 431; III, 3–Aeneas setting out to rebuild destroyed Troy].

2. **Anaxiforminges**: H, from *Anaxiphormigges hymnoi*, "Hymns that are lords of the lyre," beginning of Pindar's "Olympian Ode II," the power of poetry and recorded words. The double gamma was pronounced "ng."

3. **Aurunculeia**: Vinia A., bride praised in Catullus, *Epithalamium* LXI, 86-87. Catullus's marriage hymns echo Sappho's *Epithalamia* [cf. 5/17].

4. **Cadmus of Golden Prows**: Eponymous hero and founder of Thebes [2:24]. Like Odysseus, Cadmus set out into the unknown. He was sent by the king, his father, to discover the fate of his sister Europa, who had been abducted by Zeus. The walls of lower Thebes rose to the sound of Amphion's lyre [cf. 62:33; 90/605; 93/630; 107/761].

5. **Beat, beat, . . .** : Variation on the line in Whitman's "Drum Taps": "Beat, beat, whirr, pound . . ." [cf. Sappho 93D].

6. **Choros . . .** : L, "Chorus of nymphs" [Sappho 93D].

7. **black cock**: The cockcrow announces the rebirth of Aphrodite from the sea-foam and a rebirth of the Renaissance [FR].

8. **Ityn**: H, Itys, son of Procne and Tereus, king of Thrace [Ovid, *Meta*. VI, 652 ("Ityn huc accersite!")]. Procne killed her son Itys in order to cook and feed him to Tereus after she had discovered that he had raped Philomela, her sister, and cut out her tongue so that she could not tell what he had done. Procne and Philomela afterward escaped the vengeance of Tereus by turning respectively into a swallow and a nightingale. Philomela, the nightingale, is said to cry out the name Itys, whose death she had caused: "Itu! Itu!" [Ovid, *Meta*. VI, 426-674; cf. 78/477; 82/525].

9. Et ter flebiliter: L, "And thrice with tears" [see Horace, *Odes* IV, xii, 5].

10. Cabestan: Guillems de Cabestanh or Cabestaing, an ascetic troubadour to whom, ironically, an ancient Celtic legend was attached according to which he became the lover of the Lady Seremonda, wife of Ramon, lord of the castle of Rossillon, whom he served. According to Chabaneau, Pound's source, Raymond killed Cabestanh and served his cooked heart to Seremonda [cf. *SR*, 44]. The original legend was also attached to the Châtelain de Couci in France and the German minnesinger Reinmar von Brennenberg; see also Boccaccio, *Decamerone* IV, 9 [EH].

11. Rhodez: Earlier spelling of Rodez, a high plateau overlooking the sinuous river Aveyron. It has a cathedral whose original structure was built in 1274, and two towers remaining from the old fortification. Pound visited R on July 2, 1912, and a second time with his wife Dorothy sometime between June 6 and August 15, 1919 [cf. "The Gypsy" in *P*, 119].

12. Actaeon: By accident while hunting, he came upon the naked Diana bathing in the pool of Gargaphia. She changed him into a stag in which form he was pursued and killed by his own companions and dogs.

13. Poictiers: Refers to the church of St. Hilaire in Poitiers [cf. *GK*, 109]. Visited by Pound in 1912.

14. Diana: Or "Delia," virgin goddess of Delos, called *kallīastrágalos* ["with fine ankles"]; the Greek Artemis; "Lucina," goddess of childbirth; "Selena," goddess of the moon; of Cretan origin. Goddess of the moon, mountains, mountain lakes, woods, the hunt, and of all wildlife, the incarnation of untamed nature and its self-healing powers of renewal (hence associated with *hsin* in 110/780). Like Persephone (with whom she is associated at 76/457), Diana is also the goddess of the double gates of birth and death. Her images at Ephesus do not show her as the chaste virgin goddess, but as the Great Mother [cf. *SR*, 95-96] suckling the newborn dead at her numerous breasts. This Ephesian image of Diana later merges into the image and cult of the Virgin Mary [cf. 80/500-501], who is also depicted standing on the moon's sickle with the baby in her arms. The tradition of virgin birth is likewise linked with Artemis, who annually renewed her virginity by bathing in the pool of Gargaphia. What the "Artemis type" meant to Pound personally is expressed in *PM*, 56.

15. Vidal: The troubadour Peire Vidals of Tolosa [cf. "Piere Vidal Old" in *P*]. He dressed in wolfskins to woo his lady, Loba of Penautier, an Albigensian noblewoman. *Loba* translates as "she-wolf." Like Actaeon, Vidal in pursuit of his love becomes the prey of his own hounds. Pound translates the legend from the Provençal *vida* of Chabaneau. His English version is in *SR*, 178.

16. Pergusa: A lake [see Ovid, *Meta.* V, 386]. A deep pool suggestive of the underworld near Enna (Sicily), where Persephone was carried off by Dis [1:14, "Avernus"]. Also a parallel to Lake Nemi, where there was a temple dedicated to Diana [cf. 74/438; 77/467; *The Golden Bough*].

17. Gargaphia: A deep valley and spring in Boeotia, where Artemis was surprised by Actaeon while bathing [Ovid, *Meta.* III, 156].

18. Salmacis: [Ovid, *Meta.* IV, 285-388]. Spring near Halikarnassos (Asia Minor) belonging to the water nymph Salmacis, who attempted unsuccessfully to rape the boy Hermaphroditos.

19. The empty armour ... cygnet moves: Cygnus or "swan," the son of Neptune, comes up against Achilles, son of Thetis (a marine goddess), when defending Troy. Under the spell of Neptune, Cygnus proves invulnerable even to Achilles. But when Achilles finally throws him to the ground, crushing him bodily, his battered armor is found to be empty, Cygnus having escaped in the guise of a swan.

20. **e lo soleills plovil**: P, "thus the light rains." From Pound's rendering of Arnaut Daniel's *on lo soleills plovil*, from the last line of the song "Lancan son passat li giure," which he had earlier given as "where the rain falls from the sun" [*LE*. 122-123]. There it is meant to pinpoint an absurdity. For Pound, however, it turns into the important canto motif of the light-water-stone progression which finally ends in crystal, i.e., the transmutation of the fluid transparency of subjective experience into the objective solidity of stone through poetry, or, in another relevant terminology, the alchemist's fabrication of the philosopher's stone by palingenesis [cf. *LE*, 49; *SR*, 93-94; 23/109; 54/449; 76/456-457, 459; 91/611-613, 617; 116/795].

21. **Ply over ply**: A recurrent simile in Pound's poetry and prose originating superficially in Browning's *Sordello* V, 161-172: "The other was a scaffold. See him stand / Buttressed upon his mattock, Hildebrand / Of the huge brainmask welded ply o'er ply / As in a forge; it buries either eye / White and extinct, that stupid brow; teeth clenched, / The neck tight-corded, too, the chin deep-trenched, / As if a cloud enveloped him while fought / Under its shade, grim prizers, thought with thought / At dead-lock, agonizing he, until / The victor thought leap radiant up, and Will, / The slave with folded arms and drooping lids / They fought for, lean forth flame-like as it bids." It should be noted, however, that Browning's image of the skull of Gregory VII welded "ply o'er ply" within the scaffolding has little in common with Pound's, which recalls the layers of cloud described in "To-Em-Mei's 'The Unmoving Cloud'" (*P*, 142, a poem by T'ao Ch'ien, which begins: "The clouds have gathered, and gathered, / and the rain falls and falls, / The eight ply of the heavens / are all folded into one darkness." HK (in *Spectrum*, IX, 1967, 35-36) has shown that the last two lines derive from Fenollosa's mistranslation of *hachi hoi do kon* as "eight surface same dark," where "eight surface" should read "eight points of the compass." Proceeding

from here it is not too difficult to see how the mistake may have crept in. *Hachi hoi* (*pa mien* in the original Chinese text) is written 八面. Fenollosa correctly translated 八 as "eight" and 面 as "surface," overlooking, however, that the two characters, used together, form a compound expression meaning "eight points of the compass." Pound's rendering "ply over ply" echoes Mallarmé's *pli selon pli* in *Rémemoration d'amis belges* and *Autre Éventail*, where it describes the unfolding and folding of a fan [EH.]

22. **Takasago**: The title of a Japanese Nō play named after the legendary pine tree growing on the shore of Takasago Bay in S Honshu. The subject of the play is a Philemon and Baucis story of a couple growing old together, the couple being symbolized by two pine trees, one growing at Takasago and the other at Sumiyoshi [cf. 21/99: the "old man sweeping leaves"]. Pound, following Fenollosa, sees the Japanese Nō play as a parallel to the Greek drama [cf. *T*, 222, 246-247, 269 ff.] [EH].

23. **Isé**: A bay famous for its pine grove at Ano, mentioned toward the end of the Japanese Nō play entitled *Tamura*. Because of its association with pine trees, Pound confuses Isé with Sumiyoshi in Settsu Province, which is mentioned in the Nō play *Takasago* (see above) as the location of the legendary pine tree which forms a pair with the one growing at Takasago [EH].

24. **The water whirls**: Pound wrote in 1913: "We might come to believe that the thing that matters in art is a sort of energy, something more or less like electricity or radioactivity, a force transfusing, welding, and unifying. A force rather like water when it spurts up through very bright sand and sets it in swift motion" [*LE*, 49].

25. **"Tree of the Visages"**: Apparently a mistranslation of *seimei zyu* (生命樹), meaning "trees of life," a synonym for "pine trees" used in the Nō play *Takasago*. Fenollosa would seem to have misread the second character 命 as 臉, meaning "face," which

would explain Pound's "Visages" [cf. 22 above] [EH].

26. Gourdon: Another recollection of Pound's walking tour through Provence in 1912 as recorded in "Provincia Deserta" ["I have seen the torch-flames, high-leaping"].

27. Hymenaeus Io . . . : L, "Hymen, hail! Hymen, hail Hymen!" [Catullus LXI; cf. 3 above; 2:29]. Hymen is the god of marriage and saffron is his color.

28. Aurunculeia: [cf. 3 above].

29. scarlet flower: Fragment of another wedding hymn. This image of the virgin's loss of maidenhood on her wedding night is paralleled by the much used topos of Provençal and other medieval poetry of the knight being reminded of his beloved by blood drops in the snow [cf. 6/23; Sappho 117D].

30. So-Gyoku: Sō Gyoku. Japanese form of name of Chinese poet, Sung Yü, 4th century B.C., author of "Rhymeprose on the Wind" (Wen-Hsûan VII, 13, la) in which King Hsiang of Ch'u and the poet discuss the difference between the male and the female wind. Pound's source was the Fenollosa Notebooks. Arthur Waley's translation is to be found in *170 Chinese Poems*, 1922, 41.

31. Hsiang: King of Ch'u referred to in Sung Yü, "Rhymeprose on the Wind," noted above.

32. Ecbatan: Founded by the Median Deïoces (Herodotus I, 98), the city of Ecbatana (Agbatana, now Hamadan) was meticulously mapped out to correspond in every detail with the plan of the universe, esp. the firmament. Ecbatana is archetypal as a concept of perfect human order, a reconciliation of nature and civilization, as paralleled in other cantos by Ithaca, Troy, Mt. Segur, Thebes, Rome, Wagadu, and later Trinovant (= London). The building of the terraces of Ecbatana in correspondence with the seven planets reflects the late megalithic concept of the Mesopotamian ziggurat (or Tower of Babylon) [cf. 5/17; 74/425, 434; 80/510].

33. Danaë: Acrisius, king of Argos and father of Danaë, also tried to manipulate and control the elemental forces of nature. Having been told by an oracle that his daughter's son would kill him, he imprisoned Danaë at the top of a bronze tower. But Zeus, seeing her from above, visited her in a shower of golden light that poured into her lap [cf. 92/619]. As a result, Danaë bore him a son, the culture-hero Perseus. Learning of the birth, Acrisius cast Danaë and Perseus adrift in a sea chest. After many adventures Perseus returns and accidentally kills his grandfather. At the back of this myth is the prehistorical memory, recorded by Greek mythologists, of the transition from the fertility rites of the earth to the later cult of heaven (light = sun, moon, and stars), the great goddess representing the earth religion and the later male deities the sky religions of light [cf. 5/17]. This transition is reflected architectonically in the Tower of Babylon (the Mesopotamian ziggurat). To symbolize the new concept of the ritual consummation of a marriage of heaven and earth, a young girl was placed at the top of the tower to await the coming of the god. The golden rain of light into Danaë's lap thus symbolized the sexual consummation of the marriage of earth and heaven in the form of rain and light [cf. 32 above].

34. grey stone posts: [3:15.]

35. Père Henri Jacques: According to Pound, "a French priest (as a matter of fact he is a Jesuit)" [L, 180.]

36. Sennin: J, Japanese word for Chinese *hsien*, a genie or genies. Pound in re *sennins*: "I don't see that they are any worse than Celtic Sidhe" [L, 180]. The literal Chinese translation of *sennin* is, however, *hsin-jen*, meaning a hermit or "philosopher" (sing. or pl.) who has attained immortality by resisting desire [cf. "Sennin Poem by Kakuhaku," *P*, 139].

37. Rokku: Wrongly transcribed Japanese translation of a Chinese place-name, poss: Taipeh (Taihoku) in Taiwan. According to Pound, "either a mountain or an island" [*L*, 180].

38. Polhonac: Viscount Heraclius III of Polhonac, fl. 1180, was persuaded by the troubadour Guillems de' San Leidier (also known as Guilhem de Saint Didier) to sing to his wife a love song he had composed for her after she had refused to accept him as her knight except at the invitation of her husband. Pound comments: "Guillaume St. Leider even went so far as to get the husband of his lady to do the seductive singing" [*LE*, 94]. Ironically, in the *trobar clus* tradition, the husband did not know he was assisting in the seduction of his wife.

39. Gyges: Bodyguard of King Candaules who, for cause, killed the king and married the queen at her behest [Herodotus I, 8-14]. Gyges is a subject rhyme to the story of Polhonac, although without a happy ending, the motivation being different. Candaules, king of Lydia, secretly introduced Gyges into his bedroom so that he could admire the naked beauty of his wife. But his wife, on discovering his scheme to show her off possessively as a sex object, was offended; she seduced Gyges and made him kill Candaules and marry her.

40. Thracian platter: The platter calls to mind the story of Tereus, king of Thrace [cf. 8, 9, above].

41. Garonne: River in Provence recollected from Pound's walking tour in 1919.

42. "Saave! . . . sa'ave Regina!": L. "Hail! . . . hail Queen!" Pound, in a letter to his father (ca. 1919): "This worm of the procession had three large antennae, and I hope to develop the motive later, text clearly states that this vermiform object circulated in the crowd at the Church of St. Nicholas in Toulouse. No merely mediaeval but black central African superstitution [sic] and voodoo energy squalling infant, general murk and epileptic religious hog wash with chief totem magnificently swung over whole" [YC].

43. Adige: Italian river that rises in the Alps and flows into the Adriatic N of the Po delta.

44. Stefano: S. da Verona, ca. 1374-1451, painter of the *Madonna in hortulo*.

45. Madonna in hortulo: I, "Madonna in the Little Garden," a painting by Stefano seen by Pound in 1912 in the Palazzo Laveozzola Pompei, situated "across the Adige" from San Zeno. It is now in the Castel Vecchio at Verona. Confused by Pound with Cavalcanti's lady of Sonnet 35 [cf. *T*, 95], in which Cavalcanti explains that the miracles worked by the painting of the Madonna of San Michele in Orto (in Florence) are owing to her having been painted with his lady's face.

46. Cavalcanti: Guido C., 1250-1300, Tuscan poet and friend of Dante [cf. *LE*, 149-200; 36/177 ff.; *SR* 91]: "The rise of Mariolatry, its pagan lineage, the romance of it, find modes of expression which verge overeasily into the speech . . . of Our Lady of Cyprus . . . as we see so splendidly in Guido's 'Una figura della donna miae [sic].'" Pound corrected *miae* to *mia* in *T*, 94.

47. Centaur: Symbol of the enduring presence of the pagan elemental gods and demigods—as in Cavalcanti's sonnet. [cf. *LE*, 52: "Poetry is a centaur. The thinking word-arranging, clarifying faculty must move and leap with the energizing, sentient, musical faculties. It is precisely the difficulty of this amphibious existence that keeps down the census record of good poets"].

48. arena: The arena at Verona, to which Pound refers in order to define his position as onlooker throughout the ages and levels of time [cf. also 11/50; 12/53; 29/145; 78/481; 80/505].

CANTO V

Sources

Herodotus, Historiae I, 96-103; Dante, *Par.* XVIII, 100, 108, *Inf.* V, 107, *Rime* I, 1; John Heydon, *The English Physitians Guide: or a Holy Guide*, 1662; J. A. Symonds, *In the Key of Blue*, 1893; Giordano Bruno, *De gli eroici furori* I, V, and II, I; Catullus LXI, 86, 131; LXII, 20, 26, 32, 35; Sappho/Aldington, 98D, 120D, 132aD, 133D, 137D; F. J. M. Raynouard, *Biographie des troubadours*, 1820, Vol. V of *Choix des poésies originales des troubadours*; Ida Farnell, *The Lives of the Troubadours*, London, 1896; Camille Chabaneau, *Les Biographies des Troubadours en Langue Provençale*, Toulouse, 1885; Robert Browning, "Meeting at Night" and "Parting at Morning"; A. H. Mathew, *The Life and Times of Rodrigo Borgia, Pope Alexander VI*, 1910; Benedetto Varchi, *Storia Fiorentina* (1527-1538), III, 262-263; Aeschylus, *Agamemnon*, 1344-1345; Homer, *Iliad* I, 159, 225; William Roscoe, *The Life and Pontificate of Leo the Tenth*, 1893; Martial V, 37.

Background

EP, *P*, "Coitus," "Phanopoeia," "Provincia Deserta," "Near Perigord, II," "Ἱμέρρω," "Horae Beatae Inscriptio," "Blandula, Tenella, Vagula"; *Mauberley* (Envoi, Medallion, The Age Demanded, IV); *ABCR*, 47-48; *GK*, 128, 223, 225; *LE*, 95-97, 99, 240; Iamblichus, *On the Mysteries of the Egyptians, Chaldeans, and Assyrians*, trans. Thomas Taylor, 3d ed., London, 1968; Porphyry, *De Occasionibus*, in Marsilio Ficino, *Opera Omnia* II, Paris, 1641, fol. 1931.

Exegeses

D. H. Tritschler, *Analyst* V; J. Drummond in *Ezra Pound* (symposium, ed. P. Russell); JE, *Mauberley*, 78; D. R. Stuart, "Modernistic Critics and Translators," *Princeton University Library Chronicle*, XI; HK, *Era*, 58, 64-66; F. Moramarco, "Schiavoni ...," and EH, "Schiavoni ...," *Pai*, 4-1; S. M. Libera, "Casting His Gods Back into the NOUS," *Pai*, 2-3; CFT, in *Pai*, 6-3, 359.

Glossary

1. Ecbatan: Ecbatana (Agbatana, now Hamadan), on the Iranian plateau in N Media, founded, according to Herodotus I, 98, by Deioces as capital of Median Empire [4:32].

2. The bride [4:33]. The additional relevance here is that the transition from the fertility rites of the earth cult to the cult of the sky and the heavenly bodies marks the beginnings of astronomy and the creation of the calendar, i.e., the measuring of time by observing the stars.

3. viae stradae: L, "streets."

4. and North was Egypt . . . water-wheels: As it leaves the Nubian Desert on its way northward to Egypt, the Nile cuts through flat barren land which is irrigated to support a small nomadic population.

5. Iamblichus: fl. 4th century A.D.; Greek, Neoplatonic light philosopher, his light denoting the oneness, the single principle from which the plurality of things derive ("measureless seas and stars"). Presumed author of *On the Mysteries of the Egyptians, Chaldeans and Assyrians* (trans. Thomas Taylor, Chiswick, 1821; London, 1968). "Iamblichus' light" refers to his teaching: " . . . the whole world being partible, is divided about the one and impartible light of the Gods. But this light is everywhere one and the same whole and is impartibly present with all things that are able to participate of it" [ibid., 46]. The idea of human participation in divine creativity outlined here provides a justification of divination in Iamblichus's teaching and also has important sexual implications for *The Cantos*: "We say that the erection of the *phalli* is a certain sign of prolific power, which, through this, is called forth to the generative energy of the world. On which account, also, many *phalli* are consecrated in the spring, because then the whole world receives from the gods the power which is productive of all generation" [ibid., 53].

6. ciocco: I, "log." The game of striking a burning log and counting the sparks that fly up was used in fortune-telling, i.e., foretelling the future as a safeguard against time's treachery [cf. *Par.* XVIII, 100].

7. Et omniformis: L, "and omniform." From "Omnis intellectus est omniformis" ["Every intellect is capable of assuming every shape"], the caption of the 3-line item 10 in Marsilio Ficino's [21:10] interpretation of Porphyry's *De Occasionibus, sive causis ad intelligibilia nos ducentibus*, in Ficino, *Opera Omnia* II, fol. 1931. Pound implies in Discarded Canto 3 (1917) that he came across the quotation in John Heydon's *Holy Guide*: "Let us hear John Heydon! / 'Omniformis / Omnis intellectus est'—thus he begins, by spouting half of Psellus. / (Then comes a note, my assiduous commentator: / Not Psellus *De Daemonibus*, but Porphyry's *Chances*, / In the thirteenth chapter, that 'every intellect is omniform')" [cf. 74/425-426, 430; 80/499; *Pai*, 6 (1977), 360] [EH].

8. Topaz: For Pound the color of Hymen, just as gold, yellow, saffron, amber, and orange symbolize erotic love and sexual union. The three sorts of blue represent three different dimensions of time: azure stands for the continuum in which the gods exist, i.e., the collective memory; sapphire, for personal memory; cobalt, for oblivion [cf. *P, Mauberley*: Envoi, Medallion, The Age Demanded, IV; "Blandula, Tenella, Vagula," "Horae Beatae Inscriptio"; and Canto III]. The "three sorts of blue" is a literal quotation from J. A. Symonds, *In the Key of Blue* (1893), where the author describes how he makes Augusto, his young Venetian friend, pose "dressed in three sorts of blue," which inspires him to write a series of poems to Augusto as "a symphony in blues," referred to variously as "triple blues" and "triple azures." Symonds, however, appreciates the colors esthetically, whereas Pound uses them symbolically [see 1:29, "Orichalchi"; 3:9, "azure"].

9. barb of time: Perhaps an allusion to Giordano Bruno's motto *vincit instans* ("the instant triumphs"), of which Bruno says that the creative instant or inspiration is a barb of light which pierces the mind to give one a totally new perception beyond all mere logic chopping. This links up with Pound's notions regarding the "luminous detail" [cf. *SP*, 21-23].

10. fire . . . and vision: Reference to *Par.* XVIII, 108, the vision coming from the fire and sparks forming the head of the eagle, symbol of the so-called Holy Roman Empire and of Justice. According to Iamblichus [cf. 5 above], the sign of divine possession, and therefore also of poetic inspiration, is a divine fire: "the presence of the fire of the gods, and a certain ineffable species of light, externally accede to him who is possessed, . . . they wholly fill him, have dominion over and circularly comprehend him on all sides, so that he is not able to exert any one proper energy" [op. cit., 125; cf. *GK*, 223-224: "Iamblichus on the fire of the gods, tou ton theon pyros, etc. which comes down into a man and produces superior ecstasies, feelings of regained youth, super-youth and so forth"; cf. also 23/107, "God's fire"].

11. gold-yellow, saffron. . . . The roman shoe: [cf. 8 above, 4:3; Catullus LXI].

12. shuffling feet: [Catullus LXI].

13. Da nuces!: L, "Give nuts!" [Catullus LXI, 131]. An implied reference to the bridegroom's betrayal of his former boy concubine, who is now summarily told to "give nuts" to the young boys. The distribution of nuts in the street to celebrate a marriage was an old Roman custom.

14. Sextus: Prob. a reference to *Homage to Sextus Propertius* VII, suggesting that Catul-

lus and S. Propertius, being contemporaries, may both have known Aurunculeia.

15. Hesperus: L, "evening star" [Catullus LXII, 20, 26, 32, 35; 2:29].

16. older song: [cf. Sappho 120D, 132aD, 133D, which are older than the Catullus references noted above]. Pound repeatedly associates the poetic techniques of Sappho and Catullus so that their names often crop up together.

17. Lydia . . . Sardis: Cf. Sappho 98D and 137D via translation of Aldington, where Atthis is denounced for having turned from Sappho to Andromeda.

18. "In satieties": [cf. Sappho 137D]. "Atthis, you grew fed up with being with me in your thoughts" [cf. HK, *Era*, 54-71].

19. Atthis unfruitful: [cf. Sappho 98D]. Sappho is betrayed by her lover Atthis. The word "unfruitful" is owing to Richard Aldington's translation, in which the Aeolian ἀγάνας ["gentle"] is misread as ἄγονος ["unfruitful"] [cf. *P, 'Ιμέρρω*].

20. Mauleon: Savaric de M., d. 1236, seneschal of Peiteu [F, Poitou], professional soldier and poet, patron of Gausbertz de Poicebot and other troubadours [cf. *LE*, 95, 99; 48/243].

21. Poicebot . . . : Gausbertz de Puegsibot [F, Poicebot], a monk who became a troubadour. Roaming in search of sexual adventures, he believes his wife to be safely at home with the rest of his possessions, but finds her drifting like himself, the first to offer herself to him in a brothel, matching his betrayal with her own. "And for this grief he ceased to sing and to compose" [cf. *LE*, 96; 48/243].

22. romerya: P, *romeria*, lit. "pilgrimage," fig. "roaming, roving" ("for desire of woman he [the monk Poicebot] went forth from the monastery") [*LE*, 95].

23. Lei fassa furar a del: P, wrong transcription of *se laisset ad el* ("yielded herself to him"), a line referring to Peire de Maensac in Raynouard's *Biographie*. Pound conflates two stories: Gausbertz de Poicebot's wife was seduced by an English knight who, after abducting her, "let her go to the dogs," whereas Peire de M. seduced the wife of Bernart de Tierci who "let herself go" ("yielded herself / furar ad el"). The juxtaposition points up the opposing attitudes of the two troubadours to sex and property: the possessive Gausbertz de Poicebot, whose concern for property was already indicated in the part of the story referring to Savaric de Mauleon, loses all, including his creative powers, whereas Peire de M., careless of property, gains all and also keeps the woman he abducted [cf. *LE*, 96-97].

24. Sea-change: Another symbol of time. Perhaps an echo of "Suffer a sea-change / Into something rich and strange" [*Tempest*, I, ii, 464].

25. Hard night, and parting at morning: A combination of the titles of Browning's two poems, "Meeting at Night" and "Parting at Morning."

26. Pieire de Maensac: Peire de M. Peire and his brother Austors had too small a patrimony for both to live on, so they agreed, by means unknown (Pound invents the story of the tossed coin), that Austors should take the castle and Peire should become a troubadour [cf. "Provincia Deserta," where Peire "set on the high way to sing"]. The theme of possessiveness versus the free unencumbered poetic spirit is thus exemplified in the story of the two brothers [cf. *LE*, 96-97; 23/108-109].

27. dreitz hom: P, "an upstanding fellow" [*LE*, 97].

28. Troy in Auvergnat: The drama of ancient Troy paralleled on a smaller scale in Auvergnat, the territory of the Dalfin of Alvernhe, who protected Peire de Maensac and the wife of Bernart de Tierci from her irate husband [cf. 23, 26, 29, 30, 31]. Not a reference to Troyes in Département Aube.

29. Menelaus: Helen of Troy's husband, here used with reference to Bernart de Tierci.

30. Tyndarida: H, "Daughter of Tyndareus." The wife of Bernart de Tierci is here compared with Helen of Troy, daughter of Leda and Zeus, Leda being wife to Tyndareus, king of Sparta [2:8; "Provincia Deserta"; 23/108-109].

31. Dauphin: The Dalfin of Alvernhe, who protected de Maensac and the wife of de Tierci from her husband when he came after them "in the manner of the golden Menelaus" [cf. *LE*, 97].

32. John Borgia: Giovanni B., Duke of Gandia, son of Pope Alexander VI and Vanozza Catanei ("Vanoka" in 20/95), and younger brother of Cesare and Lucrecia Borgia. He was murdered on the night of June 14, 1497, in Rome and his body was thrown into the Tiber [cf. *Pai*, 4-1, 101 ff]. The element of treason arises here between brothers, Cesare having been suspected (wrongly) of having had Giovanni murdered.

33. Varchi: Benedetto V., 1503-1565, Italian classical scholar, wrote a history of Florence covering the years 1527-1538 [*Storia Fiorentina*, first printed 1721], in which the ruling Medici come in for objective criticism. Varchi is here turning over in his mind the possible motive behind the near-fratricidal murder of Alessandro Medici by his libertarian friend and cousin Lorenzo Medici. The juxtaposition of the Borgia and Medici murders is linked in turn with the murder of Caesar by Brutus, his protégé and supposed friend.

34. Brutus: Lorenzo was compared with the tyrannicide Brutus by his contemporaries.

35. Σίγα μαλ' αὖθις δευτέραν!: H, "Silence once more a second time." Lines 1344-1345 of Aeschylus's *Agamemnon* jumbled together: "*Leader of chorus*: Silence! Hark! Who cries he has been struck a mortal blow? *Agamemnon*: Again, I have been struck a second time." Agamemnon, returning home to his wife Clytemnestra after the long war years before Troy, gets into the warm bath she has prepared. There she stabs him ["bumped off in his bath," 96/652] [see also "Atreides" (Agamemnon, being of the line of Atreus) at 8/32, 82/523, 89/602].

36. "Dog-eye!!": A reference to Achilles' description of Agamemnon as "dog-eyed" or "dog-faced" (*Iliad* I, 159, 225). The tyrannicide Lorenzo, who was compared by contemporaries with Brutus, is compared here with Achilles; Alessandro is compared with Agamemnon [cf. *LE*, 250, "the dog-faced, chicken-hearted Agamemnon"].

37. Benedetto: B. Varchi [cf. 33 above].

38. Se pia? O empia?: I, "Whether noble / Or ignoble?" [Varchi III, 262; cf. 58 below].

39. Lorenzaccio: The name of abuse generally used for Lorenzo Medici by his contemporaries and frequently by Varchi. Also called Lorenzo and Lorenzino [cf. 7/27; 26/126].

40. Alessandro: A. Medici [cf. 33 above; 7/27].

41. O se credesse: I, "Or himself believed" [cf. 45 below].

42. Caina attende: I, "Caina is waiting" [*Inf.* V, 107]. Words addressed by Francesca da Rimini to Dante to transmit to her husband, Gianciotto Malatesta, who had murdered her and her lover, his own brother Paolo. Caina, named after the Cain who slew his brother Abel, is the first of the four divisions of the ninth circle of Hell. It is pictured as a frozen lake and reserved for traitors to kindred.

43. dreamed out beforehand: Alessandro had been forewarned of his impending assassination three times in his own dreams as well as by the horoscope worked out by the astrologer Giuliano del Carmine. Perugia is the capital of Umbria in C Italy.

44. abuleia: Abulia, a mental state characterized by the impairment of volition, so that the subject is pathologically irresolute [cf. 54/285; 93/627].

45. O se morisse, credesse caduto da sè: I, "Or if he were killed, believe he had fallen by himself." Pound's variation of Varchi III, 262, which reads: "One night he was tempted to push him from a wall, but he feared that either he would not be killed or, if killed, it would not be believed he had fallen by himself ("ma ebbe paura o che egli non morisse, o che pure morendo, *non si credesse lui esser caduto da se*"). Varchi is reporting Lorenzo's own account of his hesitations before the actual murder, which attest to the depth of his pathological hatred for Alessandro [cf. 7/27].

46. Schiavoni: I, "Slavonians." The reference is to the man on the wood barge, Giorgio of the Slavonians, a colony of Dalmatian refugees who had been allowed by Pope Sixtus IV to settle in the quarter around the Church of S. Girolamo degli Schiavoni. Giorgio had seen the body of Giovanni Borgia, Duke of Gandia, thrown into the Tiber late at night on June 14, 1497.

47. Barabello: Baraballo of Gaeta, a society poet during the papacy of Leo X who aspired to be crowned, like Petrarch, with a wreath of laurels at the Capitol. Leo X placed at his disposal the white elephant he had received as a gift from the king of Portugal. Attired in a toga palmata and latus clavus like an ancient Roman, the venerable sexagenarian set off for the Capitol on the back of the elephant. At the bridge of S. Angelo the animal was frightened by the fireworks celebrating the festival of the saints Cosmo and Damian and refused to go farther, so Baraballo was forced to descend.

48. Mozarello: Giovanni Mozzarello or Muzarelli, a talented young Mantuan poet and scholar who wrote in elegant Latin and Italian under the names Arelius Mutius and

Arelio Mutio. Leo X (1513-1521) made him governor of the fort of Mondaino, near Rimini, as a sinecure that would allow him to continue his studies. Before he could finish his epic poem *Porsenna* he was pushed by resentful local residents down a well together with his mule, where after a search lasting more than a month both were found suffocated. Ariosto placed him among the foremost scholars of his age in *Orl. Fur. Cant.* 42, st. 87: *Uno elegante Castiglione, e un culto Mutio Arelio*. The phrase "a poet's ending" could be intended to recall Horace, *Ars poetica*, 478-481.

49. Sanazarro: Sannazzaro, 1458-1530, a poet of Naples who composed a famous epigram on the murder of the Duke of Gandia implying incest as a motive: "Piscatorem hominum ne te non, Sexte, putemus, / Piscaris natum retibus, ecce, tuum" ["Sextus, let us not think that you are a fisher of men, / Behold, you catch your own son with nets"].

50. Fracastor: Girolamo Fracastoro, 1483-1553, physician and poet, author of *Syphilis sive de morbo gallico* which describes in symbolic form the symptoms, development, and treatment of the "French disease" to which he gave the name "syphilis." Escaped death as a baby in his mother's arms when she was killed by lightning. The story also recalls the birth of Zagreus/Dionysus, when Zeus appeared to the pregnant Semele as a flash of lightning.

51. Cotta: Giovanni Cotta, 1480-1510, Italian poet and scholar and a friend of Fracastoro's. Helped the general Bartolomeo D'Alviano to found an academy of the arts.

52. Ser D'Alviano: Bartolomeo D'Alviano, 1455-1515, a general in the service of the Orsini, suspected for a time of the murder of the Duke of Gandia. Founded an academy of the arts with the aid of Giovanni Cotta.

53. Al poco giorno ed al gran cerchio d'ombra: I, fig., "In the small hours with the darkness describing a huge circle" [Dante, *Rime* I, 1; the line is repeated at 116/797]. Dante was here imitating the style of Arnaut Daniel. [EH].

54. Navighero: Andreas Navagerius or Andrea Navagero, 1483-1529, a Venetian poet who wrote in Latin and Italian. When a gathering of poets praised his verses for being in the vein of Martial, he was so indignant that he publicly burned them, later recording his resentment in four distichs. According to some accounts the ceremonial burning of imitation Martials was repeated annually.

55. slavelet . . . vain: Martial mourns the death of the little slave girl, Erotion, in the three poems V, 34, 37 and X, 61. Martial's Erotion appears to have something in common with the nymphet Erotion in a poem by Lukillios in the Greek Anthology: "When a gnat kidnapped Erotion for a lark / The nymphet chirruped: 'Right on, Papa Zeus, if it's me you want'" [EH].

56. Nine wounds: The nine wounds found on the body of the Duke of Gandia in addition to his throat having been cut [cf. 32 above].

57. "Four men, white horse . . . thing!:" Testimony of Giorgio of the Schiavoni who saw the body of the Duke of Gandia thrown into the Tiber [cf. 32, 46, above].

58. Se pia, . . . O empia, ma risoluto e terribile deliberazione: Source has *risoluta*. I, "Whether noble or ignoble, certainly a resolute and terrible decision" [Varchi III, 262]. Varchi leaves the question as to Lorenzo's good or evil motives for the murder open [7:44].

59. Ma se morisse: I, "But if he were killed." Words of Lorenzo as reported by Varchi except that Pound has substituted *ma* ("but") for *o* ("or").

CANTO VI

Sources

Camille Chabaneau, *Les Biographies des Troubadours en Langue Provençale*, Toulouse, 1885; Ida Farnell, *The Lives of the Troubadours*, London, 1896; Carl Appel, *Bernart von Ventadorn*, Halle, 1915; Cesare de Lollis, *Vita e Poesie di Sordello di Goito*, Halle, 1896.

Background

EP, *P*, "Planh for the Young English King," "Provincia Deserta," "Sestina Altaforte," "Near Perigord"; *SR*, 41-42; *LE*, 34-35, 97-99, 158; *PM*, 28; *T*, 427; Giambattista Verci, *Storia degli Ecelini*, III, Bassano, 496-498; Dante, *Inf.* XII, 110, XXVIII, 134, *Pur.* VI, 58, *Par.* IX, 25 ff.; R. Browning, *Sordello*; Wace, *Brut*; Benoit de Sainte-Marie, *Roman de Troie*; William of Newburgh (chronicle of Eleanor's divorce); Richard Howlett, ed., *The Chronicle of Robert of Torigni*, London, 1889, 318-319; Lionel Landon, *The Itinerary of King Richard I*, London, 1935, 220-222; G. P. R. James, *A History of the Life of Richard Coeur-de-Lion*, London, 1864, II, 254-255; Alfred Jeanroy, *Les Chansons de Guillaume IX, Duc d'Aquitaine*, Paris, 1913, lines 8-13; Amy Kelly, *Eleanor of Aquitaine and the Four Kings*, Cambridge, Mass., 1951.

Exegeses

Thelma C. Balagot, *Analyst* III, R. Schneideman, *Analyst* IV, 1954; Dekker, *Sailing*, 51-52, 132-133; HK, *Era*, 339 ff.; CB-R, *Approaches*, 254; DD, *Approaches* 198-214; for a translation of "La Chronique de Rains," see *Three Old French Chronicles of the Crusades*, trans. E. Noble Stone, Seattle, 1939; JW, *Later*; JE, *Pai*, 8, 298.

Glossary

1. **"What have you done, Odysseus"**: Possibly a reworking or an echo of the sirens' song [*Od*. XII, 185 ff.; 1:24]. The similarity between the careers of Odysseus and Guillaume de Poitou is pinpointed by referring to the ancient biographical note on Guillaume reprinted in Chabaneau, p. 213: "Lo

Coms de Peitieus si fo uns dels majors cortes del mon, e dels majors trichadors de dompnas; e bons cavalliers d'armas, e larcs de dompneiar. E saup ben trobar e cantar; & anet lonc temps per lo mon per enganar las domnas." ["The Count of Poitou was one of the foremost courtiers in the world, one of the foremost deceivers of women; and a good knight at arms and free with women. And was a good troubadour and singer; and long roamed the world for the sake of duping women."]

2. Guillaume: William IX, 1071-1127, 9th Duke of Aquitaine and 7th Count of Poitou. His participation in the First Crusade (1101) with a large retinue of women turned into a hilarious but disastrous joyride. The canto reference appears to relate to his pilgrimage to Santiago di Compostela, whence he "brought the song up out of Spain" [cf. 8/32], thus becoming the first troubadour and the real instigator of Provençal poetry. The reference to ground rents indicates Guillaume's readiness to fritter away his fortune in order to finance his escapades. Raymond of Poitou was his second son [cf. 12 below] and Eleanor, his granddaughter. In relation to Eleanor there is the special irony that one of Guillaume's few extant songs consists of a passionate denunciation of the practice of locking up women who have given reason for jealousy. He was an "inventor" in the sense defined in *ABCR*, 39 [cf. *LE*, 94; *SR*, 39, 53; 8/32; 91/610; 100/721; 105/750].

3. Eleanor: [2:7, 9; 7:1].

4. Tant . . . vetz: Direct quotation of lines 79-80 of poem by Guillaume beginning *Farai un vers, pos mi somelh* ("I'll write a verse and take a nap"), telling of his meeting two women of noble birth who, believing him to be a mute, invited him to a week-long orgy. The lines say: "I fucked them, as you will hear, 100 + 4 x 20 + 8 times."

5. Stone . . . death year: An invocation of the prehistoric concept of kingship, where the cycle of life and death, running from sexual prowess to sacrificial regicide, is linked with the fertility of the earth just as Pound links Guillaume's sexuality with the initiation of a culture in which architecture emerges as "the first of the arts" [*PM*, 27: "Architecture consists of fitting a form to a purpose"; cf. DD, *Approaches*, on Pound's idea of "the stone alive"]. The architecture

of Poitiers is to assume a special significance for Pound later on [cf. 90/605].

6. Louis . . . Eleanor: Louis VII of France, ?1121-1180, and Eleanor of Aquitaine married on July 25, 1137, in Bordeaux, Eleanor being 15 and Louis 16 [for Eleanor, 2:7, 9; 7:1].

7. Duchess of Normandia: Since Eleanor became Duchess of Normandy and Countess of Anjou through her second marriage to Henry Plantagenet, Pound's source is in error. For "Duchess of Normandia" read "daughter of the Countess of Châtellerault," who had been one of Guillaume's more notorious mistresses. Eleanor was known as the Duchess of Normandy in her home country because she acquired that title on marrying Henry Plantagenet in 1152. Henry P. did not become Henry II of England until 1154, when he and Eleanor were crowned at Westminster. She was called the "Duchess of N." because the domain of her suzerain lord, Louis VII, was negligible and poor (the Ile-de-France, Orleans, and a part of Berry) compared with Eleanor's domain, which included the duchy of Aquitaine, the county of Poitiers, the duchy of Gascogne, and nineteen "départements" (in present parlance), combined with Henry's duchy of Normandy and the county of Anjou. From the Indre to the Basses-Pyrénées, it was all "her" territory.

8. e maire del rei jove: *P*, "and mother to the young king." The "jove rey" Henry, 1155-1183, son of Eleanor and Henry, was commonly praised as having all the virtues desirable for a ruler [cf. Pound's adaptation of Bertrans de Born's *planh* ("lament"), "Si tuit li dol e·lh plor e·lh marrimen," in *P*, 36-37]. The younger Henry was called the "young king" because Henry II had him and his young wife, Margaret (daughter of Louis), crowned in 1172, during his own reign, in order to placate Louis for the murder of young Henry's tutor and friend, Thomas à Becket. Young Henry was supposed to be king in name only, but he did not see it that way. Bertrans de Born was his friend and follower whom Dante placed in

Hell for having made strife between young Henry and his father [*Inf.* XXVIII, 134]. Altogether Eleanor bore Henry nine children, of whom only her firstborn son, William, died in childhood; all the others, daughters as well as sons, were exceptionally gifted and played major roles in history or the arts [cf. also "Near Perigord" in *P*, 151-156].

9. Went over sea . . . : An echo of the *Odyssey*. But Louis and Eleanor (aged 25), on this Second Crusade, took the land route through Hungary, Bulgaria, Byzance, and Adalia (Satalia), and traveled by sea only from there to Antioch (1147). The journey, lasting ten months and filled with hardship and mishaps, soured their relationship. Now estranged, Eleanor and Louis returned by sea separately via Sicily and Italy, where in Tusculum Pope Eugenius III (1149) temporarily patched up their marital differences.

10. Acre: Important port in all crusades, belonging to the kingdom of Jerusalem. Eleanor and Louis did not land at Acre but at Saint Siméon, the small harbor of the city of Antioch, situated at the foot of the mountain range called Jebel Accra [cf. 94/640-641].

11. Ongla, oncle: *P*, lit. "fingernail, uncle," a sexual double-entendre. From Arnaut Daniel's sestina beginning *Lo ferm voler qu'el cor m'intra* ["The longing that pierces my heart"], the first line of its three-line tornada reading "Arnautz tramet sa chansson d'ongla e d'oncle" ["Arnaut transmits his song of fingernail and uncle"].

12. Her uncle . . . : Raymond of Toulouse, younger brother of Eleanor's father, a handsome and romantic figure who had become prince of Antioch. A special relationship developed between Eleanor and Raymond, who was only eight years older than she and had been her playmate in childhood. This relationship was strengthened because the language spoken at Antioch was her native langue d'oc (incomprehensible to Louis and his men) and because Raymond had brought troubadours to the city.

13. Theseus, son of Aegeus: The exploits of Raymond, son of Guillaume, are compared here with those of Theseus, because Theseus also owed much of his success to his involvements with women. Raymond had been invited to the Holy Land by Fulco, king of Jerusalem, in order to marry the Princess Constanza, heiress to the principality of Antioch, then ruled by her widowed mother Alix. Raymond gained the confidence of the mother by first pretending he wanted to marry her, not her daughter.

14. Louis . . . not at ease: During this time Eleanor was first heard to say that she thought she had married a monk. She took to the oriental atmosphere like a fish to water, while Louis's ascetic nature was revolted by life in Antioch. Raymond pleaded for a campaign to regain Edessa, whose fall had been the real reason for the Second Crusade, but Louis insisted on continuing his pious pilgrimage to Jerusalem. Seeing the value of Raymond's strategic considerations, Eleanor strongly seconded his argument. Louis invoked his marital authority. In response Eleanor said that their marriage was null and void in the eyes of the church because of their consanguinity. The further development of the crusade bore out Raymond's argument. Louis and Eleanor returned home by sea with nothing achieved; in June Raymond had been killed by Nureddin (commander of the infidel forces) and his head cut off and sent to the caliph of Bagdad.

15. Cimier: F, "helmet." A baseless myth invented or at least recorded by the anonymous minstrel of Reims in *La Chronique de Rains*. It was Nureddin who commanded the infidel forces; Saladin at that time was a boy of 12 who was destined to reconquer Jerusalem in 1187 and to play a major role in the life of Eleanor's son Richard. Pound himself has attached Eleanor's scarf to Saladin's helmet as a luminous detail.

16. Divorced her: Another baseless myth; the opposite was true. Eleanor insisted on the annulment of her marriage on the grounds of consanguinity, as correctly recorded by the chronicler William of Newburgh. Eleanor and Louis had had only two children, Marie and Alix, in 15 years of marriage. Thus Louis lost not only Aquitaine but also, through Eleanor's marriage with Henry Plantagenet, the entire western region of his realm. Eleanor married Henry in May 1152, only two months after the annulment without the legally required permission of Louis, who was still the suzerain lord of both Eleanor and Henry.

17. Henry Plantagenet: 1133-1189, Henry II of England.

18. (that had dodged . . . suitors): After her separation from Louis had become final, Eleanor and a small train of followers took to the road to return to Poitiers. On her way she was set upon by various minor nobles who hoped to kidnap her and force her into marriage.

19. Et quand . . . fasché: F, "And when King Louis heard it he was much riled."

20. Nauphal: Territory with fort forming part of dowry of Margaret, daughter of Louis VII and his second wife, for her marriage with Henry, son of Henry II and Eleanor. Now known as Néaufles.

21. Vexis: Vexin, a territory along the border of Normandy and France, long in dispute between the two countries. To improve Franco-Norman relations and in pursuit of their common policy of uniting all the great powers of Europe through strategic marriages with their children, Henry II and Eleanor arranged for their son Henry to marry Margaret, daughter of Louis VII by a second marriage. The scheme was conceived because Louis had not as yet produced a male heir and Margaret was preceded in her claim to the French throne only by Eleanor's two daughters, Marie and Alix. Margaret's dowry included the Vexin territory and the fortresses of Nauphal, Gisors, and Neufchastel [now Neufchâtel]. Margaret was betrothed to Henry as a baby of six

months and shipped to England to be reared by her husband's family, Louis's only stipulation being that Eleanor should have no say in her upbringing. The wedding ceremony was performed when Margaret was two. Henry and Eleanor then jointly seized the Norman Vexin. Since the Templars guarding Gisors saw no reason not to surrender the keys, Louis expelled their order from Paris. When Henry, the "young king," died, Margaret was married to the king of Hungary and her dowry went to her sister Adelaide, another of Louis's daughters, who had been betrothed to Richard in 1169.

22. joven: P, "young," referring to the young king, Henry [cf. 8 above].

23. Gisors: A commanding fortress on the river Epte in Normandy. Part of Margaret's dowry [cf. 21 above].

24. Neufchastel: Neufchâtel, a fortress in the region of Rouen and part of Margaret's dowry.

25. Alix: Pound's source is in error. Alix, daughter of Louis and Eleanor, could hardly have married her half brother Richard, son of Henry and Eleanor. It was Adelaide [see 21 above] who was betrothed to Richard and shipped to England at the age of eight to become the ward of Henry II, who subsequently got her with child. Eleanor was again excluded from having any hand in the upbringing of the child. Thus Richard, now heir apparent, refused to marry Adelaide, while the French king demanded the return of either the princess or the fortress of Gisors. Estranged from his father on account of this scandal, Richard sided with the French king, now Philip II, son of Louis VII, saying: "What heretofore I could not believe, emerges now as clear as day." The French king eventually realized the need for the betrothal between Adelaide and Richard to be dissolved, and the marriage contract was annulled at Messina in 1191. Pound quotes from a text in which the scribe wrongly recorded the name of Alix in place of Adelaide.

26. Richard Plantagenet: Known as Richard Coeur de Lion, 1157-1199 [cf. 25 above; 7:1; also *P*, "Near Perigord," "Provincia Deserta," "Sestina Altaforte"; 97/671].

27. domna jauzionda: *P*, "radiant lady," from line 52 of the poem "Tant ai mo cor ple de joya" addressed by Bernart de Ventadour to Eleanor upon her return to Provence after her separation from Louis VII at the age of 30. Bernart, having been banished from the court of Eblis, went to Poitiers, where Eleanor had just arrived. From now on his poems are addressed to her.

28. Malemort, Correze: The ruins of Malemort Castle, which Pound and his wife Dorothy appear to have visited after passing the "river-marsh" of the river Corrèze and a "galleried church-porch" on July 24, 1919, during their walking tour of Provence. Occupied in 1177 by free lances and their wives and children, the castle was attacked by the combined forces of the suzerain lord of Limousin and the bishop. Those who survived the onslaught were taken prisoner and slaughtered in cold blood. The castle was henceforth given the name Malemort or Malamort, meaning "malign death." Shortly afterward it became the residence of the Lady Audiart (Na Audiart) of Malemort, the subject of the poem by Bertrans de Born translated by Pound in *P*, 8-9 [4:26, 41; "Provincia Deserta," *P*, 121-123; "Near Perigord," *P*, 151-156] [EH].

29. My Lady of Ventadour: Margarida of Torena married Eblis III of Ventadour in 1148, who shut her up in a dungeon out of jealousy. He repudiated her in 1150 in order to marry Alice of Montpellier, while she in turn married Guilhem IV of Angoulême the same year.

30. Nor watch fish rise to bait: Suggested by line 8 (*Aissi co ·l peis qui s'eslaiss' el cadorn*) ["Like the fish that rises to the bait"] in the poem of Bernart beginning *Be m'an perdut lai enves Ventadorn* ["My friends around Ventadorn have surely seen the last of me"], probably addressed to

Alaiz de Montpellier, second wife of Eblis III.

31. Que la lauzeta mover: *P*, "Quan(t) vei la lauzeta mover / de joi sas alas contral rai, / que s'oblid' e·s laissa chazer / per la doussor c'al cor li vai." A poem by Bernart de Ventadour which Pound translates [*SR*, 41]: "When I see the lark a-moving / For joy his wings against the sunlight, / Who forgets himself and lets himself fall / For the sweetness which goes into his heart." It is with this poem that Bernart is said to have won the heart of Margarida, first wife of Eblis III.

32. E lo Sordels . . . : [2:3].

33. Sier Escort: Sier El Cort, father of Sordello. Pound has misread the letter *l* as a long *s*.

34. Cunizza da Romano: 1198-1279, married (ca. 1232) Ricciardo di San Bonifazio, the Bonifazi being the leading Guelphs of the region. Her brother, Ezzelino da Romano II, 1194-1259, podesta of Verona and one of the most homicidal rulers in Italian history, is said to have been responsible for more than 50,000 executions which in many instances wiped out entire noble families. One year after Ezzelino's death, Cunizza's brother Alberic was forced by hunger to surrender unconditionally the castle of San Zeno. His sons and daughters were tortured and killed before his eyes, and he himself was dragged to his death tied to a horse. Cunizza left her husband for Sordello. Her act of releasing her brother's slaves on April 1, 1265, symbolizes for Pound her freedom from possessiveness.

35. Masnatas et servos: ML, "Domestics and slaves." "Cunizza soror Ecelini de Romano emancipat, & libertati donat Masnatas & servos fratrum suorum" [cf. Verci, III, 496].

36. Picus de Farinatis . . . : Pichinus de F., Don Elinus, and Don Lipus, mentioned in the document of manumission by which Cunizza freed her brother's slaves, were sons of Farinata degli Uberti (d. 1264), head of the Ghibelline faction, who reconquered Florence from the Guelphs in 1260. His daughter Beatrice married Guido Cavalcanti [cf. *Inf*. X]. Pound surmises that Dante consigned the elder Cavalcanti to hell because the rather free table talk in the Uberti household had shocked his orthodox mind [cf. *LE*, 158]. The descent of his Fascist friend, Admiral Ubaldo degli Uberti [78/480], from this family impressed Pound deeply.

37. A marito . . . .concubuisse: L, Sordello "took her away from her husband and is supposed to have slept with her." Direct quotation from Rolandini chronicle, lib. V, cap 3, in Chabaneau: "Sordellus de ipsius familia dominam ipsam latenter a marito subtraxit, cum qua in patris curia permanente, dictum fuit ipsum Sordellum concubuisse" ["Sordello stealthily detached from her husband and family the lady with whom he is said to have slept at her father's official residence"].

38. "Winter and Summer . . . / . . . remember her.": An adaptation of lines 2, 5, 6 and 8 of Sordello's poem beginning "Atretan deu ben chantar finamen": "D'invern com fatz d'estiu, . . . (2) / Quar la rosa senbla lei de cui chan, (5) / Aultresi es la neus del sieu senblan: (6) / Tant fort mi fai . . . el neu menbrar (8).

39. Cairels was of Sarlat: Pound's translation from the Provençal biographical

notice on the troubadour Elias Cairel, fl. 1220-1230, beginning "Elias Cairels si fo de Sarlat," given by Chabaneau. Pound translates the entire notice in *LE*, 98-99: "Elias Cairels was of Sarlat; ill he sang, ill he composed, ill he played the fiddle and worse he spoke, but he was good at writing out words and tunes. And he was a long time wandering, and when he quitted it, he returned to Sarlat and died there."

40. Theseus from Troezene: Theseus, having grown up in Troezene with his mother Aethra, was not known to his father Aegeus. Before leaving Aethra, Aegeus buried a sword and sandals under a rock, telling Aethra that his son should join him in Athens as soon as he was strong enough to lift the rock. When Theseus eventually got to Athens, he was not recognized by his father but only by Medea, whom his father had married in the interim. Jealous of the interests of Medus, her son by Aegeus, as heir apparent, Medea persuaded Aegeus that Theseus was a spy or an assassin and plotted with Aegeus to have him poisoned. But when Theseus was invited to the feast at the Dolphin Temple, where a beaker of wine poisoned with wolfsbane was set before him, Aegeus noticed from the Erechtheid serpents carved in the guest's ivory sword hilt that it had to be his son and thereupon dashed the poison to the floor.

CANTO VII

Sources

Aeschylus, *Agamemnon*, 689-690; Homer, *Iliad* III, 151-160, I, 34; Sextus Propertius; Ovid, *Ars Amatoria* I, 151, *Elegies* II, XVI, 43-46; Bertrans de Born, "B'em platz lo gais temps de Pascor"; Dante, *Inf*. IV, 112, III, 64, XII, 110, *Pur*. VI, 63, *Par*. XVIII, 100, II, 1; Flaubert, *Un Coeur Simple*; J. Joyce, *Ulysses*, Ithaca; Virgil, *Aeneid* I, IV; H. James, *The Jolly Corner, The Sense of the Past*; E. and J. de Goncourt, *Germinie Lacerteux*; Ovid, *Meta*. X,

586 ff.; Arthur Golding, *P. Ovidius Naso: The XV Bookes, entytuled Metamorphosis*, X, 586 ff.; Luiz de Camoëns, *Os Lusíadas* II, xcvii, 3-4; Arnaut Daniel, "Doutz brais et critz"; Benedetto Varchi, *Storia Fiorentina*, III.

Background

EP, *LE*; *SR*; *NPL*; *P*; "Stele," "Moeurs Contemporaines VII," "Ione, Dead the Long Year," "Dance Figure," "Liu Ch'e"; *L*, 274 (to W. H. D. Rouse); "Conversations in Courtship," *Criterion*, Jan. 1923; *Dial*, Nov. 1922, 554; *LPJ*; J. Joyce, *Ulysses*; T. S. Eliot, *The Waste Land*, "Gerontion"; Matthew Arnold, *The Study of Celtic Literature*; H. James, *The Beast in the Jungle, The Spoils of Poynton*; René Descharmes, *Autour de Bouvard et Pécuchet*, 1921; Flaubert, *Bouvard et Pécuchet*, 1881; R. de Gourmont, *NPL*, 154-155; University of Chicago Library, MSS, Dec. 3, 1912; *Observer*, London, Feb. 23, 1969; YC, no. 538; *Chelsea Mail*, London, Aug. 9, 1912; U. A. Canello and R. Lavaud, *Les Poésies d'Arnaut Daniel*, Halle, 1893; A. Stimming, *Bertrans de Born*, Halle, 1892.

Exegeses

Schneideman, *Analyst* IV and VI, 1954; Dekker, *Sailing*, 15-28 and passim; FR in *Approaches*; EH, *B. E. P.*, 99-131; HK, *Era*, 119-120, 338-339; JE, *Mauberley* (chapter on H. James and R. de Gourmont); Norman, *EP*, 114-115; CB-R, *ZBC*; Peter Makin, *Provence and Pound*.

Glossary

1. Eleanor (she spoiled in a British climate): Since this remark is in no way supported by the evidence of Eleanor's creative and active life up to the age of 82, it could perhaps be intended as (*a*) an ironical expression of the general vacuity of public opinion, which preferred Henry Plantagenet's paramour, Rosamond Clifford (Giraut de Barrie's *Rose immonde*, "impure rose"), to the emancipated and intellectual foreigner, Eleanor; (*b*) a reference to the 15 years during which Eleanor was held in durance by Henry following their break after 15 years of dynamic teamwork, in the course of which, besides bearing him seven children, she was constantly traveling between England and her own domain, Aquitaine, and shared fully in all political decision making. The break occurred because Henry found profligacy more amusing than Eleanor's Provençal concept of "creative love," which had up to then defined their relationship. After the beginning of Henry's affair with Rosamond, which coincided with the birth of his and Eleanor's youngest son, John, Eleanor returned with all her children except John, her children-in-law, and her two daughters by Louis, to Poitiers, where for 8 years she maintained a center of poetry and music. Her children, not without cause [2:9], sided with Louis VII against their father. Henry thereupon attacked Poitiers with an army of mercenaries and laid waste the land. Fleeing disguised as a page, Eleanor was recognized by Henry's men and dragged off to England for a long period of enforced inactivity. Free again at the age of 67, she ruled both England and Aquitaine for her son Richard, remaining a positive force in European affairs and culture until her death in 1204. The more likely explanation for the line is, however, Pound's sudden disregard for historical facts and justice occasioned by his disillusionment with England, which had forced him to emigrate to Paris in the winter of 1920-21, the approximate date of this canto's origin [6:2, 7; *Analyst* III, IV].

2. Έλανδρος **and** Ελέπτολις: H, "mandestroying and city-destroying," a repetition of the traditional puns on the name of Helen of Troy, which Pound here extends to Eleanor [2:8]. The line fixes the origin of the literature inspired by Helen's beauty: the *Iliad* and the *Odyssey*.

3. poor old Homer . . . : The first literary reflection of beauty via the sensibility of Homer, who transmitted it for all ages even though he never saw it with his own eyes but only "echoes it" in the terrified chatter of the old men at the Skaian gate when confronted with Helen's person. The beauty that set off all the echoes in literature is therefore actually but an echo of an echo. At the same time the episode introduces in this canto the theme of the rejection of life by the living dead [cf. *Iliad* III, 151-152].

4. Ear, ear for the sea-surge: A reference to the "magnificent onomatopoeia, as of the rush of the waves on the sea-beach and their recession" [*LE*, 250; *L*, 274, viz. the *polyphloisboio* in *Iliad* I, 34; cf. also "Stele," *P*, 181; 74/427; 92/620].

5. Rattle of old men's voices . . . : Here Pound is trying, in turn, to recapture the "authentic cadence" of the Homeric original as described in *LE*, 250 [cf. *Analyst* IV]. The Homeric passage compares the old men's voices to the chirpings of cicadas [cf. "words like locust-shells"; cf. 13, 32, 35, 37 below].

6. And then the phantom Rome: Homer's sonorous cadence echoing the sea surge is superseded by Ovid's sophisticated table talk. Roman mythology, architecture, art, and literature are commonly regarded as second-rate imitations of the Greek prototypes, but Pound finds something added to the art of writing: "we may suppose that the Romans added a certain sophistication; at any rate, Catullus, Ovid, Propertius, all give us something we cannot find now in Greek authors" [*LE*, 27].

7. "marble narrow for seats": Ovid advises the reader to pick out a shapely girl as she is about to enter the theater and follow her to a seat where they will be forced to sit squeezed together [*Ars amatoria* I, 133-142].

8. "Si pulvis nullus . . . : L, "If no dust." "And if a speck of dust should fall into your lady's lap, flick it off with your fingers; if there be no speck of dust, well, flick it off anyway" [ibid., 149-151].

9. Then file and candles, e li mestiers ecoutes: [Read *escoutes* for *ecoutes*] P, "and harkened to the crafts" or "to the mysteries." The word *mestiers* has a variety of meanings, the two most probable of which in the given context are "crafts" and "mysteries." Insofar as Pound is seeking to depict either a personally witnessed or a painted scene, the "file and candles" could refer to a file of people bearing candles in a religious procession or, as for instance in Sicily and other parts of Italy, to a detachment of craftsmen bearing candles and a large replica of a file as the emblem of their craft in a religious procession on some saint's day. Otherwise Makin (*Provence and Pound*, p. 38) could be correct in regarding the "file" (L, *lima*) as the traditional implement used by the Latin poets for polishing their verses, and the "candles" as a means of lucubration for poets too poor to afford an oil lamp.

10. y cavals armatz . . . : [Read *e* for *y*] P, "and horses in armor" (i.e. neck guard, chamfron, poitrel, flancards, rump piece). A quotation from Bertrans de Born's sirventes beginning "Be·m platz lo gais temps de Pascor [*T*, 426], in which the last line of the first stanza runs: *Chavaliers e chavals armatz* ["Knights and horses in armor"]. Cf. *SR*, 47: "Well pleaseth me the sweet time of Easter" ... "and great joy have I / When I see o'er the campagna knights armed and horses arrayed." Bertrans welcomed the arrival of spring as the season when knights can resume their warlike activities. Loving strife for its own sake, he even sang of his "Lady Battle" [*SR*, 44]. A footnote added to p. 48 of the revised edition of *SR* (1952) likens the pageantry in the above poem to the paintings of Simone Martini and Paolo Uccello that appear to be characterized by the definition "Not mere successions of [brush-] strokes, sightless narration" in the next line.

11. ciocco: I, "log" [5:6, 10]. Dante's image of the souls rising like sparks from the fifth circle (of Mars, god of war) to the sixth (of Jupiter, the sky-god) marks the transition from the medieval chronicle to Dante's *Divina Commedia*. We now leave the inventors for the "masters" [*ABCR*, 47-48]. The era of chronicled action is superseded by Dante's "imaginative vision" [*SR*, 157]. Dante's work is another reflection of Homer's for just as Virgil in the *Aeneid* was "translating" the *Odyssey* into the mentality and idiom of his time, Dante in turn was "translating" the *Aeneid* with Virgil as guide. In medieval times Virgil was commonly referred to as the "translator" of Homer. Dante, like his direct antecedents, Homer and Virgil, is seeking to present the full range of human knowledge in his age and for the first time touches critically on some of the evils of its culture. But this intellectual analysis or criticism is still caught up and neutralized by the quality of his "emotional synthesis."

12. Un peu moisi ... baromètre: F, "A little musty ... the floor being below garden level ... Against the wainscot ... a wicker armchair, ... an old piano ... and under the barometer" [Flaubert, *Un Coeur Simple*, par. 4]. "Un vestibule étroit séparait la cuisine de la salle où Mme. Aubain se tenait tout le long du jour, assise près de la croisé dans un *fauteuil de paille. Contre le lambris*, peint en blanc, s'alignaient huit chaises d'acajou. *Un vieux piano* supportait, *sous un baromêtre*, un tas pyramidal de boîtes et de cartons. Deux bergères de tapisserie flanquaient la cheminée en marbre jaune et de style Louis XV. La pendule, au milieu, représentait un temple de Vesta,—et tout l'appartement sentait *un peu* le *moisi*, car le *plancher* était *plus bas que le jardin*." Such objects begin to assume for Flaubert a dead weight that arrests the subjective movement of the mind. His genius and creative urge come up against a materialist civilization of alienation, which subsists solely on the "interest" yielded by the cultural assets of former times. Thus, Flaubert has to achieve his effects by a "greater heaping up of factual data" [*LE*, 26], as demonstrated in these lines. Flaubert's writings represent here the caesura between the epic tradition and prose, i.e. "the instinct of negation" [*LE*, 324; cf. *LE*, 31-32; FR in *Approaches*].

13. Old men's voices: [cf. 5 above and 32, 35, 37 below]. Another echo of Homer. The passage is concerned with Henry James, of whom Pound has written that although James does not "feel" as solid as Flaubert [*LE*, 305], he is sensitive to things that Flaubert did not see. James was a recorder of "atmospheres, nuances, impressions of personal tone and quality" [*LE*, 324]; his sensitivity was attuned to the "feel of the place or to the tonality of the person" [*LE*, 306]. But the action of his stories is a mere "excuse" for writing up his impressions of people so as to "show what acts, what situations, what contingencies would befit or display certain characters. We are hardly asked to accept them as happening" [*LE*, 299]. The ghostly impression of the plot thus conveyed explains James's "need of opacity" [*LE*, 321], leading among other things to his "damn'd fuss about furniture" [*LE*, 308], as demonstrated in this canto passage, and "a thickening, a chiaroscuro is needed, the long sentence" [*LE*, 304]. Hence, Pound's main criticism of James: "It is too much as if he were depicting stage scenery, not *as* stage scenery, but as nature" [*LE*, 325]. The house described in this passage is an almost compulsive leitmotif in James's writings: the "great gaunt shell of a house." It can be variously identified as (*a*) Lamb House in Surrey, where James spent his later years (Pound comments on James's bad taste in painting [*LE*, 307], but note also "a thickening, a chiaroscuro is needed'" [LE, 304]); (*b*) the London Polytechnic Institute, where Pound held his lectures on Provençal poetry in 1910 (this interpretation would explain "the old men's voices" and the "dry professorial talk"); (*c*) Leopold Bloom's Ideal Home in *Ulysses* (Ithaca), with its invented 99-year lease listing among other things the "stepped up panel dado, dressed with camphorated wax," the point being that the house remains unreal by "three squares" (panels) in spite of all of James's "thickening" [*LE*, 324; cf. *LE*, 31-32, 45, 210, 399, 403; FR in *Approaches*].

14. Con gli . . . grave incessu: I, L, "with eyes honest and slow," "solemn movement" [*Pur.* VI, 63, *Inf.* IV, 112]. The first quotation refers to Sordello; the second is a variation of Dante's *Genti veran con occhi tardi e gravi* [I, "I saw men approaching with slow and solemn eyes"], describing Homer, Horace, and Ovid, three of the four great shades of antiquity approaching Dante and Virgil (Virgil himself was the fourth). The variation incorporates Virgil's *vera incessu* [cf. *Aeneid* I, 405; *LE*, 246; 74/435]: "and from her manner of walking" and "a great goddess, Aeneas knew her forthwith" [cf. also in "Conversations in Courtship," *T*, 401]; James is thus directly associated with the grand tradition recalled from Orage's dictum: "James will be quite comfortable after death, as he had been dealing with ghosts all his life" [*LE*, 302]. The passage also sums up Pound's personal memories of

James as in *LE* [295, 311] and "*Moeurs Contemporaines* VII," where James's remark, "Oh! Abelard," regarding the castrated medieval scholar, gives the key biological clue to the indirectness of James's responses, to his perennial theme of the unlived life, and to the underlying motivation of his circuitous sentences, his oblique method, and his constant "dealing with ghosts."

15. We also . . . : Pound is referring to himself in the first person, revisiting after seven years a Paris house in search of "buried beauty," using allusively the motif of the old house, the "shell of life" in James's writings, with particular reference to *The Jolly Corner* and *The Sense of the Past*. This visit to the house of the past marks Pound's transition from the past to the present and is the first time that the present enters *The Cantos* in any real and sustained sense. Yet the "ghostly visit" emphasizes the ambivalence of what is normally called "reality" and "fact": the remembered experience has far more solidity than the objective drab shell of life, the concierge, and so on. The "flimsy partition" harks back to Flaubert's observation [cf. 12 above].

16. Empire handle: The handle of the door knocker was designed in the Empire style of Napoleon I.

17. Ione, dead the long year: Cf. Pound's poem "Ione, Dead the Long Year" [*P*, 112], first published in *Poetry and Drama* (London, Dec. 1914), seven years before the first publication of Canto VII. It has been variously pointed out that Landor used the name "Ione" as a pseudonym for a Miss Nancy Jones and also that "Ione" was the petrified maiden in Bulwer Lytton's *Last Days of Pompeii*. There was, however, among the *New Freewoman* group a beautiful 19-year-old French-born dancer, Jeanne Heyse, who used the alias Joan Hayes and the professional name Ione de Forest. She committed suicide at her home in Chelsea, London, on August 2, 1912, which can be fairly described as a "long year" before the first publication of Pound's obituary poem. She reappears in *Dance Figure* [*P*, 91; cf. Chicago MSS, Dec. 3, 1912] before its publication in *Poetry* II, 1 (April 1913), 1-12, and in *New Freewoman* I, 5 (Aug. 15, 1913), 87-88 [EH].

18. Liu Che's lintel: A reference to the poem "Lo-yeh ai-ch'an ch'ü" by Liu Che, a Chinese emperor canonized as Wu-ti, 156-187. In the Chinese poem the emperor's dead mistress, having passed through the various phases of natural decay, ends as a dead leaf clinging to the threshold, from which lowly position Pound elevates her to the lintel, the supporting beam spanning the top of the doorway. In "Liu Ch'e" [*P*, 108] she was still clinging to the threshold [EH].

19. Elysée . . . : Hotel de l'Elysée, 3 rue de Beaune in Paris, where Pound had stayed and also arranged for James Joyce and his family to stay. The name is an echo of the Elysium of antiquity, the abode of the Happy Dead. The presence of the "masters," Pound and Joyce, at this hotel would, to Pound's mind, have reinforced the assocation. Joyce might not have appreciated this to the same degree. The bus transports Pound back to the present [cf. FR, *LPJ*, 173, 176].

20. Erard . . . : Érard, a famous French make of pianos. The lines following describe Vanderpyl's Paris flat [cf. 21 below] in the style of Flaubert, using the passage from *Un Coeur Simple* (see 12 above) as a parallel just as the house in the previous passage was described in the style of Henry James. Thus "ply over ply": the present is overlapped by the past.

21. Beer bottle . . . : Another indication of the present, when the artist is confronted with the problem of the industrial mass production of artifacts and the reproduction of earlier styles. The statues in the Jardin du Luxembourg as viewed from the windows of Vanderpyl's flat are for the most part in the abominable fake style of the 19th century based on copies from antiquity and therefore examples of "dogmatized form."

22. Fritz: Fritz-René Vanderpyl, 1876-? , a Dutch writer living at 13 rue Gay-Lussac [cf. 74/435; 80/510; *L*, 151 (to John Quinn); Vanderpyl's letter in *Analyst* VI]. Vanderpyl, who knew both Pound and Joyce in Paris, was an avant-garde novelist, poet, and art critic. In his letter he writes: "I then mixed all kinds of languages in my verses . . . . In those days I took myself for a very emancipated being."

23. Smaragdos, chrysolithos . . . : L, "Emeralds, topazes." From Sextus Propertius, *Elegies* II, xvi, 43-46. S. P. is saying here that he would like to see all the modish finery, which Cynthia takes to wearing as she feels herself to be growing older, swept away by the forces of nature: "emeralds, topazes, clothes made of the finest stuffs, all of this I should like to see swept into nothingness by raging storms. Oh that they would be turned into water and dust by some sleight of the gods."

24. De Gama: Vasco da Gama, ca. 1469-1524, Portuguese navigator and explorer who discovered the sea route to India [cf. 35/175] via Africa. Allusions to the *Lusiads* of Luiz de Camoëns, 1524-1580, the tenth canto of which celebrates da Gama and other Portuguese heroes, while the second canto (xcviii, 3-4) describes da Gama's bloomers as being slashed with gold in the fashion of the time. "Mountains of the sea gave birth to troops" may parody Camoëns' grandiloquent style [*SR*, 214ff.].

25. Le vieux . . . acajou: F, "The old mahogany chest." The French should read "La vieille commode." Possibly a reference to the already quoted passage from Flaubert's *Un Coeur Simple*: "Contre le lambris, peint en blanc," taken together with later references to "un socle d'acajou" and "la commode, couverte d'un drap comme un autel"; or to E. and J. de Goncourt, *Germinie Lacerteux* (1864), fourth par. of Ch. I: "Sur la commode d'acajou, d'un style

Empire, un Temps en bronze noir et courant, sa faux en avant, servait de porte-mentre à une petite montre au chiffre de diamants sur émail bleu entouré de perles."

26. Tyro: [2:12]. Tyro, Helen, Eleanor, Atalanta, "Nicea," and Dido represent here the timeless beauty of naked humanity in the sense that Pound has ascribed to Gourmont. All are manifestations of Eros juxtaposed with the period-bound ephemera of civilization. The "But *is* she dead ... In seven years?" appears to refer to the seven years between the death of Ione [cf. 17 above] in 1912 and the composition of Canto VII in 1919 [Pound wrote to his father on Dec. 13, 1919: "done cantos 5, 6, 7" (YC, no. 538)]. The line marks the transition to Gourmont's theme of poetry as "emotional synthesis."

27. Ἐλέναυς ... : H, "ship-destroying" [2:8]. A reiteration of the original theme of beauty as reflected in the arts.

28. The sea runs: The sea and its tides, shaking the shingle [cf. 4 above re Homer's *polyphloisboio* (*LE*, 250) and "the turn of the wave and the scutter of receding pebbles" (*L*, 274), are here used to symbolize both permanence and change, analogous to the "permanent elements in human nature," one of which is for Pound the creative passion for beauty as exemplified by Eleanor's sustained impact on literature, while another is translation.

29. The scarlet curtain ... : Arthur Golding's English version of Ovid's *Meta*., particularly the passage X/586 ff. describing how, during her race with Hippomenes, Atalanta's naked beauty was enhanced by her body taking on a ruddy hue as she grew hot. Golding translates: "As when a scarlet curtaine streynd against a playstred wall / Dooth cast like shadowe, making it seem ruddye therewith all." The theme of the reflections of beauty thus enters into the image itself. This theme is emphasized where Pound [*LE*, 235] asks if Golding's translation is not "a mirror" of Chaucer, whose work in turn

"mirrors" Ovid: "Or is a fine poet ever translated until another his equal invents a new style in a later language? ... Is there one of us so good at his Latin ... that Golding will not *throw upon his mind shades and glamours* inherent in the original text.... *Or is not a new beauty created, an old beauty doubled* when the overchange is well done?" The series of echoes do not in that case fade out but intensify [cf. 102/730].

30. Lamplight at Buovilla ... e quel remir: A reference to the troubadour Arnaut Daniel, who loved the wife of Guillem de Bouvila, supposedly in vain. But his poem "Doutz brais e critz" suggests otherwise. "E quel remir" ["and that I may gaze upon her"] is from lines 31-32: "Quel seu bel cors baisan rizen descobra / E quel remir contral lum de la lampa" ["and that she should kiss me and laughingly expose her body / and I might gaze upon her in the light of the lamp"]. Pound returns here to the theme of the desire to discard the accouterments of civilization [cf. 23 above] and return to bare humanity. At the same time he is echoing the image from Ovid in the preceding line [cf. *SR*, 34; *LE*, 111, 137; 20/90].

31. Nicea ... : A recollection of the dancer, Ione [cf. 17 above, 36 below], here likened to the graceful statue of Nike of Samothrace at the Louvre. Another contrast to the fake echoes in the Jardin du Luxembourg.

32. Thin husks ... : "Shelley, Yeats, Swinburne, ... Remy de Gourmont, when he says that most men think only husks and *shells of the thoughts that have been already lived over by others*, have shown their very just appreciation of the *system of echoes*, of the general vacuity of public opinion" [*LE*, 371]. This sentence may be regarded as seminal for Canto VII. The other motifs, such as the fancy dress of history, the old men ("dry casques of departed locusts"), the "great gaunt shell of a house," the dogmatized forms, the "*idées reçues*," the reifications of life, and the consequent alienation of the living dead all hark back to this passage and to the Waste Land motif of sexual frustration, aridity, and stasis.

33. Sham Mycenian: Walls supposedly in imitation of the architectural style of Mycenae, the ancient Greek city of Argolis, seat of the kingdom of Agamemnon.

34. "Toc" sphinxes, sham Memphis columns: F (patois), *toc*, "sham, ugly." Memphis was an ancient Egyptian city said to have been built in 3110 B. C. by Menes, first king of Egypt, on the west bank of Nile about 12 miles from the present location of Cairo. It was destroyed in the 7th century A. D. by Arabs, who quarried the ruins to build al-Fustât (now Cairo).

35. Shell of the older house . . . House expulsed by this house: [cf. 32 above]. The passage is strongly reminiscent of Matthew Arnold's reference to the *Mabinogion* in *The Study of Celtic Literature*, 1867, where the *Mabinogion* myths are described as "a detritus . . . of something far older." The compilation of these tales, Arnold says [57 and 54], may be compared with the "peasant building his hut on the site of Halicarnassus or Ephesus; he builds, but what he builds is full of materials of which he knows not the history, or knows by a glimmering tradition merely—stones 'not of this building,' but of an older architecture, greater, cunninger, more majestical" [EH].

36. Square even shoulders . . . dancing woman: Another recollection of Ione [cf. 17, 31, above], dating back to 1909, three years before her suicide and exactly "ten years gone" since the canto was composed.

37. Still the old dead dry talk . . . petrifaction of air: An echo of the talk of the old men of Troy confronted with Helen's living beauty, here reflected in academic efforts to mummify the beauties of the classics, whereby they are emptied of their original content and placed under a glass dome which neutralizes the biological function of beauty by denying access to it.

38. O voi che siete: I, *Par.* II, 1, which Pound translates: "Oh you, in the dinghy astern there" [93/631; 109/774]. Dante is addressing his readers who have up to now followed the course of his big ship, telling them that from here on only the few who have applied themselves to the study of the greatest mysteries will be able to understand his meaning. Pound is picking up the original Odyssean theme of the sea voyage in order to link this canto with the preceding six.

39. Dido . . . :   The Roman *Aeneid* is an echo of the Greek *Odyssey* in that Aeneas too sets out after the fall of the archetypical city of Troy to found a new city and kingdom, Rome [1:16]. After seven years of wandering he and his remaining seven ships reach the African port of Carthage, where Dido, still grieving for her murdered husband Sichaeus, is queen. Aeneas becomes her lover ("new Eros"), but he leaves her in order to set sail for Italy. In her fresh grief Dido commits suicide [*Aeneid* I, 341 ff., IV].

40. solid as echo: In the echelonned unrealities that constitute present-day life, the echo or reverberation of an "emotional synthesis" once experienced is often more solid than reality.

41. Eros: [cf. 39 above].

42. Passion to breed . . . : Pound sees Eros as the motive force of both procreation and the artist's urge to create new forms: "The power of the spermatozoid is precisely the power of exteriorizing a form" [*NPL*, 149].

43. The live man . . . : Identified by Pound in the margin of the Faber edition of *The Cantos* as Desmond Fitzgerald, 1890-1947, London-born Irish member of T. E. Hulme's circle who took part in the 1916 Easter rising in Dublin, for which he was sentenced by the English to life imprisonment. Released on the conclusion of the treaty with England, he was appointed minister for publicity in the Irish Free State government and shortly afterward minister of external affairs (1922) and later minister of defense (1931). Fitzgerald, like Hulme, was an extreme reactionary in politics. Reviewing Fitzgerald's memoirs (1969), Christopher Hollis wrote:

"Even at the time of the rising he [Fitzgerald] violently reacted against anyone who drew a parallel between Ireland's fight and the French Revolution and in later years was to attack any smallest abridgment of the principles of absolute capitalism with a savagery that I have never heard equalled" [*Observer*, London, Feb. 23, 1969; cf. 95/644].

44. Lorenzaccio ... : [5:39, 45, 58, 59]. The allusion is to *Inf.* III, 64, i.e., to the spirits of those "who were never alive" because they "lacked energy to sin or to do good, fit neither for Hell or Heaven" [*SR*, 129].

45. the tall indifference ... : [5:44 "abuleia"].

46. Ma ... morisse: [5:59].

47. E biondo ... : I, "he is blond" [*Inf.* XII, 110]. Next to the dark head of Ezzelino, Cunizza's brother [6:34], the blond head of Obizzo d'Este (d. 1293) appears in the mire of Hell. Obizzo had been one of the most homicidal tyrants in Italy. Pound has now come back full circle to the real events that "carve a trace" in time in the same way as does the work of a poet. Action that springs from such passionate depths constitutes a "poem ... written with deeds; ... art becomes necessary only when life is inarticulate and when art is not an expression, but a mirroring, of life; it is necessary only when life is apparently without design .... *Art that mirrors art* is unsatisfactory .... No poem *can have as much force as the simplest narration of the events themselves*" [*SR*, 218]. Thus, Canto 7 leads to the straightforward account [Cantos 7-11] of the deeds of Sigismundo Malatesta, a Renaissance Odysseus.

CANTOS VIII-XI
THE MALATESTA CANTOS

Sources

C. E. Yriarte, *Un Condottière au XVe siècle*, Paris, 1882; Edward Hutton, *Sigismundo Pandolpho Malatesta, Lord of Rimini* (a novel), London and New York, 1906, and *Ravenna* (a study), London and New York, 1913; L. A. Muratori, *Annali d'Italia*, IX, 1763; Platina, *The Lives of the Popes from the time of our Savior J. C. to the reign of Sixtus IV, trans. and contd. from the year 1471 to the present time by P. Rycaut*, London,1685; A. Battaglini, "Della corte letteraria di Sigismondo Pandolfo Malatesta," F. G. Battaglini, "Della vita e dei fatti di Sigismondo Malatesta," in *Basinii Parmensis Poetae Opera Praestantiora*, II, 43-255, 259-698, Rimini, 1794; Luigi Tonini, *Storia Civile e Sacra Riminese*, II, Rimini, 1882; Luciano Banchi, *La Guerra de' Senesi col Conte di Pitigliano*, Archivio Storico Italiano, ser. 4, III, 1879; Niccolò Machiavelli, *Istorie Fiorentine*, VII; Fritz Schultze, *Georgios Gemistos Plethon und seine reformatorischen Bestrebungen*, Jena, 1874; Dante, *Inf.* V,

73-142; XXVII, 44-48, 79-90; Horace, *Odes* III, 3; Virgil, *Aeneid*
VI; Plato, *Platonic Epistles* VII; W. S. Landor, "To Ianthe"; T. S.
Eliot, *The Waste Land*, v, 430.

Background

EP, *GK* frontispiece and 159-160; T. S. Eliot, "Gerontion";
Adrian Stokes, *The Quattro Cento*, London, 1932, and *Stones of
Rimini*, London, 1934, 19-20; Byron, "Parisina," 1816;
G. D'Annunzio, *Francesca* (drama); Enea Silvio Piccolomini (Pius
II), *Commentarii rerum memorabilium*, Rome, 1584, and *Vatican
Codex Reginensis*, no. 1995; *The Commentaries of Pius II*, trans.
Florence A. Gragg with introduction and notes by Leona Gabel,
Smith College Studies in History, XXII, XXV, XXX, XXXV,
XLIII, 1939-1951; Corrado Ricci, *Il Tempio Malatestiano*,Milan
and Rome, 1925; Alberto Ricci, *Sigismondo e Isotta*, Milan,
1929; Cesare Clementini, "Vita di Sigismundo Pandolfo,"
*Raccolto Istorico della Fondatione di Rimino e dell' Origine e
Vite de' Malatesti*, II, Rimini, 1627 (facsimile in *Historiae Urbium
et Regionum Italiae Rariores*, XXXVIII, pt. 2, Bologna, 1969);
Lorenzo de' Medici, *Scritti Scelti*, Introduzione e note de Egidio
Bellorini, Turin, 1922; Roberto Valturio, *De Re Militarii*, X;
Basinio de Basini, *Le poesie liriche*, Turin, 1925; Alfonso Lazzari,
Ugo e Parisina nella realtà storica, Florence, 1915 (expanded and
reissued as *Parisina*, Florence, 1949); Giovan Battista Pigna,
Historie de' principi di Este, Ferrara, 1570; G. Boccaccio, story of
Paolo and Francesca; E. Gibbon, *Decline and Fall of the Roman
Empire*, Modern Library, 1932, chap. 66; Joseph Jay Deiss,
Captains of Fortune: Profiles of Six Italian Condottieri, London,
1966; Willibald Block, *Die Condottieri: Studien über die
sogenannten "unblutigen Schlachten*," Berlin, 1913; Geoffrey
Trease, *The Condottieri: Soldiers of Fortune*, London, 1970;
Piero Zama, *I Malatesti*, Faenza, 1956.

Exegeses

R. Mayo, *Analyst* V; A. Fang, J. Palmer, R. Ellmann, et al.,
Analyst VI; R. Mayo and S. Wuletich, *Analyst* VII; A.
Manganaris-Descavalles, *Analyst* XI; R. Mayo, *Analyst* XIII; John
Drummond, "Italian Background to the Cantos," in *Ezra Pound*,
ed. P. Russell, 104-113; FR, *P/J*, 272; DD, *Sculptor*.

Glossary Canto VIII

1. These fragments you have . . . . : The
"you" refers to T. S. Eliot, who some
months before the composition of Canto
VIII had submitted to Pound a manuscript
containing a collection of independent
poems and verse fragments for his appraisal

[cf. *L*, p. 169]. Pound indicated how many of the poems could be strung together to form a cohesive group, which subsequently came to be published under the title *The Waste Land*. Pound's own "fragments" are of course the still inchoate *Cantos*.

2. Calliope: The Muse of epic poetry. Her quarrel with "Truth" refers to the persistent denigration that has followed Sigismundo for centuries, owing mainly to the campaign of character assassination initiated against him by Pius II in his *Commentaries* [9:21; 10:25, 28].

3. sous les lauriers: F, "under the laurels."

4. Alessandro: A. de' Medici, 1511-1537, son of Pope Clement VII and a Moorish slave [5:33, 43].

5. Malatesta/Sigismund: Sigismundo Pandolfo Malatesta, 1417-1468, Lord of Rimini, Fano, and Cesena, famous condottiere, military engineer, and patron of the arts, for Pound the "factive personality." Malatesta da Verrucchio, 1212-1312, known as Mastin (the Mastiff), the first Lord of Rimini [cf. 49 below], was his great-great-grandfather, and Pandolfo Malatesta, 1377-1427, famous condottiere and patron of the arts and sciences, his father. During Pandolfo's lifetime, Pope Martin V, influenced by the Pesaro line of the Malatesta family [cf. 40 below], had dragged out his suit to have his three natural sons declared legitimate. On his death in 1427 the lordship of Rimini was taken over by his brother Carlo Malatesta [cf. 51 below] in behalf of the three young nephews. In order to plead Pandolfo's still pending suit, Carlo personally went to Rome in 1428, accompanied by Niccolò d'Este on a similar mission (cf. *tre cento bastardi* at 24/112). This time the pope, in return for certain lands and fortresses, declared legitimate the elder nephew, Galeotto, noted for his extreme piety. But within only a few months after Carlo's death in 1429 he sent troops to reclaim Rimini for the Holy See on the pretext of Carlo's failure to pay the annual levy due the Church. Though only 13 at the time, Sigismundo

with his small force succeeded in dispersing the papal troops. This incident marked the beginning of a lifelong struggle to defend his domain against all comers, a struggle that reached climactic points during the reigns of Pius II and Paul II. Above all, Pius II, a partisan of the house of Aragon against the house of Anjou, conceived a deep personal dislike for Sigismundo which is eloquently reflected in the many references to him, usually characterized by an extreme vulgarity of style, in his *Commentaries*. Sigismundo, although in many ways a heroic figure in his lifelong struggle against superior odds, was by no means without blemishes of character which can even be discerned between the lines of the Malatesta Cantos, but up to Pound's day Pius II's paranoically biased misrepresentation of him, which was parroted by later historians without the slightest attempt at verification, was still being taught in the schools even though a popular attempt to straighten the record had been undertaken by Yriarte in 1882 followed by Edward Hutton in 1906, which appears to have been the first to catch Pound's attention [cf. *GK*, 115, 159-160, 194, 261, 301].

6. Frater . . . carissime: ML, "Brother, as it were, and most dear companion."

7. Tergo: ML, "Written on the back."

8. Giohanni . . . Medici: Giovanni de' Medici, 1421-1463, youngest son of Cosimo de' Medici [10:22]. The words, which spell out "Giohanne de Medicis Fiorentia," have been partly obliterated by the wax wafer depicting Sigismundo's profile as shown facing the title page of *GK* inserted between the sheets of parchment.

9. Gianozio: Messer G., a dignitary (from Florence?) with whom Sigismundo was dealing; perhaps chancellor to Sigismundo.

10. King of Ragona: "El re de Ragona," i.e., Alphonso I of Sicily and Naples, king of Aragon (1385-1458). On the death of the Duke of Milan, Philippe Maria de Visconti, in 1447, Alphonso claimed Milan because the duke, being without male issue, had appointed him his heir. Milan was, however, also claimed both by Venice and by Francesco Sforza, while the city proclaimed itself a republic and hired Francesco Sforza [see 15], but as condottiere to defend its independence. Sigismundo had been engaged by Alphonso as condottiere to enforce his claim, but he broke the agreement by going over to the side of Florence and Venice.

11. Maestro di pentore: I, "Master of painting," prob. Piero della Francesca, ?1420-1492 [9:4].

12. buttato via: I, "chucked away" [Yriarte, 381].

13. affatigandose . . . mai: I; Pound translates: "Can work as he likes, / Or waste time as he likes / . . . / never lacking provision" [Yriarte, 385].

14. In campo . . . Cremonam: ML, "In the field of the most illustrious masters of Venice, the 7th day of April 1449, outside Cremona." Sigismundo writing, now as the leader of the Venetian forces against Sforza, and besieging Cremona, which Sforza had left in the hands of his wife Bianca Maria Sforza (a natural daughter of the late Visconti, Duke of Milan), whom he had married in 1441.

15. Duke of Milan: At the time of the agreement referred to, the duke was Francesco Sforza, 1401-1466, a peasant turned condottiere. Although lacking the military genius and versatility of Sigismundo, he succeeded in all his ventures because of his ruthless ambition. Throughout the Malatesta Cantos his career counterpoints the defeats and humiliations suffered by Sigismundo. Thanks largely to the unwavering support of the Medicis, who used him as an instrument with which to offset the power of Venice, Sforza finally achieved his ambition to become Duke of Milan in 1450 and founded a ducal dynasty [9:45; 10:17, 54].

16. Agnolo della Stufa: Negotiator sent by Florence to engage Sigismundo's services to defend the city against Alphonso's troops,

which had invaded Tuscany in 1452. Sigismundo thus suddenly found himself fighting on the side of his enemy Francesco Sforza, who was allied with Florence.

17. ten of the baily: "Dieci della Balìa." The Balìa was the emergency council of Florence, appointed during wars and rebellions when the ordinary citizen's rights were suspended.

18. gente . . . pie: I; Pound translates: "horsemen and footmen" [Yriarte, 383].

19. Penna and Billi, . . . Carpegna, . . . Marecchia: Penna and Billi are high rocks near Rimini; Carpegna is a nearby mountain; Marecchia is a river flowing into the Adriatic Sea near Rimini.

20. Lyra: An indication that the following verse should be sung to the accompaniment of a lyre.

21. "Ye spirits . . . Batsabe": Lines adapted from a poem by Sigismundo in praise of his mistress (later his third wife), Isotta degli Atti [cf. 9:59]. Pound takes the lines "O Spreti che gia fusti in questi regny / Voi ciaschaduno dalo Amor pcosso" and "Che in ver di me l'amor nascosa" and includes isolated references to *Lauti* (lutes), *Betzabé*, and *Hellena* [9:81]; Yseut is Iseult (lover of Tristan) and Batsabe is Bathsheba, one of the wives of King David.

22. Magnifico . . . carissime: ML, "most dear and honored compatriot," from a letter Sigismundo wrote to Giovanni de' Medici.

23. Johanni: Giovanni de' Medici [cf. 8 above]. Excerpt from a letter from Sigismundo dated March 4, 1449, written "in the field, outside Cremona."

24. fiorini di Camera: I, "florins of the treasury," prob. meaning coins of full weight. The gold florin of the Republic of Florence had become the basic monetary standard of Europe.

25. bombards: Early cannon for hurling rocks and other missiles. Sigismundo was renowned for his invention of military engines as well as for his ingenuity as a strategist and tactician [9:6, 10].

26. Under the plumes . . . : The siege of Cremona, which was defended by Bianca Visconti, wife of Francesco Sforza, in 1449, will have recalled to Sigismundo's mind his former alliance and friendship with Francesco Sforza. Sforza and Bianca Visconti, after their marriage in the fall of 1441, had visited Rimini in May 1442 on their way to Ancona and been received with the festivities here described. Sigismundo had in the same year married Francesco Sforza's daughter, Polissena [cf. 40 below]; Cremona was part of the dowry given to Bianca by her father, Philippo Maria de Visconti, Duke of Milan. Sigismundo had allied himself with Sforza against Sforza's father-in-law and the pope (Nicholas V), all of whom were trying to wrest the Marches of Ancona from Sforza's control. For two years (1442-1444) the two had fought unsuccessfully against Sforza's enemies, the agreement between them being that Sforza would as quid pro quo help Sigismundo regain Pesaro, a city of great strategic importance for him and part of the hereditary domain of the Malatestas which had been split off and awarded to another line of his family.

27. baldachino: I, "canopy."

28. la pesca . . . godeva molto: I, "fishing, in which he took great pleasure."

29. And the Greek emperor: John Paleologus (reign 1425-1448), who devoted his life's effort to saving Greece from the Turks, an aim that could have been accomplished only if all the European powers had combined to help the Greeks expel the Turks from Europe. But the European states were preoccupied with other interests. On May 29, 1453, Constantinople fell, ending a thousand years of Greek rule. The last Greek emperor was killed defending the city. In 1438 John Paleologus made a futile bid to enlist the aid of the Italian princes by agreeing to heal the split between the Church of Rome and the Greek Church. Thus, the unprecedented Council of Ferrara was called into being [26:39].

30. Ferrara: The remarkable meeting between the pope (Eugenius IV) and the patriarch of the Eastern Church took place when the latter debarked at Venice [25:44]. The council was attended by Sigismundo, Cosimo de' Medici, Francesco Gonzaga, and many other dignitaries. The pope planned to house and conduct the council at Ferrara because it was a central location and not subject to the pressures of any one of the strong city-states. But in 1439, when Ferrara was struck by the plague, the council was moved to Florence.

31. Gemisthus Plethon: Gemistus P., 1355?-1450?, the Byzantine Neoplatonist philosopher who attended the council at Ferrara and Florence as a delegate of the Eastern Church. Eighty-three at the time, he was steeped in Greek mythology and a Christian in name only. Under his influence Cosimo set up the Platonic Academy of Florence, which became a center of humanistic learning and of the revival of Greek studies in the Western world [GK, 160]. Gemistus returned to Greece and dièd there some ten years later. When the Venetians sent a military expedition to the Peloponnesus (Morea) under Sigismundo in 1464-1466 in order to counter the Turkish invasion, the expedition failed but Sigismundo brought back the ashes of Gemistus and had them reinterred in one of the sarcophagi decorating the outside walls of the Tempio at Rimini. His brother Novello [9:5; 11:18, 20, 27] brought back hundreds of Greek manuscripts by ship for his newly founded library, the Bibliotheca Malatestiana, at Cesena [cf. 55 below], texts that would otherwise have been lost to the Western world [cf. 26/123; 83/528; 98/685, 688, 690; GK, 224-225].

32. Delphos: One of the most sacred places of ancient Greece which Gemistus repeatedly mentioned in his conversation. He dreamed of grafting polytheistic myths onto the Christian religion, an aim with which Pound was in sympathy [9:80; 11:26, 27].

33. Poseidon: The Greek god of water [also as Neptune in 83/528; 96/795]. Gemistus's own hierarchy of the Greek gods placed Zeus first and Poseidon next in a certain correlation to the Neoplatonic hierarchy of values. Pound associates the water/stone motifs, which are so characteristic of Sigismundo's Tempio, with Gemistus's teaching about the god of water [*GK*, 224-225; DD, *Sculptor* 126 ff.].

34. concret Allgemeine: G, the "concrete universal." Pound is quoting from Fritz Schultze [p. 159], who described Gemistus Plethon as a "realist" in the medieval sense, that is, as taking the position of the *universalia in re* represented by Aristotle: "generals are known by particulars" [cf. 74/441], or as Pound [quoting Aquinas] said: "nomina sunt consequentia rerum"—not abstract and arbitrary labels pinned onto concrete things as the Nominalists would have it. A definition introduced by Hegel in order to differentiate between universals which are concrete and those which are abstract.

35. Dionysius: Dionysius I, 430-367 B.C. tyrant of Syracuse. Plato stayed at his court for a time in 388 as tutor to Dionysius the Younger, but his efforts to turn the son into a "philosopher king" failed [cf. *Platonic Epistles* 7]. Sigismundo's veneration of Gemistus is being compared by implication with Dionysius II's respect for Plato.

36. Ancona: City in the Romagna [cf. 26 above]. The described episode prob. took place during the two years of Sigismundo's alliance with Sforza.

37. church against him: Although Pope Martin V had originally tended to support the claims of the legitimate Pesaro line of the Malatesta family, he was eventually induced to accept Galeazzo, Sigismundo's elder brother, as Lord of Rimini on the death of their uncle, Carlo Malatesta of Rimini. The next pope, Eugene IV (1431-1447), similarly accepted Sigismundo as Lord of Rimini following the death of Galeazzo. In 1438 Sigismundo was even appointed chief commander of the papal

forces, while in 1445 he was invited to Rome, where he was received with full papal honors and awarded the Sword and the Hat of the Holy See. It was not until the papacy of Enea Silvio Piccolomini, as Pius II (1458-1464), that Sigismundo found the "church against him," for the simple reason that he was a supporter of the Angevine cause, whereas the material interests of Pius II lay with the Aragonese.

38. Medici bank: Cosimo de' Medici, 1389-1464, based his power on his monetary policies. By withdrawing all his capital from the market in 1464, he forced both Naples and Venice to conclude a peace with Florence. The Medici policy consisted of supporting Sforza in Milan in order to offset the power of Venice. Sigismundo had been on his own ever since Milan had fallen to Sforza in 1450. This event marked the end of 30 years of war in northern Italy, which had led to a balance of power among Venice, Milan, Florence, Naples, and the Holy See. At any rate the freedom of movement of the condottieri and minor despots was sharply restricted from 1450 on [cf. 9:48; 10:22; 21/96, 97; 26/123, 124; 93/624; 94/633].

39. wattle Sforza: A reference to the somewhat pendulous fleshy nose of Sforza [cf. 15 above].

40. Pèsaro: [cf. 26 above]. Pesaro had been part of the hereditary domain of the Malatesta family founded by Mastin [cf. 49 below]. It now belonged to Sigismundo's cousin Galeazzo, called the "Inept," who had no heirs. In order to regain Pesaro for himself, Sigismundo formed an alliance with Sforza and even married his illegitimate daughter Polissena [9:23]. But Galeazzo sold Pesaro to Sforza for 20,000 florins so that his niece Constanza could marry Sforza's brother Alessandro, who was to become Lord of Pesaro. At the same time (1445) Galeazzo sold Fossombrone to Federigo d'Urbino [11:12, 14], Sigismundo's archenemy [cf. 5 above].

41. Broglio: Gaspare B., comrade-in-arms of Sigismundo, author of "Cronaca", an unpublished account of Malatesta's campaigns [10:16].

42. bestialmente: I, 'bestially, meanly." Broglio maintained that Galeazzo had no right to sell territory that belonged to the Malatesta family collectively [cf. 40 above and 9:15].

43. templum aedificavit: ML, "he built a temple," from the *Commentaries* of Pius II [9:80], referring to the Tempio which Sigismundo had built as a monument to himself and his mistress. Pound said the Tempio at Rimini is both "an apex and in verbal sense a monumental failure" [*GK*, 159]. In order to build the Tempio, which was officially dedicated to St. Francis, Sigismundo employed the greatest artists of the age: Leon Battista Alberti, Matteo da Pasti, Simone Ferucci, Agostino di Duccio. The church was begun in 1445 and consecrated in 1450. In 1455 the work was interrupted, leaving the front incomplete and the roof not even begun. Only seven of the fourteen sarcophagi intended for the remains of humanists and philosophers were filled. The Tempio was partly destroyed in the Allied bombing raids of December 28, 1943, and January 29, 1944 [cf. 76/459; 80/497; 83/528; 90/605; 92/621; 107/758].

44. with the game lost: Prob. refers to Sigismundo's lost hopes of regaining Pesaro and Fossombrone in 1445.

45. and never quite lost till '50: The year when the treacherous Francesco Sforza became Duke of Milan [cf. 10, 15, 38 above].

46. and never quite lost . . . Romagna: Where there was life, there was always hope for the indomitable Sigismundo. But in 1468 he again fell ill of the fever he had contracted in Morea [11:21] and died at Rimini in the Romagna a few months later. He had been excommunicated in 1460 and deprived of all his possessions except Rimini in 1463 [11:15, 21, 34].

47. Poictiers: Guillaume Poitiers, Duke of

Aquitaine [6:2], believed to be the composer of the earliest troubadour lyrics extant and to have introduced troubadour music to France.

48. viels: MF, *viell(e)s*: medieval "viols": stringed instruments of the lute family.

49. Mastin: I, "Mastiff." Nickname of Malatesta da Verrucchio, 1212-1312, great-great-grandfather of Sigismundo. The "Old Mastiff" had been the original founder of the Malatesta dynasty and became the first Lord of Rimini in 1293. Earlier he had lived at Verrucchio, which had been awarded to him for his services to the city of Rimini [cf. *Inf.* XXVII, 44-46; 5 above].

50. Paolo il Bello: I, "Paul the Handsome," ?1247-1283?, second son of the "Old Mastiff." His elder brother Gianciotto was deformed and had been married to Francesca, daughter of Guido Vecchio da Polenta. Paolo and Francesca fell in love with each other and were killed by the enraged Gianciotto. Boccaccio says that Paolo tried to escape but his mantle caught on a nail [cf. *Inf.* V, 73-142; also the line *che paion' si al vent* ("who appeared so light on the wind") at 110/777].

51. Parisina: Daughter of Carlo Malatesta and cousin to Sigismundo [cf. 5 above]. In 1418 she married Niccolò d'Este, Lord of Ferrara, when she was 14 and he was 34. In 1425, after Parisina had borne him two daughters, Niccolò suspected her of adultery with his favorite son Ugo, who was of the same age, and had them both beheaded. Pound tells the story in some detail in 20/90, 91 [cf. 24/110-112; *L*, 210 to Homer Pound].

52. Atreides: H, "sons of Atreus." The violence in the house of Malatesta is compared with the internecine strife in the house of Atreus.

53. was twelve at the time: Sigismundo was 12 when Carlo Malatesta, his uncle and tutor, died. His "elder brother gone pious" was Galeotto, who had entered the Franciscan order. Wearing a monk's habit he devoted himself to prayer, fasting, and self-flagellation.

54. fought in the streets: After having become Lord of Rimini at 15, Sigismundo had been attacked on the streets of Rimini by a band of peasants led by a sixty-year-old priest, Don Matteo, who combined his support for their grievances with a desire to place the city under the jurisdiction of the Holy See. Sigismundo afterward had the priest defrocked by three friendly bishops and hanged in public on the piazza.

55. Cesena: In 1432, after Sigismundo had succeeded the dead Galeotto as Lord of Rimini, Carlo Malatesta of Pesaro (head of the legitimate side of the family), supported by the Count of Urbino, attempted to seize Rimini. Warned of the approaching forces, Sigismundo rode to Cesena, another of his possessions, where he gathered a force of 400 foot soldiers and 300 mounted men. Returning to Rimini with this force he challenged the troops of his relative outside the city walls, demanding to know whether they

came as friend or foe. They said they came as friends and thereupon withdrew. Shortly afterward Sigismundo appointed his younger brother, Domenico (Novello/Novvy), governor of Cesena [9:5; 11:18, 20].

56. Foglia: The alacrity with which Galeotto was obeying the orders of the new pope, Eugenius IV (1431-1447), to harass the Jews and investigate the practice of concubinage among the clergy gave rise to the fear among the legitimate branch of the Malatesta, headed by Carlo Malatesta of Pesaro, that Rimini would shortly be handed over to the Holy See as a gift. With the support of the Count of Urbino he decided to forestall any such action by seizing the town along with Fano, which also belonged to the illegitimate side of the family. Not long after his troops had left Pesaro and had camped for the night near Serra Ungarina, they were attacked and dispersed by a small force under the 13-year-old Sigismundo, who had crossed the Foglia (a river flowing into the Adriatic near Pesaro) at dusk.

Glossary Canto IX

1. one year . . . : The introductory lines give an impressionistic account of specific episodes in Sigismundo's career. They are also reminiscent of the lines in T. S. Eliot's description of the factive personality in *Gerontion* ("Nor fought in the warm rain / Nor knee deep in the salt marsh, heaving a cutlass / Bitten by flies, fought"). The episodes concern the flood of 1440 during which Rimini was encircled by water like Venice; the winter of 1444 when Sigismundo set out in a snowstorm and, for the sake of Sforza, caused Monte Gaudio to surrender [8:26]; the hailstorm of 1442 which wrought great destruction in Rimini and the surrounding countryside [*Analyst* VII; Hutton, 106, 129, 118].

2. Astorre Manfredi: Lord of Faenza, a condottiere like Sigismundo but an ally of the Duke of Urbino and a hereditary enemy of

the Malatestas. The lines refer to an incident when Sigismundo had to cross Astorre's territory and was ambushed by him. Sigismundo escaped the pursuing hounds by standing in marsh water up to his neck, an incident that took place near Astorre's castle of Russi on the road from Mantua to Rimini.

3. Fano: Town in the marshes of central Italy, part of the hereditary domain of the Malatestas but eventually lost to the Holy See, whence the inscription there: *Olim de Malatestis* ["Once of the Malatestas"]. Fano, originally *fanum* ["temple"], had in Roman times been the site of a temple in honor of Caesar Augustus, whence *Fano Caesaris*. It also has a triumphal arch (*l'arco d'Augusto*) left over from Roman times and thus once more associates Sigismundo with the heroes of antiquity. The incident here mentioned refers to the trouble young Sigismundo experienced in assuming lordship over the cities of Rimini, Fano, and Cesena against the resistance of their inhabitants [8:40, 54; 11:12; 11/50; 30/148, 149; 76/462; 80/501, 502; 83/529].

4. Emperor: Sigismund V, 1368-1437, Holy Roman emperor (1433-1437) of the house of Luxemburg. In the fall of 1433 he was crowned emperor in Rome by the pope. On his way back north he stopped at Rimini where, being received with elaborate ceremony, he knighted both Sigismundo and his youngest brother Domenico. Piero della Francesca depicted the event in a fresco in the Chapel of Relics of the Tempio.

5. ... knighted us: Sigismundo's youngest brother Domenico, called "Malatesta Novello," or "Novvy," by Pound, 1418-1475. He governed Cesena for Sigismundo and founded the library there [8:31; 10:58; 11:18; 16/69; 23/107].

6. wooden castle: A wooden castle designed by Sigismundo was built for use in the tourneys during the three-day fiesta celebrating his marriage to Ginevra in 1433 [cf. 8 below]. This feat of military engineering prefigures the building of La Rocca [cf. 10 below].

7. Basinio: Basinio de Basini, 1425-1457, Italian poet and humanist patronized by Sigismundo. His *L'Isottaeus*, 30 epistles in the manner of Ovid's *Heroides*, celebrates Sigismundo's love of Isotta degli Atti. After he had entered the service of Sigismundo he was challenged to a literary duel by a rival poet at the court, one Porcellio Pandone, 1405-1485, who had written a poem on the same theme, *De amore Iovis in Isottam* ["Of Jupiter's love of Isotta"]. The event, presided over by Sigismundo and Isotta, took place in the courtyard of La Rocca. Porcellio defended the thesis that one could write good Latin verse without having studied Greek (hence "the anti-Hellene"). But Basinio, who had studied Greek (a rare accomplishment at the time), defended Greek studies by showing the dependence of Latin literature upon Greek (a view shared by Pound) and the importance of Greek scholarship in the new humanistic Renaissance. Basinio was declared victor in the debate. He remained at Rimini and is buried in one of the sarcophagi outside the Tempio [cf. 82/524; 104/740].

8. Madame Ginevra: Daughter of Parisina and Niccolò d'Este, became Sigismundo's first wife in 1434 when she was 16 and he was 17. In 1437 she bore him a son who lived only a year. Unwell after the birth of the child, she died at the age of 22. Sigismundo had been away in the field during most of their marriage. Pius II [10:25] later accused him of having poisoned her.

9. Capitan: In 1437 Sigismundo, then only 20 years old, was engaged as captain by the Venetians [cf. 25 below].

10. Rocca: In the same year Sigismundo began building La Rocca, a fortress, at Rimini, a project that was to take nine years (1437-1446). Its design and execution were largely undertaken by Sigismundo himself, and the fortress was one of the main achievements of his life. In its day La Rocca was considered one of the marvels of Italy. During the past century it has been altered beyond recognition.

11. Monteluro: Site of a battle where in 1444 Sigismundo won a victory for the cause of Francesco Sforza, his father-in-law [8:26, 40]. But this victory accomplished little for Sigismundo because a few months later he broke with Sforza over the sale of Pesaro [cf. Hutton, 128].

12. Sforza: [8:15, 39].

13. March 16th: The date in 1445 when the agreement was executed between Francesco Sforza and his brother Alessandro Sforza, Federigo d'Urbino, and Galeazzo Malatesta under which Pesaro was sold to Alessandro and Fossombrone to Federigo [Tonini, v, 152; 8:40].

14. Federicho d'Orbino: Medieval spelling of Federigo d'Urbino, i.e., Federigo da Montefeltro, 1422-1482, first Duke of

Urbino, a great Italian condottiere and politician and patron of the arts. According to Pound, Federigo was "Sigismundo's Amy Lowell" [*GK*, 159].

15. bestialmente: [8:41, 42]. The account is by Gaspare Broglio.

16. per capitoli: I, "by agreement."

17. out of the Marches: Sigismundo now joined the alliance against Sforza and, in a brilliant two-year campaign, drove his enemies out of the Marches of Ancona.

18. King o' Ragona: [8:10]. Sigismundo had been engaged by Alphonso of Aragon, king of Naples, in 1447 to enforce his claim to Milan. For his services to Alphonso, Sigismundo had already received 25,000 ducats out of the 32,400 agreed upon, when the Florentines persuaded him to take service with them instead. This Sigismundo did, keeping the money already paid to him, on the advice of Valturio. For his treachery he earned the undying hatred of Alphonso [cf. F.G. Battaglini, 399].

19. Valturio: Roberto Valturio, ?1414-1489, Italian engineer and author of *De Re Militari*, 1472, one of the books on Leonardo da Vinci's library; first secretary and adviser to Sigismundo, charged with building La Rocca. He is buried in one of the sarcophagi of the Tempio.

20. haec traditio: ML, "this treachery." Pound eliminates the charge of treachery against Sigismundo by translating *traditio* as "change-over," as though the word were Latin rather than Medieval Latin [EH].

21. old bladder: Aeneas Sylvius (Enea Silvio de) Piccolomini, 1404-1464, as Pius II (1458-1462) [10:25]. Pound refers to him as *old bladder* because he suffered from gallstones [10:36].

22. rem eorum saluavit: L, "saved their cause," from the *Commentaries* of Pius II: "There is no doubt that Sigismundo's treachery saved the Florentine Cause."

23. Polixena: Polissena Sforza, natural daughter of Francesco Sforza. Sigismundo married her barely a year after the death of his first wife in return for her father's promise to help him regain Pesaro. In the following year she bore Sigismundo a son who died in his first year. Sigismundo abandoned her for his successive mistresses Vanetta Toschi and Isotta degli Atti. When the plague was ravaging Rimini in 1449, she fled to the Convent of Scolca in the hills where she choked to death one night and was hastily buried in an unmarked grave; it may thus be inferred that she fell victim to the plague. Ten years later Pius II accused Sigismundo of having strangled her [cf. 8:26, 40; 10:23].

24. old Wattle-wattle: Francesco Sforza finally entering Milan as duke in 1450 [8:15, 39].

25. Feddy: Federigo d'Urbino [cf. 14 above]. When Sforza entered Milan, Sigismundo was still in the service of Venice and therefore enjoyed a high status, since the rich republic employed only the most daring condottieri. In order to separate him from Venice, Sforza again used Pesaro as bait and induced Federigo d'Urbino to pretend that he would help Sigismundo take Pesaro from Alessandro Sforza. But when Sforza's forces came up from the rear and were welcomed in Urbino, Sigismundo knew that he had been tricked [Hutton, 197-199].

26. Foscari: Francesco Foscari, ?1372-1457, Doge of Venice (1423-1457).

27. Caro mio: I, "my dear man." Foscari writing to Sigismundo, offering to help him regain Pesaro in order to dissuade him from leaving Venetian service.

28. Classe: Refers to the great basilica of S. Apollinare in Classe, Ravenna, the most important Byzantine church in Italy, dating back to 534, the same period in which the tomb of Galla Placidia and San Vitale were built, both of which Pound praises and contrasts with the "monumental failure" of the Tempio. Sigismundo stripped the basilica of its marble decorations (porphyry, serpentine) for use in his Tempio [*Analyst* VII; Yriarte, 193-194; Hutton, *Ravenna*, 204-205; F. G. Battaglini, 431-432]. Pound's "Sant Apollinaire" comes from Yriarte's "San Apollinaire," but the original Italian form is "S. Apollinare."

29. Casus est talis: L, "that's the way it is." Sigismundo is excusing his actions to Foscari. The citizens of Ravenna, outraged at the spoliation, complained to Foscari, since Ravenna was then under the jurisdiction of a Venetian podesta. Upon pressure from the doge, the Benedictine abbot of S. Apollinare [cf. 34 below] and the commune of Ravenna agreed to accept 200 gold florins from Sigismundo in compensation for the loss. Another attempt by Sigismundo to avail himself of the treasures of the basilica, as though it were a stone quarry, took the form of obtaining a papal bull transferring jurisdiction over the Abbey of S. Apollinare to his own canon at Rimini. This caused the outraged Venetian senate to prohibit any move to take possession of the abbey. Pound has reversed the chronological order of the two events [cf. 35 below].

30. Filippo: F. Calandrini, Cardinal Bishop of Bologna, who had become "commendatary" of the Abbey of S. Apollinare. Sigismundo approached him and "easily obtained his authority to remove as much as he desired" [F. G. Battaglini, 431-432], Pound's insinuation here being that the cardinal had received "four hundred ducats" for his acquiescence, which is not borne out by the records.

31. quadam nocte: L, "on a certain night."

32. Santa Maria in Trivio: [8:43]. Name of the older church built in honor of the Madonna dell'Acqua but replaced by the Tempio Malatestiano, which was officially dedicated to St. Francis. The great Renaissance architect, Leon Battista Alberti, had decided not to destroy the older church with the tombs of Sigismundo's ancestors but to superimpose the Tempio upon it, so showing a respect for earlier achievements obviously missing in Sigismundo [cf. 54 below]. Thus the Tempio incorporates cultural layers from various periods (the Gothic church, the Renaissance shell, the Byzantine marbles), as Pound does in *The Cantos*. Pound's defense of Sigismundo from the charge of stealing is therefore not devoid of a self-serving element.

33. plaustra: L, "wagons, carts."

34. Aloysius Purtheo: Fl. 1450. Prob. Benedictine abbot of S. Apollinare in Classe.

35. corn-salve: The hasty sally of "an hundred two-wheeled oxcarts" to strip S. Apollinare overnight presumably caused considerable damage to the fields and crops. The lines are intended to show Sigismundo's concern for the peasants and the integrity of his arrangement with the abbot [cf. 29 above].

36. German-Burgundian female: The great Italian historian, Ludovico Antonio Muratori, writes in his *Annali d'Italia*: "Whether he was indeed guilty of this outrage I am unable to say, for in spite of all the investigations undertaken by the perspicacious Venetians, they were unable to discover the culprit." Pius II, on the other hand, presents the story in his *Commentaries* in the lurid denunciatory language of a cheap journalist: "Meeting not far from Verona a noble lady who was going from Germany to Rome in the jubilee year, he [Sigismundo] assaulted her (for she was very beautiful) and when she struggled, left her wounded and covered with blood" [167]. Pound, in a letter to John Quinn dated August 10, 1922, garbles both accounts and adds some trimmings of his own invention: "Authorities differ as to whether Sigismundo Malatesta raped a german girl in Verona, with such vigor that she 'passed on,' or whether it was an Italian in Pesaro, and the pope says he killed her first and raped her afterwards: . . . in fact all the *minor* points that might aid one in forming an historic rather than a fanciful idea of his character seem 'shrouded in mystery' or rather lies" [YC] [EH].

37. Poliorcetes: H, "Taker of cities," epithet linked with the exploits of Demetrius, king of Macedonia, 294-288 B.C. Demetrius's military career and his feats of military engineering show parallels with Sigismundo's. The legend on the medallions of Sigismundo executed by Pisanello read: "Poliorcetes et semper Invictus" [H, L, "Taker of cities, and always victorious"].

38. POLUMETIS: H, "many-minded," that is, versatile, stock Homeric epithet for Odysseus [*Od*. I, 1] here applied to Sigismundo [cf. 11:29; *GK*, 146].

39. Feddy: Federigo d'Urbino [cf. 14, 25 above].

40. Alessandro: A. Sforza, Lord of Pesaro [cf. 8:40, 25 above].

41. Broglio: [8:41].

42. m'l'ha calata: I [slang], "he's tricked me" [Tonini, 198-203]. Pound uses the phrase again in his translation of Sophocles' *Trachiniae*.

43. Istria: Peninsula at N end of Adriatic. Istrian marble was used in building the city of Venice [17/79]. Sigismundo had ordered a large quantity of marble from Istria for his Tempio; the delayed delivery is mentioned in Pietro di Genari's [cf. 53 below] letter [cf. Adrian Stokes, *Stones of Rimini*, 19-20; DD, *Sculptor*, 127-131].

44. Silk war: Prob. a war between Venice and Ragusa (now Dubrovnik) in Dalmatia [17/79; 77/394]. Venice and Ragusa were traditional enemies, Ragusa being the only town along the Adriatic coast that was long able to maintain its independence against Venice and to rival it in the silk industry. Venice assumed the lead in the silk industry in the 15th century. In 1423 the doge mentioned 1,600 silk weavers working there. Pandolfo Malatesta, Sigismundo's father, had unsuccessfully led the Venetians against Ragusa in 1420.

45. Wattle: Francesco Sforza. Prob. refers to the invasion of Tuscany by Alphonso

d'Aragon in 1452. Since Sigismundo had entered the service of Florence [8:10, 16], he now found himself supporting Florence and Milan, i.e., F. Sforza [8:15], against Venice and Naples.

46. Vada: Scene of one of Sigismundo's military successes. In 1453 he used his bombards to take the supposedly impregnable fortress of Vada manned by Alphonso of Aragon's troops.

47. bombards: Sigismundo is credited with the invention of various military engines, including a catapult or cannon for firing incendiary projectiles in the form of bronze balls filled with powder and fused with dry burning tinder [Valturio, 267].

48. Siena: The jobs available for Sigismundo and other condottieri were becoming scarce, forcing him to serve minor powers such as Siena, which he apparently did not take very seriously. He had been engaged by Siena to attack the Count of Pitigliano (Aldobrandino Orsini), who had seized several strongholds belonging to the commune. Sigismundo besieged his castle of Sorano: the *two lumps of tufa* describe the insignificance of the affair in Sigismundo's eyes. Venice, an ally of Siena, sent along an army under the command of Carlo Gonzago to assist him while Siena, seeing that the siege was dragging on into the winter, engaged yet another condottiere, Ghiberto da Correggio. The command was thus divided and wracked by secret hostilities, causing Siena and particularly the bishop, Enea Silvio Piccolomini [later Pius II], to suspect Sigismundo of double-dealing [8:37; 10:1, 2, 5, 6].

49. postbag: In 1454, when a breach was finally made in the fortifications of Sorano, Sigismundo, without consulting the commune, made a truce with the count and raised the siege. The commune, convinced now of Sigismundo's treachery, raided his headquarters and tried to arrest him. Sigismundo escaped, but his postbag containing the letters he had received in five months, about 50 in all, fell into the hands of the Sienese. The following are extracts from eight of these letters, discovered in the Archives of Siena in the nineteenth century. They illustrate the preoccupations of Sigismundo's mind [cf. *Analyst* VII; Yriarte, 419-423, 396-397, 443-444, 406-407].

50. Ex Arimino . . . singularissime: ML, "From Rimini, 22 December 1454, Magnificent and powerful master to me most extraordinary." This letter is written by Matteo Nuti of Fano, an architect whom Novello had lent to Sigismundo, and runs through to "roof and. . . ." The chief architect of the Tempio, Alberti, had been recalled to Rome and the plans he had left behind were giving the builders some difficulty, so Nuti was brought in to clarify them [cf. 54 below].

51. Alwidge: Luigi Alvise, overseer of carpenters and masons at work on the Tempio.

52. Magnifice . . . Mio: I, "Magnificent Excellency, My Lord" [Letter 2, dated Dec. 21, 1454]. Excerpt runs from "JHesus" to "rite." It is from Giovane, son of the overseer Alvise, who is writing at his father's dictation.

53. Genare: Pietro di Genari, Sigismundo's chancellor.

54. Albert: Leon Battista Alberti, 1404-1472, the architect of the Tempio. He was one of the universal men of the century: inventor, astronomer, athlete, poet, sculptor, painter, and Latinist, but best known as an architect. He was a Florentine and Sigismundo is thought to have met him in Florence in 1435. Alberti was under the patronage of Pope Nicholas V and it was through the pope that Sigismundo was able to obtain Alberti's services. Alberti, however, had been recalled to Rome by his patron.

55. Sagramoro: Jacopo S. da Soncino, counselor and secretary to Sigismundo. Postscript to Letter 2 saying that Sagramoro had examined all the works.

56. Illustre . . . mio: I, "My dear sir." Letter 3, dated December 21, 1454, addressed to Alberti and signed by Pietro di Genari and Matteo da Pasti. It lists material needed for the construction of the Tempio.

57. Monseigneur: Letter 4, dated December 21, 1454, addressed to Sigismundo by "D. de M.," considered by some to have been dictated by Isotta. It reports on the visit made by Isotta [cf. 59 below] to a young girl with whom Sigismundo was probably having an affair. Isotta was at that time still only Sigismundo's mistress.

58. S. Galeazzo's: Galeazzo was prob. the father of the girl who had been seduced by Sigismundo.

59. Madame Isotta: Isotta degli Atti, ?1430-1470, Sigismundo's mistress and later (1456) his third wife [8:21]. His love for her is celebrated all over the Tempio, especially in her monumental tomb, by the intertwined initials S and I. She bore him at least two sons, both before marriage: Sallustio (1448) and Valerio (1453) [cf. 61, 79, 80, 81 below].

60. Mi pare . . . chossia: I; Pound translates: "I think [she] very nearly exhausted the matter."

61. All the children: At least seven illegitimate children of Sigismundo were living in 1454. Two of them were Isotta's; Lucrezia, one of the older of the other five, was made legitimate by the pope in 1453.

62. Sagramoro: [cf. 55 above].

63. Messire Malatesta: Sigismundo's young son Sallustio, 1448-1470. Letter 5, dated December 20, 1454, signed Lunarda da Palla [cf. 66 below]. Sallustio was murdered by, or at the behest of, his half brother Roberto Malatesta [cf. 11:9; 20/94; 74/448].

64. Chateau: The fortress of Sorano [cf. 48 above].

65. Georgio Rambottom: G. Ranbutino, a stonemason.

66. Lunarda: L. da Palla, Sallustio's tutor.

67. Magnifice ac potens: ML, "to the magnificent and powerful," opening of Letter 1.

68. Malatesta ... suum: ML, "from Malatesta of Malatestis to his magnificent Lord and Father." Letter 6, dated December 22, 1454, written by Sallustio, then six years old, to his father.

69. Ex^so ... General: ML, "Excellent Lord, my Lord, and also Lord Sigismundo Pandolpho of the Malatesti, Captain General." Inscription on the outside of Sallustio's letter.

70. Gentilino da Gradara: Unknown agent of Sigismundo's.

71. Illustrious Prince: Letter 7, dated December 18, 1454, written by Iacopo Trachulo ("Servulus Trajatus"), a court poet of Sigismundo's. The advice given to Sigismundo in this letter to establish his own party in Siena and eventually take over the city must, in Pound's opinion, have clinched the matter and confirmed the Sienese in their suspicions of Sigismundo [10:2].

72. Hannibal: Famous general who led the forces of Carthage against Rome, crossing the Alps with his elephants. Sigismundo claimed to have been descended from Hannibal, so Trachulo is here addressing Sigismundo, who often used elephants as his emblem.

73. Magnifice ... premissa: ML, "Magnificent and powerful Lord, my most particular Lord, I send you my most humble greetings." Letter 8 written by Pietro di Genari [cf. 53, 56 above], dated December 18, 1454, reporting on a shipment of marble which had at last arrived and the progress of the work on the Tempio and La Rocca.

74. defalcation: Embezzlement.

75. aliofants: I, "elephants." The conventional Italian form being *elefante*, *aliofant* may have been used by Pound to emphasize the resemblance between Matteo da Pasti's black porphyry elephant heads and garlic

cloves [I, *aglio*], no one there at that time having ever set eyes on an elephant. These sculptured elephants support the columns of the Tempio [cf. HK, *Era*, 429].

76. Antonio: A. degli Atti, brother of Isotta, who had been knighted by the Emperor Sigismund.

77. Ottavian: Ottaviano, a painter commissioned to illuminate the papal bull allowing Sigismundo to erect an altar in the church of St. Sigismund.

78. Agostino: A. di Duccio, 1418-1481, Florentine sculptor who worked on the sarcophagus dedicated to Sigismundo's ancestors and on the bas-reliefs of the Tempio [cf. DD, *Sculptor*, 127-131; 20/90; 45/229; 51/250; 74/425].

79. et amava ... decus: I, ML, "And he loved Isotta degli Atti to distraction / and she was worthy of it / constant in purpose / She delighted the eye of the prince / lovely to look at / pleasing to the people (and the ornament of Italy)." This tribute to Isotta is a composite of several sources: Pius II, *Commentaries*; a 15th-century chronicle of Rimini; *constans in proposito* [L] is from Horace, *Odes* III, 3; Pound also uses it in relation to J. Q. Adams [cf. 34/171]: *Constans proposito / Justum et tenacem* ["Constant in purpose, just and enduring"] from *The Diary of John Quincy Adams*, 568 [cf. *Pai*, 6-2, 231].

80. and built a temple: From the *Commentaries* of Pius II [8:37, 43; 21 above]. The Tempio, although dedicated to St. Francis, is devoid of Christian symbols. All the allegorical figures are classical and Sigismundo himself is enthroned among Olympian deities. The temple is likewise a monument to the love of Sigismundo and Isotta; the tomb in the chapel of S. Michael Archangel is inscribed: "D. ISOTTAE ARIMINENSI. B.M. MCCCCL," where the "D" may stand for either "DIVAE" or "DOMINAE" [ML, "Sacred to the Blessed Memory of the Goddess (Lady?) Isotta of Rimini, 1450"]. Pound reads it as *Divae* [cf. *Divae Ixottae* in 76/459].

81. "Past ruin'd Latium": An echo of the line "Past ruined Ilion Helen lives" from the poem "To Ianthe" by W. S. Landor which Pound quotes to align Isotta with the archetypal Helen [8:21].

82. San Vitale: Byzantine church in Ravenna dating back to the 6th century, like S. Apollinare, and similarly full of marble, mosaics, and carved columns [cf. 28 above]. Pound compares the quiet dignity of the old sarcophagi outside San Vitale to the conglomeration of styles in the Tempio.

Glossary Canto X

1. Sorano: Sigismundo laid siege to this castle in the winter of 1454-55 [9:48, 64] while in the service of Siena. To Pound, the Siena venture was another turning point in Sigismundo's fortunes because he incurred the enmity of Enea Silvio Piccolomini [later Pius II], who was then Bishop of Siena [9:21]. According to Pound, there was no "deceit, conspiracy, treachery, slander" Piccolomini would not stoop to in order to destroy Sigismundo.

2. Orsini: Aldobrandino O., Count of Pitigliano [9:48]. From his stronghold Orsini wrote Sigismundo a taunting letter containing the same suggestions as those already made by Trachulo, namely that he abandon the siege and make himself master of Siena instead. From Sigismundo's strange truce with Orsini after he had actually breached the fortress [9:49], it would appear that he accepted Orsini's suggestions.

3. Trachulo: [9:71].

4. Fanesi: Citizens of Fano. This unknown and improbable incident, for Fano belonged to Sigismundo's own territory, was poss. invented by Pound to indicate the trivial nature of the tasks now left to Sigismundo, who had served the great powers of Naples, Florence, and Venice [8:38].

5. three men: Carlo Gonzago, Ghiberto da Correggio, and Sigismundo, officers in command of the three armies serving the Sienese [9:48].

6. Careggi: Ghiberto da Correggio, the second officer called in by the Sienese, naturally saw himself as Sigismundo's rival for the favor of the commune.

7. Carmagnola: Francesco Bussone da C., 1380-1432, one of the most distinguished condottieri of the century. In 1432 he offered his daughter in marriage to the then 15-year-old Sigismundo. The offer was accepted, but because of Carmagnola's execution shortly thereafter Sigismundo reneged on the marriage, though keeping the dowry. Bussone had long been in the service of the noble family of the Visconti of Milan, from whom he had received the title of count. In 1424 he shifted to the service of Venice, whose citizens traditionally hired professional soldiers to do their fighting while they themselves followed exclusively mercantile interests. But they were always careful to stipulate that no condottiere should ever enter Venice with his troops. The condottieri were of course little interested in bringing any armed conflict to a speedy conclusion and Carmagnola, who had been procrastinating like Sigismundo at Sorano, was therefore suspected by the Venetians of having been bribed by the Visconti. In order to set a warning example, the council summoned Carmagnola to Venice (i.e., "invited [him] to lunch") to give a progress report. On his arrival on May 5, 1432, he was seized and summarily executed, an event that left an indelible mark on other soldiers of fortune.

Thus, when Sigismundo was invited to Siena to discuss the situation, he recalled the fate of Carmagnola and declined the "invitation to lunch" [17:31].

8. the two columns: The columns (one red, one gray), brought from Syria in 1128, were set up at the Piazetta, the sea entrance to Venice and also the traditional site of executions. The red column is surmounted by a marble statue of the first patron saint of Venice, St. Theodorus, and his emblem, the crocodile [26/121], while the gray column is surmounted by his more prestigious successor, the evangelist St. Mark, and his emblem, a bronze winged lion, reputedly an ancient Chinese or Babylonian artefact. Since St. Theodorus had belonged to the lowly Eastern Church, the Venetians replaced him as their patron saint at the first opportunity (838) by St. Mark, whose remains they had pressured the padres of an Alexandrinian monastery into relinquishing to them for the trifling sum of 50 zecchini. His bones were smuggled out of the harbor under sides of bacon, which it was correctly surmised would ward off the curiosity of the Moslem officials. Thus the execution site itself came to signify a betrayal.

9. Et ... Sigismundo: ML, I, "they've got the better of Sigismundo," from a letter by Filippo Strozzi dated December 31, 1454 [Luciano Banchi in *Archivio Storico Italiano*, ser. IV, iii, 184-197] giving an account of Sigismundo's retreat after the Sienese raid on his headquarters [9:49]. Sigismundo, finding all escape routes blocked, finally requested permission from Florence to pass through its territory at Campiglia, which was granted as predicted in Strozzi's letter.

10. Filippo Strozzi: 1426-1491, member of the famous Florentine family driven into exile in 1434. Filippo became a banker in Naples, amassing a huge fortune. Later he was allowed to return to Florence. Zan Lottieri is Zanobi Lottieri [ibid.].

11. Florence ... Pitigliano: I, "Italian Historical Archives. . . . The War of the Sienese against the Count of Pitigliano," i.e., Ban-

chi's record of the Sienese affair. Identification of source of three foregoing lines.

12. Carlo Gonzago: [9:48]. Leader of the Venetian forces supporting Siena against Pitigliano; he had also outraged the commune by forcibly entering Orbetello with his troops with the intention of staying there over the winter. The Venetians had only just assuaged the Sienese on this count when Sigismundo turned up, requesting permission to take refuge at Orbetello. It certainly was an unpropitious moment.

13. Orbetello: Town situated in the middle of a muddy lagoon ca. 100 km S of Siena, whence "mud-frog."

14. Caro Mio: I, "My dear man." Gonzago addressing Sigismundo.

15. Broglio: [cf. 16 below; 8:41].

16. Gorro Lolli: Nephew of the Bishop of Siena [later Pius II, cf. 1 above], an influential man in Sienese affairs who had always defended Sigismundo. As Sigismundo had been offended by the distrust of the Sienese, Broglio had suggested that the commune placate him with the gift of a valuable charger with trappings; the horse was formally presented to him by Gorro Lolli. When Sigismundo, forgetting his upbringing, neglected to give the bearer a small present in return as custom required, the latter was deeply offended.

17. Piccinino: Giacomo P., d. 1465, a powerful condottiere released from Venetian service after the Treaty of Lodi (1454), was hanging around with his private army in the hope of establishing a dynasty as other condottieri had done (e.g., Francesco Sforza). Thus he was a constant threat to anyone in power in Italy up to the year of his death, a fact recorded by Machiavelli [quoted in 21/97: *E non avendo stato* . . ., i.e., "And as Piccinino had no property / or state, / anyone who had, felt threatened by him"]. Piccinino married Drusiana [cf. 23 below], another daughter of Francesco Sforza, at Milan and was invited to celebrate the event (another "invitation to lunch") at Naples by Alphonso of Aragon's son Ferrante [Ferdinand; cf. 44, 46, 48 below; 8:10]. Ferrante feasted Piccinino for 27 days and then had him thrown into a dungeon and strangled, afterward spreading the rumor that Piccinino had fallen out a window. This crime shocked all Italy. But it is doubtful that Francesco Sforza was a party to the plot [Muratori, IX, 236-237; 21/97].

18. the old row with Naples: [8:10; 9:18]. Alphonso of Aragon had turned Piccinino against Sigismundo, but Piccinino was diverted from his attempt to seize Rimini. Alphonso's son Ferdinand [Ferrante, 1458-1494], who succeeded Alphonso after his death in 1458, continued the old feud with Sigismundo.

19. Mantua: The most serious problem confronting Piccolomini when he became Pius II in 1458 was the Moslem threat to Europe. In 1453 Constantinople had fallen to the Turks [8:29], who had since overrun the whole of Peloponnesus (Morea), Attica, and Corinth. Hence Pius II called an international congress at Mantua in 1459. All the delegates agreed that the countries nearest the Turks should do the fighting, while the Italians should supply the funds. Sigismundo alone proposed the opposite on two grounds: (1) the countries nearest the Turks, having been defeated, were already demoralized; (2) the Italians, being more quick-witted and also better fighters, should do the fighting, while the others should foot the bill [Pius II, *Commentaries* III; 11:21; 26/125].

20. Borso: B. d'Este, 1413-1471, natural son of Niccolò d'Este [8:51], Lord of Ferrara and Modena, patron of learning and the arts, and dedicated to keeping the peace. Because of Borso's peaceful diplomacy, Ferrara was known throughout Italy during his rule as *la terra della pace* ["the domain of peace"]. Since he always strove to maintain neutrality in all conflicts, he was frequently called upon by his neighbors to arbitrate their quarrels and "keep the peace." At the same time he succeeded in increasing his

own territory without bloodshed. He was a friend of Sigismundo's [8:5] and in 1456, when Rimini was under heavy pressure, tried to mediate between Sigismundo and one of his worst enemies, Federigo d'Urbino [cf. 9:14, 25, 39; 17/78, 79; 20/91, 21/96; 24/114; 26/121].

21. Bel Fiore: Borso had arranged a meeting between Federigo d'Urbino, who was passing through Ferrara, and Sigismundo. They dined together and the next day repaired to Borso's villa Belriguardo (Pound's *Bel Fiore*). All present sought to persuade them to make peace and become friends, but according to Battaglini [468] they came close to blows instead. The exchange of vituperations given by Pound: Sigismundo: "Te cavero . . ." ["I, I'll tear your guts out"]; Federigo, "el Conte levatosi" ["the count rising"], says: "Io te . . ." ["I'll tear your liver out"] [9:14; 81/518].

22. Cosimo: C. de' Medici, 1389-1464, Florentine banker, patron of the arts, founder of the elder branch of the family, called Pater Patriae by his fellow citizens. It was his policy to work in close association with Francesco Sforza [cf. 8:15, 38; 21/96, 97; 26/123, 124].

23. Drusiana: One of Francesco Sforza's illegitimate daughters, all of whom he used to further his own political ends [cf. 17 above]. Another, Polissena, was Sigismundo's second wife [8:40; 9:23]. Yet another was married to Federigo d'Urbino. Drusiana married Piccinino in 1465, which pleased Cosimo as the alliance made Piccinino less of a threat to Florence. Drusiana, however, was soon to be widowed.

24. un sorriso malizioso: I, "a malicious smile."

25. INTEREA . . . FLAGRAVIT: ML. Quoted by Yriarte from the *Commentaries* of Pius II, this passage concerns the auto-da-fé at which Sigismundo was burned in effigy. Florence A. Gragg translates: "Meantime in front of the steps of St. Peter's there was built a great pyre of dry wood, on top of which was placed an effigy of Sigismundo imitating the [wicked and accursed] man's features and dressed so exactly that it seemed a real person rather than an image. But that no one should make any mistake about it, an inscription issued from the figure's mouth, which read: SIGISMUNDO MALATESTA, SON OF PANDOLFO, KING OF TRAITORS, HATED OF GOD AND MAN, CONDEMNED TO THE FLAMES BY VOTE OF THE HOLY SENATE. This writing was read by many. Then, while the populace stood by, fire was applied to the pyre and the image, which at once blazed up." The events leading up to this incident were the following: Sigismundo, surrounded by enemies, had ultimately been forced to come to terms with Pius II, agreeing to a treaty under which he was to pay an indemnity to Naples for his betrayal, surrender some of his strongholds to Federigo d'Urbino and Pius II, and undertake to abstain from all military activities for ten years. Sigismundo broke the treaty the following year by seizing two fortresses from Federigo d'Urbino and attacking Sinigaglia. Pius II immediately excommunicated him, declaring all his possessions forfeit and instituting legal proceedings against him. Shortly afterward (1461) the pope sent a large army against Sigismundo, who completely routed the superior papal forces [cf. 60 below]. Pius II thereupon renewed the charges against Sigismundo and issued a total interdict against anyone helping him or communicating with him; the pope also summoned Sigismundo to Rome to be burned alive (not even a pretense at an "invitation to lunch"). Since Sigismundo did not show up, Pius had two effigies made of him (the first one not having shown a sufficient resemblance) "costing 8 florins 48 bol," to be burned on the steps of St. Peter's.

26. Andreas Benzi: Of Siena, d. 1460. Fiscal agent of Pius II ordered by the latter to present the case against Sigismundo before the consistory of cardinals.

27. Papa Pio Secundo . . . : I, "Pope Pius II / Aeneas Silvius Piccolomini / of Siena,"

Piccolomini was short and stout and had a puffed face of ashen complexion which turned livid at the slightest indisposition [cf. 36 below].

28. bear's-greased latinity: Pius II was generally known for his elegant Latin, although most of his references to Sigismundo were characteristically vulgar, for which reason some of them were omitted from the official edition of his *Commentaries* [*Commentarii rerum memorabilium*, Rome, 1584] and are only to be found in the *Vatican Codex Reginensis*, no. 1995. Pound suggests that he had cooperated in writing the text of Benzi's list of charges, losing all sense of style through his personal animosity toward Sigismundo. Pius even went to the extreme of "canonizing" Sigismundo as "a devil in hell," thereby rather exceeding his sphere of jurisdiction.

29. Stupro . . . concubinarius: ML; the text of the indictment runs: "Ravisher, butcher, adulterer / murderer, parricide, and perjurer, / killer of priests, reckless [one], lecher, / . . . fornicator and assassin, / traitor, rapist, committer of incest, arsonist, and keeper of concubines."

30. and that he rejected: All present at the consistory agreed with Benzi's list of charges, but Federigo d'Urbino and Alessandro Sforza added that Sigismundo also "rejected not one or two articles of the Catholic faith but the entire Catholic Creed" and had no sense of religion. In his *Commentaries* Pius II even claimed that Sigismundo was in the pay of the Turks and had betrayed the cause of Christianity. Pound adds the charge that Sigismundo did not believe that the Church should own property or have temporal power to show how his ideas were far ahead of his age, prefiguring the criticism later to be leveled against the Church by the Reformation.

31. nisi forsitan epicureae: L, "unless perhaps a follower of Epicurus" [?342-270 B.C.]. For Pound this Greek philosopher represented an enlightened mind [cf. 31/156 where John Adams and Jefferson agree on this point in their old age, at the same time bringing up the very arguments touched upon by Sigismundo's enemies].

32. chiexa: I, *chiesa*, "church." The account of these juvenile pranks illustrates both Sigismundo's high spirits [11:34] and his enemies' lack of humor.

33. "Whence that his . . .: Pound's imitation of Benzi's rhetoric.

34. Lussorioso . . . uxoricido: I, "Lustful indulger in incest, perfidious, filthpot and glutton, / assassin, greedy, grabbing, arrogant, untrustworthy / counterfeiter, sodomite, wife-killer," Benzi's charges against Sigismundo [cf. 29 above] are here repeated with trimmings in Italian.

35. Orationem . . . filii: ML, "We have heard a most elegant and highly ornate speech of our reverend brother in Christ and most beloved son." Thus Pius II praises Benzi's indictment of Sigismundo.

36. Testibus idoneis: ML, "with fit witnesses," these being ironically Sigismundo's archenemies, Federigo d'Urbino and Alessandro Sforza. Pound associates these words with Pius's proverbial gallstones (he calls him "old bladder" [9:21]), reading *testibus* as "testicles."

37. cardinale di San Pietro in Vincoli: The cardinal at that time was Nicolas Cusanus, 1401-1464, whom Pius II had instructed to try Sigismundo *in absentia*. The adjective "kid-slapping" could refer to his recent ill-tempered behavior as Bishop of Brixen, where he banned parish fairs on feast days and ordered the excommunication of persons seen dancing in public. As a wheeler-dealer in papal politics, he amassed a fortune early by exploiting the inhabitants of church benefices awarded him in the archdiocese of Trèves and later again as Bishop of Brixen. On the other hand he was also an important philosopher who rebelled against syllogistic or Aristotelian logic by introducing the concept of the *coincidentia oppositorum*, was the first to declare the existence of a plural-

ity of worlds and to claim that the earth rotates around the sun (ideas later taken up by Giordano Bruno [cf. 114/791]), and also the first to denounce the Pseudo-Isidorus and the Constantine Donation as a forgery, for which argument Lorenzo Valla provided in 1440 the scholarly substantiation later published as *De falso credita et ementita Constantini donatione declamatio* (Basle, 1950) [cf. 89/602; *GK*, 160; *LE*, 192; *Versa prosaici*, 17] [EH].

38. tanta novità: I, "such oddities." Borso is voicing the general opinion in Italy at the time that the auto-da-fé of Sigismundo violated the humanistic spirit of the age.

39. stuprum, raptum: ML, "debauchery, rape," part of the list of charges against Sigismundo.

40. I.N.R.I. . . . Proditorum: ML, *Iesus Nazarenus, Rex Iudaeorum*, the inscription over the Cross of Jesus, here ironically placed over the head of Sigismundo's effigy: "Jesus of Nazareth, King of the Jews, General Sigismundo, King of Traitors."

41. Old Pills: Ugolino de'Pili, Sigismundo's old tutor. Benzi charged Sigismundo with having Ugolino and his sons imprisoned and murdered. The falsity of the charge was proved when Ugolino emerged alive from jail (where he had been put for conspiring against Sigismundo's life).

42. Et les angloys . . . : MF, "And the English unable to eradicate . . . poison of hatred." Poss. refers to the burning of Joan of Arc by the English 30 years before the burning in effigy of Sigismundo. The paranoiac treatment of Joan of Arc by the English reflected the hatred engendered by the Hundred Years War (1337-1453); the hatred is still evident in Shakespeare's treatment of Joan as a "Minister of Hell" in *Henry VI*, I, a play winding up with the marriage of Henry to the "she-wolf of Anjou," i.e., René of Anjou's daughter Margaret, 1430-1480 [cf. 44 below; Pound's interest in Joan of

Arc is also manifest in 80/503; 91/617; 93/630].

43. Gisors . . . : [6:21, 23]. The possession of Gisors and the Norman Vexin was one of the crucial factors in the Hundred Years War. The French regained Gisors from the English "Angevins," the Plantagenets being descended from Godfrey V, Count of Anjou.

44. Angevins: Members of the house of Anjou, here referring to the French line and particularly to René of Anjou, 1408-1480, Duke of Lorraine [cf. 42 above], whose claim to the throne of Naples and Sicily was as legitimate as that of Alphonso of Aragon [8:10]. In sending emissaries to René of Anjou in 1458, urging him to send an army to Italy to reclaim the throne of Naples, Sigismundo fatefully initiated centuries of war between Aragon and Anjou in S Italy as well as the prolonged occupation of the region by the French, Spanish, and Austrians, which accounts for the present still underdeveloped state of the S as well as its virtual separation from the rest of Italy. The "we" in "we dragged in the Angevins" refers to Machiavelli's charge in *Il Principe* that the condottieri in general were responsible for the inroads made by the French and Spanish on Italian territory.

45. Louis Eleventh: King of France, 1461-1483. Sigismundo had sought the aid of Louis against Pius II, but when Louis urged Pius II to support the Angevin cause in Naples, Sigismundo's ploy failed [18/81].

46. tiers Calixte: MF, "the third Calixtus." Pope Calixtus III and Alphonso of Aragon both died in 1458. Calixtus was succeeded by Pius II [9:21] and Alphonso by his natural son Ferrante (Ferdinand), both implacable enemies of Sigismundo [cf. 18 above].

47. this Aeneas: Pius II. Aeneas Sylvius Piccolomini chose the name "Pius" in recollection of the reference to *pius Aeneas* in Virgil's *Aeneid*, IX:21.

48. Ferdinando: King of Naples after the death of his father Alphonso of Aragon [cf. 18, 46 above].

49. Piombino: Refers to Sigismundo's defeat of Alphonso of Aragon at Piombino in 1448, Sigismundo then being in the service of the Florentine Republic. Alphonso retreated, leaving Ferdinand to drag out the war.

50. Piccinino: [cf. 17 above].

51. marriage: Alphonso once proposed that his niece marry Sigismundo's son, Roberto; on another occasion he offered Sigismundo the command of his army in the N. Both offers were declined.

52. Mantua: [cf. 19 above].

53. Tolfa: In 1462 vast deposits of alum, a mineral essential for the dyeing of wool, were discovered in the Papal States, giving the Church a virtual monopoly. Tolfa is still a center of alum mining. The discovery greatly increased the wealth of the Church, which had hitherto spent some 300,000 ducats a year to import alum from the Turks. Pius II [Pio] described the discovery as "a victory over the Turks." Pound's suggestion here is that this uncanny luck must have been the work of the devil [93/624].

54. Francesco: F. Sforza describing his interest in the division of the Malatesta territories in 1464 [8:46; 11:15, 16]. Actually Sforza disapproved of the liquidation of the Malatesta domain as a dangerous precedent that might one day jeopardize his own newly achieved status.

55. mal hecho: S, "badly done."

56. Pasti: Matteo da P., d. 1468 [9:56, 75]. Pasti, who had been commissioned by Sigismundo to paint a portrait of the Ottoman Sultan Mohammed II (1430-1481), was arrested by the Venetians on suspicion of being in league with the Turks, but he was ultimately released [21/98; 26/121; 74/437].

57. Borso: [cf. 20 above and 17/78, 79].

58. Novvy: [8:30; 9:5]. Sigismundo's youngest brother Domenico, called "Malatesta Novello," was friendly with Giacomo Piccinino and at one time promised to make him his heir [11:18]. The suggestion here that Domenico was party to a conspiracy against Sigismundo is without historical foundation.

59. Count Giacomo: I.e., Piccinino [cf. 17 above].

60. E gradment . . . annutii: I, *Grandemente li antichi e valenti romani davano fed a questi annuntii chiamati augurii* ["The an-

cient Roman knights put great faith in such omens"]. Pound is transcribing Broglio's Latin without heeding his diacritical marks. The clue to this address of Sigismundo to his captains before sending them into battle against superior papal forces in the spring of 1461 [cf. 25 above] is its allusion to the number of homosexuals among the ecclesiastical legates under the command of the Bishop of Corneto: "Though they outnumber us in heads, we have more men."

Glossary Canto XI

1. E gradment . . . annutii: [10:60].

2. Bernardo Reggio . . . : A Homeric roster of Sigismundo's officers in the battle near Vitelleschi in 1461. Piero della Bella is called a "gay bird" because the Italian (Broglio's chronicle, given by Tonini) reads *il gagliardo Piero della Bella*, where *gagliardo* can have the meaning "sturdy" or "gay." "Roberto" refers to Sigismundo's eldest son [cf. 8, 9 below; 9:61, 63; 10:51].

3. dilly cavalli tre milia: I, "of horses, three thousand," Sigismundo had only 1,300 cavalry and 500 foot soldiers to the pope's 3,000 cavalry and 2,000 foot soldiers. For *dilly* read *delli*, poss. intended as a pun.

4. mille tre cento . . . : I, "Thirteen hundred horses / . . . and barely 500 / foot."

5. spingard: I, *spingarda*, "battering ram."

6. mille . . . cavalli: I, "one thousand five hundred horses." A reference to Sigismundo's booty.

7. E li . . . trecento: I, "And the men of Messer Sigismundo were barely one thousand three hundred."

8. next August: After having taken Sinigaglia in 1462 [10:25], Sigismundo withdrew but was forced into an engagement at Mondolfo (near plains of Fano) on August 24, which he lost. Leaving his son Roberto to defend Fano he then sought to obtain help by the sea route from his Angevin allies in

the south [10:44]. *August* could also refer to the defeat of the Angevin forces at Troya [cf. 10 below].

9. Roberto: R. Malatesta, 1442-1482, Sigismundo's eldest son, made legitimate by Pope Nicholas V. At the age of 21 Roberto led the defense of Fano against Federigo d'Urbino in a manner that won the admiration of his enemies. Pius II, with heavy sarcasm, called him "a child worthy of his father." But Roberto was forced to surrender Fano in 1463. He was later disinherited by Sigismundo in favor of Sallustio, his son by Isotta. As a result Sallustio was murdered in 1470, presumably by, or at the behest of, his half brother Roberto [8:52; 9:63].

10. Tarentum: Dominant seaport of the Gulf of Taranto. Unable to withstand the superior forces of his enemies, Sigismundo turned south to seek aid via the sea from his allies, the Angevins, one of whom was the prince of Taranto [cf. 8 above]. Taranto was claimed by René of Anjou [10:44], represented by his son John, Duke of Calabria, who had been severely beaten at Troya on August 18, 1462, by Ferrante and Alessandro Sforza.

11. Anti-Aragons: [10:44].

12. Feddy: Federigo d'Urbino was beleaguering Roberto in Fano. His profile as depicted by Piero della Francesca in the bas-relief at the Bargello in Florence shows his "nick-nose." The *s.o.b.* is an allusion to Federigo's dubious parentage [9:14].

13. Par che ... mundo: I [pun], "He seems lost to the ... Sigis ... world."

14. They say he dodders ... : Refers to the siege of Rimini begun by Federigo in the winter of 1462-63 but lifted in 1463 because the plague had broken out in both the city and the countryside. The lines express the hope that Sigismundo might himself have fallen a victim to the plague.

15. rottenes' peace: Although Federigo in 1463 had taken neither Rimini nor the famous La Rocca [9:10], the peace dictated by Pius II all but ruined Sigismundo Malatesta [8:5].

16. Quali lochi ... : I, "These are the places in question." Under the peace treaty dictated by Pius II in 1463 Federigo d'Urbino was awarded the lion's share of the Malatesta domain, which had once extended across the Marches of Ancona and included many towns and fortified places. The rest were shared among Pius II's followers and captains, as well as Antonio Piccolomini, his nephew. The places listed are from a document drawn up in the name of a distant relative of Sigismundo's, Carlo de' Malatesti, a supporter of Pius II, from whom he expected to receive them as an award [F.G. Battaglini, 659].

17. salt heaps: The above list further recalls the loss of Cervia with its lucrative salt industry. Cervia had been awarded to Novello [10:58] in 1443 by the German emperor. By 1463 he had found himself forced to sell it to Venice.

18. lame Novvy: Novello was lamed in an accident at age 29, and his condition was made worse by medical treatment. He was retiring and quite unlike his warlike brother. But under the treaty of 1463 he was allowed to retain the city of Cesena for life with the proviso that if he died without issue it should revert to the Holy See, which it did in 1465 [8:31, 55; 9:5; 10:58].

19. Piero ... Vanni: These anecdotes are quoted by Tonini from the unpublished *"Cronaca"* of Gaspare Broglio at the Gambalunga Library in Rimini. *Old Zuliano* is an unidentifiable minor character; Robert is either Sigismundo's son [cf. 9 above] or Roberto Valturio [9:19]. Piero is Piero della Bella, one of Sigismundo's officers. Vanni is Giovanni Malatesta, another of Sigismundo's sons. The anecdotes suggest that as the power of the pope increased, Sigismundo was gradually reduced to meaningless activity and worrying about passing on his estate and responsibilities.

20. Sub annulo ... : ML, "Under the seal of the pope, the palace and council chamber, once of the Malatesta ... Cesena of the beautiful columns." The "z" sound and the elided "11" are supposed to reproduce Sigismundo's Romagnole accent. The inscription **OLIM DE MALTESTIS** ["once of the Lords Malatesta"] in the "long room over the arches" at Fano is frequently cited by Pound [30/149; 76/462; 80/501; 83/529]. The beautiful columns of Cesena are those of the Hospital of the Holy Cross built by Novello, who also built the magnificent library.

21. Morea: I.e., Peloponnesus [8:29, 31; 10:19]. Refers to the campaign of 1464-1466, when Sigismundo's services were once more enlisted by the Republic of Venice to recover Peloponnesus from the Turks. Sigismundo, leading an army of 7,000 which was soon reduced to 5,000, was hopelessly outnumbered by the 25,000 Turks. Frustration, defeat, and the plague forced him to disengage at Lacedaemon and go into winter quarters at a place N of Sparta, where he fell ill and was reported dead [8:46]. Hopelessly short of men and disgusted by the intrigues and suspicions at home, he sought permission to withdraw and returned to Rimini in 1466.

22. And we sit here ... : Pound and companions watching events and historical characters of all ages as if staged in the arena at Verona [cf. 4:45; 12:1; 29:41; 78/481; 80/505].

23. **And they trapped him** . . . : [9:1, 2; 10:9].

24. **And the poor devils** . . . : [9:48, 49; 10:1].

25. **Vogliamo** . . . : I, "It is our desire that the women. . . ." Sigismundo had early decreed that the womenfolk residing in his domains should dress up in all their finery. His command was in sharp contrast with the petty restrictions on the attire of women imposed in other parts of Italy at that time [cf. 22:31] in order to maintain the class barrier between aristocracy and commoners. The rising wealth and power of the commercial classes were already beginning to vex the increasingly impoverished aristocracy, especially in the republics of Florence and Venice.

26. **Platina**: Bartolomeo Sacchi, 1421-1481, a celebrated humanist known by his assumed Latin name, Platina. Pius II had made him a member of the College of Abbreviators. The college was dissolved by Pius's successor, Paul II [cf. 28 below], an act that brought him a letter of protest from Platina, who was thereupon thrown into jail for four months. Platina later became a member of the Accademia Romana [cf. 27 below]. When an alleged conspiracy against Paul II was discovered in 1468, Platina was once more cast into jail and interrogated under torture. He later avenged himself on Paul II in his *History of the Popes*. After Sigismundo arrived in Rome hoping for a chance to assassinate Paul II, he visited Platina. Later, when Platina was asked under torture whether he had conspired with Sigismundo against the pope and what they had talked about, he gave the answer translated in 29 below.

27. **Accademia Romana**: L, "Roman Academy." Being passionately devoted to the classics, the academy was accused of worshiping pagan deities such as Zeus. Like Sigismundo in his Tempio [9:32, 80] and Gemistus Plethon [8:31, 32, 33], they visualized a synthesis between the Christian religion and Greek polytheism, an idea to which Pound subscribed [cf. *L*, 30, 182,

345]. Being also confirmed republicans with regard to church authority [10:37], they were opposed to the pope's wielding absolute power. Paul II ultimately dissolved the academy, imprisoned several of its members, and declared any mention of its name to be a heresy.

28. **fatty Barbo**: Pietro B., 1417-1471, Pope Paul II (1464-1471), who succeeded Pius II. On election he chose the name "Formosus" [L, "Handsome"], which was rejected by the cardinals because it could be understood as an allusion to his good looks, a detail that to Pound pinpoints his fatheaded conceit. When Sigismundo returned from Morea in 1466 [cf. 21 above] Paul awarded him the Golden Rose as a "Champion of Christendom," an act that seemed to indicate a total reversal of the policy of Pius II. But the following year Paul, who disliked the idea of troops in the pay of Venice being stationed in Rimini, proposed that Sigismundo should exchange Rimini, the sole remaining possession he had inherited from his ancestors, for the lordships of Spoleto and Foligno. Deeply offended, Sigismundo rode to Rome firmly resolved to kill Paul II. But the pope, suspecting his intentions, summoned seven cardinals "whom he could trust" to stand by him, thus upsetting Sigismundo's plan [Tonini, 314-315, citing Broglio].

29. **de litteris** . . . : ML, "about scholarship and war, and men of outstanding genius." In a letter to John Quinn dated August 10, 1922, Pound comments: "He [S. de M.] was in Rome towards the end, the whole existence of his state depending on negotiations. . . . [He] spent most of his time in the papal library, and when they asked the librarian, Platina, what they had talked about he said 'We talked about books, and fighting, and unusual intelligence, both in the ancients, and in men of our own time, in short the things one wd naturally talk about'" [YC]. [Cf. 34/165, where the idea is used to characterize J. Q. Adams; 80/512; 83/528; Rome broadcast entitled "James Joyce: To His Memory," FR, *LPJ*, 272.]

30. sexaginta ... plures: For *tentatur* read *teneatur*. ML, "Sixty-four, nor is he to have more." The agreement that Paul II drew up for Sigismundo the following year (1468) allowed him a company of only 64 soldiers and an annual payment of only 8,000 florins, a vast comedown from the rates he had been used to. Since Paul as vicar of Rimini had the right to garrison the town himself, Sigismundo was allowed to station only half of his own company there. Paul II was eager to have his own men in Rimini in order to keep an eye on Venice, the Vatican's traditional enemy.

31. Formosus: Pope Paul II [cf. 28 above].

32. Montefiore: A stronghold in the Malatesta domain. A reference to Sigismundo's return from Morea some time between 1466 and 1468 [cf. 21 above]. Paul II, who had taken Montefiore into his own hands, is warned by the castellan to keep Sigismundo out of the district because he and his family are popular heroes. The cries of "Pandolfo" would not have been meant for Sigismundo personally, but for his whole dynasty from Pandolfo I (d. 1326) on.

33. Henry: Enrico Aquadelli, steward to Sigismundo.

34. Actum ... : ML, "Executed at the castle of Sigismundo ... in the presence of Roberto of Valturio ... freely and in clear understanding ... to Henry of Aquabello." This notarization of who was entitled to play a practical joke on whom once more illustrates Sigismundo's unquenchable spirit even in adversity. Sigismundo died at the age of 51, only three and a half months after signing the agreement with Paul II on October 7, 1466.

CANTO XII

Sources

Mostly nonliterary and personal experience. *Odyssey* I, 3.

Background

EP, "Indiscretions or Une Revue de Deux Mondes" and "Stark Realism," in *PD; SP*, 61; B. L. Reid, *The Man from New York: John Quinn and His Friends*, Oxford, 1968; NS, *Life*.

Exegeses

CE, *Ideas*, 32, 55, 114-115, 158; EH, *Approaches*, 141, 172, 264; HK, *Era*, 344, 390, 417, 425-426.

Glossary

1. **Arena romana**: L, "The Roman Arena." Pound alludes to the Theatrum in the Baths of Diocletian, situated at the junction of the Quirinal and Viminal hills in Rome, but the arena of the *Cantos* is at Verona [4:48], where Pound began his meditations on history. He used the arena as a symbolic stage where many a dramatic or significant moment of human history, past and present, is acted out. At 4/16, "there in the arena" leads into the historical events of Canto V. At 29/145, "toward sundown by the arena / (les gradins)," a linkage is established by repeating "les gradins," suggesting steps up a metaphorical Mt. Purgatory on the way to a terrestrial paradise [cf. also 78/481].

2. **les gradins ... calcaire**: F, "the steps / forty-three tiers made of limestone." At 91/614, "the steps" are 44. [Asked about the disparity in 1972, Pound affirmed 44, which would include the arena pavement. FR; cf. also picture: HK, *Era*, 344.]

3. **Baldy Bacon**: Francis S. B., fl. 1910, American businessman whom Pound met at the old Weston boardinghouse at 24 East 47th Street during his 1910 visit to America. "Baldy" was a "jobber ... living on the fringes of the business world." Pound became enthusiastic about a business proposition Baldy outlined and tried to get his father and Aunt Frank to invest in it [NS, *Life, 90*].

4. **Un centavo ...** : S, "One cent, two cents."

5. **Henry and Castano**: Private references to persons unknown. Identified in the Italian translation by Mary de Rachewiltz as "Henry Longfellow." *Index* suggests in addition to Longfellow either Henry James or Henry Newbolt as possible [cf. 74/433, and especially 80/507, where Newbolt's inverted word order is mocked].

6. **Guardia regia**: S, "royal guard."

7. **Pollon d'anthropen iden**: H, "And of many men he saw" [the cities, and knew their mind] [*Od*. I, 3].

8. **Hermes**: Messenger and herald of the gods; patron of merchants and thieves and the god of luck and wealth. Suggests Baldy arrived quickly "on the wings of Hermes [Mercury]."

9. **angelos**: H, "messenger."

10. **Habitat cum Quade**: L, "Lives with Quade."

11. **Mons Quade**: An associate of Baldy Bacon's. In "Stark Realism" [*Pavannes*] Pound wrote about Quade: "This little American went to the great city Manhattan. He made two dollars and a half per week. He saw the sheeny girls on the East Side who lunch on two cents worth of bread and sausages, and dress with a flash on the remainder. He nearly died of it. Then he got a rise. He made fifteen dollars per week selling insurance. He wore a monocle with a tortoise-shell rim. He dressed up to 'Bond St.' No lord in The Row has surpassed him. He was a damn good fellow."

12. **Dos Santos**: Prob. a Portuguese merchant. The "spoiled maize & sucking pigs" story has long been seen as an example of money lust or "usury." But since Dos Santos [S, "Two Saints"] used credit imaginatively to create real wealth [food], the story makes him a minor hero, quite in contrast with the usurious bankers in Jim X's story which follows.

13. **Tagus**: River in Spain and Portugal.

14. **nemo obstabat**: L, "nobody prevented it."

15. **e tot lo sieu aver**: P, "and all his possessions."

16. **undsoweiter**: G, "and so forth."

17. **Apovitch**: Prob. an invented name.

18. Jim X: John Quinn, 1870-1924; American lawyer; authority on modern Irish literature and drama; collector and patron of modern art.

19. S.A: South American.

20. Stambouli: Stamboul, the oldest part and main Turkish residential section of Istanbul. Although the idea of shocking the stuffed-shirt bankers with the bawdy story emphasizes the humor of the scene, the story may have another significance. Dos Santos used nature to create wealth, while the bankers, "*alias* usurers in excelsis," worked "contra naturam" with destructive effects "whining over their 20 p.c." And about sodomy, Pound wrote: "In theology, as Dante knew it, the usurer is damned with the sodomite. Usury judged with sodomy as 'contrary to natural increase,' contrary to the nature of live things" [*SP*, 61; see also *SP*, 265] .

CANTO XIII

Sources

Doctrine de Confucius: Les Quatre livres de philosophie morale et politique de la Chine, Paris, 1841, Traduits du Chinois par M. G. Pauthier. Pound uses the canonical books *Le Lun-Yu* [*The Analects*], *Le Ta Hio* [*Ta Hsüeh, The Great Digest*], and *Tchoung-Young* [*Chung Yung, The Unwobbling Pivot*] ; Chuang Tzu, XXXI. [When the standard Wade-Giles transliteration is different from Pauthier's, it is given after the Pauthier as an alternate form.]

Background

EP, *Confucius: The Great Digest, The Unwobbling Pivot, The Analects; PD*, 72-73 (EP's lively, condensed prose translation of *Le Lun-Yu*, XI, 25) "Confucius and Mencius," *SP*, 73-97; HK, *Era* 445-459; *The Complete Works of Chuang Tzu*, trans. Burton Watson, New York, Columbia University Press, 1968.

Exegeses

Little exegesis for Canto XIII exists in the published record. The indexes of most of the major books on Pound contain passing references, most of them repeating the same points. Angela Palandri, *Pai*, 3-3, 301 ff., contains new and interesting ideas; also, see David Wand, *Pai*, 3-1, 10. The lines Pound used were located by David Gordon.

Glossary

1. **Kung**: Kung Fu-tse (Confucius), 551-479 B.C., Chinese philosopher and teacher. Kung carries most of the ethical content of the *Cantos* [cf. 52/258: "Between KUNG and Eleusis"] : that is, Western ethical precepts from Aristotle on are measured against the precepts of Kung and are often found wanting. Canto 13 consists of a montage of quotations from Pauthier's translations rendered into English by Pound, who uses the French transliteration of the Chinese characters rather than the standard Wade-Giles tables. In the glosses the Wade-Giles form is given first.

2. **the cedar grove**: "the gray steps lead up under the cedars" [cf. 3/11] rhymes with "the tiered steps of the arena," the Western locus at Verona [4:48].

3. **Khieu**: Ch'iu, designation of Zan Yu, a disciple of Kung's [*Le Lun-Yu*, XI, 25; *The Analects*, 242].

4. **Tchi**: Ch'ih, surnamed Kung-hsi and styled Tsze-hwa, disciple of Kung's [*Le Lun-Yu,* XI, 25; *The Analects*, 242].

5. **Tian**: [Tien], Tsang Hsi, father of Tsang Shan, disciple of Kung's [*Le Lun-Yu*, XI, 25; *The Analects*, 242].

6. **"we are unknown"**: "Nous ne sommes pas connus" [*Le Lun-Yu*, XI, 25; *The Analects*, 242].

7. **"You will take up . . . archery?"**: "Prendrai-je l'état de voiturier, ou apprendrai-je celui d'archer? Je serai voiturier." ["Shall I take up charioteering? or shall I learn to be an archer? I will be a charioteer."] [*Le Lun-Yu*, IX, 2; *The Analects,* 228.]

8. **practice of public speaking**: No specific passage in Pauthier, but Confucius frequently condemns ornate speech and mere rhetoric.

9. **Tseu-lou**: Tze-Lu, designation of the disciple Chung Yu, often styled Yü, [*Le Lun-Yu*, XI, 25; *The Analects*, 242].

10. **". . . defences . . ."**: ". . . je pourrais faire en sorte que le peuple de ce royaume reprit un courage viril. . . ." ["I could try to make the people of this kingdom show a manly courage."] [*Le Lun-Yu*, XI, 25; *The Analects*, 242].

11. **"If I were lord . . ."**: ". . . soit préposé à son administration, en moins de trois ans je pourrais faire en sorte que le peuple eût le suffisant" ["...might propose to his administration, in less than three years I would see to it that the people were provided for"] [*Le Lun-Yu*, XI, 25; *The Analects*, 242.]

12. **"I would prefer . . . ritual"**: "Lorsque se font les cérémonies du temple des ancêtres, et qu'ont lieu de grandes assemblées publiques, revêtu de ma robe d'azur et des autres vêtements propres à un tel lieu et à de telles cérémonies, je voudrais y prendre part en qualité d'humble fonctionnaire." ["Rather than performing the ceremonies at the ancestral temples and other places of great public assemblies, adorned with my blue robe and other vestments proper for such a place and such ceremonies, I would like to take part in the rank of a humble functionary."] [*Le Lun-Yu*, XI, 25; *The Analects*, 242.]

13. **Tian said . . . mandolins**: "Le disciple ne fit plus que de tirer quelques sons rares de sa guitare; mais ces sons se prolongeant, il la déposa, et, se levant, il répondit respectueusement: Mon opinion diffère entièrement de celles de mes trois condisciples. . . . Le printemps n'étant plus, ma robe de printemps mise de côté, mais coiffé du bonnet de virilité, accompagné de cinq ou six hommes et de six ou sept jeunes gens, j'aimerais à aller me baigner dans les eaux de l'Y, à aller prendre le frais dans ces lieux touffus où l'on offre les sacrifices au ciel pour demander la pluie. . . ." ["The disciple did no more than to pluck a few occasional

notes on his lute; but with the notes still echoing, he set it down, and, rising, he answered respectfully: My opinion differs completely from those of my three codisciples.... Spring being past, my spring gown put aside, but covered with my man's hat, accompanied by five or six men and six or seven youths, I would like to go and bathe in the waters of the Y, to take the fresh air in those leafy places where one offers sacrifices to heaven to ask for rain...."] [*Le Lun-Yu*, XI, 25; *The Analects*, 242-243.]

14. And Kung smiled: "Le Philosophe, applaudissant à ces paroles par un soupir de satisfaction, dit: Je suis de l'avis de Tian." ["The philosopher praised these words by a gratified sigh and said: I agree with Tian."] [*Le Lun-Yu*, XI, 25; *The Analects*, 243.]

15. Thseng-sie: Tsang Hsi, another name for Tian [cf. 5 above].

16. Which ... nature: "Que doit-on penser des paroles de ces trois disciples? Le Philosophe dit: Chacun d'eux a exprimé son opinion; et voilà tout." ["What should one think about the words of these three disciples? The philosopher said: Each one has expressed his opinion; and that's all."] [*Le Lun-Yu*, XI, 25; *The Analects*, 243.]

17. Yuan Jang: Yüan Jang. "Youan-jang (un ancien ami du Philosophe), plus âgé que lui, etait assis sur le chemin les jambes croisées. Le Philosophe lui dit: Etant enfant, n'avoir pas eu de déférence fraternelle; dans l'âge mûr, n'avoir rien fait de louable; parvenu à la vieillesse, ne pas mourir: c'est être un vaurien. Et il lui frappa les jambes avec son bâton (pour le faire lever)." ["Yuan Jang, an old friend of the philosopher, older than he himself, was seated by the road, his legs crossed. The philosopher said to him: 'Being a child, not to have had brotherly respect; in maturity to have done nothing praiseworthy; having arrived at old age not to die: that's to be a good-for-nothing.' And he rapped his legs with his cane to make him get up."] [*Le Lun-Yu*, XIV, 46; *The Analects*, 262.]

18. And Kung said ... : "Le Philosophe dit: Dès l'instant qu'un enfant est né, il faut respecter ses facultés; la science qui lui viendra par la suite ne ressemble en rien à son état présent. S'il arrive à l'âge de quarante ou de cinquante ans sans avoir rien appris, il n'est plus digne d'aucun respect." ["The philosopher said: From the time that a child is born, one must respect his faculties; the knowledge that will come to him in the course of time will be nothing like his present state. If he lives to be forty or fifty years old without doing anything at all, he is no longer worthy of anyone's re-respect." [*Le Lun-Yu*, IX, 22; *The Analects*, 232.]

19. "When the prince ...": "... dès l'instant qu'il aura attiré près de lui tous les savants et les artistes, aussitôt ses richesses seront suffisamment mises en usage." ["From the moment that he (the Prince) has gathered about him all the savants and artists his riches will be sufficiently put to use."] [*Tchoung-Young*, XX, 12; *The Unwobbling Pivot*, 155-156.]

20. And Kung said, and wrote ... : "Les tablettes en bambou des anciennes...." ["The bamboo tablets of the ancients...."] [*Ta Hio*, 1, 7; *The Great Digest*, 35.]

21. If a man have not ... : "... ceux qui désiraient bien gouverner leurs royaumes s'attachaient auparavant à mettre le bon ordre dans leurs familles; ceux qui désiraient mettre le bon ordre dans leurs familles s'attachaient auparavant à se corriger eux-mêmes; ceux qui désiraient se corriger eux-mêmes...." ["Those who desired to govern their kingdoms well dedicated themselves first to bring good order into their families; those who desired to bring good order into their families dedicated themselves first to rectify themselves; those who desired to rectify themselves...."] [*Ta Hio*, 1, 4; *The Great Digest*, 29, 31.]

22. "brotherly deference": "La piété filiale, la déférence fraternelle, dont nous avons parlé, ne sont-elles pas le principe fondamental de l'humanité ou de la bienveillance universelle pour les hommes?" ["The filial piety and fraternal deference of which we spoke, are they not the fundamental principle of humanity or the universal benevolence for men?"] [*Le Lun-Yu*, 1, 2; *The Analects*, 195.]

23. "life after death": "Quand on ne sait pas encore ce que c'est que la vie, comment pourrait-on connaître la mort?" ["When one still does not know what life is, how can he know about death?"] [*Le Lun-Yu*, XI, 11; *The Analects*, 239.]

24. "Anyone can run . . . ": "Dépasser, c'est comme ne pas atteindre." ["To go beyond is like not hitting."] [*Le Lun-Yu*, XI, 15; *The Analects*, 240.]

25. ". . . hard to stand . . . ": "L'invariabilité dans le milieu est ce que constitue la vertu; n'en est-ce pas le faîte même? Les hommes rarement y persévèrent." ["To stand unwaveringly in the middle is what constitutes *Vertu*; is it not even the summit? Men rarely attain it."] [*Le Lun-Yu*, VI, 27; *The Analects*, 218.]

26. commit murder: ". . . le père cache les fautes de son fils, le fils cache les fautes de son père. La droiture et la sincérité existent dans cette conduite." ["The father should hide the defects of the son, the son hide the defects of the father. Rectitude and sincerity exist in such conduct."] [*Le Lun-Yu*, XIII, 18; *The Analects*, 251.]

27. Kong-Tch'ang: Kung Yeh Ch'ang, disciple and later son-in-law of Kung. "Le Philosophe dit que Kong-tchi-tchang (un de ses disciples) pouvait se marier, quoiqu'il fût dans les prisons, parce qu'il n'était pas criminel; et il se maria avec la fille du Philosophe." ["The philosopher said that Kung Yeh Ch'ang could get married although he had been in prisons, because he was not a criminal; and he married the daughter of the philosopher."] [*Le Lun-Yu*, V, 1; *The Analects*, 209.]

28. Nan-Young: Nan Yung, disciple of Kung's. "Le Philosophe dit à Nan-Young . . . que si le royaume était gouverné selon les principes de la droite raison, il ne serait pas repoussé des emplois publics; que si, au contraire, il n'était pas gouverné par les principes de la droite raison, il ne subirait aucun châtiment: et il le maria avec la fille de son frère ainé." ["The Philosopher said to Nan Yung . . . that if the kingdom was governed by the principles of right reason Nan Yung would not be fired from public office; that if, on the contrary, the kingdom was not governed by the principles of right reason, he would receive no punishment: and he married Nan Yung to the daughter of his [Confucius'] elder brother." *Le Lun-Yu*, V, 1; *The Analects*, 209.]

29. Wang: Wu Wang: 1169-1115 B.C., title under which Fa, son of Wen Wang, was canonized. Wu continued his father's battles against Cheou-Sin, assembled a huge army, and defeated him at Meng-chin in Honan and thereby ended the Shang (or Yin) dynasty. Wu ruled (1122-1115) as the first emperor of the Tcheou (Chou) dynasty. Kung said: "Les lois gouvernementales des rois Wen et Wou sont consignées tout entières sur les tablettes de bambou. Si leurs ministres existaient encore, alors leurs lois administratives seraient en vigueur . . . ." ["The governmental laws of kings Wen and Wu are completely written out on the bamboo tablets: If their ministers still existed, then their laws of administration would be in force . . . ."] [*Tchoung-Young*, XX, 2; *The Unwobbling Pivot*, 147.]

30. "And even I . . . ": "Le Philosophe dit: J'ai presque vu le jour où l'historien de l'empire laissait des lacunes dans ses recits (quand il n'était pas sûr des faits); où celui qui possédait un cheval, le prêtait aux autres pour le monter; maintenant ces moeurs sont perdues." ["The Philosopher said: I almost saw that time when the imperial historian left blanks in his writings (when he was not sure of the facts); when a person who owned a horse lent it to others to ride; now these customs are lost."] [*Le Lun-Yu*, XV, 25; *The Analects*, 267.]

31. "Without character": "Être homme, et ne pas posséder les vertus que comporte l'humanité, comment jouerait-on dignement de la musique?" ["Being man and not having the virtues appropriate to a human being, how would one play music worthily?"] [*Le Lun-Yu*, III, 3; *The Analects*, 201.]

32. "blossoms of the apricot": Chapter 31 of the Chuang Tzu starts: "Confucius, after strolling through the Black Curtain Forest, sat down to rest on the Apricot Altar."

[Watson, p. 345. A footnote explains: "the word altar here refers to a mesa or flat-topped hill rising out of the lowland."] The apricot orchard, believed to be a place where Kung lectured, is now "marked by a pavilion enclosing a stone slab with the seal characters of *Hsing T'an* ('Apricot Temple') . . . in front of the Confucian Temple in present day Ch'iu-fu of Shantung, Confucius' home town." Apricot blossoms "symbolize at once cultural florescence and Confucian teachings" [Palandri, *Pai*, 3-3, 301]. These concluding lines suggest Pound's efforts to keep Confucian thought alive and flowing from the Orient to the Occident.

CANTOS XIV-XV

The Hell Cantos

Sources

Dante, *Inf.* V, 28; Edward FitzGerald, *The Rubáiyát of Omar Khayyám*; Horace, *Ars Poetica* V, 173.

Background

EP, "The Serious Artist," *LE*, 42, and "Hell," 201-213; *L*, 191 (to Wyndham Lewis), 239 (to John Drummond), 293 (to John Lackay Brown), 210 (to his father): Preface to *CON: SR*, 127-135; *SP*, 207, 210; *A Visiting Card*, Peter Russell, London, 1952, 34; Iamblichus, *On the Mysteries of the Egyptians, Chaldeans, and Assyrians*, trans. Thomas Taylor, 3d ed., London, 1968; *The Divine Comedy*, tr. A. R. Huse, Rinehart, 1954; *The Inferno*, Italian text and trans. with commentary by Charles Singleton, 2 vols., Bollingen Series, LXXX, Princeton, 1970; Thomas Bullfinch, *Mythology*, New York, 1913; *Plotinus*, Vols. I-VI, Loeb, 1966.

Exegeses

CE, *Ideas*, passim; Dekker, *Cantos*, 7-13; LL, *Motive*, 82-83; Knox, *Pai*, 3-1, 78; JE, *Pai* 8-2.

Glossary Canto XIV

1. Io venni . . . muto: I, *Inf.* V, 28: "I came to a place mute of all light." Note rhyme with the darkness of hell in Canto I, and also "there is no darkness but ignorance" [*Twelfth Night*, IV.II.42], a favorite line of Pound's since he conceived that divinity manifested itself through intelligence [cf. preface to *CON*, 20]. In *L*, 191 (to Wyndham Lewis), Pound wrote of the "Hell Cantos": "You will readily see that the 'hell' is a portrait of contemporary England, or at least Eng. as she wuz when I left her." And in *L*, 239 (to John Drummond): "the hell cantos are specifically LONDON, the state of English mind in 1919 and 1920." And in a letter to his father [May 1925]: "I intended Cantos XIV and XV to give an accurate picture of the spiritual state of England in the years 1919 and following. Including Mr. Wilson. They were written before the Harding-Coolidge period, or I shd. have devoted a line or two to the mushiness of the former and the cant of the latter" [YC].

2. . . . . .e and . . . . .n: Lloyd George and Wilson. In *L*, 293 (to John Lackay Brown), Pound wrote: ". . . that *section* of Hell precisely has *not* any dignity. Neither had Dante's fahrting devils. Hell is not amusing. Not a joke. And when you get further along you find individuals, not abstracts. Even the XIV-XV has individuals in it, but *not* worth recording as such. In fact, Bill Bird rather entertained that I had forgotten which rotters were there. In his edtn. he tried to get the number of . . . . . . .correct in each case. My 'point' being that not even the first but only last letters of their names had resisted corruption." [For the Lloyd George, Faber has the correct 10 dots while New Directions has only 9.] Thus the name for . . . . . .f in line 22 may well be Zaharoff, the real name for Metevsky [18:12; 38:2], as Faber has the correct number of dots (7), though N.D. has only 6. Only those censored names that have been identified are glossed.

3. Profiteers: Dante puts the usurers with the sodomites at the lowest part of Cir-

cle VII, among the violent against God, and treats them as he does all mercenary souls with ultimate contempt: they are not even to be spoken to. Huse (p. 82) summarizes them: "The usurers are still competing, quarreling, rivaling, and envying each other, without honor, courage, good manners, artistic or intellectual distinction." Others in Circle VII include those who are violent against neighbors, fellowmen, and the self (suicides). They crouch at the edge of the deep canyon of Fraud which is Circle VIII. The monster Geryon [51:13, 16] carries Dante and his guide Virgil on his reptilian wings into the lower reaches of Circle VIII (the abode of panders, seducers, flatterers, simonists, soothsayers, barrators, hypocrites, thieves, evil councillors, sowers of discord, falsifiers), a place in Hell called Malebolge [*Luogo è inferno detto Malebolge*].

4. financiers: A cue to the scatological content of Pound's hell may be found in this remark: "It is said that Rabelais hid his wisdom in a mass of filth in order that it might be acceptable to his age" [*SR*, 134]. But Dante uses filth imagery at the depths of Malebolge. Although Dante translators are restrained in English, Pound's strong language can be found in such locutions as "The banks were crusted over with a mold. . . . I saw down in the ditch a people plunged in filth that seemed to have come from human privies. . . . I beheld one whose head was so befouled with ordure . . ." [*Inf.* XVIII, 106-120; Singleton trans.].

5. lashing: In Circle VIII we meet Dante's first devils who wear horns and ply the condemned with whips: "I saw horned demons with great whips beating the shades fiercely from behind" [Huse, 87].

6. betrayers of language: The occupants of Bolgia 10 are the falsifiers, who include impersonators and liars. To use words sloppily or carelessly (the opposite of Chêng Ming [51:20]) is bad enough but, in Pound's ethics, to betray the word with malice aforethought is one of the ultimate sins. Pound wrote: "Moral filth is perhaps less poisonous than intellectual filth, when it comes to considering the printed page. Moral filth, in print, poisons the reader; intellectual filth can be toxic to a whole race" [*A Visiting Card*, 34].

7. howling: Said Pound: "Hell is the state of man dominated by his passions; who has lost 'the good of the intelligence' " [*SR*, 129].

8. mysterium: L, sing. of *mysteria*, "mysteries." Secret rites in divine worship; esp. of the Eleusinian worship of Ceres [Persephone]. Later associated with alchemy.

9. acid of sulphur: Used in alchemy. Many literal-minded alchemists discounted the sacred content of the mysteries and were bent on money lust: gold. The process by which the *prima materia* (the mercury of the philosophers) was to be transmuted required the philosopher's stone which came from sulphur: "This sulphur again was not ordinary sulphur, but some principle derived from it, which constituted the philosopher's stone or elixir" [cf. *EB*, "Alchemy"].

10. jewels: Although associated with alchemy, here prob. has symbolic content related to works of art which provide "pleasures of the senses" as given in this canto, 10 lines before.

11. EIKΩN ΓΗΣ: H, "picture [or image] of the earth."

12. Pearse: Patrick Henry P., 1879-1916, Irish author and Sinn Fein leader; commander in chief of the Irish forces in the Easter Rebellion (1916); executed after surrendering his troops.

13. MacDonagh: Thomas M., 1878-1916, Irish patriot engaged in the 1916 rebellion in Ireland; executed; member of the Celtic Renaissance movement in literature.

14. Captain H.: Captain J. Bowen-Colthurst, British army officer serving in Ireland (1916) who gained notoriety for killing political prisoners in cold blood. Eventually court-martialed and confined to Broadmoor Criminal Asylum.

15. Verres: Gaius V., ca. 120-43 B.C., Roman administrator whose corruption astonished even the Romans. He plundered provinces, sold justice, avoided prosecution by selling power and influence, and corrupted and sold art treasures.

16. Calvin: John C., 1509-1564, French Protestant theologian who in Pound's view helped destroy the Mysteries of the Church and substituted fear and penance for celebration and rejoicing.

17. St. Clement of Alexandria: Titus Flavius Clemens, ?150-220?, Greek theologian of the early Christian church. His writings such as *Protrepticus* show familiarity with Greek mysteries which, after his conversion to Christianity, he rejected in favor of a Pauline, moralistic, and repressive code.

18. Westminster: District around Westminster Palace and Houses of Parliament, traditionally associated with the center of government.

19. pets-de-loup: F, "university people [scholars]"; lit., wolf farts.

20. Invidia: L, "Envy."

21. corruptio: L, "corruption."

22 Episcopus: L, "Bishop."

Glossary Canto XV

1. Grasse: City in France whose main industry, making soaps, perfumes, and the like from fats, created a noxious stench.

2. middan: Variant of midden, a dunghill or refuse heap; from ME, "myddung."

3. . . . . . .: Winston Churchill [RO].

4. USURA: The beast with a hundred legs is Pound's version of Dante's Geryon as given at the opening of *Inf.* XVII. Pound's own translation of the passage contains these lines: "Behold the wild brute with sharpened tail. ... Behold the one that fouleth all the world. ... And that uncleanly image of fraud came on, ... the rest was all a serpent's body" [*SR*, 133].

5. laudatores temporis acti: L, "admirers of bygone days" [Horace, *Ars Poetica*, 173; the original reads: *laudator temporis acti*].

6. fabians: The Fabian Society, a group of socialists, was organized in England in 1884. They espoused slow, evolutionary gradualism and were against Marxian revolution. Citing Major Douglas, Pound called Fabianism "a claim for the complete subjection of the individual to an objective" imposed on him and "a brand of poison" put forward by the intelligentsia as the ideal: "Man as a social unit. German philology with sacrifice of individual intelligence to the Moloch of 'Scholarship' " [*SP*, 207, 210].

7. et nulla . . . eos: L, "and no trust among them."

8. my guide: Virgil is Dante's guide, but since Pound uses the *Inferno* merely as a metaphor for the London of 1919-20, Virgil will be metamorphosed into Plotinus [cf. 11 below] as the Pythagorean or Neoplatonic philosopher of light who will lead Pound out of the darkness of the contemporary hell. For to both Dante and Pound, hell is a state of mind. Pound called the *Commedia* "Dante's vision of a journey through the realms inhabited by the spirits of men after death" but also "the journey of Dante's intelligence through the states of mind wherein dwell ... men before death" [*SR*, 127].

9. bolge: I, "ditches" as in Circle VIII of *Inf*. From *Malebolge* [14:3]. Pound said it contained "the violent against art, and the usurers," and, in Canto XVII, that "Dante attacks the 'unearned increment.' " Also: " 'Malebolge' is a series of concentric pits, the whole shaped somewhat like a half-opened telescope. Through the *Inferno* there is a biting satire on the aimless turmoil and restlessness of humanity ... in 'Malebolge,' only at the very root of Hell do we find the end of it, in the still malignity of the traitor's wallow" [*SR*, 133-135].

10. Andiamo: I, "Let's go." The rest of Canto XV seems to express a nightmarelike state of struggle: the kind of dream where the hero runs without progress, tries to get out of quicksand with nothing to cling to, tries to follow the directions of someone on the sidelines who cannot really help. The struggle is agonized and the scene is highly dramatic, but the hero survives the nightmare and awakes into sunlight. Yet in the last lines he drops back into an exhausted state of unconsciousness. The passage seems to be an adaptation and amalgam of materials from the Perseus-Gorgon-Medusa myth as found in several oft-used Pound sources: *Inf*. IX (an interlude between Circles V and VI which dramatizes Dante's terror at the gate of Dis); Ovid, *Meta*. IV, 743-765, 934-974; *Meta*. V, passim; the *Enneads* of Plotinus [cf. 11 below] and the Rubáiyát [cf. 16 below]. The technique of so mixing the various scenes and people seems to parallel the technique Pound used to dramatize the delirium state of Niccolò d'Este [cf. 20/90-93] as Pound described it in a letter to his father [*L*, 210]: "Then in the delirium, Nicolo remembers or thinks he is watching death of Roland. ... The whole reminiscence jumbled or 'candied' in Nicolo's delirium."

11. Plotinus: 205-270, most significant of the Neoplatonic light philosophers, and author of the *Enneads*, which were collected by Porphyry and published ca. A.D. 300. The content of the *Enneads* (so-called because the documents were arranged in six groups of nine) is similar in basics to the work of Iamblicus [5:5]. Thus Plotinus, the source of "Iamblichus' light," is an appropriate hope to lead one out of the darkness of hell. But it is also appropriate for Plotinus to be "gone" from hell as given in the last line on page 66.

12. Medusa: The worst of the three gorgons, terrifying females who laid waste the land. Bullfinch says: "She was once a beautiful maiden whose hair was her chief glory, but as she dared to vie in beauty with Minerva, the goddess ... changed her beautiful ringlets into hissing serpents. She became a cruel

monster of so frightful an aspect that no liv-
ing thing could behold her without being
turned into stone" [*Mythology*, 116]. Per-
seus, the son of Jupiter and Danaë [4:33],
was sent to slay the Medusa. Mercury lent
Perseus his winged shoes and Minerva lent
her shield which he used as a mirror so that
he would not have to look upon her directly
and be turned to stone. Says Bullfinch:
". . . guided by her image reflected in the
bright shield . . . he cut off her head and
gave it to Minerva."

13. souse: "slop." With Pound's supervision,
Mary de Rachewiltz gives "brodaglia" I,
"slops." EH, in her trans. into German, gives
"den Brei" G, "pap" or "pulp." [JE,
Pai, 8-2].

14. rast: "strip." Mary de R. gives "striscia

stretta" I, "narrow strip." EH gives "schmale
Joch" G, "narrow strip." [ibid.]

15. dern: Scot, "secret," "obscure," "dread-
ful." Mary de R. gives the phrase "the dern
evil" as "il male orrendo." EH gives it as
"dem durch unsägliche Greuel," which has
the same sense. [ibid.]

16. Naishapur: Nishapur, town in NE Iran;
birthplace of Omar Khayyám [cf. Rubáiyát,
st. 8]. Perhaps in the oblivion of the night-
marish dream, the hero is reminded of this
quatrain because of the other lines in it:
"Whether the Cup with sweet or bitter run, /
The Wine of Life keeps oozing drop by
drop, / The Leaves of Life keep falling one
by one."

17. Ἥέλιον . . . : H, "The sun, the sun."
Homeric form of Attic ' ἠλίος.

CANTO XVI

Sources

William Blake, "London," etc.; Peire Cardinal [cf. EP, *SR*, 48,
132]; Cesare de Lollis, *Vita e Poesie di Sordello di Goito* 1896;
Dante, *Pur.* VI; Arnaut Daniel [cf. EP, *LE*, 109]; J. G. Frazer,
The Golden Bough; Virgil, *Aeneid* VI, 136; Bible, Matt. 11: 18;
Propertius II, xxvi, 48.

Background

EP, *SR*, 48, 61, 132; *GB*, passim; Michael Howard, *The Franco-
Prussian War*, New York, 1961; Lincoln Steffens, *Autobiography*,
New York, 1931, 747-756.

Exegeses

LL, *Motive*, 75-76; Dekker, *Cantos*, 167, 169-170; EH, *Ap-
proaches*, 142, 172-173, 204, 206; Surette, *Pai*, 3-2, 199; JE,
Pai, 1-1, 73.

Glossary

1. hell mouth: When Dante and Virgil reach the depths of Hell at the center of the earth and the center of gravity, they turn and begin to climb back with difficulty. Just before dawn on Easter Sunday they reach the mouth of Hell and the foot of Purgatory, where Dante saw in the far distance "the beautiful things that heaven bears / and came out to see once more the stars."

2. Blake: William B., 1757-1827, English poet and visionary. Seen by Pound as a genuine religious who made heroic efforts to escape from the hell around him in his time; e.g., "The Marriage of Heaven and Hell," "Proverbs of Hell," "A Song of Liberty," "London," and such ideas as "Is the Holy Ghost any other than an intellectual Fountain?" or "What are the Pains of Hell but Ignorance, Bodily Lust, Idleness, and devastation of the things of the Spirit?" ["To the Christians"].

3. Peire Cardinal: Provençal troubadour, ca. 1185-ca. 1275, noted for his satiric attacks on evil, especially the Church in the Albigensian period in S France. Said by Pound to be "extremely lucid on the imbecility of belligerents and the makers of wars" [*SR*, 48]. Also, his "invectives against the corruption of the church temporal should be read . . ." [*SR*, 61]. And "Peire Cardinal's fable of the sane man in the city gone mad is a weaker equation for what Dante presents as a living man amongst the dead" [*SR*, 132].

4. Il Fiorentino: Dante Alighieri, 1265-1321, who as he left Hell could see Satan, as in a mirror, only backward or "upside down" [*Inf.* 34:103 ff.].

5. Sordels: Sordello [2:2; *Pur.* VI-VIII; *SR*, 57-59]. In Dante, Sordello is nowhere shown literally looking at his shield, but his main grief is over the "lack of heart" [courage] in battle of many present-day heads of cities or states. So he proposes that they eat of the heart of the hero, Sir Blancatz, to gain courage to wield their shields. Pound

translates: ". . . that they take his heart out, and have it eaten by the Barons who live un-hearted . . ." [*SR*, 58]. Thus Pound continues the metaphor of the hell men continue to create on earth.

6. Augustine: Saint A., 354-430. In the *Commedia* Augustine is mentioned twice comparatively and once incidentally [*Par.* 10:120; 12:130; 32:35], but at no point is he pictured "gazing toward the invisible." The line may then summarize the attitude expressed in *The City of God* as well as in Augustine's many other works.

7. crimen est actio: L, "crime is action."

8. Palux Laerna: L, *Palus Lernae*, the swamp of Lerna where Hercules killed the Hydra, the poisonous snake [cf. Propertius II, xxvi, 48].

9. aqua morta: L, "dead water."

10. Then light air: The scene from this line to the "one man" who "rose from his fountain / and went off into the plain" is probably based on the vision of the "Earthly Paradise" [Garden of Eden: *Pur.* 28-33]. But it is an impressionistic account in which trees become "saplings"; the two streams and the river across which Dante gazes become the "blue banded lake"; and the ten steps become the "stair of gray stone." The man who went off into the plain may rhyme with Virgil, who leaves Dante at this point since Beatrice has not become his guide. But Pound lists post-Dantean heroes in place of the "founders" Dante encounters here.

11. patet terra: L, "the earth lies open."

12. Sigismundo: S. Malatesta [8:5]. Since S. is one of the activist heroes of *The Cantos* with a vision of an earthly paradise and with a directed will [*directio voluntatis*: 77/467] rather than a paralyzed will [*abuleia*: 5:44; 54:192], he is shown contemplating his inner vision.

13. Malatesta Novello: Domenico Malatesta, 1418-1465, younger brother of Sigismundo, known popularly as "Novvy"; also a man of vision [10:58].

14. Prone in that grass: After Beatrice upbraids Dante for his sinful and childish life, he is so stung with remorse that he falls down in a faint [*Pur.* 31:85-90]. When he is restored to sense he finds himself in the river up to his throat and he hears the Lady of the Garden [Matilda] saying, "Tiemmi, tiemmi!" ["Cling to me, cling to me!"]. Beatrice has gone for the moment, but Dante is on his way "to the blessed shore" [*Pur.* 31:91-108].

15. et j'entendis des voix: F, "and I heard voices." With these words the scene of the canto switches to the hell and purgatory of contemporary wars: (1) Franco-Prussian; (2) the Silk War of Ragusa; (3) World War I; (4) the Russian Revolution.

16. Strasbourg: French city near the center of action in the Franco-Prussian War of 1870-71. Birthplace of Plarr [cf. 18 below].

17. Galliffet: General Gaston de G. Story of useless courage doomed to defeat, as in "The Charge of the Light Brigade." In the battle for Sedan, the French army, being divided and cut off from retreat, called upon Galliffet's African corps of cavalry to charge the massive German lines at Floing. He made the useless charge "leaving the carcasses of horses and the bodies of their riders lying thick in front of the German lines" [Michael Howard, *The Franco-Prussian War*, 216]. Galliffet rallied the survivors and was asked if he could try again. He said, "As often as you like, *mon général*, so long as there's one of us left." King William, seeing them plunge down the hill a second time to certain destruction, said, "Ah les braves gens!" These words were carved on a memorial erected later. A third charge led to the heaviest bloodshed of all. Legend says that Galliffet and his last followers passed exhausted within a few feet of the enemy line. "The Germans ceased fire; their officers saluted; and the Frenchmen were allowed to ride slowly away, honoured and unharmed" [ibid.].

18. Plarr: Victor Gustave P., 1863-1929, whose family settled in England after the Franco-Prussian War. The M. Verog of *Mauberley*. He told stories of that war including the famous charge of Galliffet ["For two hours he talked of Galliffet," *Mauberley*] against the Prussians and presumably the anecdote about his "Nurse." Pound knew Plarr when he worked as librarian of the Royal College of Surgeons compiling its catalog. [Pound also remarked Plarr's commemoration of the liberation of Strasbourg from the Germans in a poem, "Strasbourg," in the London *Times* of December 18, 1918 (FR)].

19. Brother Percy: Prob. Lord Algernon P., 1792-1865, British naval officer.

20. Ragusa: A port of Dalmatia which was under the control of Venice from 1205 to 1358.

21. Silk War: War between Venice and Ragusa at the beginning of the 15th century. Pandolfo led the Venetians against Ragusa in 1420 but did not capture it.

22. Lord Byron: George Gordon, 1788-1824, the English poet.

23. Franz Josef: 1830-1916, emperor of Austria, whose policies contributed to the outbreak of World War I; he rejected the Serbian note after Sarajevo and declared war on July 28, 1914.

24. Napoléon Barbiche: Charles Louis N. Bonaparte, 1808-1873, Napoleon III, known as Louis N., emperor of the French (1852-1871); called *Barbiche* because of his goatee.

25. Aldington: Richard A., 1892-1962, young associate (1912-1915) of Pound and the Imagists. Married H. D. and lived across the courtyard from Pound in Church Walk. Served as junior officer in British army (1915-1917); saw much action in trench warfare and narrowly escaped death several times. War novels: *Roads to Glory, Death of a Hero*. Poet, novelist, and critic [cf. his autobiography, *Life for Life's Sake*, 1941].

26. Henri Gaudier: 1891-1915, French sculptor who took the name of Gaudier-Brzeska. Joined with Pound, Wyndham Lewis, and others in Vorticist movement. Killed in a charge at Neuville St. Vaast, June 5, 1915. Pound used him as a prime example of the horrible waste of war. With his death a lifetime of sculpture was lost [cf. *GB*, passim, and indexes to any of Pound's volumes of collected prose].

27. T.E.H.: Thomas Ernest Hulme, 1883-1917, English philosopher and poet, killed in World War I. Original member of Imagist group. Leading mind in newly established Poets' Club which Pound joined in April 1909.

28. Kant: Immanuel K., 1724-1804, German idealist philosopher.

29. Wimbledon: Suburb of London.

30. Wyndham Lewis: Percy W. L., 1884-1957, British writer and painter. Original member of Vorticist group. Pound maintained his opinion about the superiority of Lewis's work until the end of his life [cf. 115/794]. Until 1975 edition, Faber uses the pseudonym "Maxy Larmann" in this line.

31. mitrailleuse: F, "machine gun."

32. Windeler: Donald W.

33. Aegaean: The Aegean Sea, which separates E coast of Italy from W coast of Yugoslavia.

34. Captain Baker: Guy B.; early Faber editions used Captain Corcoran.

35. Fletcher: Erroneously taken to be John Gould F., 1886-1950; American poet whom Pound met in Paris in May 1913. Associated with Imagists but turned against Pound to become "Amygist." In 1915, after World War I broke out, he returned to America, but he came back to England in 1916 to marry Daisy Arbuthnot. Was not involved in war. J. G. F. would have been 28 at outbreak of war. The 19-year-old is unidentified. Faber editions use the name "Bimmy."

36. Ernie Hemingway: Ernest H., 1899-1961, American novelist; Pound knew him well during his Paris years and promoted his work. Early Faber editions used the name Cyril Hammerton.

37. Et ma foi ... soit bien carré: F, "And really, you know, / all the nervous (or nervy) ones. No, / there is a limit; animals, animals are not / made for that, a horse doesn't amount to much. / The men of 34, on all fours, / who cried 'Mommy.' But the tough guys, / at the end, there at Verdun, there were only those big boys / and they knew exactly what the score was. / What are they worth, the generals, the lieutenant, / they weigh out at a centigramme, / they are nothing but wood. / Our captain, all shut up in himself like / the old military engineer he was, but strong, / a stronghead. There, you know, / everything, everything runs in order, and the thieves, all the vices, but the birds of prey, / there were three in our company, all killed. / They went out to plunder a corpse, for nothing, / they would have gone out for nothing but that. / And the Jerries, you can say anything you want, / militarism, etc... etc... / All that, but, BUT / the Frenchman, he fights when he has eaten. / But those poor guys / at the end they attacked each other so they could eat, / Without orders, wild animals, they took / prisoners; those who could speak French said: / 'Poo quah? Well, we attacked so we could eat.' / It's the grease, the grease / their supplies came forward at three kilometers an hour, / and they creaked, they grated, could be heard five kilometers away. / (That's what finished the war.) / The official list of dead: 5,000,000 / He tells you, well [yeah, it all smelled of oil. / But, No! I bawled him out / I said to him:] You're a jerk! You missed the war. / O Yeah! all the people with taste, I admit, / all of them in the rear / But a guy like you! / That fellow, a guy like that! / What he couldn't have taken! He was in a factory. / What, burying squad, ditch diggers, with their heads / thrust back, looking like this, / they risked their life for a shovelful of dirt. / Must be nice and square, accurate" [*Index*].

38. Trotzsk: Leon Trotsky, 1879-1940. Leading revolutionist and aide to Lenin who had returned to Russia in 1917. Trotsky was the principal negotiator of Treaty of Brest-Litovsk and accepted humiliating conditions to obtain peace with the Central Powers so that the Bolsheviks would be free to promote the revolution at home.

39. bolsheviki: R, "majority." Group led by Lenin opposed to minority party: Mensheviki. Data about unpremeditated Russian Revolution in March based on lecture given in 1924 by Lincoln Steffens in Paris which Pound attended and was excited by. Steffens incorporated these lecture notes into his *Autobiography*. The "man talking" is Lenin: ". . . when you want a government that will do socialism, then—come to the Bolsheviki" [Steffens, 761].

40. "Pojalouista": R, "if you please." "The Cossacks were summoned . . . they moved carefully, and they used the polite Russian word, 'Pajalista,' which means 'if you please!'" [Steffens, 750].

41. lieutenant: Steffens wrote: ". . . out in the great square in front of the Moscow railroad station an infantry officer was trying to command and incite his men to shoot across the open into the quiet mob. They would not. A student standing by jeered at the officer, who, in a rage, thrust the student through. A Cossack . . . saw this . . . charged . . . and drawing his sword . . . cut that officer down. There was a cry: 'The soldiers *are* with us!' and then there was another cry: 'The revolution! The revolution is on!'" [Steffens, 751].

42. Nevsky: Broad avenue that leads into a large square, the scene of the March bread riots. Square is site of station where trains leave for Moscow.

43. Haig: Douglas H., 1861-1928. British marshal, commander in chief of expeditionary forces in France and Flanders, 1915-1919.

CANTO XVII

Sources

Giambattista Pigna, *Historia de Principi di Este*, 1570; Virgil, *Aeneid* VI, 204.

Background

EP, *CON*, 183; E. A. Wallis Budge, "Isis and Osiris," in *Legends of the Gods*, London, 1912; Adrian Stokes, *The Quattro Cento*, London, 1932, *Stones of Rimini*, London, 1934, and *Colour and Form*, London, 1937; Plutarch, *De Iside et Osiride*, ed. and trans. J. Gwyn Griffiths, University of Wales, 1970; Thomas Taylor, *The Eleusinian and Bacchic Mysteries*, 4th ed., 1891; CFT, *Pai*, 2-3, 449-462; 3-1, 92-93.

Exegeses

Quinn, in LL, *Motive*, 92-95; CE, *Ideas*, 139-140; DD, *Sculptor*,
128-129; Surette, *Pai*, 3-2, 200-206.

Glossary

1. So that: A new start, in medias res, which echoes the beginning, "And then," and the end, "So that," of Canto I.

2. the vines burst: Leaving the Purgatory of Canto 16, we come to the first extended vision of Paradise. In a letter [#745, YC, D. D. Paige transcripts] Pound said of Canto 17 that it was "a sort of paradiso terrestre." The whole scene is charged with vitality from divinity operating in the world. The vines here are "bursting" in contrast with the vinestocks that lie untended, nipped by the north wind in the fading light [cf. 5/18], and the "thin husks," "locust-shells," and "dry pods" in an earlier scene of twilight and lamplight where life seems paralyzed [cf. 7/25-27] by abulia [5:44].

3. ZAGREUS: Another name for Dionysus, in late tradition the god of wine, but in Pound the god of "Orgia" [religious ecstasy] and fertility associated with the Eleusinian Mysteries, arcanum, and the rites of spring.

4. IO: H, "Hail."

5. goddess ... knees: Artemis [Diana].

6. palazzi: I, "palaces." Part of the architectural data derived from impressions of Venice.

7. The light now: Neoplatonic, primal light, "not of the sun," associated with Artemis [Diana], where the air is "alight with the goddess" but "not a ray" of sun [4:14]. Dante also uses the light imagery from Plotinus [15:10]: "... the divine light so penetrates the universe, in measure of its worthiness that nothing has power to stand against it" [*Par.* XXXI, 22-24]. Pound attributes the same metaphor to the Confucian process: "The celestial and earthly process pervades and is substantial; it is on high and gives light, it comprehends the light and is lucent, it extends without bound, and endures" [*CON*, 183].

8. Chrysophrase: Chrysoprase, an apple-green chalcedony, a semiprecious stone used in making jewelry.

9. Nerea: Prob. the Nereids, sea sprites who were the daughters of Nereus, Homer's "Old Man" of the sea.

10. she like a great shell: Suggests myth of the birth of Venus and Botticelli's *La Nascita*. Thus Venus is pictured as "between them" [the Nerea or sprites] in a "not-of-this-world" scene.

11. malachite: A green mineral from which copper is derived.

12. the light: The divine Neoplatonic light "not of the sun" [cf. *Pai*, 2-3, 449-462].

13. panthers: The hieratic animals throughout the canto are visionary [cf. *Pai*, 3-1, 92-93].

14. choros nympharum: L, "chorus of nymphs."

15. Hermes: Messenger and herald of the gods; patron of merchants and thieves and god of luck and wealth. But here he is the bearer of the golden wand used by Aeneas to enter the Elysian fields [*Aeneid* VI].

16. Athene: Pallas Athena, goddess of wisdom; patron of the arts of peace and of war; guardian of cities, especially of Athens, but here guardian of the visionary city of *paradiso terrestre*.

17. sylva nympharum: L, "wood of the nymphs."

18. Memnons: Memnon, son of Tithonus and Eos. A large statue near Thebes, Egypt (supposed to be of Memnon), was reputed to produce a musical sound when struck by the light of dawn.

19. Guiding her ... evening: For this scene see works of Stokes listed in background material.

20. Borso: B. d'Este, 1413-1471, son of Niccolò d'Este; Lord of Ferrara and patron of learning [10:20]. Here his dedication to the arts, architecture, and the advancement of peace makes him one of the canto characters with a paradisal vision.

21. Carmagnola: Francesco Bussone da C., fl. 1380-1432, Italian militarist serving under Filippo Visconti, Duke of Milan; later he led the forces of Florence and Venice against Visconti. His strange conduct led the Venetians to try him for treason before the Council of Ten, after which he was executed [10:7].

22. i vitrei: I, "makers of glass."

23. In the gloom ... : Paradisal or "otherworldly" image [cf. 11/51].

24. Zothar: Private reference [EP to FR].

25. sistrum: L, "a sort of rattle used in the worship of Isis."

26. Aletha: Prob. an invention: a sea deity.

27. Koré: H, "daughter"; a reference to Persephone [3:8]. The appearance of Koré occurs with the appearance of the gods and an evocation of the Eleusinian Mysteries, which begins with a descent into the underworld (a repeat of Canto I) where Koré is first encountered. The final 19 lines of the

canto are poss. a metaphor for the descent. But as Aeneas with the magic wand of Hermes was led, while in Hell, to a vision of the Elysian fields [the bright meadow], we descend into the darkness of Hell (as the sun descends in the West) and into the mysterious arcanum [cf. Surette, *Pai*, 3-2, 205].

28. brother of Circe: Aeëtes, king of Colchis and father of Medea.

29. Hermes: When on official assignment as a messenger of Zeus, Hermes donned a "splendid" costume, carried the magic wand, and with winged heels sped across the sky [cf. 15 above].

30. Borso: B. d'Este [10:20; 20 above; cf. 10/46]: "And they had a bow-shot at Borso / As he was going down the Grand Canal in his gondola / (the nice kind with 26 barbs on it.)" Just as Dante meets various people long dead in the *Commedia*, we meet several canto characters now dead, including Borso and the two in the glosses below.

31. Carmagnola: [cf. 21 above]. He was "invited to lunch," seized, and executed between the two columns [10:7, 8]. As Yriarte puts it: "... that this Count Carmagnola ... should be decapitated between the two columns of S. Marco, at the accustomed hour after the nones with an iron piece in his mouth and with his hands tied according to the custom followed in the Piazza ..." [cf. *Analyst* XI, 4].

32. Sigismundo: S. de Malatesta [8:5].

33. Dalmatia: Coastal region of present-day Yugoslavia, for centuries fought over by Croatia and Venice but brought under the control of Venice by 1420.

CANTO XVIII

Sources

Marco Polo, *Il Milione*, Firenze, Successori, Le Monnier, 1916; Louis Antoine Fauvelet de Bourrienne, *Mémoires sur Napoléon*, Paris, 1829.

Background

Richard Lewinsohn, *The Man behind the Scenes: The Career of Sir Basil Zaharoff*, London, 1929; Robert Neumann, *Zaharoff*, New York, 1935; Sir Henry Yule, *The Book of Ser Marco Polo*, Vol. I, 3d ed., rev. by H. Cordier, London, 1921.

Exegeses

EP, "Kublai Khan and His Currency," *New Age*, May 20, 1920, rpt. in *SP*, 204; EP, letter to Homer Pound dated Rapallo, Nov. 29, 1924, Paige collection at Yale ["As to Cantos 18-19, there ain't no key. Simplest parallel I can give is radio where you tell who is talking by the noise they make"] [cf. Nanny, *Pai*, 8-1].

Glossary

1. **Kublai**: K. Khan, 1214-1294. In 1260 he became emperor of the Mongols and in 1280 emperor of all China, giving his dynasty the name Yüan. Kublai led few military expeditions after he became emperor. In 1285 paper money in the form of bank notes was made current. Kublai was often under the influence of his ministers, particularly Ahama and Sang-Ko.

2. **Cambaluc**: Khabalik, Kublai Khan's capital city. The "City of the Great Khan" was built (1264-1267) on the site of the earlier city of Yen by Kublai Khan; site of modern Peking. Kublai's mint was in this city.

3. **hyght**: ME, past participle of *hoten,* "named." ". . . you might say he hath the Secret of Alchemy in perfection" [*SP*, 204].

4. **tornesel**: Prob. I, *tornese*, "of Tours"; a minor coin of base silver or copper, struck in many of the Italian states prior to the unification.

5. **groat**: ME, *grote*, "silver coin worth 4 pence" [Webster].

6. **bezant**: Gold coin issued by the Byzantine emperors, circulating in Europe between 6th and 15th centuries.

7. **Kahn**: Khan [cf. 1 above].

8. **Messire Polo**: Marco P., ?1254-1324?, Venetian traveler; visited Kublai Khan in 1275 and returned to Venice in 1295. In 1296 he was taken prisoner by the Genoese against whom he, with the Venetians, was fighting; he dictated his memoirs while in

prison in Genoa. He brought back information about the khan's currency given above [Yule, I, 423 ff.; *SP*, 204-206].

9. Genoa: Seaport in NW Italy.

10. Constantinople: Formerly Byzantium, now Istanbul.

11. Bourrienne: Louis Antoine Fauvelet de B., 1769-1834, French Diplomat and writer, private secretary to Napoleon (1797-1802). In his *Memoirs of Napoleon Bonaparte*, Hartford, Silas Andrus & Sons, 1856, we read (concerning Napoleon's years at the military school at Brienne): "The temper of the young Corsican was not improved by the railleries of the students, who were fond of ridiculing his name . . . and his country. He has often said to me, 'I will do these French all the mischief in my power' " [p. 17].

12. Zenos Metevsky: Sir Basil Zaharoff, 1849?-1933, European munitions magnate. He started selling arms (ca. 1876) for Nordenfeldt & Co. and later joined Maxim, an early competitor; by 1913 both Zaharoff and Maxim had joined Vickers. Zaharoff also had interests in oil, international banks, and newspapers. He had a spotty career, rising from poverty to immense wealth and spending time in prison in England and Greece. But he was able to rebound from all adversity and by extreme cunning (as well as crookedness) defeat his enemies and come out ahead. Zaharoff, who as a boy in Constantinople was kicked by a Britisher and later was imprisoned and tried in England, hated the British secretly all his life [cf. HK, *Era*, 465], a repeat in history of Napoleon's experience with the French.

13. Biers: Prob. Hiram Maxim, 1840-1916, inventor of the Maxim machine guns as well as of a smokeless powder, a delayed-action fuse, and a heavier-than-air airplane. He formed an arms company which, through the machinations of Zaharoff, consolidated with Vickers to form Vickers-Armstrong, one of the biggest producers of war materials in Europe.

14. Metevsky died . . . : An enemy of Sir B. Zaharoff, one Stephanos Xenos, wrote in his newspaper, *Mikra Ephemeris*: ". . . the convict, Zacharias Basileios Zaharoff, had made a sensational attempt to escape from the old prison in Athens called Garbola. But at the moment when he was trying to get away he was shot by a warden." But it was another prisoner who was shot. Thus, Zaharoff was able to sit in the café and watch what was supposed to be his own funeral. Later, an exhumation of the body enabled Z.'s dentist to say: "This is certainly not Zaharoff!" [Neumann, 58-59].

15. Yeiner Kafé: Poss. the Wiener Café.

16. Humbers: Pseudonym for Vickers.

17. Mr. Giddings: Pseudonym for unidentified salesman of armaments.

18. La Marquesa . . . Hurbara: Prob. Madame Maria del Pilar Antonia-Angela-Patrocinio-Simona de Muquiro y Bernete, widow of Villafranca de los Caballeros, whom Sir Basil Zaharoff, then 75 years old, married in 1924. Z. first met her in 1889 on a night train to Spain whither he was going to sell arms. According to one account she was on her honeymoon as the new Duchess of Villafranca; another report said that she literally fell into Z's arms "while flying from her sleeping-car and from the brutality of her just-wedded husband." Neumann [op. cit.] believes that since her husband was cousin to the king of Spain (Alfonso XII) and Z. was on the way to restore a large canceled order for arms, the meeting was not accidental. But the passion between Z. and the duchess became real, transformed his manner of dress and life, and lasted for years. As a devout Catholic she could not get a divorce, so they had to arrange secret meetings. But Z. was quite able to mix passion and business. "According to an entry in the *Internationale Biographische Archiv* of Berlin, the orders Zaharoff got there [Spain] amounted to thirty million pounds sterling two months after his meeting with the Duchess of Villafranca" [Neumann, 86-88].

19. **Champs Elysées**: Street in Paris inhabited by the very wealthy. Particular source of this anecdote is not known, but it is only one of many such tales circulating in Paris and London in the 1920s.

20. **las once**: S, "eleven o'clock."

21. **Este to Louis Eleventh**: Borso d'E. Louis XI, 1423-1483, was king of France from 1461 to 1483 [10:45].

22. **Mr. Oige**: Unidentified pseudonym.

23. **Gethsemane Trebizond Petrol**: Prob. a pseudonym for the Anglo-Persian Oil Company, in which Zaharoff had an interest.

24. **Manchester Cardiff**: Railroad line running from Manchester, England, to Cardiff, Wales.

25. **Hamish**: Pseudonym for Taffy Fowler, an engineer whose wife conducted a salon for young musicians and poets in Knightsbridge, London, 1908-1909.

26. **Melchizedek**: A pre-Aaronic and pre-Levitical priest-king to whom Abraham paid tithes; a prototype of the high priest. Zaharoff was the high priest of war and of preparation for war.

27. **King Menelik**: M. II, 1844-1913, emperor of Ethiopia (1889-1913). In a war with Italy (1896) Menelik freed Ethiopia from Italian control.

28. **Qu'est-ce . . .? . . . On don't pense**: F, "What do they think? . . . They don't think."

29. **"Mais . . . Metevsky?"**: F, "But, what is thought / of metallurgy in England, what do they / think of Metevsky?"

30. **MacGorvish's bank**: Poss. either Barclay's or Westminster Bank, London, but the association of banks and promoters of the international arms race is deliberate.

31. **Dave**: Unidentified. But he and Hamish [Taffy Fowler the engineer] are creative nonusurious developers of technology and wealth as opposed to the usurious and destructive kind represented by Zaharoff [cf. Baldy Bacon and Dos Santos, 12:3 12].

CANTO XIX

Sources

There are no published sources for Canto 19, which is a pastiche of memories of café talk, news-making events, and gossip drawn from pre–World War I years through the early 1920s.

Background

EP, *J/M*, 110; *SP*, 210-223; Lincoln Steffens, *Autobiography*, New York, 1931; Charles Norman, *Ezra Pound: A Biography*, New York, 1969.

Exegeses

Dekker, *Cantos*, 168, 170; Davis, *Vision*, 56-59; CE, *Ideas*, 114-115; Achilles Fang, "Materials for the Study of Pound's Cantos," Ph.D. dissertation, 4 vols., Harvard University, 1958.

Glossary

1. he: Identity unknown and unimportant. Point of anecdote is the expected response of any big company to any such challenge by an inventor.

2. Manhattan: Island and central borough of New York City, a world financial center.

3. Hudson: River in E New York State on whose banks are many old baronial mansions and estates inhabited by predatory usurers and financiers.

4. Spinder: Pseudonym for some financial wizard: the type rather than a particular person is important.

5. Marx: Karl M., 1818-1883, German political philosopher.

6. Champz Elyza: Champs Elysées, broad Parisian avenue leading up to the Arc de Triomphe, favorite haunt of tourists.

7. Das Kapital: Major document expounding Marxist doctrine, which conceives of class struggle as the only way to overthrow bourgeois democracy under capitalism to attain a socialist and thence a communist state.

8. Qui se faisait si beau: F, "who made himself so handsome."

9. old kindly professor: Unidentified, but could be Dr. Douglas Hyde. Fang says Hyde "fits the description [but] does not seem to have been in London about this time" [Fang, II, 105].

10. stubby little man: Arthur Griffith, leader of Irish Sinn Fein. In *ABCE* [1933; rpt. in *SP*, 239] Pound wrote: " 'Can't move 'em with a cold thing like economics,' said Mr. Griffiths [sic], the inventor of Sinn Fein." Pound, who met Griffith in Paris in 1924 and tried to convert him to the Douglas plan [Norman, 272], wrote later: ". . . one of the most illuminating hours of my life was spent in conversation with Griffith, the founder of Sinn Fein. We were in his room to avoid the detectives who infested the hotel. It was the time of the armistice when the Irish delegates had been invited to London. . . . Griffith said: 'All you say is true. But I can't move 'em with a cold thing like economics.' "

11. The Tatler: British magazine devoted to gossip about the upper class.

12. the slick guy: A detective, not reading but watching the scene.

13. Clio: Muse of history.

14. Prishnip: Prob. Gavrilo Princip who assassinated Archduke Francis Ferdinand at Sarajevo, June 28, 1914.

15. Vlettmann?: Unidentified.

16. Hé Sloveny!: Serb., *Hej, Sloveni*, "Up the Slavs," an old Pan-Slavic song. In 1945 it was chosen to be the national anthem of Yugoslavia [EH].

17. Birth of a Nation: Unidentified, but prob. story about the Russian Revolution.

18. Boche: Franco-British slang term for a German.

19. Naphtha: Obsolete term for petroleum or gas used as fuel.

20. Rotterdam: Trading seaport in the Netherlands connected by waterways to the Ruhr and N Germany. Famous center of transit shipping.

21. Das thust du nicht: G, "Don't you do that?"

22. Albert: Count A. von Mensdorf-Pouilly-Dietrichstein, Austro-Hungarian ambassador to London (1904-1914). Referred to below as "Wurmsdorf" [EH].

23. Nevsky: Broad avenue in St. Petersburg which leads into Alexander Nevsky Square at east end of which is the Nicolai (or Moscow) station. Along the way are "numerous pastry shops (e.g. Andrejew, Filippow, Dominique)" [Fang, II, 319].

24. Governed . . . train . . . lobby: The Mexican Revolution led by Carranza in 1914 who was running the government from traveling trains because he saw that Mexico City governments were corrupted and influenced by "foreigners and Mexican reactionaries." One day the constitutional committee [with Steffens as member] was ordered unexpectedly onto the train very early. Carranza later explained: "You foreigners are very tempting, you know. . . . The train we came on is the only train running these days; so we escaped your lobby . . . till the foreigners could get to Guadalajara on foot or a-horseback" [Steffens, 721, 731-732].

25. oil . . . map: One day the train stopped for lack of fuel . . . and Carranza came up to the constitutional committee in a rage. " 'What do you think of a situation . . . where, in an oil country like Mexico, the government cannot get enough oil to keep its own train moving? What can we do? You ought to be able to tell us that,' he blazed at me." Steffens said: "Maybe I can. Have you a map of the oil regions?" A map was brought and Steffens asked questions about the meaning of the straight lines, the wiggly lines, and so on, to find out what was government property. Then he said: "You could sink wells in them, and they'd be on your property; the oil would be your own government fuel." Carranza agreed and sent off an engine to start drilling for oil. But Steffens stopped him, saying he didn't

really have to dig: "The oil men will see what you are up to, and they will offer you all the oil you want if you will stop boring." It worked out that way [Steffens, 730].

26. Tommy Baymont: Thomas Lamont, 1870-1948, American banker, member of firm of J. P. Morgan and Co. He is the junior partner in following passage from Steffens's *Autobiography* [p. 590] concerning an article "Steff" had written for *Everybody's Magazine* (Sept. 1910) in which he charged that J. P. Morgan had absolute power and was "The Boss of all Bosses" [title of article]: "One day soon after my article to this effect was published, I was in the Morgan bank. A junior partner tapped on his glass cage and beckoned me in. He said that he had laid on J. P.'s desk the magazine, open at my article, saw him read it and read it again and then shake his head. . . . The junior partner said that J. P. had no sense of 'absolute power' . . . and he told me an incident to prove it." The incident is the anecdote about the coal mine and the railroad.

27. Jim: James Buchanan Brady, 1856-1917, known as "Diamond Jim Brady" whom J. P. Morgan could not control: "J. P. had discovered that he could not make the New York, New Haven and Hartford Railroad, which he controlled, buy its coal from a coal company he controlled, without the consent of 'Diamond Jim' Brady. He was so enraged that he was going to fight Brady. . . . But he didn't; he accepted him . . . [because] Brady represented a company in which the officers of the New Haven and other railroads held shares" [Steffens, 590].

28. My ole man: Syntax seems to indicate that this man is the uncle of "Wurmsdorf," the ambassador; thus the speaker must be the ambassador's cousin and the scene must be some family gathering just before the outbreak of World War I where all those present reflected on the "good old days." Since Russia was going with the Allies, as the dispatches doubtless showed, these people would thenceforth be divided.

29. Wurmsdorf: [cf. 22 above].

30. Ptierstoff: Aleksander Konstantinovich Beuckendorff, 1849-1917, Russian ambassador to London (1903-1916).

31. Albert: [cf. 22 above].

32. Yash (Jassy): A commercial town in NE Rumania.

33. Healthy but verminous: Although no source is known for the anecdote about the 14 girls, the point of the story seems clear: the actions and attitudes of an Englishman [or of any man] bearing the "white man's burden."

34. Kashmir: Indian state in N India on the Sinkiang and Tibet frontier.

CANTO XX

Sources

Catullus LXI; Homer, *Od*, XII, 183; Bernart de Ventadorn, no. 235 (Appel); Guido Cavalcanti, Sonnet 35; Propertius, *Elegies* II, XX; Arnaut Daniel, "Er Vei Vermeils"; EP, "Cavalcanti," *LE*, 149; Antonio Frizzi, *Memorie per la Storia di Ferrara*, 1791-1796; Giambattista Pigna, *Historia de Principi di Este*, 1570; Virgil, *Aeneid* VI; Homer, *Iliad* III, 153; *Las Almenas de Toro*; Bishop Liutprand, *Pere la Storia de Roma e del Papapo*; Heraclitus, frag. 75; Dante, *Inf. V;* Homer, *Od*. IX; St. Francis, "Cantico Secondo"; Homer, *Od*. IX, X, XII; Ovid, *Meta*. XI; *Pur*. XIV, 109.

Background

EP, *SR*, 22-38, 191-193; Werner L. Gundersheimer, *Ferrara*, Princeton, 1973; Edward Hutton, *Sigismundo Pandolpho Malatesta, Lord of Rimini*, 1906; Anthony Manganaris-Decavalles, *Analyst* XI.

Exegeses

EP, *L*, 210; CE, *Ideas*, 140-141 and passim; DD, *Sculptor*, 133-134; WB, *Rose*, 67-72; HK, *Era*, 114-117; Flory, *Pai*, 6-2, 155-165.

Glossary

1. quasi tinnula: L, "as if ringing." Adaptation of Catullus LXI. Concerned with the "singing-ringing" of wedding bells.

2. Ligur' aoide: H, "Clear, sweet song." *Od*. XII, 183: "[The sirens] raised their clear-toned song" [Loeb, 104, 445].

3. Si no'us . . . val: P, "If I don't see you, Lady for whom I must burn, / Even not seeing you can't match my beautiful thought of you." From Bernart de Ventadorn's poem, "Can par la flors," ll. 23-24 ["When the flower appears"] [Appel, 235].

4. viel: P, "a lutelike stringed instrument."

5. s'adora: I, "She [or he] is adored." Cavalcanti, Sonnet 35 [EP, *T*, 94].

6. Possum . . . tuae!: L, "Can I not remember your nature" [Propertius II, xx, 28]. From address to Cynthia; Loeb [18, 121] translates whole passage: "Many sought thee, but thou has sought me only; can I forget the kindness of thy nature? If I do, may ye, Furies of tragedy, plague me, and thou, Aeacus, pass on me the doom of hell."

7. Qui son . . .: I, "Here are Propertius and Ovid."

8. Freiburg: Freiburg in Breisgau, town in SW Germany.

9. Rennert: Hugo Albert R., 1858-1927, scholar of Romance languages, University of Pennsylvania. One of Pound's favorite professors (1905-06).

10. Provençal: Language of the troubadours in SC France.

11. Lévy: Emil L., 1855-1918, German philologist; author of *Provençal supplement dictionnaire* [8 vols., 1892-1925].

12. Arnaut: A. Daniel, 12th-century Provençal troubadour [cf. *SR*, 22-38].

13. settant . . . Ambrosiana: I, "Seventy-one R [recto] superior Ambrosian." A catalog number in the Ambrosian Library in Milan which locates a manuscript of a Daniel poem in which there is a word [*noigandres*] that prompted Pound to consult Lévy. Seventy-one is the MS number; recto is odd-numbered side.

14. noigandres: P; a word of unknown meaning which has caused much speculation and perplexity. It is known to exist only in one line of Canello's edition of Arnaut Daniel's poetry (1883) which is where Pound found it. The line is the last one of the first verse of Daniel's 13th canzone: "E jois lo grans, e l'olors de noigandres." Kenner suggests the word may not exist at all because "the manuscripts chatter a dissident babel: nuo gaindres, nul grandes, notz grandres" [HK, *Era*, 114-117]. The problem has for years been compounded for Pound scholars until Kenner discovered the actual source (Canello) that Pound used. Suggested meanings of *noigandres* range from "walnuts" to "banishes sadness." Lévy emended the manuscript text to read "d enoi gandres" [cf. 22 below] and came up with "wards off boredom." Pound does not commit himself to any translation but in effect lets the reader devise his own. But in his own translation of the song [*Instigations*], he wrote: "and pain ameises" [HK, *Era*, 114-117].

15. ranunculae: Genus of plants which includes buttercups.

16. Agostino: A. di Duccio, ?1418-1481, Italian sculptor who did the bas-reliefs in Sigismundo Malatesta's Tempio.

17. Jacopo: J. Sellaio, 1422-1493, Florentine painter.

18. Boccata: Giovanni B., ?1435-1480?, Umbrian painter.

19. Sandro: S. Botticelli, 1444-1510, Florentine painter.

20. espalier: A tree or shrub trained to grow in a flat plane against a wall.

21. e l'olors: P, "and the smell."

22. d'enoi ganres: P, "wards off boredom" [cf. 14 above].

23. remir: P, I, "I gaze" [7:30].

24. palla: I, "ball," or poss. "at a horse race"; or misprint or dialectical for *palazzo*, "palace."

25. Parisina: daughter of Carlo Malatesta [26:59] and cousin of Sigismundo Malatesta. She married Niccolò d'Este in a power play by the Malatesta family, although she was much younger than her husband. Later Niccolò discovered she was having an affair with his natural son, Ugo Aldobrandino, and had them both beheaded.

26. E'l Marchese: I, "And the Marquise." Niccolò d'Este [8:51]: N. III of Ferrara, 1384-1441, ruler of Ferrara, Modena, Parma, Reggio, Milan; father of Borso [10:20].

27. Stava per divenir pazzo: I, "Was about to go crazy." Pound in a letter to his father [*L*, 210] comments at length on Canto XX: "Nicolo ... in sort of delirium after execution of Parisina and Ugo." His turmoil explains the random associations that follow: "Various things keep cropping up in the poem. The original world of gods; the Trojan War, Helen on the wall of Troy with the old men fed up with the whole show. ... Rome founded by survivors of Troy."

28. condit Atesten: L, "founded Este." Refers to legendary founding of Este family.

29. Borso: Third son of Niccolò d'Este III, the most distinguished of the d'Este family rulers of Ferrara, a small city-state surrounded by Mantua, Padua, Verona, and Bologna with Venice and Milan near in the N. Ferrara lacked the manpower to support war and was unlike states that had a surplus of men not needed for farming and public works. "[Niccolò] realized that Ferrara owed its continuing independence to its dominion-like or semi-colonial status in relation to Venice" [Gundersheimer, 74]. Thus his continuing refrain to his sons, especially Borso, to keep the peace [10:20].

30. Ganelon: One of the 12 peers in *Song of Roland*; prompted by jealousy, he betrayed the presence of Roland's rear-guard forces to the Moslems. Pound: "... in the delirium Nicolo remembers or thinks he is watching death of Roland."

31. l'olofans: OF, *olifant*, "elephant." Refers to Roland's horn which was made of ivory. His sword broken, R. used his horn to bash in the head of the Moor who came up to finish him off.

32. Tan mare fustes: OF, "You are ill-starred." Pound: "... he smashes the moor over the head with his horn ... and then dies grumbling because he has damaged the ornaments on the horn and broken it. Tan mare fustes, colloquial: You came at a bad moment. Current cabaret song now J'en ai marre: I'm fed up" [*L*, 211].

33. Toro, las almenas: S, "The battlements of Toro," a town in Zamora Province, NW Spain. Scenes that follow are based on Lope de Vega's play, *Las Almenas de Toro*, with the characters Elvira, Sancho, Alfonso, and Ancures. Pound: "Elvira on wall or Toro (subject-rhyme with Helen on Wall [of Troy])" [*L*, 210].

34. Nic Este: Niccolò d'E. [cf. 29 above].

35. Epi purgo: H, "on wall" [*Iliad* III, 153].

36. peur de la hasle: MF, "fear of sunburn."

37. the King said: Pound writes about *Las Almenas de Toro*: "King Ferdinand had divided his kingdom at his death, leaving the cities Toro and Zamora to his daughters, Urraca and Elvira. The new King, Sancho, is not content. At the opening of the play we find the King, the Cid, and the Conde Ancures before the gates of Toro, which Elvira has closed through fear of her brother. The Cid advises the King to retire and return unarmed. He advises the King to let the sisters keep their cities. The King rejects this counsel, and the Cid is sent forward as ambassador. Elvira comes forth upon the city wall, and replies with delightful irony to the King's proposition that she become a nun. ... The king sees his sister on the battlements, and, without knowing who she is, falls in love with her. ... The Cid tells him that it is his sister" [cf. *SR*, 191-193].

38. telo rigido: L, "with rigid javelin." The sexual implication is given with typical obliquity.

39. Ancures: Companion to King Sancho.

40. Alf: Alphonso, brother of King Sancho.

41. Neestho: Pound: "translated in text: let her go back" [*L*, 211].

42. arras ...: Painting of Francesca and Paolo, adulterous lovers also murdered; a subject rhyme with Parisina and Ugo [cf. Peck, *Pai*, 3-1, 60-66].

43. Jungle ... renewals: As against the destructiveness of mankind, the proliferating energy of nature which continuously produces a new harvest, the true basis of wealth: "basis of renewals, subsistence." But seen in Niccolò's confused mind. Pound: "The whole reminiscence jumbled or 'candied' in Nicolo's delirium. Take that as a sort of bounding surface from which one gives the main subject of the Canto, the lotophagoi: lotus eaters, or respectable dope smokers; and general paradiso. You have had a hell in Canti XIV, XV; purgatorio in XVI etc." [*L*, 210].

44. Zoe: Zoë, d. 1050, a Byzantine empress who poisoned her husband, Romanus III, took the throne, and married Michael the Paphlagonian [cf. Peck, op. cit.].

45. Marozia: D. before 945, wife of Alberic I, prince of Rome; mistress of Pope Sergius III.

46. Zothar: Unidentified; prob. invented name [17:24] Niccolò's guilty wife, Parisina, suggests other guilty women to his wandering mind.

47. HO BIOS: H, "Life."

48. cosi Elena vedi: I, Pound: "(thus I saw Helen, misquote of Dante)" [*L*, 210]. *Inf*. V, 64, concerns Circle Two, Hell-abode of the Carnal. Virgil points to many women guilty of carnal acts, such as Semiramis, Dido, "sense-drugged Cleopatra," and then says, "See Helen there." Pound adds the word *cosi*.

49. Floating: Hallucinatory scene as in mind of one drugged, as were the *lotophagoi*.

50. calyx: Outer protective covering of a flower consisting of a series of leaflike segments called sepals: a funnel shape.

51. olibanum: Frankincense.

52. myrrh: An aromatic gum resin used in perfume and incense.

53. styrax: Resin or gum: storax.

54. Nel fuoco: I, "in the flame." Pound: "The 'nel fuoco' is from St. Francis' 'cantico': 'My new spouse placeth me in the flame of love.' Then the remarks of the opium smoker about the men who sailed under Ulysses" [*L*, 210].

55. Nel fuoco ... mise: I, "In the flame of love he put me."

56. croceo: I, "saffron-colored."

57. il mio sposo novello: I, "my new spouse."

58. lotophagoi: H, "lotus-eaters" [*Od*. IX, 82-104].

59. spilla: I, "pin, brooch."

60. Voce-profondo: I, "Deep-voiced."

61. Odysseus: Pound: "And then resumé of Odyssey, or rather of the main parts of Ulysses' voyage up to death of all his crew" [*L*, 210].

62. Elpenor: Companion of Odysseus who in drunken stupor fell from roof, died, and was left unburied. The first shade met by Odysseus in Hades [1:12].

63. Spartha: Sparta.

64. ingle: Gaelic, "chimney corner" where Elpenor sat in his drunken stupor.

65. Circe: Enchantress who turned Odysseus's men into swine [1:1].

66. Circe Titania: Circe, daughter of the sun [*Meta*, XIV, 382, 438].

67. Kalüpso: Calypso [*Od*. VII, 234 ff.]. Odysseus says to Queen Arete: "There is an isle, Ogygia, which lies far off in the sea. Therein dwells the fair-tressed daughter of Atlas, guileful Calypso, a dread goddess. ... There all the rest of my trusty comrades perished, but ... the gods brought me to the isle ... where ... Calypso dwells." Odysseus remained there for 7 years. Calypso

offered to make him immortal, but he re-
fused and in the 8th year she sent him on
his way bound to a raft.

68. Ear-wax: Pound: "Ear wax, ears plugged
so they couldn't hear the sirens" [*L*, 210].

69. Neson amumona: H, "excellent island."
Pound: ". . . literally the narrow island:
bullfield where Apollo's cattle were kept"
[*L*, 210].

70. Ligur' aoide: H, "clear, sweet song"
[cf. 2 above].

71. Khan: An unidentified minor khan who
must have sent the leopard to Sigismundo M.

72. Salustio: Sallustio Malatesta, 1448-1470.
Son of Sigismundo and Isotta [Pound's
Ixotta] degli Atti. Sallustio was murdered
by his half brother, Roberto [11:9].

73. Ac ferae familiares: L, "And domesti-
cated wild animals."

74. Somnus: The Roman god of sleep [*Meta*.
XI, 690 ff., which tells the story of Iris's

visit to the House of Sleep and her plea to
Somnus to prepare a vision of the Wreck of
Ceyx for his wife Alcyone].

75. chiostri: I, "cloisters."

76. le donne e i cavalieri: I, "the ladies and
the knights" [*Pur*. XIV, 109, describing past
glory of Romany].

77. hennin: OF, a high cone-shaped head-
dress with a thin veil worn by women in the
15th century.

78. Cramoisi: F, "Crimson cloth."

79. diaspre: I, "jasper."

80. barocco: I, "baroque."

81. Vanoka: Prob. an invented name. But
poss. Vannozza Catanei, mistress of Pope
Alexander VI and mother of Lucretia
Borgia. Pound may have seen a painting of
her in the classical mode suggested by the
lines.

82. Borso: [cf. 29 above].

CANTO XXI

Sources

Niccolò Machiavelli, *Istorie Fiorentine*, IV, VII, VIII, 1532;
Andrew Lipscomb and Albert Bergh, eds., *The Writings of Thomas
Jefferson*, IV, Washington, D.C., 1905; Lorenzo de Medici, *Scritti
Scelti*, Introduzione e note di Egidio Bellorini, Turin, 1922; C. E.
Yriarte, *Un Condottière au XVe siècle*, 1882; *Takasago* (Noh
play); Ovid, *Meta*. XIV, 382, 438; Homer, *Od*. XII, 127-132,
140-142.

Background

EP, *L* 269, 273; *J/M*, 33, 79; *PD*, 12-15; J. A. Symonds, *Renais-
sance in Italy*, 2 vols., Modern Library, 1935; Selwyn Brinton,
The Golden Age of the Medici, London, 1925; G. F. Young, *The
Medici*, 1909 [Modern Library, 1933; documentation in glosses

is adjusted to the page numbers of this easily available edition] ;
Edgcumbe Staley, *The Tragedies of the Medici*, New York, 1908;
Maurice Rowdon, *Lorenzo The Magnificent*, Chicago, 1974;
Ovid, Meta. VIII 621-724, and XI, 90-193; J. E. Cirlot, *A Diction-ary of Symbols*, New York, 1962.

Exegeses

EP, *J/M*, 33; CE, *Ideas*, 31-32, 108-109; GD, *Approaches*, 154-155; HK, *Era*, 343.

Glossary

1. Borso: [20:29].

2. "Keep on ...": The credo of Giovanni de'Medici [8:8], who was called "di Bicci," carried on by his son Cosimo. It was through developing their business and commercial interests that the Medici achieved power and not by aspiring to high political office.

3. res publica: L, "republic."

4. "When I was broke ...": Said by Giovanni di Bicci (1360-1429) who left his sons, Cosimo and Lorenzo, a fortune and the beginnings of a great international banking system. [*EB* (1911), Rowdon (1974), and Staley (1908) give the death date of Giovanni di Bicci as 1429, whereas Brinton (1925) and Young (1909) give 1428. Pound's source clearly agreed with the first three.]

5. cittadini: I, "citizens."

6. della gloria: I, "out of [away from] glory."

7. di sugello: I, "with seal," e.g., stamped with a seal to make official or legal.

8. "with his credit ...': ". . . in the war of 1452, in which Venice and Naples were allied against Florence, one of the chief means by which Cosimo obtained his success was by calling in such immense debts from those countries that they were deprived of resources for continuing the war" [Young, 76].

9. Cosimo: C. de' Medici, 1389-1464. Ruled 1434-1464, not as an officeholder but as the real power behind all actions of the state. Patron of the arts and learning. Called "Pater Patriae."

10. Ficino: Marsilio F., 1433-1499, son of Cosimo's physician. Cosimo had him educated "for the special purpose of interpreting Greek philosophy." In a letter to Lorenzo de' M., Ficino said: "I owe to Plato much, to Cosimo no less. He realised for me the virtues of which Plato gave me the conception" [Symonds, I, 410]. After the departure of Georgius Gemistus (sometimes called Plethon because of his dedication to Plato [8:31]) to return to the Peloponnesus, Cosimo made Ficino the head of the academy that Gemistus had run.

11. ells of red cloth: Cosimo reputedly said: "A few ells of scarlet would fill Florence with citizens" [ibid.]. Purple, because of the rarity and expense of the dye, was for centuries reserved to royalty: hence "royal purple." But any bright dye or color was a sign of wealth.

12. Col Credito ... pace: I, "With his credit ... Naples and Venice with money / Forced ... Naples and Venice ... to that peace."

13. Piero: Piero de' M., 1416-1469, eldest son of Cosimo, known as "Il Gottoso" because of the gout from which he suffered all his life. After Cosimo's death in 1464,

Piero carried on in business and affairs of state but relied on his young son Lorenzo, only 15 at the time, to assist him. Not knowing Il Gottoso's real character, the Pitti family formed a conspiracy against him which gathered strength for two years and was supported by forces from Ferrara led by Ercole d'Este.

14. Diotisalvi: Dietisalvi Neroni, d. 1482, wealthy Florentine who conspired to overthrow Medici rule after the death of Cosimo (1464). Acting as financial adviser to Piero, Neroni advised him to call in all his debts. This act caused widespread financial disaster, led to Piero's losing much of his popularity, and gave him a reputation for avarice. In 1466 Neroni's plot was uncovered and he was exiled from Florence.

15. Avignon: City in SE France; the papal see during the "Babylonian captivity" (1309-1378) and residence of several antipopes during the Great Schism (1378-1417); under papal rule Avignon became an important trading city.

16. murdered: In August 1466 the conspirators lay in wait to ambush Piero who was being carried to Florence on a litter. He was saved by the coolness of his 17-year-old son Lorenzo: "Riding on ahead, he [Lorenzo] heard of an armed party who were lying in wait for Piero on the ordinary road; with much adroitness he managed to keep their attention occupied while he sent back word to ... his father," who took a safe route to Florence and escaped [Young, 111-112].

17. Lauro: Lorenzo de' Medici, 1449-1492, son of Piero. He became known as Lorenzo the Magnificent; Florentine statesman, ruler, and patron of arts and letters.

18. Intestate: Piero died in 1469 and, despite his largesse and his generous gifts to charities, left to his son Lorenzo one of the largest fortunes in Europe.

19. In carta di capretto: I, "On rich parchment."

20. Nic Uzano: Niccolò da Uzzano, d. 1432, Florentine statesman and leader with the Albizzi clan of the aristocratic party that opposed the growth of Medici power. But he advised against a contest with the Medici family, which the Albizzi family recognized as a serious threat to their own power. At the death of Giovanni de' Medici in 1429, the Albizzi were restrained from moving against his son Cosimo by Uzzano. But at Uzzano's death in 1432, the young "hotheaded" Rinaldo degli Albizzi threw Cosimo de' Medici into jail. Cosimo fortunately had a friendly jailer, a man named Malavolti, and through him got a bribe to his judge. "The result was seen when ... his sentence, instead of death, was ten years of banishment at Padua" [Brinton, 11]. On the death of Rinaldo in 1434, the Medici returned to Florence and the power of the Albizzi family was destroyed.

21. Giuliano: G. de' Medici, d. 1478, brother to Lorenzo de' M. He was the victim of the Pazzi conspiracy: Lorenzo and Giuliano were attacked during High Mass in the cathedral. Lorenzo escaped with only superficial wounds, but "the bright and justly loved Giuliano, the idol of his family," was immediately killed [Young, 173]. The plot actually greatly increased the Medici power in Florentine politics, for the people came out in emotional support of the Medici when they learned of the murder and took it upon themselves to punish the conspirators: all the Pazzi and Salviati [a family that supported them politically] were proclaimed "enemies," and "they were pursued from house to house, whilst the peasants took up the hue and cry in the *contado*. Bleeding heads and torn limbs were everywhere scattered in the streets; doorposts and curb-stones were dashed with gore; men and women and the children, too, were all relentless avengers of '*Il bel Giulio's*' blood" [Staley, 53]. "The indignation of the people [was] not all ... on account of the attempt against the Medici, but also on account of the effrontery of such an endeavour to seize upon their state 'as if a mere spoil of war' " [Young, 173].

22. E difficile . . . in stato: I, "It is difficult / In Florence it is difficult to live like a rich man / Without having any status. / And not having any status, Piccinino / Had to fear whoever was in a high position."

23. Piccinino: Niccolò P., 1375-1444, Italian condottiere [10:17].

24. that man: Thaddeus Coleman Pound, 1832-1914, Pound's paternal grandfather. According to Pound, he built three railroads, less for personal gain than for the public good [cf. "Indiscretions" in *PD*, 12-15; *J/M*, 33].

25. Jefferson: Thomas J., 1743-1826. Letter shows dimensions of mind and character, aspects of a Renaissance man such as Sigismundo or Lorenzo de' Medici. [Complete text of original in *The Writings of Thomas Jefferson*, IV, 41.]

26. affatigandose . . . non: I, "tiring himself, for his pleasure or not" [8:13].

27. Montecello: Monticello. Residence of Thomas Jefferson near Charlottesville, VA.

28. I went up: In July 1469 Lorenzo attended the baptism of the son born to Galeazzo Sforza of Milan. "His gifts on this occasion were magnificent—a gold necklace to the Duchess, and a diamond valued at three thousand ducats—and led Duke Galeazzo to express the wish that he would stand sponsors to all his other children" [Brinton, 107].

29. Duke Galeaz: Galeazzo Maria Sforza, 5th Duke of Milan, son of Francesco Sforza [8:15].

30. the Sultan: Mohammed II. Barnado Bandini, one of the conspirators who murdered Lorenzo's brother, Giuliano, fled to Constantinople. He was captured by the sultan and sent to Lorenzo as a "gift" [cf. 21 above].

31. Soldan of Egypt: Kait Bey (Qa'it Bay), sultan, 1468-1496. Source of line unknown.

32. one pope: Giovanni, second son of Lorenzo, became Pope Leo X.

33. University: In 1472, when only 23, Lorenzo went to Pisa to found the university and stayed there to direct it for some time. In addition to state subsidies, he lavished his own money upon the institution and donated many books to it.

34. Lauro: Lorenzo de' M.

35. made peace . . . in Naples: Because of the failure of the Pazzi conspiracy [cf. 21 above] engineered by Pope Sextus IV, in which Lorenzo's brother Giuliano was murdered, the pope was so enraged that he excommunicated not only the Medici and the citizens of Florence but all Tuscany. Florence for a time was ringed by enemies called upon by the pope to conquer the city. After losing much territory, Lorenzo went alone with great courage to King Ferrante of Naples (putting himself in the power of this ally of the pope) and pursuaded the king of the justice of his cause. The visit resulted in peace and great acclaim for the young Lorenzo, whose power thereafter steadily increased [cf. Young, 182-186]. King Ferrante was the one who "invited to lunch" those he planned to dispose of, as he did with Piccinino [10:17].

36. Gold fades: [cf. 11/51].

37. Placidia's: Tomb of Galla Placidia, ca. 388-450, empress of western Roman Empire; buried in Ravenna, Italy, where her mausoleum adorned with brilliant gold mosaics rivals that of the neighboring Byzantine treasure, the church of San Vitale [cf. HK, *Era*, 343].

38. exarchate: The office of an exarch, a viceroy of a Byzantine emperor.

39. les gradins: F, "the steps" [12:2].

40. palazzo: I, "palace."

41. nel tramonto: I, "in the sunset."

42. tesserae: I, small squares used in making mosaic patterns.

43. Night of the golden tiger . . . borne in the wind: These 13 lines, which rise to a climax of passion out of which "a thing of beauty is born," present images in action which Pound associates with the Eleusinian Mysteries and the gods Dionysus, Adonis, and Helios as well as the Egyptian solar deities. As the earth turns through sunset, darkness, and into dawn, we encounter the fire of the vision [5:10] as well as the flame and light of passion [cf. *Sacrum, sacrum, inluminatio coitu*, 36/180]. In Egyptian solar myths, lions and tigers are connected with the sun chariot instead of horses, as with the Greek Helios, and they are both associated with the mystery rites [17:27]. Instead of "the lion lift over sand-plain" [17/79], we have here "Night of the golden tiger." Cirlot says that the golden tiger is solar in origin and also that "it is associated with Dionysus" and that "in China the tiger seems to play a rôle comparable with that of the lion in African and Western cultures" [*Dict. of Symbols*, 324]. But Cirlot also says that in Egypt "it used to be believed that the lion presided over the annual floods of the Nile, because they coincided with the entry of the sun into the zodiacal sign of Leo" [ibid., 180]. Here Pound seems to be assigning the functions of both the lion and the tiger to just the golden tiger, anticipating the flooding Nile later on the canto page [cf. 49 below]. The phrase "voices of the procession" evokes the image of women celebrating the death of Dionysus-Tammuz-Adonis by going down to the sea and setting their lamps afloat to go out with the tide [cf. 47/236]. As in Canto II, the "tin flash in the sun-dazzle" announces either the presence or the immediate advent of Dionysus [2/7]. The scene of passion takes place on the beach "between the sea and the mountains" and results in "a petal borne in the wind."

44. Gignetei kalon: H, "A beautiful thing is born."

45. Actium: Promontory and town, NW Acarnania, Greece; site of the battle (31 B.C.) between Octavian and the forces of Antony and Cleopatra.

46. Midas: King Midas recognized a drunk old man to be Silenus, the foster father and teacher of Dionysus. For ten days he took care of Silenus and on the eleventh restored him to the god. When offered a choice of rewards, Midas asked that everything he touched would turn to gold, as thereafter it did, including food and water. But Dionysus rescued him from his fate by telling him where to go to wash away the horrible curse. Thereafter Midas hated wealth and splendor and became a worshiper of Pan, the god of nature, and spent time listening to Pan playing music on his pipes. Thus, "the old man sweeping" suggests Silenus bewailing the bad choice of his benefactor; "Midas without Pan" suggests the coldness and the horror of a life dedicated to gathering up gold if it is not alleviated or balanced by things of the spirit [Ovid, *Meta*. XI, 90-193]. But because of the mention of the Pines of Isé, "the old man sweeping leaves" also suggests the story of Baucis and Philemon [Ovid, *Meta*. VIII, 621-724]. These good old people who served wandering travelers with the best of the food and drink they had without knowing they were gods disguised were also given a reward. Their thatched cottage was changed into a majestic temple of which they became the caretakers. After years of service they were turned into trees [cf. 48 below; 4:22].

47. Pan: Greek pastoral god of fertility.

48. Pines of Ise: Isé: the two sacred Shinto shrines to the sun-goddess, located at Ujiyamada, S Honshu, Japan [4:23].

49. Inopos: A river of Delos said to rise and fall at the same time as the Nile, so that the two rivers were supposedly connected.

50. Phoibos: Phoebus Apollo, Olympian god of light, music, prophecy, and pastoral matters.

51. turris eburnea: L, "tower of ivory" [cf. Litany of the Blessed Virgin].

52. hounds: Hieratic paradisal animals [17:13].

53. Pallas: Pallas Athena, goddess of wisdom, patron of the arts of peace and of war, guardian of cities, especially of Athens. Statues of Athena often have an owl carved into the base or otherwise shown with the goddess. Pound wrote: "Poor old Upward [author of *The Divine Mystery* who committed suicide in 1927] had a lot to say about Athene's eyes, connecting them with her owl and with olive trees. The property of the glaux, and olive leaf, to shine and then not to shine, 'glint' rather than shine" [*L*, 269]. Again: "Glaux, owl, totem or symbolic bird (gods connected with the divine animals, as stupid bitch Hera has her bull eyes), glare-eyed, owl-eyed Athena" [*L*, 273].

54. Confusion . . . renewals: [20:43].

55. Titania: Epithet of Circe [1:1; *Meta.* XIV, 382, 438].

56. Athame: Prob. invented as a daughter

of the sun, like Phaethusa in the same scene.

57. Phaethusa: Circe tells Odysseus he will come to the isle Thrinacia where fair maidens take care of the flocks of Helios, which are suspended in time. "These bear no young, nor do they ever die, and goddesses are their shepherds, fair-tressed nymphs, Phaethusa" [*Od.* XII, 127-132]. The passage rhymes with the blood drink of Tiresias [1/4] and has a similar content of prophecy. Circe tells Odysseus that if he or his crew harms the goddesses, "late shalt thou come home and in evil case, after losing all the comrades" [*Od.* XII, 140-142].

58. Dis: Roman Pluto, Greek god of the underworld whose rape of Persephone became one basis of the Eleusinian mystery rites.

59. the old man: Like the plowman in Breughel's *Icarus*, the old man is busy and indifferent to the horrendous rape of Persephone [cf. GD, *Approaches*, 154].

60. asphodel: A flower. Supposedly, a climax of the mystery rites is a vision of the paradisal Elysian fields which in classical legend are covered with asphodel.

CANTO XXII

Sources

Pound's personal experiences in 1908 at Gibraltar; Franco Sacchetti, *Le Novelle* (137), Florence, 1724.

Background

EP, *SP*, 189-263; NS, *Life*, 45; G. F. Young, *The Medici*, 1909, I, 43-44 [Modern Library, 1933, 31-32; documentation in glosses is adjusted to the page numbers of this easily available edition].

Exegeses

EP, *J/M*, 33; *LE*, 17-18; Davis, *Vision*, 59-62; CE, *Ideas*, 65, 66, 115-116; EH, *Pai*, 5-3, 413; HK, in *Italian Quarterly*, vol. 16, no. 64, 7; Klink, *Pai*, 5-1, 67.

Glossary

1. **An' that man**: Thaddeus Coleman Pound, Pound's grandfather. In *J/M* (1933) Pound wrote: "I have never believed that my grandfather put a bit of railway across Wisconsin simply or chiefly to make money or even with the illusion that he would make money, or make more money in that way than in some other" [p. 33].

2. **Warenhauser**: Pseudonym for Frederick Weyerhaeuser, 1834-1914, American capitalist known as the "Lumber King"; about 1900 he purchased approximately a million acres of timberland in Washington and Oregon from the Northern Pacific Railroad.

3. **American Curia**: United States Senate.

4. **Northwestern railway**: The Northern Pacific Railroad, running from Duluth and St. Paul, Minnesota, to Seattle, Washington, and Portland, Oregon, was chartered by special act of Congress (1864). Construction began in 1870 and the railway was opened in 1883. Of the land granted by the U.S. government for the construction of the Northern Pacific, more than 2,500,000 undistributed acres were still held by the company in 1948.

5. **he came in**: The "he" (called "Joe" a few lines later) is probably a pseudonym. But the point of the anecdote—the hazards in a profit system based on usury (price of life in the occident)—is clear no matter who "Joe" may be. In other words, Joe's shop is doing such slow and careful work that none of his "chunks" are imperfect: good work costs money. In the assembly-line system, such items must be turned out in mass which means that many of them will be rejected. The anecdote rhymes with the examples in Canto XLV, such as the price of workmanship implied by *Adamo me fecit* [45:14].

6. **C.H.**: Clifford Hugh Douglas, 1879-1952, British engineer and social economist, founder of Social Credit [38:49].

7. **Mr. Bukos**: John Maynard Keynes, 1883-1946, English economist. His early defense of the gold standard and his protest against the Versailles Treaty, expressed in *Economic Consequences of the Peace*, 1919, made him world famous. But he departed from classical free-economy concepts in 1929 and endorsed Lloyd George's programs of public works and government spending by increasing the national debt to increase employment.

8. **H.C.L.**: High cost of living.

9. **Jesu Christo ... d'Adamo**: I, "Jesus Christ! / Standing in the Earthly Paradise / Thinking as he made himself a companion of Adam," [*standu* is dialect form for *stando*].

10. **Mr. H.B.**: John Maynard Keynes [cf. 7 above].

11. **Mac Narpen and Company**: Pseudonym for the Macmillan Company, publishers.

12. **Palgrave's Golden Treasury**: Francis Turner Palgrave, 1824-1897, English poet and critic and professor of poetry at Oxford (1885-1895). He edited the poetry anthology, *The Golden Treasury of the Best Songs and Lyrical Poems in the English Language* [1861, 1897]. See "How to Read," in *LE*, 17-18, for EP's story about "something to replace that doddard Palgrave." The agent he was conferring with replied: "But don't you know that the whole fortune of X & Co is founded on Palgrave's *Golden Treasury*?"

13. Nel paradiso terrestre: I, "In the terrestrial paradise."

14. una compagna . . . fesse: I, "a mate for Adam. How to make her?" Literally *Come si fesse?* means "How did he make himself?"

15. E poi . . . volpe: I (dialect), "And then he saw a vixen."

16. e pensava: I, "and he thought."

17. Corre . . .Della volpe: I (dialect), "She runs, the vixen runs, Christ runs, the vixen runs / Christ runs, and he gave a leap, and he caught the tail / Of the vixen."

18. e di questu . . . una rabbia: I (dialect), "and from this [*questo*] / She was made, / And for this reason / Woman is a fury, / A fury-and-a-rage." Pound overheard an Italian hotelkeeper "teasing his genteel lady cashier" with this anecdote [cf. HK, *Italian Quarterly*, vol. 16, no. 64, 7].

19. Freer: Surname of Pound's great-aunt which Pound apparently used as his own during the summer of 1906.

20. Mohamed Ben Abt el Hjameed: Prob. a merchant in Gibraltar, ca. 1908.

21. Calpe (Lyceo): Mount Calpe is the Rock of Gibraltar; the Calpe Club, Church Street, Gibraltar. [*Lyceo* cannot be Spanish; it may be based on root of French *Lycée*: school or pupil. Here it seems to indicate a café or a social club.]

22. Gibel Tara: Gibraltar.

23. Jeen-jah: Ginger.

24. Mustafa: Prob. a merchant in Gibraltar, ca. 1908.

25. Yusuf: Y. Benamore, a Jewish tourist guide whom Pound met in Gibraltar in 1908 and to whom he felt greatly indebted. He wrote later: "Life saved by Yusuf Benamore." Yusuf took Pound to the synagogue where the scene described later in the canto took place [cf. NS, *Life*, 45].

26. calle: S, "street."

27. Granada: City in S Spain.

28. Edward the Seventh: 1841-1910, king of England (1901-1910), who often visited Gibraltar incognito.

29. e faceva bisbiglio: I, "and whispered [as in gossip]."

30. Down at the court-house: Pound also visited a courthouse. "Case on for rape and black-mail" may have reminded him of the difficulty of enforcing the law in the 14th century, as illustrated in *Le Novelle* (no. 137) of the Florentine writer Franco Sacchetti, source of the following anecdote about the "judge's" trouble.

31. And the judge says: The judge in *Le Novelle* was Messer Amerigo degli Amerighi of Pesaro who tried to enforce the laws prohibiting Florentine ladies from wearing ornaments and furs at the start of the 13th century. The story is retold in Isidoro del Lungo's *Women of Florence* (trans. Mary C. Steegman), London, 1907, 45-52 [EH, *Pai*, 5-3, 413].

32. lattittzo: I (dialect), *lattizo*. Defined in *Vocabulario universale italiano* as "pelle d'animale da latter' [skin of a suckling animal resembling ermine].

CANTO XXIII

Sources

Michael Constantine Psellos, *De Omnifaria Doctrina*; Porphyry *De Occasionibus, De Abstinentia*; Marsilio Ficino, *Theologia Platonica*, libre XVIII, 1561; Iamblichus, *De Mysteriis Egyptiorum, Chaldaeorum, Assyriorum*; Fritz Schultze, *Georgios Gemisthos Plethon und seine reformatorischen Bestrebungen*, 1874; Marie Curie, *Pierre Curie*, Paris, 1924; Stesichorus, fragment of a lost poem; Franz Cumont, *Textes et Monuments figurés relatifs aux mystères de Mithra*, 1894-1901; Dante, *Inf.* I; Homer, *Od.*; EP, "Provincia Deserta," in *P*; Chabaneau, *Les Biographies des Troubadours en Langue Provençale*; Plutarch, "Why Oracles Are Silent"; Homeric Hymn V, "To Aphrodite"; ΑΘΗΝΑΙΟΥ ΝΑΥΚΡΑΤΙΤΟΥ ΔΕΙΠΝΟΣΟΦΙΣΤΑΙ. *Athenaei Naucratitae Deipnosophistarum libri quindecim.* . . . Argentorati: ex typographia Societatis Bipontinae. Tomus Quartus, Anno XII, 1804, pp. 237-238 (Liber XI.469e, f) [Fang I, 44]; Yriarte, *Un Condottière au XVᵉ siècle*, 1882; *The Greek Bucolic Poets* [Loeb], trans. J. M. Edmonds, 387; Ovid, *Meta*. X.

Background

EP, *GK*, 224-225; *SR*, 101; A. A. Vasiliev, *History of the Byzantine Empire*, Madison, Wisc., 1952; H. F. Tozer, "A Byzantine Reformer," *Journal of Hellenic Studies*, VII, 2, 1886.

Exegeses

S. Libera, "Casting His Gods Back into the NOUS," *Pai*, 2-3, 368-377; J. Peck, "Pound's Lexical Mythography," *Pai*, 1-1, 5-7; J. Peck, "Arras and Painted Arras," *Pai*, 3-1, 63-66; L. Surette, "A Light from Eleusis," *Pai*, 3-2, 195-196; LL, *Motive*; CE, *Ideas*; EH, *Approaches*; DP, *Barb*; WB, *Rose*; HK, *Era*, passim; Fang, I, 41-44; *Pai*, 6-3, 359-361.

Glossary

1. Et omniformis . . . est: L, "And every intellect is capable of assuming every shape" [cf. Porphyrios, *De Occasionibus*, chap. 13, "Omnis Intellectus Est Omniformis"; *Pai*, 6-3, 359-361].

2. Psellos: Michael Constantine Psellus, 1018-1105?, Byzantine philosopher, politi-

cian, writer, and early Neoplatonist. He is one of the several Pound lists as important to the Renaissance humanism derived from Gemistus [*GK*, 224-225].

3. Gemisto: Georgius Gemistus, fl. early 15th century; Greek Platonic philosopher, sometimes called Plethon. A significant figure at the meeting of the Eastern and Western churches held at Ferrara and Florence in 1438 [8:30].

4. Peloponesus: Peloponnesus, S part of the mainland of Greece. Home of Gemistus who, to keep out Turkish barbarism and the influence of Eastern Christianity, which had become singularly corrupt, encouraged the emperor, Manuel II, to construct "a wall with numerous towers on the Isthmus of Corinth" [Vasiliev, 637]. Plethon drew up details of a new, pure-Greek society based on reorganization of all society under new laws and social classifications as well as a new religion based on his own ideas of the old polytheism of the early Greeks and Plato. He believed that Christianity made men effeminate and that a new barbarism was issuing from Rome.

5. Novvy: Domencio Malatesta, younger brother of Sigismundo, known popularly as Malatesta Novello. When 29, Novvy was lamed in an accident and turned to public works. He endowed Cesena with (1) a library, (2) a hospital for the infirm elderly and for exposed children, and (3) a school for the education of bastard boys and girls [Yriarte, 303]. He also sent an emissary to Greece to find books and manuscripts for the library, but the consignment was lost at sea [10:58, 11:18].

6. Irol: Iroline, a French motor fuel.

7. Houille blanch / Auto-chenille: F, "water power / caterpillar-tread vehicle."

8. Invention-d'entités . . . consister: F, "Invention of more or less abstract entities / in number equal to the things to be explained . . . / Science cannot be composed of it."

9. J'ai obtenu . . . guérison: F, "I got a burn . . . from which it took me six months to recover."

10. M. Curie: Pierre C., 1859-1906, French chemist and physicist. Marie Curie, his wife, writes in *Pierre Curie*: "In order to test the results announced by F. Giesel, Pierre Curie voluntarily exposed his arm to the action of radium during several hours. This resulted in a lesion resembling a burn, that developed progressively and required several months to heal" [English ed., trans. Charlotte and Vernon Kellogg, Macmillan, 1923, 117].

11. Tropismes: F, "tropisms" "responses to stimulus."

12. Ἅλιος . . . : H; the Greek and Latin lines here and on the next page are adapted from Johannes Schweighaeuser's bilingual [Greek and Latin] edition of *Athenaeus*, which reads: Ἅλιος δ᾿ ὑπεριονίδας δέπας ἐσκατέβαινε / χρύσιον ὄφρα δι᾿ ὠκεανοῖο περάσας / ἀφίκηθ᾿ ἱερᾶς ποτὶ βένθεα νυκτὸς ἐρεμνᾶς / ποτὶ ματέρα κουριδίαν τ᾿ ἄλοχον, / παῖδας τε φίλοις. δὸ δ᾿, ἐς ἄδιος ἔβαί / δάφναισι κατάσκιον / ποσσὶ παῖς Διός [Fang I, 41]. Pound has left out a few words, here translated in brackets: "The sun, Hyperion's child, stepped down into his golden bowl and then after crossing the stream of ocean [he reached] the depth of black [and holy] night and joined his mother, his faithful wife, and his dear children. [Meanwhile the son of Zeus] entered [on foot] the laurel-shaded [grove]." The son of Zeus is Heracles on his tenth labor. He is journeying to the West in the sun's boat in search of the cattle of Geryon [for sun's boat, cf. 21:43 and 91/612; for sun's journey, 17/79].

13. ima vada . . . : L, "low fords of the dark night." From the Latin version in Schweighaeuser, which reads: Sol vero Hyperionis filius in poculum inscendebat / aureum, ut per oceanum traiiciens / perveniret sacrae ad ima vada noctis obscurae / ad matrem, & Virginalem uxorem, / liberosque caros. Ipse autem in lucum se contulit lauris obumbratum / pedibus filius Iovis [Fang I, 41]. Peck [*Pai*, 1-1, 6] suggests that "The idiot" refers to Odysseus's feigned madness to keep out of the war and the derivation of ἅλιος to be "fruitless," as Liddell and Scott suggests. But Pound really thinks he has a better etymology for the word, connecting it with μάταιος, and comes up with the epithet "idiot" [Fang I, 41].

14. ἥλιος . . . μάταιος: ἥλιος, sun; ἅλιος (A), of the sea (adj.); ἅλιος (B), fruitless, idle; μάταιος, vain, empty, idle. Pound has just quoted two lines from Stesichorus, in which the Doric form ἅλιος for ἥλιος is used. Frederic Peachy shows that Pound looked up ἅλιος in Liddell and Scott's *Abridged Greek-English Lexicon* and found three definitions: (1) Dor. for ἥλιος; (2) L, marinus; (3) μάταιος: deriv. uncertain [F. Peachy, *Index*, 260; cf. Peck, *Pai*, 1-1, 5-6].

15. alixantos . . . : H, "worn by the sea, feeding in the sea [sea-reared], he went down into." Pound is here using Liddell and Scott's *Abridged Greek-English Lexicon* to construe the Stesichorus fragment on the setting sun: *eiskatebaine* is from the fragment. The other words follow immediately [F. Peachy, *Index*, 260; cf. Peck, *Pai*, 1-1, 5-6].

16. selv' oscura: I, *selva oscura*, "dark forest" [cf. *Inf.* I, 2].

17. Phrygian: Phrygia was an ancient country in WC Asia Minor.

18. 'Yperionides: H, "son of Hyperion"; Helios. The initial letter should be transliterated as *U*, not as *Y*, and what seems to be a beginning apostrophe should be transliterated from a Greek rough breathing to the letter *H*. Along with Cronos (Saturn) and Ops (Rhea), Hyperion (a child of Heaven and Earth) was one of the Titans and the father of the Sun, the Moon, and Dawn. He is the original sun-god whose functions were later assumed by his son Helios (Apollo). Thus, as the sun's boat appeared in the East, rising from the Phrygian desert, it is imaged as gaining buoyancy for the sky trip by unloading sand.

19. while I slept: The "I" may be Niccolò d'Este and the next 22 lines may return to the "arras and painted arras" delirium scene developed earlier [20:42; Peck, *Pai*, 3-1, 64-66].

20. Capriped: "goat-footed, a satyr."

21. Fa Han: Pseudonym for a female acquaintance of Pound's. Because of her "hair" Pound may associate her with Circe and certain Chinese ladies of the Confucian Odes tradition [cf. Peck, *Pai*, 3-1, 64-66].

22. Maensac: Peire de M., a poor knight of Auvergne. Pound invents the story of tossing the coin, but Austors stayed at the castle and Peire became a troubadour and ran away with the wife of Bernart de Tierci, taking her to the castle of Robert, dauphin of Auvergne. When de Tierci tried to regain his wife, the dauphin protected Peire and defeated de Tierci's attack [5:26].

23. Auvergne: Section of Provence, SE central France. Also Auvergnat [cf. next line and 5/18].

24. Chaise Dieu: F, "Seat of God." The Abbey of Chaise Dieu, founded in 1046, in Brioude, near the Languedoc-Auvergne border. Also used in general mythic sense.

25. Mount Segur: Montsegur [P, "Secure Mountain"], lofty hill and fort where the last of the Manicheans were besieged and the unrepentant were burned in 1244 during the Albigensian Crusade; now considered a symbol of Provençal glory. Because it was the site of a temple to Apollo, it has been linked to solar-force worship.

26. Simone: Simon de Montfort or Simon IV de Montfort l'Amaury, ?1160-1218, Count of Montfort and Earl of Leicester; leader of French forces against Provençals and alleged Manicheans in Albigensian Crusade; killed in battle at Toulouse.

27. they called us: Austors is speaking of himself, his brother Peire, and other troubadours and singers of *gai savoir*.

28. Manicheans: Followers of the religious system founded by Mani, a system based on the idea of a Good One and an Evil One, both of equal power, existing in the universe. Persecuted indifferently with troubadours during Albigensian Crusade by the

Church and the N French. Long a source of discontent to popes who persecuted them, the Manichaeans who had absorbed Mithraism [a doctrine derived from Mithras, Persian god of light] thrived as "Catharists" or "a pure Christian faith." Innocent III finally sent the crusade against them and destroyed the brilliant Provençal civilization. Pound condemned the mass slaughter in which 200 "Cathari" were burned in one day as well as the hypocritical purpose and result: "The Albigensian crusade, a sordid robbery cloaking itself in religious pretence, had ended the *gai savoir* in southern France" [*SR*, 101; cf. *Pai*, 3-2, 196 ff.].

29. superbo Ilion: I, "proud Troy."

30. they were sailing: Aeneas, son of Aphrodite and Anchises, en route to the founding of Rome.

31. Anchises: Father of Aeneas speaking of the destruction of Troy.

32. Tethnéké: H, "He is dead."

33. Adonis: A youth loved by Aphrodite; when he was killed by a boar, she caused the anemone to spring from his blood. Adonis is the central figure in a number of fertility rites and myths which celebrate his death and survival; Tammuz is the Babylonian equivalent of Adonis [cf. Bion, *Lament for Adonis*; Ovid, *Meta*. X].

34. King Otreus: Legendary king of Phrygia; when Aphrodite took human form to lie with Anchises, she told him that her father was King Otreus, for she wished to keep her identity a secret [cf. Homeric Hymn V, "To Aphrodite"].

35. Phrygia: [cf. 17 above].

CANTO XXIV

Sources

Luchino dal Campo, *Viaggio a Gerusalemme di Niccolò da Este*, Turin, 1861; Giambattista Pigna, *Historia de Principi di Este*, 1570; Antonio Frizzi, *Memorie per la Storia di Ferrara*, 5 vols., Ferrara, 1791-1809; Alfonso Lazzari, *Ugo e Parisina nella realtà storica*, 1915, expanded in *Parisina*, Florence, 1949; report of the librarian Cassini; Homeric Hymn IV, "To Hermes."

Background

Werner L. Gundersheimer, *Ferrara*, Princeton, 1973; E. G. Gardner, *Dukes and Poets in Ferrara*, 1904, rpt., New York, 1968.

Exegeses

EP, *SP*, 169; *J/M*, 79; D. J. Hugen, *Pai*, 3-2, 229-238; DP, *Barb*; WB, *Rose*, passim.

Glossary

1. Zohanne: Z. Giovanni, servant of Parisina Malatesta [cf. 6 below].

2. Rimini: Ancient Ariminum, seaport in Forlì Province, N Italy; seat of the Malatesta family [8:5].

3. marchesini: I, *marchisini*, "marks": lire issued by Marquis d'Este.

4. barbarisci: I, "wild horses"; associated with Barbary.

5. Modena . . . San Petronio . . . San Zorzo: Three races, the second run around a church in Bologna, the third probably around San Giorgio Maggiore in Venice. *Zorzo* is Romagnole dialect form.

6. Parisina Marchesa: P. Malatesta, d. 1425, wife of Niccolò d'Este, daughter of Carlo Malatesta. When Niccolò discovered that Parisina was having an affair with his natural son, Ugo, he had them both beheaded [8:51; 20:25].

7. un libro . . . Tristano: I, "a French book called Tristan"; Pound uses *franxese* for *francese* (dialect).

8. Carissimi nostri: I, "our dearest ones."

9. palio: I, "horse race."

10. madama la marxesana: I, "Madame the Marchioness," Parisina Malatesta.

11. Romagna: Region of Italy which now comprises the provinces of Bologna, Ferrara, Ravenna, and Forlì.

12. verde colore predeletto: I, "green color preferred."

13. ziparello: I, *zipparèllo*, a decorative, short, sleeveless tunic of the Quattrocento worn over armor. This echoes 11/52, "For a green cloak with silver brocade," which explains its costing as much as 25 ducats. [JE]

14. Ugo: Eldest son of Niccolò d'Este and stepson of Parisina Malatesta; he and Parisina were beheaded after Niccolò discovered their adultery.

15. fiolo del Signore: I, "son of the Master."

16. PROCURATIO NOMINE PATRIS: L, "procuration in the name of the father."

17. Leonello Este: Lionello d'E., 1407-1450, second son of Niccolò d'Este, who succeeded as Marquis of Ferrara after death of Niccolò in 1441.

18. Margarita: M. d'Este, d. 1452, sister of Lionello d'Este. The "dot" is F. for "dowry."

19. Roberto Malatesta: D. 1482, known as the Magnificent. His marriage to Margarita d'Este was arranged by his father Sigismundo M. for political reasons [11:9].

20. natae . . .Sponsae: L. "Margaret, daughter of the aforenamed illustrious Lord Niccolò, Marquis of Este, and his wife."

21. Gualdo: G. Tadino, town in Perugia Province, C Italy.

22. Nicolaus Marquis of Este: Niccolò d'Este, Nicholas III of Ferrara, 1384-1441, ruler of Ferrara, Modena, Parma, Reggio, and Milan; father of Borso, Lionello, and Ercole d'Este; husband of Parisina Malatesta [20:25, 26].

23. Don Carlo (Malatesta): 1368-1429, man of letters and patron of the arts; uncle of Sigismundo [26:59].

24. Illustrae Dominae Parisinae Marxesana: L, "Of the illustrious Lady Parisina, Marchioness."

25. D. Michaeli de Magnabucis: Notary public of Ferrara (1427).

26. D. Nicolaeque Guiduccioli: Prob. represented Carlo Malatesta in making arrangements for the marriage of Carlo's daughter, Parasina Malatesta, to Niccolò d'Este in 1418.

27. de Arimino: I, "of Rimini."

28. Sequit bonorum descriptio: L, "There follows a description of property."

29. And he in his young youth . . .: This passage, concluding in the middle of the next page (112), is based on a scribe's account of Niccolò d'Este's trip to the Holy Land. Pound reduces 45 pages of the "Voyage . . . " in his source for these lines [cf. Hugen, *Pai*, 3-2, 229-238, for full account].

30. Cithera: Cythera, epithet of Aphrodite, from the association of the goddess with the island of Cythera, off the SE coast of Laconia.

31. "dove fu . . . Paris": I, "where Helen was kidnapped by Paris."

32. Pola: Or Pula, a fortified seaport at S tip of Istrian peninsula.

33. Naxos: Largest island of the Cyclades, in the Aegean Sea; center of ancient Dionysus worship; a crossroads tourist stop in Renaissance times [2:14].

34. Ora vela . . . vespero: I, "Now with sails, now with oars, on to the hour of evening."

35. Zefalonia: Cephalonia, largest of Ionian Islands off Greece.

36. Corfu: Island in Ionian Sea.

37. Rhodos: Rhodes, island in Aegean Sea; in antiquity a center of trade, and later a major supply stop on route to Holy Land.

38. Paphos: Town on SW coast of Cyprus, famous as center for worship of Aphrodite.

39. backsheesh: A sort of alms or gift of money asked for by beggars: "Along the way we met streams of beggars and roisterers, some on foot, some on horseback, asking for 'baksheesh' " [Hugen, op. cit., 236].

40. groat: Grossi; one paid 7 ducats and 27 Venetian grossi to pass from Joffa to Jerusalem.

41. Jordan: River in Palestine.

42. Pilate: Pontius P., fl. A.D. 33, procurator of Judea under Emperor Tiberius. Pilate washed his hands as a gesture of innocence at the trial of Christ.

43. soldi: *Soldo*; I, "small coins."

44. Olivet: Mount of Olives, E of Jerusalem.

45. Saracens: Term commonly used in the Middle Ages to designate Arabs and, by extension, Moslems in general, whether Arabs, Moors, or Turks.

46. Judas's tree: According to tradition, the tree on which Judas hanged himself after the betrayal and the Crucifixion.

47. hic . . . mundi: L, "here is the center of the world."

48. Ego . . . : L, "I, the writer of the canto."

49. Benche niuno cantasse: I, "Although no one was singing."

50. Luchino del Campo: L. dal Campo, companion of Niccolò d'Este on a journey to Jerusalem and author of an account of the trip: *Viaggio a Gerusalemme di Niccolò da Este, descritto da Luchino dal Campo*, ed. G. Ghinassi, 1861.

51. Aldovrandino: Friend of Ugo d'Este and Parisina who was executed with them. The *Diario Ferrarese* reported: "1425, in the month of May, a Monday, at the 24th hour, the head of Ugo, son of the illustrious marquess Niccolò d'Este, was cut off, and that of madonna Parisina . . . and this because he had consorted carnally with her. And with them was decapitated one Aldovrandino di Rangoni da Modena, a familiar of the said *signore*, for having been the cause of this evil" [Gundersheimer, 79].

52. vent 'uno Maggio: I, "May 21st."

53. The Marchese: Niccolò d'Este.

54. "Signor . . . si": I, "Sir . . . yes."

55. "Fa me hora . . . Ugo": I, "Now cut off *my* head, / since you've so soon decapitated my Ugo."

56. Rodendo . . . mani: I, "Chewing with his teeth a stick he held in his hands." Trans. of source reads: "All that night the unhappy father and husband paced up and down the halls and passages of his palace in desperate grief, now gnawing his sceptre with his teeth, now calling passionately upon the name of his dead son or crying out for his own death" [Gardner, 38].

57. ter pacis . . . : L, "three times author of the Italian peace." Niccolò, one of the greatest lechers among Italian potentates, practiced seduction rather than rape. He was also known as a peacemaker: witness the recurrent refrain to his son, "Keep the peace, Borso."

58. Tre cento . . . bombardi: I, "Three hundred gun salutes . . . bombards." Although Ugo was beheaded, Niccolò ordered an elaborate state funeral; boys pulled the funeral barge from the bank. Niccolò also "sent a written report of the tragedy to all the Courts of Italy, and . . . on receipt of the news the Doge of Venice put off a State tournament" [Gardner, 39].

59. Florentine baily: Dieci Della Balia, Council of Ten of the Balia, ruling authority of Florence.

60. Madonna Laodamia delli Romei: Gardner [p. 39] writes: "The Marquis is said . . . to have ordered the execution of several noble Ferrarese ladies who were notoriously serving their husbands as Parisina had served him—'in order that his wife should not be the only one to suffer.' . . . One, Laodamia de'Romei, the wife of one of the judges, 'who was known to him,' appears to have been publicly beheaded."

61. pa della justicia: I, "palace of justice."

62. Agnesina: D. ca. 1430, a matron of Modena who, apparently, had committed adultery and poisoned her husband; under edict she was also beheaded. The point of the edict that resulted in these beheadings is that it came as a result of Niccolò's anguish following the beheading of Parisina.

63. Monna Ricarda: Ricciarda di Sallusto, daughter of Marquess Saluzzo. She married Niccolò d'Este in 1431, six years after the execution of his wife, Parisina, and bore him two legitimate sons, Ercole and Sigismundo.

64. Charles: Charles VII of France, 1403-1461 (reign 1422-1461).

65. scavoir faisans . . . Jehan Rabateau: F, "making known . . . and to come . . . to high / nobility of family and house . . . and great deeds . . . / valor . . . affection . . . our aforesaid cousin . . . / power, royal authority . . . he and his descendants . . . and / as they desire to have henceforth forever in their arms quartering / . . . three golden flower-de-luce . . . on scalloped azure field . . . / enjoy and use. [Dated] 1431, [at] council at Chinon, the King, l'Esne de la Tribouill, Vendoise, [and signed] Jehan Rabateau."

66. Marchese Saluzzo: Marquess S., father of Monna Ricciarda [cf. 63 above] and grandfather of Ercole.

67. Hercules: Ercole d'Este, 1431-1505, son of Niccolò d'Este and Ricciarda. He became the second ruler of Ferrara after Niccolò and a "Hercules" in advancing music, the arts, and the welfare of the people.

68. piccolo e putino: I, "small and boyish."

69. Polenta: Ostasio da P. Although he was an ally of the Venetians in 1441, he was deprived by them of Ravenna and exiled to Candia with his family.

70. E fu . . . : I, "And he was buried nude." In 1441 Niccolò went to serve as governor of Milan at the request of the ailing duke, Filippo Maria Visconti. He died a month later, aged 58, possibly from poison. His body was returned to Ferrara and at midnight of New Year's Day he was buried in the Church of Santa Maria degli Angeli, "nude, without any pomp, for so he did command in his will" [Gundersheimer, 91].

71. Ter pacis Italiae: L, "Three times of the Italian peace" [cf. 57 above].

72. Bondeno: Commune in Ferrara Province, N Italy.

73. Cassini: Poss. Gherado Casini, Roman publisher.

74. libraio: I, "bookseller."

75. Napoleon: N. Bonaparte, 1769-1821, emperor of the French (1805-1814).

76. Via del Po: I, "Street of the Po [River]."

77. Piacenza: Town in the region of Veneto, N Italy.

78. Marchese Niccolo: Niccolò d'Este.

79. Borso: Third son of Niccolò. The statues of both father and son were erected in the square of Ferrara, prob. in the 15th century.

80. Piazza: I, "Square."

81. Commendatore: I, "Knight of a chivalric order."

82. per diletto: I, "for pleasure" [*Inf.* V, 127], describing activities of the lustful lovers, Paolo and Francesca [cf. *Pai*, 3-2, 229].

83. Ferrara . . . stomagose: I, "Ferrara, paradise for clothiers, disgusting festivals."

84. Apollo: Phoebus A., Olympian god of light and son of Zeus and Leto whose cattle were stolen by Hermes, son of Zeus and Maia: "Born in the dawn, by midday well he harped, and in the evening stole the cattle of Apollo. . . . When he leaped from the immor-tal knees of his mother, lay not long in the sacred cradle, but sped forth to seek the cattle of Apollo." Apollo later followed the trail that led to the crib and accused the boy, who said: " . . . great marvel . . . that a new-born child should cross the threshold after kine . . . Yesterday was I born, my feet are tender" [Homeric Hymn IV].

85. A child of my age: Hermes.

86. Albert: Alberto d'Este, 1347-1393, father of Niccolò d'Este; marchese and vicar of Ferrara. Niccolò is supposedly speaking.

87. Tura: Cosimo or Cosmé T., 1430?-1495, Italian painter of murals; a leader of the Ferrarese school and court painter to Borso and Ercole d'Este; one of the Schifanoia muralists.

88. Julia the Countess: Prob. member of the Tassoni family of Ferrara, which owned the Schifanoia at one time. Text reference is to the fact that the Schifanoia once was used as a tobacco factory; the Italian verb, *conciare*, means to tan hides, or to cure tobacco, hence the confusion of *tannery* in the text. For recent history of the Schifanoia, see R. Longhi, "Il Palazzo Estense di Schifanoia dal sec. XIV al sec. XX," *Rivista di Ferrara*, July 1935.

CANTO XXV

Sources

Giambattista Lorenzi, *Monumenti per servire alla storia del Palaz-zo Ducale di Venezia*, Venice, 1868; Tibullus III, 10 (IV, iv), 15, and III, 11 (IV, v), 1; Plato, *Gorgias*; *The Epic of Gilgamesh*; Homeric Hymn V, "To Aphrodite."

Background

William Carew Hazlitt, *The Venetian Republic*: *Its Rise, Its Growth, and Its Fall, A.D. 409-1797*, London, 1915; Francis

Marion Crawford, *Gleanings from Venetian History*, New York, 1905; Gibbon, *The Decline and Fall of the Roman Empire*, Modern Library, 1932, Vol. II.

Exegeses

Dekker, *Cantos*, 31-35; EH, *Approaches*, 24-25, 30-31; HK, *Era*, 307-308, passim; S. Libera, *Pai* 2-3, 359.

Glossary

1. Council: The first two and a half pages and the last page of this canto are taken from various decrees concerning the palace of the doges. The Doge (Duke) of Venice was a nonhereditary officer elected for life by the people. In 1173 a body known as the Great Council or Council Major was set up to control the actions of the duke; it originally consisted of 480 members, but the number of members and the method of election changed frequently. The council gradually became less democratic and was dominated by a smaller body, the Council of Forty [Hazlitt, I, 495-502].

2. danari: I, "small coins."

3. loggia: I, "open gallery"; Rialto: bridge and quarter of Venice.

4. soldi: I, a small coin.

5. In libro pactorum: L, "In the book of the agreements (or 'contracts')."

6. et quod . . . : L, "and which may be publicly made known."

7. dicto millessimo: ML, from I, *millessimo* ("the year or the year and day in a formal date"), "on the said date."

8. Lord John Soranzo: Giovanni S., Doge of Venice (1312-1328). Said to be "undeniably one of the most illustrious men elected to the Dogeship in the course of its existence of exactly eleven hundred years" [Crawford, I, 292; Hazlitt, I, 562-566].

9. Curia: L, "meeting place of the Senate."

10. Palace of the Doges: On the Piazzetta, just off of the SE corner of the Piazza San Marco, Venice.

11. Castaldio: The original document has *juxta domus habitationis Gastaldionum* ["next to the habitation of the Administrators"]. *Gastaldo*, a variant spelling of *Castaldo* (I, "bailiff"), was used in Venice for a variety of administrative officers. *Castaldia* means the residence of a bailiff [Hazlitt, I, 594-595].

12. trabesilis: The original document has *de trabeselis*; neither word appears in dictionaries of classical or medieval Latin, but the word must be derived from L, *trabs* ["beam" or "timber"], so that the phrase in the document means "of small wooden beams" and Pound's "timbered" is a reasonable translation.

13. simul commorantes: L, "living together" [although *commorantes* means "abiding" or "staying," when used with *simul*, the *Index* trans. seems reasonable]. The lion, sacred to St. Mark, is the totem animal of Venice.

14. Lord King Frederic of Sicily: Frederick II of Sicily, 1272-1337, King of Sicily (1296-1337).

15. millessimo: L, "date" [cf. 7 above].

16. St. Mark's day: April 25, the day of the patron saint of Venice; the flag of St. Mark is the Venetian standard.

17. **per naturam . . . pilosos**: L, "by nature . . . alive and hairy."

18. **gyring**: "Moving in a spiral," a word often used by Yeats.

19. **John Marchesini**: Fl. 1328, ducal notary of Venice.

20. **St. Nicholas**: The Chapel of San Niccolò in the palace of the doges.

21. **gross**: Pound's translation of *grossorum*, gen. pl. of ML, *grossus* ["small coin" or "groat"].

22. **Donna Sorantia Soranzo**: Daughter of Giovanni Soranzo, Doge of Venice. Because she was married to Niccolò Querini (d. ca. 1330), a leader of a conspiracy to overthrow the government, she was exiled from Venice in 1320 and permitted to return only to attend her father when he was ill (1327). The next year he died in her arms [cf. Crawford, I, 242-243].

23. **Ascension**: Ascension Day, 40th day after Easter.

24. **ripa del Palazzo**: I, "embankment of the Palace."

25. **groats**: [cf. 21 above].

26. **Marc Erizio**: Prob. "Erizzo," a member of the Consiglio dei Dieci [Council of Ten], Venice.

27. **Nic. Speranzo**: Prob. member of the council.

28. **Tomasso Grandonico**: Prob. Grandenigo, a member of the council.

29. **the hall**: Hall of the Great Council in the palace of the doges, which was rebuilt between 1309 and 1404.

30. **because of the stink**: Three councillors were delegated to study the possibility of keeping the prisoners in a place where their odor would be less noticeable to people going up the stairs of the hall of the Great Council.

31. **Doge**: Michele Steno, Doge of Venice

(1400-1413). Money was appropriated to enlarge his private room.

32. **vadit pars**: L, lit. "a part goes." An authority at the Biblioteca Nazionale Marciana Venezia says that it is a Venetian legal formula meaning "it was decided that."

33. **da parte . . . sincere**: Original document has *De parte*. I, "on behalf of [i.e., affirmative] / of no [i.e., negative] / . . . not genuine."

34. **murazzi**: I, "dikes," embankments of the lagoon in Venice. For the same Venetian scene with palace at dawn cf. 21/98 and 17/76.

35. **Sulpicia**: Fl. 40 B.C. The niece of Messala Corvinus, she was a Roman poet whose six short pieces on her passion for Cerinthus are included in Volume III [13-18] of the works of Tibullus. An unknown author composed five poems (III, 8-12] about her or in her name; Pound is quoting from the third and fourth of these poems.

36. **Pone metum Cerinthe**: L, "Lay aside fear, Cerinthus." The author tells Cerinthus that his girl (presumably Sulpicia) will get well, since God will not harm lovers.

37. **Zephyrus**: In Greek mythology the personification of the west wind.

38. **deus nec . . .** : L, "nor does God harm lovers."

39. **Hic mihi . . .** : L, "This day a holy one for me." The day is Cerinthus's birthday.

40. **Sero, sero**: L, "Too late, too late."

41. **Pone metum . . . laedit**: L, "Lay aside fear, / fear, nor does God harm."

42. **bolge**: Pound is Anglicizing the I *bolgia*, lit. "a large wallet," Dante's word for the ten ditches in the eighth circle of Inferno [15:9].

43. **Civis Romanus**: L, "Roman citizen."

44. **vanity of Ferrara**: The seven lines culminating in *vanity of Ferrara* probably are a

comment on the central debate at the council between the Eastern and Western churches convened by Pope Eugenius IV in 1438 at Ferrara. Gibbon summarizes: "Four principal questions had been agitated between the two churches: 1. The use of unleavened bread in the communion of Christ's body. 2. The nature of purgatory. 3. The supremacy of the pope. And, 4. The single or double procession of the Holy Ghost . . . . The procession of the Holy Ghost from the Father alone, or from the Father and the Son, was an article of faith which had sunk much deeper into the minds of men; and in the sessions of Ferrara and Florence the Latin addition of *filioque* was subdividied into two questions, whether it were legal, or whether it were orthodox" [*Decline and Fall*, Modern Library ed., 1286]. And so on. Such rhetorical but dead words leading to dogma are continually contrasted in the *Cantos* with the celebration of the mysterium, the "light from Eleusis," or the "blood rite." That men presume to resolve such questions is a "vanity" [cf. 8:30 and 26:52 for more detail].

45. Phaethusa: [21:57].

46. Phlegethon: The river of fire in Hades.

47. pone metum: L, "lay aside fear" [cf. 36 above].

48. Napishtim: Prob. Utnapishtim, a character in the Babylonian epic, *Gilgamesh*. After surviving a universal flood he is granted immortality by the gods; he reveals to Gilgamesh "knowledge depth-hidden," the secret of eternal youth, a flower that was stolen away from him and eaten by a snake [cf. S. Libera, *Pai* 2-3, 359].

49. νους: H, "mind." In Neoplatonism the word is used to suggest intelligence as the active principle of deity in the universe [ibid.].

50. King Otreus: When Aphrodite appeared in disguise to Anchises, she said she was the daughter of King Otreus [23:34].

51. Tician: Titian, Tiziano Vecellio, 1477-1576, Venetian painter.

52. Tyciano da Cadore: Titian.

53. Fondamenta delli Thodeschi: I, "Embankment [in Venice 'a paved street running along a canal'] of the Germans": the "Fondaco dei Tedeschi," commerical street in Venice.

54. Ser: I, "Sir" or "Master," a title once given to notaries and simple priests.

55. Leonardus Emo: Leonardo Emo, fl. 1522, Venetian general.

56. Sapiens Consilij: L, "Reverend [member] of the Council."

57. Philippus Capello: Filippo C., fl. 1522, Venetian nobleman.

58. Sapiens Terrae Firmae: L, "Reverend [delegate] from the Mainland."

59. Zuan Bellin: Giovanni Bellini, 1430?-1516, leading painter of the Venetian school, noted for his altarpieces and Madonnas.

60. Canal Grande: I, "Grand Canal," major canal of Venice.

61. Sensaria: Original document has *sansaria*, I *senseria* means "brokerage," as trans. in second line on the canto page.

62. ducats: Italian coins of large denomination.

63. pictor: L, "painter."

64. terra . . . carta: I, "earth . . . document." Original document has *Senato Terra*, which may mean the "Senate of the Mainland" or may use the word "earth" [in a sense not recorded in the dictionary] as "year."

CANTO XXVI

Sources

Fritz Schultze, *Georgios Gemisthos Plethon und seine reformatorischen Bestrebungen*, 1874; Charles Yriarte, *Venice*, trans. F. J. Sitwell, 1896; P. Molmenti, *Carpaccio: son temps et son oeuvre*, 1893; L. A. Ferrai, *Lorenzino de' Medici*, Milan, Hoepli, 1891; L. A. Muratori, *Rerum Italicarum Scriptores*, XXII, 1733; Ludwig Schiedermair, *Die Briefe W. A. Mozarts und seiner Familie*, 5 vols., Munich and Leipzig, 1914, trans. and ed. Emily Anderson, 3 vols., 1938, as *The Letters of Mozart and His Family*.

Background

William Carew Hazlitt, *The Venetian Republic: Its Rise, Its Growth, and Its Fall, A.D. 409-1797*, London, 1915; Jacob Burckhardt, *The Civilization of the Renaissance in Italy*, London and New York, 1890; Patricia H. Labalme, *Bernardo Giustiniani: A Venetian of the Quattrocento*, Rome, 1969; G. F. Young, *The Medici*, 1909; Machiavelli, *History of Florence*, IV, xxix; Philip James Jones, *The Malatesta of Rimini and the Papal State*, Cambridge University Press, 1974; F. C. Hodgson, *The Early History of Venice*, London, 1901; Francis Marion Crawford, *Salve Venetia*, I, New York and London, 1905; Werner L. Gundersheimer, *Ferrara*, Princeton, 1973; Earl Miner, *The Japanese Tradition in British and American Literature*, Princeton, 1958, 121.

Exegeses

EP, *GK*, 45, 133, 115, 224, 241; *J/M*, 79; *ABCR*, 30; CE, *Ideas*, 31-32; HK, *Era*, 420-421; Libera, *Pai*, 2-3, 371; CFT, *Pai*, 6-3, 360.

Glossary

1. crocodile: Statue of animal bestridden by St. Theodore atop a marble column in St. Mark's Square in Venice [HK, *Era*, 421, for picture].

2. barche: I, "boats" [3:6].

3. Relaxetur: L, "Let him be released."

4. Pasti: Matteo da Pasti (d. 1468), Veronese sculptor and medalist. He was sent by Sigismundo Malatesta to Candia to paint a portrait of the Turkish emperor, Mohammed II. Because of this commission he was arrested by the Venetians, who suspected him of being in league with the Turks against them. Pasti was the artist who made the designs in Valturio's *De Re Militari* [10:56; 7 below; Hazlitt, II, 881].

5. caveat . . . : L, "let him beware of going to the Turk." The Turk is Mohammed II, Ottoman sultan (reign 1451-1481).

6. Constantinople: Capital of the Ottoman Empire, formerly Byzantium, now Istanbul.

7. Valturio: Robert de V. (d. 1489). Engineer of Sigismundo's La Rocca and his first secretary. Says Pound: "Malatesta and the late condottieri, their mouths watering over the designs, in Valturio, of war engines, tanks, superior catapults" [*GK*, 115; 9:19]

8. Nicolo Segundino: Niccolò Sagundino, spokesman at Rome for the Venetian Senate; charged by the Venetians to try to make peace between Pope Pius II and the Malatesta family.

9. omnem . . . volve lapidem: L, "turn every stone."

10. Pio: Enea Silvio Piccolomini (1405-1464), Pope Pius II (1458-1464); author, humanist, and patron of writers; in literature he is known as Aeneas Silvius [10:27]. In December 1460, Sigismundo Malatesta and his brother were both excommunicated; by January 1461 Pius II had announced the need for some process, inverting canonization, which would enroll Sigismundo as a citizen of Hell [Jones, 231]. During April 1462, effigies of Sigismundo were burned in Rome. Venice, afraid that too large an increase in the temporal power of the papacy would disturb the complicated balance of power of the city-states, tried to temper the policy of Pius and bring about peace. Much of the "diplomacy" had to be done secretly. But by the end of August 1462, with the help of Frederigo d'Urbino and others, the papal forces totally defeated the Malatestas. "From this reverse Sigismundo was never permitted to recover" [Jones, 232].

11. Malatesta: The family of Rimini, prominent from the 13th to the 16th century; in 1462 headed by Sigismundo [8:5].

12. Borso: Borso d'Este, who in the politics of the time would be sympathetic toward maintaining the power of Sigismundo as a balance wheel [20:29].

13. Ferrara: Capital city of d'Este family.

14. Bernard Justinian: Bernardo Giustiniani, 1408-1489. In 1462 he was sent by Venice to Rome to effect an agreement between Pius II and Sigismundo Malatesta, a mission he accomplished the next year. October 28 is the date of his instructions [Labalme, 174-179].

15. Senato Secreto: I, "Secret meeting of the Senate."

16. Hanibal: Annibale di Constantino Cerboni da Castello, agent of Domenico Malatesta to the Venetians.

17. Cesena: Town in Forlì Province, Emilia, Italy; controlled by the Malatestas from 1379 to 1465 [8:55].

18. flag of St. Mark: Venetian standard emblazoned with image of the city's patron saint.

19. Fortinbras: Carlo Fortebracci, Count of Montone, Venetian condottiere. During the war between Sigismundo and Pius II, Venice could not openly support Malatesta against the pope. But they gave 2,000 ducats to Fortebracci to hire Venetian soldiers and thus supported Sigismundo covertly.

20. secretissime: ML, "most secretly."

21. Henry: Henry VI of England, 1421-1471; king of England (1422-1461 and 1470-1471).

22. Inghilterra: I, "England."

23. Levant: The name given to the region extending from Egypt to Turkey along the eastern shores of the Mediterranean.

24. Corfu: Island in Ionian Sea. During the Norman expansion (England, 1066) Duke Robert (called Guiscard) led the Norman forces and cause into the Mediterranean with designs of finally conquering Constantinople, at that time under Venetian dominance. Robert occupied Corfu and, if allowed to remain there, could "keep the war ships and merchant men of Venice confined almost to their own lagoons" [Hodgson, 218]. Several battles were fought over it, one (1084) off Corfu and a critical one at sea above Corfu in which Venice, under the leadership of Doge Selvo, was seriously defeated. "The wrath of the Venetians at the ill success of their fleet in the battle led to the immediate deposition of the doge Silvio" [ibid., 222]. The continuous actions against Robert kept him out of Constantinople, at the immense pleasure of leaders of the Eastern Empire. He ameliorated the problem neatly by dying in 1085.

25. Selvo: Domenigo Selvo or Silvio, doge (1071-1084). He was married to a Byzantine princess, Theodora, daughter of the Emperor Constantine Ducas XI. She was known for "luxurious extravagance" and was "guilty of many false refinements and fantastic notions," including the use of double-pronged gold forks [Hazlitt, I, 134-142; II, 938, 982].

26. San Marco: The Basilica of San Marco, Venice. After being deposed, Selvo "retired into a convent." He "was the first to put up mosaics in the church, and also it was he who required every Venetian ship loading in the East to bring home marbles or fine stones for the basilica" [Hodgson, 227].

27. Sed aureis furculis: L, "But with golden forks."

28. Luxuria: L, "luxury."

29. Lorenzo Tiepolo: Doge of Venice (1268-1275).

30. Barbers etc.: Elaborate festivities marked the installation of Tiepolo as doge. Barbers disguised as knights-errant, furriers, smiths, skinners, glassblowers, and many other tradesmen paraded in rich costumes [Hazlitt, I, 417-420]. "The guilds of the arts and trades had been privileged to escort the wife of Lorenzo Tiepolo to the church:

... first the blacksmiths with flying banner; then the merchants of fur, dressed in their richest garments and most priceless sables . . . ; the weavers next, singing at the top of their voices to the music of trumpets and cymbals, and bearing both silver cups and flagons full of wine. After the weavers the tailors came in the dress of their trade guild, whie robes embroidered with red stars; and the wool-merchants bore olive branches in their hands and had crowns of olive leaves on their heads . . . ; and the sellers of cloth of gold, and the shoemakers, the mercers, . . . the glass-blowers, the jewellers and the barbers, all displaying the rich and fantastic costumes of their guilds in the great procession, a very splendid sight" [Crawford, 298-299]. Pound liked processions and parades of celebration. The first one is noted briefly at 4/16 [cf. also magnificent parade at 43/216-217].

31. gonfaron . . . de vin: F, "banner / and their flasks full of wine." The Venetian banner of the Lion of San Marco was called by the Old French name *gonfalon*.

32. 25th April: In 1435 Niccolò III of Ferrara, 1393-1441, had his son Leonello (reign 1441-1450) married to Margherita Gonzaga (d. 1439), daughter of Francesco Gonzaga of Mantua. Lavish festivities were held at public expense. Probably because of Niccolò's constant concern to maintain good relations with Venice, the wedding party traveled there to continue the celebrations with joustings, horse racing, and the like.

33. Ugaccion dei Contrarini: Ugaccione da Contrari, Ferrarese nobleman who was Niccolò's "constant companion, his most trusted general, diplomat, and military adviser, and his closest friend" [Gundersheimer, 84]. He ruled the city during Niccolò's trip to the Holy Land [24:29].

34. Francesco Gonzaga: 1st Marchese of Mantua (reign 1407-1444).

35. pellande: I, "loose outer garments."

36. cendato: I, *cendado*, "silk cloth."

37. **piazza**: I, "square."

38. **Mantua**: Mantova, city in Lombardy.

39. **And that year ('38)**: This line, the next 37, and the last 3 lines on page 124 concern the gathering of the delegates to the council convened by Pope Eugenius IV to explore ways to unite the Eastern and Western branches of the Church. The delegates from the East debarked at Venice, where they remained for several weeks before departing for Ferrara. The pope chose Ferrara because of its long history of peace and the cooperation he received from the Marquis of Ferrara, Niccolò d'Este, as well as for other reasons. But because of an outbreak of the plague the council, at the invitation of Cosimo de'Medici, moved to Florence [8:30; 25:44].

40. **Marquis of Ferrara**: Niccolò d'Este who came to Venice to meet his guests.

41. **Greek Emperor**: Johannes Palaeologus or John VIII, 1392-1448, Byzantine emperor (1425-1448).

42. **Archbishop of Morea Lower**: Eastern Orthodox delegate to the council, as are all those listed in the next four lines. Morea is the ancient Peloponnesus, S Greece.

43. **Lacedaemon**: District of the Peloponnesus in which the city of Sparta is located; in ancient times sometimes used as the name of the city.

44. **Mitylene**: City on island of Lesbos in the Aegean.

45. **Rhodos**: Rhodes.

46. **Modon Brandos**: Prob. Modon (Methoni), town in the SW Peloponnesus.

47. **Corinth**: City in S Greece.

48. **Trebizond**: City and so-called empire on S shore of the Black Sea, which at times included parts of Georgia and the Crimea.

49. **stonolifex**: Defined as "a Greek ecclesiastical official" in Pound's source, Sanuto, *Vitae Ducum Venetorum* [Muratori, *Rerum* *Italicarum Scriptores*, XXII]. There is no further information [BK].

50. **Cosimo Medici**: Cosimo de' Medici (1389-1464). Although the Albizzi banished Cosimo to Padua [21:20], "he was subsequently permitted to move from Padua to Venice" [Young, 764n]. Machiavelli says: "Wherever he passed, Cosimo was honorably received, visited publicly by the Venetians, and treated by them more like a sovereign than an exile" [*History of Florence*, IV, xxix].

51. **Sigismundo da Rimini**: [8/5].

52. **Trinity**: A central theological point dividing the Eastern and Western churches, derived from a statement adopted at the council of Nicaea (A.D. 325) which said that the Holy Spirit proceeded from both the Father and the Son (*Filioque*); The Eastern Church believed that the Holy Spirit came from the Father only. At the council of 1438 the Western Church tried to support its claim for the Trinity by the age of a particular document which Gemistus proved a forgery [cf. Libera, *Pai*, 2-3, 371; 25:44].

53. **Gemisto**: Georgius Gemistus Plethon [23:3; 8:31]

54. **Te fili ... anulo**: L, "Thee, my son the Duke, and thy successors / with a golden ring." The annual Venetian ceremony, "Wedding of the Sea," celebrated the domination by Venice over the Adriatic Sea. This domination goes back to the reign of Doge Pietro Orseolo II (991-1008), who conquered several cities on the Dalmatian coast. The most familiar story about the origin of the ceremony is that Pope Alexander III in 1177 gave Doge Sebastiano Ziani a consecrated ring in gratitude for the role of Venice in resolving the pope's quarrel with Emperor Frederick Barbarossa (1152-1190) to the advantage of the papacy. In the ceremony, which continued until the end of the Republic in 1797, the doge threw a ring into the sea, saying that he wedded the sea in token of his dominion over it.

55. Manuel: Manuel I Comnenus, 1120?-1180, emperor of the Eastern Roman Empire (1143-1180); his reign was marked by military victories against Italians, Venetians, Serbs, and Turks, but he was defeated by the Seljuks in Phrygia (1176) with the encouragement of Ziani.

56. Rialto: Legend says that in 809 a wooden bridge on floats, called *soleolo*, was built from the island of Rialto across the Grand Canal because it was the heart of commerce. "In 1180 . . . a permanent bridge [was made] of this temporary one" [Yriarte, 165].

57. Ziani: Sebastiano Z., Doge of Venice (1172-1178). Legend says that Pope Alexander III granted him the privilege of using lead for an official seal instead of sealing wax, an honor reserved to emperors [Hazlitt finds no evidence to support the legend (II, 490)].

58. cendato: I, *cendado*, "silk cloth."

59. Carlo Malatesta: 1368-1429, Lord of Rimini, brother of Pandolfo Malatesta, 1370-1427, and uncle of Sigismundo. Pandolfo was a vigorous general who worked with Carlo to extend the power and influence of the family by forming alliances with the popes and the major city-states, including Venice. In 1411-1412 Carlo and Pandolfo entered Venetian service and succeeded twice in defeating the Hungarians. In the second engagement Carlo "was too severely wounded to continue." In 1413 "Pandolfo and his heirs were awarded Venetian nobility" [Jones, 134; 24:23].

60. Balista: I, *ballista*, a machine like a large bow used to hurl stones.

61. Pandolfo: P. Malatesta [cf. 59 above].

62. Per animarla: I, "to enliven him."

63. San Samuele: Square in Venice where the church of the same name is located.

64. yellow kerchief: Prob. an article of dress to identify prostitutes, who were required by law in Venice to wear a peculiar motley garb [Hazlitt, II, 634].

65. ruffiane: I, "procuresses."

66. Cosimo: [21:9 and 50 above]. While in exile to Padua, Cosimo visited Venice.

67. Luigi Gonzaga: Lodovico Gonzaga, Marchese of Mantua (1444-1478).

68. Casa Giustinian: Lodovico Gonzaga was a friend of Bernardo Giustiniani's [cf. 14 above], but the *casa* ["house"] the Venetian government bought for him in recognition for his services in the war with Milan was not the same as Palazzo Giustiniani at the head of the Grand Canal but the house of another Bernardo called Bernardo della Seta [cf. Labalme, 112n].

69. Bishops of Lampascus and Cyprus: Eastern Orthodox delegates to the Council of Ferrara-Florence [cf. 39-53 above].

70. Lampascus: Lampsacus, city on the Hellespont.

71. Sigismundo: S. Malatesta. His visit to Mantua has not been identified.

72. Albizi: Albizzi, a Florentine family whose members were rivals of the Medici in the late 14th and early 15th centuries. Rinaldo degli Albizzi led the plot that exiled Cosimo de' Medici in 1433-34. The Albizzi were attempting to take over the Medici properties and commercial enterprises, but Cosimo's triumphant return ended their hopes [21:20].

73. Medici bank: Medici Bank in Florence, the foundation of the family's power and influence from the 13th century on.

74. Venetians may stand . . . Constantinople: The source of these seven lines is not known. In context they seem to concern (1) the ascent of Venice during the decline of Florence; and (2) the details of a trade treaty made between Venice and the early Ottoman Empire after the final loss of Eastern Christendom to Islam forces in 1453. Such a treaty was probably signed on April

18 in Constantinople. The significance of 6962 remains a conundrum, but it is probably an early effort to date creation similar to that of Bishop Ussher more than two centuries later.

75. Illmo ac ex^mo (eccellentissimo) princeps et d^no: L, I, "Most illustrious and most excellent [repeated in I] prince and lord."

76. Sforza: Alessandro S., 1409-1473, Lord of Pesaro and Cotignola [9:13] and brother of Duke Francesco S. Alessandro was the tricky operator who obtained control of Pesaro in 1444 by underhand means.

77. Mr. Pitro: Blacksmith in the service of Alessandro Sforza.

78. Pisanellus: Antonio di Puccio Pisano, 1395?-1455, called Pisanello, Veronese painter and medalist employed by Sigismundo in building the Tempio [8:43] and patronized by Leonello d'Este. He was also known as Vittore Pisano. In this passage he seems to be acting as an agent for Alessandro Sforza, which is possible since in 1453 Sigismundo had alliances with the Sforza family through his marriage in 1442 to Polissena, 1428-1449, daughter of Francesco Sforza, 1401-1466 [9:23]. After her death the relations between the families continued, in spite of rumors that Sigismundo poisoned her. In *ABCR* Pound discusses why Pisanello, as a painter, was a good person to buy horses [p. 30].

79. Vittor Capello: Vittore di Giorgio Capello, 1403-1466, Venetian admiral and in 1456 a member of the Privy Council of Cristoforo Moro, Doge of Venice, 1462-1471 [Hazlitt, I, 979].

80. St. George the Martyr: There has been much dispute about the identity of St. George; if he lived at all, it was before the 6th century, by which time he was recognized as a saint. What was supposed to be his skull was brought as a sacred relic to the Chuch of San Giorgio Maggiore on the island of the same name.

81. Island of Siesina: Unknown. The island of Lydda, where a huge cathedral was erected in St. George's honor, is the place to which (according to one account) his remains were taken after he was tortured and killed in 303 by order of the Emperor Diocletian [*EB*].

82. San Giorgio Maggiore: I, "Saint George the Greater." One of the islands of Venice; also the church thereon.

83. Cardinal Gonzaga of Mantua: Ercole G., 1527-1563, regent of Mantua during the minority of his nephews, 1540-1556.

84. ultimo febbraio: I, "last of February."

85. Lorenzo de Medicis: The "Lorenzaccio" who assassinated Alessandro [5:33, 39]. After his escape Lorenzo hid in a number of cities and for 11 years eluded murderers set on his trail. But finally, on the date named, he left his house poorly guarded by only "Giovanni Battista Martelli, e da Alessandro Soderini suo zio [his uncle]." The weight of conflicting evidence suggests "che la morte di Lorenzo avvenne a San Toma" ["that Lorenzo's death took place at San Toma"]. The two assassins escaped [cf. Ferrai, 380-390; *Index*, 480, for letter to Gonzaga].

86. de Mendoça: Prob. Diego Hurtado de Mendoza, d. 1575, ambassador of the Holy Roman emperor, Charles V, to Venice.

87. Marquis of Mantova: Francesco Gonzaga, Marchese of Mantua, 1484-1519. [This letter is in Molmenti, 69-70.]

88. Jerusalem: Gonzaga was trying to obtain pictures of various famous cities.

89. berettino: I, "small cap."

90. Lorenzo: Prob. Lorenzo Leonbruno, 1485-1537, a painter who in 1511 was in the service of the ruling house of Mantua.

91. Seignory: The signoria, supreme magistracy of the Republic of Venice.

92. Ancona: Italian city.

93. Victor Carpatio: Vittore Carpaccio, 1455?-1525?, famous Venetian painter, pupil to Lazaro Bastiani and follower of Bellini.

94. Zuane Zamberti: Poss. Giovanni Giamberti da Sangallo, 1482-1530, member of a famous family of architects.

95. aquarelle: I, *aquarella*, "water color" or "distemper."

96. Venetijs: L, "at Venice."

97. pictore: I (variant of *pittore*), "painter."

98. Salzburg: City in Austria famous as the home of Mozart and the site of the annual Mozart festival. The Prince Archbishop of Salzburg from 1772 to 1812 was Hieronymus Colloredo, b. 1732.

99. Wolfgang Amadeus: W. A. Mozart, 1756-1791, Austrian composer.

100. inter lineas: L, "between the lines." Pound is reading Mozart's real feelings "between the lines" of the letter which was really written (probably dictated) by his father. The real letter is firm about Mozart's desire to leave but is quite politely worded [*Pai*, 6-3, 360].

101. Miss Cannabich: Rosa, elder daughter of Christian Cannabich, 1731-1798, composer and leader of the Mannheim Orchestra. The sonata (KV 309) was composed in 1777. Of this sonata Mozart wrote to his father on December 6, 1777: "ich will es genau nach dem Caractere der Madselle Rose machen . . . wie das andante, so ist sie" ["I want it to match exactly the character of Mlle. Rose . . . she is like the andante"]. Rosa C., Mozart's pupil, was 15 at the time the letter was written [EH].

CANTO XXVII

Sources

Guido Cavalcanti, Ballata 12; Vincenzo di Chiara, "La Spagnuola" [street song popular at turn of century]; "The Wanderer"; Marie Curie, *Pierre Curie*, Paris, 1924; Francis Jammes, *Clara d'Ellébeuse; ou l'histoire d'une ancienne jeune fille*, 1899; Barrett and Davis, *Floradora* (an operetta first performed in 1899); inscription formerly over the altar in Ferrara Cathedral; Carl Appel, *Bernart von Ventadorn*, Halle, 1915; Camille Chabaneau, *Les Biographies des Troubadours en Langue Provençale*; EP, *T*, 124-125.

Background

EP, *SR*, 101; Lincoln Steffens, *Autobiography*, New York, 1931.

Exegeses

Sieburth, *Pai*, 5-2, 280; Mary de Rachewiltz, *Discretions*, 158; EH, *Approaches*, 30.

Glossary

1. **Formando . . . persona**: "Fashioning a new person from desire." [Line 17 from Guido Cavalcanti's Ballata 12: "Quando di morte mi convien trar vita," which Pound translates "If all my life be but some deathly moving" (*T*, 124-125)].

2. **Et quant . . . Pas**: F, "And as to the third / he fell into the / of his wife, [and] won't be seen again."

3. **oth fugol ouitbaer**: OE, "until a bird bore out"; adaptation of line 31 of the anonymous "Wanderer," which reads *sumne fugol othbaer* ["one a bird bore away"]. *Ouit* seems to be from no language, but it recalls the Dutch *uit* ["out"].

4. **Observed . . .** : Prob. a memory of pre-World War I report in which England quickly tried to get its navy in order.

5. **Porta-goose**: Portuguese. Early in 1914 Germany and Britain had reached a contingent agreement on the division of Portuguese colonies. But with Germany's declaration of war against the Triple Entente (Britain, France, and Russia), the British attitude toward all neutral powers changed and they began to woo Portugal as their "oldest ally."

6. **At rests . . .** : Exact source of this quote is unknown, but it is probably from a handbook used in training programs for officers in World War I.

7. **Dr. Spahlinger**: Henry S., 1882-1965, Swiss bacteriologist; inventor of an anti-tuberculosis vaccine.

8. **J'ai obtenu**: F, "I got."

9. **M. Curie**: Pierre Curie [23:10].

10. **Prince des Penseurs**: F, "Prince of Thinkers."

11. **Monsieur Brisset**: Jean-Pierre B., French philologist and writer, among whose works are *La Science de Dieu; ou, La création de l'homme*, 1900, and *Les Origines humaines*, 2d ed., 1913, in which he demonstrated that man is descended from the frog. Pound is parodying such an idea. He also considered the election of Brisset an amusing joke perpetrated by a group of French intellectuals who wanted to mock the pomposity of such an election [*Pai*, 5-2, 280; *Discretions*, 158].

12. **Deputies**: Lower house of the French national assembly.

13. **Messina**: Capital of Messina Province in NE Sicily; in the great earthquake at Messina on December 28, 1908, 90 percent of the city's buildings were destroyed.

14. **Bucentoro/"Stretti!"**: [3:5,6]. . . . "this year, '27" is the year Pound was writing Canto 27.

15. **Milan**: Capital of Milano Province, Lombardy, N Italy.

16. **Clara d'Ellébeuse**: Character in the novel *Clara d'Ellébeuse; ou l'histoire d'une ancienne jeune fille*, 1899, by Francis Jammes; the name is also found in Jammes's *De l'angelus de l'aube à l'angelus du soir, 1888-1897* (1898).

17. **Benette . . . Elfes**: F, "Benette plays the Waltz of the Elves."

18. **salotto**: I, "drawing room": main parlor or lobby.

19. **air de province**: F, "provincial air": manner.

20. **Croat**: The Croats are a south Slavic people.

21. **commercianti**: I, "merchants": commercial people.

22. **Floradora**: English operetta, music by "Leslie Stuart" (Thomas A. Barrett, 1866-1928) and book by "Owen Hall" (James Davis, 1853-1907), first performed in 1899. Published in London by Francis, Day & Hunter, and in New York by T. B. Harms.

23. **Clara d'Ellébeuse**: [cf. 16 above].

24. Sed et . . . populus: L, "And the whole population of the church, too."

25. duomo: I, "cathedral."

26. Glielmo ciptadin: I, "Guglielmo citizen." This inscription in mosaic has now been destroyed; its last two lines were *Fo Nicolao scolptore / E Gliemo fo lo auctore* ["Nicholas was the sculptor, Guglielmo was the author"]. The meaning of the last word is uncertain—perhaps "founder," perhaps "architect." Pound saw the inscription over the altar in the cathedral at Ferrara [cf. *SR*, 101]. It rhymes with the "pride of workmanship" theme in *The Cantos*, as does *Adamo me fecit* [45:14].

27. Brumaire: French Revolutionary month, October 22 to November 20.

28. Fructidor: French Revolutionary month, August 18 to September 16.

29. Petrograd: Leningrad, formerly St. Petersburg, was renamed Petrograd during World War I when the Russian Revolution broke out.

30. Tovarisch: R, "comrade."

31. Xarites: H, *Charites*, "the Graces."

32. Helios: Early Greek sun-god, whose functions were later taken over by Apollo [23:18].

33. Cadmus: Founder of Thebes. A dragon guarding a spring killed the companions of Cadmus, who in turn killed the dragon; by Athena's instruction, he sowed the dragon's teeth, and from them armed warriors sprang up; these were set fighting one another until only five remained: the Sparti (ancestors of many noble families of Thebes) who with Cadmus and his men built the city [4:4]. The great work of Cadmus in creating Thebes is compared here, as in other places [25/118], with the regret over failure.

34. Eblis: Eblis II, Vicomte of Ventadour, 12th-century Provençal nobleman. Bernart de Ventadour, Provençal poet, wrote songs to Eblis's wife. He was banished and she was locked up in a tower [6:29].

35. Ventadour: Former duchy in the department of Corrèze, S central France near Limoges. Pound visited the place in 1919 and prob. found only bees, wild grass in the courtyard, and so on.

36. acanthus: A variety of Mediterranean plant whose ornamental leaves were used as architectural decoration, especially in Corinthian columns. Suggests here the "two-way vegetation of Persephone" [cf. EH, *Approaches*, 30].

CANTO XXVIII

Sources

Current press reports of the Levine-Chamberlin transatlantic flights in, e.g., *Literary Digest*, June 18, 25, 1927, and *Current History*, July 1927; Catullus LXI.

Background

EP, *J/M*, 30; *SR*, 53, 62-63, 65; *LE*, 102-103; *L*, 153; Lincoln Steffens, *Autobiography*, New York, 1931; NS, *Ezra Pound's*

Pennsylvania, Toledo, Ohio, 1976; W. C. Williams, *Autobiography*, New York, 1951; Charles Norman, *Ezra Pound: A Biography*, New York, 1969.

Exegeses

CE, *Ideas*, 32-34, 114-116; DP, *Barb*, 108; John Drummond in Peter Russell, *An Examination of EP*, 1973, 115-116.

Glossary

1. **Boja d'un Dio**: I, "Hangman of a God"; in Romagna dialect an expletive such as "Darn it!"

2. **Romagnolo**: I, *Romagnol*, "an inhabitant of the Romagna," region of Italy now comprising the provinces of Bologna, Ferrara, Ravenna, and Forlì.

3. **Aso iqua me**: I (Romagna dialect), "This is me here."

4. **All Esimo**: I [misprint for *All' Esimio*], "To the Distinguished."

5. **Dottor Aldo Walluschnig**: Prob. an Austrian doctor in Venice, ca. 1925.

6. **Marotti, Virginia**: Venetian woman whose life and that of her son were saved by an operation performed by Dr. Walluschnig in 1925.

7. **Senni**: Seems to be the name of the hospital.

8. **San Giorgio**: Island and church in Venice [26:82].

9. **Mr. Lourpee**: Prob. a pseudonym for an unsuccessful French painter Pound saw at a pension in Madrid in 1906.

10. **Sage of Concord**: Ralph Waldo Emerson.

11. **Mrs. Kreffle**: Pseudonym for a Mrs. Kraft whom Pound knew in Madrid in 1906.

12. **Sevilla**: S, Seville, capital of Seville Province and of Andalusia, SW Spain.

13. **pesetas**: Spanish coins.

14. **West Virginia**: Miss Adah and Miss Ida Mapel, American sisters from West Virginia, were residents of the boardinghouse in Spain where Pound stayed on his trip in 1906 [91/615].

15. **Chiasso**: Town on Italian-Swiss border on the main St. Gotthard railroad line.

16. **year of the strikes**: 1920. One strike occurred in May when Pound was making his way from Como to Paris. At Milan all trains stopped at a certain midnight and he and his wife, Dorothy Shakespear Pound, "came out of Italy on a tram-car" [*L*, 153].

17. **Como**: City on Lake Como in Lombardy, N Italy.

18. **hidalgo**: S, "nobleman."

19. **Trieste**: Seaport on the Adriatic, now in Italy but formerly in Austria.

20. **the Bowery**: Section of lower Manhattan, New York, famous for its bars and its derelicts.

21. **bleeding Kansas**: The name given to the six-year period of border warfare in Kansas following the enactment of the Kansas-Nebraska Bill of 1854.

22. **Clara Leonora**: Graduate student at the University of Pennsylvania, 1906, who was in Professor Hugo Rennert's class with Pound. This line and the 16 lines following concern memories of Clara L. in Professor

Rennert's class. Her claim to authority seems to have rested on the fact that Franz Liszt, on a concert tour, had held her on his knee when she was a child, thus making her opinion about sonnets worth listening to. Pound had doubtless announced his habit of writing a sonnet a day and destroying them at the end of the year [W. C. Williams, *Autobiography*, 53; Norman, *Ezra Pound*, 6].

23. Rennert: Hugo Albert R., 1858-1927, scholar in the field of Romance languages at the University of Pennsylvania; Pound was his student, 1905-1906 [*SR*, 67n, 182].

24. Grillparzer: Franz G., 1791-1872, Austrian playwright and poet.

25. il Gran Maestro: I, "the Great Master."

26. Mr. Liszt: Franz von L., 1811-1886, Hungarian composer.

27. Rio Grande: River in the SW United States on the Mexican border.

28. Ceylon: Island in Indian Ocean; now Sri Lanka.

29. Loica: Florence Farr, d. 1917; Mrs. Edward Emery, an actress friend of Yeats who went to teach at Ramanathan College in Ceylon because she was dying of a disfiguring cancer [see Yeats, "All Souls Night"].

30. Smith: William Brooke S., a young painter Pound knew in Philadelphia, ca. 1905; Pound dedicated *A Lume Spento*, 1908, to him.

31. medico's: I, "doctor's."

32. gob: A lump of something; a mouthful of spittle. Prob. here slang for "spittoon."

33. Byers and Feigenbaum: Prob. acquaintances of Pound's in Philadelphia, ca. 1908.

34. Joe Bromley: Joseph Henry B., University of Pennsylvania class of 1905, who seems to have traveled around the world between graduation and the 1908 scene here depicted [NS, *Ezra Pound's Pennsylvania*, 32].

35. Comley: Neighbor who lived two doors away from the Pound house in Jenkintown [*ibid.*, 6].

36. Jaffa: City on the coast of Palestine.

37. Shanghaï: Shanghai, Chinese city.

38. Tribune: Prob. *New York Herald Tribune*, Paris edition.

39. Frank Robert Iriquois: Prob. an American expelled from France [identified as a Cherokee Indian by Reno Odlin]. Poss. the scene that follows was witnessed by Pound during his trip to the Pyrenees in the summer of 1919.

40. Je suis . . . le poids: F, "I am / stronger than / the Buddha / . . . I am / stronger than / Christ / . . . / I would have / abolished / weight."

41. Pyrenees: Mountain range on French-Spanish border.

42. Martinique: French island in West Indies.

43. sont . . . i-ale: F, "they are the colonial infantry."

44. voce tinnula: [cf. 3:18].

45. Ce sont . . . : F, "It's the old Marines."

46. feitz Marcebrus: P, "Marcabrun made it."

47. Marcebrus: Marcabrun, 12th-century Provençal troubadour; line 2 of his crusade song, "Pax in nomine Domini" ["Peace in the name of God"], ed. Dejeanne, no. 35, says *Fetz M. los motz el son* ["M. made the words and the sounds"]. Pound's interest in Marcabrun started early [cf. *SR*, 53, 62, 65; *LE*, 102-103].

48. Dr. Wymans: Prob. a doctor who served in Gallipoli.

49. Gallipoli: The Gallipoli campaign, 1915, in which the Allied forces made a futile attempt to capture the Dardanelles.

50. and that man: Thaddeus Coleman Pound, Pound's grandfather. The anecdote is prob. one Pound heard told in his family [22:1].

51. pornoboskos: H [from πορνοβοσκός], "a brothelkeeper."

52. Pa Stadtvolk: Unidentified. May be constructed from German as "Pennsylvania city person."

53. Prince Oltrepassimo: Prob. pseudonym for Prince Filippo-Massimiliano Massimo, 1843-1915, created Prince Lancellotti, 1865, by Pius IX; from his half brother, Prince Camillo-Carlo-Alberto Massimo, 1836-1921, he purchased the *Discobolus*.

54. saccone: I, "straw mattress"; also one of the members of an aristocratic order who wore sackcloth and were buried in it.

55. Principe: I, "Prince."

56. Discobolus: Statue of the discus thrower by the Greek sculptor Myron; only copies exist, the best known of which is the Lancelotti *Discobolus*.

57. Pope: Giovanni Maria Mastai-Ferreti, 1792-1878, Pope Pius IX, 1846-1878. In 1870, when the kingdom of Italy took over the city of Rome, Pius refused to recognize this abolition of the temporal power of the papacy and announced that he considered himself thenceforth a prisoner in the Vatican.

58. Second Baronet: Sir John Dean Paul, 1802-1868 [RO].

59. Bayle: Pierre B., 1647-1706, French philosopher and critic. His chief work, *Dictionnaire historique et critique,* 1697, was a major document behind French and German "Enlightenment."

60. Sic loquitur eques: L, "thus speaks the horseman" [or "knight"].

61. Levine: Charles A. L., American millionaire and chairman of the board of Columbia Aircraft Company. He hoped to be the first person to fly the Atlantic nonstop, but before his plane was ready Charles A. Lindbergh (probably the "official pet") flew to Paris. Levine, with Clarence D. Chamberlin as pilot, left Long Island on June 4, 1927, and on June 6 arrived at Eisleben, 110 miles SW of Berlin.

62. Azores: Islands in the Atlantic.

63. Miss Arkansas . . . : Prob. Ruth Elder, a pretty girl from a middle-class Alabama family who on October 11, 1927, at the age of 23, took off from New York with her copilot, George W. Haldeman, to fly the Atlantic by the S route. After flying for two nights and one day and weathering a severe storm, they landed in the ocean and were picked up by a Dutch tanker and taken to the nearest land, the Azores.

64. Peoria: City in NW Illinois. Prob. a reference to the familiar image of Lindbergh as a clean-cut, "all-American" boy from the Midwest.

65. Hinchcliffe: Capt. Walter G. R. Hinchcliffe, who had lost an eye in the war, was hired by Levine to fly his plane, the *Columbia*, back from Europe, but the trip was canceled. On the morning of March 13, 1928, he took off in another plane, the *Endeavour*, from an airport in Lincolnshire and was never heard from.

66. Elsie: E. Mackay, 1894-1928, English stage and screen actress. She was the daughter of James Lyle Mackay, Viscount (and later Earl of) Inchcape (1852-1932), chairman of the Peninsular and Oriental and British India Steam Navigation companies, a partner in many other businesses, and a director of two banks (prob. his claim to being a son of a bitch). Disguised as Capt. Gordon Sinclair, Elsie boarded Hinchcliffe's plane and vanished with it.

67. Dennis: D. Wyndham, English actor, married Elsie in 1917 against violent objections by her father. After their marriage was annulled in 1922 after a sensational trial, she resumed her maiden name.

CANTO XXIX

Sources

EP, *P*, "The Flame;" Giambattista Verci, *Storia degli Ecelini*, 1779; Cesare de Lollis, *Vita e Poesie di Sordello di Goito*, 1896; Dante, *Par.* IX; Psalms 42:8; Dante, *Vita Nuova*; Yeats, *A Vision*, 1925; Dante, *Par.* XXXIII, *Convivio* III; Sordello, "Ailas equem . . .," in Cesare de Lollis, *op. cit.*, 196; T. S. Eliot, recollection; "Nondum orto jubare" from "Alba Bilingalis" in *P*, 1909, and *CEP*, 91.

Background

EP, *GK*, 223; Postscript to trans. of *NPL* by Remy de Gourmont; JW, *The Cruelest Month: Spring, Nature, and Love in Classical and Medieval Lyrics*, Yale, 1965 [identified as *Cruelest* in glosses]; Drummond, "The Italian Background to the Cantos," in *Ezra Pound*, ed. Peter Russell, 1950.

Exegeses

GK, 107-108; Dekker, *Cantos*, 90-97; DP, *Barb*, 109-113; Earl Miner, *The Japanese Tradition in British and American Literature*, 1958, 149-150; HK, *Era*, 336-337; Nassar, *The Cantos of Ezra Pound: The Lyric Mode*, Baltimore, 1976, 48-49; CB-R, *ZBC*, 134-135.

Glossary

1. **Pearl . . . sunlight**: In Pound's early poem, "The Flame" [*P*, 50], these phrases are used to evoke a sense of the spiritual sources of passion: "in thy mists . . . thou eternal pearl." The lake is Garda.

2. **Pernella Concubina**: Mistress of Count Aldobrando Orsini, who was the father of Niccolò, the elder son mentioned below. The murdered younger son was named Lodovico.

3. **ainé**: F, "elder."

4. **puiné**: F, "younger."

5. **Siena**: [9:48; 10:1, 2].

6. **Pitigliano**: Town in S Tuscany ruled after 1410 by counts of the Orsini family.

7. **Nicolo**: Niccolò Orsini, 1442-1510, third Count of Pitigliano, a general in the service of Venice. In 1465 he killed his cousin Penelope Orsini, his father's mistress, and her son because she had had Niccolò's brother poisoned so that her own son could succeed the count in the rule of Pitigliano.

8. **Via Sacra**: L, "Sacred Way." The most famous one is in Rome.

9. **Tritons**: Legendary Greek mermen.

10. hippodrome: Either an arena or a track for horse races.

11. Liberans ... liberatos: L, "And freeing from every chain those who have been liberated." In Verci [III, 496-497] this passage reads "liberating the men and women who formerly belonged to her father and brothers ... she sends them away liberated and absolved from every chain" [cf. 14 below].

12. sacerdos: L, "priest."

13. Castra San Zeno: Fortification mentioned in the will of Cunizza. The castle is in the mountains between Bassano and Asolo, NE Italy.

14. Cunizza: C. da Romano, b. 1198, married to Ricciardo di San Bonifazzio, ca. 1222; she was the sixth child of Ezzelino II. Between 1227 and 1229 she had (according to tradition) an intrigue with Sordello, who was staying at Treviso with her brother Ezzelino III of Romano, 1194-1259; at his request Sordello abducted her, primarily for political reasons, though scholars are still not sure what actually happened. In 1265 she executed a deed of manumission, giving freedom to all her slaves but cursing those who had betrayed her brother Alberico [6:35].

15. Alberic: Alberico da Romano, d. 1260, podesta of Treviso and brother of Cunizza and Ezzelino III. He was besieged in his castle of San Zeno by the cities of Verona, Vicenza, Padua, and Mantua; betrayed by his own people, he surrendered and saw his whole family massacred before he himself was tortured to death.

16. Lady Cunizza: Cunizza freed her slaves while she was a guest in Cavalcante's house.

17. Cavalcanti: Cavalcante C., d. ca. 1280, father of Guido C.

18. anno: L, "in the year."

19. Eccelin da Romano: Ezzelino II of Romano, podesta of Treviso, 1191-1192, and of Vicenza, 1211, was the father of Cunizza, Alberico, and Ezzelino III.

20. Richard St. Boniface: Count Ricciardo di San Bonifazzio, podesta of Mantua and husband of Cunizza. When Ricciardo discovered the intrigue between his wife and Sordello, the poet was forced to flee to Provence.

21. Sordello: [2:2, 3].

22. Tarviso: Treviso (L, Tarvisium), city in Treviso Province, N Italy; seat of Lombard duchy in the early Middle Ages; home of Ezzelino III of Romano.

23. Bonius: Bonio, a knight from Treviso, with whom Cunizza had a long affair after Sordello was forced to flee to Provence.

24. nimium ...: L, "too much enamored of him."

25. "The light of this star ... ": Trans. of *Par.* IX, 33, where Cunizza says she was controlled by the influence of Venus.

26. Braganza: Capital of Bragança district, NE Portugal, and seat of the house of Bragança, former rulers of Portugal. When Bonio died defending Alberico, Cunizza married Amerio of Bragança. After Amerio's death she married, according to some accounts, a gentleman from Verona.

27. Juventus: L, "Youth."

28. "Passing into the point of the cone ... ": In Book V of *A Vision*, Yeats divides history roughly into 2,000-year periods, which he symbolizes by the figure of two interlocking cones; at the point of each cone the cycle reverses and is repeated in a kind of mirror image.

29. Jo Tyson: Unidentified.

30. O-hon ... vi'-a'ge: F, "It is sometimes said in the village." Imitation of colloquial language.

31. ephèbe: F, "handsome young man."

32. djassban: Jazz band.

33. Darwin: Charles Robert D., 1809-1882, English naturalist.

34. Deh! nuvoletta: I, "Alas! little cloud"; like *Deh! Violetta* ["Alas, little Violet"], in Dante's *Lyric Poetry*, ed. Foster and Boyde, no. 23, line 1. Pound's translation of this ballata in *CEP* (p. 151), entitled "La Nuvoletta," begins "Ah little cloud."

35. Wein, Weib, TAN AOIDAN: G, "Wine, Women"; H, "Song." From "Wer nicht liebt Wein, Weib, und Gesang, / Der bleibt ein Narr sein Leben lang" ["Whoever does not love wine, women, and song remains a fool his whole life long"], attributed to Martin Luther.

36. Ailas . . . vuelh: P, "Alas, and what good are my eyes / For they're not seeing what I want." Opening lines and refrain of Sordello poem [ed. De Lollis, 196].

37. "Nel . . . mente mia": I, "Inside your womb or in my mind." A combination of *Par.* XXXIII, 7, to the Virgin Mary, *Nel ventre tuo si raccese l'amore* ["In your womb love was lit again"] and *Convivio* III, Canzone Two, 1, *Amor, che ne la mente mi ragiona* ["Love, which discourses in my mind," quoted in *Pur.* II, 112].

38. Faziamo . . . : I, "Let's do it together."

39. Des valeurs . . . des valeurs: F, "Stocks and bonds, / for God's sake, and / more stocks and bonds."

40. Arnaut: A. Daniel [20:12], here a pseudonym for T. S. Eliot. A wave pattern exists in the stonework of the castle of Excideuil, where Eliot voiced his fear of death; Pound changed his name to Arnaut. The castle is associated with the troubadour Guiraut de Bornelh [HK, *Era*, 336-337].

41. les gradins: F, "the steps" of the arena at Verona [12:1].

42. nondum orto jubare: L, "before sunrise." Add P words, *Phebi claro*, for the complete opening line of an early medieval alba which is translated: "With the clear light of Phoebus not yet risen" [*P*, 1909; *CEP*, 91; JJW, *Cruelest*, 193-194].

43. Phoibos: Apollo.

44. Helios: The sun [23:18].

45. Perugia: City in C Italy, capital of Umbria.

46. San Piero: San Pietro, church and monastery on S edge of Perugia.

47. Brookwater: Used of eyes in "Yeux glauques" [*P*, 192].

48. prore: I, "prows."

CANTO XXX

Sources

Luiz de Camoëns, *Os Lusíadas*, 1572; Chaucer, "Complaint unto Pity"; Giambattista Pigna, *Historia de Principi di Este*, 1570; Antonio Frizzi, *Memorie per la Storia di Ferrara*, 1791-1796; G. Fumagelli, *Dictionnaire géographique d'Italie pour servir a l'histoire de l'imprimerie*, 1905; Hieronymos Soncino, *Petrarca*, 1503.

Background

Simon Harcourt Smith, *The Marriage at Ferrara*, 1952; J. A. Symonds, *Renaissance in Italy*, 2 vols., Modern Library, 1935; Edmund G. Gardner, *Dukes and Poets in Ferrara*, 1904, rpt., New York, 1968.

Exegeses

EP, *SP*, 83; DP, *Barb*, 115-131; GD, "Persephone's Ezra," in EH, *Approaches*, 160-161; Dekker, *Cantos*, 65-70, 170-171; CE, *Ideas*, 120-123; HK, *Pai*, 8-1, "Interview"; CFT, *Pai*, 7-1 & 2, 141-154.

Glossary

1. Compleynt . . . hearde upon a day: Poss. variation of Chaucer's "Complaint unto Pity."

2. Artemis: Greek name of Diana, goddess of wildlife and the hunt [4:14].

3. Paphos: Town on SW coast of Cyprus; famous as site of Aphrodite worship.

4. Mars: Roman god of war. He was the lover of Venus [Aphrodite], who was married to the lame smith, Vulcan [Hephaestus], "a doddering fool."

5. Pedro: Pedro I, 1320-1367, king of Portugal, succeeded his father, Alfonso IV, in 1357; he was the "husband" of Inés de Castro [3:23].

6. Lisboa: Lisbon.

7. ῟ΥΛΗ: H, *hule*, "wood," "material," "slime," "shit." Pound says of *hule*: ". . . the stuff of which a thing is made, matter as a principle of being" [*SP*, 83; 35/175; *Pai*, 7-1 & 2, 141-154].

8. Madame Hule: Lucrezia Borgia, 1480-1519, daughter of Rodrigo Borgia, 1431-1503, who became Pope Alexander VI (1492-1503). For political reasons the pope, at the behest of his son Cesare Borgia, 1476-1507, arranged for Lucrezia's marriage to Alfonso d'Este, grandson of Niccolò d'Este and young heir of Ercole I, Duke of Ferrara. Cesare, who as Duke of Valentinois [Valentino] had been extending the power of the Borgia family and the Papal States, first arranged for the assassination of Lucrezia's second husband. In view of Lucrezia's dubious reputation, the d'Este family had no enthusiasm for the match and negotiated long and hard for an excessively large dowry; they demanded it be paid in hard ducats before the ceremony, which was performed by proxy in Rome. Finally, Lucrezia set off for Ferrara with a large entourage on a journey that took more than a month because she was feted by a number of important personages on the way; she arrived at the end of January 1502.

9. Light of the altar: With the sanction of her father, the pope.

10. Honour? Balls . . . : When the d'Este family found the pope pressuring for the marriage, they said the "honor" of the family required the large dowry. These two lines probably reflect the attitude of Cesare Borgia toward their honor (?) and the dowry.

11. Messire Alfonso: Lucrezia's husband, who visited her secretly by night a few days before her arrival. The story goes that he looked at her long and hard and, being a man of few words, departed. He spoke to no one either coming or going. Although Lucrezia made the last stage of her journey on a large ducal barge, Alfonso came and returned on horseback [Smith, *Marriage at Ferrara*].

12. Caesar's fane: The city of Fano in the province of Pesaro e Urbino. Pound is punning on the original meaning of the Latin word *fanum* ["shrine"]. At that time the city was in the territory of Cesare Borgia. Called *Fano Caesaris* below.

13. Duke of Valent: Another title of Cesare Borgia's [5:32].

14. Aemelia: Emilia, district in N Italy.

15. Fano Caesaris: L, "the Fano of Caesar."

16. Francesco da Bologna: A type designer brought to Fano by Soncino [see 18 below] to found a press to publish books in Hebrew, Greek, Latin, and Italian [cf. Fumagelli].

17. Aldous: Aldus Manutius (Aldo Manuzio, 1449-1515), famous Venetian printer who founded the Aldine press and for whom Francesco cut new typefaces. He is usually credited with inventing italic type.

18. Hieronymous Soncinus: Hieronymos Soncino, ca. 1460-1534, one of a family of Jewish printers, who came to Fano in 1501.

19. the text taken: Petrarch's *Rime* which Soncino printed for Cesare Borgia in 1503.

20. Laurentius: Lorenzo de' Medici [21:17, 33, 35], founder of the Laurentian Library in Florence.

21. Malatesta: Family of Sigismundo [8:5].

22. Pope Alessandro Borgia: [cf. 8 above]. One widely accepted legend about the death of the pope says that he and Cesare, who had invited themselves to dine with the Cardinal Adriano Castellesi of Corneto, sent ahead a gift of poisoned wine intended for the host. But either by accident or by someone else's design, they were hoisted by their own petard and became grievously ill. Some days later, after a long struggle, "Alexander died, a black and swollen mass, hideous to contemplate" [Symonds, I, 215-217]. Some contemporaries say both were stricken, not by poison, but by a malignant fever. Whatever happened, the death of the pope brought the efforts of the Borgias in the advancement of art, the spread of Renaissance culture, and the unification of Italy to a quick and dramatic end. Cesare, stricken by the same disease at the same dinner party, never recovered completely enough to exercise significant influence from then on until his death in 1507.

23. Il Papa mori: I, "The Pope died."

24. Explicit Canto XXX: L, "Canto XXX is ended."

CANTO XXXI

Sources

Andrew Lipscomb and Albert Bergh, eds., *The Writings of Thomas Jefferson*, V, VI, X, XIII, XIV, Washington, D.C., 1905; Philip R. Fendall, ed., *Letters and Other Writings of James Madison*, II, 495-506, Philadelphia, 1865; inscription on tomb of Isotta degli Atti.

Background

EP, "The Jefferson-Adams Letters as a Shrine and a Monument,"
SP, 147-158; *J/M*; "An Introduction to the Economic Nature of
the United States," *SP*, 167-185.

Exegeses

Knight, "Thomas Jefferson in Canto XXXI," *Pai*, 5-1, 79-93; DP,
Barb, 142-151 and passim.

Glossary

1. Tempus loquendi, Tempus tacendi: L, "There is a time to speak, there is a time to be silent," the personal motto of Sigismundo Malatesta [Ecclesiastes 3:7] which he had inscribed on the tomb of Isotta degli Atti in Rimini. (It is a reversal of the Vulgate's *Tempus tacendi, et Tempus loquendi*.)

2. Jefferson: Thomas J., 1743-1826, 3d president of the United States (1801-1809). Born in Virginia, graduated at William and Mary (1862), and studied law. He became a leader in the House of Burgesses, esp. of the patriot faction, and helped form and served with the Virginia Committee of Correspondence. Served in Continental Congress and wrote Declaration of Independence. While president he espoused agrarian democracy. During the years covered by Canto 31 (1785-1798) he was U.S. minister to France.

3. modern dress: Some believed that the statue of Washington should be done in a classical mode. Washington agreed with the recommendation that it be done in modern dress.

4. Congress: Continental Congress. The First Continental Congress (September 5-October 26, 1774) met in Philadelphia. The Second Continental Congress met in Philadelphia on May 10, 1775. It issued the Declaration of Independence (July 4, 1776) and carried on the Revolutionary War. Mentioned here is the so-called Congress of the Confederation (1781-1788), succeeded in 1789 by the Congress of the United States.

5. Annapolis: Port in Maryland; seat of Congress of the Confederation, 1783-84.

6. Big Beaver: River in W Pennsylvania.

7. Cayohoga: Cuyahoga River, E Ohio. Jefferson, in his correspondence about a possible canal linking Lake Erie and the Ohio River, spelled it both Cayahoga and Cayohoga.

8. Lake Erie: Easternmost of the Great Lakes. Buffalo, at E end of the lake, was W terminus of the Erie Canal, opened in 1825.

9. T.J.: Thomas Jefferson.

10. General Washington: George W., 1732-1799, 1st president of U.S. (1789-1797). Served with British forces during French and Indian Wars (1752-1758), with rank of colonel; retired (1759) to Mount Vernon, Virginia. Member of Continental Congress (1774-75); elected to command all Continental armies (1775); resigned commission (1783).

11. Maryland: Middle Atlantic state whose border with Pennsylvania was the Mason-Dixon line, often used to mark the division between North and South.

12. Connecticut: Southernmost of the New England states.

13. screw: TJ went to see a ship propelled over water by a blade which he said "operates on the air, as a screw does." Because of "the thinness of the medium," he concluded that it would work better under water [V, 37; unless otherwise noted, all Jefferson quotes in glosses for this canto are from *The Writings of Thomas Jefferson*].

14. Bushnell: David B., ?1742-1824, American inventor noted for invention of a submarine.

15. Adams: John A., 1735-1826, 2d president of the U.S. (1797-1801). Delegate to First Continental Congress (1774); served as commissioner to France (1777-1778), minister to United Provinces (1780-1782), envoy to Great Britain (1785-1788). Elected vice-president (1788, 1792), serving under George Washington.

16. Franklin: Benjamin F., 1706-1790, American statesman, printer, scientist, and writer; member of committee that drafted Declaration of Independence (1776); appointed sole plenipotentiary to France (1778); negotiated Treaty of Paris (1781-1783) with John Adams and John Jay. In 1785, when Congress sent Jefferson as an additional minister plenipotentiary to Paris, Franklin returned to America.

17. Paine: Thomas P., 1737-1809, political philosopher. The letter to Paine is dated March 18, 1801.

18. Dawson: John D., 1762-1814, member of House of Representatives (1797-1814) and bearer to Paris of the ratified convention with France (1800).

19. "English papers . . .": Source of quote is TJ letter to James Monroe (Paris, August 2, 1785): "The English papers are so incessantly repeating their lies about the tumults, the anarchy, the bankruptcies and distresses of America, that these ideas prevail very generally in Europe" [V, 99].

20. "Their tobacco . . .": The actual figures in source are only Jefferson's estimate and vary from those used by Pound. The point is that selling the privilege of tax collection to a private monopoly is costly to everyone except those who own the monopoly [V, 68-76].

21. livres: F, "pounds," French monetary unit.

22. Maison Quarée: Maison Carrée. TJ's proposed model for new Capitol to be built in Richmond, VA. In a letter to Madison dated at Paris, September 20, 1785, he calls it "one of the most beautiful, if not the most beautiful and precious morsel of architecture left us by antiquity" [V, 135].

23. Nismes: Nîmes, manufacturing and commercial city, capital of Gard department, S France, noted for its ancient Roman buildings, among them a Corinthian temple (Maison Carrée) restored in 1789 and converted into a museum in 1832.

24. Madison: James M., 1751-1836, fourth president of U.S. (1809-1817), member of the Continental Congress (1780-1783) and the Constitutional Convention (1787). As a member of the House of Representatives (1789-1797), Madison led the Democratic-Republican party opposition to Hamilton's financial measures. Secretary of state (1801-1809). Source of Madison note is *Letters and Other Writings of James Madison* [II, 495-506], a memorandum account of Madison's differences with his secretary of state, Robert Smith.

25. Robert Smith: 1757-1842, secretary of the navy (1801-1809) and secretary of state (1809-1811). President Madison requested Smith to resign the latter post because of his poor conduct of business at the State Department, "particularly in the foreign correspondence . . . which was almost always so crude and inadequate, that I was in the more important cases generally obliged to write them anew myself." Madison also accused Smith of divulging secrets to political enemies and opposing the whole course of U.S. foreign policy toward Great Britain [ibid., II, 499].

26. that country: Holland. Jefferson, believing that Holland would rather have its money in the U.S. than in France, is proposing that Adams borrow enough money from Holland to pay off U.S. debts to France.

27. This country: France, the country from which TJ is writing to James Madison, August 2, 1787.

28. XTZBK . . . : Source reads: "This country is really supposed on the eve of ****." Pound hit typewriter keys at random. Paul Leicester Ford, in his edition of *The Writings of Thomas Jefferson*, deciphered the letters in the original to mean "a bankruptcy" [*Pai*, 5-1, 86].

29. Beaumarchais: Pierre Augustin Caron de B., 1732-1799, French playwright and man of affairs. Line starting "I hear . . ." comes from letter of TJ to John Jay, not to Washington. In the whole letter TJ is recommending that foreign officers should be paid hush money. It seems that B. is among them: "I hear also that Mr. Beaumarchais means to make himself heard, if a memorial which he sends by an agent in the present packet is not attended to, as he thinks it ought to be" [VI, 248-249]. A secret agent of the king, Beaumarchais provided arms, ammunition, and supplies for the American Revolution. Such pains were taken to keep the operation under cover that Beaumarchais never got paid for war supplies he sent, and by 1787 he was threatening to make trouble if he did not receive payment. Although he was paid nothing, years later the Congress finally made some settlement to his heirs [32:2, 10].

30. Potomac: River in Virginia. TJ's letter to Washington, dated 1788, reads: "It will infallibly turn through the Potomac all the commerce of Lake Erie" [VI, 447]. Jefferson is arguing for the construction of the Ohio Canal [32:12].

31. a crowned head: These three lines ["I can . . . parish"] are preceded in same letter by: "I was much an enemy to monarchies before I came to Europe. I am ten thousand times more so, since I have seen what they are. There is scarcely an evil known in these countries, which may not be traced to their king, as its source" [VI, 454].

32. Lafayette: Marie Joseph Paul Yves Roch Gilbert du Motier, Marquis de L.,

1757-1834, French statesman and officer; commissioned major general in Continental army (1777); supported American interests in France. Letter from John Adams to TJ is dated at Quincy July 13, 1813 [XIII, 308].

33. John Quincy Adams: 1767-1848. In 1784 he was secretary to his father, John Adams.

34. Cul de Sac: The cul-de-sac Tête-bout in Paris. TJ leased the town house known as *l'hôtel Tête-bout* from October 16, 1784, to October 17, 1785, when he moved to *l'hôtel du Comte de Langeac*, Grille de Chaillot.

35. Turgot: Anne Robert Jacques T., 1727-1781, French economist and disciple of the Physiocrats, who based their theories on the idea that agriculture was the sole source of wealth.

36. La Rochefoucauld: François Alexandre Frédéric, Duc de La R., 1747-1827, French politician and philanthropist; member of the States-General (1789).

37. Condorcet: Marie Jean Antoine Nicholas de Caritat, Marquis de C., 1743-1794, French philosopher, mathematician, and politician.

38. Monticello: TJ's residence near Charlottesville, VA. The correspondence cited in rest of this canto was written during TJ's retirement there.

39. Barlow: Joel B., 1754-1812, American writer and diplomat. Appointed U.S. consul to Algiers (1795), he succeeded in releasing American prisoners and negotiating treaties with Algiers. In 1811 he was sent to Europe to negotiate a commercial treaty with Napoleon.

40. Gallatin: Abraham Alfonse Albert G., 1761-1849, Swiss-born financier and statesman who came to the U.S. in 1780; member of House of Representatives (1795-1801); member of committee negotiating with England after War of 1812; U.S. minister to France (1816-1823); U.S. minister to Great Britain (1826-1827). In a letter to William Wirt, prompted by Madison's dismissal of

Robert Smith [cf. 25 above], TJ is trying to get Wirt to reconcile William Duane (editor of the influential *Aurora*) and President Madison. TJ knew that one of the causes of Smith's disaffection was his intense rivalry with Gallatin, then secretary of the treasury [*Pai*, 5-1, 89; XIII, 54].

41. Adair: James A., 1709?-?1783 18th-century trader in Georgia and the Carolinas; author of *The History of the American Indians* (1775) in which he advanced the theory that the Indians were descendants of the Jews. Interesting as one of numerous examples in the early 1930s of Pound's attitude about anti-semitism: he obviously agreed with TJ that it is "kinky."

42. Eppes: John Wayles E., 1773-1823, nephew and son-in-law of TJ and, at time of letter, a member of Congress. TJ is attacking the National Bank proposal then before Congress. The proponents of the bill argued that increasing the public debt would be a good thing for business and would lead to increase of commerce and thus to increase of public revenues. The letter concludes: "That our debt was juggled from forty-three up to eighty millions, and funded at that amount, according to this opinion was a great public blessing, because the evidences of it could be vested in commerce, and thus converted into active capital, and then the more the debt was made to be, the more active capital was created. That is to say, the creditors could now employ in commerce the money due them from the public, and make from it an annual profit of five per cent., or four millions of dollars. But observe, that the public were at the same time paying on it an interest of exactly the same amount of four millions of dollars. Where then is the gain to either party, which makes it a public blessing?" [XIII, 421].

43. "Man, a rational creature!": In his letter John Adams introduces the anecdote by saying that Franklin was "unusually loquacious" the morning in 1775 when he told it.

44. Gosindi: Pierre Gassendi, 1592-1655, French philosopher, theologian, and physi-

cist; author of *Syntagma philosophiae Epicuri* (1649). In all his works he staunchly defended experimental science.

45. Epicurus: Greek philosopher, ?342-270 B.C. The two lines concerning Gosindi and Epicurus are from TJ letter [not Adams] to Charles Thomson dated January 9, 1816, in which he says he has made "a paridigma of His [Christ's] doctrines" and arranged "them on the pages of a blank book." He adds: "And I wish I could subjoin a translation of Gosindi's Syntagma of the doctrines of Epicurus, which ... is the most rational system remaining of the philosophy of the ancients" [XIV, 358-386].

46. Patrick Henry: American "firebrand orator" and patriot, 1736-1799. In 1773 he was a delegate to the House of Burgesses of Virginia. TJ is talking about the "close of the session" of this house. After the session, the people mentioned agreed that they would propose to their house "the appointment of a committee of correspondence" whose business would be to contact other such houses in the colonies so that they could "promote a harmony of action salutary to all" [XIV, 398-399].

47. Frank Lee: Francis Lightfoot L., 1734-1797, American statesman; member of Continential Congress (1775-1779) and signer of Declaration of Independence.

48. Henry Lee: Virginian also known as Light-Horse Harry L., 1756-1818. American soldier and statesman best known for his abilities as a cavalry commander in the Revolutionary War when he covered Greene's retreat across North Carolina and Virginia (1781); member of Continental Congress (1785-1788); member of House of Representatives (1799-1801).

49. D. Carr: Dabney C., 1773-1837, American jurist; nephew of TJ; justice of the Virginia Supreme Court of Appeals (1824-1837). The five lines from this letter concern the controversy about who proposed the "Committees of Correspondence" as a channel of communication among the colonies before the Revolution. In the early 1880s renewed interest in the history of the Revolution created controversies. Massachusetts claimed that Adams proposed the committees; TJ is explaining how he remembered the events [XIV, 398-401].

50. St. Peter: St. Peter's Church in Rome. John Adams to TJ, February 2, 1816: "That stupendous monument of human hypocrisy and fanaticism, the church of St. Peter at Rome, which was a century and a half in building, excited the ambition of Leo the Xth, who believed no more of the Christian religion than Diderot, to finish it; and finding St. Peter's pence insufficient, he deluged all Europe with indulgences for sale, and excited Luther to controvert his authority to grant them" [XIV, 423-424].

51. human reason ... : TJ had asked Adams "How the apostasy from national rectitude of France and England can be accounted for?" In reply, Adams says that he does not know, but, he adds, "human reason, and human conscience, though I believe there are such things, are not a match for human pas-

sions, human imaginations, and human enthusiasm" [XIV, 424].

52. A tiel ... scripture: [Source reads *tiels*] OF, "according to such laws; in old handwriting." In a detailed letter about how far common law agrees with ecclesiastical law, TJ shows that an early "falsification" led to historical error. He then writes: "... here then we find *ancien scripture*, ancient writing, translated 'holy scripture.' ... Thus we find this string of authorities all hanging by one another on a single hook, a mistranslation" [XIV, 73-74].

53. Bonaparte: Napoleon B., 1769-1821, emperor of the French (1805-1814). TJ to John Adams, June 5, 1814: "But *Bonaparte* was a lion in the field only. In civil life, a cold-blooded ... usurper, without a virtue; no statesman, *knowing nothing of commerce*, political economy, or civil government, and supplying ignorance by bold presumption" [XIV, 145-146].

54. Hic Explicit Cantus: L, "Here the Canto ends."

CANTO XXXII

Sources

Charles Francis Adams, ed., *The Works of John Adams*, X, 182-184, Boston, 1856; Andrew Lipscomb and Albert Bergh, eds., *The Writings of Thomas Jefferson*, XI, XII, XV, XVI, Washington, D. D., 1905; Dante, *Pur.* VI.

Background

Charles J. Stillé, *Beaumarchais and the Lost Million*, Philadelphia, 1887; George L. Clark, *Silas Deane: A Connecticut Leader in the American Revolution*, New York and London, 1913; Elizabeth S. Kite, *Beaumarchais and the War of American Independence*, Boston, 1918; Cynthia Cox, *The Real Figaro*, London, 1962; Alfred Martineau, *Bussy et l'Inde Français, 1720-1785*, Paris, 1935.

Exegeses

There is little exegesis for Canto XXXII in the literature, but passing references may be found in most of the major books on Pound. Consult, for example, indexes in DP, *Barb*; HK, *Era*; and DD, *Sculptor*.

Glossary

1. Mr. Adams: In 1815 John Adams, former president, responded to a request for information about the causes and course of the Revolution (to be used in a history of the period) with a letter to Dr. J. Morse which starts: "A history of military operations . . . is not a history of the American Revolution, any more than the Marquis of Quincy's military history of Louis XIV . . . . is a history of the reign of that monarch. The revolution was in the minds and hearts of the people, and in the union of the colonies; both of which were substantially effected before hostilities commenced" [*Works*, X, 182-184].

2. Amphitrite: French ship belonging to Beaumarchais [cf. 31:29] which carried supplies to the colonists during the Revolutionary War. Details of its cargo and sailing are from a report of an American agent in France who arranged to buy the materials. Silas Deane, one agent, reported the sailing and arrival of the *Amphitrite* and other ships with details of the cargo. But the exact source of Pound's figures is not known.

3. Merchants of Morea: The Morea is in the Peloponnesus, S Greece, but the merchants named and the details given in the next nine lines are from an unidentified source.

4. et des dettes . . . sur les moyens: F, "and of the debts of the said Echelles . . . / . . . in the principal decrees of the Council, December [17] 66 / weapons and other implements which can only be for / the government's account . . . M. Saint-Libin / well versed in the languages of the country, known by the Nabobs / . . . to excite him, and to follow hot upon the enemy (to the) English / not very delicate about the means."

5. Echelles: The Echelles du Levant, commercial ports of the Near East on the Mediterranean, were long under Turkish control.

6. Saint-Libin: Palle-Bot de Saint-Lubin, sent by the French government to India to establish relations with the Mahrattas, who were effectively opposing the British. Haidar Ali [cf. 8 below] had already led the Indian princes to victory earlier and in 1778, while the British were at war with the French, he was opposing the British in India again. In 1780 the French sent a fleet to help him [Martineau, 327-330; BK].

7. Nababs: Nabobs. Name first given to governors in India under the Mogul Empire. In 18th or 19th century an Englishman who had acquired a fortune in India was called a nabob.

8. Hyder Ali: Haidar Ali, 1722-1782, Indian maharaja of the Hindu state of Mysore. At times he effectively opposed the British by joining forces with their enemies.

9. Portagoose: Portuguese. A possible explanation of the line: In 1762 Great Britain assisted King Joseph of Portugal in its war with Spain by sending Brigadier General John Burgoyne at the head of 50,000 troops. Together they defeated the Spanish by 1763. During this time Britain had strong bonds with Portugal. After King Joseph's death in 1777, Pombal (his prime minister who had for 20 years brought about dramatic reforms) was dismissed. Under Queen Maria (who was believed to be insane) the ancien régime and the Jesuits tried to break the bonds with Protestant Britain in favor of Catholic France and Spain.

10. Beaumarchais: This famous French dramatist was a natural for secret intrigue as well as an enthusiast for the cause of the American Revolution. Without his unceasing efforts, the colonies would prob. not have received arms and other war supplies. Using a fake import-export firm, Roderique Hortalez & Co., as a front, Beaumarchais tried to conceal his shipments from the English [31:29].

11. Burr: Aaron B., 1756-1836, American Revolutionary officer and political leader; U. S. senator (1791-1797). In 1800, running for the presidency, he received the same number of electoral votes as did Jefferson; the election was thrown into the Congress and Burr withdrew from the race to become vice-president under Jefferson. He was tried for treason and accused of conspiring to seize territory from Spanish America to form a new republic in the SW, but he was acquitted (1807).

12. Ohio Canal: George Hay, State's attorney for Virginia, was chief prosecutor of Aaron Burr in the treason trial. In a letter to Hay (June 19, 1807), TJ says that Burr had tried to get a man named Latrobe to employ a number of men supposedly to work on a canal opposite Louisville. A postscript to the letter reads: "Since writing the within I have had a conversation with Latrobe. He says it was five hundred men he was desired to engage. The pretexts were, to work on the Ohio canal, and be paid in Washita lands. Your witnesses will some of them prove that Burr had no interest in the Ohio canal" [XI, 236; unless otherwise noted, all Jefferson quotations in glosses in this canto are from *The Writings of Thomas Jefferson*.] TJ believed that Burr wanted the men to conduct an armed rebellion against the U. S.

13. coram non judice: L, "not in the presence of a judge."

14. as usual . . . solid: In a letter to Hay (June 20, 1807), TJ outlines what is probably the first declaration of executive privilege by a president: "I did not see till last night the opinion of the Judge on the *subpoena duces tecum* [a requirement to produce certain documents in court] against the President." TJ says that since the document was produced *"coram non judice"* he paid little attention to it, but adds: "Yet I saw readily enough, that, as is usual where an opinion is to be supported, right or wrong, he dwells much on smaller objections, and passes over those which are solid" [XI, 240].

15. Oryzia mutica: *Oryza mutica* L, "short-grained rice." TJ mentions what he knows of this upland rice in a letter to Dr. Benjamin Waterhouse. It was of interest because it would grow "without any more water than the common rains" [XII, 204].

16. Sweden: In a letter to John Hollis, TJ mentions the seed of both "perennial succory" and the "famous turnip of Sweden": the first was received by General Washington from the Board of Agriculture of London and the second was received by TJ himself from a member of the same board at a later time [XII, 253].

17. rectus in curia: L, "right in point of law." In a letter (March 8, 1809) to William Short telling him that the Senate had "negatived your appointment," TJ adds: "I pray you to place me *rectus in curia* in this business with the emperor, and to assure him that I carry into my retirement [from the presidency] the highest veneration of his virtues." Short was TJ's minister plenipotentiary to Russia. It was his nomination for reappointment by President Madison which was "negatived"; "this business" refers to the problem of the appointment [XII, 264-265].

18. Alexander: Alexander I, 1777-1825, emperor of Russia (1801-1825). The new American government was at pains to develop good diplomatic and trade relations with Russia but to keep out of continental entanglements and wars.

19. shepherd dogs: TJ wanted "the shepherd's dogs" because they would be "a valuable possession to a country now beginning to pay great attention to the raising [of] sheep" [XII, 260].

20. war: In a letter to President Madison (March 17, 1809) shortly after the latter took office, TJ warns him that war must be avoided: "I know no government which would be so embarrassing in war as ours" because of "the lying and licentious character of our papers" and "the wonderful credulity of the members of Congress in the floating lies of the day" [XII, 267].

21. Ronaldson: James R., 1768-1842, American printer and typographer who established a type foundry in Philadelphia in 1796. He carried a letter from TJ to Spain to obtain "antimony" needed to make type so that the U. S. would not have to obtain its books from England.

22. indians: The following ten lines are adapted from a TJ letter (April 7, 1809) to Governor James Jay concerning the right way to civilize Indians. He recommended the raising of cattle and education so that the Indians could run their own affairs, followed by religious training [XII, 270-271].

23. Creeks: American Indian confederacy in SE United States.

24. Cherokees: Later in 1820 this Indian tribe, the largest and most important in SE United States, formed the Cherokee Nation. The tribe was deported to the Indian Territory (Oklahoma) in 1838 [34:83].

25. and as many . . . : After his retirement to Monticello, TJ heard of a libel suit against a clergyman who had defamed him when he was president. He requested the charges be dropped because, he said, respectable men present would swear on both sides of the question [XII, 288-289].

26. Johnson: William J., 1771-1834, appointed associate justice of the U. S. Supreme Court (1804) by TJ. The 10 lines beginning " . . . deem it necessary," written to Johnson in 1823, concern TJ's analysis of the Monarchist party and its ideas during the

early years of the Republic. He traces these ideas of government to Europe and describes the ways in which the party sought to "constrain the brute force of the people." Johnson had asked for the information because he was writing a history of political parties in the U. S. [XV, 440].

27. whether in a stye . . . animals: TJ equates the training of kings with the training of animals: "Now, take any race of animals, confine them in idleness and inaction, whether in a stye, a stable or a state-room, pamper them with high diet, gratify all their sexual appetites . . . they become all body and no mind . . . . Such is the regimen in raising Kings" [XII, 377-378].

28. Cannibals: [cf. 44 below].

29. Marshall: John M., 1755-1835, American jurist; one of the American commissioners to France (1797-1798); member of House of Representatives (1799-1800); secretary of state (1800-1801); chief justice of Supreme Court (1801-1835). Marshall established the basic principles of constitutional interpretation by his decisions, but TJ says that in one particular he was unwise: "This practice of Judge Marshall, of travelling out of his case to prescribe what the law would be in a moot case not before the court, is very irregular and very censurable" [XV, 447].

30. animal . . . thought: In a letter from TJ to John Adams [Pound has it reversed], dated January 8, 1825, he discusses the latest scientific theories about the function of the brain and wonders if an animal deprived of that organ would be entirely without thought [XVI, 91].

31. Louis Sixteenth: 1745-1793, king of France (1774-1792). He and all the monarchs mentioned in next 10 lines are named at the end of the letter to Judge Johnson quoted above. TJ's opinion of monarchs had not been tempered by time. The letter reads: "While in Europe, I often amused myself with contemplating the characters of the

128   32/159

then reigning sovereigns of Europe. Louis
the XVI. was a fool, of my own knowledge,
and in despite of the answers made for him
at his trial. The King of Spain was a fool,
and of Naples the same. They passed their
lives in hunting, and despatched two couriers
a week, one thousand miles, to let each
other know what game they had killed the
preceding days. The King of Sardinia was a
fool. All these were Bourbons. The Queen of
Portugal [the queen of Portugal is the Maria
in 9 above and 36 below], a Braganza,was
an idiot by nature. And so was the King of
Denmark. Their sons, as regents, exercised
the powers of government. The King of
Prussia, successor to the great Frederick, was
a mere hog in body as well as in mind.
Gustavus of Sweden, and Joseph of Austria,
were really crazy, and George of England,
you know, was in a straight waistcoat. There
remained, then, none but old Catharine, who
had been too lately picked up to have lost
her common sense" [XII, 378-379].

32. King of Spain: Charles IV, 1748-1819,
king of Spain (1788-1808); subservient to
Napoleon; forced to abdicate (1808).

33. King of Naples: Ferdinand I of Naples
and Sicily, 1751-1825; king of Naples
(1759-1806; 1815-1825) as Ferdinand IV;
because he remained hostile to Napoleon, he
fled to Palermo while the French established
the short-lived Parthenopean Republic at
Naples (1799); in 1806 Ferdinand fled to
Sicily where he ruled as Ferdinand III while
Naples was ruled by Joseph Bonaparte and
Murat; he was restored to the throne of
Naples in 1815 and was made king of the
Two Sicilies in 1816 as Ferdinand I.

34. King of Sardinia: Victor Amadeus III,
1726-1796; king of Sardinia (1773-1796).

35. Bourbons: Royal family of France,
branches of which ruled Spain, Sicily, and
Parma at various times.

36. Portuguese Queen: Maria Francisca,
1734-1816; Maria I, queen of Portugal
(1777-1816); she was considered by many to
be sickly, weak-minded, or insane, and to be
a tool of the Jesuits.

37. Braganza: Capital of Bragança district,
NE Portugal; seat of the house of Bragança,
former rulers of Portugal.

38. Frederic of Prussia: Frederick II or
Frederick the Great, 1712-1786, king of
Prussia (1740-1786).

39. Gustavus: Gustavus III of Sweden,
1746-1792; king (1771-1792).

40. Joseph of Austria: Joseph II, 1741-
1790; king of Germany (1764-1790) and
Holy Roman emperor (1765-1790).

41. George III of England: 1738-1820; king
of England (1760-1820).

42. Catherine: Catherine II, 1729-1796;
empress of Russia (1762-1796).

43. a guisa [di] . . . posa: I, "like a lion . . .
when he crouches" [*Pur.* VI, 66, describing
Sordello, guard of Vale of Princes (note list
of kings and queens preceding)].

44. Cannibals . . . : At the end of a letter to
John Adams (June 1, 1822), TJ uses this
phrase as he turns to "the news of the day."
He judges that mankind acts like an animal,
devouring his own kind, and in doing so dis-
plays a "pugnacious humor [which] seems
to be the law of his nature" [XV, 371-373].

CANTO XXXIII

Sources

Charles Francis Adams, ed., *The Works of John Adams*, X, Boston, 1856; Julian P. Boyd, ed., *The Papers of Thomas Jefferson*, II, IV, Princeton, 1950; Karl Marx, *Capital: A Critique of Political Economy*, trans. Samuel Moore and Edward Aveling, 1906, I; Paul Wilstach, ed., *Correspondence of John Adams and Thomas Jefferson, 1812-1826*, Indianapolis, 1925; Grigory Bessedovsky, *Revelations of a Soviet Diplomat*, London, 1931; *Congressional Record, Senate*, February 25, 1931.

Background

EP, *Impact: Essays on Ignorance and the Decline of American Civilization*, 1960; *J/M*; E. C. Mullins, *The Federal Reserve Conspiracy*, Hawthorne, CA, 1971; Arthur Kitson, *A Fraudulent Standard*, London, 1917, *The Bankers' Conspiracy!*, London 1933; John Kenneth Galbraith, *Money, Whence It Came and Where It Went*, Boston, 1975.

Exegeses

William Chace, "The Canto as Cento: A Reading of Canto XXXIII," *Pai*, 1-1, 89-100; Davis, *Vision*, 124-125; CE, *Ideas*, 35, 36, 55-56.

Glossary

1. **Quincey**: Quincy, city in E Massachusetts, eight miles south of Boston; birthplace and home of John Adams and John Quincy Adams. The first nine lines are from the letter of John Adams to TJ on date given.

2. **the gent**: Col. William Finnie, quartermaster of the Albemarle County (VA) prisoner-of-war camp, whose inept administration caused many English and German prisoners to be improperly fed and cared for.

3. **P. Henry**: Patrick H., Revolutionary War patriot from Virginia.

4. **Versailles**: City S of Paris where Louis XIV built the palace known as Versailles.

The menagerie was a zoo on the palace grounds. The thrust of the whole letter (JA to TJ, July 13, 1813) is that democracy cannot be based on a population "where only two-percent of the people can read and write."

5. **Napoleon**: N. Bonaparte. The same letter expresses the idea that Napoleon's word, ideology, "is meant to define that particular madness in which a great many men, thinking themselves all equal, practice democracy" [Chace, *Pai*, 1-1, 90].

6. **Theognis**: T. of Megara, aristocratic elegiac poet of the sixth century B.C. His best-known work is *Elegies to Kyrnos*, in

which he considers the values of the aristo-cratic man in human affairs and cites as exemplum purebred stallions that sire better offspring.

7. Livingston: Robert R. L., 1746-1813, American lawyer and statesman; member of Continental Congress (1775-1777; 1779-1781); member of committee that drafted Declaration of Independence; first U. S. secretary of foreign affairs (1781-1783); minister to France (1801-1804).

8. Humphries: David Humphreys, 1752-1818, colonel in the American army during the Revolution; aide-de-camp to George Washington; minister to Spain (1794). He was recognized as an expert on raising merino sheep.

9. Merino: Breed of sheep, originating in Spain, which was known for its fine, heavy wool. Thrust of argument in letter: If these men can introduce an aristocracy of sheep, can one not arrange some control of the aris-tocracy of America other than the one based on money lust and land lust?

10. AGATHOS: H, "good, wellborn." Ap-plied to Plato's philosophy. Correct date of letter to TJ is September 15, 1813.

11. kalos k'àgathos: H, "a perfect gentle-man." Lit., "beautiful and wellborn." In Karl Marx, *Capital* (259-260), the passage in which this Greek phrase occurs says that the owner of the means of production lives off surplus labor no matter what he is— Athenian, theocrat, or whatever.

12. bojar: R, *boja*, member of the Russian aristocratic order that owned most of the serfs and the land.

13. difference . . . : TJ to Giovanni Fab-broni (June 8, 1778), explaining why colo-nial Revolutionary soldiers suffered fewer casualties than those of England by "about one half." He explains that "this difference is ascribed to our superiority in taking aim when we fire; every soldier in our army hav-ing been intimate with his gun from in-fancy" [Chace, 91].

14. Grand Duke: Charles Bellini, a known moneygrubber. After the Declaration of Independence the colonies needed to borrow money abroad to promote the Revolution. In a letter dated August 2, 1777, TJ pro-posed to John Adams (who was trying to obtain money from almost any source in Europe) that he try Bellini, but that it would be wise to get a letter of introduction from Franklin who was much favored in the courts of Europe.

15. Condorcet . . . Pharisees: JA to TJ (June 1815). Condorcet's ideas led Adams to con-clude that "philosophers have shown them-selves as incapable of governing mankind, as the Bourbons or the Guelphs."

16. "Outline . . . Human Mind": *Esquisse d'un tableau historique des progrès de l'esprit humain* (1801-1804) by Condorcet, in which he traces the human development through nine epochs to the French Revolu-tion and predicts that the tenth epoch will be the ultimate perfection of man. JA reached other conclusions.

17. Pharisees: The Jewish religious party that insisted on strict adherence to laws, both written and oral. It was a Christian as-sumption in the 18th century that in their struggles with the Sadducees, who accepted only the teaching of the Torah, the Pharisees practiced casuistry and the arts of deception to maintain their position.

18. Lexington: Town in Massachusetts. Lo-cation of opening engagements of the Ameri-can Revolution, April 19, 1775. Revolution took place in the minds of the people [32:1].

19. T. J. on provisions: Part of letter to Patrick Henry [cf. 3 above].

20. Bonaparte . . . Jefferson: JA to TJ, August 1815, letter in which Adams mistak-enly predicts a similar fate for Wellington.

21. Cromwell: Oliver C., 1599-1658, lord protector of England (1653-1658).

22. Wat Tyler: Or Walter T., d. 1381, English leader of the Peasants' Revolt (1381) in protest against the Statute of Laborers and the poll tax.

23. Jack Cade: D. 1450, English rebel leader of the Kentish rebellion (May-June 1450) protesting corruption at court.

24. Wellington: Arthur Wellesley, 1st Duke of Wellington, 1769-1852, British general and statesman; defeated Napoleon at Waterloo (1815).

25. Litterae nihil sanantes: L, "Literature curing nothing." The line is from JA letter to TJ, June 28, 1812. But the "melancholy . . . snow-storm" lines are from JA to TJ letter, November 15, 1813. The phrase "serpents' teeth" refers to Cadmus sowing the dragon's teeth which led to the building of Thebes [27:33].

26. Whigs: The Whig party was one of the dominant political parties in the U. S. during the second quarter of the 19th century. Letter from JA to TJ, September 1816, recalls the reaction to the death of Washington.

27. $75,000 . . .: From letter of TJ to Nathanael Greene, commander of Southern army, about military requisitions and prisoners. Quote may concern plan to reward Revolutionary War veterans with Western land grants.

28. Das Kapital: The ten-line quote is based on Vol. I, Part IV, of Marx's *Capital*, entitled "The Production of Relative Surplus-Value." It concerns the horrors of child labor which was the subject of a parliamentary commission report in 1842. One commentator said it was "the most frightful picture of avarice, selfishness and cruelty on the part of masters and of parents, and of juvenile and infantile misery, degradation and destruction ever presented" [Chace, 94].

29. Rogier: Charles Latour R., 1800-1885, Belgian statesman; premier of Belgium (1847-1852). The five lines are from a Marx footnote illustrating that even a supposedly advanced labor country such as Belgium had difficulty passing child-labor laws.

30. Brussels: City in C Belgium.

31. Lord H. de Walden: Charles Augustus Ellis, 6th Baron Howard de W., 1799-1868, English diplomat; minister to Stockholm (1832-1833), Lisbon (1833-1846), and Brussels (1846-1868).

32. Factory Act: The British act passed in 1825 shortened the hours of child labor; it was amended (1829, 1831) specifically to regulate child employment in cotton mills. The Factory Act of 1848 was resisted by vigorous propaganda. Marx says: "They denounced the Factory Inspectors as a kind of revolutionary commissioners like those of the French National Convention ruthlessly sacrificing the unhappy factory workers to their humanitarian crotchet" [Chace, 95].

33. Hobhouse: John Cam H., Baron Broughton de Gyfford, 1786-1869, British administrator, liberal pamphleteer, and sponsor of an act to control child labor. A Marx footnote says about the Hobhouse Act: " . . . it was forbidden to any owner of a cotton-spinning or weaving mill, or the father, son or brother of such owner, to act as Justice of the Peace in any inquiries that concerned the Factory Act" [ibid.].

34. Leonard Horner: 1785-1864, English geologist and educational reformer; appointed in 1833 to a commission on child employment and until 1856 was a chief inspector under the Factory Act.

35. avénement [avènement] . . . (allemand): F, "beginning German revolution posed some new problems, / commercial routine to be replaced by the creation of two / funds (of) gold and wheat destined to the victorious (German) proletariat." Source of this quote and the rest of page 163 is *Revelations of a Soviet Diplomat* by Grigory Bessedovsky.

36. bureaucrat . . . sanguinaire: F, "a peaceful bureaucrat, Van Tzin Vei showed himself completely incapable of assuming the role of chief of a bloody revolution."

37. Van Tzin Vei: Wang Ching-wei, 1885-1944, Chinese statesman; disciple of Sun Yat-sen who, after Sun's death, led the left wing of the Kuomintang. He later broke with Chiang Kai-shek and the Kuomintang and, in March 1940, became president of the National Government of China at Nanking, a puppet regime under the control of the Japanese government. Bessedovsky [cf. 38, 39 below] said that a personal friend of Stalin's tried to educate Wang but could not because he was "a peaceful bureaucrat, [and] proved himself quite incapable of leading a bloody revolution" [*Revelations*, 165].

38. Bessedovsky: Grigory Zinovevich B., former Soviet diplomat.

39. Midland: Midland Bank in England. Source shows that corrupt Soviet functionaries, by discounting bills in the right places, pocketed the difference and cheated their own government. But worse, Stalin feared that by taking trade advantage of up to 15 million pounds in Midland Bank short-term credits, the Soviets might fall into a trap that would lead "into an economic, and so political, impasse." Bessedovsky, who believed the Soviets should take the loans, negotiate long-term credits, and develop trade, described the opinions of his opponents: "These fears of the Politbureau coincided with interests of certain English companies, and of quite a number of high officials of the U. S. S. R. Soviet bills, in London as elsewhere, were discounted at exorbitant rates of interest, three or four times higher than that fixed by the Midland Bank" [ibid., 232].

40. 150 millions: Bessedovsky complained about the destructive effect of Stalin's economic policies: "Soviet trade was at a standstill, solely because of these exorbitant rates

of discount. According to my estimates, we were spending more than 150 million roubles a year merely on usurious discounts" [ibid., 235].

41. he even: The "he" is W. P. G. Harding, governor of Federal Reserve Board.

42. Federal Reserve banks: The U. S. Federal Reserve Bank is a privately owned corporation organized to serve as a bank of reserve and rediscount for member banks (all national banks and many state banks and trust companies). Federal Reserve banks have the power to issue currency even though they are independent of the United States treasury. The U. S. government has no currency other than the few greenbacks issued by Lincoln which are still in circulation.

43. Brookhart: Smith Wildman B., 1869-1950, U. S. senator from Iowa (1928-1932). The remaining lines of the canto, after "to change the subject," are focused on Brookhart's speech to the Senate on February 25, 1931. The message is that a small businessman is injured, to the advantage of giant corporations, through manipulation of government agencies; private information, denied to the general public, allows a few entrepreneurs to make fortunes [Chase, 98-99].

44. Swift amoursinclair: Swift and Armour are American meat-packers. They, along with the Sinclair Oil Company, were privy to the deliberations of the Federal Reserve Board and knew that the depression was coming, but nevertheless they could make huge loans because of anticipated deflation of interest rates.

CANTO XXXIV

Sources

Allan Nevins, ed., *The Diary of John Quincy Adams,*
1794-1845: American Political, Social and Intellectual
Life from Washington to Polk, New York, London,
Toronto, 1928.

Background

Charles Francis Adams, *The Memoirs of John Quincy*
Adams, 12 vols., 1874-1877; Josiah Quincy, *Memoir of*
the Life of John Quincy Adams, Boston, 1859; Leonard
Falkner, *The President Who Wouldn't Retire*, New
York, 1947; George Lipsky, *John Quincy Adams: His*
Theory and Ideas, New York, 1950.

Exegeses

CFT, "Canto 34: The Technique of Montage," *Pai*, 6-2,
185-232; DD, *Sculptor* 135-138.

Glossary

1. Mitchell: Dr. Samuel Latham M.,
1763-1831, author and former professor at
Columbia College. The conversation took
place at a dinner with President Jefferson on
November 3, 1807, which John Quincy
Adams [JQA] attended.

2. black manservant: On August 5, 1809,
JQA left for Russia, with some of his family
and a black manservant named Nelson, to
serve as minister plenipotentiary for the
newly inaugurated President James Madison.

3. Consistent . . . : At his first meeting with
the Emperor Alexander, JQA assured him
that the "political duty of the United States
towards the powers of Europe was to for-
bear interference in their dissensions" and
that the U. S. would support the liberal prin-
ciples of the emperor in all ways "consistent
with their peace and their separation from
the political system of Europe."

4. auf dem Wasser: G, "on the water."

5. En fait . . . étourdi: F, "In regard to com-
merce this [Bonaparte] is a scatterbrain."

6. Romanzoff: Count Nicholas Petrovitch
R., 1754-1826, minister of foreign affairs for
Alexander I. R. assured JQA that Russians
had for years been "Anglomanes" but that
England's "exclusive maritime pretensions"
made it necessary that Russia support a rival
commercial state and that the emperor
hoped the U. S. would be such a state.

7. Freedom of . . . : JQA thought both
England and France were impolitic in re-
stricting commerce and that all the U. S.
wanted was freedom of the seas and of com-
merce.

8. corps diplomatique: F, "diplomatic
corps." The "only members" were "General

Pardo, a Spaniard, and Count Maistre, a Savoyard."

9. Shakespeare etc.: JQA talked with Count Romanzoff about literary men until 2 o'clock, when the court was over.

10. "Monsieur Adams...": F, "Mr. Adams ... I haven't seen you for a hundred years." The remark was made when JQA encountered the emperor on his morning walk.

11. treaty of commerce: An idea JQA broached to Romanzoff.

12. ambassador (french): Armand Augustin Louis, Marquis de Caulaincourt. He had a bantering conversation with JQA, who said that France would probably make peace between England and the U. S. because the French had promised to repeal the Berlin and Milan decrees which had closed French ports to American trade.

13. Tilsit: East Prussian city where, on a raft in the middle of the Neman River, Napoleon and Alexander concluded a peace, July 7-9, 1807. The peace was broken in 1812.

14. two empresses: (1) The dowager empress (wife of Alexander's father, Paul I, who had been assassinated), and (2) Alexander's wife.

15. un peu interessantes: F, "somewhat interesting." Ironic restraint. Much excitement surrounded Napoleon's new acts of war in 1812. Nevins added a footnote to his text giving approximate number of troops on both sides and commenting: "Alexander could not mobilize more than 200,000 [sic]." He added, however, that Alexander rightly "counted on space and time to win his victories for him." Napoleon, because of his military difficulties, is said to have added to the old list of elements, "earth, air, fire, and water," a fifth element: mud [51/250; 51:2].

16. Claud Gabriel: On returning to Russia, Gabriel said "he was obliged to lay aside his superb dress and sabre, which he had been ordered to wear [in America] but which occasioned people to insult and even beat him."

17. Oranienbaum: Town near Petrograd, site of an imperial residence, 1727-1914.

18. Ld. Cathcart: William Schaw, 1st Earl of Cathcart, 1755-1843; English soldier and diplomat. As ambassador to Russia (1813-1821) he organized and brought Russia into the last coalition against Napoleon (1813).

19. Madame de Stael: Anne Louise Germaine Necker, baronne de Staël-Holstein 1766-1817, cosmopolitan French-Swiss woman of letters who always gathered a group of brilliant people around her.

20. Qu'il fit . . .: F, "that he committed the folly of Moscow."

21. Gallatin: Albert G. and James A. Bayard joined JQA in negotiating with England the end of the War of 1812. The five lines concern details of the negotiations which were concluded in 1815 [31:40].

22. Tamerlan: In Paris, after the Treaty of Ghent had been signed, JQA recorded reactions to Napoleon's arrival in the French capital following his escape which opened the Hundred Days. At the Opéra on the night of March 14, 1815 JQA heard *Tamerlan* (with score by P. Winter and libretto by E. Morel De Chéfdeville, based on Voltaire's *Orphelin de la Chine*) and saw the ballet drawn from A. Boieldieu's *Télémaque*.

23. Auxerre: Capital of Yonne department, NE central France; it was on Napoleon's route to Paris.

24. Ney: Michel N., 1769-1815, marshal of France. Distinguished French commander, a commoner who in the 1805 campaign against Austria attained a brilliant victory at Elchingen and was created Duke of E. by Napoleon. After Napoleon and Murat deserted the army in Russia, Ney worked valiantly to save the remnants. After Napoleon's abdication he swore allegiance to the

Bourbons, and upon Napoleon's return from Elba he was put in command of the king's guard with orders to stop him. Ney intended to do so, but when he saw that the army dramatically preferred Napoleon he considered the Bourbon cause lost and joined Napoleon at Lyons, thus clearing the way to Paris.

25. King of Rome: François Charles Joseph Napoleon, 1811-1832, son of N. and Marie Louise, whom N. had made titular king of Rome.

26. Tuilleries: Tuileries, Palace in Paris which both N. and Louis XVIII used as chief residence.

27. Beauvaise: Capital of Oise department, N France.

28. Seance Royale: F, "Royal Interview."

29. Ah, voui, Vive le Roi: F, "Ah, yeah, Long Live the King."

30. Bourbon: [32:31].

31. Sir James Mackintosh: On May 25, 1815, JQA reached London with Gallatin and his friends to negotiate a trade treaty with Great Britain. At a dinner held at Holland House on June 2, 1816, Sir James M. (a scholar and a member of Parliament) asked if Dr. Franklin was sincere when "he lamented the revolution." The three lines are JQA's response.

32. Samuel Adams: 1722-1803; activist in Revolution; instigator in Boston Tea Party; signer of Declaration of Independence.

33. Sir James Otis: 1725-1783; American lawyer and patriot; Revolutionary activist.

34. Gouverneur Morris: 1752-1816. When JQA stopped in New York on his way to Washington to serve as James Monroe's secretary of state, Governor De Witt Clinton and Morris attended a dinner at Tammany Hall to honor him.

35. Mr. Astor: John Jacob A., 1763-1848, American merchant who made a fortune in fur trading and commerce.

36. Tammany Hall: New York City headquarters of the Tammany Society, founded in 1786, a major force in New York politics until 1932.

37. Mr. Onis: Don Luis de O., Spanish minister at Washington in 1819. He negotiated treaty with Spain which ceded Florida to the U. S. in 1821 when there was much popular sentiment against Spain.

38. Mr. Jefferson: Return to TJ's conversation with Dr. Mitchell [cf. 1 above].

39. Mr. Bagot: Sir Charles B., 1781-1843, minister to the U. S. (1815-1820) when he negotiated the Rush-Bagot Convention limiting armaments on the Great Lakes.

40. De Witt Clinton: 1769-1828, New York lawyer and politician whose political fortunes ebbed and flowed. U. S. senator (1802-1803); unsuccessful candidate for president in 1812; for two terms governor of New York.

41. Banks breaking: On June 10, 1819, JQA recorded: "Crawford told me much of the information which he is receiving with respect to the operations of the Bank, and the gigantic frauds practicing upon the people by means of those institutions. The banks are breaking . . . . "

42. Colonel Johnson: Richard Mentor J., 1780-1850, from Kentucky; in House of Representatives (1807-1819), 1829-1837); in Senate (1819-1829); vice-president (1837-1841). Johnson proposed to JQA that the U. S. sell arms to South American countries so that his friend Duane, a journalist, could be a U. S. agent in the deal. Both President Monroe and JQA opposed such chicanery.

43. Duane: William D., 1760-1835, for 25 years the editor of the *Aurora* which, according to JQA, was "the most slanderous newspaper in the United States." JQA wrote: "As to sending Duane as an Agent to South America, he [Monroe] had no confidence in him, and believed him to be as unprincipled a fellow as lived" [31:40].

44. moral considerations . . . : These eight lines are JQA's comments on the behind-the-scenes project of selling, secretly, "any number short of twenty thousand stand of arms" to Colombia to extend the South American revolution into Peru and Mexico, despite the U. S. policy of neutrality.

45. secretissime: ML, "most secretly."

46. vice-presidency: In the spring of 1820 President Monroe seemed destined for re-election in the fall. The vice-presidency seemed the only question. A number of men including Henry Clay were jockeying for position. As JQA wrote, "But the Vice-Presidency is, to call things by their proper names, in the market . . . ."

47. Henry Clay: 1777-1852, lawyer and statesman; House of Representatives (1811-1814, 1815-1821, 1823-1825); supported JQA in election of 1824; secretary of state (1825-1829); senator (1849-1852). First half of sentence Pound uses reads: "In politics, as in private life, Clay is essentially a gamester, and, with a vigorous intellect, an ardent spirit, a handsome elocution."

48. Mr. Calhoun: John C., 1782-1850; representative from South Carolina (1811-1817); secretary of war (1817-1825); vice-president (1825-1832); senator (1832-1843); secretary of state (1844-1845); senator (1845-1850); champion of slavery and the Southern cause. JQA: "We conversed upon politics past, present, and future . . . a vague but wide-spread discontent . . . . The primary cause is that which has been the scourge of this country from its Colonial infancy—speculations in paper currency, now appearing in the shape of banks."

49. Mr. Noah: Mordecai N., 1785-1851, American journalist and diplomat; founder and editor of several New York newspapers; surveyor of port of New York (1829-1833). When consul at Tunis he was "recalled for indiscretions" and "published a book of travels against Mr. Madison and Mr. Monroe. He has great projects for colonizing Jews in this country, and wants to be sent as Chargé d'Affaires to Vienna for the promotion of them."

50. George: George Washington Adams, 1801-1828, eldest son of JQA.

51. George Clinton: 1739-1812, New York lawyer and statesman; member of Continental Congress (1775-1776); governor of New York (1777-1795); vice-president (1805-1812). On December 27, 1820 JQA attended a funeral and conversed with Calhoun about the casual way in which the great men of the nation were honored at their deaths.

52. Elbridge Gerry: 1744-1814, American statesman, member of Continental Congress; signer of Declaration of Independence; delegate to Constitutional Convention (1787); member of XYZ mission to France; governor of Massachusetts (1810, 1811); vice-president of U. S. (1813-1814).

53. half-educated: "Clay is an eloquent man, with very popular manners and great political management. He is, like almost all the eminent men of this country, only half educated."

54. Calhoun . . . concerns: The issue was whether the U. S. should follow the lead of Britain and object to the interference of the Holy Alliance on behalf of Spain to get back their South American colonies. JQA's stand that the U. S. act unilaterally led to the Monroe Doctrine.

55. General Lafayette: In October 1824 JQA went to a party attended by Lafayette and his son. Also present were the "two Misses Wright, maiden ladies, who have followed General LaFayette to this country."

56. So that . . . Washington: Anecdote told twice at cabinet meeting by William Crawford, candidate for president along with JQA and Jackson in 1824.

57. They (congress) . . . : JQA's election by the House of Representatives after his failure to gain a majority of the electoral college prevented his programs for education and other matters from being adopted.

58. Black walnut: On May 23, 1828, JQA visited his nursery: "I discovered also several black walnuts, planted the 22d of March; several almond trees . . . . The black walnut, therefore, and the almond, planted in spring, vegetate to the surface in precisely two months." The presidential election took place in the fall of 1828.

59. May 26th: The day was harassing because most of it was devoted to problems of the military and Generals Scott and Macomb. Mr. Mercer, a member of the House, proposed that "at the demand of General Scott, a Court-martial should be assembled, and that General Macomb and General Scott should engage to abide by their decision. This has been a harassing day; but I perceived a tamarind heaving up the earth in the centre of tumbler No. 2; and I planted in tumbler No. I three whole Haut-boy strawberries."

60. Interfere . . . : William Wirt, attorney general, had been asked for his professional services by the Baltimore Railway Company against the Ohio Canal Co. and asked JQA if acting in a private case would interfere with his official duties.

61. Evelyn: John E., 1620-1706; English writer and diarist; author of *Sylva*, a book on practical arboriculture.

62. Clay: Henry C. [cf. 47 above]. After Jackson's inauguration Clay, JQA's secretary of state, called on Adams to say good-bye, since both were leaving government service.

63. Shakespeare: Upon reading *Antony and Cleopatra*, a few days after he left the presidency, JQA made these observations [Diary entry of March 17, 1829].

64. lost relish: On September 24, 1829 JQA reflected at length on a lifetime of reading and added: "But of late years I have lost the relish for fiction. I see nothing with sympa-

thy but men, women, and children of flesh and blood."

65. Dec. 13th: Diary dated December 30, 1829. Margaret Eaton, known as Peggy, 1796-1879, daughter of a Washington, D. C., innkeeper; married John B. Timberlake (d. 1828) and then John Henry Eaton in 1829. When Eaton became secretary of war (1829) the wives of the other cabinet members refused to accept Mrs. Eaton socially. Although President Jackson tried to quiet the matter, Eaton was forced to resign in 1832 [37:6].

66. Mrs. Calhoun: Wife of the vice-president. "Mrs. Calhoun, being of the virtu-ous, and having then declared that rather than endure the contamination of Mrs. Eaton's company she would not come to Washington this winter; and accordingly she remains in the untainted atmosphere of South Carolina."

67. Quarterly Review: Issue of November 1829. One of the two articles was against America and the other, against Russia. "They are both full of rancorous English passions; but I had not time to read them through" [Diary entry of January 27, 1830].

68. Mr. Van Buren: Jackson's secretary of state who approved Jackson's defense of Mrs. Eaton. "Calhoun heads the moral party, Van Buren that of the frail sisterhood; and he is notoriously engaged in canvassing for the Presidency by paying his court to Mrs. Eaton" [Diary entry of February 6, 1830].

69. President Jackson's spittin' box . . . : Part of scene in a political cartoon calling for Jackson's resignation.

70. Nicholas Biddle: 1786-1844; American financier; appointed director of Second National Bank of the U. S. in 1819; became its president in 1822. Biddle was Jackson's chief antagonist in the "bank war" [cf. 88/583].

71. seat Number 203: At the behest of Massachusetts friends, JQA, after leaving the presidency, ran for the House of Representatives in 1830 and was elected. He took seat number 203 in the House.

72. Mr. Webster: Daniel W., 1782-1852; American lawyer and statesman; opposed Jackson on the Second National Bank issue.

73. Miss Martineau: Harriet M., 1802-1876; English novelist and economist; author of *Illustrations of Political Economy* (1832-1834). JQA visited her and her friends on January 18, 1835 [JQA has the title incorrect].

74. L'ami de tout le monde: F, "The friend of all the world."

75. in the yard: Demonstration of some hundred laborers in front of the White House to protest against working more than ten hours a day. President Van Buren said he could not parley with them if they presented themselves in that manner.

76. Queen Victoria: In 1837, at age 18, she had just ascended the throne.

77. Legaré: The speech made in the House was actually given by Andrew Pickens of South Carolina, who said that "if the abolitionists of the North would preach insurrection to the Southern slaves, he would retort upon them by preaching insurrection to the laborers against the capitalists of the North."

78. battling with each other: On August 2, 1840 JQA reflects that Calvinists and Unitarians have for many years been fighting over religious issues.

79. Tippecanoe: The procession at the inauguration of William Henry Harrison in 1841 included "Tippecanoe clubs." Harrison gained fame in wars against the Indians (1811-1812) and was known as "Tip" for his successful battles against the Indians at Tippecanoe.

80. The world ... slave trade: Entry for March 29, 1841.

81. Adminstration: Harrison died of pneumonia after exactly one month as president, and Vice-President Tyler assumed office. The line concerns expectations of his term in office.

82. haec sunt infamiae: L, "these are the infamies."

83. Cherokee nation: Of the Creeks and Cherokees, JQA wrote on June 30, 1841: "Georgia extended her jurisdiction over them, took possession of their lands, houses, cattle, furniture, negroes, and drove them out of their own dwellings. All the Southern States supported Georgia in this utter prostration of faith and justice; and Andrew Jackson, by the simultaneous operation of fraudulent treaties and brutal force, completed the work."

84. Buchanan: James B., 1791-1869, president (1857-1861). On April 3, 1843, in commenting on the approaching elections, JQA wrote: " ... prospects of Henry Clay irretrievably gone .... Those of Tyler, Calhoun, Cass, are equally desperate. Buchanan is the shadow of a shade, and General Scott is a daguerreotype likeness of a candidate—all sunshine, through a camera obscura."

85. Scott: Winfield S., 1786-1866; American soldier; Whig candidate for president in 1852.

86. City of Ararat: On a trip to the Middle West taken during the summer and autumn of 1843, JQA's party stopped at Grand Island on the way to Buffalo by boat and "inspected the pyramid announcing in Hebrew and in English the city of Ararat, founded by Mordecai M. Noah" [cf. 49 above].

87. Firemen's ... : At most places on JQA's Midwestern trip, the people celebrated by joining a "torchlight procession" run by local firemen.

88. Morse: Samuel Finley M., 1791-1872; American artist and inventor. "Electromagnetic" refers to the Morse code.

89. Constans proposito ... : [Source has "Constans Propositi" from Horace, *Odes*,

III, iii, 1]. Julius Pratt & Co. in April 1844 presented to JQA an ivory cane with a gold ring around it on which was engraved: "To John Quincy Adams Justum et Tenacem Proposito Virum." L, "The man tenacious of his purpose in a righteous cause" [Loeb].

90. 信: C, "Integrity" [M2748: The num-ber of the Ideogram in *Mathews' Chinese-English Dictionary*, Harvard Univ. Press, Rev. Ed., 1943; or any of the various reprints through 1972]. Pound sees the two charac-ters together as "Fidelity to the given word. The man here standing by his word" [*CON*, p. 22].

CANTO XXXV

Sources

Il Monte dei Paschi di Siena e le Aziende in Esso Riunite, 9 vols., ed. Narciso Mengozzi, Siena, 1891-1925; personal memories and experiences from the 1920s and early 1930s.

Background

EP, *L*, 246, 268, 326, 343; *GK*, 79; Alfred Perlès, *Le Quatuor en Ré Majeur*, Paris, 1938.

Exegeses

Douglas Stone, "Pound's 'Mr Corles': Canto XXXV," *Pai*, 2-3, 411-414; EH, *Pai*, 5-2, 345-348; *Pai*, 7-3, 620.

[Some details of the glosses identifying the pseudonyms in this canto were supplied by Reno Odlin. Sometime in 1957-58 he asked Pound about some of the names and wrote notes into his text of *The Cantos*. Some of his notes were supplied, not by Pound, but by others who had asked the poet similar questions. Still other notes had other sources. Mr. Odlin is no longer sure what the original source was; he knows only that he would not have written a note without good authority.]

Glossary

1. Mitteleuropa: G, "Central Europe," esp. that part of Europe which the advocates of Pan-Germanism proposed to form into an empire.

2. Mr Corles: Alfred Perlès, Austrian-born writer whom Pound met at a restaurant in 1934. During lunch Perlès told the anecdote about his World War I experience as a line officer [*Pai*, 2-3, 411-414].

3. Mr Fidascz: Tibor Serly, Hungarian musician whom Pound knew in the early 1930s. He assisted in efforts to start a publishing venture in 1933 [cf. *L*, 246, 268, 326, 343]. Pound eventually gave Serly all his music MSS [*Pai*, 7-3, 620].

4. Nataanovitch: Leopold Stokowski [RO].

5. Mattias Passion: *Passion According to St. Matthew* by Johann Sebastian Bach (1729).

6. Fraulein Dokter: Prob. Marie Stiasny, who is referred to as *Fraülein Doktor* in letters at the Yale archive. She was a friend of Mr. S. Schwarzwald, a Viennese banker, and worked at the Wilhelm Braumüller Bookstore in Vienna. She helped Pound find books on Frobenius and others. Pound may have met her during a trip to Vienna in 1928 [M de R].

7. Tyrol: Former Austrian, now Italian, province; it includes Bavarian Alps on N border and the Ötztaler Alps in center.

8. Francois Giuseppe: I, Franz Josef [16:23].

9. Tsievitz: Unidentified.

10. Mr Lewinesholme: Richard Lewinsohn, author of several books about munitions makers, including a biography of Sir Basil Zaharoff, *The Man behind the Scenes*, London, 1929. Lewinsohn was financial editor of *Vossische Zeitung* [18:12].

11. young lady: Prob. Judith Cohen. RO says there is a Pound letter that starts: "CAN I see Ma Cohen giving him all the choice bits of the chicken and shoving off the neKK and tail on Pa Cohen because I praised their Judith 'si tante' " [S, "so much"]. RO's notes do not tell him anything more about the letter or where it is now.

12. Mister Axon: Unidentified.

13. Dortmund: A German beer, Dortmunder Aktien Brauerei.

14. Alexi: Unidentified.

15. Murphy: Unidentified.

16. Potemkin: Grigori Aleksandrovich P., 1739-1791, Russian statesman, first the paramour and then the husband of Catherine II. He was not divorced and no biography mentions the death of his grandmother. Prob. the name is used here as pseudonym for a Russian acquaintance of Pound's who was as practiced in lust as the original Potemkin.

17. Egeria: Nymph who in Roman legend gave advice to King Numa in the Arician wood [cf. Livy I, xix, 5]; also classical idealization of a mistress. Thus the Potemkin "cover" was probably a painter.

18. Mr Elias: Unidentified, but Pound, tracing the name through Ulysses to the Greek Odysseus, speaks of a current Elias as "identified with the prophet" [*GK*, 79]. RO's notes say simply "Abrams Elias."

19. Hall Caine: Sir Thomas Henry Hall C., 1853-1931, English novelist, friend of Dante Gabriel Rossetti.

20. East End of London: Section of London lying east of the Bank of England, generally occupied by laboring classes.

21. dixit ... ? : L, "thus spoke the happy Elias?"

22. schnorrer: Yiddish, "panhandler" or professional beggar; from G, *schnurrer*, "whirr" or "purr," suggesting the musical instruments traveling mendicants used to play.

23. a peautiful chewisch poy: A young artist. Pound gave him work space at Rapallo where he produced "a fairly good imitation Gaudier and then went rapidly down hill." RO believes his name was Heinz.

24. Eljen! Eljen Hatvany!: Magyar, "Hail! Hail Hatvany!"

25. Hatvany: Prob. Bernhard and Joseph Deutsch, Jewish bankers from the town of Hatvan, titled January 15, 1879, as Deutsch de Hatvany. Bernhard Deutsch de Hatvany was director of the Osterreich-Ungarische

Bank in 1888. The sons were made barons in June 1908.

26. Comment! . . . bas?: F, "What! You have fallen so low?"

27. Franchet de Whatshisname: Louis Félix Marie, Franchet d'Esperey, 1856-1942, marshal of France; commanded the French 5th Army in battle of the Marne (1914); in 1918 he led the Allies to victory in the Balkans.

28. Jewish Hungarian baron: Hatvany [cf. 25 above].

29. bojar: Member of Russian aristocracy which owned most of the land and the serfs and formed an advisory council to the czar.

30. Virtusch: Uncertain. Perhaps the Italian *Virtu* [used in the sense of "power"] pronounced with a German accent.

31. fontego: I, "chamber." This and the next several "Items" [21 lines] concern petitions made to the duke to form the Monte dei Paschi ["Bank of the Pastures"] at Siena, the central subject of Cantos 42-44 [cf. 42:1-10].

32. scavenzaria: I, "special sale."

33. a schavezo: I, "at special price."

34. Brescians . . . Resanesi: People from Brescia, Cremona, Parma, and Resana in N Italy.

35. inficit umbras: L, "tinges with a darker shade" [Ovid, *Meta*. X, 596].

36. Romagnols: People of Romagna district of N Italy which comprises the present-day provinces of Bologna, Ferrara, Ravenna, and Forlì.

37. March folk: People from the Marches, the region in C Italy extending from the E slopes of the Apennines to the Adriatic coast.

38. una grida: I, "a proclamation, ban."

39. stars: Small flowers of the olive tree, which blooms in late spring and loses its petals in midsummer [49:23].

40. St. John's eve: June 23.

41. Madame $\dot{\upsilon}\lambda\eta$: H, "Matter," the physical as opposed to the spiritual. Epithet applied to Lucrezia Borgia [30:8].

42. Madame la Porte Parure: F, "Madame the Wearer of Adornment."

43. Romancero: I, neologism of Pound's. May suggest "aura of romance."

44. luogo di contratto: I, "place of contract."

45. the Dominant: Traditional term applied to Venice: Venezia Dominante.

46. De Gama: Vasco da G., ca. 1460-1524, Portuguese navigator [7:24].

47. omnes de . . . : L, "all from overseas regions."

48. Victoria? Where . . . : Pound saw an unpublished cartoon by Max Beerbohm with this caption.

49. undersell . . . rags: Exact source of these data is unknown. But they prob. concern details of a trade treaty made between Venice and one of her overseas trading partners.

50. Wazir: Vizier, high executive officer, usually a minister of state, of various Mohammedan countries, esp. the former Turkish Empire.

51. Mocenigo: Tommaso M., 1343-1423, doge of Venice (1414-1423).

52. Tola, octroi . . . decime: *Tola*: ML, "toll, tribute"; *octroi*: F, "dues, taxes"; *decime*: I, "tithes, imposts."

CANTO XXXVI

Sources

Guido Cavalcanti, "Donna mi priegha," 5th ed., 1527; rpt. *LE*, 163-167; Cesare de Lollis, *Vita e Poesie di Sordello di Goito*, 1896.

Background

EP, "Cavalcanti," *LE*, 149-200; *GK*, 304-341.

Exegeses

CE, *Ideas*, 14-15, 185-186; Dekker, *Cantos*, 125-128; DP, *Barb*, 154-159; HK, *Era*, 451; CB-R, *ZBC*, 236-237 and passim; JW, *Epic*, 59-85; Bradford Morrow, "De Lollis' *Sordello* and Sordello: *Canto 36*," *Pai*, 4-1, 93-98.; William Tay, *Pai*, 4-1, 37-54.

Glossary

1. A Lady asks ... no will to make company: Complete trans. of Cavalcanti's canzone, "Donna mi priegha" a project Pound had in process for some 25 years [cf. *LE*, 149-200].

2. virtu: I, "power." Perhaps "latent power" is a more accurate trans. of this difficult medieval word. Although present-day English "virtue" [meaning sexual chastity] comes from same root, the canzone word has a different meaning. It is distinguished from *potenza* ["force"] in the same line.

3. Where memory liveth: Trans. of *dove sta memoria* which Pound uses as a sort of leit-motif elsewhere in *The Cantos* [63:54; 76/452, 457].

4. diafan: I, "diaphanous substance," translucent. Albertus Magnus writes in *De Anima*: "For we see light not by itself but in a certain subject, and this is the diafane" [cf. JW, *Epic*, 78].

5. Mars: Roman god of war, but here a metaphor for the male principle in love and in contradistinction to Venus [Aphrodite] as a metaphor for the female principle. Pound said concerning the Italian *Da Marte*: "I suppose as 'impulse.' At any rate there is a Neoplatonic gradation of the assumption of faculties as the mind descends into matter through the seven spheres, *via* the gate of Cancer: in Saturn, reason: in Jupiter, practical and moral; in Mars, the 'spirited'; in Venus, the sensuous" [*LE*, 184].

6. name sensate: An attempt to render Cavalcanti's hard surface [*e a sensato / nome*]. Said Pound: "Unless a term is left meaning one particular thing, and unless all attempt to unify different things ... is clearly abandoned, all metaphysical thought degenerates into a soup. A soft terminology is merely an endless series of indefinite middles" [*LE*, 185].

7. He is not vertu but ...: Love [He] flows from virtu just as in the epigraph to Canto 90 [90:1] love is said to flow from the soul. Thus, perhaps, virtu can be called an attribute or function of the soul.

8. "Called thrones ... ": A pastiche from *The Divine Comedy* prefiguring the attainment of Paradise. The Thrones (to be used as the title for Cantos 96-109) are the angels in control of the seventh sphere (*voi dicete Troni* ["which are called Thrones"], *Par.* IX, 61), the reference to whom is shortly followed (69) by a passage mentioning the ruby (*balasso*, mod. I, *balascio*). Later, and again in connection with the Thrones, Dante refers to rubies (*rubin, Par.* XXX, 66), following ten lines later with a description of the surrounding brilliance of gleaming water and light (*Il fiume, e li topazii ch'entrano ed esconso* [" ... and the topazes that plunge in and leap forth"]) [JE].

9. Eriugina: John Scotus Erigena, ca. 800-ca. 877, medieval philosopher, theologian, and early Greek scholar. His works on the Eucharist (calling it only a symbol) and on "predestination" marked him as unorthodox [see *EB* for excellent account]. Pound, in *SP* [p. 61], attributes to Scotus the line, "authority comes from right reason," and sees him as an important link in Neoplatonic light philosophy. It was not Scotus whom they dug for, but a disciple of his, Amaury de Bène [cf. HK, *Era*, 451; 74/429; 83/528; *Pai*, 4-1, 49 ff.].

10. Manicheans: Christian sect considered heretical [23:28].

11. Aquinas: St. Thomas A., 1225-1274, scholastic philosopher; author of *Summa Theologica*. Since he seemed to rely on logic, rhetoric, and rationalized dogma and to neglect the *mysterium*, Pound sees him as getting things backward, "head down," and to have no means of support and thus to be "in a vacuum."

12. Aristotle: Cf. *GK*, 304-341, for EP's analysis of the *Nichomachean Ethics* and his suspicions about "Arry's" logic.

13. Sacrum ... coitu: L, "Sacred, sacred, the illumination in coitus." Scotus Erigena and Cavalcanti saw sex as revelatory, as an expression of the sacred mystery.

14. Lo Sordels ... : P, "Sordello is from Mantua" [2:3].

15. Goito: Name of castle and town (10 miles from Mantua) where Sordello was born.

16. Five castles: Gift to Sordello from Charles I, king of Naples and Sicily, for service in the battles at Benevento and Tagliacozzi.

17. dye-works: Later Sordello found himself possessed of another village, Palena, "famous well into the 19th century for its fabrics and dyes" [Morrow, *Pai*, 4-1, 98]. When S. found himself responsible for a major industry, his reaction was "what the hell!"

18. His Holiness: In 1266 Pope Clement IV wrote a letter to King Charles reprimanding him for his cruel and "inhuman" treatment of his subjects, even of soldiers who had served him faithfully, including Sordello: "And now your soldier Sordello ... at least should be redeemed in keeping with his worth." Maybe the pope's letter worked, but not rapidly: three years later, in 1269, Charles began to distribute awards and fiefs, including the five castles, to Sordello [ibid., 94-95].

19. Dilectis ... Thetis: *Dilectus ...* L, "Most beloved and familiar soldier ... the fort of Monte Odorisio / Monte San Silvestro with Pagliete and Pila ... / In the region of Thetis." Pound's *pallete et pile* are the names of castles in the source as indicated by capitals [ibid., 97].

20. Thetis: Locality in the Abruzzi, Italy.

21. land incult etc.: Paraphrased from same decree as above.

22. pratis nemoribus pascius: L, "meadows, woodlands, pastures."

23. sold the damn lot: [For details of Sordello's transactions, cf. ibid. and De Lollis, op. cit.].

24. Quan ... pensamen: P, "When I think deep in my rich thought" [line 17, Canso 21, of Sordello; De Lollis, 180].

CANTO XXXVII

Sources

George Bancroft, *Martin Van Buren to the End of His Public Career*, New York, 1889; Edward M. Shepard, *Martin Van Buren*, American Statesmen Series, Boston and New York, 1899; *The Autobiography of Martin Van Buren* (Annual Report of the American Historical Association for the Year 1918, in two volumes; Vol. II, *The Autobiography*, ed. John C. Fitzpatrick); Allan Nevins, ed., *The Diary of John Quincy Adams, 1794-1845*, New York, London, Toronto, 1928; review in Boston *Herald* entitled "Peggy Eaton's Own Story," March 30, 1932.

Background

The Autobiography of Peggy Eaton, with preface by Charles F. Deems, New York, 1932; Arthur Schlesinger, Jr., *The Age of Jackson*, Boston, 1946.

Exegeses

No exegesis has been published for this canto, but most of the major works on Pound have passing references to it. See also LL, *Motive*, 67-68; CE, *Ideas*, 35, 37; Dekker, *Cantos*, 168, 171; Davis, *Vision*, 90-91, 126-127.

Glossary

1. Martin Van Buren: 1782-1862, 8th president of the U.S. (1837-1841). A practicing lawyer who early in life became an active Democrat in state politics. MVB is one of the Odyssean, *directio voluntatis*, heroes of *The Cantos* because he supported Andrew Jackson in his war against the banks and he defended Petty Eaton [34:68, 8 below], and also because he fought for the welfare and liberty of the common man and maintained a vigorous antislavery position. After Vice-President Calhoun's faction had paralyzed Jackson's government for two years because of the Peggy Eaton affair, Van Buren resigned as secretary of state; his action led the way for the rest of the cabinet, including Major Eaton, Jackson's secretary of war, to

resign, thus making it possible for Jackson to appoint a new cabinet and get the government operating. Jackson responded to these good offices by supporting Van Buren for president in the 1836 election. His enemies accused him of playing politics in these moves; Pound believes Van Buren's actions were morally based.

2. debt: As a New York state senator, MVB was faithful to his campaign promise and in 1813 introduced a "Bill for the Relief of Small Debtors." In 1818 he reported a "Bill to Abolish Imprisonment for Debt, and to Punish Frauds," which was adopted by a 21-5 vote [Bancroft, 54; cf. 44/223].

3. immigrant: During a brief term (Jan. to

March 12, 1829) as governor of New York, MVB sponsored a safety fund to protect people against bank failures. It was an insurance scheme requiring banks to contribute to the fund. In his inaugural address MVB cited many examples of the need for such a fund, including instances of monetary injustice to the poor and powerless as well as that of the immigrant made penniless [Bancroft, 160; Shepard, 168 ff.].

4. rich patroon: In colonial times governors had issued numerous royal patents which ceded to individuals "hundreds of thousands of acres" in New York with loosely defined boundaries. Those who fell heir to the patents interpreted them as broadly as possible and in MVB's time were "encroaching on a humble class of freeholders" and driving them off their land. "In defending their rights against encroachments, Van Buren stood alone . . . having the ablest of his seniors at the bar arrayed against him" [Bancroft, 8-9]. Under old Dutch law, a patroon was a holder of entailed estates and had certain manorial rights.

5. High judges: As a U.S. senator, MVB opposed extension of the powers of the Supreme Court into the jurisdiction of states. In 1826 he said: "I believe the judges of the Supreme Court (great and good men as I cheerfully concede them to be) are subject to the same infirmities, influenced by the same passions, and operated upon by the same causes that good and great men are in other situations. I believe they have as much of the *esprit de corps* as other men" [Bancroft, 133].

6. The Calhouns: Mrs. Calhoun let it be known that she would not associate with Peggy Eaton because Mrs. Eaton lacked the virtue one should expect in the wife of a cabinet member. As the wife of the vice-president, Mrs. Calhoun rallied most Washington wives to the "standard of feminine virtue" [34:65, 66].

7. Mr. Adams: John Quincy A., defeated for reelection by Jackson in 1828, recorded [*Diary*, Dec. 30, 1830] his understanding of the Eaton affair: "This question has occasioned a schism in the party. . . . Mrs. Calhoun . . . declared that rather than endure the contamination of Mrs. Eaton's company she would not come to Washington this winter."

8. Peggy Eaton: After retiring from public life some 45 years later, Mrs. Eaton left a manuscript for posterity telling her side of the story. Scribner's published it in 1932 under the title: *The Autobiography of Peggy Eaton*. An unsigned review of the book in the Boston *Herald* of March 30, 1932, says: "All the trouble, in the judgment of Mrs. Eaton, was due to 'the Calhounites.' [Calhoun] . . . was Vice-President in the early part of Jackson's first term, as he had been in the term of Jackson's predecessor, John Quincy Adams, and expected to follow Jackson in the presidency. In the cabinet were two or three men whom Calhoun could not control, especially Eaton. The Calhoun men, therefore, must break down Peggy's husband, and the way to do it was to attack Peggy's character. Says Mrs. Eaton: 'I was the victim of these political machinations.' The results were the disruption of the cabinet and the blocking of the political ambitions of Calhoun. Jackson saw to it that Martin Van Buren and not Calhoun should be his successor." The reviewer concludes: "It is hard to believe that Mrs. Eaton did not write the truth in this apologia."

9. muncipal government: Source unidentified.

10. Ambrose: A. Spencer, 1765-1848, significant political figure in Governor De Witt Clinton's Republican party in New York. He opposed all efforts of MVB to extend the franchise at a time when only half the population were entitled to vote. "Ambrose Spencer . . . would not extend the franchise to 'those who work in factories, and are employed by wealthy individuals in the capacity of laborers' " [Bancroft, 78].

11. Van Renselaer: Stephen Van Rensselaer, 1764-1839, New York Republican. As "one of the committee on the elective fran-

chise ... [he desired] to confine the suffrage to tax-payers who had been longer resident in the state" [ibid.] .

12. State Convention: In 1821, as leader of the Democratic party, MVB called a convention for the express purpose of extending the franchise from "freeholders and actual tenants" [ibid., 62-63] to as many citizens as possible.

13. dixit Spencer: L, "said Spencer." To give the vote to those who worked for the wealthy might "in reality give it to their employers. The man who feeds, clothes, and lodges another has a real and absolute control over his will" [ibid., 80] .

14. Kent: James K., 1763-1847, judge of New York State Court of Chancery (1814-1823). He said: "I wish to preserve our Senate as the representative of the landed interest." He warned that if the Senate was not so preserved, "our posterity will have reason to deplore in sackcloth and ashes the delusion of the day.... The tendency of universal suffrage is to jeopard the rights of property and the principles of liberty" [ibid., 81-82] .

15. Tompkins: Daniel D. T., 1774-1825, governor of New York (1807-1817); vice-president (1817-1825). He said: "Property, when compared with our other essential rights, is insignificant and trifling. Life, liberty, and the pursuit of happiness, not of property, are set forth in the Declaration of Independence.... How was the late war sustained? Who filled the ranks of your armies? Not the priesthood, not the men of wealth, not the speculators. The former were preaching sedition, and the latter decrying the credit of the Government to fatten on its spoil" [ibid., 83-84] .

16. Two words: Said MVB: "There are two words which came into common use with our Revolutionary struggle.... They are, taxation and representation" [ibid., 88] .

17. Spencer: At the end of a long speech MVB turned to Chief Justice Spencer (whose argument that workers would be influenced by employers put him in a dilemma) and said: "If they are so influenced, they will be enlisted on the side of property which you propose to promote; if they are independent of their employers, they will be safe depositaries of the right" [ibid., 94-95] .

18. turnpike: As U.S. senator, MVB opposed federal funding of highways and canals on the grounds that it was an unconstitutional intrusion into the jurisdiction of the states, would extend federal power, and would lead to abuses: "... but when the turnpike before the farmer's door depends on Congress or the Cabinet at Washington, the opportunity of local supervision is lost" [ibid., 115] .

19. foreign associations: As U.S. senator, MVB vigorously opposed the slave trade, but he rejected the right of England [also opposed to the slave trade] to seize and search U.S. ships. "He opposed every attempt to surrender the 'control of our conduct in the support of our rights, or the discharge of our duties to foreign associations' " [ibid., 144] .

20. working ... stock: In 1836, as vice-president during Jackson's second term and a candidate for president himself, MVB strongly opposed the chartering of the national bank and argued for specie as a circulating medium: "Gold and silver should constitute a much greater proportion of the circulating medium of the country than they now do. To protect the working-classes (who ... have no control over a paper currency, and derive no profit from bank stock) against losses arising from depreciation ... should be our 'first object,' as it is our 'imperative duty' " [ibid., 189-190] .

21. merchants: In June 1836 a federal surplus resulting from high tariffs was distributed by the Congress among the states, thus exhausting the Treasury. By the time of MVB's inauguration, "every financial evil at once gathered round" his administration. Debts of merchants to Great Britain and the speculation of banks led to massive deflation: "The whole community was involved in the great disaster. The merchants of New

York, unwilling to confess over-trading; the speculators, refusing to condemn themselves for yielding to the bad counsels of eager cupidity . . . all sent their committees to the General Government for relief" [ibid., 199-200].

22. **revenue**: To deal with the disaster, MVB called a special session of the Congress in September 1837 and set forth a new principle in the use of public funds: "The system was a strict recurrence to the principles of the Constitution and to the general laws that regulate commerce. He advised to collect only revenue enough for the wants of the Government; to collect that revenue not in uncertain promises, but in real money, and to keep such revenue under public responsibilities for public purposes" [ibid., 205-206].

23. **banks of deposit**: Part of MVB's plan was to establish an "independent treasury," which would separate the government from all involvement in the credit system of banks and businesses. The act of 1840 "tended to make the flow of credit steady; not adding, in seasons of ardent speculation, new fuel to the flame by throwing the national revenue into banks of deposit to be loaned out for the gain of the banks" [ibid., 211, 220].

24. **patronage**: "By forbidding loans of public money, it diminished the patronage of the General Government, which no longer could select from among eight hundred banks its few favored ones" [ibid., 221].

25. **sailor**: "The evils of arbitrary power in the navy . . . were alleviated and circumscribed; . . . by an order [of MVB] in March, 1839, the sailor before the mast was protected against the lash, except as a punishment ordered by a court" [ibid., 226-227].

26. **land . . . Mr. Clay**: MVB proposed to deed public land to settlers. Henry Clay opposed the plan: "The men for whose benefit it was designed he characterized as a lawless rabble of intruders, as a class entitled to no consideration" [ibid., 227].

27. **Mr. Eaton**: Before the death of Peggy E.'s first husband, her "father had become deeply involved . . . [with well-known merchants] in a contract to furnish the government with pork." By the merchants' chicanery, the estate of Peggy's father was threatened. John Eaton stepped in, assumed all debts, bought the estate at auction in his own name, and then secured the property back to Peggy's father and mother. Said Peggy: "God bless his memory! for God knows that John H. Eaton had no other reason for his munificence towards my dear father and mother than the promptings of his own generous heart" [*Autobiography*, 59]. Washington society thought otherwise. They chose to believe that Peggy's continual munificence to Eaton in her husband's absence had much to do with the promptings of his heart [cf. 8 above].

28. **loose morals . . . uncivil**: JQA wrote [*Diary*, 483]: "There are many features in the character of Mr. Van Buren strongly resembling that of Mr. Madison—his calmness, his gentleness of manner, his discretion, his easy and conciliatory temper. But Madison had none of his obsequiousness, his sycophancy, his profound dissimulation and duplicity. In the last of these he much more resembles Jefferson, though with very little of his genius. The most disgusting part of his character, his fawning servility, belonged neither to Jefferson nor to Madison."

29. **"No where . . . "**: In his second annual message to the Congress, Jackson said that "the resources of the nation beyond those required for the immediate and necessary purposes of government can nowhere be so well deposited as in the pockets of the people" [Shepard, 204-205].

30. **union five years**: Source unknown.

31. **Bank . . . currency**: Recalling that the charter of the Bank of the United States would come up for renewal in 1836, Jackson said in his first annual message to the Congress: "Both the constitutionality and the expediency of the law creating this bank are well questioned . . . ; and it must be admitted by all that it has failed in the great

end of establishing a uniform and sound currency" [ibid., 203].

32. import grain: Within two months after the inauguration of MVB as president, the greatest commercial disaster ever to hit the country occurred. The Panic of 1837 was caused in part by an "explosion" of commercial paper and notes issued by banks. MVB called the Congress into special session and met it "with a message which marks the zenith of his political wisdom" [ibid., 326]. Among the many causes of the panic, he cited "the diversion to other pursuits of labor that should have gone to agriculture, so that this first of agricultural countries had imported two millions of dollars worth of grain in the first six months of 1837" [ibid., 328].

33. Bank of England: During the crisis MVB faced many demands to reestablish the national bank. He said such an act would do nothing: " . . . the same motives would operate on the administrators of a national [bank] as on those of state banks, . . . the Bank of the United States had not prevented former and similar embarrassments, and . . . the Bank of England had but lately failed in its own land to prevent serious abuses of credit" [ibid., 328-329].

34. Mr. Webster: Standing against Jackson and MVB and, in Pound's mind, for the forces of usury, Daniel Webster was one of the most vocal defenders of banking interests. But it was Henry Clay who actually spoke the lines attributed to Webster. In a speech to the Senate [Sept. 25, 1837], Clay said he saw no remedy for the panic which did "not comprehend a national bank as an essential part of it." He further asserted that in banking corporations, indeed, "the interests of the rich and poor are happily blended" [ibid., 337].

35. Maccoboy: In 1832-33 Jackson gradually removed $10 million in government deposits from the chartered Bank of the United States for deposit in different state banks, an act that caused an uproar among the bank's supporters. In a Senate speech

Clay implored Vice-President Van Buren to go to President Jackson "and tell him without exaggeration, but in the language of truth and sincerity, the actual condition of this bleeding country, . . . of the tears of helpless widows no longer able to earn their bread, and of unclad and unfed orphans." Van Buren's response at the end of the harangue was a rebuff: he "went up to the eloquent and languishing Kentuckian, asked him for a pinch of his fine maccoboy snuff, and walked away" [ibid., 253].

36. In Europe: Part of MVB's argument in refusing to support a national bank was that it was not necessary: "Throughout Europe domestic as well as foreign exchanges were carried on by private houses, and often . . . without the assistance of banks" [ibid., 329].

37. Relief: In the continual financial crises caused by bad banking practices and speculation, MVB stood firm against those who advised him to solve the problem by increasing the public debt. "We must not turn for relief to gigantic banks . . . . Relief was to be sought, not by the increase, but by the diminution of debt . . . let it be indelibly engraved on our minds, that relief is not to be found in expedients. Indebtedness cannot be lessened by borrowing more money, or by changing the form of the debt" [ibid., 373-374].

38. Justice Marshall: A reference to Jefferson's judgment that John Marshall erred when he sought to make legal distinctions on "for instances" that were outside the case he had in hand [32:29]. The suggestion is that MVB, in citing European practice and the Bank of England, lost contact with the people and consequently was defeated in the 1840 election.

39. Tip an' Tyler: General Benjamin Harrison (with John Tyler for vice-president) ran as the Whig candidate against MVB in 1840. Harrison was elected because of his fame as an Indian fighter in the battle of Tippecanoe. A campaign slogan was "Tippecanoe and Tyler too." A campaign song ran: "Farewell, dear Van, / You're not our man; / To guard the ship, / We'll try old Tip. / With Tip and Tyler / We'll burst Van's biler" [Shepard, 389].

40. luxuria ... furculis: L, "luxury but with golden forks" [26:25, 27]. This "vice" was attributed to MVB as opposed to Harrison, who provided for his followers a barrel of cider and told his soldiers that his door would never be shut. "Van Buren meantime, with an aristocratic sneer upon his face, was seated in an English carriage, after feeding himself from the famous gold spoons bought for the White House" [ibid., 388].

41. Mr. Lee: MVB did not approve of ostentation. He wrote later: "As far back as ... Mr. Monroe's administration, a quantity of very extravagant French furniture was purchased for the Presidential mansion, through the agency of Consul Lee, himself an ostentatious man; and among the rest, a parcel of spoons, which were alleged to be of pure gold" [*Autobiography*, 769].

42. doughface: In 1835 a bill was introduced in the Senate forbidding postmasters to deliver antislavery material. MVB's political enemies skillfully contrived to achieve a tie so that MVB would have to cast the deciding vote. If he voted for the bill, they believed he would lose some of his Southern support. Recognizing the nature of the plot against him as political, MVB cast a "political" vote for the bill. Shepard says: "Van Buren never deserved to be called a 'Northern with Southern principles'" [278]. "Doughface" was an epithet for Southern whites who defended slavery. Shepard's index refers to the vote by the phrase: "Not a 'doughface,' 278" [Shepard, 494].

43. Authorized: Anticipating the possible veto by President Jackson of any congressional act extending the charter of the Bank of the United States, Nicholas Biddle [34:70], president of the bank, began, in the last half of Jackson's first term, to build a political campaign in the press. The idea was to prevent Jackson's reelection if he exercised his veto power. MVB wrote: "The

exercise of that power was the obstacle most feared by the bank. . . . Authorization of its President to employ the funds of the institution at his discretion to influence the Press . . . had been provided for" [*Autobiography*, 620].

44. veto power: MVB wrote: "The possession of majorities in both branches of the national Legislature enabled the bank to drive the Executive to resort to the extreme power [of the veto] . . . . This power . . . had been used with marked hesitation and reserve by his predecessors and was nowhere favorably received" [ibid.].

45. charter existing: Nicholas Biddle had intimations of Jackson's attitude from remarks made in his first two annual messages: "These intimations and declarations went no further than to announce objections to the bank under its existing charter" [ibid., 619].

46. Friendly feeling ... November: The editor of MVB's *Autobiography* wrote: "It is well-nigh impossible for natures like Andrew Jackson and Nicholas Biddle to understand each other and that Biddle misunderstood the situation does not seem to have occurred to Van Buren even as a remote possibility" [ibid., 619n]. But Biddle did misunderstand, as shown by letters he wrote after a meeting with Jackson: "I found with great pleasure a friendly feeling towards the Bank in the minds of the President & his particular friends" [letter to Robert Lennox, 1759-1839, New York merchant and president of the New York Chamber of Commerce, 1827-1839]; "The rumor to which you allude, I have not heard . . . & I believe it is entirely without foundation . . . . I had much conversation of a very full & frank character with the President. . . . [He] spoke in terms the most kind & gratifying towards the institution—expressed his thanks for the services it had rendered" [letter to Aexander Hamilton; for Hamilton cf. 56 below and 62:134].

47. Victoria: Source of the line about Jackson's autograph to the future queen of England has not been identified.

48. line of discounts: One of Biddle's ploys to prevent a Jackson veto was to increase the bank's credit line, especially in the Midwest, so much that financial disaster would ensue if the charter was not renewed: "Forty millions had been for years the average amount of the loans of the bank. In October 1830 they stood at $40,527,523. Between January 1831 and May 1832 they were increased to $70,428,007: the highest figure ever reached" [MVB, *Autobiography*, 621].

49. Sorrento . . . : In 1854, at the age of 71, MVB retired to the Italian coast to rest and write his memoirs. In the first chapter he wrote: "With these scanty preparations, but under the stimulus imparted by high health, the exhilaration of this beautiful situation and salubrious climate in the mountains of Sorrento, and the thought-stirring vicinage of Vesuvius . . . the island of Capri, and the exhumed cities of Pompeii and Herculaneum, I have once more determined . . . [to write the autobiography]." He worked from many documents and from memory [ibid., 9].

50. Dan Webster . . . : No one supported the bank more vigorously than Webster. MVB, though granting Webster "consummate ability" in oratory, shows that the materials he used came directly from Biddle and his henchmen. The bill to renew the charter of the bank passed both branches of Congress, but Jackson "interposed his *veto*, and the Bill failed for want of a two-thirds vote." To get that two-thirds vote, Webster had pulled out all his stops. MVB commented: "Thirty millions of the capital of the bank (said he) are now on loan and discount in States on the Mississippi. These will all have to be called in within three years and nine months if the charter is not extended . . . . 'I hesitate not to say,' he continued, 'that as this *Veto* travels to the West it will depreciate the value of every man's property from the Atlantic to the Capital of Missouri. Its effects will be found in the price of land, the great and leading article of Western property, in the price of crops, in the produce of labor, in the repression of enterprise and in embar-

rassments of every kind of business and occupation' " [ibid., 622-623].

51. de mortuis: L, "about the dead." In avowing to tell the whole truth about the fight over the bank charter, MVB saw that he would have to tell about acts less than good done by people now dead: "The aphorism *'de mortuis nil nisi bonum'* [about the dead nothing except good] is doubtless founded in the most humane principles . . . ; it does not however apply to a case of this character" [ibid., 629].

52. 4 to 5 . . . secret service: MVB cites figures to show the enormous monetary power wielded by the president of the bank, compared with the limited control of the president of the country over federal funds; then he shows how the bank deliberately used its power to cause financial chaos and panic: "The balance of the National Treasury, at the commencement of the 'panic session' was between four and five millions, the receipts from all sources for the year between 31 and 32 millions and the estimate of the accruing revenue for the year, from which it did not vary much, amounted to between 32 and 33 millions, whilst the annual operations of the bank in discounts and foreign and domestic exchanges and according to its own published statements, at the same period amounted to three hundred and forty one millions of dollars, and it had on deposit a yearly average in its vaults of six millions of dollars belonging to the Federal Government, besides the deposits of individuals. The revenue of the United States was in due time appropriated by law to specific purposes, but whether this was or was not done the President could not use a cent of it, until after the passage of the law authorising him to do so, without exposing himself to the penalties of impeachment; and of the national legislature, by which alone such an act could be passed, it is not too much to say that a majority in one of its branches—the Senate—were the devoted partisans of the bank. The public money subject to the individual control of the President was that portion constituting the secret service fund, which was limited to fifteen or twenty thousand dollars" [ibid., 633].

53. employing . . . : It was MVB's opinion that after Jackson's veto the bank and its defenders deliberately devised a plan to create panic and financial distress, so that the Congress would submit the Act of Renewal again and Jackson would be forced to sign it: "Hence the origin of the plan which was carried out with such unrelenting vigor,—that of employing the vast means at the disposal of the bank in deranging the credits of the Country and of embarrassing business concerns to an extent sufficient to create wide spread distress and to infuse intense alarm for the safety of its every interest into all the ramifications of a great community—to excite public indignation against the Executive branch of the Government by imputing these disastrous occurrences to the interposition of the President's *Veto* and to the necessity he had wantonly imposed on the bank of preparing to wind up its affairs" [ibid., 639-640].

54. Bank's directors: One of Biddle's acts was to appoint a special committee with power to supersede the actions of the authorized board of directors: "most important . . . was . . . the 'Exchange Committee,' composed of only five directors, of whom the President of the bank was one and the other four were selected by him, and the bestowment of all but unlimited power on this Committee, whose doings were confidential and from whose councils the Government directors were invariably excluded" [ibid., 641].

55. Bank president—thirties: These phrases may be found in random order in the source [ibid., 648-649].

56. Mr. Hamilton: MVB does not impute to Biddle any design "to feather his own nest." Biddle was as innocent of acting for his own monetary gain as was Alexander Hamilton; he, like "Hamilton, who never hesitated to jeopard the general for the support and encouragement of special interests . . . would never have countenanced the application of the public money in direct bribery and would not have . . . permitted a dollar of it to reach his own pocket unworthily" [ibid., 650].

57. Bank curtailed: As part of its program of creating panic, the bank managed a "total reduction in thirteen months, including that which took place before the first of December, $17,100,851 upon a discount line of sixty four millions" [ibid., 654].

58. Mr. Taney . . .1834: Roger P. T., secretary of the treasury, was praised by Churchill C. Cambreleng, a representative from New York: "Armed with these millions in Western drafts, with balances steadily accumulating, the branch at New York would have drawn from our city banks their last dollar and would have broken every bank in the Union had not the Secretary of the Treasury . . . prevented that branch from collecting $8,760,000—had he not armed our city institutions with near nine millions to defend the whole Country in this war upon its trade and currency. (*Extra*-Globe, 1834, page 181.)" [ibid., 656].

59. Peggy Eaton: [cf. 8 above].

60. Marietta: Unidentified.

61. Dolores: Unidentified.

62. Placuit oculis: L, "She pleased the eyes."

63. Irritable . . . life: Source unknown.

64. Sorrento: MVB stayed at an inn named Villa Falangola at Sorrento while writing his memoirs [cf. 49 above].

65. Judge Yeats: Joseph C. Yates was a jurist MVB knew during his years in state politics. Yates was elected governor of New York after De Witt Clinton retired and just before MVB took his seat in the U.S. Senate. Upon his transfer to federal service, MVB found he could still be held responsible for state affairs, an "inconvenience . . . very disagreeably illustrated by bringing me very early into disfavour with the new Governor whose nomination I had preferred and aided in effecting. Judge Yates was an honest man, possessed of a good understanding, who always designed to do what he thought was right. He warded off too strict a scrutiny into his mental capacities by a dignified and prudent reserve—a policy that long practice had made a second nature" [*Autobiography*, 113].

66. Alex Hamilton: When a man named Reynolds intimated that he possessed information that would inculpate Hamilton's administration of the Treasury Department, Hamilton revealed to an investigating committee a full exhibition of documents showing that "his connection with Reynolds grew out of a criminal intercourse between himself and Mrs. Reynolds" [ibid., 119]. Eventually Hamilton published the full documents, but his friends were at great pains to have the book destroyed. MVB read it early in life "with great interest, and could not but be strongly and favorably impressed by the readiness with which Gen. Hamilton exposed his moral character to just censure ... while vindicating his official conduct from unmerited reproach" [ibid., 120-121].

67. Marshall, said Roane: MVB took a trip to Richmond, VA to visit Spencer Roane [1762-1822, American jurist and political writer] and found him on a sickbed from which he never rose, but he also found Roane to be "a root and branch Democrat, clear headed, honest hearted, and always able and ready to defend the right regardless of personal consequences." The two men talked for several hours: "Mr. Roane referred ... to the course of the Supreme Court, under the lead of Chief Justice Marshall, in undermining some of the most valuable clauses of the Constitution to support the pretensions of the Bank of the United States" [ibid., 126].

68. Tom Jefferson: As MVB was leaving, he referred to the way Roane had arranged the busts of Jefferson, Madison, and Monroe in the room, and said that "if there had been

anything of the courtier in his character he would have placed Mr. Monroe, he being the actual President, at the head instead of the foot. He replied with emphasis, 'No! No! No man ranks before Tom Jefferson in my house!'" [ibid., 126-127].

69. wool-buyers ...: A number of New York woolgrowers had succeeded in having a "Woollens Bill" introduced into Congress as a protectionist measure. Since MVB was a fervent free-trade Democrat, a number of his opponents sought to humiliate him publicly by passing a vote of censure against him for his course of action in regard to the bill. At a public meeting at the Capitol arranged for this purpose, MVB listened to all that anyone else had to say and then "addressed the meeting for nearly two hours." His friend Benjamin Knower was in the audience; and the meeting ended without taking up the question of censure. MVB thought the speech one of his best speeches, though admitting a defect: "Mr. Knower came to me in the evening and told me that, on his way home from the Capitol, Mr. Wood, one of his wool buyers and a sensible man, said to him—'Mr. Knower! that was a very able speech!' 'Yes, very able!' he answered. 'Mr. Knower!' again said Mr. Wood, after a considerable pause,—'on which side of the Tariff question was it?' 'That is the very point I was thinking about when you first spoke to me, Mr. Wood!' replied Knower.

"I have frequently been told and have always believed that I rendered much service to the cause of truth by that speech, but this conversation between two intelligent and interested men would seem to indicate that directness on all points had not been its most prominent feature" [ibid., 170-171].

70. James Jones ... compromise: Because of a series of contretemps caused by several well-intentioned but inept politicians, MVB's party was in a shambles: "I left Albany for Washington as completely broken down a politician as my bitterest enemies could desire. On board of the small steamer that took us to the larger one that waited for her passengers below the *overslaugh* it was my luck to meet Mrs. Clinton (the Governor's wife) and her brother James Jones. The latter said to me whilst we were seated at the breakfast table, 'Now is the time admirably fitted for a settlement of all difficulties between Mr. Clinton and yourself.' I thanked him for his friendly suggestion—the sincerity of which I did not in the least doubt—But replied that my fortunes were at too low an ebb to be made the subject of a compromise, and that when they improved a little I would remember his generous offer" [ibid., 149].

71. John Adams: MVB reflects in several pages on "Mr. Adams's subsequent failure in public life" and concludes that it "was, in no [in]considerable degree, owing to an overweening self esteem and consequent impatience under honors conferred on his contemporaries." He adds: "These well known circumstances, in connection with his after expressed admiration of the English system, always excepting its corruptions, gave rise to the imputation, undoubtedly unjust, that his resistance to the Crown did not arise so much from opposition to Monarchy in the abstract as to a natural preference for the House of Braintree over that of Hanover" [ibid., 189-190].

72. his son: John Quincy Adams, sixth president [34:passim], was seen by MVB to be burdened by the unpopularity of his father as well as by an insensitivity to political realities. To make his point, MVB quoted from JQA's first annual message in ironical tone to show the fantastic nature of his program, which "embraced among several other specified objects a University and Astronomical Observatories, describing the latter as 'light houses of the skies!' " He implied that JQA had a deficient sense of the meaning of the democratic process by citing the end of his first annual message: it "closed with an admonition as to the consequences of attempting to excuse our failure in duty by proclaiming to the world that we had allowed ourselves 'to be paralized by the will of our Constituents' " [ibid., 195].

73. publicly answered: MVB tells an anecdote illustrating the effect political labels had on his reputation. He was accused of not taking clear-cut stands on controversial issues. When asked about the content of a letter, a colonel said to a general: "Upon that point his letter is quite *Van Buren-ish* and leaves us altogether in the dark!" MVB denied the validity of the label, saying: "I publicly answered . . . " [ibid., 196-197].

74. Mr. Webster: MVB says that perhaps Webster's enthusiastic support of the bank was really disinterested, but if so his "superiority to the influence of money in the discharge of public functions" was not supported by the facts: " . . . his eagerness to borrow and the recklessness with which his loans were made were very generally known and his being largely in debt to the bank and . . . within its power, was undoubted" [ibid., 661].

75. Damned . . . : In 1826 Henry Clay accused someone of accepting bribes in issues involving Spanish claims. Clay said: "I think we can pay these people with land." Mr. Buchanan dissented. Then Clay said: "that yellow rascal is to have $70,000 of the money." When asked if he meant Webster, Clay said that he did [ibid., 662].

76. Taney: Roger T., secretary of the treasury [cf. 58 above], ordered that government deposits be withdrawn from branches of the Bank of the United States and placed in state banks. For months the adherents of the bank challenged Taney's power to do so just to keep the issue alive, but they never proposed any legislation: "It was, in fact, debated *de die in diem* three months and a day, a duration unprecedented in this or, I believe, any Country and that without the introduction . . . of a solitary proposition which . . . would have reversed the action of the Secretary of the Treasury or have afforded redress to the bank or have relieved the distress of any one" [ibid., 716-717].

77. HIC . . . LIBERATOR: L, "Here / Lies / the Liberator of the Treasury."

CANTO XXXVIII

Sources

Dante, *Par.* XIX, 118; EP, articles in *New English Weekly* [*NEW*],
1932-33; Richard Lewinsohn, *The Man behind the Scenes: The
Career of Sir Basil Zaharoff*, London, 1929; Dexter Kimball,
Industrial Economics, New York, 1929; Cary T. Grayson,
Woodrow Wilson: An Intimate Memoir [*Wilson*], New York,
1960; J. Q. Adams, *Diary*, ed. Allan Nevins, New York, 1928;
Charles W. Beebe, *Beneath Tropic Seas*, New York, 1928; Leo
Frobenius, *Erlebte Erdteile*, V. Frankfurt, 1925-1929; Lucien
Lévy-Bruhl, *How Natives Think*, London, 1926; Lorin Blodgett,
The Textile Industries of Philadelphia, 1880; Clifford Hugh
Douglas, "Credit Power and Democracy," serial in *New Age*,
beginning in 1920, and published as a book, *Social Credit*, 1924;
Robert Pinot, *Le Comité des Forges de France au service de la
nation*, 1919; Franco Sacchetti, *Le Novelle* (181), Florence,
1724; Fenner Brockway, *The Bloody Traffic*, London, 1933.

Background

Leo Frobenius, 1873-1973, ed. Erik Haberland, Wiesbaden, 1973.

Exegeses

GD, "Pound and Frobenius," *Motive*, 33-59; EH, *Pai*, 1-1; CE,
Ideas, 81-82, *passim*; EH, *Pai*, 5-2, "Answers to Queries"; HK,
Era, 113-114, 306-307; Witemeyer, in *Occident*, 7-1 (1973),
51-53, rpt. in *Pai*, 8-1.

Glossary

1. il duol ... la moneta: I, "the woe
brought upon the Seine [Paris] / by falsify-
ing the coinage [*Par.* XIX, 118]. Outcry
against false manipulation of currency which
Dante attributes to Philip the Fair, of
France, who debased the coinage to a third
of its value to finance his Flemish campaigns
in 1302.

2. Metevsky: Sir Basil Zaharoff, Greek-born
arms salesman for Vickers, British arma-
ments and shipbuilding firm, and later one

of its directors; he owned shares, also, in
Schneider-Creusot [cf. 57 below] and sev-
eral other armaments firms. "That year"
seems to have been 1894, and the two South
American belligerents, mentioned in lines 1,
11, 13, 19-23, are Bolivia and Paraguay
[18:12].

3. the Pope: Achille Ratti, Pius XI. Pound
met him when he was subprefect at the
Vatican library (1911-1918).

4. **Mr. Joyce**: James J., Irish novelist.

5. **Marconi**: Marchese Guglielmo M., Italian engineer who perfected wireless telegraphy.

6. **Jimmy Walker**: Irish Catholic mayor of New York (1925-1932), involved in Tammany Hall scandals and accused of all kinds of political and religious hypocrisy.

7. **Lucrezia**: L. Borgia, sister of Cesare Borgia and daughter of Pope Alexander VI, who married Alfonso d'Este, heir to the Duke of Ferrara. Possibly she wanted the rabbit's foot as a charm against conception since she had "three children, five abortions, and died of the last" [30:8].

8. **(thus cigar-makers ... Kimball 1929)**: Dexter Kimball, op. cit., 79-80, verbatim; the context defends the routine manual task imposed by the division of labor on the ground that it leaves the mind free for thought.

9. **Don't buy ... etc.**: Sales ploy used by Zaharoff to governments of nations: he sold happily to both sides and liked war because it was good for business.

10. **Akers**: Fictional name for Vickers.

11. **gentle reader ... before**: Not in *The Cantos*; perhaps the "reader" is that of *NEW*, in which Pound first published Canto 38 and to which he had been contributing articles and letters during the year before the poem appeared.

12. **Mr. Whitney**: Richard W., New York banker and stockbroker.

13. **short sellin'**: Selling shares or commodities not yet owned in anticipation of a fall in price.

14. **two Afghans**: Five Afghans went to Europe in 1921 and signed a treaty with Soviet Russia; later that year a peace treaty signed with Great Britain restored the right of Afghanistan to import munitions through India. Committee work on the Geneva disarmament conference began in 1920, under the aegis of the League of Nations; preparation for the conference took 12 years; the conference itself ran from 1932 to 1934 and was never formally concluded.

15. **secretary of something ...**: Prob. Albert B. Fall, secretary of the interior, who in 1929 was found guilty of accepting bribes in 1922 to transfer government oil fields from the Navy Department to private oil companies. The action led to a Senate investigation and the resulting Teapot Dome scandal.

16. **In the name ... this date**: In 1901 William Knox d'Arcy, an Australian oil explorer, obtained from the shah of Persia the sole right to most of the Persian oil fields for 60 years; he founded the Anglo-Persian Oil Company, in which both Zaharoff and the British government later took an interest and which Zaharoff used to help penetrate the French oil market.

17. **Mr. Mellon**: Andrew M., American banker who was secretary of the treasury at the time of the Wall Street crisis (1929); in 1932 President Hoover (1928-1932) made him ambassador to Great Britain to provide him a graceful exit from the treasury, but his term expired with Hoover's.

18. **Mr. Wilson ... prostatitis**: Admiral Grayson, Wilson's personal doctor, who lived at the White House and attended Wilson until his death, has a chapter in his book (*Wilson*) on the president's medical history. Minor diseases such as measles and hemorrhoids are mentioned as well as major ones such as neuritis and phlebitis. Prostatitis is not.

19. **new Messiah**: A label applied to President Wilson who was received with great acclaim in both England and France for his visionary stands in the conferences following World War I which led to the Treaty of Versailles.

20. **Her Ladyship**: Emerald Cunard, 1872-1948, née Maud Burke, usually referred to as

"Her Ladyship" by her daughter, Nancy Cunard.

21. Jenny: Pseudonym for Nancy Cunard, 1896-1965, contemporary American poet and patron of the arts.

22. Ipswich, Agot: Prob. Margot Asquith, 1864-1945, second wife of Herbert Henry A., 1st Earl of Oxford and Asquith, British statesman; prime minister, 1908-1916. The countess was a celebrated London wit whose autobiography became such a *succès de scandale* in 1920-1922 that she went on to write a novel and several volumes of reminiscences, including *Places and Persons* (1925) and *More Memories* (1933).

23. And that year: 1914, when World War I began.

24. louse in Berlin: Kaiser Wilhelm II of Germany.

25. François Giuseppe: Franz-Josef, emperor of Austria.

26. Will there . . . May 1914: An anecdote prob. relating to Violet Hunt, English novelist who lived with, and later married, Ford Madox Ford. Pound saw them frequently when he lived in London before and during the war.

27. Mr. Gandhi: Mohandas Karamchand G., 1869-1948, Indian religious and political leader and architect of his country's independence from the British (1947).

28. if we don't buy . . . : I.e., armaments and cotton cloth from the British. Gandhi's idea was that the money so saved could be spent on food and the cause of peace.

29. Monsieur Untel: F, "Mr. So-and-so."

30. Jockey Club: A smart social club in Paris; cf. Pound, "By All Means Be Patriotic," *NEW*, I, 25 (Oct. 6, 1932), 589: "When somebody, for purely social reasons, hunts up Mr Whatshisname, the French toy-maker, and doesn't find him in the Jockey Club, but does ultimately locate him

in Japan, some weeks before the Manchurian shindy, this either is, or ought to be, news."

31. Mitsui: Japanese holding company whose interests include shipping and armaments; one Mitsui company was a subsidiary of Vickers; also the name of a (related) central bank in Japan.

32. "The wood . . . gunstocks": J. Q. Adams experimented with black walnut seedlings [*Diary*, 374-375, 551]; he also recorded a visit to the Springfield, MA, armory, where "we saw the various processes of making the gun-barrels and the black walnut gun-stocks" [ibid., 552; 34:58].

33. Muscou: Moscow (cf. F, Moscou).

34. Italian marshes: The Pontine Marshes, drained and reclaimed by the Fascists, one of the projects that inclined Pound to favor Fascist social programs.

35. Tiberius: T. Claudius Nero Caesar, 42 B.C. to A.D. 37, 2d Roman emperor. He was adopted as the heir of Emperor Augustus and succeeded him without difficulty in A.D. 14. Pound sees him as an intellectual: "And there are Italian intellectuals, and from the time of Tiberius the Italian intelligentzia has been *talking* about draining the swamps" [*J/M*, 23].

36. Beebe: Charles William B., American zoologist who dived to a record depth in a bathysphere in 1934; his book, *Beneath Tropic Seas*, is a beautifully written description of tropical fish.

37. Rivera: Miguel Primo de R. y Orbaneja, Marqués de Estella; his dictatorship (1923-1930) of Spain, based on the Italian model, was supported by the king.

38. Infante: Prob. eldest son of last king of Spain, Alfonso XIII, who supported Rivera's revolution.

39. gothic type . . . type: Cf. Pound, "Orientation and New Sense," *NEW*, II, 12 (Jan. 5, 1933), 273-274: "Vienna is tragicomic. . . . Herr Baur [Otto Bauer, Austrian Social Democrat and advocate of the Anschluss, the political merger of Austria and Germany] is (or was a few months ago) still printing his 'advance guard' journal in Gothic type. And they explained to me at the party headquarters . . . that they kept this type because the old people were used to it. Every shop sign in Vienna that is intended to be read, to convey information to the by-passer that something in particular is for sale, is printed in Roman or block letters."

40. Schlossmann: Unidentified, but prob. a U.S. correspondent Pound met in Vienna in 1928. The Anschluss refers to Hitler's attempts and final success in forming a political union with Austria. Some, but not many, Austrians were against the union.

41. Baluba: Should read Biembe; refers to an incident between an African tribe and the German anthropologist Leo Frobenius, whom Pound was reading and admiring in the early thirties; the tribe threatened to attack Frobenius's party, but were deterred by a thunderstorm; next morning Frobenius's interpreters heard the tribe refer, in a drum signal, to the "white man who made the thunderstorm in Biemba"; but Frobenius [op. cit., V, 53] says: "Der Weisse, der in Biembe das Gewitter gemacht hat" [cf. EH, *Pai*, 1-1, 85].

42. The country: Presumably Austria; this and the "Schlossmann" episode appear to be private reminiscences. The "hungarian nobleman" is prob. Bernhard Deutsch [35:25].

43. Kosouth: Ferenc Kossuth, 1841-1914, leader of Hungarian Independence Party.

44. losing the Tyrol: The Austrians lost the Tyrol to Italy in the peace settlement following World War I.

45. Frobenius: Leo F., 1873-1938, German cultural anthropologist whom Pound met in 1927. F. spent some 17 years doing fieldwork all over Africa and knew Africans from

the Mediterranean to the far reaches of the south. Pound preferred Frobenius's work to Frazer's. In a letter to T. S. Eliot, 1940, he said: "However, for yr. enlightenment, Frazer worked largely from documents. Frob. went to *things*, memories still in the spoken tradition, etc." [*L*, 336]. Frobenius became even more important to the Africans. Leopold Senghor, African poet and first president of Senegal (from 1960), said: "For no one did more than Frobenius to reveal Africa to the world and the Africans to themselves" [*Leo Frobenius*, ed. Erik Haberland, VI].

46. Bruhl: Lucien Lévy-B., professor of philosophy at the Sorbonne (1899-1927), took an interest in the "prelogical mentality" of primitive peoples and paid close attention to the details of their languages. Pound's summary may be a paraphrase of Lévy-Bruhl [op. cit., 125-127], but Pound "improves" the thesis to fit his aesthetic theory more closely; Lévy-Bruhl argues, not that natives are incapable of generalization, but that they generalize according to different criteria from those of modern Europeans, including traditional anthropologists like Sir James Frazer.

47. Romeo and Juliet: Pseudonyms given to cover a contemporary death and suicide case Pound knew about. Newspaper (or other) cutting unknown.

48. Mr. Blodgett: Prob. Lorin B., American economist; his prediction may appear in his book, *The Textile Industries of Phildelphia*.

49. Douglas: Clifford Hugh D., 1879-1952, British engineer and economist who founded Social Credit, an economic system championed by Pound, published in *NEW* a five-part essay answering some of his academic critics. "The New and Old Economics" ran in *NEW*, II, nos. 6-10; Pound's "I have of course . . . prices at large" is drawn from the first installment of the essay [Nov. 24, 1932, 126-127]. Douglas wrote: "I have, of course, never said that the cash (by which in Great Britain is meant not merely 'till' money, but deposits of the Joint Stock Banks with the Bank of England) is constant in amount no matter what may be the amount of deposits which the banks acquire as the result of creating loans. The ratio of cash to loans . . . is simply a result of an actuarial estimate of the percentage of 'till' money in a given country which is required to meet the ordinary habits of the population. On August 4, 1914, as a result of a panic, the population of Great Britain suddenly demanded cash for an unusual proportion of its deposits, with the result that, in the ordinary meaning of the word, all the banks became bankrupt simultaneously. When the depositors had drawn out all the *cash*, about eight hundred millions of *deposits* remained, which were only satisfied by printing Treasury notes."

50. A factory . . . large: These 19 lines, taken from Douglas's paraphrase of his A & B theorem in "Credit Power and Democracy" [21-23], form his central critique of the capitalist system of distribution.

51. per forza: I, "by force."

52. and the light . . . bewildered: [*Par.* XXVIII, 16-19]: "Un punto vidi che raggiava lume / Acuto sì, che'l viso ch'egli affuoca / Chiuder conviensi per lo forte acume" ["I saw a point of light so sharp that I had to close the eyes it burned, so strong was it"].

53. Herr Krupp: Alfred K., 1812-1887, who took over his father's small Prussian foundry and turned it into one of the largest steel and armaments firms in the world; Krupp started making musket barrels and breastplates in 1843 and produced his first cannon four years later.

54. 1847 orders . . . Crimea: Krupp built his first cannon in 1847 [cf. above] and in 1855 took a larger version of it to the Paris Exhibition; Emperor Napoleon III ["Barbiche"] made Krupp a knight of the Legion of Honor, but no one bought his cannon until 1857, when the viceroy of Egypt

ordered 36. By that time Krupp had already sold gun bores to France and later supplied guns to both Britain and Russia for the Crimean War, 1854-1856 [Brockway, 53-55].

55. Pietro il Grande: I, Peter the Great (1672-1725); czar of the Russians (1682-1725). An honor and decoration bestowed upon Herr Krupp by the Russian government was the Order of Peter the Great.

56. Command . . . Honour: At another Paris world's fair, 1867, Krupp was made an officer of the Legion of Honor.

57. Creusot: Schneider-Creusot, French steel and armaments firm.

58. Sadowa: Battle of Sadowa, also called Königgrätz, between the Austrian and Prussian forces in 1866.

59. The Emperor . . . Schneider: In 1868 Krupp sent Napolean III a catalogue "exhibiting steel cannon which I have supplied to *several powerful European Governments*" [his italics]; the reply, which Pound summarizes, came from General Leboeuf, a relative of the Schneider family; despite the gracious tone, the sale was not made [Brockway, 56-57].

60. Leboeuf: Edmond Leboeuf (1809-1888), French statesman, minister of war (1869-1870), marshal of France (1870); disgraced in Franco-Prussian War.

61. Schneider: Joseph Eugène S., 1805-1875.

62. operai: I, "workers."

63. 53 . . . country: The figures are from Brockway [58].

64. Bohlem und Halbach: Gustav Krupp von Bohlen und Halbach (Alfred Krupp's son-in-law) took the family name and directed the firm during World War I.

65. Herr Schneider: Charles-Prosper-Eugène S., grandson of Joseph Eugène Schneider, directed Schneider-Creusot during World

War I when the firm dominated French armaments production.

66. Eugene, Adolf: Joseph Eugène and Adolphe Schneider, brothers who established the Schneider company in 1836.

67. Alfred: A. Pierrot Deseilligny, 1828-1875, son-in-law of Joseph Eugène Schneider and comanager of the iron works with Henri Schneider, son of Joseph Eugène.

68. Soane et Loire: I.e., he was a member for Saône-et-Loire, the region in France in which the city of Le Creusot is situated.

69. always . . . a conservative: Charles-Prosper-Eugène Schneider was also a conservative deputy for Saône-et-Loire.

70. Schools . . . children: Established by the Schneiders for their workers at Le Creusot; Krupp's, too, built housing, schools, bars, public baths, a church, and a cemetery for their workers; even Zaharoff financed homes for soldiers and sailors in France.

71. Herr Henri: Prob. H. de Wendel, director, with his brother Robert, of an old French steel company that cooperated with the Schneiders in 1880 to build a steel mill capable of processing the phosphorus-heavy iron ore of Lorraine.

72. Chantiers de la Gironde: Shipyard in Bordeaux partly owned by the Schneiders.

73. Bank of the Paris Union: Partly owned by the Schneiders; Eugène was its director. Zaharoff, too, owned shares in it.

74. franco-japanese bank: Eugène Schneider was on its board.

75. François de Wendel: Son of Henri, president of the Comité des Forges, the powerful French industrialists' union, of which the Schneiders' company was the most important member.

76. Robert Protot: Prob. R. Pinot, secretary-general of the Comité des Forges in World War I, serving under the presidency of François de Wendel; author of *Le Comité des Forges de France au service de la nation (Août, 1914–Novembre, 1918).*

77. 'And God . . . Hawkwood: Sir John de H., 14th-century English mercenary captain who finally settled in Florence. An Italian story tells of two mendicant friars greeting Hawkwood with their customary "Monsignor, God give you peace," to which he answered, "and God take your living from you, too"; when questioned about his rebuff to their benevolence, he replied: "How can you believe you wish me well when you come to me and say, may God make you die of hunger? Don't you know that I live by war, and that peace would undo me?" [cf. Sacchetti, *Le Novelle*, 181; *SR*, 70];

78. Journal des Débats: French nationalist newspaper in which François de Wendel had a controlling interest.

79. Le Temps: French popular newspaper in which François de Wendel had a controlling interest.

80. Echo de Paris: French newspaper that campaigned vigorously against disarmament after World War I; Brockway claims [159] the paper received several large "gifts" from armaments firms to finance the campaign: In "Orientation and New Sense" [*NEW*, II, 12, 273-274] Pound says that the *La Stampa* articles "explain why the 'Comité des Forges' can afford to pay out subsidies measured by the million in francs to the 'Temps,' 'Journal des Debats,' "Echo de Paris,' 'Ordre,' etc."

81. Polloks: Unidentified.

82. Mitsui: [cf. 31 above].

83. "faire passer . . . la nation": F, "to put these matters before those of the nation."

CANTO XXXIX

Sources

Homer, *Od.* X; *Pervigilium Veneris* [Loeb]; Ovid, *Meta.* XIII, XIV; Dante, *Par.* XXIII, 129, XXX, 62; Catullus XXXIV; Virgil, *Aeneid* VI; *Lyra Graeca* [Loeb], 11, 84; 14th-century lyric, "Alisoun"; *Odyssey*, Latin trans. by Clark and Ernestus, 1804.

Background

EP, "Translators of Greek: Early Translators of Homer," *LE*, 249-275.

Exegeses

EP, *SP*, 53; FR, "A Man of No Fortune," in *Motive*; DP, *Barb*, 161-164 and passim; Dekker, *Cantos*, 171-172 and passim; Surette, *Pai*, 3-2, 204, 211.

Glossary

1. the cat: Conflation of three memories: (1) the sound of the looms on the hill path leading up from Rapallo; (2) the guard railing at Lake Garda; and (3), most important, the sound of Circe's loom overheard by Odysseus's men as they approached her house of "polished stone" [*Od.* X, 211].

2. song: "They heard Circe singing with sweet voice, as she went to and fro before a great imperishable web" [*Od.* X, 221-223].

3. ingle: Gaelic, "chimney corner." The "I" is taken to refer to Elpenor [1:12].

4. Circe: Elpenor seems to be remembering scenes in Circe's house after Odysseus and his men had fallen into her snares. Thus we have a flashback to events that took place before the exodus dramatized in Canto I.

5. panthers etc.: *Od.* lists "mountain wolves and lions."

6. tisane: F, "a decoction of herbs."

7. Kaka . . . edóken: H, "She gave them evil drugs" [*Od.* X, 213].

8. lukoi . . . leontes: H, "mountain wolves and lions" [*Od.* X, 212].

9. Helios: H, Apollo, god of light, father of Circe.

10. Perseis: H, Perse, mother of Circe and Pasiphaë [*Od.* X, 138-140].

11. Pasiphae: Pasiphaë, sister of Circe who became wife of Minos, king of Crete, and mother of the Minotaur.

12. Venter . . . cultrix: L, "Belly beautiful, cunny tender."

13. Ver . . . novum: L, "New spring singing, new spring." From *Pervigilium Veneris* [Loeb, 348].

14. KALON AOIDIAEI: H, "She sings beautifully." So Polites describes Circe's voice [*Od.* X, 227].

15. e theos ... thasson: H, "either a goddess or a woman ... let us quickly call to her" [*Od.* X, 228]. Last line of Polites' speech.

16. honey ... acorns: Details of what Circe fed the men before and after she administered the "evil drugs" [*Od.* X, 233-243].

17. illa ... vocem: L, "She hushed with grief, and her voice likewise." Hecuba's reaction to the death of her last child, Polydorus, whose corpse is washed ashore [*Meta.* XIII, 538 ff.].

18. Ἀλλ' ... Περσεφόνεια: H, "But first you must complete another journey, and come to the house of Hades and dread Persephone, to seek soothsaying of the Theban Teiresias, the blind seer, whose mind abides steadfast. To him even in death Persephone has granted reason, that he alone should have understanding" [*Od.* X, 490-494]. Pound does not give the last line he indicated in margin.

19. Hathor: Egyptian fertility goddess, usually imaged as either a cow or a cow and woman combined.

20. Mava: Unidentified.

21. Che mai ... diletto: I, "So that never will the delight part from me" [*Par.* XXIII, 129, where past tense ("did part") is used in talking of heavenly bliss].

22. Fulvida di folgore: I, "dark [or reddish yellow] in its splendor [lightning]" [*Par.* XXX, 62]; *fulvido* describes the light (*lume*) shaped like a river in a spring setting.

23. Glaucus: G. of Anthedon. Made immortal by a magic herb, he jumped into the sea and became a sea-god famous for gift of prophecy.

24. nec ivi ... sum: L, "Nor went I to the pigsty / Nor into the pigsty did I enter." Since Eurylochus did not enter the house of Circe, as did the rest of his men, he was free to report back to Odysseus [*Od.* X, 255-260]. Pound uses *harum* rather than *haram*

for "pigsty" because the word occurs thus in his source: Clark and Ernestus Latin version, 1st printing, 1804 [cf. *LE*, 249 ff.].

25. Euné ... Kirkh: H, "Making love in bed, said Circe." Pound elides *Od.* X, 335-336, and transliterates the Greek *eta* as *h* in Circe's name.

26. es thalamon: H, "into the bedroom" [*Od.* X, 340].

27. Eurilochus: Odysseus's lieutenant who led first party of men to explore Circe's island [1:4].

28. Macer: Prob. Macareus, a companion of Eurylochus's [*Meta.* XIV, 223 ff.].

29. Kirke: H, Circe.

30. "I think ...": What Circe says when her evil drug and wand did not work on Odysseus [*Od.* X, 330].

31. feel better ... past: [*Od.* X, 460-465].

32. Ad Orcum ... pervenit: L, "Has anyone ever been to hell in a black ship?" [*Od.* X, 502].

33. Sumus ... sub nocte: L, "We have the protection / and girls, let us sing / beneath the night" [cf. Catullus XXXIV, 1-4, for two lines and *Aeneid* VI, 268, for the last line]. These lines start a celebration of the "rites of spring" or the rebirth of the god in the vegetation rites.

34. Flora: Roman goddess of fertility and flowers.

35. ERI ... KUDONIAI: H, "In the spring the quinces," first words of a fragment by Ibycus [*Lyra Graeca*, II, fr. 1, 84; *OBGV*, no. 164]. The line is used as epigraph to "The Spring" [*P*, 87].

36. Betuene .... Merche: From 14th-century lyric "Alisoun": "Bytuene Marsh and Averil / When spray beginneth to spring."

37. Goddess: Aphrodite.

38. Circeo: A mountain near Terracina which forms N arm of a bay on W coast of Italy.

39. Terracina: Seaport in C Latium, SE of Pontine Marshes (some 5 miles S of Circeo), where the ruins of a temple to Jupiter still stand. In "Credo" Pound wrote: "Given the material means I would replace the statue of Venus on the cliffs of Terracina" [*SP*, 53].

40. "Fac deum! ... Est Factus": L, "Make god! . . .He is made."

41. Ver novum!: L, "new Spring!" [cf. 13 above].

42. A traverso le foglie: I, "through the leaves."

43. sic ... nupta: L, "So the bride speaks / So the bride sings."

CANTO XL

Sources

Lewis Corey, *The House of Morgan* [*Morgan*], New York, 1930; *The Periplus of Hanno*, trans. Wilfred A. Schoff, 1912.

Background

Davis R. Dewey, *Financial History of the United States*, New York, 1922; EP, "Civilization, Money and History," *SP*, 187-355; *GK*, 227.

Exegeses

CFT, *Pai*, 1-2, 223 ff.; WB, *Rose*; Davis, *Vision*, 62-67, 128-130; DP, *Barb*, 165-166.

Glossary

1. Smith, Adam: Adam S., 1723-1790, Scottish economist; author of *Inquiry into the Nature and Causes of the Wealth of Nations* (1776). Pound discusses this oft-quoted squib from Smith in several places; e.g., "The Trade Unions are naïve seekers of plunder offering no solution, but presenting rather an extended demonstration of Adam Smith's basis of 'Economics' to the effect that 'Men of the same trade . . .' " [*SP*, 209].

2. Independent use . . . : The general thesis of those who were against the Bank of the United States [37:33], as well as the theses of those who founded the Sienese bank [42:9].

3. De banchis . . . : ML, "From the exchange mart" [the word should be *banchiis*].

4. Venice 1361: The event in Venice for the year referred to here is not known.

5. Toward producing: The vision of seigneurial splendor which motivated the robber barons who desired to create a financial "royalty" with all the trappings; "undsoweiter": G, "and so forth."

6. Peabody: George P., 1795-1869, a shrewd yankee who made a fortune in commercial ventures but finally went into banking and international finance with headquarters in London. In 1854 Junius Spencer Morgan became a partner in the firm, Peabody and Co., which, upon George Peabody's retirement in 1863, became J. S. Morgan and Co., the origin of the house of Morgan. Peabody and Co. were several times racked by the severe financial panics that occurred every few years in the U.S., and were almost wrecked by the panic of 1857. During that year money could be secured only through the Bank of England. "Junius Morgan . . . negotiated with the Bank for a loan of £800,000 and was crushed by the answer: The Bank would make the loan providing Peabody & Co., agreed to cease business in London after 1858. But George Peabody was a fighter; he dared the Bank to cause his failure, mobilized powerful British support, received the loan and survived the crisis" [*Morgan*, cf. 21 below].

7. D'Arcy: William Knox d'A. [38:16].

8. '62 report . . . : During the Civil War a "committee of the House of Representatives in 1862 reported large frauds in the purchase of ordnance. . . . J. Pierpont Morgan appeared in a case as financing the sale to the government of the government's own arms at an extortionate profit. The facts are in the Congressional Reports, 'Case No. 97' " [*Morgan*, 58-59].

9. Morgan: John Pierpont M., 1837-1913, built the family fortune into a vast network of holding companies and demonstrated the supremacy of finance over industry and commerce as well as over the U.S. government. He developed vast interlocking directorates which reached across the whole industrial world. Pound's source [*Morgan*, passim] demonstrates that Morgan's operations, though often crooked or downright

corrupt, sometimes gave him the power to assist the nation during financial crises, but they were crises that the house of Morgan had helped to create.

10. forcing up gold: "The price of gold was intimately affected by military events" [*Morgan*, 65]. Gold speculation, however, was considered unpatriotic; it was practiced in a place called the Coal Hole, "a dark, repulsive basement" [ibid]. Morgan with all his foreign connections was in an excellent spot: "In one spectacular coup forcing up the price of gold, Morgan and an accomplice reaped a profit of $160,000–" [*Morgan*, 66].

11. After Gettysburg: With "unscrupulous" partners, Morgan took advantage of the Civil War emergency to reap vast profits in gold speculation. If the South seemed to be winning, the price of gold would rise: "Early in 1863 gold was selling at 163. A series of Union victories produced considerable price declines. The Gettysburg victory sent the price down five points in one day" [*Morgan*, 66-67].

12. Bulls . . . : The New York *Times* ascribed "the enormous and unprincipled speculation in gold" to "a knot of unscrupulous gamblers who care nothing for the credit of the country." It was urged that "Congress at once order the erection of scaffolds for hanging" them. But Morgan and his henchmen had it both ways. Concludes Corey: "The speculators were bulls on gold and bears on the Union" [*Morgan*, 69].

13. Business . . . : Congress attempted to curb or control the speculation and passed the Gold Bill in 1864. But the bankers screamed that the bill was "only one more instance of the utter lawlessness of Congress" [*Morgan*, 70]. The bill did not work, for the money-making facts of life were clear to many big businessmen: If business prospered because of war failures, then war failures would have to go on [*Morgan* 66-73].

14. If a nation: A sort of summary statement of Pound's money pamphlets [cf. *SP*, 187-355].

15. Boutwell: George S. B., 1818-1905, of Massachusetts; secretary of the treasury (1869-1873). Boutwell's policy was to refinance the government debt, created during the Civil War at high interest rates, by a new issue of bonds, some as low as 4 percent [cf. Dewey, *Financial History*, 352 ff.]. Boutwell would have liked the treasury to sell directly to the public. "The Ways and Means Committee of the House of Representatives held meetings on the new loan, there being considerable sentiment in Congress for the direct sale of bonds by the Treasury." But the bankers won. "Levi Morton, appearing for the Morton syndicate . . ., [said] 'I do not know of any other method of negotiating a government loan except by bankers' " [*Morgan*, 119-120].

16. Republican party: Some big financiers gave large sums to the Republican party in the hope that by "sweetening up" politicians they would get government business, but they discovered that politicians were "as unreliable as their principles." Morgan made no such mistake; he was "contemptuous of politics and politicians," though he kept on "contributing generously to the Republican party" [*Morgan*, 119].

17. Beecher: Henry Ward B., 1813-1887, Congregational minister who achieved national fame by using his pulpit in Brooklyn as a political platform from which to discuss important questions of the day. He was an abolitionist, preached woman suffrage, and was converted to the theory of evolution. Later on, however, he became the tool of reactionaries. Says Corey: "Henry Ward Beecher, himself the recipient of $20,000 a year and whose church had been organized as a profit-making enterprise by real-estate speculators, sermonized against labor amid the applause of Plymouth's congregation." Said Beecher: " 'Is the great working class oppressed? Yes, undoubtedly it is. God had intended the great to be great and the little to be little. . . The trade union, originated under the European system, destroys liberty. . . . I do not say that a dollar a day is enough to support a working-

man. But it is enough to support a man! Not enough to support a man and five children if a man insist on smoking and drinking beer. . . . But the man who cannot live on bread and water is not fit to live' " [*Morgan* 123-124].

18. Belmont: August B., 1816-1890, head of one of the largest financial houses, August Belmont and Co. He dealt in international money markets and often represented in the U.S. the house of Rothschild, Morgan's competitor in international money markets. In 1876 Morgan's company organized a syndicate to secure "a government issue of $5,883,000 5% bonds against the competition of August Belmont representing the Rothschilds." Morgan won [*Morgan*, 124].

19. specie payment: The banking community after the Civil War made a great killing by defeating the Greenback party, which wanted to pay the national debt in greenbacks rather than to resume the redemption of Civil War Bonds in gold. "As after the Revolution redemption of the worthless paper currency enriched a clique of speculators . . ., so the resumption of specie payments enriched a small group of bondholders—while depression oppressed the people" [*Morgan*, 125].

20. stock subscription: Stock manipulation, "watering," in the financing of railroads was dominated by banking buccaneers: "The buccaneers plundered investors as much as they plundered business and the public. . . . In 1876, railroad bonds in default represented 39 percent of the total" [*Morgan*, 145].

21. Corey: Lewis C., pseudonym for Louis C. Fraina, 1894-1953, political scientist and author of numerous books, including *The House of Morgan*, 1930. The central institution in London is the Bank of England.

22. Pujo: Arsène Paulin P., 1861-1939, American lawyer and legislator, chairman of the House Committee on Banking and Currency (1911-1913) and head of the money-trust investigations that led to the formation of the Federal Reserve Bank.

23. Mr. Morgan: Samuel Untermeyer directed the investigation of the money trust for the Pujo committee. He asked J. P. Morgan, who appeared before the committee, " 'Do you approve of short selling?' Morgan: 'I never did it in my life, that I know of' " [*Morgan*, 405]. Earlier Corey writes: "J. P. Morgan & Co. were in shipshape condition to meet the crisis [1907 panic] having learned from the experience of 1903-4 to maintain a high degree of liquidity in their resources" [*Morgan*, 342].

24. Mr. Baker: George Fisher B., 1840-1931, one of the founders of the First National Bank of New York and closely associated with the house of Morgan. " . . .Baker . . .unquestioningly accepted Morgan's authority" [in measures taken to meet the 1907 panic]. Morgan told his son later: " 'Of course, you see, it could not have been done without Mr. Baker; he is always ready to do his share—and more' " [*Morgan*, 343].

25. government's arms: Pound cites this anecdote in his economic writings: "The great Morgan, during the Civil War, bought on credit a certain quantity of damaged rifles from the War Department in Washington, and sold them to a Military Command in Texas, and was paid by the latter before he had to pay the former" [*SP*, 171; cf. 8 above].

26. Ionides: Prob. Luke Ionides. Pound wrote: "Note, when I got to London the men who were old *enough* were all right. Col. Jackson, Luke Ionides represented something hearty, pre-Victorian, they had something that Palmerston might have recognized as appertaining to men" [*GK*, 227].

27. Palladio: Andrea P., 1518-1580, Italian architect who adapted the principles of Roman architecture to the requirements of the Renaissance. These eight lines are a reprise of the motivation of the great robber barons and a list of the trivial things they

used their money to buy. These items of conspicuous consumption imply a cultural wasteland. The list is as significant for what it does not include as for what it does [note echoes of the 2d baronet, 28/139].

28. AGALMA: H, ἄγαλμα, "ornament" or "statue" or any beautiful object.

29. ormoulu: F, *or moulu*, "ormolo," brass made to imitate gold.

30. brocatelli: I, "types of brocade."

31. HANNO: Ca. 470 B.C. The Carthaginian navigator who led an expedition through the Strait of Gibraltar and founded seven towns on the Atlantic shore of Morocco. The account of his voyage is *The Periplus of Hanno*. Although Hanno was a common name in Carthage at the time, a consensus says that this Hanno was either the father or the son of the Hamilcar who led the expedition to Sicily ca. 470 B.C. All but the last six of the remaining lines of Canto 40 are adapted from *The Voyage of Hanno, King of the Carthaginians*, trans. Schoff [*CFT*, *Pai*, 1-2, 223 ff.].

32. pillars of Herakles: Strait of Gibraltar.

33. 60 ships . . . provision: The source reads: "And he set forth with sixty ships of fifty oars, and a multitude of men and women, to the number of thirty thousand, and with wheat and other provisions" [cf. ibid. for this quote and all those below for Canto 40]. Pound gets the idea of Phoenician cities from his source: "It pleased the Carthaginians that Hanno should voyage outside the Pillars of Hercules, and found cities of the Libyphoenicians."

34. Gibel Tara: Gibraltar.

35. Thumiatehyon: The first city Hanno founded, identified as "Mehedia at mouth of Sbou River."

36. Solois: Prob. Cape Cantin.

37. Entha hieron P.: H, "there a temple of Poseidon."

38. Karikon, etc.: The Phoenician cities founded by Hanno.

39. Lixos: The river at which Hanno stopped and also the town, the modern Larache.

40. High Libya: Roughly present-day Algeria.

41. lixitae: Name of the nomadic people who lived on the banks of the river.

42. aethiopians etc.: Source reads: "Above these folk lived unfriendly Aethiopians, dwelling in a land full of wild beasts, and shut off by great mountains, from which they say the Lixus flows, and on the mountains live men of various shapes, cave-dwellers, who, as the Lixitae say, are fleeter of foot than horses."

43. Cyrne: Island of Cerne, or Herne, in the mouth of the Rio de Oro.

44. Xrestes: The modern St. Jean River.

45. West Horn: The modern Bay of Bissau, chief port of Portugese Guinea.

46. fires etc.: Source reads: " . . . we came to a great bay. . . . In it there was a large island, and within the island a lake of the sea, in which there was another island. Landing there during the day, we saw nothing but forests, but by night many burning fires, and we heard the sound of pipes and cymbals,

and the noise of drums and a great uproar. The fear possessed us, and the soothsayers commanded us to leave the island."

47. One pillar etc.: Source reads: "After a journey of four days, we saw the land at night covered with flames. And in the midst there was one lofty fire, greater than the rest which seemed to touch the stars. By day this was seen to be a very high mountain, called Chariot of the Gods."

48. carroch: I, *carroccio*, "flag car of an army" or "chariot."

49. Gorillas etc.: Source reads: " . . . the interpreters called them *Gorillae*. When we pursued them we were unable to take any of the men; for they all escaped, by climbing the steep places and defending themselves with stones; but we took three of the women, who bit and scratched their leaders, and would not follow us. So we killed them and flayed them, and brought their skins to Carthage. For we did not voyage further, provisions failing us." Thus ends the last section of *The Voyage of Hanno*.

50. baily: Bail, the outer walls of a feudal castle or the court thereby enclosed.

51. NOUS: H, νους, "mind, intellect, spirit."

52. Karxèdonión . . .: H, "the King of the Carthaginians."

CANTO XLI

Sources

EP, *J/M*; EP, *GK*; Wilhelm Baur, *Geschichts-und Lebensbilder aus der Erneuerung des religiösen Lebens in den deutschen Befreiungskriegen*, 2 vols., Hamburg, 1864; Andrew Lipscomb and Albert Bergh, eds., *The Writings of Thomas Jefferson*, V, IX, Washington, D.C., 1905; George Seldes, *Iron, Blood, and Profits*, New York and London, 1934.

Background

EP, *A Visiting Card*, 15; *SP*, 314, 325; NS, *Life*, 306.

Exegeses

Davis, *Vision*, 130-131; DP, *Barb*, 140-141; WB, *Rose*, 88, 141; Knight, *Pai*, 5-1, 83.

Glossary

1. Ma questo . . . è divertente: I [Romagnol dial.], "But this is amusing."

2. Boss: Benito Mussolini, 1883-1945, Italian founder of fascism and head of government (1922-1945). Pound met M. on January 30, 1933, at the Palazzo Venezia. While leafing through *A Draft of XXX Cantos*, M. made the above remark. Pound probably took politeness to indicate quick comprehension by a genius [NS, *Life*, 306].

3. Vada: Village in Livorno Province, Tuscany, C Italy. Its nearby swamps were drained by M. and planted to crops. Pound wrote: ". . . from the time of Tiberius the Italian intelligentsia has been *talking* about draining the swamps" [*J/M*, 23]. Hence the line: "Waited 2000 years . . ." [38:35].

4. Circeo: Town near Vada.

5. vani: I, "rooms." Accomplishments of M.'s leadership: increased housing and the water supply.

6. XI of our era: The 11th year of the Fascist state, 1933.

7. mezzo-yit: I, Yiddish, "half (or rotten) Jew." *Mezzo* can mean either "half" or "rotten." The anecdote seems to show that the person telling it is partly of M.'s [and Pound's] opinion that such "consortiums" formed by "hoggers of harvest" are not for the public good. In time a "yit" in Pound comes to mean one guilty of "usurious" practices. In 1933 it seems to have had another meaning.

8. confine: I, "border" or "boundary." The meaning of this word in context is unclear. Perhaps "confino" was intended, or possibly Pound used an incorrect plural. Around 1933, he wrote: "Get it into your head that Italy was, even in 1900, immeasurably ahead of England in so far as land laws and the rights of the man who works on the soil are concerned. Some of the follies and cruelties of great English owners would not now be permitted in Italy. Certain kinds of domestic enemy would be shipped to the *confino*" [*J/M*, 70]. The context here suggests a prison or concentration camp.

9. Noi ci facciam sgannar . . . : I, "We would let ourselves be butchered [*scannar*] for Mussolini." It was a hotelkeeper in Rimini who made this remark to Pound "years ago, thinking I knew nothing about the revolution and wanting to get it into my head." The hotelkeeper was also the *commandante della piazza*. He cut through red tape to help Pound see a manuscript he had come to Romagna to look at [*J/M*, 26].

10. commandante della piazza: I, "commander of the square." Title of a local official in Italian government.

11. "Popolo . . . ignorante!": I, "The people . . . ignorant!" Pound wrote: "Gigi aged two used to stand up on his chair after lunch and say 'Popolo ignorante!' as a sort of benediction, one day he added the personal note 'And the worst of all is my *nurse* [*donna*]' " [*J/M*, 53].

12. Messire Uzzano: Niccolò da U., d. 1432,

Florentine statesman, "a truly disinterested man" [21:20].

13. Orbe: Town in Vaud Canton, W Switzerland, on Orbe River.

14. Eleven hours . . . : Working hours and wages in pre-Fascist Italy, apparently when "the boss" [Mussolini] was young.

15. documento: I, "document."

16. Geschichte und Lebensbilder: G, "history and pictures of life."

17. Erneuerung des Religiosen Lebens: G, "revival of religious life."

18. In den Deutschen Befreiungskriegen: G, "In the German wars of liberation."

19. Wilhelm Baur: 1826-1897. Author of *Geschichts- und Lebensbilder aus der Erneuerung des religiösen Lebens in den deutschen Befreiungskriegen*, Hamburg, 1864.

20. Uhlan officer: Fritz von Unruh, 1885-1970, German playwright, poet, and novelist; officer in World War I.

21. Augusta Victoria: Augusta Viktoria von Schleswig-Holstein, 1858-1921, wife of last German emperor, Wilhelm II.

22. ordine, contrordine e disordine: I, "order, counterorder, and disorder."

23. una pace qualunque: I, "some kind of peace or other."

24. San Casciano: Hospital [?] in Val di Peas, town in Firenze Province, near Florence in C Italy.

25. Corriere di Domenica: I, *Sunday Courier*, a newspaper.

26. Hindenburg: Paul von H., 1847-1934; German general in command on E front early in World War I; president of Weimar Republic (1925-1934).

27. Fritz' father: Fritz's father was Karl von Unruh, German military officer [cf. 20 above].

28. Herr Nvon so Forth: Karl von Unruh.

29. Battle of Waffenschlag: Invented battle; G. *Waffle* = "weapon," and *schlag* = "strike."

30. Udine: City in NE Italy used in World War I as a military base for Italian operations against Austria; occupied by Austrian troops in October 1917.

31. Hun: Slang for "German."

32. french vacation: French leave, or AWOL: absent without leave.

33. Winston's mama: Jennie Jerome, [1854?-1951] who married Lord Randolph Henry Spencer Churchill in 1874 and became mother of Winston Churchill.

34. his cousin: Of Shane Leslie (1885-1971) Pound wrote: "Shane Leslie was greatly bedazzled by his stout cousin Winston. He wrote a book to tell it to dh' woild. Winston once said to Leslie apropos of thinking and having ideas (in the sense of making ideas for oneself): 'Don't waste your time making munitions, be a GUN and shoot off other people's munitions.' Leslie, as a journalist, of sorts, was overwhelmed by this brilliance. Both cousins are half-breed Americans, determined to succeed, just like the cheapest of Mr. Lorimer's heroes" [*J/M*, 64].

35. M. Crevel: René C., 1900-1935, French author who wrote *Les Pieds dans le Plat* (1933). Speaking of Crevel's work as a novelist and the work of poets such as Cros, Vlaminck, and Bunting, Pound wrote: " . . . it may be said that they are better than the foreign crap currently displayed [1941] on the bookstalls" [*SP*, 325].

36. Esperanza...: Esperanza (Duchess of Monte Putina), Lady Primrose (Marquise of Sussex), and Augusta (an Austrian archduchess) are the three principal characters in Crevel's *Les Pieds dans le Plat*.

37. Bill Yeats: William Butler Y.

38. Pig and Piffle: Prob. English journal *Sport and Country*.

39. Times: London *Times*.

40. censorship: Pound wrote: "As the Duce has pithily remarked: 'Where the Press is *"free"* it merely serves special interests' " [*J/M*, 41].

41. Cosimo First: C. de'Medici [21:9].

42. Monte dei Paschi: I, "the mountain of the pastures": Sienese bank founded in 1624 and still running. It was established by a grant from Ferdinand II of Tuscany and its credit was based upon the Sienese public lands: the pastures of Maremma. Pound refers to it by a number of names: Bank, Monte, Monte Nuovo, Monte Paschale, Mount, New Monte, New Mount, and New Mountain [42:7].

43. CH: C. H. Douglas [38:49].

44. Woergl: Wörgl, small town in Austrian Tyrol which in the early 1930s issued the form of stamp scrip proposed by Silvio Gesell and created a miniboom in the midst of the depression that surrounded it [cf. *A Visiting Card*, 15; *SP*, 314].

45. Vergennes: Charles Gravier, comte de V., 1717-1787, French statesman; minister of foreign affairs under Louis XVI (1774-1787) and during the years when Thomas Jefferson was U. S. ambassador to France. The anecdote is repeated from Canto 33 [cf. 33/154; Knight, *Pai*, 5-1, 83].

46. Mrs. Trist: Eliza House, friend of Jefferson who cared for his daughter while he was in Europe. In a letter to her from Paris, August 18, 1785, Jefferson wrote: "Indeed, it is difficult to conceive how so good a people ... should be rendered so ineffectual ... by one single curse,–that of a bad form of government.... Of twenty millions of people supposed to be in France, I am of opinion there are nineteen millions more wretched, more accursed in every circumstance of human existence than the most conspicuously wretched individual of the whole United States" [Jefferson, *Writings*, V, 81].

47. Public debt . . . Colonel Monroe: These 12 lines are excerpted from Jefferson's letter to Colonel James Monroe, the future president, who was U.S. ambassador to France in 1796 when Jefferson wrote: "Congress have risen....I had always conjectured, from such facts as I could get hold of, that our public debt was increasing about a million of dollars a year. You will see by Gallatin's speeches that the thing is proved. You will see further, that we are completely saddled and bridled, and that the bank is so firmly mounted on us that we must go where they will guide. They openly publish a resolution, that the national property being increased in value, they must by an increase of circulating medium furnish an adequate representation of it.... All the imported commodities are raised about fifty per cent. By the depreciation of the money.... Lands had risen within the vortex of the paper, and as far out as that can influence.... Mechanics here get from a dollar to a dollar and a half a day, yet are much worse off than at the old prices" [ibid., IX, 337-338].

48. Gallatin: At time of letter (TJ to Col. James Monroe, June 12, 1796), Gallatin was a member of House of Representatives [31:40].

49. 120 million german fuses . . . : The Krupp armaments firm in Germany sold its patented fuses to Germany, England, or to any country that would buy, during the years when it and other great companies such as Vickers in England and Schneider-Creusot in France, armed Europe for World War I. "After the war, Krupps, with cynical effrontery, sued the British firm for 123,000,000 shillings, one shilling royalty for each Krupp patent fuze (Kpz 96/94) used on the British hand grenades to kill German soldiers" [Seldes, *Iron, Blood, and Profits*, 69].

50. Jena: City in Thuringia, Germany.

51. Schneider Creusot: [38:57, 59].

52. Hatfield: Pseudonym for unknown person.

53. ad interim: L, "in the meantime" or "for the time being."

CANTOS XLII-XLV

Sources

Il Monte dei Paschi di Siena e le Aziende in Esso Riunite, 9 vols., ed. Narciso Mengozzi, Siena, 1891-1925; Herbert C. F. Bell, *Lord Palmerston*, London, 1936; Antonio Zobi, *Storia civile della Toscana dal MDCCXXXVII al MDCCCXLVIII*, 5 vols., Firenze, 1850-1852; MSS inedit. concerning Il Monte dei Paschi preserved in the Archivio di Stato, Palazzo Piccolomini, Siena [referred to as Archivio-Piccolomini].

Background

EP, *GK*; *Social Credit: An Impact*, London, 1935, 112, 115; *SP*, 61; *America, Roosevelt, and the Causes of the Present War*, London, 1951; "Civilization, Money and History," *SP*, 187-355; HK, *Era*.

Exegeses

John Drummond, "The Italian Background to *The Cantos*," in *Ezra Pound*, ed. Peter Russell, London, 1950; Giuseppe Galigani, "Montis Pascuorum," *Yale Literary Magazine*, 127 (1958), 18-23; JE, *Pai*, 4-3, 547; Witemeyer, *Pai*, 4-1, 85-88.

[Most of the glosses for Cantos 42, 43, and 44 (the Leopoldine Cantos) were written by Ben Kimpel and T. C. Duncan Eaves and were based on their detailed study of the sources published in *Pai*, 6-3; 7-1 & 2; 8-3].

Glossary Canto XLII

1. Palmerston: In 1863 the British prime minister, Lord Palmerston (1784-1865), wrote to the foreign minister, Lord John Russell (1792-1878), that though he was going to detain ironclads ordered by the Confederate States on the insistence of the American minister, Charles Francis Adams (1807-1886; "H" should read "F," as in the older Faber edition), he considered that the American demands should be resisted.

2. H.G.: The novelist Herbert George Wells (1866-1946) delighted Pound by asking why the monument of Queen Victoria was still allowed to stand in front of Buckingham Palace.

3. Lex salica: L, "the Salic law," a law in France that prevented women from succeeding to the throne. The Germanic law [*lex Germanica*], in England and other countries, permitted women to reign.

4. Antoninus: Antoninus Pius, Roman emperor, 137-161; Antoninus confirmed the fact that at sea the customary law of

Rhodes, designed by commercial interests, rather than Roman law, should be followed.

5. nell' anima: I, "in the mind or soul."

6. Illustrious College: the ruling magistracy of the Tuscan city of Siena, the Collegio de Balìa. Later in this canto Pound translates Balìa as "Bailey."

7. Monte: I, literally "mountain"; here a "fund of money" or a "bank."

8. banco di giro: I, "a bank for transfer of credits."

9. With paternal affection . . .: Like most of this canto and a good deal of the next two cantos, what follows is translated from *Il Monte dei Paschi di Siena e le Aziende in Esso Riunite*, 9 vols., Siena, 1891-1925. The document quoted in this passage is a report of the decisions of the General Council of Siena, March 4, 1622-23, in reference to the foundation of a new bank, Il Monte dei Paschi ["Mountain of the Pastures"], whose funding was guaranteed by the income from grasslands south of Siena.

10. S.A.: I, *Sua Altezza*, "Your Highness."

11. dei ministri: I, "of the administrators."

12. scudo: I, coin, usually translated as "crown."

13. id est, piú [piu] utilmente: L, I, "that is, most usefully."

14. contrade: I, "the divisions of a city."

15. Loco Signi: L, "Place of the Sign." The original reads *Loco Sigilli*, "Place of the Seal."

16. cross: The source actually has a cross for the seal in the margin.

17. benché [benchè]: I, "however."

18. idem: L, "the same."

19. Consules, Iudices: L, "Consuls, Judges."

20. pro serenissimo: I, "for the most serene" [the Most Serene Grand Duke of Tuscany, Ferdinando II, 1610-1670].

21. Mount of Pity: Pound's translation of *Monte de Pietà* [I, "pawnshop"]. What follows is from another document, a report of the Florentine Council to the grand duke about the request of the Sienese Balìa to erect a new bank, December 29, 1622.

22. AA VV: I, *Altezze Vostre*, "Your Highnesses." The plural refers to the Grand Duke and his two guardians or regents, his mother, the Grand Duchess Maria Maddalena, 1591-1631, and his grandmother, the Grand Duchess Christina, 1565-1636.

23. Universities . . .: In the source, *Universita* is probably used to include all the people of a given region [that is, the congregations of the region]. But Pound uses it in a modern sense [Kimpel, *Pai*, 6-3, 336]. *Luoghi* literally means "places." But Pound gives his interpretation as "companies . . ." etc.

24. Mallevadoria: I, "Security."

25. 'The Abundance': I, *L'Abondanza*, a magistracy charged with provision of grain.

26. fruit: I, *frutto*, means also "interest on money."

27. Xember: December. Siena was still on the old calendar (Julian), under which December was the tenth month of the year, which began at the spring equinox (March 23).

28. Nicolo de Antille: Misprint for Niccolò Dell'Antella.

29. Horatio Gionfiglioli: Misprint for Horatio Gianfigliazzi.

30. Tutrice: I, "female guardian."

31. Horᵒ della Rena: Horatio della Rena, secretary of the grand ducal government.

32. Fabbizio bollo vedo: Misprint for *Fabrizio Colloredo*, member of the Tuscan council of four who were to act as advisers to the regents during the minority of the grand duke.

33. Governatore: I, "Governor."

34. Cenzio Grcolini: Misprint for Orazio Ercolani.

35. ACTUM SENIS: L, "transacted at Siena," from a third document (Nov. 2, 1624), the formal instrument founding Il Monte dei Paschi.

36. Parish of San Joannij: Parish of San Giovanni (or John).

37. Marquis: The two marchesi are Giovanni Cristoforo de Malaspinis, son of Antonio Maria, and Giovanni de Binis, son of Andrea.

38. Ego . . . filius: L, "I . . . son of."

39. Pavia . . . Adige: Pavia and Vicenza are cities in NE Italy; San Zeno Maggiore in Verona on the Adige River is one of Pound's favorite Romanesque churches. He is probably referring to the triptych in that church painted by Andrea Mantegna, which shows three medieval Italian cities.

40. I Nicolaus . . . Senensus: I, "I Nicholas Ulivis [misprint for Ulixis (Ulisse or Ulysses)] of Cagnascis [misprint for Magnanis] citizen of Pistoja, a Florentine notary of public countersigning [for the] Senate and people of Siena." Kimpel and Eaves say of the passage starting "ACTUM SENIS": "Pound is partly joking about the names,

partly giving the impression of reading a crabbed legal document, and perhaps partly puzzled" [Kimpel, *Pai*, 6-3, 358].

41. OB PECUNIAE SCARCITATEM: L, "because of the scarcity of money."

42. Monte non vacabilis: L, "a bank whose shares do not expire but have an unlimited duration"; *publico* goes with the following Latin phrase in the document, *publico eorum commodo* ["for the public convenience"].

43. cauteles: L, "guarantees."

44. die decima ottava: I, "on the eighteenth day."

45. Don Ferdinandus Secundus Dux Magnus: L, "Lord Ferdinando II, Grand Duke."

46. Chigi: The four members of the Balìa designated to sign the agreement were Agostino Chigi; Alessandro de Sozzini; Marcello de Augustini [*Illuri* is perhaps a deliberate misreading of the original's "Ill^{m,i}," an abbreviation for Latin "Most Illustrious," which modifies the name of his father], Lord of Caldana; and Cesare de Marescotti, Lord of Mont'Albano.

47. Loca Montis: L, "Shares of the Mountain."

48. ex certe scientia et: L, "from certain knowledge and."

49. de libris septeno: The original reads *de Libris septem*, Latin for "of seven pounds."

Glossary Canto XLIII

1. serenissimo . . . Domino: L, "most serene Lord." Pound continues to quote from the third document [42:35].

2. et omnia alia juva: L [the original reads jura], "and all other rights."; "juva" means "aid" (imperative of *juvo*) [See Kimpel, *Pai*, 8-3, 514 for the confusion of *r* and *v* in the Sienese documents.]

3. Pawn Shop (Mount of Pity): [42:21].

4. eiusdem civitatis Senén: L, "of the same city of Siena."

5. Most Serene M Dux and serenest (feminine) tutrices: The Grand Duke Ferdinando II, the Grand Duchess Maria Maddalena, and the Grand Duchess Christina [42:22].

6. Bailey: Collegio de Balìa [42:6].

7. videlicet alligati: L, "evidently under obligation," or ML, "evidently leagued together."

8. Tuscanissimo Nostro Signore: I, "Our Most Tuscan Lord," This superlative for Tuscan is doubtless a Poundian joke about the grandiose honorary titles in Italian. The word is not in the source. Pound was also puzzled by the word *Inditione* in the source. It means "indication" or a fiscal cycle. Thus the translated source would read: "In the Name of Omnipotent God and of the Glorious Virgin Mary Our Advocate, and to the honor and exaltation of the Most Serene Grand Duke of Tuscany our Lord. The year of the Lord 1622, Sixth Fiscal Period, Saturday the 4th day of March" [Kimpel, *Pai*, 6-3, 343].

9. dilettissimo: I, "most beloved."

10. siano soddisfatti: I, "that they be satisfied."

11. Ob pecuniae scarsitatem: L, "Because of the scarcity of money."

12. S.P. SENENsis **... civitatis:** L, "The Senate and the People of Siena and in its behalf the Most Illustrious College of the Balìa to whose watchfulness over all the state" [*amplissim* is an abbreviation for *amplissimum*, and *civices* is used instead of the original *cujus* ("whose"); *civices* seems to be a cross between the Latin *civicus* ("civic") and *cives* ("citizens")].

13. Urban VIIIth: Pope, 1623-1644.

14. Ferd. I: In both instances this should be *Ferd. II*: Ferdinand II, 1578-1637, the Holy Roman emperor—elect, and *mag duce dᵒ nᵒ* ["Our Lord the Grand Duke"], Ferdinando II of Tuscany [42:20]. The Latin words *felcitatem dominante et* mean "ruling happiness and," but the source reads: *feliciter dominante*, "happily ruling."

15. 1251 ... arabic: Mengozzi's Volume III contains the notary's copies of the three documents concerning the founding of Il

Monte dei Paschi. On the spine is printed: "Stanza Prima. Scaffale No. XII Lettera F N.° 4." Pound renders this information in these two lines.

16. To the end: The next 17 lines mostly concern a parade and a celebration by the people, who after so many years finally got their bank; Pound enjoys all the sense impressions (sound, sight, color) as well as the pomp and ceremony with the animals and triumphant chariot: *carroccio*. St. George and the Unicorn and prob. others were pictured on flags or banners carried by different craft guilds in the parade. *Hokeypokey* means ice-cream stands and by extension any hucksters who appear at carnivals and fairs or on feast days to sell their wares. *Nicchio* is not a particular person, but the voice of some mother whose young son is doubtless lost in the crowd. The *one box* is doubtless a box of candles and *200 lire* is prob. the price, for traditionally parades ended at a cathedral where candles were used as votive offerings.

17. contrade: I, "divisions of a city."

18. kallipygous: H, "with beautiful buttocks."

19. salite: I, "hill paths."

20. 'laudate pueri': L, "praise, boys."

21. palio: Sienese horse race held annually on July 2 and August 16. Pound is presumably describing his own memories of this famous festival.

22. Duomo: I, "Cathedral."

23. quocunque aliunde: L, "from anywhere else."

24. obligatio: L, "obligation."

25. scudi: I, coins, usually translated as "crowns."

26. Maister Augustino Chisio equites ... holy): The original Latin reads *Domino Augustino Chisio, equiti Sacrae III.ᵐᵃᵉ Religionis Divi Stephani papae et martiris* ["Lord Agostino Chigi, Knight of the Sacred and Most Illustrious Order of St. Stephen pope and martyr"] [for Chigi, see 42:46].

27. ducatorum? no. ducentorum: L, "of ducats? no. of two hundred thousand."

28. parish of San Giovanni (Joannis): Parish in Siena. L, *Joannis*, "of Giovanni or John."

29. libris septem: L, "seven pounds" [lire].

30. summam, scutorum: L, "the sum, of scudi [crowns]."

31. Out of Syracuse: Pound is referring to Demosthenes' oration "Against Zeno-themes," prosecuting an attempt to defraud creditors by trying to sink a ship supposed to be loaded with borrowed money.

32. S.O.: The older Faber edition reads "Standard Oil." Presumably this passage describes a modern instance of commercial chicanery similar to the ancient Greek one.

33. Loca Montis: L, "Shares (literally 'Places') of the Mountain."

34. Il Banditore: I, "The Town Crier."

35. Ill^us Balia eseguisca in tutto: I, "The Illustrious Balìa executes in everything."

36. ACTUM SENIS in Parochia [Parocchia] S. Giovannis [Joannis]: L, "transacted at Siena in the Parish of San Giovanni."

37. hoc die decim' octavo: L, "on this eighteenth day."

38. Celso: Celso Cittadini, 1555-1627. Before the founding of Il Monte dei Paschi Cittadini had proposed increasing the cultivation of grain and hemp.

39. stati fatti Signoria: I, "was made a Lordship." Paris Bolgarini was the first supervisor of Il Monte dei Paschi.

40. cancellarius: ML, "chancellor."

41. Luoghi: [42:23].

42. fondo: I, "fund," "base," "deep."

43. 'entrate': I, literally "entrances"; here "incomes." Such incomes are given in the next lines. "M" equals 1,000—thus 150 to 200 thousand scudi (a unit of currency]. But the source indicates the incomes are the costs of management. Kimpel and Eaves translate thus: "And to this end it is reported that the administration and management of this Mountain will not, it is believed, turn out to be more than one-hundred-and-fifty to two-hundred thousand crowns (scudi). And therefore it is enough to assign it a certain and sure income of eight to ten thousand crowns yearly on the incomes of the Excise Taxes [gabelle] or Customs [dogana] or other safe organ of that city [gabelle]" [Kimpel, *Pai*, 6-3, 336].

44. Epifany: Epiphany, the feast celebrated on January 6 commemorating the coming of the Magi.

45. Off^o de Paschi: I, "Office of the Pastures" [42:9].

46. Donna Orsola: An official prostitute. The documents are unclear about the heinous crime that deprived her of her official sanctions. The source has a blank space (probably an erasure) which accounts for Pound's words "of wherever" [cf. Kimpel, *Pai*, 8-3, 515]. The "book" becomes the "register" where Mrs. Gallo's (next canto page) crime of thievery is made crystal clear.

47. black money: Defined as lead money [bottom of next canto page]. The source shows the Balìa instructing customs officers to be more diligent because "of the introduction into this state of so much foreign black money with injury to the public." The reader should note the content of *hilaritas* and outright comedy in the admixture of business, ranging from the sacred through the profane to the brilliant trivia that come before this high council and are somberly recorded by the secretary and given legal sanction by the notary. One of the points obviously is to show that human nature changes but little. The comic point can be nothing but devastatingly clear to professors who have served on high academic councils. In 1626 the Sienese Balìa kept getting into more of a "stew" [cf. next canto page] about the black money. Finally on May 19,

1626, a prohibition against *quattrini neri* ["black pennies"] was promulgated [Kimpel, *Pai*, 8-1, 516].

48. Monte de Firenze: I, "Bank of Florence."

49. vacabile: I, "the shares of which do expire." The Bank of Florence was so eager to get money that it announced that even bandits could contribute.

50. Pietro de Medici: Pietro de' Medici, 1554-1604, youngest son of Cosimo I. This member of the grand ducal house had a reputation for profligacy, and the government refused to allow his bastards to be recognized, but it was arranged that they would be recognized as the bastards of the secretary, Orazio della Rena. [For della Rena, see 42:31].

51. Orbem . . . implevit: L, "Urban VIII filled the world with wars, the city with taxes."

52. Monte Nuovo: I, "New Bank" (literally "New Mountain").

53. Xbre: I, *dicembre*, "December."

54. Monte Paschale, fatto Signoria: I, "Mountain of the Pastures, made a Lordship."

55. Grosseto: A city in the Maremma, S of Siena.

56. 1676 ambassadors to Firenze: Ambassadors from Siena to the government in Florence are protesting the devaluation of Spanish pieces of eight.

57. non intendeva di quella materia: I, "did not understand that matter."

58. Buonuomini: I, literally "Good Men," a Florentine tribunal.

59. Tolomei: Celso Tolomei had left money to found a college to which Il Monte dei Paschi made a loan in 1678.

60. fruitage: I, *frutto* means both "fruit" and "interest."

61. LL AA: I, *Lora Altezze*, "Their Highnesses" [42:28, 29].

62. prestare: I, "lend."

63. Paschi di detta Città: I, "Pastures of the said City." They were located in the Maremma [cf. 55 above].

64. cautele: I, "guarantees."

65. Hor⁰ della Rena: [cf. 50 above].

66. Orazio Grcolini: Misprint for Orazio Ercolani.

67. Stile senese: I, "in Sienese style," i.e., according to the old calendar [42:27].

68. S. Gionni, in palatio: I, "San Giovanni, in the palace."

69. Firenze 1749 . . . 12,000: This is one of several examples of useful public works financed by Il Monte dei Paschi.

70. the end of the Medici: The grand ducal house of Medici became extinct in 1743.

71. lire pre-war: Value of the lire in pre–World War I currency [cf. 50/246 on debt; 50:4].

Glossary Canto XLIV

1. Pietro Leopoldo: 1747-1792; member of the Austrian house of Hapsburg-Lorraine, became Leopoldo I, Grand Duke of Tuscany, 1765-1790, and Leopold II, Holy Roman emperor, 1790-1792. The lines above his name are one of the various decrees with which his government tried to

alleviate the economic hardships of Tuscany [note rhyme with 37/181].

2. Heavy grain crop unsold: Under the Medici there were many restrictions on free trade, and in 1721 and 1723, when the harvests were unusually rich, the government prohibited the importation of grain ("shut down on grain imports").

3. never had the Mount . . . investments: Very often an excess of capital forced Il Monte dei Paschi to cut down the interest rate. The date of the first reduction mentioned was 1680; the other dates are correct.

4. that trade . . . impediments: The government of Pietro Leopoldo was strongly in favor of free trade; this decree was issued in 1781.

5. motu proprio: I, *motuproprio*, "voluntary decree."

6. Ferdinando EVVIVA!!: I, "Long live Ferdinando!!" Ferdinando III, 1769-1824, the second son of Pietro Leopoldo, was grand duke of Tuscany from 1790 to 1799 and again from 1814 until his death.

7. Flags trumpets horns drums . . .: This and the following lines describe a celebration at Siena in 1792 in honor of Ferdinando III's restrictions on the exportation of grain and his regulation of small hucksters.

8. the chapel of Alexander: The Capella di Alessandro VII in the Cathedral of Siena.

9. St. Catherine's chapel in S. Domenico: The Capella di Santa Caterina in the Church of San Domenico in Siena. Saint Catherine is the patron saint of Italy.

10. Fonte Giusta: Fontegiusta, a church in Siena.

11. contrade: I, districts of the city.

12. Palace of the Seignors: The Palazzo Pubblico or town hall of Siena, located in the Piazza del Campo.

13. the tower in the piazza: The Torre del Mangia, which rises from the Palazzo Pubblico.

14. procession: Pound loved a parade [43:16].

15. e di tutte le qualità: I, "and of all kinds."

16. mortaretti: I, "little mortars."

17. chapel of the Piazza: The Capella di Piazza, at the foot of the Torre del Mangia.

18. Evviva Ferdinando il Terzo: I, "Long live Ferdinando the Third."

19. Piazza del Duomo: I, "Cathedral Square."

20. Dovizia annonaria: I, "abundance of provision," specifically a reference to the annual income in natural products, mostly corn or grain, and the body of restrictive laws shaped to provide Florentine industry with cheap food in order to undercut the prices of Florence's competitors. Enforced by the office of the Abbondanza [I, "abundance"], these laws exploited and ruined the peasantry by fixing the prices of commodities, prohibiting the import and export of food, and disallowing all free exchange. Offenders were prosecuted as common criminals.

21. Frumentorum . . . conservit: L, "freedom of grains restrained of provision reduced for the good of poor and of rich preserves (or retains)." This quotation is not only altered from the original, but makes no sense as it stands: among other things, none of the nouns can be the object of the final verb, which has an impossible ending. The original refers to Ferdinando and asks the people to pray for him "quod / frumentariorum licentia coercita / Re annonaria laxata / Pauperum aeque ac divitum bono / consylverit" ["because when the freedom of grain dealers was restrained and the supply of provisions expanded, he had consideration for the good of the poor and equally of the rich"].

22. refused . . . nation: When driven out by the French armies in 1799 [Pound's date is wrong], Ferdinando did not take valuable and easily portable treasures.

23. il più galantuomo del paese: I, "the most honest man in the country."

24. Fr Lenzini: Under the French occupation the Sienese clergy, among them the archbishop, who like everyone in Revolutionary France was called simply "citizen," took part in the ceremony of erecting a tree of liberty. *Fr* stands for "Francesco." Abram was the French commissioner.

25. from 750 . . . April: This rise of prices took place in 1799, soon after the beginning of the French occupation.

26. and on June 28th . . . little powder: An uprising that began in the city of Arezzo drove the French out of Tuscany for a while; when the liberators took Siena, they let the French escape to the fortress and turned their attention to burning Jews. Traitors tried to ruin the cartridges of the liberators from Arezzo. The Roman Gate [Porta Romana] was the gate one used when journeying to Rome.

27. semolina: I, "coarse meal."

28. Respectons les prêtres: F, "Let us respect the priests." It was actually Napoleon who wrote to his foreign minister, Charles Maurice de Talleyrand-Périgord, 1754-1838, that the only way to live at peace with the peasants of Italy was to respect the priests.

29. Premier Brumaire: F, the first day of the French Revolutionary month, October 22 to November 20.

30. Vous voudrez citoyen: F, "You will, citizen." This order was delivered by the French forces to Il Monte dei Paschi.

31. fraternité: F, "brotherhood."

32. Delort: Jacques-Antoine-Adrien, Baron Delort, 1773-1846, French officer, later general.

33. Dupont: Pierre D., Later Comte Dupont de L'Etang, 1765-1840.

34. Louis King of Etruria, Primus: Luigi, Duke of Parma, 1773-1803, was in 1801 made Louis I of Etruria, a new kingdom formed by Napoleon which included Tuscany.

35. Gen. Clarke: Henri Jacques Guillaume Clarke, 1765-1818, had been a general under Napoleon, and when he made this sarcastic remark about the taxes of the king of Etruria at the time of his death, he was French ambassador to that state.

36. Ministro degli [Affari] Esteri: I, "Foreign Minister."

37. Whereas . . . expenses: This low percentage was the difference between the rate of interest paid to shareholders and the rate of interest paid by borrowers.

38. Madame ma soeur et cousine: F, "Madame my sister and cousin." This letter, down through the signature "NAPOLEON," was written to Maria Luisa, 1782-1824, infanta of Spain and widow of Louis I of Etruria. On the death of her husband she became regent for their infant son, Louis II, but in 1807 she was informed that Napoleon had made a treaty with Spain under which Tuscany was to become an integral part of France and that she had to leave the country. She appealed to Napoleon and this letter was his answer. The French original sometimes addresses her in the second person and sometimes in the third; a footnote points out that it was probably written by a secretary.

39. General Reile: Honoré Charles Michel Joseph Reille, 1775-1860. He was at this time a general in the French army and later became a marshal of France.

40. Lisbon: The original has *Livourne* (Livorno or Leghorn); "that capital" in the next line is Lisbon.

41. And those men . . . prepared: In 1809 Napoleon granted the grand duchy of Tuscany to his sister Maria Anna Elisa Bonaparte (Mme Felice Bacciocchi), 1777-1820, princess of Lucca and of Piombino. The diarist Bandini reports that when she entered Siena men took the horses from her carriage and pulled it themselves, but that he was sure their action was not based on genuine enthusiasm.

42. "Artists . . . Napoleon: Napoleon believed that Tuscany under his sister was favorable to the arts and that artists of high rank were the only aristocrats not over-turned by the recent events.

43. 'Semiramis': Semiramis was the queen of Assyria who was renowned in legend as the builder of Babylon. Elisa was called "Semiramis of Lucca." She was forced to leave Florence in January 1814.

44. her brother's law code: The writer of *Il Monte dei Paschi* [42:9] praises several results of the French administration, especially the Code Napoléon, which he called a *monumento di civile sapienza* ["monument of civil wisdom"]. He quotes another writer who remarked that Napoleon was one of those men whom we must take pride in and admire, but it is the grace of God that he sends such men very rarely.

45. And before him ... Habsburg Lorraine: The writer of *Il Monte dei Paschi*, by way of contrast with the very mixed blessing of Napoleon, lists for three pages the reforms of Pietro Leopoldo. Pound has brought his effort to abolish the state debt from the middle of the list to the beginning.

46. gabelle: I, "excise taxes."

47. Val di Chiana: I, "Valley of Chiana."

The Chiana is a river in Tuscany which rises in the Apennines and used to flow for some 60 miles to the Tiber. In the Middle Ages the valley was swampland, but in the late 18th century Count Fossombroni moved the watershed some 25 miles south so that the Chiana now flows partly into the Arno and partly into the Tiber. This engineering feat made it possible for the third Ferdinand to improve tillage of the now arable land; note rhyme with Mussolini's drainage of the Pontine marshes [41:3] and the Emperor Yü's controlling of the Yellow River [53:15].

48. porto franco: I, "free port." On his restoration Ferdinando III protected the interests of the free port of Livorno in addition to accomplishing several other reforms, but Pound has exaggerated the size of his tax cuts.

49. Letizia: Maria Letizia Ramolino Bonaparte, 1750-1836, mother of Napoleon.

50. Niccolò Piccolomini, Provveditore: Piccolomini called himself the *provveditore* ["supervisor"] of *Il Monte dei Paschi*. The book does emphasize the effort to combat usury.

Glossary Canto XLV

1. Usura: L, I, "Usury." Pound defines the way he uses the word at the end of this canto. Usury functions in *The Cantos* to dramatize the forces at work in human nature which prevent the human race from creating a paradise on earth—or realizing the vision first announced in Canto V. The man without a paradisal vision will have no "painted paradise on his church wall."

2. harpes et luz: OF [*luthes*], "harps and lutes"; part of line 896 from Villon's *Testament* in the ballad for his mother, where she speaks of seeking paradise painted.

3. virgin receiveth: Prob. a reference to various paintings entitled *The Annunciation*.

4. Gonzaga: Any of the great patron lords from Mantua, but in particular Francesco G. who married Isabella d'Este and encouraged her in her patronage of the great artists of the day. She was painted by both Leonardo and Titian who spent much time in residence at her court in Mantua.

5. thy bread: First protest against the adulteration of bread which since Pound's time has become a continuously louder clamor [cf. 74/428 where "white bread" is so bad even birds won't eat it, and 80/493 where it is said Spanish bread used to be "made out of grain"].

6. line grows thick: Pound wrote: "I suggest that finer and future critics of art will be able to tell from the quality of a painting the degree of tolerance or intolerance of usury extant in the age and milieu that produced it" [*GK*, 27].

7. Pietro Lombardo: 1435-1515, Italian architect and sculptor. His most famous work is Dante's tomb at Ravenna.

8. Duccio: D. di Buoninsegna, 1278-1319, Italian painter and leader of the Sienese school.

9. Francesca: Piero della Francesca, 1420?-1492, Italian painter from Umbrian region who is famous for his portraits and altarpieces [8:11].

10. Zuan Bellin': Giovanni Bellini, 1430?-1516, Venetian painter known for his altarpieces and Madonnas [25:59].

11. 'La Calunnia': I, "The Slander." Title of painting by Sandro Botticelli, 1444?-1510, now in Uffizi Gallery, Florence.

12. Angelico: Fra [Brother] A. Known also as Giovanni da Fiesole, 1387-1455; Italian painter from Florence.

13. Ambrogio: A. de Predis, 1455?-1508, Italian portrait and miniature painter from Milan.

14. Adamo me fecit: L, "Adam made me."

Inscription on pillar in Church of San Zeno, Verona. Pound makes much of this column, which the artist was proud enough of to sign, and contrasts it with columns turned out by the hundreds in modern times [cf. HK, *Era*, 324, who gives a picture of the column; the full inscription reads: ADAMINUS DESCO GEORGIO ME FECIT; see also *Pai*, 4-1, 85-88].

15. St. Trophime: Beautiful church in Arles, France, noted for its cloistered courtyard with sculpted columns [cf. HK, *Era*, 328-329].

16. Saint Hilaire: Church in Poitiers, France [cf. ibid., 327].

17. cramoisi: F, "crimson cloth."

18. Memling: Hans M., 1430?-1495, religious painter and portraitist of Flemish school.

19. CONTRA NATURAM: L, "against nature."

20. Eleusis: Town in Attica where the Eleusinian Mysteries were celebrated. One of the major poles of *The Cantos*: "Between Kung [an ethical system] and Eleusis [celebration of the mysteries]." Thus usury debauches what is most sacred: "the love of money is the root of all evil" [cf. 52/258].

CANTO XLVI

Sources

Personal experiences and memories of Pound; Christopher Hollis, *The Two Nations*, London, 1935; Dante, *Inf*. XVII.

Background

EP, *GK*, 184, 35-36; *A Visiting Card*, Peter Russell, London, 1952; *SP*, 311, 272-273, 57, 280, 437-439.

Glossary

1. Eliot: Thomas Stearns E., 1888-1971, poet and critic and lifelong friend of Pound's. Called "Reverend" because in 1927 he became a devout Anglo-Catholic churchman. Also before and during the time when Pound was writing Canto 46, Eliot was writing on religious subjects.

2. natural language: A language close to nature and therefore mythic or "paideumatic." Eliot's language in *The Waste Land* drew on primitive myth via Christianity. Pound sought to infuse his language with the European myths of Eleusis.

3. hell: Because Pound sees hell as the locus of greed, Geryon, and usury as the dominating thrust of Western civilization, he does not believe anyone will traverse it quickly: "Abomination of desolation ... lasting on into our time in the infamy which controls English and U.S. finances and has made printing a midden, a filth, a mere smear, bolted down by the bank racket. ... The first step toward a new Paideuma is a clearance of every prelate or minister who blocks, by diseased will or sodden inertia, a cleaning of the monetary system. There is no mediaeval description of hell which exceeds the inner filth of these mentalities" [*GK*, 184].

4. Zoagli: Town on the Ligurian coast, NW Italy, a few miles S of Rapallo.

5. Seventeen ... nineteen ... ninety: Writing in "a.d. 1935" [cf. 46/235], Pound is recalling the formal beginning of his economic struggle when he met and listened to Major Douglas in *The New Age* offices in 1918 or 1916. "Ninety" prob. refers more generally to the *bellum perenne* against Geryon and Usura.

6. the fuzzy bloke: Pound referring to himself ironically as he listened and responded to Major Douglas.

7. The major: C. H. Douglas, the Social Credit economist. Social Credit proposed a national dividend as one instrument to keep purchasing power equal to the goods and services being marketed.

8. Decennio: Tenth anniversary celebration of Italian fascism (1932).

9. Il Popolo: *Popolo d'Italia*, newspaper started by Mussolini in 1914.

10. Mills bomb: Mills hand grenade, invented by Sir William Mills and used by British and Allies in World War I.

11. the teapot: Poss. Pound talking so that the *ours* refers to the celebration of 1932, which had no such record to contend with as the Teapot Dome Scandal of the late 1920s. But the lines, *Waal ... brown one*, may refer to the first meeting with Major Douglas in Orage's office. Pound's obituary for Orage [*New English Weekly*, Nov. 15, 1934; rpt. *SP*, 437-439] discusses the number of years Orage fought for the truth about the monetary system [cf. 38/190; 38:49]. If so, the *teapot* may have been a real pot sitting next to a Mills bomb on some table, all part of the scene.

12. 5 millions: "Liste officielle des morts 5,000,000," i.e., in World War I [cf. 16/73].

13. Debts ... New York: Source reads: "Owing to the tariff, the whole South was going into debt. We must never forget the important statistic which Horace Greeley ... gave at the outbreak of the Civil War, that southern debtors owed at least $200,000,000 to money-lenders in New York City alone" [Hollis, 208]. Thus the Civil War was more over money than over slavery.

14. Max's drawings: The drawings of Max Beerbohm, who caricatured the Victorian, Edwardian, and Georgian eras.

15. Balfour: Arthur James B., 1848-1930, British statesman; foreign minister (1916-1919); author of the Balfour Declaration which pledged British support to the founding of a Jewish state in Palestine as part of the solution to Middle East problems.

16. Johnny Bull: Nickname for Great Britain.

17. Orage: Alfred Richard O., 1873-1934, English journalist; editor of *The New Age*.

18. G.B.S.: George Bernard Shaw, 1856-1950, Irish playwright.

19. Mr. Xtertn: Gilbert Keith Chesterton, 1874-1936, English journalist, writer, and defender of Catholicism; a brilliant representative of Edwardian England.

20. Mr. Wells: [42:2].

21. John Marmaduke: Marmaduke William Pickthall, 1875-1936, English novelist living in the Near East and, like Pound, a writer for *The New Age*, was converted to Mohammedanism. His racial slurs against the Greeks were prob. meant to document his ignorance, because Pound's own opinions about the Greeks, including their art and religion, were quite different. The more Marmaduke talks the more he shows his true character.

22. Abdul Baha: Sir A. B. Bahai, 1844-1921, leader of the religion known as Bahaism, founded by his father Baha Ullah. Bahaists believe in the unity of all religions, universal education, world peace, and equality of the sexes.

23. Camel driver said: Presumably Pound heard this anecdote directly from Pickthall.

24. Uberton, Gubberton: Prob. refers to Surbiton, a town on the Thames, in Surrey.

25. Mohammedans: Followers of the prophet Mohammed.

26. Paterson: William P., 1658-1719, British financier, chief founder of the Bank of England (1694). Source reads: "As Disraeli put it, 'the principle of the system was to mortgage industry in order to protect property,' or, as Paterson, the originator of the Bank [of England], himself explained with charming simplicity, 'The bank hath benefit of the interest on all moneys which it creates out of nothing' " [Hollis, 30].

27. Mr. Rothschild: Prob. Junius R. or John Pierpont R., Sr. In *A Visiting Card*, Pound says: "It was a Rothschild who wrote: 'Those few who can understand the (usurocratic) system will be . . . busy getting profits, . . . while the general public . . . will probably never suspect that the system is absolutely against their interests,' (From a letter of Rothschild Bros., quoting John Sherman, addressed to the firm of Ikleheimer, Morton and Van der Gould, dated 25 June 1863)" [*SP*, 311].

28. anno domini: L, "in the year of the Lord."

29. Foundation of Regius Professors: Royal endowment of professorships at Oxford and Cambridge universities. Leading 18th century Whigs became alarmed at the "unpopularity of the debt-system among the gentry who had to pay the taxes to meet its charges." Therefore a "Whig" history was written [*History of Our Own Times*] and a deliberate campaign to subvert the faculties of Oxford and Cambridge was undertaken: 12 fellows from each university were invited to preach a sermon and receive a £ 30 emolument. None could hope to receive a share of this bounty "but they who are staunch Whigs and openly declare themselves to be so." The sermons worked so well that Townshend [a famous Whig leader], thinking they should be permanently endowed, proposed to George I that a regius professorship be established at both Oxford and Cambridge. The professors' real business would be to propagandize Whig political and economic views. So that there would be no mistake, wrote Townshend, "George himself [meaning the Whig prime minister] is to put in the professors" [Hollis, 35-52].

30. Whiggery: Prob. the doctrines of laissez-faire economics.

31. Macmillan Commission: MacMillan Committee, a British committee on finance and industry (1929) under the chairmanship of Lord MacMillan. Since the committee placed major blame for the depression not on the maintenance of the gold standard itself, but upon the shortsighted handling of it by, major nations and upon the gold-hoarding policies of the U.S. and France, it agreed that the gold standard should be replaced. Pound's source adds: "That policy [return to stable price level] had already been recommended by the MacMillan Report which said: 'The ultimate aim should be the stability of the international price-level, meaning by this the composite price at wholesale of the principle foodstuffs and raw materials entering into international trade as measured by the best known wholesale index numbers' " [Hollis, 243].

32. ex nihil: L, "from nothing." Refers to the statement attributed to William Paterson [cf. 26 above; *A Visiting Card*, 9].

33. Mr. Marx, Karl: Pound wrote: "Marx and La Tour du Pin were equally deaf, dumb and blind to money.... And the amazing history of the 19th century is summed up in: 'Marx found nothing to criticize in money' " [*SP*, 272-273]. Pound seems to be using the L *monumental* (which means lit. "a memorial" or "a monument") in the sense of "enormous" or "monumental."

34. St. Peter's: [31:50].

35. Manchester: Manufacturing city, Lancashire, NW England.

36. Si requieres Monumentum?: L, "If you require a memorial?"

37. Hic est hyper-usura: L, "This is hyper-usury."

38. Mr. Jefferson: The source is unknown, but the prohibition epitomizes Jefferson's economic thought.

39. Replevin: In law, the return to, or recovery by, a person of goods or chattels wrongfully taken or detained, upon giving security to try the matter in court and return the goods if defeated in the action.

40. estopple: Estoppel. In law, a bar to alleging or denying a fact because of one's own previous action by which the contrary has been admitted, implied, or determined.

41. VanBuren: Martin V. B. That the lender must have the money to lend was a recurrent theme in Van Buren's and Jackson's long fight against the renewal of the charter of the Bank of the United States in the mid-1830s [37:passim].

42. Antoninus: [42:4]. A. Pius, Roman emperor (137-161), famous for early work on maritime law. Significant because Pound associates the beginnings of usury in the Occident with events in his reign: "The archeologist and serendipidist can ... find the known beginnings of usury entangled with those of marine insurance, sea lawyers, the law of Rhodes; the disputed text of Antoninus Pius on the limits of his jurisdiction. Even then the dealers in metal appeared to be privileged over other merchants, and the insurance risk mainly paid by the takers of greater risk" [*SP*, 272-273].

43. lex Rhodi: L, "the law of Rhodes."

44. usura: L, I, "usury." Concerning usury, Pound wrote: "The 'Church' declined and fell on this issue. Historians have left the politics of Luther and of Calvin in the blurr of great ignorance .... The Church slumped into a toleration of usury. Protestantism as factive and organised, may have sprung from nothing but pro-usury politics" [*SP*, 273].

45. Athens: As opposed to Sparta, where "the true nature of money was comprehended," Pound sees Athens as the home of monetary fraud: "... you might make out a fairly good case against Athens as the mother of rascality, did one not see her as the grand-daughter of a long line of markets and mediterranean trading posts. Every form of fraud flourished there in perfection, nothing is added in ingenuity.... There sat the scoundrel ... lending out his shilling a day.... Further along a bloke with a table performing the next grade of usury" [*GK*, 35-36].

46. Luther: Martin L., 1483-1546. Pound wrote: "I take it that the Catholic Church broke from the top, as Paganism had possibly broken. I mean to say that the Church was no longer interested in theology, it no longer believed or even knew what it meant. Leo X was interested in administration, in culture, in building St. Peter's. It simply never occurred to him that anyone would take Luther seriously. No one in his set did take Luther seriously, I mean as a writer or thinker. He was merely a barbarian bore. Protestantism has no theology. By which I mean it has nothing that a well grounded theologian can possibly consider salonfähig" [*SP*, 57].

47. 1527: . . . art thickened: Pound wrote before 1931: "Certainly the metamorphosis into carnal tissue becomes frequent and general somewhere about 1527. The people are corpus, corpuscular, but not in the strict sense 'animate,' it is no longer the body of air clothed in the body of fire; it no longer radiates, light no longer moves from the eye, there is a great deal of meat, shock absorbing, perhaps—at any rate absorbent. It has not even Greek marmoreal plastic to restrain it. The dinner scene is more frequently introduced, we have the characters in definite act of absorption; later they will be but stuffing for expensive upholsteries." [*LE*, 153].

48. 'Hic nefas' . . . 'commune sepulchrum': L, "Here is infamy . . . the common sepulcher."

49. Aurum est . . .: L, "Gold is a common sepulcher. Usury, a common sepulcher."

50. helandros . . . helarxe: H, "destroyer of men, and destroyer of cities, and destroyer of governments" [2:8; 7:2].

51. Hic Geryon . . .: L, "Here is Geryon. Here hyperusury." Geryon was (1) a three-headed or three-bodied monster living on the island of Erythia, killed by Heracles; (2) the symbol of fraud and guardian of the eighth circle of hell in the *Inferno*; (3) sometimes a symbol of usury and violence against nature and art [*Inf*. XVII, passim].

52. FIVE million . . .: The state of the U.S. economic system as reported variously in the press in 1935. Pound's thesis is that an economic system that produces such results is sadly deficient.

53. F. Roosevelt, signed F. Delano: Franklin Delano R., 1882-1945, president of the U.S. (1933-1945). Pound wrote: "In contrast to the idiotic accumulation of debt by Roosevelt, observe that *if* such government expenditure be necessary or advisable, the direct payment of workers, etc., in stamp scrip would in eight years consume itself, and leave the next decade *free* of all debt. The Roosevelt system is either a fraud or a selling of the nation's children into slavery without the ghost of excuse" [*SP*, 280].

54. Eunited: Pun on "United," with Greek prefix *eu-*, meaning "done well."

55. foetor: L, "stench."

56. Mr. Cummings: Homer Stillé C., 1870-1956, American lawyer and politician; attorney general (1933-1939).

57. Farley: James Aloysius F., 1888-1976, American politician, who was rewarded by being made postmaster general. The irony of the headline under the conditions of the economy is obvious.

CANTO XLVII

Sources

Od. X, 250 ff., XI, 1-150, XII, 80-100; Frazer, *The Golden
Bough*, 1890 and many later editions [references in the glosses
are paged to the easily available Gaster abridgment of 1959, 286-
296]; Bion, "The Lament for Adonis" [Loeb, 387-395]; Hesiod,
Works and Days [Loeb, 31-45].

Background

EP, *GK*, 146; Ovid, *Meta*. III.

Exegeses

Dekker, *Cantos*, 36-46 and passim; DP, *Barb*, 172- 192; EH,
Approaches, 167-168, 198-199; Rosenthal, *Pai*, 6-3.

Glossary

1. Who ... entire: Tiresias. [*Od*. X, 493;
1:7]. Pound believed that the Greeks
thought intelligence in man manifested div-
inity in man. Zeus said of Odysseus, "A chap
with a mind like THAT! The fellow is one of
us." Pound follows this free translation from
the *Odyssey* with the remark: "I hope that
elsewhere I have underscored and driven in
the greek honour of human intelligence
'Who even dead yet hath his mind entire'
[*GK*, 146].

2. First. . . end: Circe gave directions to
Odysseus in the dark: "But when the sun set
and darkness came on . . . I went up to the
beautiful bed of Circe" [*Od*. X, 480]. He
asked that she let him and his men go home.
In consenting, Circe said: "Odysseus . . .
abide ye now no longer in my house against
your will; but you must first complete
another journey, and come to the house of
Hades and dread Persephone, to seek sooth-
saying of the spirit of Theban Teiresias, the

blind seer, whose mind abides steadfast"
[*Od*. X, 488-494; 39:18].

3. Ceres: Latin name of Demeter, goddess
of the harvest and central figure in the
Eleusinian Mysteries.

4. Tiresias: Greek seer who was struck blind
by Hera, wife of Zeus. Since Zeus could not
undo the act of the goddess, he compensated
for the loss of sight by giving Tiresias the
power of prophecy [Ovid, *Meta*. III].

5. beefy men: Men in the flesh, before
death.

6. phtheggometha thasson: H, "let us raise
our voices without delay." Transliteration of
the Greek words in next line [cf. 39/193;
39:15].

7. The small lamps: During the July festival
of Montallegre Madonna, Pound could see at
Rapallo local women set votive lights adrift
in the Golfo Tigullio. He relates the cere-

mony to early vegetation rites held to celebrate the death of "Tammuz-Adonis."

8. Neptunus: L, Neptune. Roman god of the sea.

9. Tamuz: Tammuz, Babylonian name of Adonis.

10. By this gate: Janus ruled the two gates, one into life and the other into death. Here it is the gate into the underworld, rhyming with the Persephone- Adonis myth. See repetition of line below followed by "Thy day is between a door and a door" [cf. also "And that all gates are holy," 94/634].

11. Scilla: Scylla, according to Greek myth, was a sea monster who lived in a cave opposite Charybdis. She had six heads, each with a triple row of teeth, and barked like a dog [cf. *Od*. XII, 80-100].

12. TU DIONA: H, "You Dione." Aphrodite. In myth, she fell in love with Adonis who after his death spent part of the year with Persephone in Hades and returned to earth (with spring) to be with Aphrodite for the rest of the year.

13. *Kai* **MOIRAI' ADONIN**: H, "And the fates . . . Adonis." From Bion's "Lament for Adonis." The complete line reads: "The fates cry over Adonis."

14. The sea is streaked red: Spring freshets used to bring red-stained water from the mountains into the sea. Eastern Mediterranean people related the color to the blood of Adonis, the yearly slain [*Golden Bough*, 286-296].

15. Wheat shoots rise: Reference to "Gardens of Adonis" in which pots were filled with earth and the seed of "wheat, barley, lettuces, fennel. . . . Fostered by the sun's heat, the plants shot up rapidly . . . and at the end of eight days were carried out with the images of the dead Adonis, and flung with them into the sea" [*Golden Bough*, 293].

16. Two span: Source unknown.

17. Moth . . . bull: Answering blind sexual call through odors in the air.

18. naturans: L, "obeying its nature." Creative nature was called *natura naturans* by Johannes Scotus Erigena.

19. Odysseus: Called to the "lair" of Circe [*Od*. X, 300 ff.].

20. Molü: Herb given to Odysseus by Hermes to resist the evil potion of Circe [ibid.; 39:7].

21. Begin thy plowing . . . time: Most of this 14-line passage is adapted from Hesiod's *Works and Days*: "When the Pleiades . . . are rising begin your harvest, and your ploughing when they are going to set. Forty nights and days they are hidden and appear again. . . This is the law of the plains, and of those who live near the sea. . . . Get two oxen, bulls of nine years; for their strength is unspent . . .they are best for work. . . . Mark when you hear the voice of the crane who cries . . . above for she gives the signal for ploughing" [Hesiod, 31 ff.].

22. Pleiades: The seven daughters of Atlas who became a cluster of stars in the constellation Taurus.

23. small stars: Olive-tree blossoms are shaped like small stars, but they do not fall at the time of spring plowing. Perhaps the stars of the Pleiades going "down to their rest" are to be seen through the olive-tree branches. But the falling stars may be phosphorescent insects [48:53].

24. Tellus: Roman goddess of the earth.

25. Scylla: [cf. 11 above].

26. cunnus: L, "female sex organ."

27. Io: H, "Hail."

28. Zephyrus: West wind.

29. Apeliota: East wind.

30. Adonis falleth: At the harvest or in the waning year when the god of the vegetation myths dies.

31. KAI MOIRAI' etc.: [cf. 13 above].

32. almond bough . . . flame: Rebirth of Adonis in the vegetation myths. The coming of spring makes the sap run and the almond "flame" with flower.

33. Tu Diona: [cf. 12 above].

34. power over wild beasts: Attribute of the god Dionysus-Adonis-Tammuz [cf. 2/8]. A power also attributed in myth to special humans, as to Apollonius of Tyana in *The Cantos* [91/616; 93/623].

CANTO XLVIII

Sources

Personal experiences and memories of Pound; Remy de Gourmont, *The Natural Philosophy of Love*, New York, Boni and Liveright, 1922; rpt., New York, Collier Books, 1972, 39-40.

Background

Mary de Rachewiltz, *Discretions*, Boston and Toronto, 1971, 72-73; EP, *J/M*, 18.

Exegeses

HK, *Pai*, 2-1, 41; DG, *Pai*, 4-2, 3, 225 ff.; CE, *Ideas*, 38, 39, 114, 116; WB, *Rose*, 60.

Glossary

1. money be rented: Exact source unidentified, but the four lines are a Poundian paraphrase of Jackson's and Van Buren's ideas in their fight in the mid-1830s against renewal of the charter of the Bank of the United States [37:passim].

2. Mahomet VIth Yahid Eddin Han: Mohammed VI, 1861-1926, last Ottoman sultan (1918-1922); deposed in 1922 when Turkey became a republic.

3. San Remo: Seaport in Imperia Province,

NW Italy, on Ligurian Sea, a resort where the exiled sultan died.

4. Abdul Mejid: 1823-1861, Ottoman sultan (1839-1861), father of Mohammed VI.

5. At beatification: The Paris edition of the *Herald Tribune*, June 12, 1930, contained an item about the electric illumination in St. Peter's for the beatification of Paula Frasinetti, 1809-1882, founder of the Sisters of St. Dorothy, a religious teaching order for poor children. The last line of the

Tribune story reads: "For the beatification ceremony 80 loudspeakers were used" [HK, *Pai*, 2-1, 41]. A rhyme with other items concerning growth of scientific inventions [cf. "Electro-magnetic" at 34/171, and "Marconi . . . electric shakes" at 38/187].

6. Turkish war: When Kara Mustafa came to the Turkish throne, he wanted to memorialize his regime by some "great exploit." Thus, in a quite unjustifiable war, he marched a vast Turkish army (more than 200,000) to the walls of Vienna from which the emperor and his court fled. Because of the fantastic ineptness and military stupidity of Mustafa, John Sobieski, king of Poland, put the entire Turkish army to flight with a force of 20,000 men and saved the cause of Christianity. In Austrian history, the siege of Vienna in 1683 looms as large as the battle of Waterloo does in the West.

7. Mr. Kolschitzky: Georges François Koltschitzky de Szombor, fl. 1683, interpreter for a commercial company of the East who was employed to spy on Turkish forces during the siege of Vienna (1683). As payment he was granted a patent to open the first coffeehouse in Vienna and was given a quantity of coffee found in the Turkish camp.

8. (de Banchiis cambi tenendi): L, "concerning banks for carrying on exchange" [40:3].

9. Von Unruh: Fritz von U., 1885-1970, German playwright, poet, and novelist; officer in World War I [41:20].

10. Kaiser: Wilhelm II, 1859-1941, German emperor and king of Prussia (1888-1918).

11. Verdun: Scene of the longest and bloodiest battle of World War I; 2 million men were engaged and 1 million were killed.

12. Mr. Charles Francis Adams: 1807-1886, American statesman, minister to Great Britain (1861-1868). Traveled widely in Europe, graduated Harvard in 1825, studied law with Daniel Webster. Became famous

writer and editor of his grandfather's letters, diaries, and papers [62:29]. Where Charles Francis A. made this remark is unknown, but the thought rhymes with similar statements made by his father, John Quincy Adams, who complained that only the "corps diplomatique" had any interest in conversation [cf. 34/165].

13. Browning: Robert B., 1812-1889. In addition to his "hearty" opinions, it was the vigor and cacophony in his verse which at first made Browning seem un-English to the English.

14. Van Buren: Martin V. B. Pound came to believe that Van Buren's *Autobiography*, written in 1854 but not published until 1918, was deliberately suppressed ("kept in the cellarage").

15. J. Adams: John A. Source of the words he supposedly said is unknown.

16. Marx: In his discussions of the ill effects of child labor, Karl Marx was concerned not only with the horrors the children suffered at the moment but also with lasting ill effects, since some of them would grow up to "become fathers of the next generation" [cf. 33:28, 32, 33].

17. Bismarck: Otto von B., 1815-1898, German soldier and statesman. Source of line is unknown.

18. Rothschild: Source of line is unknown.

19. Disraeli: Benjamin D., 1804-1881, 1st Earl of Beaconsfield, British statesman and author; prime minister (1874-1880).

20. DIGONOS: H, [Δίγονος], "twice-born." Associated with Dionysus who was twice-born, once from his mother, Semele, and then from the thigh of his father, Zeus [74/425]. Leopards and all animals in the cat family are sacred to Dionysus [2: passim].

21. Your Highness: Prob. Queen Victoria. Neither the writer nor the source of the letter is known.

22. **Cawdor**: Prob. Cawdor Castle, Nairnshire, N Scotland.

23. **Dhu Achil**: Gaelic, "Black Achilles," prob. a dog.

24. **Mr. Rhumby**: Pseudonym for Bainbridge Colby, secretary of state under Wilson (1920-1921). The juxtaposition of the lines in parentheses makes an ironic contrast: British royalty choosing a pedigreed dog with an American president choosing a secretary of state.

25. **Mr. McLocherty**: Doubtless a Scottish friend of the royal agent who is writing the letter.

26. **Galileo**: G. Galilei, 1564-1642, Italian mathematician and astronomer.

27. **'Garry Yeo'**: Galileo.

28. **err' un' . . . mondo**: I, "he was an imbecile; and he has made imbecile / . . . the world." Prob. official attitude of Church toward theories of Galileo.

29. **Salem**: City in Massachusetts, once an important center of fishing, shipping, and shipbuilding. Similar ironic comment on the reasonable requirements for a trustee of the Salem Museum as opposed to politicians making appointments in the smoke-filled backroom: ". . . three senators: four bottles of whiskey."

30. **Good Hope**: The cape at tip of S Africa.

31. **The Horn**: Cape Horn at the tip of S America.

32. **Bithynia**: Bythnia, ancient country of NW Asia Minor; it became a Roman province in 74 B.C. when Nicomedes IV willed his kingdom to Rome.

33. **theign**: OE, one of a class of free attendants on a lord; later, a baron.

34. **Athelstan**: D. 940; king of the English (924-940) who introduced guilds. Pound considers him to be one of the wisest of early English kings. The ironic contrast continues.

35. **'A little more stock'**: In the early days of uncontrolled stock speculation, the so-called robber barons could (and did) print any amount of stock and sell it without regard to the assets of the company.

36. **Norse engineer**: Unidentified. But Pound is prob. using a story told him about "this amazing navigational feat."

37. **'while she bought . . . Sunday shoes?'**: The first four lines in this 24-line passage are based on a letter to Pound from Olga Rudge who [according to Pound's daughter, Mary de Rachewiltz] at the time was in Paris where she had escorted a lady of means on a shopping expedition. The 20 following lines are based on a letter written by Mary herself from her foster parents' home in the Italian Tyrol [*Discretions*, 72-73]. Thinking about such celebrations as the ones depicted, she wrote later: "But time was never grudged for Church activities and we had grand processions and parades when the Bishop came for the confirmation ceremony or when one of the village boys came to officiate at his first Mass. No greater blessing or honor could have befallen the village; the grown-ups rejoiced and we children were wildly excited. . . . The new pair of shoes I needed when the Bishop came and I had to recite a poem."

38. **una nuova . . . festa**: I, "a new mass / (12th year of the Fascist era) / beautiful ceremony."

39. **full of fires**: Apparently an annual celebration of the founding of fascism included religious observances, parades, fireworks in the mountain villages, music, etc. Rhymes with mountain fires in *The Periplus of Hanno* [40:31, 46].

40. **in giro . . .**: I, "around the countryside."

41. **carrozze**: I, "carriages."

42. **orchis**: H, "a testicle." Prob. a metaphor for "chrysalis" as a step in the process of metamorphosis into the *farfalla* ["butterfly"], a creature of wings. The metaphor is

much elaborated in the Pisan cantos [cf. 83/532]. It appears as a leitmotiv in later cantos, such as "the king-wings in migration" [cf. 106/754] and "the kings meet in their island, / where no food is after flight from the pole" [cf. Drafts/802; for insect themes in summary cf. DG, *Pai*, 4-2 & 3, 225 ff.].

43. Mt. Segur: The last stronghold of the Catharists and Albigensians which, when they were persecuted by Innocent III, became their graveyard [23:25].

44. Val Cabrere: Valcabrère, village in S France on road to Mt. Segur.

45. San Bertrand: Saint B. de Comminges in Pyrénées, a department in S France on way to Mt. Segur.

46. Terminus: An altar, in Provence, to the great god Terminus, the sacred boundary stone that stood in the great temple of the Capitoline Jupiter in Rome.

47. Savairic: Savaric de Mauleon, whose native town is near Mt. Segur [5:20].

48. Gaubertz: G. de Poicebot, who traveled by Mt. Segur on his way to Spain [5:21].

49. Paris: The Church in N France, coached by Innocent III, insisted that the Christians in Provence (S France) come under its jurisdiction and help wipe out heretical sects such as the Manicheans. But the Manicheans, insisting they were the true Christians, would not accept the authority of Paris.

50. Falling Mars: Poss. a metaphor [derived from Gourmont] for a male insect armed for sexual consummation: "Everyone knows the flying-stag ... which flies through the summer evening buzzing like a top. ... He is the male, his war-gear pure ornament ... females are devoid of warlike apparatus. ... The glow-worm is a real worm. ... The male of this female is a perfect insect, provided with wings which he uses to seek in the darkness' [Gourmont, 39-40]. Here Pound also associates "direction of the will" with

"instinct" and sees them, acting in concert, to be superior to conventionalized intellect. He wrote: "The flying ant or wasp or whatever it was that I saw cut up a spider at Excideuil may have been acting by instinct, but it was not acting by reason of the stupidity of instinct" ["Directio Voluntatis," in *J/M*, 18]. The whole amalgam of images here becomes a mosaic of one of the most important themes in *The Cantos*: the way that divinity manifests itself as intelligence in process, the kind of intelligence that makes the cherrystone become a cherry tree [51:8; 113/778].

51. ox ... spire-top: Poss. details of place where Pound saw and was struck by the mating of a certain flying insect which dramatically illustrated precise descriptions by Remy de Gourmont.

52. jet avenger ...: Another insect, prob. a flying wasp, gets its prey while, nearby, the ants get theirs.

53. Mars in the air ...: The conclusion. Many an insect in Gourmont exists for a brief moment to be used (for generation) and then dies; it becomes a "was": "There is a kind of lamprey of which both sexes are equally phosphorescent, one in the air, the male, the other on the ground where she awaits him. After coupling they fade as lamps when extinguished. ... When the female sees the small flying star descend toward her, she gathers ... exults in fear, trembles in joy. The fading light is symbolic of the destiny of nearly all insects ... coupling accomplished ... life vanishes from them" [Gourmont, 40; cf. 47:23].

54. Lido: Town at N end of the island, outside the Lagoon of Venice, which has a famous beach.

55. an old man ... placed a stone: I.e., on beach cloths to keep them from blowing away. His sexual potency gone, he has become in the universal process (or "the way") a kind of death-in-life [cf. "the old man sweeping leaves," etc., 21/99-100].

CANTO XLIX

Sources

A manuscript of *Sho-Sho Hakkei* [eight paintings of scenes along
the Sho-Sho River] in Pound's possession; notes [inedit.] Pound
took from verbal translations and comments on the Chinese
poems; Fenollosa Notebooks (inedit.), University of Virginia
Library; Sasaki Genryu, *Poems in Chinese and Japanese on the
Eight Famous Scenes by Genryu*, 1683; H. A. Giles, *A History of
Chinese Literature*, London and New York, 1901.

Background

Ichisada Miyazaki, *Prosperity of the Empire of Shin*, Tokyo,
1967; Shigeki Kaizuka, *A History of China*, 3 vols., Tokyo, 1971.

Exegeses

Sanehide Kodama, "The Eight Scenes of Sho-Sho," *Pai*, 6-2,
131-145; Angela Jung Palandri, "The 'Seven Lakes Canto' Re-
visited," *Pai*, 3-1, 51-54; HK, "More on the Seven Lakes Canto,"
Pai, 2-1, 43-46; DP, *Barb*, App. B; Dekker, *Cantos*, 179-181;
Fang, Ph.D. dissertation, Harvard University, I, 77.

Glossary

1. **seven lakes**: Because of this first line,
Canto 49 has come to be known as "The
Seven Lakes Canto." Kenner says it "con-
sists of (1) [eight] anonymous poems much
rearranged; (2) the Emperor's poem; (3) a
folk song; (4) a terminal Poundian distich
and four interpolated Poundian lines" [HK,
Pai, 2-1, 46]. Kodama identifies the source
of the poems as eight famous paintings of
scenes along a river in C China which pours
into Lake Dotei. Ezra Pound's parents
owned an old Japanese manuscript book
which contained the eight Chinese and eight
Japanese poems illustrated by the paintings.
The book is entitled *Sho-Sho* [the river]
Hakkei [Kodama, *Pai*, 6-2, 131-145; unless
otherwise noted, quotations in the following

glosses are from this article]. "Sho-Sho" is
Japanese for Chinese "Hsiao-Hsiang"
(M2622-M2565); the river Hsiao flows into
the Hsiang, a major tributary of the Yangtze,
at Lingling in S Hunan province. "Hakkei" is
Japanese for Chinese "pa ching" (M4845-
M1129), traditionally defined as the "eight
classes of scenery."

2. **Rain . . . weeping**: These five lines are
based on a poem for Scene 6, entitled
"Night Rain in Sho-Sho." The poem con-
cerns events after the legendary emperor Yü
Shun died, causing his wives such grief that
their tears dyed the bamboo leaves purple;
dappled purple bamboos still grow in the
area. "Later [the wives] killed themselves,

and their shrine is said to be near the River. The narrator of the poem is on his way to the shrine, and is filled with sorrow."

3. **Autumn . . . reeds**: These six lines are based on a poem for Scene 5, entitled "Autumn Moon on Lake Dotei." "Lake Dotei" is the Chinese "Tung-t'ing Hu" (M6609-M6405, M2168), long anglicized as "Tungting Lake", a large shallow body of water in N Hunan province. The Hsiang, after being joined by the Hsiao, drains E Hunan, flowing north into this natural reservoir of the Yangtze.

4. **Behind . . . wind**: From Scene 7: "Evening Bell of a Misty Temple." Kodama writes in a footnote: "According to one interpretation, the poem refers to the ruin of a Buddhist temple on top of Mt. Kyugi in the Sho-Sho area, and the bell the narrator hears is from a nearby temple." "Kyugi" is prob. "Chiu-chi" in Hunan province.

5. **Boat fades . . . river**: Based on Scene 2: "Sailboats Returning to Far-off Shores," which evokes a feeling of loneliness and yearning.

6. **Where wine flag . . . light**: Based on Scene 3: "Mist over a Mountain Town." Kodama renders some of the lines as "A wine flag on the pole is in the slanting sun / Some houses are in the mist."

7. **Comes . . . cold**: Based on Scene 4: "Evening Snowfall over the River." Key words and phrases in original are "colorless clouds," "low sky," "jewel dust flying," "small leaflike boat."

8. **San Yin**: Pound's notes show this originally transcribed as "Sai Yin." The two Chinese characters "shan yin" (M5630, M7444)—"san yin" in the dialects of C China—form a phrase meaning "the north side of the mountain"; but Pound turned them into a place name. [See Kodama, *Pai*, 6-2, 136, n. 6 for another view].

9. **Wild geese . . . autumn**: Scene 1: "Wild Geese Plummeting to the Flat Sands,"

10. **Rooks . . . sky line**: Scene 8: "Sunset Glow over a Fishing Village." Some phrases are "Twilight bewilders the crows," "clamors of fish and shrimps," "the waves are colored in the track of the setting sun."

11. **Tsing**: Ch'ing, name of the 22d dynasty, 1616-1912. It was prob. K'ang-hsi, the 2d Ch'ing emperor (1662-1722), who visited the hill lakes. Kodama says that he seems to have visited the Seven Lakes area with the empress in 1699. His reign is the subject of Cantos 58-61; the *Sacred Edict* of K'ang-hsi is the main subject of Cantos 98-99.

12. **State . . . debt?**: Attitude of Presidents Thomas Jefferson, Andrew Jackson, and Martin Van Buren [cf. 37/183: "Relief is got not by increase / but by diminution of debt"].

13. **Geryon**: [46:5].

14. **TenShi**: Prob. a village to which Yodai's canal went.

15. **old king**: Yodai [Yang-ti], 605-618, a king who found that building canals gave pleasure to himself and to his people; the canals became economically useful.

16. **KEI . . . KAI**: These four lines are a transliteration of Japanese pronunciation of a classical Chinese poem Pound found in the Fenollosa Notebooks. Translations are many and varied. Kodama gives: "The auspicious clouds bright and colorful / Twist and spread. / The sun and the moon shed their rays / Morning after morning."

17. **sun up . . . what is it?**: These five lines are based on the translation of an ancient Chinese poem to be found in a Fenollosa Notebook as well as several other places. The intent or tone of the poem is controversial. Fang calls it the well-known "Clod-Beaters Song" [Chi-jang-ko] "supposedly sung by contented peasantry of the time of Shun's predecessor Yao" [53:14]. Others have translated it as "a coolies' song": the lazy king does nothing and lives off the sweat of the laboring man. A Fenollosa note says of it:

"This is called an earth beating song, because old folk beat the ground (for music) in singing this song." Kodama believes Pound achieves "the simplicity of a folk poem" by consulting Fenollosa [*Pai*, 6-2, 144].

18. The fourth ... beasts: Pound told a

visitor that in Canto 49 he intended to present "a glimpse of Paradiso" [Palandri, *Pai*, 3-1, 51]. The paradisal thrust of the lines is suggested by stillness ["the still point of the turning world" in Eliot] as well as the Dionysian power over wild beasts [cf. 2/8]. Note also rhyme with Apollonius [94/635].

CANTO L

Sources

Antonio Zobi, *Storia civile della Toscana dal MDCCXXXVII al MDCCCXLVIII*, 5 vols., Firenze, 1850-1852; Christopher Hollis, *The Two Nations*, London, 1935; Charles Francis Adams, ed., *The Works of John Adams*, X, Boston, 1856; Andrew Lipscomb and Albert Bergh, eds., *The Writings of Thomas Jefferson*, XIV, Washington, D.C., 1905; *Il Monte dei Paschi di Siena e le Aziende in Esso Riunite*, 9 vols., ed. Narciso Mengozzi, Siena, 1891-1925.

Background

Fang, Ph.D. dissertation, Harvard University, I, 80; any of the standard biographies of Napoleon, Wellington, and Metternich.

Exegeses

Kimpel and Eaves, *Pai*, 8-1.

Glossary

1. Revolution' said Mr. Adams: John Adams in a letter about the history of the Revolution [32:1].

2. Peter Leopold: Pietro Leopoldo, Duke of Tuscany, who worked hard to improve conditions in his land. A rhyme with what the early Revolutionists were doing in New England [44:1].

3. Count Orso ... place: The source shows that on December 23, 1624, Count Orso and "suoi figli et descendenti maschi legittimi et naturali ["his sons and male descendants legitimate and natural"] were enfiefed with the territory of Monte Pescali and entrusted by the Grand Duke of Tuscany with the ... administration of Civil and Criminal Justice in the said Place" [Kimpel and Eaves, *Pai*,

8-1]. According to Kimpel, the lines are "almost certainly" meant to describe the situation under the old rulers of Tuscany, the Medici, who became extinct in 1737.

4. debt when the Medici: [43:70]. The debt of the Medici recorded from Il Monte dei Paschi in the last lines of Canto 43/222 Pound found also in Zobi, who noted: "When the Medici came to the throne, the debt of the Republic calculated all together did not exceed five million ducats; and at the time of their extinction the Tuscan debt has grown to fourteen million scudi, the interest on which absorbed the best incomes of the State" [Zobi, I, 118; trans. Kimpel, *Pai*, 8-1].

5. the first folly ... : Zobi says [I, 120] that the germ of the decay of the commercial prosperity of Tuscany was the avidity of Florentine merchants, which caused them to establish wool factories in Flanders, England, and elsewhere in order to save the cost of transportation of raw materials; the English, who produced the raw wool, soon prohibited its export.

6. the arts ... : Zobi [I, 153-163, esp. 160] laments the decay of letters and the graphic arts in Tuscany.

7. and Leopoldo ... : [cf. 2 above]. Pound had stressed the wise reforms of the Grand Duke Pietro Leopoldo of Tuscany toward the end of Canto 44. Here he adds, from Zobi, the abolition of many taxes [II, 99, 182, 269-270], the refinancing and reduction of the national debt [II, 104-107, 441-446], the expulsion of the Jesuit order [II, 133], and the abolition of the Catholic Inquisition [II, 305].

8. 'Un' abbondanza che affamava': I, "An abundance which famishes," a play on the name of the Abbondanza ["Abundance," the office in charge of relief works]. Zobi reports [I, 403] that before Pietro Leopoldo's reign it had no funds and was called "l'affamatrice Abbondanza." Pietro Leopoldo created a new office to replace the old

Abbondanza, "che facevano l'ufficio d'*affamare*" ["whose office it was *to starve*"]. Thus, Leopold becomes one of the minor heroes of *The Cantos*, a man, *directio voluntatis*, who gets things done [II, 60].

9. Mr. Locke's / essay on interest: Pietro Leopoldo entrusted the direction of finance to Angelo Tavanti, one of the very few Italians who had studied French and English writers on politics and economics; he collaborated on a translation of *Several Papers Relating to Money, Interest and Trade, ... Writ upon Several Occasions and Published at Different Times*, by John Locke (1632-1704), the famous philosopher and political theorist [Zobi, II, 267-268n].

10. but Genoa took our trade ... : Because of the close connection between the grand duke and the royal family of Austria, the trade of the Tuscan port of Livorno (Leghorn) suffered when Austria got involved in a war with Turkey, and its old rival the independent city of Genoa took advantage of the situation; similarly, the grand duke refused to have relations with the American Colonies while they were at war with England, and when they became independent they preferred to trade with Genoa, which had had early commercial ties with them, so that trade from Livorno had to pass through Genoa [Zobi, II, 388-389].

11. Te, admirabile, O VashinnnTTonn! ... Voi, popoli transatlantici admirabili!: I, "You, Oh admirable Washington! ... You, admirable people across the Atlantic." Zobi seizes the occasion described in the above note for a digression [II, 389-390], which he hopes his readers will pardon, on the virtues of the Americans and their leader. He calls America the daughter of Italy and contrasts her independence and hopeful future with the servile state of Italy after the failure of the revolutions of 1848.

12. two thirds of state debt: The public debt in 1788 was 12,330,000 crowns; Pietro Leopoldo, who wanted to abolish the whole debt, had arranged for the cancellation of 8,256,343 crowns [Zobi, II, 444n].

13. they sent him off ... and Paris exploded: [44:1]. When he became Holy Roman emperor on the death of Josef II in 1790 (just as the French Revolution was starting), Pietro Leopoldo necessarily went to Vienna [Zobi, II, 509]. Pound had expressed his dislike of the Austrian Empire and especially of Franz Josef, 1830-1916, who became emperor in 1848, in Cantos 16 and 35 [16:23; 35:8]. In 1790 Franz Josef was not yet born, and Klemens Wenzel Nepomuk Lothar, Prince von Metternich, 1773-1859, the dominating figure of the reactionary period following the fall of Napoleon, did not become chancellor until 1809, but Pound is looking ahead. Pietro Leopoldo's son, the Grand Duke Ferdinando III, prevented the union [Anschluss] of the crowns of Austria and Tuscany, which were declared to be absolutely separated [Zobi, II, 554-555]. The Austro-Hungarian Empire, which succeeded the Holy Roman Empire, prided itself on its multinational nature ("embastardized cross-breeds"); *merdery* is a coinage from the French word for excrement. The explosion was the French Revolution.

14. 'certain practices called religious' ...: In discussing the reasons for the success of the American Republic and the failure of the Roman Republic set up at the time of the French Revolution, Zobi mentions [III, 230] that the Italians were too much given to such practices "by scoundrels," which served only to weaken mind and body "and in short make man less than man." He also mentions the Italian ignorance of economics.

15. Pius sixth: Giovanni Angelo Braschi, 1717-1799, elected pope in 1775. He followed an ultrareactionary policy even before the French Revolution; Zobi gives [III, 39] several examples of his unwise actions, such as his "excessive imprudence" in writing a letter to Louis XVI congratulating him on his escape from France before Louis had in fact got out of the country (he was caught and brought back). The letter was intercepted by the National Assembly and helped induce France to persecute the Gallican church and to invade Italy. The French took Rome in 1798, a republic was set up there, and the pope died a prisoner.

16. MARENGO ... a.d. 1800: Marengo, near Alessandria in Piedmont, NW Italy, was the site of Napoleon's great victory over the Austrians on June 14, 1800, which gave him effective control of Italy. Napoleon had been in control of France, as first consul, since his coup d'etat of 18 "Brumale" or Brumaire [Nov. 9, but Zobi says Nov. 10], 1799. Zobi remarks [III, 406] that Napoleon thereby disposed the national representatives, so "1791" may be a misprint for 1799; or Pound may be thinking of the short-lived Constitution of 1791, which ended the power of the king and replaced the Constituent Assembly with a legislative assembly. The latter, a little more than a year later, was dominated by the radical Jacobin party, as the first step toward the end of representative government. "I left peace ... to yr enemies" is from a speech, quoted by Zobi, which Napoleon made to his soldiers in Paris after his return from Marengo; Zobi says the speech was most truthful (as to the state of France) and most seditious (in giving Napoleon a reason to increase his power).

17. interest at 24 ...: Zobi reports [III, 440-441] the scarcity of money caused by the impositions of this war period, with the resulting rise in interest rates and decline of commerce.

18. 1801 the triumvirs ...: The three men governing Tuscany tried to restore some of the reforms of Pietro Leopoldo but were overthrown by a French army under Murat [Zobi, III, 461-463].

19. A thousand ... English frigate descended: In 1814 Napoleon, forced by the allied armies to abdicate, was made king of the small island of Elba, off the Tuscan coast, the capital of which is Portoferraio.

On May 3 a British frigate landed him on Elba, where he was soon joined by a thousand men of his old guard. Pound states the income the allies granted him. Napoleon claimed to have chosen the island because of "the sweetness of their [the inhabitants'] customs and the goodness of their climate" [Zobi, III, 757-759].

20. **Ferdinando Habsburg**: Ferdinando III [44:6, 18; Zobi, III, 762] makes the remark about the state of his finances when he was restored as Grand Duke of Tuscany after the fall of Napoleon.

21. **England and Austria . . . bloody oppression**: A brief summary of the peace terms imposed by England and Austria, along with Russia and Prussia, in the Treaty of Vienna after the fall of Napoleon [the treaty is printed in Zobi, IV, 40-78]. The powers attempted to restore the pre-Revolutionary status, but went even further in extinguishing three old Italian republics: Venice went to Austria, Genoa to Sardegna (Sardinia), and Lucca to Maria Luisa, former queen of Etruria [44:38].

22. **Rospigliosi**: In 1814, before Ferdinando III could take charge of Tuscany, the state was temporarily administered by Prince Rospigliosi, who issued to the independence-loving Tuscans a proclamation containing "the enormous indecency that the Grand Duchy was the patrimony of foreign lords, as if states could be an allodial property and their inhabitants serfs" [Zobi, IV, 24].

23. **throne of England**: In 1814-1815 the English king, George III, had been insane for a number of years and his son, the future George IV, was regent.

24. **Austrian sofa**: The Austro-Hungarian emperor was Franz I, 1768-1835.

25. **four Georges**: The first four Georges ruled England from 1714 to 1830.

26. **Spain**: In 1814 the Bourbons were restored to Spain in the person of Fernando VII, 1784-1833.

27. **Wellington**: Arthur Wellesley, Duke of Wellington, 1769-1852, the victor of Waterloo. The conferees at the Congress of Vienna [including Wellington] are regarded by Hollis [*Two Nations*, 134-136] as not seeing the facts as they were. Pius the VI and the monarchs were persuaded that the old order had been restored. "Metternich and Stadion . . . were the rulers of Austria [they thought] because they were called the rulers of Austria. . . . The papacy [cf. 15 above] saw Metternich and Stadion in their seats of office. They did not see Stadion pocketing the loans of the Rothschilds and Metternich creeping down into the Frankfort ghetto to learn their latest will" [Hollis gives as sources *Rise of the House of Rothschild* (1928) and *Reign of the House of Rothschild* (1928) by C. E. Corti and *Metternich* (1933) by Algernon Cecil]. In the mid-thirties Pound saw Wellington as one of many willing victims of the usurers: "For fifty years after Waterloo Papal policy was directed by pious and simple men. They preached sincerely the Church's doctrine against usury . . . because in their innocence of the world they did not know they were usurers." It is important to note that in this canto Pound distinguishes "Jew" and the Jewish God from "jew" as "Rothschild usurer," saying that no Jew God would be foolish enough to keep a man like Pius VI in office [cf. 15 above]. But by the early 1950s he began to see other sides of Wellington's character [cf. "Wellington's peace after Vaterloo," 85/543].

28. **'Leave the Duke, Go for gold!'**: As evidence that a few bankers could plunge England into chaos, Hollis writes that when Earl Grey resigned as prime minister in 1832 because the king refused to create enough new peers to pass the first reform bill, the Duke of Wellington made an effort to form a Tory government. The watchword among the reformers was, "To stop the Duke, go for gold," that is, corner gold and thus create a run on the banks. Because of this threat the Whigs regained power [Hollis, 106].

29. Metternich: [13, 27, above].

**30. 'From the brigantine Incostante'...
into Flanders:** A description of the Hundred
Days during which Napoleon tried to recover
his empire. Zobi tells [IV, 62] how Napo-
leon left Elba on the brigantine *Incostante*
and landed at Cannes, in S France, on March
1, 1815. France quickly rallied behind him
and his armies advanced into Flanders, but
there, at the battle of Waterloo, on June 18,
he was finally defeated, partly because Mar-
shal Michel Ney, Prince de La Moskova,
1769-1815, was thrown from his horse and
Emmanuel, Marquis de Grouchy, 1766-1847,
did not bring up his troops in time [IV, 89].

31. Bentinck's word ... Sardegna: In 1814
Lord William Cavendish Bentinck, 1774-
1839, commander of the British forces in
Sicily, led an expedition against Genoa and
declared the republic there restored [Zobi,
IV, 10, 102-103]. But the republic did not
remain restored.

32. 'Not' / said Napoleon ... : Zobi quotes
[IV, 223n-224n] Earl Grey as reporting a
statement made by Napoleon (after his final
imprisonment on the island of St. Helena)
that he "had fallen not because of the league
formed against him but because he contra-
dicted the spirit of the century."

33. Zeitgeist!: G, "Spirit of the times!"

34. OBIT, aetatis 57: L, "He died, aged
57." Napoleon died in 1821, and Dante
Alighieri in 1321; but Napoleon was born in
1769 and died at the age of 51.

35. il sesso femminile: I, "the female sex."
Zobi [IV, 273], describing the death of
Napoleon's second wife, Maria Luisa of
Parma, 1791-1847, is of the opinion that she
was "certainly not distinguished for that
which most embellishes the female sex and
makes it estimable."

36. Italy ever doomed: Zobi, describing the
enthusiasm for Pius IX [37 below] before
1848 but writing just after the failure of the
revolutions of 1848, which attempted to

unify the peninsula and cast out the Aus-
trians who dominated much of it, laments
[IV, 618] the fall of "this poor Italy, always
destined to be ruined by pursuing brilliant
abstractions and deceptive purposes."

37. Mastai, Pio Nono: Giovanni Maria
Mastai-Ferretti, 1792-1878, became Pope
Pius IX ("Pio Nono") in 1846. After giving
early hopes of a more liberal policy [Zobi,
V, 21], he was forced to flee from Rome in
1848, and on his return in 1850 he became
steadily more conservative [for a later stage
of his career, cf. 28:57].

38. D'Azeglio: Massimo, Marchese d'Azeglio,
1798-1866, was one of the leaders of the
Italian nationalist revival and fought against
Austria in 1848. Zobi reports [V, 27] that
he was exiled from Tuscany in 1847 because
of his liberal sentiments.

39. Lord Minto: Gilbert Elliot, 2d Earl of
Minto, 1782-1859, lord privy seal, was sent
by the British government to Sardinia, Tus-
cany, and Rome in the autumn of 1847 to
encourage a policy of reform and to report
on the state of Italy. Zobi describes [V,
236-237n] his enthusiastic reception on
October 30 in Arezzo (on the road from
Florence to Rome) as representing the
friends of Italian liberation and of a customs
union. He responded with a salute to Leo-
poldo II [cf. 42 below] and to Italian
independence, which gave unjustified en-
couragement, since the British government
favored a policy of slow but sure, not
revolutionary, reform.

40. Bowring had preceded: Sir John B.,
1792-1872, English writer and traveler, vis-
ited Italy in the autumn of 1836 and the
next year reported to Lord Palmerston's
government on the state of trade in Tuscany
as well as in other regions [Zobi, V, 36-37].

41. EVVIVA ... INDIPENDENZA: I, "Long
live ... independence."

42. Leopoldo: Leopoldo II, 1797-1870, suc-
ceeded his father, Ferdinando III, as Grand
Duke of Tuscany in 1824 and abdicated in

1855. The old Leopoldo is of course Pietro Leopoldo, Leopoldo I [cf. 2 above].

43. Lalage ... Dirce: Classical names of women, prob. not used with reference to any specific personages. Lalage was a common name for a courtesan; Dirce was the wife of Lycus, king of Thebes, but Pound is probably thinking of the beautiful Dirce in one of his favorite poems, Landor's "Stand close around, ye Stygian set."

CANTO LI

Sources

Guido Guinicelli, "Al cor gentil repara sempre amore"; Charles Bowlker, *The Art of Angling, Greatly Enlarged and Improved* ... , Ludlow, 1829; Dante, *Inf.* VII, 97-98.

Background

EP, *LE*, 186, 211; *SR*, 101-117; *T*, 441; Francesco De Sanctis, *History of Italian Literature*, trans. Joan Redfern, New York, 1931; John Hill, *A History of Fly Fishing for Trout*, New York, 1921; Charles Fox, *Rising Trout*, 1967.

Exegeses

EP, *GK*, 172; HK, *Era*, 431; Robert Demott, "Ezra Pound and Charles Bowlker: Note on Canto LI," *Pai*, 1-2, 189-198; DP, *Barb*, 216-220.

Glossary

1. Shines ... eye: Trans. of part of stanza 4 of "Al cor gentil repara sempre amore" ["Love always repairs to the noble heart"] by Guido Guinicelli, ca. 1230-1276; it is an important Neoplatonic poem which links the poet's lady with angels and also serves as a model for Dante's school. As the first image in this canto which, at the time it was written (ca. 1936), Pound considered central to his design of probably 100 cantos, these lines are most significant: they emphasize light as the major Neoplatonic symbol of divine intelligence operating in the created universe as opposed to the darkness of ignorance which Pound associates with hell as in Cantos I, XIV, and XV.

2. Fifth element ... Napoleon: The same Guinicelli canzone (1 above) has a stanza that starts, "Fère lo sol lo fango tutto 'l giorno: / vile riman, né il Sol perde calore. / Dice uom altier:—Gentile per schiatta torno:— / lui sembra il fango, e 'l Sol gentile valore," which Redfern translates as "The Sun shines on the mud the whole day long: the mud remains vile and the Sun keeps its heat. When a proud man says, 'I am noble because of my race,' he is like the mud, the true nobility is like the Sun" [De Sanctis, 32]. The word "mud" is thus carried from the Guinicelli context into a Napoleonic one, repeating a motif stated earlier [34/116]. "Mud" for Pound seems to be a metaphor for the basic stuff of the universe through which mind can operate. He wrote: "mud does not account for mind" [GK, 172]. The significance of the fifth element is controversial. Some believe that because of his experience in military campaigns, Napoleon added to the classical list (earth, water, fire, and air) the combination that caused him the most trouble: "mud."

3. **usura**: L, I, "usury" [for this and the remaining names on p. 250, see 45:1 ff.].

4. **looms are hushed**: "Japan's quest for foreign markets hushed all the looms in those hills" around Rapallo [HK, Era, 431].

5. **Blue dun**: One of the two most popular fly patterns dressed by experts for use in fishing. Although "Number 2" in Pound's source [Bowlker, The Art of Angling] refers to the number of an illustration, he uses it accurately enough as the size of a hook. The first eight lines contain data on making the fly and suggest the best and only times to use it. The next ten lines contain similar data on another popular fly, the Granham [Demott, Pai, 1-2, 189 ff.].

6. **Hen pheasant's ... Granham**: Bowlker's heading is "Granam, or Green-tail. No. 6" Pound has selected his data from this passage: "It derives the name of Green-Tail from a bunch of eggs, of a green colour, which it deposits in the water while floating on the surface. The wings lie flat on the body, and are made of a shaded feather from the wing of a partridge, or hen pheasant; the body of the dark fur of a hare's ear, and a

yellowish grizzled cock's hackle for legs; a small quantity of bright green wax (or green harl from the eye of a peacock's tail) about the size of a pin's head." One of the amazing things revealed in The Art of Angling is the precision of nature in process. Trout will rise for a dressed fly only if it duplicates exactly a natural fly that can be expected not only that season of the year but also the right time of day. Any variation from nature and the fish will not take the bait: "As long as the brown continues, no fish will take Granham."

7. **light of the doer** ... : The juxtaposition of the fly-fishing sequence and usury is not casual; since fly-fishing is an art that depends on nature's increase as well as profits from it, it has none of the destructive effects of usury, which is CONTRA NATURAM [45:19].

8. **Deo ... adeptus**: L, "Godlike in a way this intellect that has grasped." Adapted from Albertus Magnus [cf. LE, 186]. "Light" in the doer is divinity manifested through the intelligence of man and nature: central Neoplatonic concept of The Cantos. Other metaphors of the idea are "the kind of intelligence that makes the cherrystone become the cherry tree" [48:50] or "the weasel eat rue, / and the swallows nip celandine" [cf. 92/618].

9. **Grass**: Like "the brown marsh fly" which after eleven "comes on," grass is nature's increase and is "nowhere out of place."

10. **Königsberg**: Rudolf Hess, Hitler's deputy and Reichsminister, used the following German and Latin phrases in a radio message broadcast from Königsberg in East Prussia, July 8, 1934 [EH].

11. **Zwischen ... wird**: G, "Between the [two] peoples a modus vivendi is achieved."

12. **modus vivendi**: L, "way of life."

13. **circling etc.**: Dante and Virgil climb on the back of Geryon [14:3] who circles down with them into the depths of fraud. Virgil said: "Geryon, move now; fly in big

circles and descend slowly" [*Inf*. XVII, 97-98]. After he set them down "he darted off like an arrow from the bow." As opposed to art, where "Slowness is beauty" [cf. 87/572], usurers are in a hurry: "Time is money!"

14. the 12: Unidentified.

15. the regents: Pound told Daniel Pearlman that the regents are "bankers" [DP, *Barb*, 218n].

16. Geryone: Geryon, the Dantean personification of usury [46:51]. Says Pound: "We . . . see more clearly the grading of Dante's values, and especially how the whole hell reeks with money. The usurers are there as against nature, against the natural increase of agriculture or of any productive work. Deep hell is reached via Geryon (fraud) of the marvellous patterned hide, and for ten cantos thereafter the damned are all of them damned for money" [*LE*, 211].

17. help . . . aged . . . peace: Prob. satirical note on the international gnomes and usurers who say their stock supports widows and orphans and who promote wars and arms sales in order to obtain "universal peace," as witness Zaharoff, the house of Morgan, etc. The international gang speaks in many languages.

18. eel-fishers basket: This obscure phrase occurs also in Fragments/799. Perhaps the eel is the tail of Geryon. Someone told me that on the Mediterranean they fish for eels by dragging a basketlike instrument as if it were a net. But this possibility has not been documented. [CT]

19. League of Cambrai: A brief (1508-1510) alliance of states, led by Maximilian and Louis XII, which tried to crush Venice. The league, joined by England and Spain, succeeded briefly, but Venice recovered [DP, *Barb*, 220].

20. Ideograms: Chêng⁴ [M351]: "right"; Ming² [M4524]: "name."

CANTO LII

Sources

S. Couvreur, *Li Ki, ou mémoires sur Les Bienséances et les Cérémonies. Texte Chinois avec une Double Traduction en Français et en Latin*, Ho Kien Fou, 1913.

Background

S. Wells Williams, *The Middle Kingdom*, 2 vols., New York, 1883; EP, *SP*, 84, 87, 300n, 159; *GK*, 181; *L*, 250; M. Beer, *An Inquiry into Physiocracy*, London, 1939.

Exegeses

John Drummond, "The Italian Background to *The Cantos*," in *Ezra Pound*, ed. Peter Russell, London, 1950, 100-102; CE, *Ideas*, 40-41; Davis, *Vision*, 98-99, 135-136; DP, *Barb*, 222-223; HK, *Era*, 171, 426, 465.

Glossary

1. Duke Leopold: Leopold II, 1747-1792, Holy Roman emperor (1790-1792). As Leopold I of Tuscany, he carried out many reforms in administration, taxation, punishment for crime [44:1, 4].

2. abundance etc.: Pound's central thesis, deriving with additions and modifications from the Physiocrats, a French economic group that developed in reaction to "mercantilism": "They generalized their views in the economic doctrine that agriculture was the only source of riches or the only productive occupation, while manufacture and traffic were sterile. . . . The inordinate fostering of 'sterile' manufacture at the expense of productive tillage; the striving for a monetary balance of trade; the restrictive regulations imposed on trade and commerce, and, finally, the agelong restrictions on the marketing and exportation of grain, formed . . . the source of the misery of the French people, and were the cause of all social distempers and devastating wars between nations. They believed that those policies and restrictions . . . were in conflict with the moral basis of economic life, that is, with equality of exchanges, just prices, or commucative justice" [Beer, 14]. The Physiocrats' theories developed and flowered during the century before the French Revolution and may be seen in Jeffersonian agrarianism. Physiocratic theories also formed the basis of Duke Leopold's activities in Siena. As were the Physiocrats, Pound would be opposed to such characteristics of mercantilism as: "(i) Conception of money (coin, and bullion or treasure) as the essence of wealth. . . . (ii) Regulating foreign trade with a view to bringing in money by the balance of trade," etc. [ibid., 13n].

3. Schacht: Horace Greeley Hjalmar S., 1877-1970, German financier who became president of the Reichsbank under Hitler and presided over the financial operations of the Nazi state.

4. anno seidici: I, *anno sedici*, "year six-teen." Refers to 1938, the sixteenth year of the Fascist era.

5. commerciabili beni: I, "goods for commerce."

6. neschek: Heb., "usury." The serpent: Geryon [51:16].

7. Vivante: Leone V., 1887-   , Italian writer and critic, author of *English Poetry* (1950) (issued with a preface by T. S. Eliot), lived in a villa on a hill near Siena. Author of *Note sopra la originalità del pensiero*. Pound mentions him twice in "Mang Tsze," *The Criterion*, 1938 [*SP*, 84, 87; *GK*, 181].

8. yitt: From German *Jude*, slang for "Jew." Usually applied to poor Jews as opposed to financial operators such as the Rothschilds.

9. goyim: Heb., "gentiles." Pound's apparent intent is to deplore the way anti-Semites in the 1930s blamed all Jews, including poor ones, for the destructive financial practices of a very few. At least, in a letter to T. C. Wilson in 1934 [*L*, 250], Pound wrote: "Don't be an anti-Semite." And later, on November 21, 1935, he said: "Usurers have no race. How long the whole Jewish people is to be a sacrificial goat for the usurer, I know not" [*SP*, 300n].

10. Miss Bell: Gertrude M. L. B., 1868-1926, British authority on the Near East, where she served as military intelligence agent and political secretary.

11. Stalin: Joseph [Iosif] Vissarionovich Dzhugashvili, 1879-1953, seized power over the Soviets after Lenin's death.

12. Litvinof: Maksim Maksimovich Litvinov, 1876-1951, Russian revolutionary who in various roles became a powerful figure in Stalin's government during the 1930s.

13. entrefaites: F, "events."

14. Johnnie Adams: Adams said: "All the perplexities, confusion, and distress in America arise, not from defects in their constitution or confederation, not from want of honour and virtue, so much as from downright ignorance of the nature of coin, credit, and circulation" [cf. *SP*, 159; 31:15].

15. Ben: Benjamin Franklin. The document on which this line was based has been exposed as a forgery; Franklin never said anything of the kind.

16. chazims: Yiddish, *chaseirim*, "pigs."

17. Black lines: To avoid possible libel suits, the publishers wanted to delete six lines of names from the text; Pound would not consent but said they could be blacked out to show the censorship. Both New Directions and Faber made the same deletions.

18. KUNG: Kung Fu-tse [Confucius; see 13:1]. Two major ingredients of *The Cantos* are the ethical system of Kung and the sacred mysteries represented by Eleusis: everything takes place between these poles [45:20].

19. Golden Roof: Church of La Daurade, Toulouse, France.

20. la Dorata: I, "the Golden One," the French *La Daurade*. The church was visited by Guido Cavalcanti.

21. baldacchino: I, "canopy."

22. Riccio: Guido R., Sienese hero at the siege of Montemassi; a fresco of him on horseback (1328) is in the Palazzo Pubblico in Siena.

23. Montepulciano: Erroneous for Montemassi, a town in C Italy SW of Siena.

24. groggy church: A thesis of *The Cantos* is that the Church, which used to forbid usury [*neschek*], began to decline when it changed this policy and joined the money-makers.

25. Burgos: Capital of Burgos Province, N Spain, in Old Castile, the home and burial place of El Cid [3:16]. The firm song is *The Epic of the Cid*.

26. Cortona: Town in Tuscany, C Italy.

27. Gregory: Pope Gorgory I, who initiated the Gregorian chant.

28. Know then: The remainder of the canto is based on *Li Ki* [*Book of Rites*], one of the five Chinese classics. *Li Ki* is held in special esteem because people believe it contains Confucius's views on government and manners. *Li*, usually translated as "rites" or "ceremonies," cannot be conveyed in English by one word, for the Chinese idea of *li* includes "not only the external conduct, but involves the right principles from which all true etiquette and politeness spring. The state religion, the government of a family, and the rules of society are all founded on the true *li*, or relations of things" [S. Wells Williams, I, 645]. *Li* is both the spirit and the substance of Confucianism.

29. Hyades: A cluster of stars in the constellation Taurus. When they rose with the sun, it was supposed to rain.

30. Lord of the Fire: A spirit in the religion of ancient China.

31. Son of Heaven: Title of Chinese emperor.

32. Gemini: The third zodiacal constellation represented by the twins, Castor and Pollux. The sun enters Gemini about May 21.

33. Virgo: The Virgin: the constellation (due S of the handle of the Dipper) represented as a woman holding a spike of grain in her hand.

34. Hydra: A southern constellation having the form of a serpent.

35. Antares: The brightest star in Scorpio (called Scorpio's Heart), a southern constellation.

36. Andromeda: A northern constellation, between Pegasus and Perseus, represented as a chained woman.

37. Ming T'ang: The "Temple of Light" (or "Wisdom") where the imperial family of China worshiped its ancestors.

38. manes: L, "spirits of the dead."

39. Lords of the Mountains: Spirits in ancient Chinese religion.

40. Sagittarius: The southern constellation represented as a centaur shooting an arrow.

41. Orion: The constellation on the celestial equator represented as a hunter.

42. Houai: Hwai River in S Honan and NW Anhwei provinces in E China flows into the Hwang Ho, or Yellow River, above Hungtze Hu.

43. Heaven's Son: The emperor.

44. archer's shoulder: Prob. the archer is the constellation Orion.

45. Spirit of Mountains: Spirit of the ancient Chinese religion.

46. Lord Palmerston: One of the minor *directio voluntatis* people celebrated in *The Cantos*, who worked for the people and got things done [cf. 42:1].

47. Sligo: Seaport of county Sligo in N Eire on Sligo Bay. When Palmerston was prime minister, he promoted such public works as are listed for Sligo and London.

48. chih[3]: M939, "to stop."

CANTOS LIII-LXI

THE CHINESE CANTOS

Sources

J. A. M. de Moyriac de Mailla, *Histoire Générale de la Chine*, 13 vols., Paris, 1777-1785; A. de Lacharme, *Confucii Chi-King*, ed. Julius Mohl, Stuttgart and Tübingen, 1830, XI-XII; Homer, *Od.* X, 305; I, 3; Robert Grosseteste, "De Luce seu de inchoatione formarum," in L. Baur, *Die philosophischen Werke des Robert Grosseteste*, Münster, 1912.

Background

Henri Cordier, *Histoire Générale de la Chine et de ses Relations avec les Pays Étrangers*, 4 vols., Paris, 1920; Homer H. Dubs, *The History of the Former Han Dynasty*, 3 vols., London, 1938-1955; Burton Watson, *The Records of the Grand Historian of China*, 2 vols., New York, 1961; René Grousset, *The Empire of the Steppes*, New Brunswick, NJ, 1970; H. A. Giles, *A History of Chinese Literature*, London and New York, 1901; H. G. Creel, *What Is Tao-ism?* Chicago, 1970; EP, "Mang Tsze," *SP*, 81; EP, *CON*, 83; EP, *LE*, 161; EP, *GK*, 215, 249.

Exegeses

DG, "The Sources of Canto LIII," *Pai*, 5-1; Tay, "Between Kung and Eleusis," *Pai*, 4-1; JW, "Two Heavens of Light and Love," *Pai*, 2-2; JN, "The Sources for Canto LIV," *Pai*, 5-3, 6-1; JN, "The Sources for Canto LV," *Pai*, 7-1 & 2; JN, "The Sources for Canto LVI," *Pai*, 8-2, 3; HK, *Era*, 468, 435.

Pound's adaptation of Mailla's French transliterations as they appear in *The Cantos* is used for all items glossed and indexed; this form is followed by the Standard Wade System according with Karlgren's tables. For Mongolian or Turkic words which have no established form, Pound's usage is followed without a list of variants. B.C. is given for dates before the common era. To save space A.D. is used through the 1st century only.

Glossary Canto LIII

1. Yeou: Yu Tsao-chi, mythical king of China. He followed the reign of the great trinity of powers (the three august ones) who ruled 18,000 years each. Yu is said to have taught men to build houses, and his name means "nest having." Source says that Yu stopped vagabondage and showed the people how to make bird's-nest huts with branches [DG, *Pai* 5-1, 123; all references in the glosses to this article in *Pai* are by volume and page numbers.]

2. Seu Gin: Sui Jen-chi, mythical king of China who followed the reign of Yu. He is said to have introduced the use of fire and wood; accounting, by tying knots in string; and the beginnings of trade. His name means "producer of fire and wood."

3. Fou Hi: Fü Hsi, reigned 2852-2737 B.C., first of the five emperors of the legendary period of China. He is said to have taught his people to hunt, fish, and keep flocks. He invented a calendar, formed musical instruments, developed marriage contracts, invented writing, and taught people to cook flesh. His name means "to be humble, to hide."

4. ante Christum: L, "before Christ."

5. Chin Nong: Shên Nung, reigned 2737-2698 B.C., second of the five emperors of legendary China. He introduced a system of barter. He taught the art of agriculture and was known as the "Prince of Cereals." Through his glass-covered stomach he could watch his own digestive processes and thus studied the properties and effects of herbs. His name means "divine agriculturalist."

6. gros blé: F, "coarse wheat."

7. Kio-feou-hien: Chüeh-fou-hsien, near city of Yen-chou-fu in Shantung Province.

8. Souan yen: Hsuan Yen, fl. 2722 B.C., one of the favorite governors serving under Emperor Shên Nung.

9. Hoang Ti: Huang Ti, reigned 2697-2597 B.C., the "Yellow Emperor" from whom all later kings and princes of China claimed descent. A practical and beneficent ruler, he fought successfully against barbarians. He started official historiography, invented bricks, introduced calendar reform, invented carts and musical instruments, and devised the "well-field" method of dividing up a plot of land into a "latticework" system, with the outer sections tilled by individual families and the center by all in common.

10. Syrinx: Nymph pursued by Pan; when she changed into a tuft of reeds, Pan fashioned the reeds into pipes, the pipes of Pan.

11. Kiao-Chan: Chiao-shan, mountain in the district of Chung-pu, in Shensi Province.

12. Ti Ko: Ti Ku, reigned 2436-2366 B.C., was noted for administering justice to and evincing interest in his people. He attained fame by being the first emperor to have more than one wife. His name means "imperial communication."

13. Tung Kieou: Tung-chiu, a place near the department of Ta-ming-fu in Chihli (or Hopei) Province, NE China.

14. Yao: Son of Ti Ku, reigned 2357-2259 B.C.. He was so benevolent a ruler that even the weather was favorable toward him. He commanded the royal astronomers to create an agricultural calendar. Like Shun, Yao was one of the ideal emperors of China against whom all emperors were measured; at his death there were three years of mourning before Shun took the throne. On the eve of his death Yao passed over his own incompetent son and named Shun as his successor.

15. Yu: Ta Yü or Great Yü, reigned 2205-2197 B.C.; founder and first emperor of Hsia dynasty. It was Shun who first brought Yü to the attention of Emperor Yao, and Yü was assigned the task of controlling the floodwaters of the Yellow River. He was so successful that Shun had him serve as his vice-regent and offered him the throne in place of his own son. Like Yao and Shun, Yü is one of the standards by which all Chinese emperors are measured.

16. Shantung: Province in NE China; one of the Five Northern Provinces.

17. Ammassi: I, "grain pools," for careful collection with an eye to the future; the plan was backed by Mussolini.

18. Siu-tcheou: Siu-ch'ou, department in the province of Kiang-Nan, E China.

19. Yu-chan: Yü-shan, mountain in the province of Kiang-Nan.

20. Se-choui: Se-shui, river in Kiang-Nan which joins the Yangtze.

21. Tsing-mo': *Tsing-mao*, a Chinese herb.

22. molü: H, the magic herb Hermes gave Odysseus to counteract the drugs of Circe [cf. *Od*. X, 305].

23. Chun: Shun, reigned 2255-2205 B.C.. After serving a 28-year apprenticeship Shun was selected to follow Yao as emperor. He was noted as a governor, an astronomer, and as one who regulated the order and ceremony of religious service.

24. Chang Ti: Shang Ti, Supreme Ancestor or Ruler of Heaven: the active divine force as opposed to T'ien, the passive divine force. Shang Ti, a personalized deity, is associated with an abode of or "haven" for departed spirits.

25. que . . . conforme: F, "that your verses express your intentions and that the music conform."

26. Yao: Ideogram across from name [M7295] : "Eminent" [cf. 14 above].

27. Chun: Ideogram across from name [M5936] : "Wise" [cf. 23 above].

28. Yu: Ideogram across from name [M7620; name of founder of Hsia dynasty [cf. 15 above].

29. Kao-Yao: Ideograms across from name [M3285, M6156] : "Bless" + "Kiln." A famous minister under Emperor Yü of Hsia, Kao-Yao, who died in 2204 B.C., was said to have been the first to introduce laws for the repression of crime.

30. Empress: Min, wife of Emperor Ti-hsiang. When he was killed by the usurper, Han-tsuo, she fled and gave birth to Shao Kang, who grew up during the interregnum.

31. Chao Kang: Shao Kang, reigned 2079-2055 B.C. This emperor, Min's son, came to the throne after the interregnum of forty years, which began when Han-tsuo, the usurper, was deposed by the people. Shao Kang quelled disorder in the empire and gave the state of Hsia its first prominence.

32. Fou-hi: [cf. 3 above].

33. Chin-nong: [cf. 5 above].

34. Hoang Ti: [cf. 9 above].

35. Chan: Shan. Prob. a reference to Shao-Hao [M5675 + M2072]: "little-vast." Fourth of the legendary five emperors; son of and successor to Huang Ti. His reign was weakened by poor judgment and neglect.

36. Tchuen: Tchuen-hio, Chuan Hsü, reigned 2513-2436 B.C. The grandson of Huang Ti, he was the fifth of the legendary emperors of China.

37. Chun: [cf. 23 above].

38. Yu: [cf. 15 above].

39. Chang Ti: [cf. 24 above].

40. Tching Tang: Ch'êng T'ang, who reigned 1766-1753 B.C., founded the Shang dynasty (1766-1122). He was a model king who subordinated every passion and feeling to the good of his people. In time of drought he coined money so the people could buy grain, but there was no grain to buy until his sacrifices were accepted by Heaven and rain fell. On his washbasin he inscribed the admonition, "Make it new."

41. der . . . hat: "[The white man] who made the tempest in Baluba." Just as "magic" was attributed by the Biembe to Frobenius, so here Tching's "magic" [prayer] brought rain [38:41].

42. hsin[1]: [M2737], "new."

43. jih[4]: [M3124], "sun." The four characters mean: "make new, day by day, make new." This "spirit" of Emperor Ch'êng T'ang describes the regenerative and ethical metamorphoses effected by the Shang dynasty and functions at all neo-Confucian periods in the dynastic cantos [cf. *Pai*, 5-1, 130; 4-1, 45; 2-2, 188; Pound, "Mang Tsze," *SP* 81].

44. Hia: Hsia [M2521]: "Summer" [cf. ideogram in middle of canto page]. With the fall of Hsia, the first dynasty of China, 2205-1766 B.C., the Middle Kingdom was ruled by the Shang-Yin Dynasty, 1766-1122, which is the first historically verifiable state. The dynastic title was changed to Yin by Pan Keng in 1041.

45. Chang Ti: [cf. 24 above].

46. Tang: [cf. 40 above].

47. Yu: [cf. 15 above].

48. Yin: The Shang dynasty (1766-1122); the name of the dynasty was changed to Yin ca. 1401 B.C.

49. Wen Wang: Wên Wang [M7129 + M7037]: "Elephant king," 1231-1135 B.C. Wên Wang ruled the principality of Chou in the W reaches of the Shang Empire. Called "Chief of the West," he was glorified by historians as an ideal administrator. Because the Shang rulers degenerated into love of pleasure and cruel treatment of the people, Wên Wang tried to overthrow their last king, Chou Hsin. He was captured and imprisoned but was released on payment of a fine. Although he failed to overthrow the Shang-Yin dynasty [a feat eventually achieved by his son, Wu Wang], he is celebrated as the father of the Chou dynasty and was later honored by Confucius as a model for good kings. The entire *Shih Ching* [*Book of Odes*] is a four-part tribute to his greatness as founder of the Chou dynasty.

50. Uncle Ki: Chi Tzŭ, fl. 1153 B.C., was the uncle of Chou Hsin, the depraved emperor of Yin. Because he bravely criticized his nephew, saying, "You drink only out of jeweled vases and eat bear's paw and leopard's blood," Chi was degraded and imprisoned [cf. *Pai*, 5-1, 131].

51. Lou Tai: Lü-t'ai, the "Stag Tower" built by the last Shang emperor, Chou Hsin, as a palace for his mistress, T'a Chi. It was the scene of torture, sexual orgies, and crime.

52. Tan Ki: T'a Chi, d. 1122 B.C., concubine of Emperor Chou Hsin, was an evil woman. After Wu Wang's victory at Mou Ye, she was executed, "to the delight of nearly everyone who knew her."

53. Kieou's daughter: Chiu Hou, ca. 1147 B.C., was a noble who served Emperor Chou Hsin. His daughter disapproved of the evil emperor and his concubine, T'a Chi, so they had her killed, quartered, cooked, and served up to her father for dinner. Repeat in history [4:8].

54. Y-king: *I Ching*, [*Book of Changes*], one of the five classics, was written by Wên Wang while in prison at Yu-li.

55. Mou Ye: Battlefield in N Honan, in the country of K'i, where the forces of Wu Wang and Chou Hsin met (1122 B.C.). Chou Hsin was defeated and the Shang dynasty brought to an end [cf. *Classic Anthology*, ode 236].

56. Cheou-sin: Chou Hsin, who reigned 1154-1122 B.C., was the last emperor of the Shang (or Yin) dynasty. His career was marked by extravagance, lust, and cruelty. The *Odes* say that when he went to battle, his hosts "were as a forest on route." After his defeat Chou Hsin set fire to his own palace and perished in the flames.

57. Wu Wang: 1169-1115 B.C., son of Wên Wang, continued his father's battles against Emperor Chou Hsin. Wu Wang assembled a huge army and defeated the emperor at Mou Ye, in Honan, ending the Shang (or Yin) dynasty. Upon entering the city Wu Wang ordered that all grain be given to the people and the immense riches in the treasury be given to the army [cf. *Pai*, 5-1, 133].

58. Nine vases of Yu: "When Wu Wang was preparing to return to the capitol . . . after conquering Shang, he took with him the nine vases that the Emperor Yu had cast in bronze which displayed the geographic description of each of the nine provinces of the empire" [ibid.].

59. Hoa-chan: Hoa-shan, mountain in Shensi Province.

60. South Chariot: More commonly called the "south-pointing chariot." The ancestor of the mariner's compass, the chariot is said to have been invented by Chou Kung, the Duke of Chou. It was not a magnetic compass, as Mailla supposes, but rather a system of gear wheels which would keep an original pointing. Chou Kung presented the chariot to the court as it prepared to move to Loyang.

61. Lo Yang: Loyang, city in N Honan Province, E central China. Founded in 1108 B.C., it served as capital through several dynasties.

62. Middle Kingdom: One of the many names for the Chinese Empire. Others are "Flowery Kingdom" and "Celestial Empire."

63. Tcheou Kong: Chou kung, d. 1106 B.C. Duke of Chou, adviser to his brother Wu Wang and regent for his nephew Chêng Wang. His activities, devoted wholly to the welfare of the state, aided greatly in establishing the Chou dynasty. Credited with inventing the south-pointing chariot, Chou Kung is one of the measuring sticks for the greatness of any ruler.

64. eleven o six ante Christum: 1106 B.C., the year in which the Duke of Chou died.

65. Tching-ouang: Chêng Wang, son of Wu Wang, reigned 1115-1078 B.C. as the second ruler of the Chou dynasty. He fostered cultivation and reclamation, brought good men into government, and regulated the measure of money and cloth.

66. tchu: Chu, 1/24 of a tael.

67. tchang: Chang, a unit of measurement equal to 141 inches.

68. Chao Kong: Shao Kung, d. 1053 B.C., the Duke of Shao, kinsman to Wu Wang. He was a counselor famous for dispensing justice from his seat under a wild pear tree. The next 23 lines give details of the celebration Shao arranged for the coronation of K'ang Wang, son of Wu Wang.

69. Tching-ouang: [cf. 65 above].

70. Hong-pi: *Hung-pi*, a precious stone.

71. Yuen-yen: *Yuan-yen*, a precious stone, perhaps jade.

72. Mt. Hoa-chan: [cf. 59 above].

73. Chun: [cf. 23 above].

74. In: Yin, name given to the Shang dynasty [85/543].

75. Ouen Ouang: Wên Wang [cf. 49 above].

76. Kang: K'ang Wang, third Chou ruler, 1078-1052 B.C. Though apparently weak, he was supported by strong ministers.

77. Tcheou: Chou, the third dynasty (1122-255 B.C.).

78. Confucius: K'ung Ch'iu or K'ung Fu-tse, or K'ung, ca. 551-479 B.C., Chinese philosopher and statesman. Confucianism is an organized series of precepts dealing with morals, the family system, social reforms, statecraft, and ceremonials. It considers action, directed by right thinking, to be the highest good. It postulates the innate virtue of man. It opposes the passivity of Buddhism and the mysticism of Taoism. A philosophy of reason, it influenced the thought of the French Enlightenment [52:18].

79. Chao-Kong: Shao Kung, the great minister who served both Wu Wang and K'ang Wang. Next several lines list his activities.

80. Yao and Chun: Great kings of the Hsia dynasty [cf. 14, 23, above].

81. Chou: [M1293]: "To encircle." Ideogram for the Chou dynasty.

82. Kang Ouang: [cf. 76 above]. In the 16th year of his reign he lost his most valuable minister, Pe Chin.

83. Pé-kin: Pe Chin, d. 1063 B.C. Ruler of the principality of Lü (Lou). Son of Shao Kung, the Duke of Shao, he succeeded his father as chief minister to K'ang Wang.

84. Prince of Lou: Pe Chin.

85. Kang Ouang: K'ang Wang. In the 26th year of his reign . . . .

86. Kang Wang: He died the same year as Shao Kung, his great minister.

87. Tchao-ouang: Chao Wang, fourth Chou ruler, reigned 1052-1001 B.C. He allowed the government to become weak and the prosperity of the country to decline. He was drowned while crossing the river Han, prob. the victim of a plot.

88. Mou-Ouang: Mu Wang (1001-946 B.C.), fifth ruler of Chou dynasty, was famous for his military campaigns. He decreed that punishments might be redeemed by money payments, and some 3,000 offenses were made expiable by this method.

89. Chun: [cf. 23 above].

90. Law of Mou: [cf. 88 above].

91. Lin hing: *Lü-Hsing*. Sec. 21, Chap. XXVII of *Shu Ching*, the history classic, records the foregoing idea about "Riches. . . ."

92. Chu King: *Shu Ching* [*Book of History*], supposedly collected and edited by Confucius.

93. governor's daughters: The three beautiful daughters of Mi, governor of a province during the reign of Kung Wang, who became enraptured over them.

94. King-Ho: King or Ching, river of China rising in NE Kansu Province, N central China, and flowing to the Wei River in C Shensi.

95. Kong: Kung Wang, sixth ruler of Chou dynasty, reigned 946-934 B.C. Enthralled by Mi's daughters, Kung waited for them for a year (*un an entier*) and then, being denied, destroyed the town, an act he came to regret.

96. Y-wang: I Wang, son of Kung Wang and seventh ruler of Chou dynasty (934-909 B.C.). During his reign barbarian tribes frequently invaded China.

97. Hiao wang: Hsiao Wang, eighth Chou ruler (909-894 B.C.) known as "The Filial," brother of I Wang. He was a weak ruler whose reign was marked only by the appearance of Fei Tzŭ, whose descendants were later to overthrow the Chou dynasty.

98. Han-kiang: Han River, which flows through Shensi and Hupeh provinces and into the Yangtze River at Hankow [*kiang*, "river"].

99. Fei-tsei: Fei Tzŭ, fl. 900 B.C., ancestor of Yih, an official in the government of the great Shun. Fei Tzŭ was given charge of Hsiao Wang's studs. His appointment as head of his clan was followed by a heavy hailstorm in Shensi; many oxen and horses died and the Han River was frozen. These omens seemed to be unlucky for the Chou dynasty. Fei Tzŭ, given a small portion of land in Kansu Province, whose chief town was Ch'in, became the Prince of Ch'in.

100. Pe-y: Pe I, ancestral house of Fei Tzŭ, who became Prince of Ch'in and founder of the house that was to become the Ch'in dynasty.

101. Li Wang: Tenth Chou ruler (878-841 B.C.), known as the "Stern One." Remorseless in his treatment of those who opposed him, he was avaricious in seeking money to carry out his cruel plans. When his people finally rose in rebellion, Li Wang fled to Shensi.

102. à ce que l'argent circule: F, "that money circulate."

103. Heou-Tsie: Hou Chi, fl. 2357 B.C., chief minister of agriculture and animal husbandry under Emperor Yao.

104. Youi-leang-fou: Yü Liang-fu, fl. 860 B.C., was one of the first officers of the empire under Emperor Li Wang.

105. Chao-kong: Shao Kung, Duke of Shao during the reign of Li Wang (878-841 B.C.); not to be confused with the earlier Duke of Shao. He is said to have advised Li Wang that to suppress the feelings and the speech of his people would lead only to disaster.

106. Lord to the four seas of China: Prob. refers to the Chou ruler, Li Wang.

107. Interregnum of Cong-ho: *Kung-ho*, historical name for the interregnum (841-827 B.C.) between the reigns of Li Wang and Hsüan Wang, his son.

108. west tarters: A western tribe of barbarians, the Ch'iang, lived to the W of Kansu. They defeated the forces of Hsüan Wang in the battle of "The Thousand Acres" (788 B.C.).

109. Siuen-ouang: Hsüan Wang (827-781 B.C.), eleventh ruler of Chou dynasty. He was a good ruler who chose trustworthy counselors. Although the kingdom was bothered by attacks from barbarians, Hsüan managed for some time to repel them with royal troops.

110. contra barbaros / legat belli ducem: L, "against the barbarians / he appoints a leader in war" [cf. Lacharme, 308].

111. Chaoumoukong: Shao Mu-king, fl. 826 B.C. The name, which means "Mu, Prince of Shao," was given to Shao Hu after his death. He was a general in the service of Hsüan Wang.

112. Hoailand: Hwai, territory roughly identical with the old province of Kiang-nan. It is a rich agricultural area watered by the Hwai Ho, S Honan and NW Anhwei provinces of modern E China.

113. Hoai river: Hwai Ho, river in S Honan and NW Anhwei provinces in E China which flows into the Hwang Ho above Hungtze Hu.

114. Tchang wine: Chang, river that rises in Shensi Province and flows NE, parallel to the Hwang Ho, joining it on the Great Plains.

115. Juxta . . . mora: L, "By the river Hwai the battle line is drawn up without delay" [cf. Lacharme, III, 3, ode 9, st. 4; *Classic Anthology*, p. 192].

116. Yangtse: Yangtze, principal river of China.

117. agit considerate: L, "he leads with deliberation" [Lacharme, III, 3, ode 9, st. 3].

118. Han: Han Hu, fl. 800 B.C., military officer during the time of Hsüan Wang. For his services in battle Han Hu was given the districts of Yüeh and Me, which he developed into important principalities.

119. Yuei: Yüeh or Yü-yüeh, kingdom or principality in S China.

120. Siuen: Hsüan Wang [cf. 109 above]. He began his reign with so successful a defense against the attacks of the Tartars that he was praised in the *Shih Ching*. In praising Hsüan, Pound conflates Lacharme's translation and notes for odes 262 and 263 [cf. *Pai*, 5-1, 141].

121. Sié: Sie, town in the principality of Chin, in Shansi Province, NE China.

122. RITE is: The Chinese rites of spring, a rhyme with the vegetation rites of Dionysus [47:7], include the ceremonial duties of the emperor recorded in the next several lines. Since Hsüang did not observe the rite [*so did not Siuen*], famine ensued.

123. hac . . . alluit: L, *haec loca* . . . : "these places the river washes."

124. Campestribus locis: L, "in country places."

125. Lady Pao Sse: Pao Ssŭ, ca. 8th century B.C., concubine of Chou ruler, Yu Wang. Earthquakes preceded her coming to the throne and the great eclipse of the sun on August 29, 775, followed it. She enslaved the emperor and incited him to the wildest acts of folly: "[She] usurped the queen's throne and led the emperor a reckless dance to his ruin. . . . Rivers trembled and boiled; Mt. Ki-shan, the cradle of the emperor's family, split apart; eclipses (ode 193), comets, and frozen rivers appeared" [cf. *Pai*, 5-1, 143].

126. Tcheou: Chou, the third dynasty (1122-255 B.C.). Surrounded by barbarians, Yu Wang was overwhelmed in 771 B.C., his palace was destroyed, and he and his concubine, Pao Ssŭ, were killed, thus bringing the western Chou dynasty to an end.

127. Mount Ki-chan: Chi-shan, mountain in China destroyed by the earthquakes that appeared as evil omens during the reign of Yu Wang.

128. Yeou Ouang: Yu Wang (781-771 B.C.), a thoroughly bad and unprincipled ruler who was under the influence of Pao Ssŭ. Before Yu's death many of his feudal chiefs, outraged by his wickedness, refused to obey his orders and began to act as independent lords. After Yu and the end of the western state, the whole Chou dynasty began to decline.

129. Tçin: Ch'in. "A prince of Tçin [Weng Kung] dreamed of imperial aspirations and broke away from the declining Chou empire in 749 B.C." [ibid. This Ch'in is not to be confused with the later Ch'in dynasty 255-206 B.C.].

130. Tartar: Tartars, Tatars, northern barbarians, were nomadic tribes on the borders of Chihli, Shansi, and Kansu provinces. When they began to demand the empire in payment for their services, the Prince of Ch'in helped drive them out.

131. tombs fallen: The fall of Chou could be seen in spreading neglect, including that of dynastic temples and tombs. In 745 B.C. each prince asserted independence and the nine original states of the Chou empire were split into 21 parts. This fragmentation began the "Spring and Autumn" period of unrighteous wars described by Confucius as "a rain of stars," because "9 Tcheou wd / not stand together."

132. Siang: Hsiang, territory in central Hunan Province, SE central China, watered by the Hsiang River.

133. Ouen Kong: Wên Kung, d. 609 B.C., Prince of Lü, was a benevolent and capable ruler who distributed grain to the people in time of famine.

134. Sung: Important Chinese state that occupied (1113-285 B.C.) the lower part of the valley of the Hwai River. Confucius's ancestors are said to be of the royal house of Sung.

135. Siang: Tchao- Kung, brother of Wên Kung, spurned the people, which caused the Princess of Hsiang to have him murdered on a hunting trip.

136. Ouen: [cf. 133 above] But Wên died early so that the "states of Lou were still unfortunate" [*Pai*, 5-1, 144].

137. States of Lou: Lü, a state established by Tan, the Duke of Chou, in 1122 B.C. His son established his capital at Chieh-fu (in Shantung Province, NE China) about 1115 and was called Duke Lü. Lü was the birth-place of Confucius.

138. Their Richards: Like Richard III of England who murdered the princes in the Tower, the followers of Wên Kung's second wife [Hsüan-kung] hatched a plot to murder the two sons of his first wife.

139. Ling Kong: Ling Kung (d. 608 B.C.) was a depraved and homicidal Prince of Ch'in whose only pleasure lay in shooting people and eating bears' paws. He died in his own snare at a banquet when he was trying to murder someone. "Without virtue, without sense, his heart turned naturally to evil" [*Pai*, 5-1, 145].

140. Nine Urns of Yu: The nine vases that Emperor Yu had cast in bronze and engraved with geographical descriptions of the nine provinces of the empire. The vases were to be found in the capital of Chou, the principality.

141. King Kong: Ching Kung (d. 578 B.C.), Prince of Ch'in, was a powerful warrior who became the leader of the other princes. In 584 B.C., hearing a prisoner play the dynastic music of Chou, he was so affected that he sent the prisoner home loaded with gifts, an act that led to a peace pact.

142. Cheou-lang: K'ung Shu Liang-ho (d. 548 B.C.), father of Confucius, was chief magistrate of Tsu in Shantung Province. He was remarkable for his gigantic stature and great strength. After fathering nine daughters by his first wife, he remarried at seventy and his second wife, Cheng Tsai, bore him Confucius in 551 B.C.. A year before Confucius's birth there were two eclipses of the sun.

143. portcullis: Refers to an episode ca. 562 B.C. when Confucius's father saved his troops by holding up a portcullis that had trapped them during the siege of a city.

144. hillock: It is said that Confucius's father was given the name Ch'iu ("hillock") because of a "protubérance qu'il avait sur la tête" [Cordier, I, 146; cf. Mailla, II, 81].

145. Man of Sung: Refers to Confucius's father, Shu Liang-ho, whose ancestors may have come from the ancient state of Sung.

146. Lou land: Land of the state of Lü, where Confucius was born.

147. Kung-fu-tseu: K'ung Fu-tse: Confucius.

148. Chung Ni: [M1505 + M4654], Confucius's cognomen. It literally means "second in order of birth."

149. Taught and the not: Prob. Pound is pointing out that in both the Confucian and the Greek patterns virtue must be learned and is part of a process of initiation.

150. Eleusis: Town in Attica where the Eleusinian Mysteries of Demeter were held. Originally an agrarian festival, the mysteries came to be concerned with underworld deities, the descent into Hades, and mystic visions of future life. In *The Cantos*, the phrase "Between Kung and Eleusis" names the two most important poles between which human value systems must be established: "the ethical life and the sacred mysteries" [52:18].

151. catechumen: The word *alone* is placed ambiguously; perhaps it is used in the sense of "only": only the student can hope to achieve the Confucian ethic or the knowledge of the mysteries.

152. **Kung was poor**: When he was only 19 years old, Kung had a great reputation in the kingdom of Lü although he was very poor. Thus Chao Kung "le fit intendant des vivres" ["made him supervisor of victuals"], a job of little importance which paid enough [Mailla, II, 190; all references to this source are referred to hereafter by volume and page numbers only].

153. **Pien's report**: In 552 B.C., when 18 or 19, K'ung married Pien-kuan-chi, a woman of Sung. He did his job with so much wisdom that he was promoted to be "l'intendance des bestiaux" [ibid.].

154. **Scorpio**: In the winter of 525 B.C. a great comet in "le coeur du *scorpion* ou *antares*" spread across the west as far as the Milky Way [II, 193].

155. **Kiang**: Yangtze River on which, in 525 B.C., a terrible battle was fought between the forces of the princes of Chou and Wu which lasted without interruption for a whole day and night [ibid.].

156. **King Wang**: Ching Wang, in 524 B.C., thinking he could make a big profit by changing the base of the currency, did so even though warned by his council that it would ruin commerce and impoverish the people [cf. *Pai*, 5-1, 147].

157. **μεταθεμένων . . .** : H, "of change of moneys." An act in opposition to all the principles of Confucius.

158. **Fen-yang**: Fên Yang, fl. 520 B.C., general and adviser to Ching Wang. He was honored because he refused to carry out orders to murder an innocent prince [ibid.].

159. **King Kong**: Ching Kung, a feudal prince of Tsi [Chi]. He asked Confucius how a king could be a good ruler and was told "by being a ruler acting like a ruler." Later Kung said the advice was good but that he was too old to start following it.

160. **Kungfutseu**: In 497 B.C., Confucius, aged 54, was promoted to the rank of minister of state.

161. **C. T. Mao**: Shao Ching-mao, who, because he was causing serious disorder, was arrested and put to death on Confucius's order. When the latter's disciples asked about his severity, he replied that "Mao's five kinds of deceit and improbity in government made him more criminal than a thug" [ibid.].

162. **LOU rose**: Lü. Because of the morality Confucius brought to the state in 497 B.C., the state's significance increased.

163. **Tsi sent girls**: The Prince of Chi, jealous of Lü's success, tried to corrupt its prince by sending him beautiful singing girls.

164. **Kungfutseu**: The Prince of Lü was corrupted by the singing girls (he did not leave his palace for three days); hence Confucius left Lü and went to the state of Wei.

165. **Tching**: Ching, feudal state in E central China. When Confucius was strolling near the East Gate of the city, someone saw him and told the king that a man, wandering about like a lost dog, had the forehead of Yao [cf. 14 above], the neck of Kao-Yao [cf. 29 above], the shoulders of Tsé Chin, and the height of Yü [cf. 15 above; II, 211].

166. **Confucius**: K'ung denied his similarity to great emperors but admitted to the lost-dog description [ibid.].

167. **Tchin**: Chin, feudal principality in NE China.

168. **Yng P**: Ying Pi, illegitimate son of Ling Kung, who wanted to make Ying his heir. "But Yng refused the honor because it would have sullied their ancestors" [*Pai*, 5-1, 148].

169. **Tsai**: Feudal state in Honan Province, E central China. When Confucius was on his way to the Prince of Chu in 489 B.C., "he was intercepted and driven into an arid and rocky desert by the princes of Tchin and Tsai who feared his wisdom" [*Pai*, 5-1, 149]. There he went without food for seven days. Most of his disciples were sick with

hunger, but K'ung, seeming not to be sad, sang the odes and played music more than before [II, 214].

170. Tcheou: Chu, feudal state in NE China whose prince sent troops to rescue Confucius and then received him with great honor.

171. Tsao: A small state created in 1122 B.C. which lasted until 501 B.C.. It was finally lost by its prince, Yang Kung, because he followed the advice of an extravagant minister.

172. odes: Because the princes of the states would not follow his advice, K'ung in 493 B.C. retired to work on the odes.

173. Yng star ... Sin: The stars Mailla names *Yng* and *Sin* have not been identified with certainty.

174. King Ouang: Ching Wang, 25th ruler of Chou dynasty [not to be confused with the Ching Wang who changed the currency (cf. 156 above)]. Since he ruled from 519 to 475 B.C., 479 was the 40th year of his reign. In that year K'ung, aged 73, died.

175. Min Kong: Min Kung, d. 478 B.C., created great disorder in the land.

176. Fan-li: Fan Li, fl. 474 B.C., a minister who connived to reduce the power of rival princes. Afterward he withdrew secretly to the five lakes.

177. Snow ... Apricots ...: Strange portents in nature are seen to signal the decline of the Chou dynasty: eclipses, comets, snow in summer, fruit in winter, etc. "In the sweltering summer of 435 B.C. snow fell, and in mid-winter of 428 apricots bore fruit" [*Pai*, 5-1, 150].

178. Tai-hia: *Tai Hsia* high mountains.

179. Hoang-ho: Hwang Ho, the Yellow River, second largest in China. About 387 B.C. Wu Chi said that rivers and mountains were not impregnable barriers: "a state's power is its humanity. Neither high cliffs nor torrents will defend an inhumane ruler" [ibid.].

180. douanes: F, "customhouses" or "custom duties."

181. Kong-sung-yang: Kung Sung-yang, d. 338 B.C., chief prince or noble. Also known as Wei Yang or Shang Yang, he became minister of the state of Ch'in in the middle of the 4th century B.C. Under his direction, Ch'in's laws and administration were reorganized and the foundations were laid for the eventual victory of Ch'in over its rivals and the founding of the first Chinese Empire. Note that the Faber edition reads "280 died Hao tse." The "280" refers to the page number in Mailla, II. "Hao tse" may be Pound's abbreviation of "hao Han tzu" ["tse" in Mailla], meaning "a true Chinese man," literally "a good son of Han"; or he may have intended "good prince," Mailla using "tse" frequently in this sense.

182. Sou-tsin: Su Ch'in, d. 317 B.C., Taoist philosopher who was for a time minister of the state of Ch'in. He was one of the wandering scholar-diplomats of the time. Mocked by a prince of Ch'in, Su turned [as a Taoist in Mailla would] to revenge, intrigue, warmongering, etc. Finally dishonoring himself by having an affair with the "dowager queen," he was murdered in 317 B.C.

183. Tchan-y: Chang I, d. 309 B.C., Chinese condottiere who served the states of Wei, Ch'in, and Chou during the feudal wars near the end of the Chou dynasty.

184. Tsin: Ch'in [*Sou-tsin* in text].

185. POLLON IDEN: H, *Pollon d'anthropon iden*, "And of many men he saw" [*Od.* I, 3].

186. Tchao Siang: Chao Hsiang, who fl. 288 B.C. King Chao Hsiang of the state of Ch'in, in his many wars with contending states, did much to bring the Chou dynasty to its final demise and prepare the way for the Ch'in empire. In 288 B.C. Chao Hsiang assumed for himself the title of emperor of the West. He gave to the Prince of Chi the title of emperor of the East.

187. Sou Tsi: Su Chi, fl. 288 B.C., was a general in the court of Chao Hsiang. He carried the message about the new emperor titles to the Prince of Chi. It was the prince, not Su Chi, who called the title "un simple badinage."

188. Yo-Y: Yo I, fl. 285 B.C., minister of the feudal state of Yen, which lasted from 1122 to 265 B.C., near Peking.

189. corvées: F, "forced labors."

190. Hillock: [cf. 144 above].

191. Chou: The dynasty K'ung said he was for [cf. 81 above].

Glossary Canto LIV

1. Tien-tan: T'ien Tan, fl. 279 B.C., a soldier and later a commander of the forces of Chi.

2. dragons . . . : These first nine lines describe a battle ploy practiced by T'ien: he let loose 1,000 oxen with daggers attached to their horns and torches burning on their tails and drove them into the camp of Ch'i Chieh whose men fled into the night [JN, *Pai*, 5-3, 421; further references to this article give *Pai* with volume and page numbers].

3. Ki-kié: Ch'i Chieh, fl. 279 B.C., commander of the forces of the Prince of Yen. He was killed in the battle of the thousand oxen, his army was dispersed, and the inhabitants of Chieh-me were set free.

4. Tsié-mé: Chieh-me, town in Shantung Province.

5. For three hundred years . . . : During the last 300 or 400 years of the Chou dynasty, intermittent warfare was carried on by the various states of feudal China; thus the period came to be known as the time of the warring states.

6. Wall: Great Wall of China. Begun at various places by rulers of several frontier states, the wall was finally put together as a unit by the first Ch'in emperor, Shih Huang Ti. It extends for approximately 1,250 miles from Mongolia to the Yellow Sea.

7. Tsin Chi: Ch'in Shih Huang Ti, reigned 246-209 B.C. Fourth ruler of the state of Ch'in, he subdued all his enemies and established himself as the first emperor of a unified Chinese empire. His name means "First Emperor of the Ch'in."

8. Tcheou: Chou, third dynasty (1122-255 B.C.).

9. Tsin: Ch'in, fourth dynasty which lasted only until the death of Erh Shih Huang Ti in 206 B.C.

10. China: During the centuries prior to Shih Huang Ti's time, rulers of the Chinese states had the title of Wang ["king"]. Shih Huang himself was known as King Cheng. But after he unified all China, he assumed the title of Huang Ti ["sovereign emperor"], indicating that he now held sway over all the Chinese states, each ruled by a lesser prince. But to warn the princes not to take too much pride in their rank, "when he spoke of himself, he made a point of using Tchin, which means the surplus, as you might say the surplus in the empire" [*Pai*, 5-3, 423].

11. Li-ssé: Li Ssŭ, d. 208 B.C., prime minister under Emperor Shih Huang Ti. Li Ssŭ convinced the emperor that all the unrest in the kingdom was the result of scholarly research and writing. He also suggested that it might be useful to destroy all history so that Shih Huang Ti could be recorded as the "first emperor" of China. All existing literature, except for works on agriculture, medicine, and divination, was ordered destroyed.

12. Han: Fifth dynasty, or Earlier Han dynasty, from 206 B.C. to A.D. 25.

13. some fishin' . . . : Unidentified.

14. some cook . . . : Dorothy Pound made a marital stipulation that she not be required to cook, a condition about which she was adamant, as Pound came to see.

15. Tse-Yng: Tzŭ Ying, who reigned 206 B.C., was the grandson of the Ch'in Shih Huang Ti, nephew of Erh Shih Huang Ti, the last emperor of the Ch'in dynasty. After holding the throne for only 29 days, he was seized by a rebellious prince, who eventually had him decapitated.

16. Siao-ho: Hsiao Ho, d. 193 B.C., adviser to Liu Pang, Prince of Han. Much of Liu Pang's success in founding the Han dynasty was owing to the efforts of Hsiao Ho, who kept the army supplied, provided accurate maps, and helped to create a new penal code and a stronger administration. The first Han emperor named Hsiao Ho chancellor of state, and so great was the respect for him that the title was not used again during the Han dynasty.

17. Lieou-pang: Liu Pang, 247-195 B.C., one of the two leaders of a revolt against the Ch'in dynasty. The two had agreed that the first to reach the capital would gain the principality of Ch'in; Liu Pang arrived first and Emperor Tzu-Ying surrendered. The second general, Hsiang Yü, now not satisfied with the bargain he had made, fought Liu Pang from 206 to 202. In 202 Liu Pang defeated Hsiang Yü and became emperor, founding the Han dynasty and taking the title of Kao Huang Ti, or Han Kao-Tse, the "Exalted One."

18. Eulh: Erh Shih Huang Ti, who reigned 209-206 B.C., was extremely inept as emperor. He was controlled by the eunuch Chao Kao, who finally contrived a plot that, according to modern scholars, led to Erh Shih's suicide. Mailla says both Erh Shih and Chao Kao were murdered [*Pai*, 5-3, 425].

19. Hiang-yu: Hsiang Yü, 233-202 B.C., a general who at first fought with Liu Pang against the Ch'in dynasty and then turned against his ally after the dynasty was overthrown. Hsiang Yü's forces were crushed in 202 and their leader was killed [cf. 17 above].

20. bloody rhooshun: This epithet is not in the *Histoire* which has the other details of the passage including: "He showed no less repugnance when they tried to teach him fencing which placed (one) in the position to resist only one man; but it was altogether different for the art which teaches one person to defeat ten thousand, an art in which he made very great progress" [*Pai*, 5-3, 426].

21. Kao: Kao Huang Ti, also known as Han Kao-Tse, who reigned 202-195 B.C., was founder and first emperor of the Han dynasty. Known formerly as Liu Pang, he was an able emperor who had many wise ministers to whom he listened most of the time. He established a firm foundation for the Han dynasty.

22. "when the quarry . . . ": Said by a loyal general who was plotted against.

23. "It appears . . .: The response of Kao when asked how he was able to gain the empire: "[Because] . . . of using everyone according to his talents" [*Pai*, 5-3, 428].

24. Lou-kia: Lü Chia, fl. ca. 200 B.C., adviser to and confidant of Emperor Kao Huang Ti, was sent by the emperor as his envoy to Ch'ao T'o, ruler of the state of Nan Yüeh in SE China (modern Kwangtung), in an effort to gain Ch'ao's allegiance. After Lü Chia's return he was scolded by the emperor for referring to the Chinese classics. The emperor said: "I got the empire on horseback, why should I bother with the Book of Odes or the Book of History?" To which Lü Chia replied: "You got it on horseback, but can you rule it from horseback?" Lü Chia left a treatise on government called *New Discourses* [Dubs, I, 21].

25. Nan-hai: The name often used for the state of Nan Yüeh in SE China.

26. Chu king: *Shu Ching* [*Book of History*], supposedly collected and edited by Confucius but probably pieced together both before and after his time.

27. Chi king: *Shih Ching* [*Book of Odes*], supposedly collected and edited by Confucius but probably pieced together both before and after his time.

28. Lou: [see 24 above].

29. "The New Discourse" (Sin-yu): Hsin Yu. The Han emperor commissioned his adviser Lü Chia to write a treatise on good government. Lü "accordingly set out to describe, in a work with twelve sections, the keys to political survival and defeat. As each section was presented to the throne, the emperor never failed to express his delight and approval, while all those about him cried 'Bravo!' " The book was given the title *New Discourses* [cf. 24 above].

30. Kung fu tseu: Confucius.

31. videlicet: L, literally *videre licet*, "it is permitted to see," "namely," "that is."

32. Fan-kouai: Fan Kuai, d. 189 B.C., a dog butcher of P'ei (in modern Kiangsu) who early attached himself to Liu Pang and joined his group of advisers when Liu became emperor. After the last battle against the Ch'in, Liu Pang (Kao Huang Ti) entered the royal Ch'in palace, where he found treasure and waiting women. Fan Kuai, however, admonished him and urged him to return to the field with his troops, which he did. The anecdote is a flashback to days following the collapse of the Ch'in dynasty [cf. 17 above].

33. Hien-yang: Hsien-yang, capital city of the Ch'in dynasty, where Kao Huang Ti finally defeated the last Ch'in emperor. Today it is Sian, capital of Shansi Province in NE central China.

34. Siao-ho: Hsiao Ho, the most respected chancellor of state of the first Han emperor [cf. 16 above].

35. Au douce . . . pascor: OF, P, "In the sweet season of spring." Echo of troubadour verse, esp. Bertrans de Born's "B'em platz lo gais temps de pascor" ["How I Like the Gay Time of Spring"].

36. Tchang-tsong: Chang Ts'ang, fl. 202-195 B.C., a member of the court of Emperor Kao Huang Ti who studied the theory of music.

37. Sun-tong: Shu Sun-t'ung, fl. 202-195 B.C., member of the court of Emperor Kao Huang Ti, whose task it was to write on the ceremonies and usages of the rites. Upon the urging of the emperor he devised a set of protocol rules which were much more simple and less ostentatious than those of the Ch'in. As the emperor said: "But make it easy to learn! Keep in mind that it must be the sort of thing that I can perform" [Watson, I, 293].

38. Imperial Seal: The seal of the emperor of China during the Earlier Han dynasty.

39. Hiao Hoei Ti: Hsiao Hui Ti, who reigned 194-187 B.C., was the second son of Kao Huang Ti. He was a kindhearted, but rather feeble-minded, youth who was completely controlled by his mother, the Empress Lü. His name means "Beneficial Rule."

40. Y-yang: I-yang-hsien, town and region near the modern city of Loyang in Honan Province, E central China. It is recorded that in April, 191 B.C., Hui Ti, the emperor-to-be was "capped" (came of age) and "in Y-yang it rained blood." It is also recorded that in late 190 B.C. "peach and plum trees flowered" [Dubs, I, 103].

41. Liu-heou: Lü Hou, wife of Kao Huang Ti. She dominated her son during his reign and after his death she continued to rule the empire by placing puppet rulers on the throne. She was an adept murderess but an able ruler.

42. Hiao Ouen: Hsiao Wên Ti, who reigned 179-156 B.C., was famous for his generosity, humanity, and economy. He decreed that a man's family should not suffer for his crimes. He established the unit of money in the empire and reserved to the government the sole right to coin money. For the punishment of mutilation he substituted flogging and made beheading the only severe penalty. He also ordered that the classical books be hunted out again and that scholars start studying them. His name means the "Literary Ruler." The eldest son of Kao Huang Ti and prince of the state of Tai, he succeeded the ineffectual Emperor Hui Ti after some intricate maneuvers following Empress Lü's death.

43. Chief of the Southern Barbarians: The southern barbarians were the tribes of the region of Yüeh, a state in SE China.

44. Nan-yuei: Nan Yüeh, state in SE China and part of Annam. The ruler of Nan Yüeh, Ch'ao T'o, had been enfeoffed by Kao Huang Ti, but during the days of Empress Lü he had reason to believe that the Han court had reneged on its promises. He thereupon assumed the title of Emperor Wu of Nan Yüeh. The Emperor Wên Ti, how- ever, was able to mend this fence on his S frontier. Ch'ao T'o gave up the title of emperor and Nan Yüeh continued as before in a tributary status.

45. Kia-Y: Chia I, fl. 178 B.C., member of the court of Emperor Hsiao Wên Ti and head of office of tax collection.

46. Hiao Ouen Ti: [cf. 42 above].

47. Chang Ti: Shang Ti, Supreme Ancestor or Ruler of Heaven, was involved in the controversy between Chinese and Jesuits about the name of God. One question was: could the "God" in the Mass be equated with Shang Ti as Ruler of Heaven? [53:24].

48. Tchao-tso: Ch'ao T'so, fl. 170 B.C., minister at the court of Emperor Hsiao Wên Ti.

49. Li-kouang: Li Kuang, fl. 144 B.C., commander of forces on NW frontier of China whose task it was to guard against Tartar tribes, or Hsiung-Nu. In one battle Li Kuang fooled them into thinking his small band was really the vanguard of a larger force. The Hsiung-Nu withdrew and Li Kuang and his small force escaped.

50. Hiong-nou: Hsiung Nu, one of the no- madic tribes on China's NW frontier which posed a continuous threat to the security of the empire. They were prob. related to the Huns who burst into Europe in the fifth century A.D.

51. Yu: Ta Yü or Great Yü [53:15].

52. Chun: Shun [53:23].

53. Yao: [53:14].

54. Hiao King: Hsiao Ching Ti, reigned 156- 140 B.C. In his second year as emperor the feudal lords rebelled but said they would disband their forces if the emperor would execute his chief counselor, Ch'ao Tsu, who had urged the emperor to abolish all feudal dependencies. The peace terms were met, but the feudal lords attacked again and were not defeated until later. The emperor's name means "Luminous Ruler."

55. Ideogram: [M2737] "new."

56. Sin/jih/jih/sin: Hsin Jih Jih Hsin: "make new, day by day, make new" [53:43].

57. Hia: Hsia [53:44].

58. Han Ou: Han Wu Ti, who reigned 140-86 B.C., was perhaps the greatest of the earlier Han emperors; the dynasty reached the peak of its power under his rule. The half century of his reign is noted both for extensive foreign conquests and for signifi- cant developments in internal administra- tion. Above all he was instrumental in establishing Confucianism as the basis for Chinese government. His name means "Martial Ruler."

59. Prince of Hoai-nan: Lieou-ngan or Liu An, Prince of Huai-nan, was fond of reading books and playing the lute. He seems to have spent most of the rest of his time plotting revolts against the Han emperor.

60. Hoai-nan: Huai-nan, princely state south of the Hwai River.

61. Prince of Ho-kien: Lieou-te or Liu Te, d. 130 B.C., was Prince of Ho-chien and son of Emperor Hsiao Ching. The prince spent much money and effort to recover and restore the Chinese classics.

62. Ho-Kien: Ho-chien, state in the province of Hopeh.

63. Chu King: *Shu Ching, Book of History* [53-92].

64. Tcheou-li: *Chou-li, Rites of the Chou Dynasty.*

65. Li-ki: *Li Chi, Book of Rites* compiled by the Elder and Younger Tai (fl. second and first centuries B.C.) from documents said to have come from Confucius and his disciples. The text, frequently revised, was not completed until the second century B.C.

66. Mencius (Mong-tsé): Méng-tzu or Mêng K'o, 372-289 B.C., Chinese philosopher who was a follower of Confucius; he was author of the second of the Chinese classics, the *Book of Mencius.*

67. Chi-King or Odes of Mao-chi: *Shih Ching* [cf. 27 above].

68. Tchun-tsiou: *Ch'un Ch'iu [Spring and Autumn Annals]*, the last of the five classics, is a chronological record of the chief events in the state of Lü between 722 and 484 B.C. It is generally regarded as the work of Confucius, whose native state was Lü.

69. Tso-kieou-min: Tso Chiu-min, fl. fifth century B.C., was a disciple of Confucius. He wrote a commentary on the *Spring and Autumn Annals [Ch'un Ch'iu]* of Confucius. Tso has been canonized as the "Father of Prose," for he expanded the brief entries of Confucius into dramatic episodes. His commentary is known as *Tso Chuan*.

70. Li-yo: *Li Yu*, Chinese treatise on ceremonies and music.

71. Han Tchao Ti: Han Chao Ti, reigned 86-73 B.C. In the second year of his reign he remitted the land tax in impoverished areas. When crops failed in 80 B.C. the emperor's ministers said he should "pay more attention to the good government of the people." The people said they wanted taxes on salt, iron, spirits, and property abolished. Han Chao Ti compromised and abolished taxes on spirits and property. His name means "Illuminating Ruler." Emperor Chao came to the throne at the tender age of eight. During the first ten years of his reign affairs of state were handled by the regent, Ho Kuang. Most of the economic reforms noted were undertaken on Ho Kuang's initiative.

72. Han Sieun (or Siun): Han Hsüan Ti, reigned 73-48 B.C., was an able emperor who in 65 sent out Kung-Su to deal with the many men who had become brigands during a famine. Kung-Su said that every man with a hoe on his shoulder would be treated as an honest man. Every poor man was invited to present his case to the emperor, and farmers without seed were assisted. One of the most able and compassionate of the Han emperors, Hsüan Ti did much to ease the burdens of his people. During his reign the Hsiung Nu (Tartars) were a continuing problem. But in 60 B.C. an internal struggle for power prompted the Hsiung Nu king to come to the Han capital in Ch'ang-an in search of help. He was well received, was treated as a guest, and became a loyal vassal to the Han emperor. His name means "Proclaiming Emperor."

73. Tchang-ngan: Ch'ang-An, the modern city of Sian in Shensi Province, NE China. It was the capital of the empire under the Han dynasty.

74. Mandarins: Members of the mandarinate, the scholar ruling class, or civil service, of China which came into being about 600 B.C. The mandarins were disliked, but respected, by the people of China. Trained in the Confucian classics, by Emperor Hsüan Ti's time they had become the core of the Chinese administrative system.

75. Ouan-soui!: *Wan-sui*, "Ten thousand years!" A traditional Chinese phrase for "a long time!"

76. Tchen-yu: Shan yu, title the Tartars gave their kings.

77. Prince of Hiong-nou: The Tartar prince who because of all the celebrations in his honor "came into the empire."

78. Si-yu: Hsi-yu, large region in W China outside the limits of Shensi Province. Once the territory of the Tartar tribes, it is now modern Sinkiang Province.

79. Tchang-ngan: [cf. 73 above].

80. Bay of Naples: An exhibition of submarine warfare was put on by Mussolini for Hitler in the Bay of Naples in 1938, year 16 of the Fascist state [HK, *Era*, 435].

81. Ngan: Chang-an. The assumption here is that since the Hsiung Nu (Tartars) were now vassals of the Chinese emperor, the emperor controlled everything from the Han capital, Ch'ang-an, to the Caspian Sea. The assumption, of course, was not true.

82. Fong-chi: Fêng Shih, fl. 6 B.C., concubine of Emperor Han Yüan Ti. During the reign of his grandson, Han Ai Ti, she emerged as the grand empress dowager née Wang.

83. Fou-chi: Fü Shih, fl. 6 B.C. Another concubine of Han Yüan Ti, she may have been the mother of Emperor Han Cheng Ti and the grandmother of Emperor Han Ai Ti. She was known as the empress dowager née Fu.

84. Han Yuen: Han Yüan Ti, emperor 48-32 B.C., started his reign by cutting taxes and forcing the court to be economical, but he later came under the control of the eunuch Shih Hsien who "seduced the emperor into immoral habits." His name means "Foremost Emperor."

85. Fong faced him: The bear escaped while the emperor was walking with his wives, all of whom fled except Fêng. The emperor asked why such courage. She said her life was worth nothing, but "the days of your majesty are precious to the state, and there was no reason for me to hesitate" [*Pai* 5-3, 445].

86. bhuddists: Buddhists. The neo-Confucian bias against Buddhism is recorded faithfully in Mailla's *Histoire*. But Mailla, a good Jesuit, deplores Buddhism: "It is at this time that the sect of *Foe* came to infect China with its pernicious doctrines" [*Pai*, 5-3, 445].

87. Han Ping: *Han Ping Ti*, emperor A.D. 1-6. Since he was only nine when he came to the throne, the empire was ruled by Wang Mang, a scheming minister who usurped all

power and may have murdered Han Ping Ti. His name means "Peaceful Emperor."

88. tael: Chinese coin. The scheming Wang Mang served the people well. At a time of drought he won their favor by suggesting to the empress "that she decrease her expenses and wear simpler clothes.... Only the most common foods were to be served at his table.... He ordered up to one million taels to be distributed to the poor" [*Pai*, 5-3, 446].

89. Tseou-kou: Ch'ou Ku, fl. A.D. 73. He and Tchong [Ching Ch'ang] were generals during the reign of Emperor Han Ming Ti.

90. Prince of Ou-yen: Wu Yen, fl. A.D. 73, was a Tartar chief during the reign of Emperor Han Ming Ti. Mailla's *Histoire* says "they met the Prince of Ou-yen, whom they defeated, killing him and more than a thousand soldiers.... They went on to capture Y-ou, and after having placed a strong garrison there, they employed the rest of their troops in cultivating the land" [*Pai*, 5-3, 445].

91. Kouang Ou: Kuang Wu Ti, reigned 25-58, first emperor of the Later Han dynasty. His reign was marked by a series of wars, as rebellions arose within the empire and Tartars attacked from without. Kuang Wu Ti was a successful warrior and also had sympathy for scholars and literary men. His name means "Luminous Martial Emperor."

92. Han Ming: Han Ming Ti, reigned 58-76, is known for having introduced Buddhism, and consequently idolatry, into China. Having dreamed that there was a holy man in the West named Foé, he sent ambassadors to discover his teachings and bring back books of his doctrines. His name means "Brilliant Emperor."

93. Yang Tchong: Yang Chung, fl. A.D. 76, was a member of the privy council of Emperor Han Chang Ti (76-89).

94. Tartar war: Wars between the Chinese Empire and the Tartars during the first century A.D.

95. **Empress Ma Chi**: Ma Shih, fl. A.D. 77, mother of Emperor Han Chang Ti (76-89). Her wisdom and virtue aided the young emperor when he took the throne at the age of 18.

96. **Empresses' relatives**: In A.D. 77 Empress Ma Shih advised her son the emperor that only trouble could ensue should relatives of empresses be elevated to high positions.

97. **Ouang Chi**: Wang Shih, fl. A.D. 15. She was a scheming empress during the time of Wang Mang who arranged that her five brothers be raised to high office.

98. **Han Ho Ti**: Emperor 89-106; during his reign the military fame of China was higher than ever before. At this time eunuchs were raised to the rank of mandarin, thus setting a precedent that led to many seditions and intrigues in later years of the empire.

99. **Han Ngan**: Han An Ti, reigned 107-126, was a very just emperor. Unfortunately he elevated women to the rank of court officials, and from that time on there was widespread corruption, justice was perverted, and honest men were driven from the government. His name means "Peaceful Emperor."

100. **Empress**: Wife of Emperor Han An Ti.

101. **Teng-tchi**: Têng Chê, fl. A.D. 107. He refused to be made a prince, but later returned to the court to aid the government of Emperor Han An Ti.

102. **Yang-tchin**: Yang Chên, fl. 107, was a philosopher of Shensi Province who came to be known as the "Confucius of the West." At the age of 50, yielding to repeated requests to come out of retirement, he became a governor in Shantung. His old friend Huang-mi came, bringing the usual present of money to a superior, but Yang Chên refused.

103. **Léang-ki**: Liang Chi, d. 159. Uncle of Emperor Han Chung Ti (145-146); Liang Chi and the queen dowager, Liang, became great powers in the empire. Liang Chi served as prime minister under Han Huan Ti; he sent poisoned cakes to those who insulted him and was not very well liked. Finally Han Huan Ti sent 3,000 men to put Liang Chi to death. Liang Chi, realizing what was happening, ate one of his own cakes. All the members of his house were slain and his treasure became the emperor's.

104. **Huon**: Han Huan Ti, reigned 147-168. In 158 he did away with his corrupt prime minister, Liang Chi, and confiscated his estate, which amounted to 300 million taels. Because he had so much money, Han Huan Ti remitted the land tax for a year. He also built a temple to honor Lao-tzŭ. Unfortunately Huan Ti had to rely on the palace eunuchs in his successful plot to destroy the Liang family, a policy simply perpetuating the political instability that led to the downfall of the dynasty.

105. **Taoists**: Followers of Lao-tzŭ.

106. **Téou-Chi**: T'ou Shih, fl. 168. As queen dowager she was appointed regent over Emperor Han Ling Ti.

107. **Han Ling**: Han Ling Ti, emperor 168-189. His reign was distinguished while T'ou Shih was regent and her father Tou Wu (d. 167) was prime minister. But the chief eunuch persuaded the emperor that Tou Wu was dangerous, so Han Ling Ti executed him and banished the queen dowager. In 184 an outbreak in the northern provinces started the series of calamities that brought the downfall of the Han dynasty in 221.

108. **Han**: The Later Han dynasty (25-221).

109. **three kingdoms**: The fall of Han was followed by the period of the Three Kingdoms (221-263), when China was divided into three parts: Wei (north), Wu (south), and Shu-Han (west). It was during this period that certain Taoists who called themselves the "Seven Wise Men of the Bamboo Forest" said happiness came from wine and that everything came from the void [*Pai*, 6-1, 46].

110. Lieou-Tchin: Liu Chin, fl. 263, son of the Minor Han emperor, Han Hou-chu (223-264). The Minor Han was also called the Shu-Han, from its base in Szechwan Province.

111. Tçin: Chin, seventh dynasty (265-420), was divided into the Western Chin (265-317) and the Eastern Chin (317-420).

112. Tou-yu: Tu Yu, fl. 247, an officer serving Emperor Chin Wu Ti who proposed to build a bridge over the Hwang Ho [Yellow River]. He also led an attack against the kingdom of Wu.

113. Tçin Ou Ti: Chin Wu Ti, emperor 265-290, also known as Ssu-Ma Yen, founded Western Chin dynasty. His most important act was to overthrow the kingdom of Wu, one of the Three Kingdoms.

114. Yang-Hou: Yang Hu, d. 278, was an important general serving Emperor Chin Wu Ti. Since the emperor needed to take the kingdom of Wu in order to control all China, Yang Hu was directed to plan the campaign, but he died before accomplishing his task.

115. Ouang-siun: Wang Hsün, fl. 280, was a general serving Emperor Chin Wu Ti. He engaged in campaigns against the kingdom of Wu.

116. San-chan: San-shan, mountain in the province of Kiang-nan.

117. Kiang: Chiang, a general term for "river," but here meaning the Yangtze.

118. Sun-hao: Sun Hao, d. 283, was ruler of the kingdom of Wu, which controlled the territory south of the Yangtze. Emperor Chin Wu Ti spent many years trying to bring the kingdom under his rule, finally succeeding in 280. Sun Hao was a cruel king, and his people finally revolted to join the emperor.

119. Tçin Ou: Chin Wu Ti [cf. 113 above].

120. Ou: Wu, one of the Three Kingdoms; it controlled the territory south of the Yangtze. After its conquest by Chin Wu Ti, taxes were remitted for those who would submit to the new ruler.

121. Emperor: Chin Wu Ti.

122. Quindicennio: I, Fifteenth anniversary celebration of rule.

123. Lieou-Y: Liu I, fl. 289, was a highly respected adviser to Emperor Chin Wu Ti, who had begun his reign well but had let the government decline in favor of dancing girls. When asked by the emperor what former rulers he should be compared with, Liu I said Huan [cf. 104 above] and Ling Ti [cf. 107 above], with one difference. They sold offices as Chin did but they put the money into the public coffers while Chin put the money into his own pocket.

124. Yang Siun: Yang Hsün, fl. 289, father-in-law of Emperor Chin Wu Ti. When the emperor became occupied with the entertainments of the court, which had originally belonged to Sun Hao, he told Yang Hsün to govern the kingdom.

125. Tchang: Wang Chang, fl. 290, was a Tartar chieftian who refused to accept a high post from the infamous Yang Hsün.

126. prince Imperial: Refers to the heir apparent during the reign of Chin Hui Ti, second emperor of the Chin dynasty who reigned 290-307. While amusing himself, the prince went in for moneymaking and "operated taverns where he collected the profits from selling wines" [Pai, 6-1, 52].

127. Lao Tse: Lao-tzŭ, ca. 604-531 B.C., one of China's most famous teachers, popularly regarded as the founder of Taoism. His teachings centered on the need to become one with tao, "the way." He professed to have found the clue to all things human and divine. Central to his teaching is the doctrine of inaction which states: "Do nothing, and all things will be done." Later, pure Taoism became mixed with magic, astrology, alchemy, and the search for an elixir of life.

128. Hoai Ti: Chin Huai Ti, reigned 307-313, was a very intelligent emperor who was versed in the arts of government, but he had no success in war with the prince of the Eastern Sea (who was to bring the Eastern

Chin into prominence). Because the emperor was so poor a commander in battle, he was eventually deposed.

129. Min Ti: Chin Min Ti, emperor 313-317. His reign was disturbed by attacks of Tartars who in 317 captured the capital and made the emperor a prisoner.

130. Lieou-Tsong: Liu Tsung, fl. 317, was the son of the Tartar prince Liu Yuan, who had invaded N China about 308. Liu Tsung launched an attack against the Chin capital at Loyong, conquered the city, and made the Chin emperor his prisoner. Liu Tsung considered himself the heir to the Han dynasty, and all China N of the Yangtze came under Tartar control.

131. Tçin Tching: Chin Ch'eng Ti, emperor 326-343, was not himself a bad man, but he came to the throne at the age of five and had incompetent and cruel advisers.

132. Tçin Ngan: Chin Ai Ti, emperor 362-366. "His health had been ruined by the potions which the followers of Lao-tse . . . had given him." He died in the fourth year of his reign [*Pai*, 6-1, 53].

133. Tçin Hiao: Chin Hsiao Wu Ti, emperor 373-397. His reign was plagued with civil wars, for Chin was declining in power and the Liu Sung dynasty was about to appear. This emperor is noted for his poor knowledge of female psychology. He told one of his wives that as she was nearing 30 she should think of retiring so that he could replace her with a younger girl. He was making a joke, but the wife didn't think it was funny. She got him drunk and then strangled him [*Pai*, 6-1, 53].

134. piquée de ce badinage: F, "stung by this banter."

135. Sung: Liu Sung, eighth dynasty (420-479).

136. Lieou-yu: Liu Yü, 356-423, founder of Liu Sung dynasty. In 399 he enlisted in the imperial army and was given a command of 70 men. So able was he that by 416 he was made commander in chief and Duke of Sung. In 419 he caused Emperor Chin Ai Ti to be strangled and set up the latter's brother, Chin Kung Ti, as emperor. After sixteen months Chin Kung Ti abdicated and Liu Yü took the throne with the title Kao Tsu.

137. Kao-Tsou: Kao Tsu Wu Ti, reigned 420-423, formerly Liu Yü, known generally as Wu Ti, founder of the Liu Sung dynasty. He proved to be a good emperor but he did not live long enough to be effective.

138. Li-Chan: Liu-shan, mountain in Kiangsi Province near Lake Po-yang. It was the residence of the scholar Lei Tzu-tsung who refused to leave his mountain once he had seen to the courses of study at the academies founded by Wen Ti in 438.

139. Et les Indiens disent que Boudha: F, "And the Indians say that Buddha." Refers to a folktale which says that Buddha was the result of the miraculous union of a chaste queen and a white elephant.

140. Queen Nana: In the legends that gathered about the historical Buddha, Nana is said to have been a virgin who miraculously gave birth to Buddha after the figure of the Supreme Being appeared to her in the form of a white elephant.

141. Prince of Ouei: Toba Tao, d. 452, prince of the kingdom of Wei. An important and powerful ruler, he paid much attention to education in his domain. Because he once entered a Buddhist monastery and found the priests all drinking whiskey and the monastery full of women, he banished Buddhists from his kingdom.

142. hochangs: *Ho-shang*, Buddhists.

143. shamen: Shamans, those who practice shamanism, here meaning Buddhists.

144. Taotssé: Taoist, a believer in Taoism, supposedly founded by Lao-tzŭ [cf. 127 above].

145. Ouen Ti: Wên Ti, reigned 424-454 as ruler of the Liu Sung state. In spite of the opposition of the state of Wei, he extended the power of the emperor over a large territory. As he was fond of literature and the arts and interested in education, he established national colleges. He was eventually killed by his own son.

146. To-pa-tao: Prince of Wei [141 above].

147. placet: F, "petition." Derived from L, *placet*, "it pleases."

148. Yupingtchi: Yü Ping-chih, fl. 448, president of the judicial tribunal under Emperor Wen Ti. He sought after justice so ardently and with such severity that he ruined multitudes of poor people. The emperor finally had to remove him from office.

149. Oueï land: Wei, principality in the general region of the modern Sian, a city in Shensi Province, NE central China, on the Wei River where it joins the Hwang Ho.

150. à la Valturio: F, "in the manner of Valturio" [9:19].

151. Ou Ti: Wu Ti, ruler (483-494) of the state of Ch'i, which replaced the Liu Sung. He paid attention to the laws of the kingdom and cut down the number of retainers at court. While worrying about rebellion within the empire, however, he forgot to consider the threat of the powerful kingdom of Wei to the north.

152. Yen Yen: Yen Yen-chih, d. 456, although of peasant stock, rose to be prime minister of the empire under Emperor Wu Ti. He was a model of modesty, frugality, and disinterestedness.

153. Oueï prince: The Wei Tartars attacked, but since Sung reacted strongly "the Wei forces withdrew" [*Pai*, 6-1, 60].

154. Tien: *T'ien*, "heaven." It was an old tradition that in the "spring rites" the emperor should plough a furrow to ask heaven for a good harvest; and that the empress set a good example by the ceremony of feeding silkworms.

155. Ou: Hsiao Wu Ti, emperor 454-465. Little happened during his reign, and he had no able minister to spur him to activity. The emperor was very frivolous, giving people of the court nicknames and having his servants chase mandarins with a stick. Thus, no respect was paid Hsiao Wu Ti, and he became known as the "Discarded."

156. Kao: Kao Ti, first emperor (479-483) of the Ch'i dynasty (479-502). He is said to have been deficient in heroic qualities.

157. Siao: Hsiao Tzŭ-liang, son of Emperor Wu Ti, 483-494, ruled less than a year after his father died. He collected antique vases.

158. Topas: The people of Topa, of Turkic origin, who founded the kingdom of Wei (386-534).

159. Tan Tchin: Fan Chên, fl. 484, Chinese scholar, one of a group that gathered about Hsiao Tsu-liang, son of Emperor Wu Ti. The prince was a Buddhist, but Fan Chên took it upon himself to discourse on the methods Buddhist monks (bonzes) used to deceive the people.

160. Ou Ti: Wu Ti, reigned 502-549, overthrew the Ch'i dynasty and founded the Liang dynasty. A good emperor who helped his people during the famine and purged the court of corruption, he became a Buddhist and imported 3,000 Buddhist priests. During his reign more than 13,000 Buddhist temples were built in the empire. In 527 Wu Ti became a Buddhist monk. So seriously did he adhere to his Buddhist vows that he became an ineffectual statesman and was overwhelmed by a rebellious general.

161. Ping Tching: P'ing-ch'êng, capital of the kingdom of Wei (386-534).

162. Crown Prince: The son and heir apparent of Emperor Wu Ti.

163. Topa Hong: To Pa Hung, ruler of the kingdom of Wei from 466 to 471, also known as Hsien Wen Ti, became a Buddhist. In 471 he abdicated in favor of his son, who, while adhering to many Buddhist teachings, also gave support to Confucian precepts and required his officials to use the Chinese language and wear Chinese dress.

164. Yuen: Yüan. In 496 To Pa Hung, ruler of Wei, changed the name of his family from To Pa to Yüan. The northern Wei was also known as the Yüan Wei.

165. Kung-fu-tseu: Confucius.

166. Ou Ti: Wu Ti, first ruler of the Liang dynasty [cf. 160 above].

167. 46 tablets: "The Stone Classics," a basic Confucian document. In 517, when Hu Hsi was empress, they were torn down and used to build a Buddhist temple.

168. Yo Lang: Lo Yang. In 494 the ruler of the northern Wei (the son of To Pa Hung) moved his capital from P'ing-ch'êng to the ancient Chinese capital of Lo Yang [53:61].

169. Foé: Fu, the name of Buddha and more commonly the name given to Buddhist priests [*foés, foéist*, in French transliteration] and to Buddhism.

170. Hou-chi: Hu Hsi, the dowager queen who ruled the kingdom of Wei from 515 to 528. An unscrupulous but able woman, she perpetrated the most horrible crimes but also, as a devout Buddhist, did much to further the Buddhist cause in N China.

171. Ou Ti: Wu Ti, founder of the Liang dynasty, finally became a Buddhist monk [cf. 160 above] and left the kingdom to its fate.

172. Ouen Ti: Prob. Shang Ti, "Spirit of Heaven" [53:24].

173. Yang-kien: Yang Ch'ien, emperor 589-605, reunited China, founded the Sui dynasty, and became one of the greatest Chinese emperors. He ruled under the name of Sui Wên Ti until 604, when he was assassinated, apparently by his son.

174. Soui: Sui, a minor state that later became a dynasty.

175. Sou-ouei: Su Wei, fl. 580, adviser to Yang Ch'ien.

176. Heou: Hou Chu, reigned 583-589, was the last of the rulers of the small state of Ch'en. Not heeding the signs that his rule was at its end, this prince pursued a course of extravagance and debauchery. He built three huge buildings [the three Towers] for his favorite concubines. When he was told that Yang Ch'ien was about to overthrow his dynasty, he told his ministers not to worry because the rebellion would probably be unsuccessful; but it wasn't.

177. Soui: Sui, twelfth dynasty (589-618).

178. Yang-Kien: Yang Ch'ien, personal name of Sui Emperor Wên Ti.

179. Mt. Taï Chan: T'ai Shan, sacred mountain of China in W Shantung Province, 32 miles S of Tsinan. There are many shrines on the road to the top where temples were built.

180. Gin Cheou: Name of palace built by Sui Emperor Wên Ti in 593.

181. Touli-Kahn: Tuli Kohan, fl. 593, leader of Kohan, of the Tu-chüei, a Turkic tribe that had established its power in what is now Mongolia. He was given a daughter by the first Sui emperor, Wên Ti [Yang Ch'ien], which eventually led to Sui domination over this border territory.

182. Ouen: Wên Ti, reigned 589-605, known as Yang Ch'ien, was the first emperor of the Sui dynasty (589-618). He concerned himself with agriculture, but was unable to control his scheming brothers.

183. Yang (kouang) Ti: Yang Ti or Yang Kuang, reigned 605-618, son of Wên Ti. He moved the imperial capital to Lo Yang and began building palaces, gardens, and canals, employing, it is said, 2 million men. His canals in the provinces of Hupeh, Shantung, and Honan were designed primarily to facilitate state progress, and they greatly improved commerce in the N. But Yang Ti's methods were harsh, leading to a rebellion; he was soon overthrown and the Sui dynasty came to an end.

184. Kou-choui: Ku-shui, river in Shantung Province which was part of Yang Ti's canal system.

185. Hoang Ho: Yellow River.

186. Wall: Great Wall of China: Chang-chêng. A defensive wall extending 1,250 miles from Mongolia to the Yellow Sea. It was started in the third century B.C. and finished during the reign of the Chin emperor, Shih Huang Ti. In the early seventh century Yang Ti repaired the section between Yü-lin and Tzü-ho.

187. Yu-lin: Yü-lin, city in N China on N border of Shensi Province.

188. Tsé-ho: Tzü-ho, city on N border of Shensi Province.

189. Pei-kiu: Pei Chü, fl. 607, was sent by Emperor Yang Ti to be governor in Hsi-yu and turned his journey to good account by mapping the country.

190. Si-yu: Hsi-yu, large region in W China outside the limits of Shensi Province in the territory of the Tartars.

191. Kong: Kung Ti, who reigned 618-619 as the last emperor of the Sui dynasty, was one of the two puppets who were set up as emperors after the death of Yang Ti. Both were killed within the year.

192. abuleia: L, "paralysis of the will." One of two poles in *The Cantos* [the other: *directio voluntatis*] used to describe the "paideuma" of persons or periods. Thus the Sui dynasty died out because it no longer could put "ideas into action" [5:44].

193. Tang: T'ang, thirteenth dynasty (618-907).

194. Kao Tseu: Kao Tsu, reigned 618-626, known as Li Yüan, was the first emperor of the T'ang dynasty. As the Count of T'ang he had served as governor of a military district in Shansi. A rather timid man and a dedicated Confucianist, he was extremely reluctant to participate in the revolt against the corrupt Sui dynasty. It was his son, Li Shih-min, who actually led the revolt and succeeded in overthrowing the Sui. By a bit of clever intrigue Li Shih-min brought his father into the revolt so that the latter would become the first T'ang emperor.

195. Li-Chi: Li Shih, d. 623, daughter of Emperor Kao Tsu. In 617 she raised an army and came to the aid of her father and brother in their struggles to gain the empire.

196. Tou-kou-hoen: Tu-Yü Hun, Tartar tribe that occupied the territory around Lake Koko Nor in Tsinghai Province, W central China.

197. Fou: Fü I, fl. 626, served as minister under Emperor Kao Tsu. He petitioned that all Buddhist establishments be abolished and that all Buddhist monks and nuns be sent to their homes because, he argued, Buddhism demoralized the empire by de-emphasizing the proper relationships between ruler and people, between parents and children.

198. foé: Fu, Buddhists.

199. Taï Tsong: T'ai Tsung, reigned 626-649. T'ai Tsung was the title adopted by Li Shih-min when he replaced his father on the T'ang throne. He was one of China's most remarkable emperors. A disciple of Confucius, he noted that emperors who embraced Taoism or Buddhism brought about the downfall of their dynasties: "Just as wings are necessary for the birds and water for the fishes, so I put my trust in the teachings of the sages of our country." He cut government costs, reduced taxes, built libraries, aided scholars, and saw that his people had more than enough for their daily needs. He greatly expanded the empire to the west. In 645 he invaded Korea but could not bring it completely into the empire. In 649 he composed *Notes on Conduct*.

200. Fou-Y: [cf. 197 above].

201. Kung: Confucius.

202. Ouëi-Tching: Wei Chêng, d. 643, was an astute minister who served Emperor T'ai Tsung. He was noted for the frankness with which he criticized the emperor.

203. Tchang-sun Chi: Chang Sun-shih, d.

636, empress of T'ai Tsung, was one of the great queens of China. Like her husband she was a foe of Taoism and Buddhism. At her death she asked the emperor not to build her an elaborate tomb because it would cost the people too much. She, like Wei Chêng, was not loath to criticize her husband.

204. "Notes for Princesses": Work by Empress Chang Sun-shih on the lives of the princesses of the Chinese Empire before her time.

205. denar: Coin. From L, *denarius*; variant of I, *denaro*, or F, *dener* or *denier*.

206. palatio: L, "palace." Rhyme with the various intrigues and plots in the palaces of the Italian city-states.

207. Corea: Korea. Only in Korea was T'ai Tsung's foreign policy unsuccessful.

208. Caspian: Caspian Sea.

209. Koulihan: Ku-li-kan, nation NW of China and N of Caspian Sea. It was said they lived so far north that "the days are very long and the nights very short." They sent an embassy to China in 647.

210. Kieï-kou: Chieh-ku, barbarian tribe, obviously European, living W of China. These people had red hair and blue eyes. They were tall and had a martial air. "The such like had never been seen in China before." They sent an embassy to China in 648.

211. Atchen (Atkins) Chélisa: Shih Pu-chü Atchen, fl. 647, first officer of Che-li-sa [Shih-li-sa] of the Chieh-ku. As ambassador to the court of Emperor T'ai Tsung, he demanded that the emperor give him the title of grand mandarin. Since titles cost nothing, the emperor made him grand general of the army as well.

212. "Notes on Conduct": Treatise with twelve sections on "How a king should conduct himself," written by Emperor T'ai Tsung for his son.

213. Hempire: Chinese Empire.

214. Empress Ou-heou: Wu Hou, 625-705, one of the concubines of Emperor T'ai Tsung. In 656, after his death, she became the empress consort of Kao-Tsung and for the next forty years was one of the most important figures in Chinese political history. Cruel and unscrupulous, she controlled two emperors and became virtual ruler of the empire. She forced her husband to make her coruler (they were know as "The Two Holy Ones") and finally took over all his power. During the years 684-705 her son Chung Tsung was nominally the emperor, but the period is often known as the reign of Empress Wu Hou.

215. Contraption: The administrative machinery set up by T'ai Tsung was run by good people he brought into government. Because it worked in spite of Wu Hou, the empire was at peace for several years.

216. Tching-gintai: Chêng Jen-t'ai, fl. 662, was a general of the imperial troops serving Emperor Kao Tsung (650-684). He was sent to deal with the Tartar tribes that had been attacking the borders of the empire. His campaign was a success, but on the return journey snow raised havoc: ". . . almost the entire army died of misery and fatigue, so that barely eight hundred men were able to reach the Chinese frontier" [*Pai*, 6-1, 86].

217. hochang: Buddhists. During the T'ang period their power and influence increased. One of their leaders gave the empress a book in which they pretended to prove that she was the daughter of Buddha and that she should succeed to the T'ang dynasty.

218. Tartars: A Tartar chief refused to give his daughter in marriage to a nephew of Wu Hou and threatened to invade China and restore the house of T'ai Tsung.

219. Tchong: Chung Tsung, reigned 684-710, was a weak emperor who was controlled by women. His mother, Wu Hou, ruled the empire until 705; from 705 to 710 the emperor was dominated by his wife, Wei, who wanted to be a second Wu Hou. Wei was murdered in 710.

220. Hieun: Hsüan Tsung, reigned 713-756, was one of the most celebrated emperors in Chinese history. He paid strict attention to governing his people and made sumptuary laws for the court in order to cut down state expenses. In 740 he ordered that Confucius be elevated to the rank of prince. But his reign ended in rebellion and palace politics, and Hsüan Tsung resigned in favor of his son, Su Tsung. Hsüan forbade display at court: "He ordered the precious stones and the clothes embroidered with gold and silver to be burned" [*Pai*, 6-1, 88].

221. Lang-tchéou: Lang-ch'ou, city in Honan Province, was one of the places where mathematicians implemented Hsüan Tsung's orders to make accurate astronomical observations. Pound gives the results in the text.

222. Tsiun-y: Chün-i, village in Honan Province, N of Lang-ch'ou.

223. Lou-tchéou: Lu Chou, home village of Hsüan Tsung who traveled there in 723 and exempted it from taxes for five years "to let it be known that he did not forget his home country" [*Pai*, 6-1, 89].

224. Chépoutching: Shih-pu-chêng, city in N China.

225. Ngan-yong: An-Yang, city in N China and ancient capital of Shang dynasty.

226. Tou-san: T'u-fan. Prob. refers to the T'u-fan people of Tibetan stock. The Chinese lost two cities to the T'u-fan but later recaptured them.

227. taozer: In 741 a Taoist named Chang-ko came to court claiming to have the secret of immortality. The emperor seemed convinced until the "Taozer" suddenly died.

228. Koué-fei: Yang Kuei-fei, d. 756, was the favorite concubine of Emperor Hsüan Tsung and second in importance to the empress. During the An Lu-shan rebellion in 756 the soldiers demanded her death because of her political intrigues. The em-

peror finally consented and she was strangled. When her body was shown to the soldiers, they promptly returned to their posts. But because she was innocent and the victim of a plot, the emperor became so sad that he resigned the throne that same year.

229. Tchang-siun: Chang Hsün, fl. 756, was a commander of imperial troops serving Emperor Su Tsung. He is best known for his defense of Yung-Chiu during a siege. It was he who devised the arrows ploy that resulted in defeat for the Tartars.

230. Sou Tsong: Su Tsung, reigned 756-763. At the start of his reign the barbarians held both the E and W capitals of the empire. His reign was one of continual wars, but he was served by able generals.

231. Yong-kieu: Yung-chiu, city in Honan Province.

232. Li-yen: Li Yen, fl. 779, was a mandarin serving in the government of Emperor Te Tsung.

233. Té Tsong: Te Tsung, reigned 780-805, was a weak but amiable emperor. His ministers urged him to obtain revenue by imposing new taxes and to abolish the three existing taxes: land tax, compulsory labor, and payment in kind. The new tax was an annual collection in money. Once the emperor became aware of the condition of the peasants, he gave special attention to making their lot easier, but his ministers prevented him from accomplishing many of his aims. He was a poet and wrote his imperial decrees in verse.

234. Nestorians: Members of the Nestorian church, originally the ancient church of Persia. It is related to Catholicism but is not part of the Catholic communion. Its period of greatest expansion was from the seventh to the tenth century, when missions were sent to India and China. In 631 the Nestorians brought Christianity into China. The famous Nestorian tablet (in Sian, Shensi Province) is a record, in Chinese and Syriac, of the progress of Christianity in China from 631 to 781, when the tablet was erected.

235. Kouo-tsé-y: Kuo Tsu-i, 697-781, was one of the most famous Chinese generals. He served four emperors: Hsüan Tsun, Su Tsung, Taï Tsung, and Te Tsung. His campaigns against the rebel An Lu-shan and the Tartars were successful. He proved an able governor of various cities and provinces. His loyalty to the empire, unlike that of most officials, was never questioned. His name is mentioned in the famous Nestorian tablet.

236. Li-ching: Li Shêng, fl. 787, was a captain in the imperial troops who enjoyed great success against the Tartars. It was he who said that war with them was better than peace. In 787, when it was discovered that he was having an affiar with a daughter of Emperor Su Tsung, the latter became so angry that he exiled Li Shêng to Kwangtung.

237. Sintien: Hsin-tien, prob. a town close to Ch'ang-an, capital of the T'ang dynasty, in Shensi Province. The rest of the canto concerns an anecdote that Pound neatly summarizes from the *Histoire*, VI [*Pai*, 6-1, 96].

239. bé: F, "well!"

240. corvée: F, "labor required by the state." Te Tsung did nothing about taxes in general, but he relieved the peasants he visited from required labor.

Glossary Canto LV

1. Orbem bellis, urbem gabellis / implevit: L, "Filled the world with wars, the city with taxes." Said of Pope Urban VIII.

2. Tchun: Shun Tsung, reigned 805, a mild and good man, was ill with an incurable disease when he came to the throne. After eight months he abdicated in favor of his son, who ruled under the name of Hsien Tsung.

3. Li-Chun: Hsien Tsung, reigned 806-821, son of Emperor Shun Tsung whom he succeeded.

4. Ouie-Kao: Wei Kao, d. 805, was a general of the imperial troops who won significant victories over Tartars and Tibetans. As governor of Szechwan Province for 21 years he gained more fame, for during that time the people of his province paid exactly the tax demanded by the emperor from the province—and no more.

5. Lin-Yun: Lin Yün, fl. 806, was a military officer serving under the rebel Liu Pi. When he objected to the rebellion Liu Pi ordered him beheaded, but Lin Yün was so brave that he was given his freedom.

6. Lieou Pi: Liu Pi, d. 806, succeeded the illustrious Wei Kao as governor of Szechwan Province. He raised a rebellion because the territory he ruled was not expanded. Defeated in his first major battle against imperial troops, Liu Pi, with all his family, was sent to the capital and executed.

7. Liki: Li Chi, fl. 807, was governor of a department in the province of Kiang-nan who accumulated and hoarded the treasure of six departments. The emperor ordered that the money be put back into circulation to stimulate commerce. Li Chi launched a revolt, was defeated, sent to the court, and executed.

8. Hien-Tsong: Hsien Tsung, reigned 806-821. He started his reign by regulating the revenue of the empire, ending the practice of giving presents, forbidding slavery, and remitting taxes. In a series of wars (814-819) he reestablished imperial control over the provincial governors. The emperor, however, was controlled by the court eunuchs, who often opposed his reforms. Toward the end of his reign he became a Buddhist and died suddenly after taking some pills that were supposed to ensure his immortality.

9. Ideograms: From top to bottom, right column first, the 13 characters read: *Jên*

[M3099]: "Humane"; *chê* [M263]: "who"; *i* [M293]: "take"; *ts'ai* [M6662]: "wealth"; *fâ* [M1768]: "to develop"; *shên* [M5718]: "themselves"; *Pu* [M5379]: "Negative." The rest of the characters are repeated in different order: *Jên, chê, i, shên, fâ, ts'ai.* The literal sense of this Confucian saying is: "Humane men use wealth to develop themselves; inhumane men use themselves to develop wealth." Pound translates it: "The humane man uses his wealth as a means to distinction, the inhumane becomes a mere harness, an accessory to his takings" [*CON*, 83].

10. eunuchs: Usually placed in charge of the royal harem, they were able to observe, and perhaps influence, the sexual activities of the royal family. From this unique position they found it possible to bring tremendous influence to bear upon royal decisions. In times of weak emperors, such influence was usually malevolent and had disastrous consequences for the dynasty.

11. tao-tse: Taoists [54:105, 127].

12. hochangs: Buddhists [54:217].

13. Hien: [cf. 8 above].

14. Hoai: Hwai [53:112].

15. Li Kiang: Li Chiang, fl. 812, was a minister serving Emperor Hsien Tsung.

16. Tien Hing: T'ien-Hsing, fl. 812, a minister serving Emperor Hsien Tsung.

17. Tching-Ouang: Chêng Wang [53:65].

18. Kang: K'ang Wang [53:76].

19. Han-Ouen: Hsiao Wên Ti [54:42].

20. Han King Ti: Hsiao Ching Ti [54:54].

21. Tou-san: Tu-fan [54:226].

22. Mou-Tsong: Mu Tsung, reigned 821-825. He thought it likely that his father had been poisoned, but he didn't make a big thing over it: he had the Taoist who promised his father immortality put to death and banished the rest of the Taoists [VI, 430].

23. Ouen-Tsong: Wên Tsung, reigned 827-841. He began his reign by cutting government expenditures, dismissing 3,000 women from the royal harem, and giving audiences to his ministers every other day. But he lacked firmness of purpose, and soon the power of the court was usurped by the eunuchs. The latter thus became a national danger, but all efforts to get rid of them failed.

24. Ou-Tsong: Wu Tsung, reigned 841-847. His one important decree was that all Buddhist priests and nuns in the empire should return to their homes and stop living in idleness and immorality. He also proscribed the Christian cult of Manicheism.

25. bonzes: Buddhist monks.

26. Tsaï-gin: Wang Tsai-jen, d. 847, was the favorite concubine of Emperor Wu Tsung. She hanged herself as soon as Wu died.

27. Siuen: Hsüan Tsung, reigned 847-860. An emperor of intelligence and decision, he became known as the "little" T'ai Tsung.

28. 'Gold Mirror': *Chin-ching*, or *The Mirror of Gold*, a work by Emperor T'ai Tsung. This work may be the same as T'ai Tsung's *Notes on Conduct*.

29. Tai Tsong: T'ai Tsung [54:199].

30. Hien: Hsien Tsung [cf. 8 above].

31. Y Tsong: I Tsung, reigned 860-874, was an emperor with little common sense; he preferred his own pleasures to the responsibility of governing his people. During his reign there were rebellions and barbarian invasions.

32. Hi-Tsong: Hsi Tsung, reigned 874-889. He left the government to eunuchs while he devoted himself to sport, music, and mathematics. During his reign the most serious rebellions of the T'ang dynasty occurred; they devastated much of China and led to the ruin of the dynasty.

33. Sun Te: Sun Tê-chao, fl. 901, was first general of the empire during the reign of

Emperor Chao Tsung (889-905). He freed the emperor from the control by the eunuchs and had several of them executed. In gratitude, the emperor made his family an affiliate of the royal house and gave him the honorary name of Li Chi-chao.

34. Prince of TçIN: Li K'o-yung, d. 908. Of Turkic origin, he became a distinguished commander of the imperial troops. His campaigns against the T'u-fan invaders (barbarian tribe in the province of Sinkiang, W China) were so successful that Emperor Chao Tsung (889-905) made him Prince of Chin in 895.

35. TçIN: Chin, principality in the province of Shansi.

36. Li-ké-Yong: Li K'o-yung [cf. 34 above].

37. Tchu: T'ai-tsu, reigned 906-913. Known as Chou Wên, he was first emperor of the Later Liang Dynasty (907-923). When the last emperor of the T'ang dynasty made him Prince of Liang, T'ai-tsu assumed much of the emperor's power and assassinated him in 907. Tai-tsu's reign was troubled by rebellions and invansions of the Ch'i-tan Tartars.

38. Hiu: Li Ts'un-hsü, d. 926, son of Li K'o-yung, overthrew the Later Liang dynasty and in 923 set himself up as the first emperor of the Later T'ang dynasty, ruling under the name Chuang Tsung (923-926). He waged successful wars against the Ch'i-tan Tartars, regaining the province of Szechwan for the empire. Finally he gave himself up to sensuality and was assassinated by an actor.

39. douanes: F, "custom duties."

40. chançons de gestes: F, *chansons de geste*, "songs of heroic deeds."

41. Khitans: Ch'i-tans, Mongol tribe N of China, near Korea. By 907 they had become very strong under the chieftain Yeh-lü A-pao-chi, who proclaimed himself emperor of an independent kingdom with the dynastic title of Liao ["iron"]. The Ch'i-tans en-

croached on the empire until China was divided at the Yellow River. Kai Feng became the capital of the empire, and Peking became for the first time a metropolis and the Ch'i-tan capital.

42. Yeliou Apaoki: Yeh-lü A-pao-chi, d. 926, chieftain of the Ch'i-tan Tartars.

43. Chuliu: Shulu, d. ca. 953. Also known as Empress Ying T'ien, she was queen of the Ch'i-tan chieftain, Yeh-lü A-pao-chi. She was a woman of great beauty and wisdom, and her husband often depended on her advice in matters of state and military operations.

44. Tching-tcheou: Poss. city of Ting-ch'ou in Hopeh Province, N China.

45. Prince Tçin: Chin [cf. 35 above].

46. Ouang Yeou: Wang Yu, fl. 921, was a rebel commander of the troops of Li Ts'un-hsü, Prince of Chin. He invited the Ch'i-tan Tartars to attack some cities in China, which they did.

47. Khitan of Apaoki: Ch'i-tan, Tartars.

48. TçIN: Chin [cf. 35 above].

49. Tang: T'ang: The Later T'ang, the fifteenth dynasty (923-936). Founded by Li Ts'un-hsü, Prince of Chin.

50. Chou: A principality in the province of Szechwan, S central China.

51. Prince . . . but no Emperor: Son of the Later T'ang Emperor Chuang Tsung who died in 926 and was replaced by Tartar general Li Ssu-yuan [VII, 251-254].

52. Tartar Yuen: Li Ssu-yuan, 866-934, adopted son of Li K'o-yung. Like his father, he was a brilliant general and did much to preserve the Later T'ang dynasty. After the death of his half brother, Li Ts'un-hsü, he was proclaimed emperor by the army. He ruled under the name Ming Tsung.

53. Ming Tsong: Ming Tsung, reigned 926-934, proclaimed emperor by the army but refused for a time to function as anything but regent. By 932 the art of printing had been invented and the nine classics were printed by imperial orders from wooden blocks and sold to the public.

54. Li Tsongkou: Li Ts'ung-k'o, 892-936, commanding general of the imperial guards who in 934 came to the throne as the fourth emperor of the Later T'ang dynasty, ruling under the name Liu Wang (934-936). His dynasty fell to the Ch'i-tan Tartars.

55. Kungfutseu: Confucius.

56. Chéking-Tang: Shih Ching-t'ang, 892-944, general and governor of Shantung Province under the Later T'ang. He bribed the Ch'i-tan Tartars with a promise of half of Chihli and Shansi to help him to the throne. In 936 he proclaimed himself emperor, ruling under the name of Kao Tsu (936-944). He was the founder of the Later Tsin [Chin] dynasty.

57. Apaoki son of Chuliu: Yeh-lü-Tê-kuang, d. 947, second son of Ye-Lü-A-pao-chi. In 927 he succeeded to the throne of the Ch'i-tan Tartars (the Liao dynasty) as Emperor T'ai Tsung and in 936 he agreed to help Shih Ching-t'ang gain the empire in return for territory in Chihli and Shansi provices. The revolt was successful, and Yeh-lü-Tê-kuang, the "Father-Emperor," received a yearly tribute from Shih Ching-t'ang, the "Child Emperor" of the Later Chin.

58. Chuliu: [cf. 43 above].

59. Te Kouang: [cf. 57 above].

60. Ouan soui!!: [54:75].

61. evviva, evviva: I, "hurrah!"

62. Lieou-Tchi-Yuen: Liu Chih-yüan, d. 948, was a distinguished general and governor of Shansi Province under Emperor Chi Wang of the Later Chin (943-947). When the emperor ordered his troops to attack the Ch'i-tan Tartars, Liu Chih-yüan refused, knowing the imperial troops could not withstand the barbarians. After the Tartars withdrew from Kaifeng, the imperial capital, Liu Chih-yüan was proclaimed emperor by his army. He ruled under the name Kao Tsu

(947-948) and founded the Later Han dynasty.

63. Turk . . . of Chato: Prob. refers to Liu Chih-yüan whose family was of Sha T'o Tartar descent and thus of Turkic origin.

64. Caïfon fou: K'ai Feng, city in Honan Province, E central China. It served as the capital of various Chinese states during the period of the Five Dynasties (907-960).

65. Sung: Nineteenth dynasty (960-1280). It is divided into two parts: the Sung (960-1127), sometimes called the Northern Sung, and the Southern Sung (1127-1280).

66. Teoui-tchéou: Ts'ui Ch'ou-tu, fl. 952, was an officer of the imperial troops, serving Emperor T'ai Tsu of the Later Chou dynasty.

67. Taï-Tsou: T'ai Tsu, reigned 951-954, founder and first emperor of the Later Chou dynasty. Although his reign was disturbed by the rebellious Prince of Han, T'ai Tsu proved to be an able administrator and leader. He was a patron of literature and honored the memory of Confucius by saying, "Confucius is the master of a hundred generations of emperors."

68. Kung: Confucius.

69. Ou-tchao: Wu Chao-i, fl. 953. Wishing to start a college, he requested permission of the Prince of Chou to have *Shu Ching* [*Book of History*] and *Shih Ching* [*Books of Odes*] printed (953). The permission was granted.

70. Chi-Tsong: Shih Tsung, reigned 954-959, was a benevolent and generous emperor of the Later Chou. He waged successful wars against the Ch'i-tans and the Northern Han and enlarged the empire. When there was a scarcity of money, he ordered all copper utensils given up for imperial uses. He also seized all the bronze images of Buddha and converted them into coin, remarking that Buddha, who had given so much to mankind, was not likely to object.

71. Tçé-tchéou: Tz'u-ch'ou, city near Liuchow in Kwangsi Province, SE China. In 954

the Northern Han attacked Liuchow and Emperor Shih Tsung engaged the Han troops near Tz'u-ch'ou.

72. Han: Later Han dynasty.

73. Chi: Shih Tsung [cf. 70 above].

74. hochang: Buddhists.

75. bonzes and bonzesses: Buddhist monks and nuns.

76. Chou: Later Chou dynasty (951-960).

77. Tang: T'ang. The southern T'ang, a principality in the province of Kiangsu, E China. Formerly this region was the principality of Wu, but in 937 the princes of Wu changed their name to T'ang.

78. Hoaï-ho: Hwai Ho, river in S Honan and NW Anhwei provinces in E China. It was on the Hwai River that a naval battle was fought between the armies of Emperor Shih Tsung and those of the ruler of the Later T'ang [cf. Cordier, II, 52].

79. Kiang: Yangtze River.

80. Hoaï-nan: City on the Hwai River.

81. devast: F, "ravaged."

82. Ouang-po: Wang Po, d. 959, was statesman, mathematician, and personal counselor to Emperor Shih Tsung.

83. pourvou que ça doure: F, "provided that it lasts."

84. Han: Prob. Later Han dynasty (947-951); Yin Ti, the last emperor of the Later Han, was 18 when he came to the throne.

85. Tchao Kouang: Chao K'uang-yin, founder of the Sung dynasty (960-1127) who ruled as Emperor T'ai Tsu [cf. 90 below].

86. South Han: Nan-han, roughly the area of the provinces of Kwangsi and Kwangtung in SE China; this principality lasted from 905 to 971.

87. douanes: F, "custom duties."

88. Tsiuenpiu: Wang Ch'uan-pin, fl. 965, was a general serving Sung Emperor T'ai Tsu. He was in charge of the expedition that overcame the remnants of the Later Chou dynasty.

89. Chou: Hou Chou, Later Chou dynasty (951-960).

90. emperor: T'ai Tsu, reigned 960-976, founded Sung dynasty. He was serving as a general under Emperor Shih Tsung when his troops invested him with the yellow robe of emperor. His greatest accomplishment was the restoration of the empire. He reclaimed the lands of Southern Han, the Later Chou, Szechwan, and other provinces for the throne, and only Northern Han resisted his attacks. He encouraged the study of literature, revised the law courts, improved the criminal code, and stabilized the economy.

91. this general: Wang Ch'uan-pin. He received the emperor's robe with tears of happiness. The emperor sent a message with the robe saying he wished he was able to send one to all his generals. Because of such acts the troops loved the emperor and for him rapidly conquered the states of Chou.

92. Koué: C, *Kue*, the constellation Andromeda.

93. Tai Tsong: T'ai Tsung, reigned 977-998, was a mild but decisive emperor who governed with economy. His first important act was to suppress the state of Northern Han (979), a task his brother, T'ai Tsu, had not completed. But T'ai Tsung was unable to check the Ch'i-tan Tartars or to stop a dangerous alliance between the Ch'i-tan and Nü-chên Tartars. He was a student of history, honored Confucius, and studied the classics.

94. true BOOKS: Prob. refers to a multi-volume work, *T'ai-Ping Yu Lan*, prepared under the direction of Emperor T'ai Tsung.

95. Ssétchuen: Szechwan, province in W central China.

96. Ouang Siaopo: Wang Hsiao-po, fl. 993, was a man of the people who roused Szechwan province to revolt against its governor in 993. There was little money in the province because the conquering Sung troops had carried it away a few years before. The mandarins were fleecing the people. The rich were buying up small farms and depriving the poor of land and food. Imperial troops soon put down the rebellion, and Emperor T'ai Tsung appointed a governor who improved the condition of the poor.

97. Tsing-chin: Ch'ing-shên, city in Szechwan Province, later known as Koan-hsien.

98. Pongchan: Peng-shan, district and city in the province of Szechwan.

99. Jelly Hugo: Yeh-lü Hsiu-ko, d. 998, was governor of the region of Yen, which surrounds the city of Peking (once called Yen as well). He was a general of the Ch'i-tan Tartars and is known for his humanity and his just and liberal administration.

100. Ghengis: Genghis Khan, 1162-1227, Mongol emperor. His personal name was Temujin or Temuchin and his imperial title was Tai-Tsou [T'ai-Tsu]. He proclaimed himself emperor of the Mongols in 1206. By 1214, through a series of wars with various Tartar tribes (mainly Ch'i-tan and Nü-chên), he became master of all the territory north of the Hwang Ho, except for Peking, capital of the Chin dynasty of the Nü-chên. He conquered Korea, and by 1221 he controlled much of C Asia. During his career of conquest he established the power of the Mongols in a large part of Asia.

101. Tchin-Song: Chên Tsung, reigned 998-1023, was a capable emperor but a devout Taoist, whose superstition led him to disgrace. K'ou Chun, a brilliant general and statesman, forced the emperor to fight the Ch'i-tan Tartars and to make peace with them by promising an annual tribute of 100 ounces of silver and 200 pieces of silk. When court intrigues led to the ouster of K'ou Chun, the emperor fell into the hands of ministers who used his superstition to their advantage. Three books, reputed to be from heaven, were presented to the emperor, who

was so impressed by this supposed honor that he ordered a huge temple built; the project took seven years to complete and cost so much that some historians date the decline of the Sung dynasty from this extravagance. By 1020 the emperor was insane and his power had passed to eunuchs.

102. marte zibbeline: F, *martre zibeline* "sable."

103. Tchin-Tsong: Chên Tsung.

104. King of Khitan: Yeh-lü-Lung-hsü, d. 1031, was king of the Ch'i-tan Tartars. After leading his troops into the empire and taking over a large area in 1004, he was met by imperial troops and after several battles was persuaded to make a peace that was honorable both for himself and for Emperor Chên Tsung.

105. Tchongking: Chung-ching-fu, modern city of Chungking in Szechwan Province.

106. Tchin: Chên Tsung. "Going mumbo" suggests the ravings of his insanity [cf. 101 above].

107. Gin Tsong: Jen Tsung, reigned 1023-1064. Internal rebellions and invasions weakened the empire, and in 1042 Jen Tsung was forced to make a humiliating peace with the Ch'i-tan Tartars to keep them quiet. As a patron of literature he encouraged a golden age of Chinese literature in which many of China's most noted poets, historians, and scholars emerged.

108. Fou-Pié: Fü Pi, d. 1085, was a scholar and diplomat serving Emperor Jen Tsung. In 1042 the Ch'i-tan Tartars demanded ten counties of the empire and threatened war if the emperor refused. Fü Pi was sent to negotiate, and the resulting treaty enjoined the Ch'i-tan to keep peace and promised them an annual tribute of 100,000 ounces of silver and 100,000 pieces of silk in addition to the tribute promised in 1006 by Emperor Chên Tsung. Fü Pi's treaty, though humiliating to the empire, was a masterpiece of diplomacy.

109. Chin-Tsong: Shên Tsung, reigned 1068-1086, was an able administrator, ambitious for his empire, his people, and himself. His chief ally was the minister, Wang An-shih.

110. Ngan: Wang An-shih, 1021-1086, became Emperor Shên Tsung's confidential adviser and minister of state in 1069. He and the emperor instituted reforms based on Wang's new and "more correct" interpretations of the classics: state administration of commerce, state support for farmers, compulsory military service, a state system of barter, a new land tax system. In the face of strong opposition, the emperor put Wang's reforms into practice, but Wang tried to move too rapidly and lived to see all his reforms abolished. After his death he was disgraced and his tablet was removed from the Confucian temple.

111. Tcheou emperors: Chou [cf. 53: passim].

112. douanes: F, "custom duties."

113. Yao: [53:14].

114. Koen: Kun, fl. 2297 B.C., Earl of Ch'ung and father of the Great Yu. He was minister of works under Emperor Yao and was appointed to drain the empire after the disastrous overflow of the Hwang Ho in 2295. In 2286, after he had worked for nine years but had accomplished little, his son was given the task. After another nine years, Yu succeeded.

115. confino: I, "in exile."

116. Liu-hoei: Liu Hui-ching, 1031-1111, a minister serving Emperor Shên Tsung who originally opposed the reforms of Wang An-shih.

117. Ngan: Wang An-shih. The word "twister" comes from the idea of a soul that seemed simple and open on the outside but was full of detours on the inside.

118. Hoei: Liu Hui-ching [cf. 116 above].

119. Tengtcheou: Têng-ch'ou, city on the N coast of Shantung Peninsula in Shantung Province, NE China.

120. denar: Coin [54:205].

121. Fan-chungin: Fan Chun-jen, fl. 1069, was the minister sent by Emperor Shên Tsung to inspect the progress of Wang An-shih's reforms in the province of Shensi. Fan Chun-jen complained of the new regime because it did away with the traditional form of government in China.

122. Heoi-king: Liu Hui-ching [cf. 116 above].

123. Ssé-ma: Ssŭ-ma Kuang, 1019-1086, was a distinguished statesman, historian, and scholar. He was minister of state under Emperor Jen Tsung (1023-1064) and an important minister under his successor, Emperor Shên Tsung. Ssŭ-ma Kuang zealously opposed the reforms of Wang An-shih and, when Shên Tsung refused to part with the latter, retired to private life. In 1085 he returned to the government, but died a few months later. His greatest work was *Tzu Chih T'ung Ch'ien* [*A Comprehensive Mirror for the Aid of Government*] which was finished in 1084 after more than 20 years of work. Ssŭ-ma Kuang also wrote a history of 35 centuries of Chinese culture, a dictionary, and a number of miscellaneous papers.

124. Tsong of Tang: T'ai Tsung [54:199].

125. Chin: Shên Tsung [cf. 109 above].

126. Ngan: Wang An-shih [cf. 110 above].

127. Ssé-ma Kouang: Ssŭ-ma Kuang [cf. 123 above].

128. Fan Tsuyu: Fan Tsu-yu, fl. 1084, was a historian at the court of Emperor Shên Tsung. He was one of those who helped Ssu-ma Kuang compile *Tzu Chih T'ung Ch'ien.*

129. Lieou Ju: Liu Ju, fl. 1084, was a historian at the court of Emperor Shên Tsung. He helped Ssu-ma Kuang compile *Tzu Chih T'ung Ch'ien.*

130. Tsé-tchi tong kien hang mou: *Tzu Chih T'ung Ch'ien,* commonly called *T'ung Ch'ien* or *Mirror of History*, is a history of China from the fifth century B.C. to the beginning of the Sung dynasty, A.D. 960. Ssŭ-ma Kuang was editor and chief author. The work, begun before 1064, was completed in 1084 and presented to Emperor Shên Tsung. Later abridged and cast in a new form, it was given the title *Tzŭ-chih t'ung-ch'ien kang-mu* or *Kang-mu.*

131. Tso kieou ming: Tso Chiu-min [54:69].

132. Ouëi-Lie: Wei-Lieh Wang, reigned 425-401 B.C. The reign was uneventful except that the tripods of Yu began to make noises, thus signaling that the end of the Chou dynasty was near.

133. Tcheou dynasty: Chou [53:77]

134. Chin-Tsong: Shên Tsung [cf. 109 above].

135. Lux ... partem: L. "For light of herself into every region" [Grosseteste, *De Luce seu de inchoatione formarum*, ed. Baur, 51; cf. *LE*, 160-163].

136. Tcheou Tun-y: Chou Tun-i, 1017-1073, scholar and philosopher, held small posts in the government. His chief works are elucidations of the mysteries of the *Book of Changes*, or *I Ching*, which is ascribed to Wên Wang. Chou Tun-i is considered one of the forerunners of the neo-Confucian movement led by Chu Hsi.

137. seipsum ... diffundit: L, "itself, it diffuses itself."

138. risplende: I, "it gleams," key verb from line 26 of Cavalcanti's "Donna mi priegha," trans. in 36/177 as "shineth out," describing the action of loving is here related to Chinese views of reason and the Latin of Grosseteste [cf. *LE*, 161].

139. et effectu: L, "and in effect."

140. Yao: [53:14].

141. Chun: [53:23].

142. Nenuphar: F, "water lily." Refers to Chou Tun-i who, because he lived by a

stream full of water lilies, was called "Master of the Water Lily" [*Pai*, 7-1, 2, 235].

143. Caïfong: K'ai Feng [cf. 64 above].

144. Ssé-kouang: Ssŭ-ma Kuang [cf. 123 above].

145. anti-tao, anti-bhud, anti-Ngan: Refers to the anti-Taoist, anti-Buddhist, anti-Wang An-shih thought of Ssŭ-ma Kuang.

146. Kung: Confucius.

147. Tsaï King: Ts'ai Ching, 1046-1126, partisan of Wang An-shih. In 1107 he became lord high chamberlain under Emperor Hui Tsung and gained control of the administration. He filled all posts with his own men, made oppressive changes in the salt tax and the coinage, and led the empire into expensive wars. He was several times degraded but always managed to work his way back to power. Ts'ai Ching is known in Chinese history as "Chief of the Six Traitors."

148. Ngan: Wang An-shih [cf. 110 above].

149. Hoeï: Hui Tsung, reigned 1101-1126, was a clever artist and collector of antiques, but not much of an emperor. He was dominated by his minister, Ts'ai Ching, who led him into Taoism. Unable to resist the Chin Tartars, the emperor abdicated and surrendered himself to the invaders. They gave him the title of "Besotted Duke."

150. Tsaï: Ts'ai Ching [147 above].

151. Akouta: Akuta, 1069-1123, was chieftain of the Chin Tartars. In 1114 he rebelled against the Liao dynasty of the Ch'i-tan Tartars and entered into an agreement with Emperor Hui Tsung. He attacked the Liao and then invaded the empire, forcing Hui Tsung off the throne. The Chin withdrew to Peking and made it their capital.

152. Kin: Chin, Tartar tribe formerly known as Nü-chên. In 1114 Akuta, chieftain of the Nü-chên, proclaimed himself an emperor and gave the name of Chin ("gold") to his dynasty, which lasted from 1115 to 1234.

153. Hoang-ho: Hwang Ho, or Yellow River.

154. old Turk's country: Refers to tribes of Turkic origin which controlled the territory N and W of China during the last years of the T'ang dynasty.

155. Leao: Liao, dynasty of the Ch'i-tan Tartars which lasted from 907 to 1125 and controlled much of N China from their capital at Peking. After the capture of Peking by the Chin Tartars, the house of Liao was diminished to a minor dynasty known as the Western Liao (1125-1168).

156. Nutché: Nü-chên, Tartar tribe formerly of N Korea near the headwaters of the Yalu River. It was long dominated by the Ch'i-tan Tartars, but in A.D. 1114 it defeated them. The tribe's chieftain, Akuta, proclaimed the Chin dynasty of the Nü-chên Tartars.

157. Corea: Korea.

158. Ghengiz: Genghis Khan [cf. 100 above].

159. Tai-Tsou: T'ai Tsŭ, imperial title of Genghis Khan.

160. Témouginn: Temuchin, personal name of Genghis Khan.

161. Chi-Tsou: Shih Tsu, name taken by Kublai Khan when he began his reign over China (1280).

162. Koublai: Kublai Khan [18/80].

163. Hoang ho: Hwang Ho, or Yellow River.

164. Sung: [cf. 65 above].

165. shagreen: Rough skin of the shark; shagreen leather.

166. Oulo: Shih Tsung, also known as Wanyen P'ou, fifth emperor of the Chin dynasty of the Nü-chên Tartars. During his reign (1161-1190) the Chin gained much territory in China, mainly in Honan Province. An ex-

ceptional man, wise and benevolent, he was sometimes called "Little Yao and Shun."

167. Hia: Hsia, minor kingdom or principality (fl. ca. 1150) near the Ordos Desert, a territory bordered on one side by the Hwang Ho [Yellow River] and on the south by the Great Wall. The territory is on N border of Shensi and was occupied by Tartars.

168. Ghingiz: Genghis Khan [cf. 100 above].

169. Tchinkis: Genghis Khan. It is said that *Tchinkis* is an imitation of the cry of a celestial bird which no one has ever seen but which will herald great happiness when it does appear.

170. mores: L, "customs."

171. fumée maligne: F, "evil smoke."

172. Yéliu Tchutsaï: Yeh-lü Ch'u-ts'ai, 1190-1244, a Ch'i-tan Tartar, served as adviser to Genghis Khan and to Ogotai Khan. Yeh-lü was largely responsible for the establishment of a regular administration among the Mongols, for a system of taxation, and for a code of criminal law. When paper money was issued in 1236 it was owing to Yeh-lü's advice that the issue was limited to 100,000 ounces of silver. As a patron of literature and a student of Confucius, he did much to civilize the Mongols. Some of his contemporaries suspected that he had grown rich in government service, but when his house was searched after his death, all that could be found were musical instruments, pictures, and several thousand books.

173. Sung: [cf. 65 above].

174. Antzar: Antsar, fl. 1231, was a Mongolian general who served under Emperor Ogotai Khan during the great Mongol campaigns against the Chin Tartars in Honan Province.

175. Tang and Teng: T'ang and Têng are villages in the province of Honan, near the modern city of Nanyang.

Glossary Canto LVI

1. **Billets, biglietti**: F, I, "paper currency."

2. **Ou-Kiai**: Wu Ch'ieh, fl. 1135, captain of the imperial troops who served Southern Sung Emperor Kao Tsung (1127-1163), had some success against the Tartars.

3. **tartars**: Here the Chin Tartars.

4. **Yu-Tchong**: Yü Chung, fl. 1081, governor of Ching Ch'ou, department in Shensi Province.

5. **Kingtcheou**: Ching Ch'ou, capital and seventh department of Shensi Province.

6. **Chensi**: Shensi Province, NE central China, one of the Five Northern Provinces.

7. **Sung**: Nineteenth dynasty [55:65].

8. **Hoei**: Hui Tsung [55:149].

9. **Tchinkis**: Genghis Khan.

10. **Tartary**: Indefinite region in Asia and Europe extending from Sea of Japan to Dnieper River, controlled at different times by various Tartar tribes. The Tartars who invaded China occupied the area beyond N boundaries of Shensi, Shansi, and Hopeh provinces.

11. **Yeliu-Tchutsai**: Yeh-lü Ch'u-ts'ai [55: 172].

12. **Yeliou apaoki**: Yeh-lü A-pao-chi [55: 42].

13. **Ouanyen**: Wan-yen, family name of rulers of Chin Tartars.

14. **akouta**: Akuta [55:151], a chief of the Chin Tartars [Grousset, 134], succeeded in the early 12th century in uniting all China N of the Yangtze River [ibid., 516].

15. **Kin**: Chin Tartar tribe formerly known as the Nü-chên [55:152].

16. **Khitan**: Ch'i-tan, Tartar tribe [55:41].

17. **Genghis**: Genghis Khan.

18. **Yuen**: Yüan, twentieth dynasty (1206-1368). This dynasty of Mongol emperors was proclaimed in 1206 by Genghis Khan. By 1280, under Kublai Khan, the Yüan had extended its control over the entire Chinese Empire.

19. **Ogotai**: Ogotai Khan, 1185-1241, second khan of the Mongols, succeeding Genghis Khan in 1228. With the help of his minister, Yeh-lü Ch'u-ts'ai, he gave to the Mongols and the people they conquered a stable administration, taxation, and criminal jurisprudence. In 1236 he issued paper money and started a system of government examinations. He campaigned in Korea, China, and C Asia and managed to extinguish the Chin Tartars in 1234.

20. **Bojars**: R, *bojas*, members of a Russian aristocratic order favored with certain exclusive privileges [33:12].

21. **Hoang Ho**: Hwang Ho, or Yellow River.

22. **Mt Kuai**: Mt. Kuei-ki. Japanese pronunciation of Kuei-Chi [Fang, I, 136].

23. **Taozers**: Taoists, followers of Lao-tzŭ. Their idea of an "elixir of internal life" was anathema to neo-Confucians [54:127].

24. **li Sao**: *Li Sao* ["Falling into Trouble" is a collection of poems by Ch'ü Yüan, 343-290 B.C. [cf. Giles, 50-53].

25. **Mt Tai . . . carpet**: Three lines from a poem by Li Po.

26. **Mongols**: Nomadic barbarian tribes that occupied a vast territory N of China [55:41]. A royal prince of Chin, submitted to barbaric torture, suffered it all with a constancy that astonished the barbarians. "Plusieurs versèrent à terre du sang de cavalle, & prièrent qu'un si brave homme renaquit parmi les *mongous*" [Mailla, IX, 156].

27. **Ouen yan Tchin hochang**: Wan-yen Chen Ho-shang, d. 1232, prince royal of the Chin dynasty and an officer leading Chin troops in the battles between the Chin and

the Mongols. He suffered the torture noted in 26 above.

28. Yao, Chun, Yu: The ideograms are for these emperors [53:14, 23, 15].

29. Han: Prob. Later Han dynasty, 947-951 [55:84].

30. Sung: Nineteenth dynasty [55:65].

31. mogul: Mongol.

32. mus ingens . . . comedere: L, "huge, huge mouse, don't eat my grain" [cf. Lacharme, Pt. I, Bk. 9, ode 7, p. 47; *GK*, p. 215; in *Classic Anthology*, Pound translates it: "RATS, big rats, lay off our wheat" (113, p. 54)].

33. Kin Lusiang: Chin Li-hsiang, 1232-1303, scholar at the court of the Sung. After the fall of the Southern Sung dynasty in 1280, he retired to Mt. Jen where he attracted many disciples. He wrote a history of early China and many commentaries on the classics.

34. Pa Yang: Pan-yang, poss. P'ing-yang, city in Shansi Province. Mailla says that 2,410,070 mulberry trees perished there in the frigid spring weather [IX, 485].

35. I-Tching-tcheou: Ching-ch'ou, village near city of Kai Feng Fu.

36. Ogotai: [cf. 19 above].

37. Nik-ia-su: Nin-chia-ssu, reigned 1225-1234 as last emperor of Chin dynasty. His reign was marked by almost continuous war with the Mongols of Ogotai Khan.

38. Ozin (Wodin) Youriak: Unidentified.

39. Ghenso: Genghis Khan.

40. chi: C, "winnowing basket," used as measuring device.

41. denar: Coin [54:205].

42. ZinKwa: Prob. the Nestorian Chingai, of Turkic origin, an adviser to Ogotai and his successors ca. 1250 [cf. Grousett, 257].

43. Ten Bou: Prob. Wu Tu Pu, reigned 1213-1224, emperor of Chin dynasty. His reign was marked by almost continuous war with Genghis Khan's Mongols.

44. Yeliu Tchutsai: Yeh-lü Ch'u-ts'ai [55: 172].

45. Meng Kong: Meng Kung, d. 1246, was an officer of imperial troops serving Sung Emperor Li Tsung (1225-1265). Meng Kung was the leader of several imperial campaigns against the Mongols.

46. Han: Han-ch'ou, large town in Szechwan Province.

47. Lang: Lang-ch'ou, modern city of Langchung [formerly Paoning], Szechwan Province.

48. Ouen: Wen-chiang-hsien, district in Szechwan Province.

49. Kong: Chiung-ch'ou, large town in Szechwan Province.

50. Mie: Mei-ch'ou, large town in Szechwan Province.

51. Kien: Ch'ien-ch'ou, large town in Szechwan Province.

52. Tchong, King Fou: Chung-ching-fu, modern Chungking [55:105, 54 below]. The comma after *Tchong* is an error.

53. Pong: Pêng-shui-hsien, district in Szechwan Province.

54. Chun King: Chung-ching-fu, modern city of Chungking in Szechwan Province.

55. Vendome: Vendôme, town in Loir-et-Cher department, N central France.

56. Beaugency: Town in Loire department, on Loire River, France. An old French song runs: "Orleans, Beaugency! /Notre Dame de Cléry! / Vendôme, Vendôme / Quel chagrin, quel ennui / De compter toute la nuit / Les Heures—les heures!"

57. Notre Dame de Clery: Church of Our Lady in Cléry, town in Loire department, SW of Orléans.

58. Kujak: Kuyuk, reigned 1246-1248, son of Ogotai Khan, was a Mongol king who held a magnificent court in Tartary. A footnote in Mailla [IX, 245] says that Kuyuk raised two armies to fight Hungary and Poland and declared his intention to send another one against Livonia and Prussia. The first armies were to depart for E Europe in March 1247, but the premature death of Kuyuk halted the preparations.

59. Mengko: Mangu Khan, 1251-1259, Mongol emperor who put down all feudal opposition to his rule, reduced the tax burden, and curbed the power of the nobles. In 1259 he invaded Szechwan Province and besieged Ho-Chou (60 miles N of Chungking). The city resisted, plague broke out in the Mongol ranks, and Emperor Mangu died of the disease [Grousset, 284].

60. Caï Fong: K'ai Feng, city in Honan Province which at times served as the Chinese capital [55:64].

61. ammassi: I, "grain pools" to be available in times of bad harvest [53:17].

62. Yao, Shun, Yu: Early emperors [53:14, 23, 15].

63. Kung: Confucius.

64. Tchin Ouang: Chêng Wang, second ruler of Chou dynasty [53:65].

65. Ouen: Wên Wang, the elegant king called "Chief of the West" [53:49].

66. Ghengiz Khan: Genghis Khan.

67. Bagdad: Baghdad, city in Iraq, on Tigris River. The brother of Mangu Khan, Hulugu, was ordered to attack Baghdad in 1254 [cf. Grousset, 282].

68. Kukano: Koko Nor, large lake in W China in what is now known as Chinghai Province.

69. Ho-tcheou: Ho-ch'ou, city on Kialing River, 60 miles N of Chungking, where Mangu Khan died in 1259.

70. Ogotai: [cf. 19 above].

71. Kublai: Kublai Khan [18:1]. As a great general serving his brother Mangu, he consolidated the victories over the Sung and extended the power of the empire not only to the S into Tibet and the Na-khi territories but also into the NW. When Mangu died in 1259, Kublai ascended the throne and led the empire into its most illustrious and powerful period. By 1280 the last of the Sung emperors, Ti Ping, drowned himself and Kublai's power was no longer resisted. He built a new capital, Khanbalik "City of the Khan", known in European chronicles as Cambaluc and later as Peking. All Mongol princes became his vassals and paid him tribute. Marco Polo visited Kublai Kahn during his reign [18:8]. Although he ruled discreetly and munificently, relieving the distress of the poor, undertaking public works, and patronizing art and literature, the Chinese never forgot that he was both an alien and a barbarian. Few regretted his death in 1294 when his grandson, Timur, succeeded him with the title of Yüan-chêng.

72. Mt Hianglou: Hsiang-lu, prob. a mountain near the Yangtze River, in Honan Province.

73. Kiang: Yangtze River.

74. Sung: The Southern Sung, second part of nineteenth dynasty (1127-1280).

75. Li Tsong: Li Tsung, reigned 1225-1265, fifth emperor of Southern Sung dynasty. He broke his treaty with the Mongols and attacked them in 1234. Thereafter his reign was marked by almost continuous warfare with the Mongols.

76. Kiassé: Chia Ssu-tao, fl. 1273, minister and military officer serving Sung Emperor Li Tsung. He made a secret treaty with Kublai Khan in 1259, representing the emperor as willing to pay a tribute to the Mongols to ensure peace. Kublai accepted the treaty and turned his troops north, but Chia Ssu-tao attacked the rear of the Mongol troops. For this treachery, Kublai vowed to ruin the Sung dynasty. Chia Ssu-tao was minister to two other emperors: Tu Tsung (1265-1275) and K'ung Ti (1275-1276). His attempts to deal with the Mongols, either by diplomacy or by armed force, never seemed to do the Sung much good. He died disgraced.

77. Pasepa: Phags-pa, Tibetan lama who provided the Mongols with an alphabet [cf. Cordier, II, 337-338]. Kublai Khan raised him to a princely title [Grousset, 298].

78. Yai: Yai-shan, small island in a bay 30 miles SW of Canton, Kwangtung Province, which served as the last stronghold of the Southern Sung dynasty. In 1279 the Mongol fleet attacked the island, defeating the Sung fleet and prompting Emperor Ti Ping (1271-1279) to drown himself. Thus ended the Southern Sung. Kublai Khan became ruler of all China.

79. Yuen: Dynastic name adopted by the Mongols [cf. 18 above].

80. Hoang-ho: Hwang Ho, or Yellow River.

81. Ouang tchi: Wang Chu, d. 1282, chief officer of city of Peking. He led the conspiracy to assassinate Ahmed, the corrupt financial minister under Kublai Khan. Wang Chu lured Ahmed to the palace late at night and killed him with an iron mace. Kublai had Wang Chu executed [cf. Cordier, II, 315], a deed he later regretted.

82. Ahama: Ahmed Fenaketi, d. 1282, Kublai Khan's finance minister who used his power to enrich himself. Alarmed at his excesses, several members of the court, led by Wang Chu, formed a conspiracy and assassinated him [cf. Grousset, 297].

83. Ouen Tiensiang: Wên T'ien-hsiang, 1236-1283, one of the most patriotic men in Chinese history. He served the last five emperors of the Southern Sung dynasty as minister and general. All his efforts to stem Mongol invasions failed, and when the dynasty fell he was taken prisoner (1279). Unlike most others he refused to pledge his loyalty to the Mongols. The general who captured him did not want to execute a man so loyal to his own country, but he was pressured into doing so by courtiers.

84. Lou-chi: Lü Shih-chung, d. 1285, was so dishonest a minister that he was known as the "second Ahmed." He made so many enemies by his intrigues that he was finally condemned to death and butchered; his body was thrown into the street.

85. Tchin-kin: Chên Chin, d. 1286, son of Kublai Khan and prince royal of the empire. He was a model of all virtues and manners, learned in the humanities and the arts of war and ruling. His early death was a serious loss to his father and to the empire.

86. L Sieuen: Liu Hsuan, fl. 1286, was the minister who persuaded Kublai Khan to give up his plans to conquer Japan and Annam.

87. Annam: Part of present-day Vietnam.

88. Yeliu: Yeh-lü Yiu-shang, fl. 1287, was a scholar who received permission from Kublai Khan to reopen the Imperial College, which had not been in operation since the time of Ogotai Khan.

89. Sangko: Sang Ko, d. 1291, served as finance minister to Kublai Khan (1288-1291). A villain who was clever and apt at flattery, he sacrificed the honor of the empire to his own interests. He was executed in 1291 [cf. Grousset, 297].

90. Ouantse: Wan Tzŭ, fl. 1291, one of Kublai Khan's ministers of state. One of Kublai's great accomplishments was the creation of an effective administrative system and the introduction of a systematic code of law, projects in which Wan Tzŭ played a part.

91. Timour: Timur Khan, reigned 1294-1308, was the grandson of Kublai Khan, whom he succeeded on the throne. He ruled as Emperor Ch'eng Tsung. Timur was an honest ruler who tried to promote the welfare of his people. He improved the administration, reformed the system of selecting officials, curbed the power of the nobility, expelled dishonest officials, and cut down bribery. When mandarins wanted to move strongly against thieves and brigands in many provinces, and Timur found that the latter stole because they were hungry and not to gain wealth, he ordered that they be fed instead of being hunted down and killed. In 1303 he was confined to his bed and the government was run by palace ladies and corrupt officials.

92. Sung: The last Sung emperor was Ti Ping, who drowned himself [cf. 78 above].

93. Ghengiz: Genghis Khan.

94. Hia: Hsia, first dynasty [53:44].

95. Chang: Shang, ancient Chinese dynasty (ca. 1766-1121 B.C.) which preceded the great Chou dynasty.

96. Tcheou: Chou, third dynasty [53:77].

97. Kungfutseu: Confucius.

98. Han: Former Han dynasty, 206 B.C. to A.D. 25 [54:12].

99. Tcin: Chin, Western Chin dynasty, A.D. 265-317 [54:111].

100. Tang: T'ang, thirteenth dynasty [54:193].

101. Sung: Nineteenth dynasty [55:65].

102. Yuen: Yüan, twentieth dynasty [cf. 18 above].

103. Isle of Yai: Yai-shan, island where the last Sung was defeated [cf. 78 above].

104. Ming: Twenty-first dynasty (1368-1644).

105. (Cambuskin): Cambyuskan or Cambiuskan, the Tartar king in Chaucer's "The Squire's Tale" (line 12) and usually identified as either Genghis Khan or Kublai Khan.

106. Tchin Tiaouen: Chên Tiao-yen, fl. 1297, was a brigand in S China who gathered a large band of vagabonds. He attacked the city of Chang-chou and killed Kang Wên-hsing, its commander.

107. Tchang tcheou: Chang-chou, city in Fukien Province, SE China.

108. Ouang Chi: Wang Shih, d. 1297, was the wife of Kang Wên-hsing, commander of Chang-chou. Rather than become the wife of Chên Tiao-yen, murderer of her husband, Wang Shih threw herself onto her husband's funeral pyre. Emperor Timur, deeply impressed by the deed, built a memorial to her.

109. Kanouen: Kan Wên-hsing, d. 1297, Wang Shih's husband.

110. corvée: F, "forced labor."

111. Gin Tsong: Jen Tsung or Ayuli Palpata, reigned 1312-1321 as eighth emperor of the Yuan dynasty; he was also known as Buyantu (Ayur paribhadra) [Grousset, 321]. An able administrator, well read in Confucius and Buddha and averse to war, he tried to improve the government by abolishing abuses brought to his notice, but the practice of giving the highest government posts to Mongols was not effective and the people were oppressed. He enacted sumptuary laws and established regular examinations for officials.

112. Miao Haokien: Miao Hao-chien, fl. 1318, wrote a treatise on cultivation of mulberry trees and silk production. Emperor Jen Tsung had copies of the work circulated in the provinces.

113. Aiülipata: Ayuli Palpata, personal name of Emperor Jen Tsung, who was also known as Aïyulipalipata.

114. Algiaptou khan: Prob. Aïyulipalipata, Emperor Jen Tsung. In 1313 he restored the ceremonies instituted to honor Confucius.

115. Tiemoutier: Tiehmutiehr or Temudar, d. 1322, minister of state under Emperor Jen Tsung and prime minister under his son Emperor Ying Tsung (1321- 1323). Tiehmutiehr was an unscrupulous minister who grew rich through official robberies. After his death, Ying Tsung abrogated all his honors and started to put his followers to death; some of them plotted to assassinate the emperor and succeeded in 1323.

116. lamas: Tibetan priests. Pound links them with anti-Confucians and with Buddhists [foés] and Taoists.

117. Jason: Pound's name for Yesun-Temour: like the Greek Jason, he killed assassins.

118. Chunti: Shun Ti, reigned 1333-1368, was also known as Timur, last Mongol emperor of the Yüan dynasty. Weak and pleasure loving, he was incapable of action and his reign was marked by continual rebellion of the Chinese as well as by famine among the people. Among the wonders that augured the end of the dynasty was "une pluie de sang qui teignit les habits de tous ceux qui l'essuyèrent." At the third moon there fell "des filamens de couleur verte qui ressembloient à des cheveux" [Mailla, IX, 563].

119. Hanjong: Han Jung, fl. 1347, imperial inspector serving Emperor Sung Ti. When Han Jung found temples on land needed for cultivation, he had them destroyed. When he found young people who wanted to learn, he had schools established.

120. Kung's epigon: Poss. "Confucius descendant" [ibid., 575].

121. Pleiades: In 1350 a star as large as the moon exploded in the "constellation des sept étoiles" with a noise like thunder [ibid., 590].

122. Hoang-ho: Hwang Ho, or Yellow River.

123. Milé Buddha: Mille (or Maitrêya) Buddha, the goddess of mercy, a reincarnation of Buddha. The reign of Emperor Shun Ti was marked by unrest, famines, earthquakes, and heavenly disturbances. When the emperor started work on the diversion of the Hwang Ho, there was a surge of popular resentment, and it was rumored that Buddha was soon to descend to save China from the Mongol dynasty. This rumor was used for political purposes by the White Lotus Society.

124. pseudo-Sung: White Lotus Society, a secret society that arose in China (1351) in opposition to the Mongol dynasty. Ostensibly the society was organized to worship the Mille Buddha, or goddess of mercy, who was

to free China from the Mongols, but actually it was used to raise a rebellion against Emperor Shun Ti. The leader of the White Lotus pretended to be a descendant of the Sung dynasty, and at a large meeting he sacrificed a white horse and a black cow and had all those who would follow his standard wear a red cap.

125. Tienouan: T'ien-wan, name of the dynasty that Hsü Chou-hui attempted to found (1351-1357). His revolt against Shun Ti was successful for a time, but he was captured and killed (ca. 1357). The name of the general who "beat the rebels" was Tung Pu-hsiao.

126. Taipou: T'ai Pu-hoa, d. 1352, scholar and military officer serving Emperor Shun Ti. He successfully encountered the rebels on several occasions but finally died in battle.

127. Singki: Hsing Chi, d. 1352, commander of imperial troops serving Emperor Shun Ti. His sudden death from a wound gave the rebels an unexpected victory in Kiangsi Province.

128. Tang dance: Called T'ang because the dancers wore headdresses like those used by the T'ang dynasty.

129. Kongpei: Kung Pe-sui, fl. 1353, officer in imperial troops under Emperor Shun Ti.

130. Toto: T'o-t'o, 1313-1355, minister of state under Emperor Shun Ti, was one of the latter's few honest ministers. T'o-t'o attempted to quell the rebellions of the rising Ming, but court intrigue hindered his efforts. His campaign against the rebels was stopped by a decree stripping him of all honors and sending him into exile. In 1355 he was poisoned, but by 1363 his reputation was again being honored. He is also known for his historical studies, particularly for his history of the Chin Tartars.

131. Red Caps: The Red Turban Society which raised the standard of revolt in 1356. Its leader proclaimed himself Emperor Ming Wang [Cordier, II, 355].

132. **Ming Ouan**: Ming Wang, dynastic title assumed by Han Lin-êrh, d. 1367. In 1355, when the Red Turban Society proclaimed him emperor of a new Sung dynasty, he set up his capital at Po-chou in Honan Province. This new Sung dynasty, created in opposition to Emperor Shun Ti of the Yüan dynasty, was one of many such ventures during the reign of this last Mongol emperor. As a symbol of revolt, Han Lin-êrh's dynasty was effective, but it was not permanent.

133. **Yuentchang**: Chu Yüan-chang, 1328-1399, founded the Ming dynasty. He was a Buddhist novice, but when the Buddhists were forced to abandon some monasteries, Chu Yüan-chang offered his services to Kuo Tzǔ-hsing (d. 1355), a rebel leader. He later parted from Kuo Tzǔ-hsing and proclaimed himself Prince of Wu (1364). After that he led the major force seeking the overthrow of Emperor Shun Ti and the Mongol dynasty. In 1367 he proclaimed himself emperor of China, founded the Ming dynasty, and called himself Hung Wu.

134. **Ito Yen**: Poss. Ho Yen, town in what is now Anhwei Province. It was taken by Chu Yüan-chang forces in 1355 without suffering pillage.

135. **Kiang river**: Yangtze River.

136. **Taiping**: Poss. a city on the right bank of the Yangtze River in present-day Anhwei Province. It was taken by Chu Yüan-chang without plunder.

137. **Tchang star**: Chang, Chinese name for the constellation Hydra.

138. **Tai Ming**: Geographical region, poss. in C China.

139. **South Country**: Prob. the area comprised by the modern province of Anhwei which was the birthplace of Chu Yüan-chang, founder of the Ming dynasty.

140. **Yukiou**: Yu Chiu, d. 1358, commander of the city of Ngan-king (Anking) in Anhwei Province. He was killed while defending the city against the rebels fighting Emperor Shun Ti.

141. **Chang-tou**: Shangtuho, city in Mongolia not far N of China border. The city that Coleridge called Xanadu, it was the famous summer residence of Kublai Khan and other Mongol emperors, from 1260.

142. **Kouetchin**: Fang Kuei-chên, fl. 1358, Chinese pirate during the reign of Shun Ti. He operated a fleet of junks off the S China coast and added his bit to the general rebellion that ended the Mongol dynasty.

143. **Corea**: Korea.

144. **Peyen**: P'eyen Temur, d. 1362, king of the Koreans.

145. **lake Peyan**: Poyang Hu, lake in N Kiangsi Province, SE China; it is China's second-largest lake, into which flows the Han River.

146. **Hoang Ho**: Hwang Ho, or Yellow River.

147. **Yeougin**: Ch'ên Yu-jen, fl. 1363, brother of Ch'ên Yu-liang, took part in the battle of Lake Poyang (1363) in which his brother was defeated by Chu Yüan-chang, founder of the Ming dynasty.

148. **Tching brothers**: Ch'ên Yu-jen and Ch'ên Yu-liang. Ch'ên Yu-liang (d. 1363) was commander of an independent rebel force during the general uprisings against Shun Ti. In 1358 he proclaimed himself Prince of Han and styled himself emperor of a "Han" dynasty. By 1363 his power in China was second only to that of Chu Yüang-chang, the great rebel leader who founded the Ming dynasty. In 1363 the two forces met in a battle at Lake Poyang, and Ch'ên Yu-liang was killed by a stray arrow and his army was routed. His two brothers, Ch'ên Yu-jen and Ch'ên Yu-kuei, were associated with him in his career.

149. **Leou Lean**: Ch'ên Yu-liang, leader of the brothers.

150. **Tchin-li**: Ch'ên Li, fl. 1363, second son of Ch'ên Yu-liang. After his father was defeated in battle at Lake Poyang, Ch'ên Li

was allowed by Chu Yüan-chang to retain the family estates.

151. KianKing: Prob. error for Nanking.

152. Timour: Timur Khan [cf. 91 above].

153. Yuen: Yüan, twentieth dynasty: the Mongols.

154. Yuentchang: Chu Yüan-chang, founder of Ming dynasty [cf. 133 above].

155. suis fils d'un pauvre laboureur: F, "I am the son of a poor workingman." He was, in fact, from a poor family.

156. Ssetcheou: Ssŭ-ch'ou, town near modern city of Feng-yang in Anhwei Province.

157. Kiangnan: Chiang-nan, an old province, roughly the area of the present provinces of Anhwei and Kiangsu.

158. Tsehing: Kuo Tzu-hsing, d. 1355, was one of the more successful rebels in the reign of Emperor Shun Ti. He captured Anhwei Province and proclaimed himself generalissimo. His nephew, Chu Yüan-chang, served under his flag for a time but later left to raise an independent rebellion of his own; thereby he became the founder of Ming.

159. Schicksal: G, "destiny."

160. Li: Li Hsiang-kuei, fl. 1355, fighting companion of Chu Yüan-chang's.

161. Su: Su Hsiang-kuei, fighting companion of Chu Yüan-chang's.

162. Tong: Tung Ping-chang, fighting companion of Chu Yüan-chang's.

163. Chantong: Shantung, one of the Five Northern Provinces.

164. Pekin: Peking, in Hopeh Province, NE China, was the capital of China during the Yüan and subsequent dynasties.

165. Su Ta: Hsu Ta, d. 1385, was a lieutenant serving under Chu Yüan-chang during his struggles to found the Ming dynasty. When Chu became emperor (using the name Hung Wu), Hsu Ta became his adviser.

166. Chang Shang: Chou, Han, important early dynasties.

167. Chung Ni (Confucius): [cf. 53:148].

168. Yuen: Yüan, twentieth dynasty.

169. Tai Tsong: T'ai Tsung [54:99].

170. Kao Tsue: Kao Tsu Wu Ti [54:137].

171. Tai Tsou: T'ai Tsu, reigned 960-976, founder of the Sung dynasty. While he was serving as a general under Emperor Shih Tsun, of the Later Chou, his troops invested him with the yellow robe of emperor. His greatest accomplishment was the restoration of the empire. He encouraged the study of literature, revised the law courts, changed the criminal code, and stabilized the economy.

172. Hong Vou: Hung Wu, reigned 1368-1399, founder of the Ming dynasty. He started his career as a rebel against Emperor Shun Ti. In 1368 he overthrew the Yüan dynasty, took the throne, and adopted the reign title of Hung Wu. Once emperor, he showed himself an able administrator. He reformed the law code and the system of taxation, reestablished government coinage on a sound basis, prohibited eunuchs from holding office, and patronized literature and education [cf. 133 above].

173. Ideograms: Yao, Shun, Chou [53:26, 27, 81]; Han [M2039].

174. Ninghia: Ninghsia, province in far NW China.

175. Yé-ouang: Yeh Wang, fl. 1375, admiral serving Emperor Hung Wu. He won several victories over the Mongols.

176. Yuen: Yüän, Mongols or Tartars.

177. Coreans: Koreans.

178. Emperor: Ai Yu Shih Litala, d. 1378, king of the Mongols. He succeeded Emperor Shun Ti.

179. Li-ouen: Li Wen-chung, d. 1384, one of the best military officers serving Emperor Hung Wu.

180. Su Ta: Hsu Ta [cf. 165 above].

181. Et / En l'an . . . funérailles: F, "And / In the thirty-first year of his Rule / the year sixty of his age / Hong Vou, seeing his strength weaken / said: May virtue inspire you, Tchu-ouen, / you faithful mandarins, cultivated people, soldiers / Help my grandson sustain / the dignity of this power, the weight of his office / And just as for Prince Ouen Ti of Han in former times, / make the obsequies for me" [Mailla, X, 104].

Glossary Canto LVII

1. Kien Ouen: Ch'ien Wên Ti, reigned 1399-1403, second emperor of Ming dynasty and grandson of Hung Wu. A weak emperor, he was unable to deal with rebellions led by his uncle, the Prince of Yen, fourth son of Hung Wu. In 1403 the prince took Nanking, the capital, and assumed the throne as Emperor Yung Lo. Ch'ien Wên Ti was about to kill himself, when he was told of a chest that Hung Wu had left to be opened in such an emergency. In the chest were the dress of a Buddhist priest, a diploma, a razor, and money. So, dressed as a Buddhist monk, Ch'ien Wên Ti escaped to a monastery in Yunnan. After wandering for 35 years he was discovered during the reign of Ying Tsung (1436-1450).

2. Tcheou-kong: Chou Kung [53:63].

3. Tching-ouang: Chêng Wang [53:65].

4. Hong Vou: Hung Wu, founder of Ming dynasty and grandfather of Ch'ien Wên Ti [56:172].

5. Kouémen: Kuei-men, gate of Nanking, or perhaps the underground passage through which Emperor Ch'ien Wên Ti escaped from the city in 1403.

6. Chin Lo-koan: Shen-lo-Kuan, Buddhist temple outside Nanking.

7. Ouangchin: Wang Shên, Buddhist priest serving in the temple of Shen-lo-Kuan, outside Nanking.

8. Ouan Soui: C, *wan-sui*, "Ten thousand years". A cheer in honor of an emperor or king.

9. Yang-long: Yang Ying-lung, member of the court of Emperor Ch'ien Wên Ti, one of the nine who helped the emperor escape from Nanking.

10. Yé Hihien: Yeh Hsi-hsien, member of the court who also helped the emperor to escape.

11. Kien Ti: Ch'ien Wên Ti, the young emperor.

12. Yng-tsong: Ying Tsung, reigned 1437-1450, 1457-1465. He came to the throne at the age of eight and, although his mother tried to provide a responsible guardian, the young emperor was much influenced by the eunuch Wang Chin. In 1449 Wang Chin precipitated a war with the Mongols, who invaded Shansi, defeated the troops commanded by Wang Chin, and captured the emperor. Ching Ti was made emperor in his brother's place, but in 1457 Ying Tsung returned to the throne and executed many who had served his brother.

13. Yong Lo: Yung Lo, reigned 1403-1425. As the Prince of Yen, he dethroned his nephew, Ch'ien Wên Ti, in 1403 and took the throne himself. He repopulated areas devastated by war, drew up a penal code, and sent missions to Java, Sumatra, Siam, and Ceylon. A patron of literature, he compiled a gigantic encyclopedia, known as *Yung Lo Ta Tien*, which included many commentaries on the classics.

14. Bengal: State on NE coast of India. A tribute mission from Bengal arrived at the Ming court in 1415.

15. Malacca: Roughly, the area of the Malay Peninsula. A tribute mission from Malacca arrived at the Ming court in 1409.

16. **Yang Lo**: Yung Lo [cf. 13 above].

17. **summa**: L, "the whole," a treatise covering the whole of a field. Here it refers to the encyclopedia *Yung Lo Ta Tien* commissioned by Emperor Yung Lo.

18. **Mahamou**: Mahamu, d. 1418, chief of the Oirat Mongol tribe. In 1416 he sent a tribute gift of horses to Emperor Yung Lo.

19. **Gin Tsong**: Jen Tsung, reigned 1425-1426, came to the throne at the age of 47 and ruled only a little more than nine months.

20. **Yng Tsong**: [cf. 12 above].

21. **Hong Vou**: Hung Wu, founder of Ming dynasty.

22. **Yukien**: Yü Ch'ien, 1398-1457, minister serving Emperor Ching Ti, was the only person who kept his head when Emperor Ying Tsung was captured by Mongols in 1450. He defended Peking, the capital, against the invaders and succeeded in driving them beyond the Great Wall. On the death of Ching Ti in 1457, Ying Tsung returned to the throne and had Yü Ch'ien executed for supporting Ching Ti. This act was an injustice, for Yü Ch'ien had done great service for the empire and had made Ying Tsung's return from captivity possible. The execution of Yü Ch'ien was engineered by Shih Hêng [cf. 27 below].

23. **King Ti**: Ching Ti, reigned 1450-1457, came to the throne after his brother, Ying Tsung, was captured by Mongol invaders. Ching Ti regarded his position as a permanent one and did not wish to give it up when his brother was rescued by General Yü Ch'ien. But before he could establish the succession on his son, Ching Ti died and Ying Tsung returned to the throne.

24. **Fan-kuang**: Fan Kuang, fl. 1450, commander of imperial troops defending Peking from Mongol warriors.

25. **Yésien**: Yeh Hsien, d. 1454, commander of Mongol forces that invaded the empire in 1449. He captured Emperor Ying Tsung and attacked Peking in 1450. In 1453 he seized supreme power over the Mongols but was killed in a battle with a rival.

26. **Péyen**: P'eyen T'iehmur, fl. 1450, Mongol general who took charge of the captured Emperor Ying Tsung. He also participated in the Mongol attack on Peking in 1450.

27. **Che-heng**: Shih Hêng, d. 1460, one of the generals serving Emperor Ching Ti who defended Peking against the Mongols in 1450. He later plotted against the empire and died of poison.

28. **Honan**: Province in E central China.

29. **Shantung**: Province in NE China.

30. **carroch**: I, *carroccio*, "army flag car" or "triumphal car."

31. **vide Valturio**: Roberto de Valturio [9:19].

32. **li**: C, measure of length, ca. one-third of a mile.

33. **Hien Tsong**: Hsien Tsung, reigned 1465-1488, a weak emperor, was ruled by his concubine and by eunuchs. Despite rebellions in the northern provinces, he did repair the Great Wall, improve the Grand Canal, and restore the reputation of Yü Ch'ien with posthumous honors.

34. **Kungfutseu**: Confucius.

35. **Hoai-ngan**: Huai An, fl. 1487, palace eunuch who became president of the tribunal of mandarins and then minister of state under Emperor Hsiao Tsung.

36. **Ideogram**: P'ien [M5245], "Metamorphosis," a subject rhyme with alchemy in the West.

37. **Hoai of Sung**: Hui Tsung. He and Hsien Tsung of T'ang were earlier emperors done in by Taoists [55:8, 149].

38. **Ou Ti of Léang**: Wu Ti [54:151] economized and advanced the rule of law.

39. **Hoeï-Tsong**: Hui Tsung [55:149].

40. **Laoist**: Follower of Lao-tzǔ, founder of Taoism.

41. **foéist**: Follower of Buddha.

42. **Yao and Shun**: Early great emperors [53:14, 23].

43. **Tcheou Kong**: Chou Kung [53:63].

44. **Hiao Tsong**: Hsiao Tsung, reigned 1488-1505, had able ministers and instituted several administrative reforms, stopped internal rebellions, dealt with Mongol invasions, and curtailed the power of eunuchs.

45. **Lieu**: Liu Chin, d. 1510. He and seven other palace eunuchs conspired to gain control over the young Emperor Wu Tsung by pandering to his tastes and enjoyments. So successful was the scheme that in 1508 the emperor decreed that all petitions had to pass through the hands of Liu Chin. Then the emperor's uncle raised a rebellion and demanded Liu Chin's death as the price of peace. The emperor consented to imprison the eunuch, but when large amounts of treasure were found in the latter's house, the emperor ordered his execution.

46. **Hong Vou**: Hung Wu, founded Ming dynasty [56:172].

47. **Ou Tsong**: Wu Tsung, reigned 1506-1521, a weak and childish emperor who was persuaded to execute the eunuch Liu Chin [cf. 45 above]. He then chose Chiang Ping, a military adventurer, as his chief adviser. Wu Tsung came to the throne as a minor, but as he grew older he did not grow wiser. He devoted himself to leisure and frivolity and left no heir.

48. **Manchu**: Tartar tribe originally descended from the Nü-chên Tartars. The Manchu power was established in present-day Manchuria in 1587 by Nurhachi. In 1644 the Manchu brought about the fall of the Ming dynasty and established the Ch'ing dynasty (1644-1912).

49. **Lieou-kin**: Liu Chin [cf. 45 above].

50. **Chi-tsong**: Shih Tsung, reigned 1522-1566. Like many other Ming emperors, Shih Tsung consistently picked peer advisers and refused to listen to the most able men in his kingdom.

51. **Hien Tsong**: Hsien Tsung [cf. 33 above].

52. **Tchang Chi**: Chang Shih, fl. 1521, empress dowager, mother of Emperor Wu Tsung. At the death of her son, who left no heir, she called a council to name the next emperor. Shih Tsung, grandson of Emperor Hsien Tsung, was chosen.

53. **Kiang-ping**: Chiang Ping, d. 1521, military adventurer who became the favorite of Emperor Wu Tsung. He corrupted the emperor by providing him with pleasures and, in 1520, attempted to murder him. After Wu Tsung's death Chiang Ping was ambushed and killed by order of Emperor Shih Tsung. His entire family was also killed and his property was confiscated. Chiang Ping, like Liu Chin before him, had amassed a huge fortune.

54. **Mansour**: Mang Su Erh, fl. 1522, prince of the Tartar tribes that occupied the area of Turfan, in Sinkiang Province, W China.

55. **regnicoles**: F, "inhabitants of a kingdom."

56. **Yng-che**: C, *Ying-shih,* "the Five Sisters."

57. **Mt. Tien-cheou**: T'ien-shou, range of hills NW of Peiping where the tombs of the Ming emperors were located.

58. **Hai men**: Hai Men, department of what is now Kiangsu Province.

59. **Oua-chi**: Wa Shih, fl. 1559, princess in Kwangsi Province who led Chinese troops against Japanese pirates attacking SE coast of China.

60. **wolves of our Lady**: The troops led by Princess Wa Shih were called *Lang Ping,* "Loups soldat" [Cordier, III, 60].

61. **Fou-kien**: Fukien, province in SE China.

Glossary Canto LVIII

1. **Sinbu**: Jimmu Tenno, first of the legendary emperors of Japan, reigned 660-585 B.C. Jimmu is regarded as a direct descendant of the sun-goddess and as the founder of the Japanese imperial dynasty, which has remained unbroken since his accession to the throne. The Japanese Era is dated from the beginning of his reign (Feb. 11, 660 B.C.).

2. **Sun land**: Japan.

3. **Nippon**: Japan.

4. **Dai**: J, "great." The term is used to refer to the Dairi dynasty of Japan and, by extension, to Japanese emperors.

5. **Shogun**: Japanese title of commander in chief or generalissimo. The title originated in the eighth century during the wars against the Ainu. Shoguns became military dictators who held the real civil and military power in Japan, while the imperial dynasty was theoretically and ceremoniously supreme.

6. **Joritomo**: Or Yoritomo, 1146-1199, who assumed power in 1185, was the first true shogun in Japanese history. A great statesman, he inaugurated a system of military government which ran the affairs of Japan until the dissolution of the shogunate in 1868.

7. **reges sacrificioli**: L, "priests with kingly functions."

8. **Miaco**: Present city of Kyoto. It was established as the capital of Japan in A.D. 784 and remained the official capital until 1869, when the imperial government was moved to Tokyo.

9. **Ten Seo Daisin**: Tensio Dai Sin or, in Japanese, *Amaterasu-o-mi-kami*, Japanese sun-goddess and chief goddess of the Shinto religion. Her descendants became the emperors of Japan.

10. **jeu de paume**: F, "court tennis."

11. **escrime**: F, "fencing."

12. **Messire Undertree**: Hideyoshi Toyotomi, d. 1598. In Japanese his name means "the man found under a tree." He was known to the Chinese as Ping Hsiu-chi. Born of poor parents, he rose through his military exploits to be the greatest power in Japan. In 1586 he was named *kwam paku* ["regent"] and became far more powerful than the emperor. He is noted for his toleration of Christianity, but in 1587 he expelled the Portuguese Jesuits from Japan because he thought they might make his country a vassal of Portugal. In 1592 he declared war on Korea, hoping to destroy Korean control of the sea and to reopen trade with China, but he was unable to subdue Korea completely.

13. **Sa Mo**: Satsuma, feudal fiefdom on Kyushu Island, Japan.

14. **Portagoose prelates**: Portuguese Jesuit missionaries in Japan.

15. **Xtians**: Christians.

16. **Ouan Li**: Wan Li, title used by Emperor Shên Tsung, whose long reign (1573-1620) brought about the end of the Ming dynasty [cf. 38 below].

17. **Lord Lipan**: Li Pan, d. 1618, king of the Koreans.

18. **Pinyang**: Pyongyang, ancient capital of Korea.

19. **Ku ching**: Chang Chü-chêng, scholar and statesman who was tutor to Emperor Mu Tsung (1567-1572) and regent for Emperor Shên Tsung (1573-1620). He centralized the government, promoted peace and order in the empire, and tried to balance the budget. Often accused of taking bribes, he was deprived of his titles and property in 1584.

20. **Chin Song**: Shên Tsung [cf. 38 below].

21. **Nutché**: Nü-chên, Tartar tribe from which came the Chin dynasty [55:156].

22. Kaiyuen: Kai-yüan, city in S Manchuria.

23. Pe: P'ei-k'ou, the North Pass, which is N of Nan-kuan. The work may also refer to the Nü-chên Tartar tribe which takes its name from the region of the pass.

24. Nan-koan: Nan-kuan, the South Pass, a few miles N of Nankow, Hopeh Province, in NE China. The word may also refer to Nü-chên Tartar tribe which takes its name from the region of the pass.

25. Ming: Twenty-first dynasty.

26. martes zibbeline: F, *martre zibeline*, "sable."

27. Nankoen: Nan-kuan [cf. 24 above].

28. Suen Te: Hsüan Teh, 1426-1436, fifth emperor of Ming dynasty.

29. ginseng: Herb prevalent in Manchuria and Korea which, when dried, was thought to have medicinal properties.

30. Père Ricci: Mathieu or Matteo Ricci, 1552-1610, founder of the Jesuit Catholic missions in China, arrived at Macao in 1582. He tried to show that Christian doctrines were not antithetical to the teachings of the Confucian classics. Ricci died in Peking in 1610, having made a considerable impact on many of the scholar-officials at the Chinese capital.

31. Emperor: Shên Tsung [cf. 38 below].

32. Ku Tchang: Chang Chü-chêng, scholar and statesman, regent for Shên Tsung [cf. 19 above].

33. cabal: "Secret plot." Princesses of the palace and many others joined in the plot against Chang Chü-chêng, and finally the emperor was forced to dishonor him and exile his family. His eldest son hanged himself from grief rather than finish his days in ignominy.

34. Tientsin: City of E Hopeh Province in NE China, at junction of Pei River and Grand Canal.

35. Père Mathieu: Mathieu Ricci [cf. 30 above].

36. Rites: A tribunal of rites was set up by Emperor Shên Tsung in 1601, after the Jesuit mission had been in China almost 20 years, to consider the merits of Christianity. The tribunal, particularly offended by the idea of relics, rejected Christianity. Although its members recommended that Ricci be sent back to his own country, the emperor allowed him to remain at court. The report of the tribunal was made by the eunuch Ma Tang, who said that on a similar occasion Han Yü had reported the ruin brought to the empire by Buddhists [cf. next gloss]. Pound has confused Ma Tang with Han Yü [Mailla, X, 390].

37. Han Yu: Han Yü, 768-824, investigated Buddhism in the empire during the reign of T'ang Emperor Hsien Tsung. In a memorial to the emperor, Han Yü said that the Buddhists had been the ruin of many dynasties, that they had perverted the old ways of the Chinese, that they exercised a pernicious influence in the empire, and that they and their temples should be stamped out.

38. Chin Tsong: Shên Tsung, reigned 1573-1620. Under the title of Wan Li, his long reign ushered in the ruin of the Ming dynasty. After the death of Chang Chü-chêng, the regent, Shên Tsung abandoned himself to sensuality and extravagance. From 1585 to 1610 no one except the court eunuchs saw the emperor. High taxes ruined the people, Manchu hordes raided from the N, and Japanese attacked from the SE. The damage wrought by floods, droughts, and famines was not alleviated by the corrupt officials.

39. ghazel: Arabic, *ghazila*, a form of Persian love poetry in couplets rhyming on the same sound: *aa, ba, ca*, etc.

40. hoang miao: *Hung-mao*, "redheads," was the term used by the Chinese to designate European barbarians, especially British and Dutch.

41. TO KALON: H, "the beautiful."

42. Ti Koen: Pound has incorrectly taken Tien-ki [T'ien Ch'i], the reign title of Emperor Hsi Tsung, as a person. Mailla wrote: "Au commencement de l'an 1622, deuxième de *Tien-ki*, on entendit des cris effroyables du Côté de cette forêt." He gets the phrase "bull tanks" from *grandes machines* [X, 423].

43. Tchu-yé: Chu Yeh-yuan, fl. 1622, was commander of imperial forces in Shantung serving Emperor Hsi Tsung (1621-1627). His clever ruse of throwing *petards*, "firecrackers," *sur les boeufs* led to the defeat of the rebel forces in 1622 [X, 423].

44. Hoai Tsong: Huai Tsung, reigned 1628-1644, last true emperor of the Ming dynasty. He tried to rule well, but heavy taxes and poor harvests drove the NW to revolt. The emperor managed to keep peace with the Manchus, but Chinese rebels, led by Li Tzŭ-ch'eng, captured the province of Honan and by 1642 had advanced into Shensi. When Peking fell in 1644, the emperor killed himself.

45. ly: C, *li*, about a third of a mile.

46. Tsunhoa: Tsun-hua, fortified city in the province of Hopeh, fell to the Manchu forces in 1629 during their march on Peking.

47. Tai Tsong: T'ai Tsung or T'ien Ts'ung, 1591-1643, reigned 1625-1643, son of T'ai Tsu (1559-1625) who founded Manchu power. In 1635 T'ai Tsung proclaimed himself emperor of China, although the Ming dynasty still held Peking. In 1636 he established the Manchu rule as the Ch'ing dynasty, conquered Mongolia, and gained control over much of the empire. He modeled his government after that of the Chinese, especially in the matter of holding public examinations, but offended the Chinese by abolishing some of their customs. T'ai Tsung's Manchu name was Abahai. His father, T'ai Tsu, was known as Nurhachi.

48. Manchu: T'ai Tsung not only continued Chinese law for the Chinese, but he also established it for the Manchu who were forbidden to marry "leur belle mère, leur belle-soeur ou leur nièce." The Manchu were not accustomed to marrying their sisters. Pound's source covers only mother-in-law, stepmother, sister-in-law, stepsister, and niece [X, 449].

49. Li koen: Li-chiu-chêng, fl. 1631, was not a viceroy but an officer in command of Ming troops during the Manchu invasion. He stole the money the viceroy, Sun Yuan-hua, gave him to pay the soldiers; the unpaid troops mutinied and the general turned traitor and highway robber [X, 455].

50. Suen fou: Hsuan-hua-fu, city near Peking, in province of Hopeh.

51. Spirit of Heaven: Shang Ti [53:24].

52. Kong Yeou: Kung Yu-teh, fl. 1633, rebelled against Ming dynasty and joined forces with the Manchu leader T'ai Tsung.

53. hetman: Headman, chieftain.

54. Aba tchan, Maen tchan, Tihali tchan: Manchu general officer ranks.

55. Berlitz: School of language studies founded by Maximilian Delphinus Berlitz (1852-1921). T'ai Tsung started such a language school [X, 462].

56. Kourbang tourha: Kur-bang-turha, town in Inner Mongolia.

57. Mongrels: Mongols. As T'ai Tsung established his dynasty, many tribal chieftains came to pledge allegiance.

58. Ho-che: Hoshih Te-kelei, fl. 1643, a Mongol prince who allied himself with T'ai Tsung during one of the many raids on Shansi Province, was ordered "pénétrer par la gorge de Tou-ché-kéou" [X, 463].

59. Ton: Tu-shih-k'ou, gorge N of Shansi Province, leading from Inner Mongolia into China.

60. Tai chen: T'ai Shên, fl. 1634, another Mongol prince who allied himself with T'ai Tsung, was ordered to get to Sou-Tcheou by "passant à l'ouest de Tai-Tong" [X, 463].

61. **Taitong**: Tai-tung, city in Shansi Province, just inside N border between China and Inner Mongolia.

62. **Chensi**: Shensi [56:6].

63. **Tai Tsou**: T'ai Tsu or Nurhachi (1559-1624), reigned 1616-1625, was the real founder of Manchu power. He consolidated the tribes of Inner Mongolia and brought most of the territory NE of the Great Wall under his control. In 1625 he established the Manchu capital at Mukden.

64. **Mougden**: Mukden, city in S Manchuria which controls the N-S trade there. It became the Manchu capital in 1625 and later (1644) served as the base for the Manchu invasion of China.

65. **Yao, Shun . . . Yu**: Early great emperors [53:14, 23, 19].

66. **Kungfutseu**: Confucius.

67. **Tartary**: Land of the Mongols.

68. **Suen-hoa-fou**: Hsuan Fu, city near Peking in province of Hopeh.

69. **Tengyun**: Lü Tên-yün, fl. 1635, officer in the imperial army serving Ming Emperor Huai Tsung. He fought engagements against the Manchu forces then invading China. According to Mailla, a dispatch he wrote to the emperor fell into the hands of T'ai Tsung, who was outraged by the lies it contained. In reality, the lying general was Ts'ao Wen-chao, and it was not to him but to another general, Chang Tsung-heng, that T'ai Tsung addressed his challenge [Fang, I, 155].

70. **Princes of Manchu**: Princes of Manchu tribes who owed their loyalty to T'ai Tsung.

71. **Hong Vou**: Hung Wu [56:172].

72. **Kin**: Chin dynasty, 1115-1234 [55:152].

73. **Yuen**: Yüan, twentieth dynasty, 1206-1368 [56:18].

74. **Princes Mogul**: Princes of the Mongolian tribes that formed a confederation in 1635 under the hegemony of T'ai Tsung, the Manchu leader.

75. **Ming**: Twenty-first dynasty (1368-1644), now coming to an end because of misrule and corruption.

76. **(gallice Chantong)**: L, "in French, Shantung."

77. **Kiangnan**: Chiang-nan [56:157].

78. **Ousan**: Wu San-kuei, d. 1678, commander of imperial forces during last years of Ming dynasty. In 1643 Wu San-kuei received news that Peking had fallen to the rebel Li Tzŭ-ch'eng and that the emperor had committed suicide. After stipulating conditions for the treatment of the Chinese, Wu San-kuei gave his allegiance to the Manchus. As a result the Manchus captured Peking and established their dynasty in China.

79. **Kai fong**: Kaifeng, capital of Honan Province. In a footnote Mailla gives details of a terrible famine, worse than that caused by the siege of Jerusalem: "On vendoit publiquement de la chair humaine, & on croyoit faire un acte de piété en jettant dans les rues les corps morts, pour servir de nourriture à ceux qu'un même sort attendoit" [X, 477].

80. **Litse**: Li Tzŭ-ch'eng, 1606-1645, rebelled against the Ming dynasty. Leading an army of brigands, he overran parts of Hupeh and Honan provinces (1640) and captured Shensi Province (1642). In 1644 he proclaimed himself first emperor of the Great Shun dynasty and marched on Peking. The city fell and Ming Emperor Huai Tsung killed himself. But Wu San-kuei enlisted the aid of the Manchus and drove Li Tzŭ-ch'eng out of Peking. When Li was slain in battle, the Manchus, left in control of China, established the Ch'ing dynasty (1644-1912).

81. **Li Sao**: [56:24].

82. **Kientsong**: Chang Hsien-chung, fl. 1643, rebel chieftain with a reputation for extreme cruelty, tortured and killed all the residents of villages he captured [X, 479].

83. HOEI: Huai Tsung, last Ming emperor [cf. 44 above].

84. Likoue: Li Kuei-cheng, fl. 1644, commander of Peking. After the death of Emperor Huai Tsung, Li Kuei-cheng was forced to surrender the city to Li Tzŭ-ch'eng, but he first demanded permission to give the emperor and the empress a full imperial funeral.

85. Atrox MING, atrox finis: L, "frightful Ming, frightful end."

86. Ousan: Wu San-kuei [cf. 78 above].

87. OUAN SOUI: C, *wan-sui*, "ten thousand years."

88. A NOI: I, "ours."

89. eijen: Unidentified. Poss. misspelling of *Eljen* (Magyar), "Hail!"

90. Litse: Li Tzŭ-ch'eng [cf. 80 above].

91. τάδ' ῶδ' ἔχει: H, "that's how it is" [*Agamemnon*, 1413]. From Clytemnestra's line: "This is Agamemnon, my husband, dead by my right hand, and a good job. That's how it is."

Glossary Canto LIX

1. De libro . . . censeo: "Concerning the book, *Shih Ching*, I think thus" [Lacharme, XI-XII; the other Latin phrases on 324 are from the same place; cf. *GK*, 249].

2. Chi-King: *Shih Ching, Book of Odes.*

3. Chun Tchi: Shun Chih [cf. 20 below].

4. Ut animum . . . rationis: L, "To purge our minds, Confucius says, / and guide [them] to the light of reason."

5. perpetuale effecto: I, "perpetual effect." Part of line 26 of Cavalcanti's "Donna mi priegha" [36:1] describing the action of love, or perhaps of "love in action" [meaning process]. Here associated with reason as intelligence in process [cf. *LE*, 161].

6. Chi King . . . servat: L, "the *Shih Ching* shows and exhorts. But the just man and the one free from lust so serve their masters" [source: *domino*].

7. obsequatur . . . deflectat: L, "obeys his parents / never turns aside" [source: *obsequitur parentibus*].

8. igitur . . . enconomiis: L, "therefore, in my praises."

9. anno undecesimo: I, "eleventh year" [source: *undesimo* and *1654*; Lacharme's date is wrong]. The year in the reign of Shun Chih, the first Manchu emperor (1644-1661) [cf. 20 below].

10. periplum: H, "circumnavigation." Used by Pound in objective case as a coastal voyage.

11. tarters: Mongols N of Great Wall [53:130].

12. sojers with lanthorns: Soldiers with lanterns.

13. Nanking: City in Kiangsu Province, E China, on S bank of Yangtze. It served as the Ming capital from 1368 to 1403. The name means "Southern Capital."

14. Tchinkiang: Chinkiang, city and port of Kiangsu Province, E China.

15. Kouei: Kuei or Kuei Wang, d. 1662, was the last person to be proclaimed emperor of the Ming dynasty. About 1648 he set up a government in the S provinces. The Manchus, however, were determined to destroy all Ming power, and Kuei Wang was soon overthrown. In 1651 he fled to Burma, and in 1663 the Burmese returned him to the Chinese authorities. The Manchu Emperor K'ang Hsi had him strangled.

16. utilité publique, motif trop élevé: F, "public usefulness, too elevated a motive" [source has *rélevé* (X, 511)].

17. Young Manchu: Shun Chih, the young emperor, only 14 years old in 1649, was controlled by his uncles. They arranged his marriage for reasons of state [XI, 9].

18. **hong-mao**: C, *hung-mao*, "redheads," term designating certain European barbarians.

19. **Macao**: Portuguese colony on a peninsula W of mouth of Pearl River in Kwangtung Province, S of Canton.

20. **Chun Tchi**: Shun Chih, reigned 1644-1661, first emperor of the Manchu dynasty to rule over China. He consolidated Manchu power by crushing what remained of the Ming dynasty. In 1645 Manchu troops took Nanking, a stronghold of Ming power, and in 1651 the "last" emperor of the Ming dynasty, Kuei Wang, was defeated. A wise and generous ruler, Shun Chih eliminated eunuchs from the court, set up a civil administration, and treated Catholic missionaries with favor.

21. **Kang Hi**: K'ang Hsi, reigned 1662-1723, second emperor of Manchu dynasty to rule over China. In 1675 the Manchu dynasty was threatened by the revolt of the three feudatories (one of them was Wu Sankuei), but by 1681 K'ang Hsi had reestablished a firm rule over all China and, two years later, over Formosa. He extended the empire to the borders of Kokand and Badakhshan and into Tibet. He was a patron of the Jesuits, whom he employed (especially Verbiest) to survey the empire, study astronomy, and cast cannon. Later, fearing the Jesuits' propaganda and the possible influence of the pope on the government of China, he restricted missionary activities. A great patron of literature and scholarship, the emperor directed the writing of the *Imperial Dictionary* and the great *Concordance* of all literature. K'ang Hsi was an emperor in the tradition of Yao, Shun, and Yu.

22. **Johnnie Bach**: Johann Sebastian Bach, 1685-1750, German organist and composer.

23. **portagoose**: Portuguese.

24. **frog**: Reference to French people.

25. **Pereira**: Thomas Pereyra, d. 1708, Jesuit missionary in China, served with the French Jesuit Gerbillon on the Manchu-Chinese Commission to negotiate the Treaty of Nerchinsk between China and Russia (1689).

26. **Gerbillon**: Jean-François G., 1654-1707, Jesuit missionary to China, was a skilled linguist and mathematician. He arrived in Peking in 1688 and his talents at once impressed Emperor K'ang Hsi. He served with Pereyra on the commission to negotiate a border treaty between China and Russia in 1689, the Treaty of Nerchinsk. He wrote an account of his journeys in Tartary.

27. **Mt. Paucity**: Desolate mountain range in Manchuria called the "Mountains of Poverty" by the Chinese.

28. **ho fo**: C, *huo-fu*, "living Buddha."

29. **assez mal propre**: F, "rather slovenly."

30. **Hans of Kalkas**: Kings of the Khalkhas, Mongol tribe to the NW of China. Khalka chiefs were known as khans.

31. **Eleutes**: Or Eleuthes, Mongol tribe to the N and NW of China. The period of their greatest power was 1680-1696, when they were led by Galdan.

32. **Oros**: Russians.

33. **Selinga**: Selenginsk, town on the border between Russia and China, SE of Lake Baikal.

34. **Nipchou**: Nerchinsk, town on the upper Amur River, on the Chinese-Russian frontier, where the treaty between China and Russia was signed in 1869. The treaty, requiring Russia to withdraw from the Amur Valley, served for a while to check Russian colonization in that area.

35. **Cha houkoen**: Shan Hai Kuan Pass, near the place where the Great Wall reaches the Yellow Sea.

36. **Kang**: K'ang Hsi.

37. **ly**: [cf. 58:45; source says 200 *li*].

38. **Amur**: River in NE Asia forming boundary between Manchuria and the Chita Region and Khabarovsk Territory of Russia.

Glossary Canto LX

1. **Jesuits**: Members of the Society of Jesus, founded by St. Ignatius Loyola in 1534. Jesuit missionaries established the modern Roman Catholic missions in China. First to arrive was Matteo Ricci (1582), followed by Johann Adam Schall von Bell (1619). The period of most intensive missionary effort began in 1688 when Gerbillon and Verbiest gained the favor of Emperor K'ang Hsi (1662-1722).

2. **Galileo**: Galileo Galilei, 1564-1642, Italian mathematician and astronomer. No works of Galileo were specifically listed in the *Index Librorum Prohibitorum*, but many of his thoughts were considered heretical and he was subjected to enormous pressure by the Church.

3. **Grimaldi**: Philippe G., fl. 1691, Jesuit missionary to China, aided the Manchu in calendar reform.

4. **Intorcetta**: Fl. 1691, Italian Jesuit missionary to China.

5. **Verbiest**: Ferdinand V., 1623-1688, Jesuit missionary to China, arrived in Peking in 1660 and introduced the Chinese to the astronomical systems of Copernicus and Galileo. He was also employed by Emperor K'ang Hsi as a mathematician and a cannon founder. Verbiest's plea that Chinese priests be ordained, that they be allowed to say a vernacular Mass, and that ancestor worship be tolerated was not granted by Rome. The disagreement led to the famous rites controversy of the 18th century [cf. 59/327].

6. **Koupelin**: Philippe Couplet, fl. 1680, Jesuit missionary to China, arrived in Peking with Verbiest (1660) and served as procurator of the China missions. In 1682 he returned to Rome, carrying Verbiest's plea for ordination of Chinese priests and a vernacular Mass.

7. **Orosians**: Russians.

8. **lama**: Tibetan priest.

9. **hochang**: C, *ho-shang*, Buddhist priests.

10. **taotsé**: Taoists: followers of Lao-tzŭ.

11. **Kang Hi**: K'ang Hsi [59:21].

12. **Emperor**: K'ang Hsi. Thus, the year 1691.

13. **Gerbillon**: Jean-François G. [59:26].

14. **Fourtères**: Jean de Fontaney, Jesuit missionary to China.

15. **Bournat**: Joachim Bouvet, Jesuit missionary to China. With Gerbillon and four other Jesuits, he arrived in Peking in 1688. Bouvet and Gerbillon were made professors of mathematics by K'ang Hsi and translated several Tartar works on mathematics into Chinese. Bouvet also served as surveyor and cartographer in the Chinese provinces.

16. **Hoang Tchang**: Huang-chêng, region within the walls of the imperial palace at Peking. In 1693 the first permanent church and residence of the Jesuits in China was established there at the expense of Emperor K'ang Hsi.

17. **Feyenkopf**: Fei Yang-ku, d. 1701, Chinese general in the service of Emperor K'ang Hsi. His greatest military feat was the part he played in the campaigns against Galdan, chief of the Eleuthes. In 1696 he pursued Galdan's forces through the Gobi desert and defeated them at Chao-modo, S of Urga. In 1697 Galdan died and his followers submitted to the emperor all the country E of the Ordos.

18. **Kaldan**: Galdan, d. 1697. Chief of the Eleuthes, a nomadic tribe NW of China. In 1680 Galdan became khan of his people and invaded the territory of the Kalkas. When Emperor K'ang Hsi declared himself on the side of the Kalkas, Galdan, daring the emperor's power, invaded China in 1691. He was beaten but not crushed. When he invaded China again (1695), his forces were destroyed by the imperial troops, who used cannon.

19. Eleutes: Eleuthes, Mongol tribe led by Galdan [59:31].

20. Mohamedans: Mohammedans, tribes that were making incursions on the SW borders of the empire.

21. de suite: F, "consecutively."

22. Crown Prince: Prob. the future Emperor Yung Ch'eng.

23. Kalkas: Mongol tribe that traced itself back to Genghis Khan.

24. Hoang Ho: Hwang Ho, or Yellow River.

25. Ortes: Ordos, Tartar tribe occupying the territory of Ordos, a desert region S of the Hwang Ho in Suiyuan Province, C Inner Mongolia.

26. Taouen: Ta-wan, principality in Shensi Province. According to legend, the horses of Ta-wan were celestial (*Tien ma*) and their sweat was the color of blood. "Blood sweating" probably came from small lesions caused by parasites [Creel, 176].

27. Tien ma: C, *T'ien-ma* "Heavenly horse." A term dating back at least to Han times [ibid.].

28. Tchaomed: Chao-modo, town N of the Gobi desert, where Fei Yang-ku defeated Galdan, leader of the Eleuthes.

29. Tipa: Or "Dezi," title of the viceroy who governs Tibet for the Grand Lama. After some years of patient listening to the protests of the Tipa about peace and allegiance to the emperor, K'ang Hsi finally concluded that all the lamas were liars and traitors [XI, 272].

30. the sun . . . : K'ang Hsi was an amateur astronomer. These figures were added to the letter [Mailla says in a note (XI, 273): "one degree twenty minutes less"].

31. Paichen: Hsin-a-pai-cheng, prob. modern city of Sining (or Hsining) in Tsinghai Province, N central China.

32. Kalda: Galdan [cf. 18 above].

33. Samarkand: City in Soviet Central Asia.

34. Bokara: Bukhara city in W Uzbek Republic, USSR, once a center of Moslem worship.

35. Grimaldi: [cf. 3 above].

36. Pereira: Thomas Pereyra [59:25].

37. Tony Thomas: Antoine T., fl. 1691, Jesuit missionary to China.

38. Gerbillon: [59:26].

39. placet sic: L, "it is agreed, thus." Formula phrase used on the petition sent in.

40. Kung-fu-tseu: Confucius.

41. Material Heaven: Prob. refers to the Christian concept of a physical heaven. The Jesuit missionaries wanted to adapt Chinese religious ritual into Christianity. A big bone of contention was the noise one made when he said "God." Could a different sound in a different language mean the same thing? In a footnote, Mailla says that the four Jesuits wanted to know what the Chinese intended by the words "T'ien" and "Shang Ti." Did they intend "le ciel matériel ou le Seigneur du ciel"? Although such questions mightily perplexed the Jesuits, the Chinese seemed not to understand why they should. A part of the rites controversy.

42. Changti: Shang Ti. An all-pervasive force which the Christians tried to equate with their God [53:24].

43. manes: L, "spirits of the dead."

44. cartouche: Scroll or tablet in ornamental form.

45. wallahs: Slang expression for VIPs.

46. archbish of Antioch: Charles-Thomas Maillard de Tournon, 1668-1710, titular patriarch of Antioch who, in 1704, was sent to China by Pope Clement XI with the title of papal legate and charged with the task of studying the merits of the rites controversy [59/327]. He arrived in Canton in 1705 and had an interview with Emperor K'ang Hsi in Peking. After making a complete fool of himself, he returned to Canton; he was arrested and imprisoned, upon the emperor's orders, by the Portuguese in Macao. He died there in 1710.

47. Canton: City and port in Kwangtung Province, SE China.

48. Monseigneur Maillard de Tournon: Patriarch of Antioch [cf. 46 above].

49. Clemens: Clement XI; 1649-1721, pope (1700-1721). He condemned the custom of Chinese ancestor worship and denied the Jesuit petition that the Mass might be said in Chinese, or that the Chinese could be ordained as priests.

50. papa: I, "pope."

51. Kiao Hoang: C, *chiao-hua huang*, "the sovereign pontiff of the prosperous religion." Chinese term for the pope.

52. Portagoose king: John V, 1689-1750, king of Portugal (1706-1750).

53. Kang Hi: K'ang Hsi. In 1709 the emperor contracted an illness that grew worse each day. It reached a point where no hope could be expected from Chinese doctors. Then Europeans, asked for help, brewed up an "Alchemical Confection" which they gave to the emperor with wine from the Canary Islands. It worked; and little by little his strength returned [XI, 320].

54. Batavia: City on NW coast of Java. In 1716 the emperor was told that money-makers were shipping large quantities of rice out of the country by liaisons with Chinese established in Batavia. K'ang Hsi stopped the exporting.

55. Tommy Juffusun: Thomas Jefferson. In 1716 Jefferson was yet to be born [21:25; 31 passim].

56. tsong-ping: C, *tsung-ping*, "brigadier general."

57. Tching mao: Ch'en Mao, mandarin of the second rank, held a military command in Kwangtung and served as viceroy of Canton. In 1717 he memorialized Emperor K'ang Hsi, recommending that Christian missionaries be expelled from the empire and European merchants from Macao. The emperor, insulted by the actions of Clement XI, proclaimed that no missionaries could stay in China unless they agreed to follow the "Rites of Ricci." Those who did not were to be expelled.

58. Ming: The struggles toward the end of the Ming dynasty [56:104].

59. Siam: Country in SE Asia, modern Thailand.

60. Tonkin: Tongking, region in N French Indo-China, once a part of China; now N Vietnam.

61. Hong-mao: C, *hung-mao*, "redheads" [58:40].

62. Yenkeli: C, prob. Pidgin English for Englishmen in China.

63. Yntsa: C, prob. Indians, or Eastern Indians, though Pound takes it to refer to the French.

64. froggies: Slang reference to French people.

65. Holans: C, "the Dutch."

66. Manilla: City of Manila on SW Luzon, Philippine Islands.

67. Tching Mao: Ch'en Mao, mandarin who signed the petition to the emperor [cf. 57 above].

68. edict of '69: The emperor gave the petition about dealing with European barbarians to his tribunal with orders to report on it. On April 16, 1717, the chiefs of the tribunals "united in general assembly" adopted a resolution and sent it to the emperor. It was based on an edict of 1669. There is no mention of a sea captain in Mailla [XI, 325].

69. Verbiest: One of the earlier Jesuit missionaries [cf. 5 above]. He and his colleagues had been permitted to practice their religion. Since that time the Christians had continued to spread and build churches all over China.

70. Peter of Russia: Peter I, or Peter the Great, 1672-1725, emperor of Russia (1682-1725), founder of the modern Russian state. The embassy referred to is that of L. V. Izmailoff.

71. Kiao-hoang: *chiao-hua huang*, Chinese name for the pope.

72. Haitse: Hai-tzŭ, game preserve near Peking where Emperor Kang Hsi "caught a cold" while hunting in 1722.

73. Yong Tching: Yung Chêng, reigned 1723-1735, fourth son of Emperor K'ang Hsi. His first act was to degrade and confine his brothers in order to reduce contention for the succession. He then turned against the Christian missionaries, some of whom had supported other candidates for the throne, and confined them to either Peking or Macao. In 1732 he tried to expel all Christians, but finding that they taught filial obedience (a central doctrine of Confucius) he left them alone, stipulating, however, that no more missionaries should enter the country. He was concerned with the people's wel-

fare and avoided wars, although he did expand the empire to the Laos border.

74. Tartary: Area N of the Great Wall inhabited by Mongols.

75. Verbiest: [cf. 5 above].

76. Pereira: [59:25].

77. Gerbillon: [59:26].

78. Bouvet: Joachim B., Jesuit mathematician [cf. 15 above].

79. mémoires . . . Paris: F, "memoirs of the Academies / of Sciences of Paris" [XI, 364].

80. qu'ils veillèrent . . . termes propres: F, "that they looked to the purity of the language / and that one should use only suitable terms" [XI, 365].

81. Ch'ing ming: C, *chêng-ming*, "to regulate the names"; "to define the correct term"; a precise definition.

82. Ideograms: Chêng, M351: "right"; Ming, M4524: "name."

83. En son Palais divers ateliers: F, "in his Palace various workrooms."

Glossary Canto LXI

1. Yong Tching: [Yung Chêng], fourth son of K'ang Hsi [60:73].

2. hochang: ho-shang, Buddhists.

3. sic in lege: L, "thus in the law."

4. Gerbillon: Jean-Francois G., Jesuit missionary [59:26].

5. Kung: Confucius.

6. Tientsing: Tientsin [58:34].

7. Lieu-yu-y: Liu Yü-i, fl. 1725, imperial examiner for the province of Shansi. He dealt successfully with a famine in his province and gained the approval of Emperor Yung Chêng.

8. magazines: F, *magazins*, "stores."

9. Chan-si: Shansi Province in NE China; one of the Five Northern Provinces.

10. fontego: I, "chamber," used by Pound as a place that lends money [35:31].

11. AMMASSI: I, "grain pools" [53:17].

12. 8th degree button: The Chinese civil service was divided into nine ranks, each having two grades. The highest was 1a and the lowest, 9b. Each rank carried with it the right to wear special insignia, or "buttons" [XI, 426].

13. One . . . painter: "Un seul d'entre-eux, qui passoit pour un excellent peintre, étoit employé au palais; les autres n'y avoient aucun accès . . . ." (Only one among them [the Europeans allowed to reside in Peking], who had the reputation of being an excellent painter, was employed in the palace; the others had no access to it . . . [XI, 428-429] .

14. **Pope's envoys**: Envoys of Pope Benedict XIII (1724-1730). At the end of their audience in the imperial palace each envoy was given a melon by the eunuchs. The emperor sent bolts of silk, some gold-brocaded, and gin-seng root to the pope [XI, 431-432] .

15. **Lon Coto**: Lung Kodo, fl. 1725, cousin of Emperor Yung Chêng and a prince of the empire. In 1725 he was accused of conspiring against the emperor and sentenced to exile in Ninghsia, in the remote NW. In 1727 he was recalled by the Tribunal of Criminal Affairs and sentenced to death. The sentence was later commuted to life imprisonment [XI, 481-483] .

16. **confino**: I, "in exile."

17. **Kang Hi**: K'ang Hsi [59:21]. It was the emperor who said he couldn't resign.

18. **Victor Emanuel**: V. Emmanuel II, 1820-1878, king of Italy (1861-1878).

19. **Count Cavour**: Camillo Benso di C., 1810-1861, Italian statesman, premier (1852-1859). In 1851, shortly after Charles Albert, king of Piedmont, abdicated in favor of his son, Victor Emmanuel II, Cavour got into an argument with the president of the chamber which prompted his resignation. Since Cavour was technically only a minister, the new king was bound to accept the resignation. Cavour used the brief period to travel to the major courts of Europe, including those of England and France. A new crisis in Piedmont resulted in his appointment as prime minister, a position he maintained with two short interruptions until his death.

20. **Old Worker's Hill**: Shen Nung Tan, "Altar dedicated to Shen Nung," the mythical emperor of China who invented the plow. Commonly known as the Temple of Agriculture, situated in Peking directly across from the T'ien Tan, or "Altar of Heaven." In 1726 Emperor Yung Chêng revived the ancient rites connected with the Altar of Agriculture [XI, 442-443] .

21. **Li Ki**: *Li Chi*, or *Book of Rites* [52:28] .

22. **Christers**: Christians.

23. **Dom Metello**: Alexandre Metello-Souza-y-Menezes, fl. 1726, Portuguese emissary to Emperor Yung Chêng. Metello and the Jesuit Antoine Magalhaens reached Peking in 1727 and tried to negotiate a treaty that would provide for more lenient treatment of missionaries. The emperor assumed, however, that the two had merely come to pay tribute to him, and the talks had no result.

24. **Portagoose boss**: John V of Portugal [60:52] .

25. **Sounou**: Sunu or Sourniama, 1648-1725, a prince of royal blood descended from Nurhachi and from an older branch of the Manchu princes than was Emperor Yung Chêng. Sunu was regarded as a threat to the throne and at the age of 77 he was banished to exile in Shansi. Several of Sunu's sons were Christians, and he, too, may have been baptized before his death.

26. **Yun-nan**: Yunnan, province in SW China.

27. **button 8th class**: [cf. 12 above] .

28. **arpens**: F, "acres."

29. **cramoisi**: F, "crimson cloth."

30. **Governor**: Viceroy of Honan Province in 1728.

31. **Chiyeou**: Shih Yu, fl. 1727, a poor laborer of Shensi Province who found a purse and gave it back to its owner without accepting a reward. Emperor Yung Chêng was so impressed when he heard of this that he rewarded the man with 100 ounces of silver and used the honesty of Shih Yu as the text of a long letter to his people, urging them to reform their morals.

32. **muggin' up**: British slang for "cramming," as for an exam.

33. Kien: Ch'ien Lung, reigned 1736-1795, fourth son of Emperor Yung Chêng. He was an excellent administrator and is often compared with his grandfather, K'ang Hsi. After ten years spent in reorganizing the government, Ch'ien Lung put down a revolt of the aborigines in W China, forced Burma and Nepal to pay tribute, established Chinese supremacy over Tibet, and maintained friendly relations with Western nations. The emperor was an indefatigable poet and published a total of 33,950 pieces. His work is very correct, but rather mediocre. Under his patronage, historical works, encyclopedias, and library catalogues were printed. His reign began 40 years before the American Revolution of 1776.

34. canaglia: I, "rascals."

35. FU: C, *fu*, "happiness, prosperity" [M1978].

36. Coupetai: Gubadai, d. 1709, was a Manchu general and president of the Tribunal of Rites. He had been picked by K'ang Hsi to tutor Yung Chêng.

37. Cai Tsong Hien Hoang Ti: Shih Tsung Hsien Huang Ti, dynastic title of Emperor Yung Chêng.

38. Kien Long: Ch'ien Lung [cf. 33 above].

39. Adamses: The Adams family in the U.S. John Adams was born in 1735, during the last year of Yung Chêng's reign.

40. haskai: Hashar, a petty court in the khanate of Bukhara region, C Asia.

41. yerqui: Yerquen, a petty court in the khanate of Bukhara region, C Asia.

42. hotien: Khotan, town in C Asia on far W border of China. It was important as a caravan junction.

43. teuke: Piece of money used by Russians in W Asia.

44. tael: Chinese coin containing about one and a third ounces of silver.

45. Tchao-hou: Chao Hui, 1708-1764, a general serving Emperor Ch'ien Lung, was responsible for the success of the campaigns to put down the Eleuthes. Under the leadership of Amursana they revolted against the empire and attempted to take the district of Ili in Sinkiang Province in 1757.

46. Kasgar: Kashgar, city in W Sinkiang Province, W China, which became a part of China in 1759. It was the chief city of Chinese Turkistan, now known as Sinkiang.

47. Boucaria: Bukhara, city in W Uzbek Republic, USSR, formerly Chinese Turkistan.

48. EMPRESS Hiao Ching Hien Hoang Heou: Hsiao-shêng, Hsien-huang-hou, 1693-1777, empress dowager, mother of Emperor Ch'ien Lung. After her death she was accorded great honors by her son.

49. Beauties of Mougden: "The Eulogy on Mukden," a poem written by Emperor Ch'ien Lung in 1743 after a visit there to honor the tomb of his ancestors.

50. Ming histories: *Ming Shih Kang Mu*, a history of the Ming dynasty. This work, finished in 1742, did not receive imperial approval, and *T'ung Chien Kang Mu San Pien* was substituted for it in 1775. Emperor Ch'ien Lung's redaction of the Ming histories was published under the title *Yu Chih Kang Chien*.

CANTO LXII

Sources

Charles Francis Adams, ed., *The Works of John Adams*, I, Boston, 1850 (citations from this basic source are given simply by volume and page numbers); Frederick K. Sanders, *John Adams Speaking*, Orono, Maine, 1975, pp. 50-107.

Background

L. H. Butterfield, ed., *Diary and Autobiography of John Adams*, 4 vols., Cambridge, Mass., 1961; Catherine Drinker Bowen, *John Adams and the American Revolution*, Boston, 1950; Page Smith, *John Adams*, 2 vols., Garden City, N.Y., 1962; Clinton Rossiter, "The Legacy of John Adams," *Yale Review*, 46 (1957), 528-550; Peter Shaw, *The Character of John Adams*, Chapel Hill, N.C., 1974; EP, "The Jefferson-Adams Letters as a Shrine and a Monument," *Impact*, 166-183; EP, "Civilisation, Money, and History," passim, in *SP*.

Exegeses

Vasse, "American History and the Cantos," *Pound Newsletter*, no. 5, 13-19; EP, *L*, 319, 322; EP, *GK*, passim; CB-R, *ZBC*, passim; DD, *Sculptor*, passim; Dekker, *Sailing*, passim; CE, *Ideas*, passim; Fraser, *Ezra Pound*, 70; HK, *Poetry*, passim, *Era*, passim; DP, *Barb*, passim; NS, *Exile*, passim; NS, *Reading*, passim.

[Little exegesis has been done for the Adams cantos. Most Pound scholars mention them in passing or with only a generalized comment. Thus under the exegeses heading for these cantos, the major authors who comment are listed with page numbers for readers who would like to know typical attitudes or changes of opinion over the years, though no extended comment should be expected.]

Glossary

1. **'Acquit ... Europe'**: In the summer of 1829, after leaving the presidency, John Quincy Adams started a biography of his father, John Adams, later taken up by Charles Francis Adams. Aware of the inherent difficulties, CFA knew the account would contain errors, but he hoped that he might be "acquitted of evil intention" and

he promised to "correct any errors with cheerfulness." He was particularly concerned over judgments about motives which were subject to interpretation [preface, vi-vii].

2. **To The Governor And The Companie**: In these words ["planting ... ruling," etc.] Charles I granted land to the Massachusetts

Bay Company in a charter dated "the 4th of March, 1629" [not 1628].

3. Thomas Adams: One of the grantees of the charter.

4. 18th assistant: At a meeting on October 20, 1629, John Winthrop was elected governor; 18 assistants to the governor were also elected "of whom Thomas Adams was the last" [I, 4].

5. Merry Mount: By 1627, the new name of Mount Wollaston.

6. Braintree: Town in Massachusetts (now Quincy), home of the Adams family; incorporated 1640.

7. Weston: Thomas W., ?1575-1644?, English merchant and adventurer; organized the expedition of colonists who settled an area near Mount Wollaston in Massachusetts (1625). Perhaps ancestor of Pound's maternal grandfather.

8. Capn Wollanston: Wollaston, English adventurer and colonist who settled an area within the limits of what is now Quincy, Massachusetts, and gave it the name of Mount Wollaston (1625); neither his dates nor his Christian name survives.

9. ten head . . .: The records of Boston read: "24th day, 12th month, 1640. Granted to Henry Adams, for ten heads [members of a family], forty acres, upon the same covenant of three shillings per acre" [I, 5 n. 4].

10. brewing: Henry's son, Joseph, ran the brewery business as his life's work and "after a lapse of more than forty years, left the malting establishment to his youngest son" [I, 11].

11. Henry: H. Adams, founder of Adams family in America [cf. 9 above]. During the six years before his death, Henry Adams may have started the brewing business.

12. Joseph Adams: ?1626-1694, youngest son of Henry Adams, great-grandfather of John Adams and Samuel Adams.

13. old style . . . new style: In 1752 England adopted, by act of Parliament, the Gregorian (New Style) calendar to replace the Julian (Old Style) calendar which did not accurately measure the length of the solar year. Eleven days were dropped from the 1752 calendar (September 2, Wednesday, was followed by Thursday, September 14) and the beginning of the new year was changed from March 25 to January 1.

14. John Adams: 1735-1826; graduated from Harvard at age 19. Charles Francis Adams [CFA] says: "His condition, as the teacher of a school . . . could not be permanent . . . . Its emoluments gave but a bare and scanty subsistence" [I, 22; 31:15].

15. Calvinism: JA considered and rejected "the study of theology, and the pursuit of it as a profession," for reasons Pound gives [I, 42].

16. order than liberty: JA believed that "Parliament could not lawfully tax the colonies. His whole soul was in the cause. But to him it was not less the cause of order and of justice than of liberty" [I, 80].

17. Burke: Edmund B., 1729-1797, British statesman and writer; prominent Whig under George III; favored liberal treatment of American colonies. CFA says of him and Gibbon: "Such a beautifier of imperfect figures is the illusive mirror of national pride!" [I, 92].

18. Gibbon: Edward G., 1737-1794, British historian.

19. tcha: *ch'a* [M101], "tea." The character is given in the margin.

20. Lord North: 1732-1792, 2d Earl of Guilford, English statesman. As prime minister under George III (1770-1782), North made himself the agent of the king's plans to control the American colonies; he supported the Stamp Act and the tax on tea. JQA assigns him, next to the king, the heaviest responsibility for the Revolution and says he followed "the same middle path, the perpetual resource of second-rate statesmen" [I, 94]. During the French and Indian Wars, British troops were welcome protectors of the colonists. North's policies changed their attitudes toward the redcoats [British soldiers, so-called because they wore red uniforms].

21. Rapallo: Town of Liguria, NW Italy, on Gulf of Rapallo; residence of Pound, 1924-1945.

22. Lard Narf: Lord North. Spelling (as in other instances) is an effort to reproduce the Boston accent. Source says: "At about nine o'clock of the night on which Lord North declared himself impassible to menace, a single sentry was slowly pacing his walk . . . in King Street . . . . It was moonlight, and a light coating of fresh snow had just been added to the surface of the ground" [I, 97].

23. King St.: Street at Boston's commercial center.

24. Styschire: Invented by Pound as a pun on the naming of British regiments by counties, such as Wiltshire and Hampshire. It seems to imply that soldiers were pigs living in a sty. Both the 14th and 29th regiments were stationed in Boston at the time.

25. Brattle St: Street in Boston on which John and Abigail Adams lived (1768) and on which Murray's barracks were located.

26. Murray's barracks: Barracks on Brattle Street where British soldiers were quartered (1770) at time of Boston Massacre.

27. barber's boy: Source reads: "In this case, it was a barber's boy whose thoughtless impertinence [in tormenting the lone sentry] opened the floodgates of passion in the town. The resentment of the sentinel and the complaints of the boy drew the attention of stragglers . . . to the soldier's isolated condition, which soon brought his fears to the point of calling upon his comrades for support" [I, 98].

28. Capn Preston: Thomas P., captain of the British troops involved in the Boston Massacre (March 5, 1770). Source says: "A cor-poral and six men of the guard, under the direction of Captain Preston, came to his releif . . . . The movement could not take place without exciting observation, the effect of which was the collection around them [the sentinel and other men] of forty or fifty of the lower order of town's people, who had been roving the streets armed with billets of wood" [ibid.].

29. Chawles Fwancis: Charles Francis Adams, 1807-1886, son of John Quincy Adams and editor of *The Works of John Adams*. Spent much of his youth in European capitals, graduated from Harvard in 1825, and studied law under Daniel Webster. He became a leader of the Whigs. In 1848 he was the Free-Soil party candidate for vice-president; during the Civil War he was minister to Great Britain. In writing about the Boston Massacre and the 40 rowdies who gathered around the sentinel, "scarcely averse to . . . a quarrel," he said it "was the first protest against the application of force to the settlement of a question of right" [ibid.].

30. Louses of Parleymoot: Houses of Parliament.

31. sojers aiming?: The 40 or 50 men who had gathered began to throw snowballs and rocks at the nine members of the guard, who became frightened and fired their muskets. Although they apparently intended to fire over the heads of the crowd, some of the bullets miscarried. But CFA writes: "So fatal a precision of aim, indicating not a little malignity, . . . is one of the most singular circumstances attending the affray" [I, 99].

32. Gent . . . five deaders: Source reads: "Five men fell mortally wounded, two of them receiving two balls each. Six more were wounded, one of whom, a gentleman, standing at his own door, observing the scene, received two balls in his arm" [ibid.].

33. 'never Cadmus': Source continues: "The drops of blood then shed in Boston were like the dragon's teeth of ancient fable—the seeds, from which sprung up the multitudes who would recognize no arbitration but the deadly one of the battle-field" [ibid.]. After slaying the dragon, Cadmus was told to scatter its teeth over the ground. From each tooth a fully dressed warrior sprang out of the earth. They fought one another to the death until only five were left. Then they declared a truce and founded with Cadmus the city of Thebes [27:33].

34. legal advisor: Source says: "It was not as a politician, but as a lawyer, that John Adams was first drawn into public life. The patriotic party stood in need of a legal adviser at all times, but never more than now . . . . John Adams was looked to as a guide in those measures in which questions involving professional knowledge were to be discussed with the authorities representing the crown" [I, 107].

35. Blaydon: Colonel Bladen, member of the Board of Trade and Plantations, objected, around 1740, to the enacting form used for provincial laws. The wording, "Be it enacted by the Governor, Council, and House of Representatives *in General Court assembled, and by authority of the same*," he believed implied an authority outside that of the king. So he arranged to have the standing instructions of the governor of Massachusetts include a prohibition against the use of the objectionable words, and they had not been used for thirty years when, in JA's time, the House reinstated them. In the ensuing debate between the House and Governor Hutchinson about the reintroduction of the former wording, JA played an influential role in shaping the argument for the House [I, 108].

36. Encourage arts: A committee with JA as a member "was directed to mature a plan for the encouragement of arts, agriculture, manufactures and commerce" [I, 109].

37. not suggest . . . 1770, Bastun: These 22 lines concern JA's defense of Captain Preston and the British soldiers, an exceedingly unpopular job he undertook in the name of justice. Feelings were running high in the colony, and Adams was seen by some to be no less than a traitor. Most people wanted the British soldiers hanged. But reason prevailed. JA said that until abandoned by the administration of England, "we must try causes . . . by the law of the land." Since the very small guard had been attacked by all kinds of missiles thrown by an angry mob which was gathering force, JA argued that in human nature they were entitled to defend themselves: "If an assault was made to endanger their lives, the law is clear; they had a right to kill in their own defence. If it was not so severe as to endanger their lives, yet if they were assaulted at all, struck and abused by blows of any sort, by snowballs, oyster-shells, cinders, clubs, or sticks of any kind, this was a provocation, for which the law reduces the offence of killing down to manslaughter, in consideration of those passions in our nature which cannot be eradicated" [I, 113].

38. brand 'em in hand: Two of the soldiers, found guilty of manslaughter, prayed for benefit of clergy (an old form of English law) which was granted. They were publicly "burnt in the hand" and then were "suffered to depart" [I, 114].

39. mens sine affectu: L, "a mind without feeling [passion]" a phrase JA quoted from a work by Algernon Sidney. It is a favorite quotation in defense of the "rule of law" instead of the "rule of men," who are likely to be controlled by their feelings [ibid.].

40. Burke: [cf. 17 above]. He said: "Bad laws are the worst sort of tyranny. In such a country as this, they are of all bad things the worst." It was not Burke but an unknown person who "disputed the right . . . of seizing the lands occupied by the heathen, by virtue of authority vested in the head of the Catholic Church, and granting them to any Christian monarch whose subjects might be the first to discover them" [I, 120; 121-122].

41. feudatory: JA wrote: "If our government be ... merely feudatory, we are subject to the king's absolute will, and there is no authority of Parliament, as the sovereign authority of the British empire" [I, 126]. And later: " 'Every subject is presumed by law to be sworn to the king, which is to his natural person,' says Lord Coke. 'The allegiance is due to his natural body;' and he says: 'In the reign of Edward the Second, the Spencers, the father and the son, to cover the treason hatched in their hearts, invented this damnable and damned opinion, that homage and oath of allegiance was more by reason of the king's crown, that is, of his political capacity, than by reason of the person of the king; upon which opinion, they inferred execrable and detestable consequents' " [I, 127].

42. 'The Spensers': Hugh le Despenser, 1262-1326, Earl of Winchester, and his son supported Edward II and were beheaded as traitors.

43 Coke: Sir Edward C., 1552-1634, English jurist, best known for his four *Institutes* (1628-1644), the first of which is called *Coke upon Littleton.*

44. Mercantile ... : CFA said: "The mercantile and manufacturing temper of Great Britain regarded the people of the colonies not as friends and brethren, but as strangers who might be made tributaries" [I, 132].

45. Oliver: Peter O., 1713-1791, Massachusetts loyalist. When, as chief justice of Massachusetts colony (1771-1776) Oliver agreed to accept special monetary grants from the English Crown to the Massachusetts judiciary, the legislature tried to impeach him. JA drafted the articles of impeachment, but Governor Thomas Hutchinson blocked the proceedings. In 1774, after Adams's articles of impeachment had appeared in the newspapers, several Massachusetts grand juries refused to serve under Oliver. The Oliver case was critical. The Crown had offered to assume the payment of the salaries to judges. Most judges seemed willing to accept the "steady

patronage of the crown" in lieu of the possible acts of "an uncertain and capricious legislative assembly." JA's idea was that if the Crown paid the judges, the Crown would own them [I, 135 ff.].

46. wigs: Massachusetts judges who, in the English manner, wore wigs when presiding in court.

47. Governor: Thomas Hutchinson, 1711-1780, American colonial administrator; member of Massachusetts governor's council (1749-1766); accepted legality of the Stamp Act (1765); royal governor of Massachusetts (1771-1774). Hutchinson was a firm believer in British authority, and his policies in Massachusetts did much to hasten the American Revolution.

48. Abigail: A. Adams, 1744-1810, wife of John Adams. On May 12, 1774, when she was at Braintree, JA wrote to her from Boston expressing despair over his trials and the trials of the colony: "The town of Boston, for aught I can see, must suffer martyrdom. It must expire." He also spoke of his money troubles: "It is expensive keeping a family here, and there is no prospect of any business in my way in this town this whole summer. I don't receive a shilling a week [not month]." But he ended the letter on a spirited note: "Don't imagine, from all this, that I am in the dumps" [I, 143].

49. June 7th: On June 17 [not 7th], 1774, a town meeting was held at Faneuil Hall with JA acting as moderator. It voted not to pay for the tea thrown into the sea at the Boston Tea Party the preceding December. Later that day the House of Representatives, meeting in Salem, adopted a motion that a "General Congress of deputies meet at Philadelphia to consult together upon the present state of the Colonies." This action, taken in the greatest secrecy, was critical in the history of the Revolution. After the motion was adopted, "five delegates from Mass. were named and agreed on" [Bowen, op. cit., 444].

50. Bowdoin: James B., 1726-1790, American statesman. He was nominated to the Continental Congress in 1774 but was too ill to serve. Later he became a leading figure in the Massachusetts councils during the American Revolution and became governor of the state in 1785.

51. Cushing: Thomas C., 1725-1788, American political leader; member of Boston Committee of Correspondence (1773) and of Continental Congress (1774-1776).

52. Sam Adams: Samuel A., 1722-1803, 2d cousin of John Adams, was one of the most active of the Revolutionaries. As colonial resistance to the Crown stiffened, Sam Adams took a lead in expressing the case of the discontented. He helped organize the Sons of Liberty and assisted the cause by his writings. He signed the Declaration of Independence.

53. Paine: Robert P., 1731-1814, American jurist; member of Continental Congress (1774-1778) and signer of Declaration of Independence; judge of Massachusetts Supreme Court (1790-1804).

54. mope . . . : Phrases JA confided to his diary, along with the reflection: "I am often in reveries and brown studies. The objects before me are too grand and multifarious for my comprehension. We have not men fit for the times" [I, 148].

55. le / personnel manque: F, "the personnel is lacking." A phrase Pound adds to the text. Because the colonies do not have men competent to meet the needs of the time, JA sees only bad times ahead. Thus he exhorts Abigail to watch the money and cut down on expenses in every way [I, 150].

56. non importation . . . : The Congress at Philadelphia believed the colonies could force England into bankruptcy by cutting off all trade of any kind with the motherland. JA believed that such an act would not work, but he went along with it, looking to better action in the future. His caveat was reinforced by examples from the orient.

CFA said that inconvenience might result from a total embargo, but not bankruptcy of a whole community: "The history of countries like China and Japan proves clearly enough that it is by no means essential to national existence that they should trade with outside nations at all" [I, 163].

57. Boston Gazette: Newspaper, published 1719-1798, which strongly favored the American Revolution.

58. Lexington: Here, on April 19, 1775, the first shot was fired in the Revolution. Thereafter, JA stopped writing for the *Boston Gazette*.

59. Novanglus: JA used the pen name Novanglus ["New Englander"] to sign a series of articles (*Boston Gazette*, 1774-75) in which he sought to demonstrate that the laws of England could not be made to apply to the American colonies; the articles were an answer to a series of loyalist papers by Daniel Leonard (*Massachusetts Gazette and Post Boy*, 1774-75), who signed himself "Massachusettensis."

60. Taking a side: CFA, analyzing the situation, said that in all civil convulsions a certain group will wait to see who is likely to win before taking sides: "This naturally leads them [such fence-sitters] to oppose, with all their might, any and every measure likely to precipitate their decision. Already, at the first congress, both the Adamses had been marked by these persons as partisans of extreme, if not treasonable opinions" [I, 171].

61. bills of credit: Among the exertions CFA attributes to JA were "the selection of . . . general officers, . . . maturing the form of commission and the instructions for the commander-in-chief; and, lastly, in superintending the preparation of the continental bills of credit which were to serve the purposes of money during the earlier stages of the struggle" [I, 178].

62. navee . . . ridicule: JA strongly believed that the colonies should "procure the establishment of a fleet .... This naked proposition was at once met with a storm of ridicule" [I, 187].

63. Guided pubk mind: JA created public support by such pamphlets as "Thoughts on Government" and other writings not formally published: "In this way his sentiments were so extensively diffused as materially to guide the public mind in the construction of many of the State constitutions. The immediate effect was particularly visible in those adopted by New York and North Carolina, the last of which remained unchanged for sixty years" [I, 209].

64. retain ... despotism: These five lines give the gist of CFA's analysis of JA's temperament and education: "... he [JA] applied his mind to the task of saving whatever experience had proved to be valuable in the British constitutional forms, and cutting off only those portions which were not adapted to the feelings, manners, habits, and principles of a young nation oppressed by no burdens transmitted from a ruder age." JA believed in "the States as nations wholly independent of each other, and needing no bond of union stronger than a single federal assembly of representatives fairly apportioned, with authority sacredly confined to cases of war, trade, disputes between the States, the post-office, and the common territories." CFA avers, however, that JA needed to do more thinking so that he could see that "republican jealousy which seeks to cut off all power from fear of abuses, sometimes does quite as much harm as if it created a despotism" [I, 210-211].

65. 9th Feb.: ... Nation: CFA makes a judgment: "It is probable that the period embraced between the 9th of February, the day of his return to Philadelphia, and the end of this year [1776], was the most laborious and exciting of Mr. Adams's long life.... He felt, not that three millions of men were to declare their own emancipation, but that a nation was to come into being for a life of centuries" [I, 213].

66. Birth of a Nation: Pound's comment, emphasizing the role of JA in the Continental Congress of 1776 in bringing about the creation of a new, independent nation. Poss. refers to D. W. Griffith's 1914 film of the same name, a story of the Civil War and Reconstruction. The Poundian view thus challenges a popular 20th-century view that regards the Civil War as the real crucible in which the nation was formed and regards Abraham Lincoln as the true founding father; instead Pound asserts that the story of the nation's founding must begin at the beginning, and it is especially important that at the beginning were Jefferson and JA [cf. "The Jefferson-Adams Letters as a Shrine and a Monument"].

67. privateers ... : JA wrote to Abigail on April 12, 1776: "The ports are opened wide enough at last, and privateers are allowed to prey upon British trade. This is not independency, you know. What is? Why, *government in every colony, a confederation among them all, and treaties with foreign nations* to acknowledge us a sovereign State, and all that" [I, 213].

68. Brit. majesty: JA helped draft the preamble of a resolution which began: "Whereas his Britannic Majesty, in conjunction with the lords and commons of Great Britain, has, by a late act of parliament, excluded the inhabitants of these United Colonies from the protection of his crown ..." [I, 218].

69. May 12th: Source states: "The committee reported a draft [of the resolution] on the 13th, which was debated and passed on the 15th [of May 1776]." Perhaps Pound assumed it was written on May 12 [I, 218].

70. 12 months ago: On May 16 Adams wrote to a friend about the resolution: "Yesterday the Gordian knot was cut. If such a resolution had been passed twelve months ago, as it ought to have been, ... how different would have been our situation!" [ibid.].

71. June 7th: Congress finally agreed to a formal discussion of independence. CFA states: "The movement took place, accordingly, on the 7th of June." Since treason was an idea in the air, caution was necessary; thus CFA adds about the motion: "It appears on the journal, recorded with the customary caution, as follows:—'Certain resolutions respecting independency being moved and seconded,—..." [I, 221].

72. spies . . . punished. JA was a member of a group called in his journal the "Committee on Spies." It reported resolutions on June 17 which were adopted in part a week later. In part, the resolution reads: "Resolved, that it be recommended to the several legislatures of the United Colonies to pass laws for punishing, in such manner as they shall think fit, persons who shall counterfeit, or aid or abet in counterfeiting, the continental bills of credit, or who shall pass any such bill in payment, knowing the same to be counterfeit" [I, 225].

73. orationem . . . elegantissimam: L, "oration . . . most elegant." The line is Pound's and is not in the source.

74. Routledge: Edward Rutledge, 1739-1800, American lawyer; member of Continental Congress (1774-1777) and signer of Declaration of Independence; member of South Carolina legislature (1782-1796) and governor of South Carolina (1798-1800); brother of John Rutledge. Patrick Henry described him "as the most elegant speaker in the first congress" [I, 228].

75. hackneyed: The debates in the Congress on the Declaration of Independence may have impressed others, but in a letter to Samuel Chase, JA said: "... nothing had been said which had not been hackneyed in that room for six months before" [I, 229].

76. Chase: Samuel C., 1741-1811, American patriot; signer of Declaration of Independence; delegate to First and Second Continental Congresses; appointed associate justice of Supreme Court (1796).

77. Schicksal, sagt der Führer: G, "Destiny, says the Führer [leader]."

78. (sero): L, "too late."

79. Cavalier: Virginian, from CFA's passage comparing the New England and Virginian attitudes concerning loyalty to the Crown of England and finding citizens of both colonies, though having origins in different social classes in England, committed to the "spirit of personal independence" [I, 243].

80. Impassible: "The army, although at heart patriotic, was all the time filled with personal jealousies and discontents, which nothing kept within reasonable bounds but the impassible moderation of Washington" [I, 265].

81. Clearest head: An unidentified member of Congress wrote about JA: "In a word, I deliver to you the opinion of every man in the House, when I add that he possesses the clearest head and firmest heart of any man in the congress" [I, 273].

82. Thumon: H, "Soul, life, strength, courage, mind."

83. Bordeaux: JA was appointed a member of the commission to arrange the purchase of war materials from France and solicit the favor of the French toward the American cause. He reached Bordeaux safely, "was received with honors, and immediately passed on to Paris, where he arrived on the 8th of April, 1778" [I, 277].

84. Franklin: Benjamin F. [31:16]. JA did not think much of BF's ethics, which seemed to allow him to enjoy advantages "obtained at the expense of others." In defense of his expression of opinion about Franklin, JA wrote: "Yet if rigid moral analysis be not the purpose of historical writing, there is no more value in it than in the fictions of mythological antiquity" [I, 319].

85. Leyden Gazette: Dutch newspaper published in 1782 by John Luzac, with whom JA had established permanent relations when he was in Holland trying to negotiate a loan from the Dutch government.

86. **Magazine Politique Hollandais**: Dutch magazine established ca. 1782 by a man named Cerisier. JA wrote out the answers to many questions the Dutch had about America. His responses, published in this magazine and in the *Leyden Gazette*, counteracted information previously published in Holland which came only from English sources.

87. **Calkoen**: Hendrik C., 1742-1818, Amsterdam lawyer; instrumental in swaying Dutch opinion in favor of the American colonies during the Revolution. At his request JA wrote "Twenty-six Letters upon interesting subjects respecting the Revolution of America," and Calkoen arranged to have them published in the Dutch press in October 1780.

88. **Amsterdam**: Dutch city where JA served as American minister to the Netherlands (1780). While there, Adams cultivated as many of the most reliable bankers as he could because they would be a factor in his efforts to negotiate loans for the newly established and independent United States.

89. **Cornwallis**: Charles C., 1738-1805, British general who surrendered to the Americans and French at Yorktown, Virginia, in 1781. His defeat bolstered the cause of the colonies in Europe and helped make it possible to borrow money to carry on as well as to persuade the Dutch to acknowledge "the independence of the United States" [I, 346].

90. **De Ruyter**: Michel Adriaanszoon de R., 1607-1676, Dutch admiral and naval hero; active in cause for Dutch freedom.

91. **doivent... de la France**: F, "they ought always to cry Liberty—friends of France." Source reads: "Les amis de la France devaient toujours *crier* la liberté." In referring to this description of French policy under Louis XV, CFA [I, 345n] remarks: "From that quarter it was a cry and nothing else, as well in Holland as in America."

92. **Flassans**: Jean Baptiste Gáetan de

Raxis de Flassan, 1760-1845, French diplomat and historian; author of *Histoire Générale et Raisonée de la Diplomatie Française* (1808).

93. **Van Capellen**: Joan Derk, Baron van der Capellen tot dem Pol, Dutch statesman; friend of American interests during late 18th century.

94. **der Haag**: The Hague, capital of the Netherlands. JA undertook the bold policy of insisting that the U.S. be recognized as an independent nation. Thus he began (on Jan. 8, 1782) "a series of formal visits, in person, to the chief officers ... at the Hague, in which he respectfully reminded them of the memorial he had addressed to them, asking for the recognition of his country .... He then stated the object of his visit to be to demand a CATEGORICAL ANSWER" [I, 347].

95. **Leyden**: Industrial town in South Holland, SW Netherlands.

96. **Harlem**: Haarlem, city in North Holland, W Netherlands, near Amsterdam.

97. **Zwol**: Zwolle, city in Overijssel Province, E Netherlands, on Ijssel River.

98. **Zeland**: Zeeland, province, SW Netherlands, composed of several small islands. Source reads "Zealand."

99. **Overyssel**: Overijssel [cf. 97 above].

100. **Gronye**: Groningen, province in NE Netherlands.

101. **Utrecht**: Province in C Netherlands and its capital city.

102. **Guilderland**: Gelderland, province in E Netherlands. In many Dutch towns and provinces "petitions were gotten up, setting forth ... reasons why the provincial States ... should be instructed early to declare in favor of granting Mr. Adams's demand" [I, 347].

103. **U.S.N.A.**: United States of North America.

104. Birth of a Nation: [66 above]. JA received a favorable categorical answer and was "acknowledged in quality of envoy of the United States of North America" and "as the accredited minister of the new nation." Later JA was presented to the ministers of other European states "as a new and recognized member of the *corps diplomatique* at the Hague" [I, 348-349].

105. corps diplomatique: F, "diplomatic corps."

106. Dumas: Charles William Fredrick D., d. 1796, Swiss man of letters whom Franklin employed as an agent to promote American affairs in Holland (1775), he acted as JA's secretary in Holland (1780-1782) and remained there as American chargé d'affaires, though he never officially held that title. Adams found him completely trustworthy.

107. Willink: Wilhem and Jan W., directors of Dutch banking house bearing their name (ca. 1780).

108. van Staphorst: Nicholas and Jacob van S., fl. 1780, directors of Dutch banking house bearing their name.

109. Fynje: De la Lande and Fynje, Dutch banking house (ca. 1780).

110. guilders: Amount of the first loan JA negotiated with Dutch bankers. From that time until he returned to America in 1788, he kept up relations with the bankers of Amsterdam and through them received successive advances [I, 351].

111. Adam Street: Street in C London. On October 20 JA set out, for reasons of health, with his son [the young JQA who was acting as his secretary] and one servant for London. On his arrival a postboy told him he was being carried to the best inn in London. JA wrote: "Whether it was the boy's cunning, or whether it was mere chance, I know not, but I found myself in a street which was marked John's Street. The postilion turned a corner, and I was in Adam's Street. He turned another corner, and I was in John Adam's Street! I thought, surely we are

arrived in Fairy land. How can all this be?" [I, 403].

112. Adelphi: Adelphi Hotel on the Strand, London, where JA stayed in 1783.

113. Hired!: A bookseller told JA: "Sir, the men of learning are all stark mad. There are in this city at least one hundred men of the best education, the best classical students . . . any one of whom I can hire for one guinea a day to go into my closet and write for me whatever I please, for or against any man or any cause. It is indifferent to them whether they write *pro* or *con*" [I, 404].

114. Ice, broken ice . . . : JA's return trip from England to Holland was the worst experience he ever had. He gives comparative details of bad trips, such as "once, in 1777, in the dead of winter, from Braintree to Baltimore, five hundred miles, upon a trotting horse," and in 1778 "in a furious hurricane . . . which struck down our men upon deck, and cracked our mainmast"; he concludes that he never suffered "so much . . . as in that jaunt from Bath to Amsterdam" [I, 412].

115. fundamentals: JA went to England as a visitor for his health. As a guest auditor in Parliament, he heard George III confess that "he had thrown away an empire." The king, far from dishonoring the name of his American auditor, said that the Adams "name was henceforth to go out indelibly graven by his act upon the list of those who, by upholding fundamental principles at critical moments, originate the beneficial movements of the world!" [I, 413].

116. literature . . . : Mrs. Adams joined JA in Paris in the summer of 1784. JA wrote that the place had changed. "Literature and philosophy had become the rage even in fashionable circles" [I, 415].

117. Frederick: Frederick II (the Great) of Prussia adopted a trade treaty with the U.S. which was different from any such treaty yet made: "Free trade, freedom of neutrals, respect for individual property of enemies at sea, the abolition of privateering, and the limitation over the power to confiscate contraband of war, were new and bold steps in the progress of international civilization" [I, 416].

118. philanthropy: Since the treaty would protect the U.S. from British sea power, JA was bound to add: "Hence their [the Americans'] philanthropy was not wholly free from suspicion of incidental benefit to ensue to themselves" [I, 417].

119. The Duke: John Frederick Sackville, 1745-1799, Duke of Dorset; English ambassador extraordinary and plenipotentiary to France (1783-1789). In February 1785 the Congress made JA the envoy to the Court of St. James's. The duke remarked to him in Paris that "he would be stared at a great deal" [I, 418].

120. to make gain . . .: JA wrote: "The pamphlet of Lord Sheffield [which in 1783 got the U.S. excluded from trade with other British colonies] had its effect upon the formation and adoption of the federal constitution of 1788. Thus it often happens with nations that think to make a gain out of the embarrassments and miseries of their neighbors . . . . Lord Sheffield's interference must be classed among the secondary misfortunes which befell Great Britain in the disastrous record of the American war" I, 423].

121. Euclid: Greek mathematician, 3d century B.C. JA said that the "infallible truth" of the doctrines of the Constitution was as clear as any demonstration in Euclid.

122. taste and elegance: In order to defend the Constitution to New Englanders and others, JA published *A Defence of the Constitution of the United States of America against the attack of M. Turgot*. He wrote the treatise hastily because it had to be published immediately to do any good, and people complained that it lacked "taste and elegance." JA said that such things would have to come after "substance."

123. Libertatem Amicitiam Fidem: L,"Liberty, Friendship, Loyalty" [*Tacitus* I.XV (Loeb, no. 111, p. 28)]. The sentence from which these words are taken reads: "Fidem, libertatem, amicitiam, praecipua humani animi bona, tu quidem eadem constantia retinebis." ["Honour, liberty, friendship, the chief blessings of the human mind, you will guard with the same constancy as before" (Loeb trans.).] CFA writes: ". . . the passage from Tacitus . . . became such a favorite with Mr. Adams that he selected the first three words and the governing verb *retinebis*, as a motto for himself, which he caused to be engraved in various forms for his private use" [I, 433].

124. a new power: In talking about national prosperity, JA wrote: "The commercial and moneyed interests, which were the first to feel it, at once rallied around Mr. Hamilton [Washington's secretary of the treasury] as their benefactor, and they never deserted him afterwards. A new power arose, that of the fundholders, the rapid increase of which inspired Mr. Jefferson with alarm and a determination to resist it" [I, 452].

125. rotation: In a letter to his wife [Jan. 2, 1794], JA wrote: "Our anti-federal scribblers are so fond of rotation, that they seem disposed to remove their abuse from me to the President" [I, 460].

126. To be punctual . . . unmercantile: In a letter to Abigail [Feb. 8, 1794], JA wrote of his boredom after presiding over the Senate for two months: "I . . . am wearied to death with *ennui*. Obliged to be punctual by my habits, confined to my seat, as in a prison, to see nothing done, hear nothing said, and to say and do nothing." And later: "Borrowing of banks for a trading capital is very unmercantile" [I,465-466].

127. war: In a letter dated March 27, 1794, JA wrote: "I have one comfort; that in thought, word, or deed I have never encouraged a war" [I, 469].

128. horror: In an April 19 letter JA wrote: "You cannot imagine what horror some persons are in, lest peace should continue" [I, 471].

129. DEBT: In a letter of May 5, JA wrote: "While I confess the necessity of it . . . I lament the introduction of taxes and expenses which will accumulate a perpetual debt and lead to future revolutions" [I, 473].

130. Adet: Pierre-August A., 1763-1834, French envoy to U.S. (1795) with rank of minister plenipotentiary. He represented the Directory whose short-lived regime began after the execution of Robespierre.

131. Jay: John J., 1745-1829, American jurist and statesman; member of Continental Congress (1774-1777, 1778, 1779); aided in peace negotiations with Great Britain (1782-83); chief justice of Supreme Court (1789-1795); negotiated Jay's Treaty with Great Britain (1794-95). That Jay was elected governor of New York before the treaty was published JA thought a happy circumstance, "for the parties against him would have quarrelled with the treaty, right or wrong, that they might give a color to their animosity against him" [I, 479].

132. J.Q.A.: John Quincy Adams [34: passim].

133. nominatim: L, "namely."

134. King: Rufus K., 1755-1827, American statesman, member of Continental Congress (1784-1787) and of U.S. Senate (1789-1796, 1813-1825); minister to Great Britain (1796-1804). He was a strong supporter of Alexander Hamilton. He, and the others named, refused to be secretary of state after the resignation of Edmund Randolph, who had been compromised by revealing a secret correspondence with the French envoy. The comments about "good men and true" are taken from letter to Abigail [Jan. 7, 1796; not 1795]. [I, 483].

135. Henry: Patrick H. refused to accept office of secretary of state [31:46].

136. Cotsworth: Charles Cotesworth Pinck-

ney, 1746-1825, American statesman. He was sent to France on a special mission (1796) but when the French refused to recognize his status he went to Amsterdam, where he was approached by members of the French government who offered terms under which negotiations might start (the main point was Jay's Treaty); this incident became the famous XYZ Affair [70:16].

137. War Office: U.S. Department of War.

138. expenses etc.: In a letter to Abigail [Jan. 7, 1796], JA spoke of the difficulty of filling the cabinet: "The expenses of living at the seat of government are so exorbitant, so far beyond all proportion to the salaries, and the sure reward of integrity in the discharge of public functions is such obloquy, contempt, and insult, that no man of any feeling is willing to renounce his home, forsake his property and profession for the sake of removing to Philadelphia, where he is almost sure of disgrace and ruin. Where these things will end, I know not. In perfect secrecy between you and me, I must tell you that now I believe the President will retire." JA believed that he should not serve as vice-president under a new president whose sentiments might differ from his own or be "so opposite . . . as to endanger the peace of the nation. It will be a dangerous crisis in public affairs, if the President and Vice-President should be in opposite boxes" [I, 483-484].

139. Philadelphy: Philadelphia was the meeting place of the First Continental Congress (1774), of the Second Continental Congress (1775-76, 1777, 1778-1789) and of the Constitutional Convention (1787). It also served as the capital of the U.S. (1790-1800).

140. hate speeches: In a letter to Abigail [March 1, 1796], JA listed the things he hated about government. In addition to those Pound lists, he said: "I hate to speak to a thousand people to whom I have nothing to say. Yet all this I can do" [I, 487].

141. Amphion: A musician, so excellent that he drew stones after him with the music of his lyre. JA wrote: "Alas! I am not Amphion. I have been thirty years singing and whistling among my rocks, and not one would ever move without money. . . . I cannot sing nor play. If I had eloquence, or humor, or irony, or satire, or the harp or lyre of Amphion, how much good I could do to the world" [I, 488] .

142. House: House of Representatives. JA wrote: "If Mr. Jefferson should be President, I believe I must put up as a candidate for the House. . . . I declare, however, if I were in that House, I would drive out of it some demons that haunt it" [I, 489] .

143. Washington's: Washington declined to run for a third term in the election of 1796, a decision that created violent partisan politics. CFA wrote: "The retirement of President Washington removed the last check upon the fury of parties. . . . The individual whom the opposition would sustain, with marked unanimity, was Thomas Jefferson. . . . The federalists . . . enjoyed no such advantage. A portion of them . . . reposed implicit confidence in Alexander Hamilton. But they were . . . compelled to admit that that confidence was not shared by the people at large, and that an attempt to oppose him to Mr. Jefferson would be futile" [I, 490-491] .

144. Mr. Hamilton: Alexander H., 1755-1804, American statesman, member of Continental Congress (1782, 1783, 1787, 1788) and first U.S. secretary of the treasury (1789-1795). The proponent of a strong federal government, he was instrumental in securing the ratification of the Constitution, especially in New York. In Washington's administration Hamilton established a national fiscal system and placed public credit on a sound basis. But from Pound's point of view, his decision to model the U.S. banking system on the Bank of England has had destructive effects ever since. Pound also pillories him for the "scandal of the assumption" [*SP*, 169] and for being anti-John Adams,

anti-Jefferson, and anti-Andrew Jackson in their struggles for the people versus financial interests [*SP*, 338] . Here Hamilton quarreled with JA primarily because he was a threat to Hamilton's control of Federalist party policies. Knowing that in the controversies of partisan politics Adams would not necessarily be a strict party man, Hamilton [69:67] sought to diminish Adams's influence by working behind the scenes to deny him party support. In the presidential campaign of 1796, Hamilton encouraged Federalist electors to vote unanimously for Thomas Pinckney for vice-president, hoping that Pinckney would receive enough additional electoral votes to become president, with Adams as vice-president. But Adams was elected president and, partly as a result of Hamilton's maneuverings, Thomas Jefferson of the opposition Republican party was elected vice-president. During Adams's presidency Hamilton contrived to have Secretary of State Timothy Pickering, Secretary of the Treasury Oliver Wolcott, and Secretary of War James McHenry report to him behind Adams's back the confidential business transacted at cabinet meetings. In May 1800, when Adams finally recognized the intrigues against him, he dismissed Pickering and McHenry and reorganized his cabinet. Hamilton made a treacherous attack on JA in the presidential campaign of 1800 by writing a pamphlet entitled *Letter from Alexander Hamilton, concerning the Public Conduct and Character of John Adams, Esq., President of the United States*, which contributed to Adams's defeat in his bid for a second term [71:60] . Ironically, Hamilton, who approved of Adams's politics much more than he did those of Jefferson, ended up throwing his support to Jefferson in the 1800 election, seeing him as a lesser evil than Aaron Burr, who, in July 1804, was to kill Hamilton in their famous duel [37:56, 66] .

145. '96 till 1854: Pennsylvania deserted New England and voted for Jefferson. Adams received 71 electoral votes, only one more than necessary. But in all subsequent elections until 1854, Pennsylvania voted for the nominee who was elected.

146. Giles: William Branch G., 1762-1830, American statesman, member of House of Representatives (1790-1798); member of Senate (1804-1815). Giles opposed the founding of the first Bank of the United States and brought charges of corruption against Hamilton (1793), which were dismissed. After the election of 1796, JA reported to Abigail what Giles had said: " 'The point is settled. The V.P. will be President. He is undoubtedly chosen. The old man will make a good President, too. . . . But we shall have to *check* him a little now and then.' . . . There have been manoeuvres and combinations in this election that would surprise you" [I, 495-496].

147. Constitution: JA's inaugural address emphasized ideas whose time had not come. He referred in part to "a love of science and letters, and a wish to patronize every rational effort to encourage schools, colleges, universities, academies, and every institution for propagating knowledge, virtue, and religion among all classes of people, not only for their benign influence on the happiness of life in all its stages and classes, and of society in all its forms, but as the only means of preserving our constitution from its natural enemies" [I, 505].

148. Elleswood: Oliver Ellsworth, 1745-1807, American statesman and jurist, delegate to Continental Congress (1777-1784); chief justice of Supreme Court (1796-1799). Ellsworth was appointed to the second peace mission to France by John Adams and, with William Vans Murray and William Davie, concluded the convention with France at Mortefontaine (1800). He "administered the oath of office to JA with great energy."

149. Napoleon: Napoleon I [31:53]. Napoleon made a separate peace with Sardinia in May 1796; entered Milan on May 14; laid siege to Mantua in July; and negotiated favorable armistices with the king of Naples

and the pope. Victories at Arcole, Rivoli, and Mantua followed, after which Napoleon crossed the Alps toward Vienna and soon became the idol of Europe.

150. Miranda: Francisco de M., 1750-1816, Venezuelan revolutionist and leader of the Venezuelan struggle for liberty; in 1806 he sought foreign aid and led an expedition to the Venezuelan coast, but the military venture was a failure; he was a commander of the forces during the revolution of 1810 and was dictator for a short time. During JA's term in office, Alexander Hamilton became involved with Miranda in South America in the hopes of conquering the American [South and North] possessions of Spain. Secretary of War McHenry reported sub rosa to Hamilton on actions by Adams's cabinet. CFA says: "Mr. Hamilton had become a party to a grand project of revolution in South America, conceived years before in the fertile brain of Francisco de Miranda" [I, 523].

151. Talleyrand: Charles Maurice de Talleyrand–Périgord, 1754-1838, French statesman; minister of foreign affairs (1797-1807). Implicated in the XYZ Affair [70:16]. The Hamilton party was all for war with France; it was JA's policy to follow any lead to prevent war. Thus a dispatch of Talleyrand's which indicated a hope of "a good understanding with America" was picked up by Adams, who had to undertake the most delicate kind of political maneuvering to get a new envoy sent to France. JA's success in preventing a war with France was the most important accomplishment of his term in office. But the war-mongering press, led by Hamilton's Federalists, saw America's backing down from open conflict as a weakness; thus Adams's cause was not popular in the nation at large.

152. Murray: William Vans M., 1760-1803, minister to The Hague (1798) replacing John Quincy Adams. Murray was instrumental in preparing the way for recognition of an American minister to France; in

February 1799 JA appointed him envoy to France on the second peace mission. Adams later added Oliver Ellsworth and Patrick Henry to the mission but Henry, who was unable to go, was replaced by William Davie. Murray had been the person through whom Talleyrand's dispatch was transmitted to the U.S. government. Hence he was JA's nominee to be the special envoy to France.

153. vindictive: In a letter to Abigail [Feb. 22, 1799], JA said: "I do not remember that I was ever vindictive in my life, though I have often been very wroth. . . . [Murray's] mission came across the views of many, and stirred the passions of more. This I knew was unavoidable" [I, 545]. CFA commented on the problem with France: "He roused the country to war, solely as a measure of defence, and to deter France from further persevering in her aggressions" [I, 541]. "Ready for war, if France continued faithless, he was not less ready for peace the moment she showed signs of returning reason" [I, 550].

154. Fries: John F., ?1750-1818, American insurgent who, opposed to a federal property tax, led a force of Pennsylvania Germans against assessors and collectors in 1799; Fries was arrested by government troops, tried, and found guilty of treason under the Sedition Act; JA pardoned him in 1800. CFA says about the case: ". . . the cabinet could not complain that they had not been consulted at every step. But that seems to have made no difference in the feeling with which at least one of the disaffected viewed the direction of the President . . . that a pardon should be made out for all the offenders" [I, 573].

155. Snot: James McHenry, 1753-1816, American politician; aide to General Washington and to Lafayette during the Revolution; member of Continental Congress (1783-1786); delegate to Constitutional Convention (1787); secretary of war (1796-1800). While secretary of war in JA's cabinet, McHenry remained loyal to the interests of Alexander Hamilton.

156. Bott: Prob. Timothy Pickering, 1745-1829, American general and statesman; during the Revolution member of the Board of War (1777) and quartermaster general (1780-1785); postmaster general (1791-1795); secretary of war (1795); secretary of state (1795-1800). JA dismissed Pickering from his last office because his anti-French attitude was not in line with Adams's foreign policy and because of his intrigues on behalf of Alexander Hamilton. JA's foreign policy was to maintain neutrality in all European conflicts. The Federalists wanted to align the U.S. with Britain against France.

157. Cott: Prob. Oliver Wolcott, 1760-1833, American lawyer and politician. He succeeded Alexander Hamilton as secretary of the treasury in Adams's cabinet (1795-1800) and during that time cooperated with Hamilton in his efforts to control and manipulate Adams's policies. Fang [I, 176] believes that Snot, Bott, Cott refer to Cabot [69:68] and Wolcott.

158. ego scriptor . . . : L, "I, writer of the canto."

159. pater patriae: L, "father of his country."

160. arriba: S, "hail!"

CANTO LXIII

Sources

Charles Francis Adams, ed., *The Works of John Adams*, I, II;
Frederick K. Sanders, *John Adams Speaking*, Orono, Maine,
1975, 108-127; Guido Cavalcanti, "Donna mi priegha," 5th ed.,
1527; rpt. *LE*, 163-167.

Background

L. H. Butterfield, ed., *Diary and Autobiography of John Adams*,
I, Cambridge, Mass., 1961; Catherine Drinker Bowen, *John
Adams and the American Revolution*, Boston, 1950; Gilbert
Chinard, *Honest John Adams*, Boston, 1964 (first publ. 1933);
Peter Shaw, *The Character of John Adams*, Chapel Hill, N.C.,
1974; Page Smith, *John Adams*, 2 vols., Garden City, N.Y., 1962.

Exegeses

CE, *Ideas*, 43; Dekker, *Cantos*, 179, 186-187; DP, *Barb*, 233;
CB-R, *ZBC*, 240.

Glossary

1. Ellsworth ... Fries: [62:148, 152, 154].
JA, in sending Oliver Ellsworth to join
William Vans Murray on a second peace
mission to France (1799) and in pardoning
John Fries, charged with treason under the
Sedition Act and sentenced to death for
leading a tax rebellion, had acted contrary
to the wishes of Alexander Hamilton and
his followers. Hamilton, in his *Letter ...
concerning the Public Conduct and Charac-
ter of John Adams* (1800), referred to both
incidents in his efforts to discredit JA's
influence in the Federalist party, despite
JA's 25 years of public service.

2. General Pinckney: Charles Cotesworth P.
[62:136, 144]. Alexander Hamilton wanted
to use General Pinckney to challenge the
leadership of JA in the Federalist party as
the election of 1800 approached, but
Pinckney, when he realized what Hamilton

was doing, insisted that he would partici-
pate only on a ticket that included JA.

3. Mr Hamilton: [62:144]. CFA's opinion
about Hamilton's morals was based on
Hamilton's reaction to being blackmailed
by a Mr. Reynolds with whose wife he had
had an affair. Rather than be thought
guilty of mishandling the nation's finances,
Hamilton wrote out a complete statement of
his marital infidelity and faced the ensuing
scandal bravely. CFA thinks he would have
done better to remain silent.

4. they effect ... flourish: Words from JA's
last speech to the Congress [Nov. 22, 1800],
delivered at the new Capitol in Washington.

5. Washington 4th March 1801: On this day
Thomas Jefferson was inaugurated president,
at the first inauguration held in Washington.

6. in ardour ... good deed: Pound's source reads "a great deal" for the last phrase [I, 607]. The reference is to the election of 1802 in which J. Q. Adams [JQA] was nominated, despite the hostility of certain Massachusetts Federalists, to run for a seat in the House of Representatives. JQA lost this election.

7. Pickering: [cf. 62:156]. The reference here is to the election of 1803 to fill two vacancies in the U.S. Senate. After an unsuccessful attempt to elect Timothy Pickering to one of the vacant seats, support swung to JQA; after he was elected the way was clear for Pickering to take the other seat.

8. J. Adams: John Quincy Adams, elected to the Senate (1803) in an election that saw Timothy Pickering, his father's former antagonist, win the other Massachusetts seat.

9. rights ... treaty of peace: From a resolution in which the Massachusetts Convention paid tribute to JA for revising the state constitution (1820-21) which JA had been so influential in drafting forty years earlier; JA, then 86, declined the honor of serving as presiding officer at this convention.

10. Chas Holt: Editor of the *Bee*, Republican newspaper in Connecticut, who was imprisoned under the Sedition Act (1798) for his attacks on the administration of JA. In a letter of March 4, 1825, Holt congratulated JA on the election of his son JQA as sixth president.

11. John Quincy Adams: Upon being elected president by the House of Representatives in February 1825, JQA wrote to JA a note that began: "My dear and honored father" [I, 632].

12. Scott's fictions ... Ld / Byron: JA enjoyed having the writings of Scott and Byron read to him, in his 90th year, by members of his family.

13. property: CFA wrote: "In Mr. Adams's vocabulary, the word *property* meant land.

He had no confidence in the permanence of any thing else" [I, 639].

14. From Fancy's dreams: These lines are inscribed on the tomb of John and Abigail Adams: "From lives thus spent thy earthly duties learn; / From fancy's dreams to active virtue turn: / Let Freedom, Friendship, Faith, thy soul engage, / And serve, like them, thy country and thy age." [I, 644].

15. cats: Catholics.

16. Franklin: [31:16]. JA, writing in the *Boston Patriot*, May 15, 1811, of Benjamin Franklin's attitude of "unlimited toleration in matters of religion" [I, 661].

17. Eripuit caelo fulmen: L, "He snatched the lightning from the sky." Turgot's epigram on Franklin reads: *Eripuit coelo fulmen; mox sceptra tyrannis* ("He snatched the lightning from the sky; next the sceptres from the tyrants"). JA, in the *Boston Patriot*, May 15, 1811, recalled that the compliment paid to Franklin in the motto *Eripuit coelo fulmen sceptrumque tyrannis* ("He snatched the lightning from the sky and the sceptre from the tyrant") acknowledged Franklin's experiments with electricity and his opposition to Great Britain's oppression of the colonies; but when Turgot changed the second part of the motto, the implication was that "Mr. Franklin was soon to destroy or at least to dethrone all kings and abolish all monarchical governments" [I, 662].

18. and all that: A reference to Franklin's efforts, in 1780, with the encouragement of the French foreign minister, Vergennes, to discredit JA as commissioner to France and to have his role substantially reduced. A good account of the quarrel between JA and Franklin, and of the question of the devaluation of American paper money which precipitated it, is found in Shaw, chap. vi.

19. No books ...: JA writing in his diary, April 24, 1756, at age 20.

20. even bagpipe: JA heard the bagpipers in

the army of Sir Geoffrey Amherst when it passed through Worcester, Mass., after the capture of Fort Louisburg, Nova Scotia, in 1758.

21. Mrs Savil: Wife of Dr. Elisha Savil, a friend of JA's in Worcester; JA occasionally read Ovid's *Art of Love* to Mrs. Savil [JA's diary, Oct. 5, 1758].

22. Ars Amandi: L, for *Ars Amatoria*, "The Art of Love," by Ovid.

23. half after three: Pound's source reads "half after ten" [II, 45].

24. Court House: On October 24, 1758, JA traveled from Braintree to Boston to visit the courthouse to be sworn in as a member of the bar.

25. Saml Quincy: Samuel Q., 1735-1789, American lawyer and JA's friend; became solicitor general of Massachusetts under the Crown; a loyalist, he left the country in 1776. Quincy went to Boston with JA to be sworn.

26. Dr Gordon: Sylvester Gardiner, 1708-1786, American physician; he was a loyalist and fled America when the Revolution started.

27. Gridley: Jeremiah G., 1702-1767, American lawyer and attorney general of Massachusetts Bay Province; in 1761 he defended the legality of the Writs of Assistance. JA visited him in October 1758 to ask his advice about studying law. The advice Gridley gave had a permanent effect on JA, which is summarized in the next 10 lines of the canto. JA asked Gridley if he should study Greek. Gridley replied, "It is a matter of mere curiosity" [II, 47].

28. Reeve: Sir Thomas R., d. 1737, English jurist; author of *Lord Chief Justice Reeve's Instructions to his Nephew concerning the study of law.*

29. Judge Leighton: Robert Lightfoot, 1716-1794, loyalist of Rhode Island; judge of the British Court of Vice-Admiralty for the southern district of North America.

30. Institutes: *Institutes of the Laws of England* (London, 1628-1644), a work containing Sir Thomas Littleton's *Tenures* with commentary by Sir Edward Coke, "long the standard authority on real property in England and America" [Butterfield, I, 56 n. 3].

31. Coke: [62:43].

32. Littleton: Sir Thomas L., ?1407-1481, English jurist and writer on law. His *Tenures* is the earliest printed treatise on English law; the text is the basis of Coke's commentary known as *Coke upon Littleton* [major source of Cantos 107-109].

33. Mr Thatcher: Oxenbridge Thacher, 1720-1765, American lawyer and member of the Massachusetts General Court; associated with James Otis and Stephen Sewall in the controversy over the Boston Writs of Assistance (1761). On October 25, 1758, when JA visited Thacher to ask if he would concur in sponsoring JA before the bar, Thacher talked about many subjects before finally coming around to the subject most on JA's mind.

34. country: Pound's source reads "county" [II, 47]. Meaning full of lawyers.

35. Van Myden: Van Muyden's *Short Treatise on the Institutions of Justinian*, which Jeremiah Gridley lent JA in a Latin edition [JA's diary, Oct. 26, 1758].

36. editio terza: I, "third edition."

37. Ideogram: Chêng [M351], "upright, true."

38. of technical terms: JA's comment on Hoppius's *Commentaries on Justinian*: "The design of this book is to explain the technical terms, and to settle the divisions and distributions of the civil law. By the way, this is the first thing a student ought to aim at, namely, distinct ideas under the terms, and a clear apprehension of the divisions and distributions of the science. This is one of the principal excellencies of Hawkins's Pleas of the Crown, and it is the very end of this book of Van Muyden" [II, 48]. Pound underlines the Confucian concern for terminology here expressed by JA, by including the ideogram.

39. Hawkins: William H., 1673-1746, English lawyer, author of *Treatise of the Pleas of the Crown* (1716).

40. Bracton: Henry de B. (or Bratton), d. 1268, English jurist; author of the first systematic treatise of law in England, *De legibus et consuetudinibus Angliae.*

41. Britten: John le Britton (or Breton), d. 1275, bishop of Hereford; author of *Britton*, a treatise on English law.

42. Fleta: Name of a Latin textbook on English law: *Fleta, seu Commentarius Iuris Anglicani* (ca. 1290); believed to have been written in Fleet prison by one of the corrupt judges imprisoned by Edward I.

43. Glanville: Ranulf de G., d. 1190, English statesman and jurist; adviser to Henry II of England.

44. Fleta on Glanville: Pound's source reads "Fleta and Glanville" [II, 50 n. 2].

45. must dig . . . : JA's comment on the difficulties of starting a law practice [*Diary*, Dec. 18, 1758].

46. Tully: Marcus Tullius Cicero, also known as Tully, 106-43 B.C., Roman orator and philosopher. JA noted the value of reading Cicero aloud [*Diary*, Dec. 21, 1758].

47. Cataline: Lucius Sergius Catilina, ?108-62 B.C., Roman politician. In 63 he entered into a conspiracy to assassinate the consuls and plunder Rome, but his plot was stopped by Cicero.

48. Ruggles: Timothy R., 1711-1798, prominent loyalist. The reference is to JA's assessment, in April 1759, of Ruggles as a lawyer.

49. practising law: Biographical note on Ruggles quoted from *Sabine's American Loyalists* [II, 67n].

50. Sandwich: Town in SE Massachusetts.

51. Novascotia: Nova Scotia, province in E Canada.

52. 1788: Pound's source reads "1798" [II, 67n].

53. tory: Member of the loyalist party in America during the Revolution.

54. in quella . . . memora: I, "in that part / where memory is" [Cavalcanti, "Donna mi priegha"; cf. 36:3].

55. Colonel Chandler: Leader of Boston pre-Revolutionary troops with which JA sometimes served.

56. Mr Quincy: Edmund Q., 1703-1788, friend of JA's; father-in-law of John Hancock and Jonathan Sewall [II, 81].

57. Franklin . . . : Benjamin F. The episode mentioned in these nine lines is found in JA's diary, May 26, 1760; it is a very complimentary account of Franklin's kindness in response to Edmund Quincy's expression of interest in viniculture for his province [II, 81-82].

58. Timon of Athens: JA read this Shakespeare play on a rainy day, June 6, 1760.

59. Ira: L, "Anger." JA noted in his diary on June 10, 1760, that "the mind must be agitated with some passion, either love, fear, hope, &c., before she will do her best" [II, 87-88].

60. la qual manda fuoco: I, "which sends fire." In *LE*, 157, Pound translates this phrase from "Donna mi priegha" as "that breaketh into flame" and, in Canto 36 [p. 178], as "rouseth the flame."

61. Braintree: [62:6]. JA, disturbed at the excessive number of lawsuits in his town, wrote in his diary (June 19, 1760): "The town is become infamous for them throughout the country" [II, 90].

62. fraud . . . into system: JA's opinion of an institute of the canon law, which he borrowed from Jeremiah Gridley and read at Gridley's recommendation. He said that he was glad he read it for it would "explain many things in ecclesiastical history, and open that system of fraud, bigotry, nonsense, impudence, and superstition, on which the papal usurpations are founded" [II, 116].

63. 'Our constitution'... laugh: A quotation from an anonymous newspaper article JA recorded in his diary on March 21, 1761. The year 1760 mentioned by Pound may be an error.

64. hoarse laugh: Pound's source reads "horse laugh" [II, 121].

65. Cockle: James C., customs officer in Salem, Mass., who petitioned the court to grant him Writs of Assistance to let him search for prohibited merchandise. James Otis and Oxenbridge Thacher represented the protesting Boston merchants; Jeremiah Gridley appeared for Cockle in support of the writs. Cockle won his case (1761) but Otis's speech against the writs crystalized for JA the nature of the conflict to come

[see II, App. A, 521-525, for an abstract of the arguments presented at the trial and for a version of Otis's speech].

66. Writ(s) of Assistance: Writs of Assistance, authorized by the statute of 12 Charles II (1672), were issued to officials to aid them in the search for smuggled or uncustomed goods; in practice, a writ was a general search warrant. Writs of Assistance were issued in Boston (1760) to allow English port agents to discover smuggled goods; they were not very effective and served to stir up discontent against the British [71:9].

67. Mr Sewall: Stephen S., 1702-1760, American jurist; judge of the Supreme Court of Massachusetts in 1739 and chief justice from 1752; he opposed the British Writs of Assistance.

68. Oxenbridge Thayer: O. Thacher [cf. 33 above].

69. Otis: James O. [34:33].

CANTO LXIV

Sources

Charles Frances Adams, ed., *The Works of John Adams*, II; Frederick K. Sanders, *John Adams Speaking*, Orono, Maine, 1975, 128-173; EP, *SP*, 21.

Background

L. H. Butterfield, ed., *Diary and Autobiography of John Adams*, I, II, Cambridge, Mass., 1961; Catherine Drinker Bowen, *John Adams and the American Revolution*, Boston, 1950; Peter Shaw, *The Character of John Adams*, Chapel Hill, N.C., 1974; Page Smith, *John Adams*, 2 vols., Garden City, N.Y., 1962; Bernard Bailyn, *The Ordeal of Thomas Hutchinson*, Cambridge, Mass., 1974.

Exegeses

CE, *Ideas*, 43; DD, *Sculptor*, 163-164, Davis, *Vision*, 139; DP, *Barb*, 233.

Glossary

1. John's bro, the sheriff: Peter Boylston Adams, 1738-1823, who, as a result of JA's efforts, was appointed deputy sheriff of Suffolk County in the summer of 1761 as part of JA's campaign against pettifoggers, amateurs who dabbled in legal affairs. Of his brother, JA wrote in his *Autobiography*: "He was young, loved riding, and discharged his duties with skill and fidelity; but his disposition was so tender, that he often assisted his debtors with his own purse and credit, and upon the whole, to say the least, was nothing the richer for his office" [II, 129n].

2. Cromwell: Oliver C. [33:21]. This judgment was expressed to JA by the Reverend Anthony Wibird, Congregational minister at Braintree, September 10, 1761.

3. Prayer ... crown: JA's reflections on the application to his own situation of the following passage from Pope's "Fourth Satire of Dr. John Donne, Dean of St. Paul's, Versifyed": "Bear me, some god! Oh! quickly bear me hence, / To wholesome solitude, the nurse of sense, / Where contemplation prunes her ruffled wings, / And the free soul looks down to pity kings" [II, 132].

4. George: George III of England [32:41].

5. Louis: Louis XV, 1710-1774, king of France (1715-1774).

6. Frederick: Frederick II of Prussia [32:38].

7. Palmer: Joseph P., 1718-1788, American soldier. As a colonel in the colonial militia Palmer helped defend the coast near Boston; in 1777 he was appointed brigadier general and given command of the Massachusetts militia defending Rhode Island. JA visited him in October 1762 at his home in German-

town, Massachusetts, and took a particular interest in his husbandry.

8. 1752: Prob. 1762, the year JA visited Deacon Palmer.

9. Gridley of Abingdon: Pound's source reads "Greenleaf of Abington" [II, 137].

10. ramshorn of straw: Pound's source reads "ram's-horn or straw" [II, 137].

11. sub conditione fidelitates: L, "under condition of faith" or "on trust" [cf. II, 149, where the phrase is quoted from a work of Strykius]. Source reads "*Sub conditione ... fidelitatis*." This quotation came up at a meeting of a sodality of lawyer friends informally organized by Jeremiah Gridley to improve their familiarity with the law. JA hosted, at Blodget's in Boston, on this occasion [*Diary*, Feb. 21, 1765].

12. Oliver: Andrew O., 1706-1774, secretary of the province of Massachusetts and later lieutenant governor. On August 14, 1765, in response to reports that Secretary Oliver would distribute stamps when the Stamp Act went into effect, a Boston mob hanged him in effigy. Later that day the mob burned Oliver's office building, burned him in effigy, and vandalized his house and garden. When Lieutenant Governor Hutchinson tried to restore order, the mob drove him and the sheriff away. In his diary [Aug. 15, 1765] JA condemned the behavior of the mob: "But to be carried through the town in such insolent triumph, and burned on a hill, to have his garden torn in pieces, his house broken open, his furniture destroyed, and his whole family thrown into confusion and terror, is a very atrocious violation of the peace, and of dangerous tendency and consequence." But JA also believed that the people had a measure of provocation because of the powerful offices controlled by Lieutenant Governor Hutchinson: Andrew Oliver was Thomas Hutchinson's brother-in-law and Andrew's brother, Peter Oliver, was chief justice of the superior court of the colony.

13. Lieutenant Governor: Thomas Hutchinson [62:47].

14. By 40 towns: In 1765 JA drafted the "Braintree Instructions," a document directing Braintree's representative to the provincial assembly, the General Court, to give the stated reasons for Braintree's refusal to accept the terms of the Stamp Act. JA's document was printed in Draper's *Massachusetts Gazette and Boston News Letter* (Oct. 10, 1765) and was subsequently adopted by 40 other towns as instructions to their representatives.

15. instrument: Pound's source reads "instructions" [II, 153].

16. Sam Adams: [34:32]. Chosen by the town of Boston to prepare instructions for its representatives, Samuel Adams, upon reading what JA had written for Braintree, incorporated some parts of the "Braintree Instructions" into his own document.

17. Stamp Act: A revenue law passed by Parliament (1765) which extended the British stamp tax to America and required all publications and legal documents issued in the colonies to bear a stamp. The violent opposition throughout the colonies culminated in the Stamp Act Congress, which met on October 7, 1765, in New York City and petitioned the king and Parliament to remove the tax. Fearing loss of trade with the colonies, the British repealed the act in 1766.

18. Stamp Act . . . America's: JA's description of the effects of resistance to the Stamp Act [*Diary*, Dec. 18, 1765].

19. To renounce under tree: JA noted that Andrew Oliver had been compelled "to renounce his office of distributer of stamps, by a declaration under his hand and under his oath, taken before Justice Dana in Hanover Square, under the very tree of liberty, nay, under the very limb where he had been hanged in effigy, August 14th, 1765" [*Diary*, Dec. 19, 1765].

20. Gridley: [63:27]. On December 18, 1765, Gridley, Otis, and JA were chosen counsel for Boston to argue before the governor of the province, Francis Bernard, that the courts, closed since November 1, when the Stamp Act had gone into effect, be reopened. Since legal documents had to carry stamps indicating payment of the tax, and since the citizens of Massachusetts refused to accept the validity of the Stamp Act, no legal business could be conducted.

21. Jas Otis: James O., one of JA's senior mentors in the law [34:33; 71:89, 91].

22. Lord Bacon: Sir Francis B., 1st Baron Verulam, 1561-1626, English philosopher and statesman. JA's reflections on the events of December 18 "call to mind my Lord Bacon's observation about secret, invisible laws of nature, and communications and influences between places that are not discoverable by sense" [*Diary*, Dec. 19, 1765].

23. Coke: Lord C. To Pound's mind one of the greatest writers on the law for all time [62:43]. His Institutes are the source of Cantos 107-109/756-774.

24. 3rd Inst.: Pound's source reads "2 Inst." [II, 159]. JA wrote: "The law is the subject's best birthright." Coke wrote: "It is called, right, because it is the best birthright the subject hath" [*Magna Charta*, cap. 29, sec. 11, sub. 3, p. 56].

25. actus . . . injuriam: L, "an act of law does harm to none" [II, 159].

26. Governor in council: On December 20, 1765, JA, Gridley, and Otis appeared before Governor Bernard to argue that the law courts should be reopened without imposition of the stamp tax, JA saying that the act was invalid, "it not being in any sense our act, having never consented to it," and that in any event the dispute over the act should not justify a failure to make justice available to citizens through the courts. Governor Bernard, evading the issue, responded that his office had no power to act on the request to open the courts and that the petitioners should therefore approach the judges directly so that they could decide the question for themselves. When asked his opinion of the best response to Governor Bernard's decision, JA suggested that the petitioners follow the governor's advice and first call upon the governor-in-council, as the supreme court of probate; then ask the judges of the superior court their opinion on the question of opening the courts for business without stamps; then consult with the judges of the inferior courts; and if there is still no satisfactory response to the petition, then request that the governor convene the two houses of the colonial legislature and, if he refuses, attempt to convene the two houses themselves [II, 158, 162].

27. by more ... plague: JA's opinion of office seekers who desired appointment from the Crown [*Diary*, Dec. 25, 1765].

28. tendency of the act: Stamp Act.

29. Ipswich Instructions: The instructions given by the people of Ipswich to Dr. John Calef, their representative in the Stamp Act Congress (1765), argued that the colony would be bound to the laws of England under three conditions: that the emigration of the original colonists be a national act; that the original emigrating be at national expense; and that the place settled be land already belonging to the Crown. JA thought the questions raised were debatable [II, 171-172].

30. waddled: "A great storm of snow last night; weather tempestuous all day. Waddled through the snow driving my cattle to water at Doctor Savil's;—a fine piece of glowing exercise" [*Diary*, Jan. 2, 1776; II, 173].

31. Shutting courts: James Otis, using the pseudonym Hampden, wrote a newspaper essay answering Pym (pseudonym of an English writer who supported the Crown) with arguments from Grotius and other writers, that "shutting up the courts is an abdication of the throne, a discharge of the subjects from their allegiance, and a total dissolution of government and reduction of all men to a state of nature" [II, 174].

32. Louisburg: Port city of E Nova Scotia. On January 13, 1766, the day the inferior Court of Common Pleas reopened at Boston, JA took a case involving rum stolen from a vessel in Louisburg.

33. Pitt: William, "the Elder Pitt," 1708-1778, English statesman who opposed the Stamp Act and British taxation of the American colonies. In March 1766 JA learned that Pitt had appeared before the House of Commons to argue that "the House granted taxes in their representative capacity, not in their legislative, and, therefore, that the Parliament had not the right to tax the colonies" because they were not represented in the House of Commons [II, 190-191].

34. Grenville: George G., 1712-1770, prime minister under George III (1763-1765). His most famous act was writing the Stamp Act (1765); he was also responsible for the Quartering Act of 1765 which required colonists to furnish lodging for British troops if barracks were not available.

35. Thatcher: Thacher [63:33].

36. Goffe: Edmund Trowbridge, 1709-1793, Massachusetts jurist who used the surname of his guardian, Edmund Goffe, during most of his early life. He presided at the Boston Massacre trial in 1770 and in 1774 renounced the royal salary grant. During the Revolution he remained neutral.

37. Eaton: Joseph E., Massachusetts laywer of doubtful character. JA wrote: "This Eaton, Goffe set up, as Pynchon tells me, to be a justice, but Thacher got him indicted in the county of Essex for a barrator, which defeated the scheme of Goffe, and he came near conviction. Goffe grew warm, and said that Eaton's character was as good as any man's at the bar." The same entry in the diary [Nov. 5, 1766] continues: "Spent the evening at Mr. Pynchon's ... very agreeably. Punch, wine, bread and cheese, apples, pipes and tobacco" [II, 201].

38. Martin's: An inn between Salem and Boston. The money in specie (i.e., silver dollars) JA sees going to England is a "luminous detail" [*SP*, 21]. Taxes due England had to be paid in metal, so that over a period of time most metal would be drained from the colonies. If they were not allowed to print paper money, they would be left with no means of transacting business.

39. Salem: [48:29].

40. lopping ... : "Went up to my common pasture to give directions about trimming the trees." About the misshapen pines JA said: "These I fell without mercy, to open the prospect and let in the sun and air" [II, 201].

41. case between negro ... : [cf. 48 below].

42. Hutchinson: [62:47].

43. Dr Tuft: Cotton Tufts, 1732-1815, American physician; friend of JA, whose affairs he administered while JA was in London. JA dined with him on April 8, 1767.

44. White House: The first house of John and Abigail Adams in Boston, to which they moved in April 1768.

45. office lucrative: In 1768 Governor Bernard arranged to have JA's friend Jonathan Sewell offer JA the office of advocate general in the Court of the Admiralty, a position that promised prosperity, royal favor, and promotion, but JA refused the offer "on account of the unsettled state of the country and my scruples about laying myself under any restraints or obligations of gratitude to the government for any of their favors" [II, 211].

46. new statutes: The Townshend Acts, passed by Parliament in June 1767, placed a tax upon glass, lead, tea, and paper.

47. J.Q.A.: John Quincy Adams. JA wrote in his *Autobiography*: "The year before this, that is, in 1767, my son John Quincy Adams was born, on the eleventh day of July, at Braintree; and at the request of his grandmother Smith, christened by the name of John Quincy, on the day of the death of his great grandfather, John Quincy of Mount Wollaston" [II, 210].

48. between negro ... : While attending the 1768 session of the superior court at Springfield, JA was engaged "in a cause between a negro and his master." He says he argued it "in such a manner as engaged the attention of Major Hawley, and introduced an acquaintance which was soon after strengthened into a friendship that continued till his death" [II, 213].

49. Mr Hawley: Joseph H., 1723-1788, American political leader who was associated with James Otis, Samuel Adams, and JA. He was one of the first to urge a declaration of independence and unified colonial administration.

50. 100 towns: A convention was proposed at a regular town meeting in Boston and, with only one week's notice, a hundred towns sent representatives. This show of support for the colonists' cause probably influenced General Gage's decision to quarter the majority of his troops in Boston rather than at the castle in Boston harbor.

51. 10 o'clock: Pound's source reads "one o'clock at noon" [II, 213 n. 2].

52. Byles: Mather B., 1707-1788, American Congregational clergyman and writer of light verse. On his return from the legal circuit JA said: "I found the town full of troops [British redcoats], and, as Dr. Byles, of punning memory, expressed it, our grievances red-dressed. Through the whole succeeding Fall and Winter, a regiment was exercised by Major Small, in Brattle Square, directly in front of my house. The spirit-stirring drum and the ear-piercing fife aroused me and my family early enough every morning, and the indignation they excited, though somewhat soothed, was not allayed by the sweet songs, violins and flutes, of the serenading Sons of Liberty under my windows in the evening" [II, 213].

53. Sons of Liberty: Groups organized throughout the American colonies to resist enforcement of the Stamp Act (1765); Samuel Adams was a prominent leader.

54. Boston Gazette: [62:57]. JA was chosen in 1768 and 1769 to draft the "Instructions" for the Boston representatives [III, 501-510, where these "Instructions" are reprinted].

55. Madeira: Largest island of the group W of Morocco, N Africa.

56. Mr Hancock: John H., 1737-1793, American merchant and statesman; member of Continental Congress (1775-1780; 1785, 1786); first signer of Declaration of Independence; governor of Massachusetts (1780-1785; 1787-1793). On June 10, 1768, John Hancock's sloop *Liberty* was seized in Boston harbor for carrying a cargo (wine) not listed on its loading permit. The *Liberty* was sold, and Hancock was subsequently charged with an earlier offense of smuggling wine: i.e., not paying British customs duty. The case dragged on for months, but JA finally won for his client what is generally regarded as a masterful courtroom victory. The 12 lines following "a cargo of wines" are from JA's reflections upon the case [II, 215].

57. Battle of Lexington: [33:18]. JA's long struggle in the courts stopped when the Revolution began, for, he said, the "battle of Lexington . . . put an end, forever, to all such prosecutions" [II, 216].

58. Mt Wollanston: Wollaston [62:8].

59. East chamber: The view from the home of Norton Quincy, uncle of Abigail Adams, whom JA visited on August 13, 1769.

60. Liberty Tree: An elm that stood on Washington Street in Boston, on which unpopular persons were hung in effigy during the Stamp Act agitation. Where Pound got "buttonwood" tree is unknown. Bowen (op. cit., 270) says it was an elm.

61. Brackett's: Bracket's Tavern, the Cromwell Head Inn, Boston.

62. Case of a whale: JA represented Joseph Doane in a suit versus Lot Gage tried in the Court of Vice-Admiralty: "Doane had sunk the first iron, but Gage had taken the whale. The question was whether Doane had been 'fast' when Gage struck; if so, Doane was entitled to a one-eighth share of the value of the whale" [Butterfield, I, 344].

63. British Statutes: Prob. *State Trials and Statutes at Large*, ed. John Selden, from which JA cited a law (6 Anne, chap. 37, sec. 9) prohibiting impressment of seamen in America. In 1769 JA defended four sailors accused of killing Lieutenant Panton of the British frigate *Rose* while he was attempting to impress them. When Governor Hutchinson saw that JA had the statute before him, he refused to allow the public trial to continue; a verdict of self-defense was given, and the statute was subsequently repealed.

64. 1769: Refers not to the repeal of the statute prohibiting impressment but to the occasion of JA's thoughts about the case.

65. 9 o'clock: March 5, 1770, the evening of the Boston Massacre, in which British soldiers, shooting into a crowd, killed five Boston citizens [62:31, 32]. Source reads "barber's boy" [62:27].

66. Mr Forest: James Forrest, Boston merchant and loyalist, born in Ireland, who asked JA to defend Captain Preston and the British soldiers involved in the Boston Massacre.

67. Captain Preston: [62:28].

68. Mr Quincy: Josiah Q., Jr., 1744-1775, American lawyer, younger brother of Samuel Quincy, the loyalist. He is known

for his political pamphlets written in support
of the Revolution. With JA, he served as
counsel for Captain Preston in the Boston
Massacre affair of 1770; he doubtless was
willing to defend the British soldier because
of his loyalist sympathies. JA defended the
British because of his firm belief in the
principles of law and justice.

69. Mr Auchmuty: Robert A., d. 1788,
colonial jurist and loyalist; appointed
judge of the Court of Vice-Admiralty for
Massachusetts and New Hampshire. With
JA, he was counsel for Captain Preston in
the Boston Massacre case (1770). He re-
turned to England in 1776.

70. But he must ... accepted: These five
lines express part of JA's response to Mr.
Forrest when he said he would take the
Preston case and Mr. Forrest's response of
giving him a retaining fee.

71. Hutchinson: [62:47]. CFA in an edi-
torial note wrote: "Hutchinson, who in his
third volume has done much to embody, in
a permanent form, these floating insinu-
ations of the day, ... alludes to this affair
[JA's defense of Capt. Preston] in the
following insidious manner: 'Captain Preston
had been well advised to retain two gentle-
men of the law, who were strongly attached
to the cause of liberty, *and to stick at no
reasonable fees for that purpose.' "* The
passage implies that JA made a great deal of
money on the defense. JA himself wrote:
"Forrest [the man who persuaded him to
take the case] offered me a single guinea as
a retaining fee, and I readily accepted it.
From first to last I never said a word about
fees ... and I should have said nothing
about them here, if calumnies and insinu-
ations had not been propagated that I was
tempted by great fees and enormous sums
of money" [II, 230-231].

72. ego ... : L, "I, writer of the Cantos."
"Scrofulous," meaning "morally degenerate,"
is Pound's judgment of Hutchinson.

73. 10 guineas ... and 8: Total fees JA re-
ceived for his defense of the British, but he

said he did not ask any fee and would have
handled the case for nothing.

74. But where the devil: Words attributed
to Governor Shirley, former governor of
Massachusetts province, while he was living
in retirement in Roxbury [II, 233].

75. Oxenbridge Thatcher: Pound's source
reads "Thacher." The reference is to CFA's
note that by the time of the Boston Massacre
(1770) JA had superseded Thacher and
James Otis as legal adviser for the patriot
cause [II, 233n].

76. Beccaria: Cesare, Marchese di B., ?1735-
1794?, Italian economist and jurist; author
of *Tratto dei Delitti e delle Pene* [*Essay on
Crimes and Punishments*]. In his defense of
Captain Preston JA began with the following
quotation from Beccaria: "If, by supporting
the rights of mankind, and of invincible
truth, I shall contribute to save from the
agonies of death one unfortunate victim
of tyranny, or of ignorance equally fatal,
his blessing and tears of transport will be a
sufficient consolation to me for the con-
tempt of all mankind" [II, 238].

77. He went out: Reference to an anony-
mous citizen JA met on June 28, 1770.

78. nihil humanum alienum: L, "nothing
human is alien." Refers to a man charged
with rape whom JA defended; acquitted, the
man was promptly held on a charge of
assault with intent to ravish. "This was a
worthless fellow," in JA's opinion, but
"nihil humanum, alienum." The phrase is
from "The Self-Tormentor" by Terence,
l. 77.

79. When he came away: Pound's source
reads: "... when I came away, took a view of
the comet ..." [II, 243].

80. to roll and cool: "Rode to Patten's, of
Arundel, and Mr. Winthrop and I turned
our horses into a little close to roll ..."
[II, 244].

81. Subillam ... apothanein: L, "Sibyl /
at Cumae I with my own eyes...." H, "What

do you want?" L, "She replied." H, "To die." [cf. Petronius, *Satiricon* XLVIII, 8. Pound alludes to this passage in reference to a lady named Poke, said to be 110 or 115 years old, whom JA visited on July 2, 1770. Cf. also the epigraph to Eliot's *The Waste Land*, based on the same source.] With several others JA walked a quarter of a mile to see Mrs. Poke: "We looked in at the window and saw an object of horror." When told who had come, she said: "Gentlemen . . . I am glad to see them; I want them to pray for me; . . . I have been praying so long for deliverance" [II, 244-245].

82. Nantasket: A point on Beacon Island, where Boston Light stands, opposite Nantasket; JA visited the island on August 19, 1770.

83. non vi sed saepe legendo: L, "not by violence, but by frequent reading" [II, 248]. JA relates a story about how he and some friends were trying to recollect an old Latin distich. They remembered the first line, 'Gutta cavat lapidem, non vi, sed saepe cadendo" ["The drop wears away the stone, not by force, but by constant dripping"], but couldn't remember the second; but JA recollects it and records it later: "Sic homo fit doctus, non vi, sed saepe legendo" ["So man becomes learned, not by violence, but by constant reading"].

84. Severn Ayres: S. Ayers, member of the Virginia House of Burgesses in 1770, visited Cambridge with JA on August 22, 1770.

85. Mr Bull: William B., 1710-1791, colonial lieutenant governor of South Carolina, visited Cambridge with JA on August 22, 1770.

86. Mr Trapier: An acquaintance who visited Cambridge with JA on August 22, 1770.

87. Chas Second's time: Reference to a tax, dating from the reign of Charles II. JA says Ayers told him about it: ". . . two shillings a hogshead upon all tobacco exported from the Colony, to his Majesty forever. This duty

amounts now to a revenue of five thousand pounds sterling a year, which is given, part to the Governor, part to the Judges, &c. to the amount of about four thousand pounds, and what becomes of the other one thousand is unknown. The consequence of this is, that the Governor calls an Assembly when he pleases, and that is only once in two years" [II, 249-250]. The reference to *Carolina* may be a misprint for *Virginia*, the home colony of Colonel Severn Ayers.

88. which wd / render: JA's reaction to stories about new policies regarding law in the colonies [II, 252].

89. green tea: Served at a dinner JA attended at John Hancock's home on February 14, 1771. JA: ". . . and spent the whole afternoon, and drank green tea, from Holland, I hope, but don't know" [II, 255].

90. recovered at Braintree: JA's reference to fatigue from his journey from Northborough to Boston to Braintree on May 1, 1771.

91. Stood by . . . : A diary entry for May 2, 1771: "I have very cheerfully sacrificed my interest, and my health, and ease and pleasure, in the service of the people. I have stood by their friends longer than they would stand by them. I have stood by the people" [II, 260].

92. 1771 make potash: JA's reference to commerce in Connecticut.

93. Hartford and Middletown: JA's diary (June 8, 1771) contains a detailed account of these two Connecticut towns which he visited.

94. just as we got there: At Bissell's in Windsor, Connecticut, JA on his journey home June 10, 1771.

95. One party . . . 13th, Thursday: JA is concerned about implications of reports in that day's paper on new harmony between Governor Hutchinson and the leadership of the patriots. He feels that everyone else has returned to "confidence and affection" for the governor except himself, and so he feels "quite left alone in the world" [II, 279].

96. landlady: At Treadwell's in Ipswich, where JA boarded June 22, 1771, he found preoccupation with Puritan emphasis on sin.

97. Governor Endicott: John E., ?1589-1665, one of six persons who bought the patent from Plymouth Council in England for territory on Massachusetts Bay; acted as first governor of the colony (1628) until Winthrop took charge (1630); served as assistant governor, deputy governor, and governor at various times (1630-1664).

98. Indian preacher: JA recorded this anecdote after an unremarkable day in court: "The Indian preacher cried, Good God! that ever Adam and Eve should eat that apple, when they knew in their own souls it would make good cider" [II, 289].

99. Mrs Rops: Pound's source reads "Mrs. Ropes." JA had tea at Judge Ropes's on November 9, 1771.

100. Tells old stories: Refers to a Colonel Pickman with whom JA spent the evening of November 9, 1771.

101. Always convinced that the liberties: JA's reflections on Governor Shirley's remarks about the "brace of Adams." John and Samuel Adams believed Hutchinson was most dangerous because they had direct knowledge of "his character, his unbounded ambition, and his unbounded popularity" [II, 295].

102. 'Is mere impertinence a contempt?': James Otis's explanation of the question he would raise in court concerning the proposal that "your Honors are to be paid your salaries, for the future, by the Crown out of a revenue raised from us without our consent" [II, 298-299, 300]. The controversy over the independence of the judges was to occupy JA's attention in 1773-74 and would lead him to draw up articles of impeachment against Chief Justice Peter Oliver for his refusal to renounce the salary grants from the Crown [62:45].

103. Hutchinson: In the three years after 1770, the year of the Boston Massacre and the repeal of the Townshend Acts (in which duties on all items except tea were eliminated), Massachusetts province had enjoyed a measure of tranquility, and Governor Hutchinson, thinking that the patriot movement was fading, addressed the General Court in January 1773, declaring that "the Parliament of Great Britain had an authority supreme, sovereign, absolute, and uncontrollable over the Colonies, in all cases whatsoever," and especially in matters of taxation. To JA the presumption of such a speech clearly exhibited Hutchinson's "plenitude" of "vanity and self-sufficiency" [II, 311].

104. Moore: Sir Francis M., 1558-1621, English law reporter; his most important work, often called "Moore's Reports," is *Cases Collect and Report* (1663). When JA was consulted to help frame a reply to Governor Hutchinson's speech of January 1773, he contributed passages "from a law authority which no man in Massachusetts, at that time, had ever read. Hutchinson and all his law counsels were in fault; they could catch no scent. They dared not deny it, lest the book should be produced to their confusion.... The book was Moore's Reports. The owner of it, for alas! master, it was borrowed, was a buyer, but not a reader, of books. It had been Mr. Gridley's" [II, 313].

105. Mr Gridley: Jeremiah G., 1702-1767 [63:27]. Gridley had been JA's legal patron.

106. N/Y state has done: In early 1773 JA began publishing in the *Boston Gazette* a series of eight letters, arguing the necessity of the independence of the judges, in response to a General Brattle, who approved of salary grants from the Crown for the judges. Some of the principles JA espoused in these letters were later incorporated in the New York state constitution, in the Massachusetts state constitution, and in the federal constitution of 1787.

107. Hutchinson's letters: On December 2, 1772, Benjamin Franklin, then London agent of the Massachusetts House of Representatives, sent a letter to the speaker of the House, Thomas Cushing, and included with it seventeen letters from the years 1767-1769 written by Hutchinson, Andrew Oliver, Moffat, Paxton, and Rome. How Franklin secured the correspondence was not revealed, but after the letters had been made public Franklin lost his position as postmaster general; in England Sir John Temple, the person suspected of delivering the letters to Franklin, fought a duel with Thomas Whately, to whom the letters were originally sent; and the Massachusetts House of Representatives petitioned for the removal of Hutchinson and Andrew Oliver from their offices. Hutchinson's letter of January 20, 1769, contained the passages most offensive to the colonists, including the statement, "There must be an abridgement of what are called English liberties" [a detailed account of this episode is in Butterfield, II, 80 n. 1].

108. Oliver: Andrew O. Oliver was secretary and lieutenant governor of Massachusetts and stamp officer to enforce the Stamp Act in Massachusetts. He advocated the dispatch of British troops to America and the prosecution of Samuel Adams for his political agitation [cf. 12 above].

109. Moffat: Thomas Moffatt, d. after 1779, loyalist of Rhode Island; comptroller of the customs at New London (ca. 1770). He left America in 1775.

110. Paxton: Charles P., 1704-1788, British commissioner of customs at Boston and head of the Board of Commissioners. He left America in 1776.

111. Rome: George R., d. after 1788, loyalist merchant of Newport, Rhode Island; during the Revolution he served as a contractor for the royal forces.

112. Sir John Temple: According to CFA, Sir John Temple was responsible for delivering the purloined letters to Benjamin Franklin; Temple fought a duel with Thomas Whately in England over this allegation [II, 319 n. 1].

113. Col. Haworth: Colonel Howarth. On August 30, 1773, JA dined at the home of his wife's uncle; an inconspicuous guest on this occasion was a Colonel Howarth.

114. Bohea: A kind of tea, a reference to the Boston Tea Party of December 16, 1773.

115. House: The Massachusetts colonial legislature consisted of a lower house, the House of Representatives, and an upper house, the Council.

116. Gridley: Benjamin G., b. 1732, d. before 1800; nephew of Jeremiah Gridley [63:27], a loyalist who went to England in 1776. The reference here is to the winter of 1773-74 when JA was assisting Major Hawley and other members of a committee to draft articles of impeachment against Chief Justice Peter Oliver for his refusal to renounce salary grants from the Crown.

CANTO LXV

Sources

Charles Francis Adams, ed., *The Works of John Adams*, II, III; Frederick K. Sanders, *John Adams Speaking*, Orono, Maine, 1975, 174-264; EP, *SR*, 42.

Background

L. H. Butterfield, ed., *Diary and Autobiography of John Adams*, II,III; Cambridge, Mass., 1961; Samuel Flagg Bemis, *A Diplomatic History of the United States*, New York, 1936; Richard B. Morris, *The Peacemakers: The Great Powers and American Independence*, New York, 1965; Peter Shaw, *The Character of John Adams*, Chapel Hill, N.C., 1974; Page Smith, *John Adams*, 2 vols., Garden City, N.Y., 1962; Carl Van Doren, *Secret History of the American Revolution*, New York, 1941.

Exegeses

CE, *Ideas*, 43, 176, 177; Dekker, *Cantos*, 185-186; Davis, *Vision*, 122, 139-140; DP, *Barb*, 232.

Glossary

1. Chief Justice: Peter Oliver. JA, in his *Autobiography*, refers to jurors in Massachusetts who refused to serve under Chief Justice Oliver while he faced articles of impeachment drawn by JA in 1774 [62:45].

2. Moses Gill: Lieutenant governor of Massachusetts (1794-1800), here mentioned by JA's friend, Justice Samuel Pemberton, as another example of how justices can be controlled by money [JA's diary, March 13, 1774].

3. (His Majesty): George III of England. JA's diary [Aug. 20, 1774] included a description of this statue and other sights observed on a tour of New York City made by JA when he stopped there on his journey to the First Continental Congress in Philadelphia.

4. the Province: Royal province of New York, established 1685-1717; area of the present state of New York.

5. Hakluyt: Richard H., ?1552-1616, English historian and geographer.

6. J. Cabot: John C. Pound's source, JA's diary [Aug. 23, 1774], refers to "the Voyage of Sebastian Cabot." Sebastian Cabot, ?1476-1557, was the son of John Cabot,

1450-1498, erroneously mentioned by Pound. JA recommended this account to Ebenezer Hazard, a New York bookseller who was seeking advice about documents concerning early American history. Hazard eventually published a collection of such documents under the title *Historical Collections; Consisting of State Papers ... Intended as Materials for an History of the United States*, Philadelphia, 1792-1794.

7. Hudibras tavern: Tavern near Nassau Hall College in Princeton, New Jersey, where JA stopped on August 27, 1774. The president of the College of New Jersey, John Witherspoon, D.D., later to sign the Declaration of Independence for New Jersey, suggested to JA the employment of writers favorable to the cause of the colonists in English newspapers.

8. Washington: In Philadelphia, JA heard from Thomas Lynch, Sr., of South Carolina the widely reported story (now regarded as apocryphal) of George Washington's offer, in a speech at the Virginia Convention, to help Boston.

9. Patrick Henry: Pound begins his redaction of JA's notes of the debates of the First Continental Congress with Patrick Henry's declaration of a new national identity (Sept. 6, 1774).

10. in capite: Refers to the holding of land under direct grant of the lord or king; lit., "in chief" [cf. 11 below].

11. Galloway: Joseph G., ?1729-1803, American lawyer and loyalist; member of Pennsylvania colonial legislature (1756-1764; 1765-1775); member of Continental Congress (1774-75). Galloway's first remarks, in JA's notes on the debates, argued that the English Constitution was founded on the ancient principle that landholders, tenants in capite, had a right to vote. Thus the ancestors of the present colonists, when they came to America, would have been bound by laws made before they left England but not by laws subsequently passed by Parliament since they, the landholders in the New World, tenants in capite, had had no vote on those laws. According to JA's notes [Sept. 8, 1774], Galloway said: "I have ever thought we might reduce our rights to one—an exemption from all laws made by British Parliament since the emigration of our ancestors." But although Galloway recognized that these sentiments identified him with the independence movement, he was a loyalist who believed the solution to the current grievances was a "British American legislature" under the Crown, as his Galloway Plan proposed (Sept. 28, 1774).

12. Bill of Rights: A reference to the committee selected by the Congress "to prepare a bill of rights or a declaration of the rights of the Colonies." JA was appointed to the committee.

13. Mr Rutledge: John R., 1739-1800, American statesman; member of Continental Congress (1774-1776; 1782-83); governor of South Carolina (1779-1782); associate justice of U.S. Supreme Court (1789-1791); appointed chief justice (1795) but appointment not confirmed [II, 373-375].

14. Turtle . . .: JA dined at Mr. Willing's. "A most splendid feast, again—turtle and

every thing else." Afterward he went to the Moravian evening lecture [*Diary*, Sept. 11, 1774] where the audience heard "soft, sweet music, and a Dutchified English prayer and preachment."

15. 17th of September: On this day in 1774 the Continental Congress endorsed the "Suffolk Resolves" of Suffolk County, Massachusetts. Parliament, during the summer of 1774, had passed the so-called Intolerable Acts, whose most important provision was that the port of Boston should be closed until the tea destroyed the preceding December had been paid for. The "Suffolk Resolves" declared the Intolerable Acts null and void. JA was happy with sentiments expressed: "This day convinced me that America will support the Massachusetts or perish with her" [II, 380].

16. American legislature: The preceding quotation refers to Patrick Henry's criticism of the Galloway Plan which proposed the creation of an American legislature under the British Crown. Henry believed the Crown would try to bribe any assembly under its authority.

17. Domenica: Dominica, island and British colony in British West Indies, mentioned in a committee resolution concerning a non-importation policy.

18. Philadelphy: The First Continental Congress adjourned on October 26, 1774, and two days later JA left Philadelphia to return home.

19. 2nd petition: The second petition to the king, the "olive branch petition" proposed by John Dickinson in an effort at reconciliation to head off independence. JA saw it as a delaying tactic and was extremely disappointed when Congress approved it in July 1775 and sent it to the king.

20. Mr Hancock: When the Second Continental Congress convened in May 1775, JA recognized that, in addition to factional disputes over independence or loyalty to

England, there was a strong sectional division between representatives of the northern and southern colonies. To get unified support in the Congress for the army before Boston, JA decided that a Southerner should be appointed its commander. He nominated George Washington, Samuel Adams seconded, and the Congress voted its approval. But John Hancock, who was presiding officer of the Congress at the time, wanted the position of commander-in-chief for himself and was bitterly disappointed when he realized that JA had turned his back on a fellow citizen of Massachusetts.

21. Dickenson: John Dickinson, 1732-1808, American statesman; member of Continental Congress (1774, 1775, 1779) and delegate from Delaware to federal Constitutional Convention. In 1767 Dickinson had begun publishing *Letters from a Farmer in Pennsylvania to the Inhabitants of the British Colonies* to protest the Townshend Acts passed in the summer of 1767. But at the Continental Congress Dickinson worked tirelessly for reconciliation with England, proposed the second petition (the "olive branch petition"), and resisted independence until he saw his position decisively defeated in July 1776.

22. alum: JA, on January 28, 1776, noted in his diary how alum could be extracted from a certain stone found in Brookfield, Massachusetts, according to his host, Mr. Upham.

23. yr/ladyship: Abigail Adams, as JA addressed her in his letter of October 11, 1776, explaining that he had obtained leave from the Continental Congress to return home.

24. Red Lion: An inn between Philadelphia and Bristol, Pennsylvania, where JA stopped on October 13, 1776, on his way home.

25. Bethelehem: Bethlehem, town in Pennsylvania. Almost a year had elapsed since JA stopped at the Red Lion [cf. 24 above]. On September 19, 1777, JA and other members of the Continental Congress left Philadelphia, fearing that the city would fall to

the British army commanded by Sir William Howe. During his absence JA visited the Moravian community at Bethlehem where he saw the mills and works described [II, 440].

26. sharing house: Pound's source reads "shearer's house."

27. no account of the powder: Pound's source reads "produced an account of the powder" [II, 448 n. 2].

28. Cushing: [62:51]. Cushing said: "I . . . winter." R. R. Livingston [33.7] said: "Ammunition cannot be had, unless we open our ports. I am for doing away our non-exportation agreement entirely." Chase [62:76] said: "We can't support the war and our taxes without trade. . . . We must trade with foreign nations . . . export our tobacco to France, Spain or any other foreign nation" [II, 453-455].

29. Rutledge: Edward R. [62:74]. He said: "Take . . . precarious," [II, 455]. Livingston said: "The Americans are their own carriers now, chiefly."

30. Mr Zubly: John Joachim Z., 1725-1781, clergyman, delegate to Continental Congress from Georgia (1775), although he was more a loyalist in sentiment than a Revolutionary. He published several political pamphlets: *The Stamp Act Repealed* (1766) and *The Law of Liberty* (1775). He said: "The navy can stop our harbors and distress our trade; therefore it is impracticable to open our ports" [II, 457]. Pound has changed the word "impracticable" to "imperative" which reverses the meaning of the line in the source.

31. Spain: Lee said: "Suppose provisions should be sold in Spain for money, and cash sent to England for powder." Prob. Richard Henry Lee, 1732-1794, delegate from Virginia to Continental Congress and signer of Declaration of Independence [II, 461; cf. 53 below].

32. Livingston: Robert R. L., member of Continental Congress [33:7]. He said: "We are between hawk and buzzard; we puzzle ourselves between the commercial and war-like opposition" [II, 461].

33. pleased that: CFA has a headnote saying that on October 10, 1775, the Congress adopted a resolution recommending that the Convention of New Jersey raise two battalions, composed as stated in the four canto lines.

34. Who to appoint ...: JA posed the question of appointment.

35. Personal friends: Chase [62:76] said: "In my Province, we want officers. Gentlemen have recommended persons, from personal friendships, who were not suitable" [II, 467]. Ward [Samuel W., Rhode Island delegate] said: "I would rather take the opinion of General Washington [about the appointment of officers] than of any convention" [II, 468].

36. Trade ... houses: These seven lines are Pound's summary of the issues raised and commented on by JA in "Notes/Debates" (Oct. 10, 1775) in the Continental Congress.

37. Mr Zubly: [cf. 30 above]. The 17 lines from "Everything we want" through "*in terrorem*" [L, literally "in terror"; in law, "as a warning"] are a précis of Zubly's speech on October 12, 1775 [II, 469-470].

38. (commerciabili?): I, "for trade."

39. Deane: Silas D., 1737-1789, member of Connecticut legislature and later of Continental Congress (1774-1776); served as one of American commissioners in Paris. Charged with profiteering during this mission (1778), he was unable to clear himself and spent the rest of his life in exile. In 1842 Congress granted restitution to his heirs. As Deane's successor in Paris, JA found his records as commissioner very confusing. On October 20, 1775, Deane said: "I would have traders prohibited from importing unnecessary articles, and from exporting live stock, except horses." Chase [62:76] said: "We have letters from Guadaloupe, Martinique,

and the Havana, that they will supply us with powder for tobacco."

40. Guadaloupe: Guadeloupe, name applied to two islands in French West Indies, Basse-Terre and Grande Terre; separated by a narrow channel.

41. Martinique: [28:42].

42. Jay: [62:131]. The four lines give the sense of what Jay said.

43. Wythe: George W., 1726-1806, American jurist and statesman; member of Continental Congress from Virginia (1775-76); signer of Declaration of Independence. His speech, summarized in the two lines, led to the formation of a committee which brought in a resolution: "That two more vessels be fitted out with all expedition" [II, 484n].

44. 6th April: CFA comments: "This discussion was continued from time to time until the sixth of April [1777], when the Congress came in to sundry resolutions taking off the restrictions on trade" [II, 485].

45. oblige Britain: It was JA's idea that an American navy would "oblige Britain to keep a navy on foot, the expense of which will be double to what they will take from us."

46. FAECE ... republica!: L, "in the dung of Romulus, not in Plato's republic!" [cf. Cicero, *Epp. ad Atticum* II, i, 8]. Wythe [cf. 43 above] used the Cicero quotation and gave the substance of the next five lines, except that he said: "By inviting foreign powers [not "powders"] to make treaties of commerce with us" [II, 486].

47. Bristol: Port city, Gloucestershire, England.

48. Liverpool: Port city, Lancashire, England.

49. Resolved ... sail cloth: The Continental Congress adopted four different resolutions embodying the sense of these seven lines.

50. France: From JA's notes for a speech given on March 1, 1776. He adds to the

question Pound uses in the canto line:
"... to join with Britain, or to join with
the Colonies? Is it not her interest to dis-
member the British empire?" [II, 488].

51. Resentment ... without it: From JA's
notes for a speech given on March 4, 1776.

52. Hooper: William H., 1742-1790, mem-
ber of Continental Congress (1774-1777)
and signer of Declaration of Independence.

53. Lee: Richard Henry L., 1732-1794,
American statesman; with Patrick Henry and
Thomas Jefferson he initiated the intercolo-
nial Committees of Correspondence (1773);
delegate from Virginia to Continental Con-
gress (1774-1780) where he supported JA's
proposal to negotiate a treaty with France;
signer of Declaration of Independence; again
a member of Congress (1784-1789); member
of Senate (1789-1792).

54. Sherman: Roger S., 1721-1793, Ameri-
can jurist and statesman; judge of Connecti-
cut superior court (1766-1767; 1773-1788);
member of Continental Congress (1774-
1782; 1784) where he supported JA's pro-
posal to negotiate a treaty with France;
signer of Declaration of Independence;
member of House of Representatives (1789-
1791) and of Senate (1791-1793).

55. Gadsden: Christopher G., 1724-1805,
American Revolutionary leader; delegate
from South Carolina to Continental Con-
gress (1774-1776) where he supported JA's
proposal to negotiate a treaty with France;
served as brigadier general in Continental
Army (1776-1778).

56. Rush: Benjamin R., ?1745-1813, Ameri-
can physician and political leader; member
of Continental Congress from Pennsylvania
(1776-77) and signer of Declaration of
Independence; surgeon in Continental Army
(1777-78); member of Pennsylvania Consti-
tutional Ratification Convention (1787);
treasurer of U.S. mint (1797-1813). JA, in
a letter dated August 6, 1822, is relating
his memory of events leading up to the
Declaration of Independence. He wrote that
he and some friends met Rush and the

others listed with him here on a trip from
Massachusetts to Philadelphia. During that
meeting Rush told him of the rumors being
spread that the Sons of Liberty in Boston
were being represented "as four desperate
adventurers" [II, 512-515n].

57. Franklin: Pound's addition; Benjamin
Franklin is not mentioned as being present
in the source [II, 512n]. Pound appears to
have transcribed *Frankfort*, the place where
Dr. Rush, Mr. Mifflin, and Mr. Bayard met
the Massachusetts delegation, as *Franklin.*

58. Bayard: John Bukenheim B., 1738-
1807, Philadelphia merchant; colonel in
Philadelphia Volunteers during Revolution;
member of Continental Congress (1785-86).

59. Mifflin: Thomas M., 1744-1800, Ameri-
can Revolutionary officer and statesman;
member of Continental Congress from
Pennsylvania (1774-1776; 1782-1784) and
its president (1783); aide-de-camp to Gen-
eral Washington (1775) and later major
general; member of Constitutional Conven-
tion (1787).

60. Mr Jefferson ... slavery: These six lines
are from JA's recollections, in a letter
written to Timothy Pickering on August 6,
1822, of how the Declaration of Indepen-
dence came to be written by Thomas Jeffer-
son and approved in its present form by the
Continental Congress.

61. Board of War: Special committee
selected by the Continental Congress and
headed by JA in the summer and fall of
1776 to act as intermediary between Con-
gress and the military. It was activated by a
resolution adopted on September 18, 1775.
JA said it kept him "in continual employ-
ment ... from the 12th of June, 1776, till
the 11th of November, 1777, when I left
Congress forever." The board was charged
specifically to do the things listed, beginning
with "To contract ..." [III, 3, 6].

62. had conversed ... plundah': Letters
from London prompted the Congress, on
October 5, 1775, to appoint a committee
of three "to prepare a plan for intercepting

two vessels ... on their way to Canada, laden with arms and powder." JA says that his experience talking with the fishermen in New England convinced him that "if they were once let loose upon the ocean, they would contribute greatly to the relief of our wants, as well as to the distress of the enemy." JA was all for such action. Those who opposed the idea used the argument that its implementation would have a bad effect on the words and characters of the seamen [II, 6, 7] .

63. Lord Howe: Richard H., 1726-1799, 4th Viscount and 1st Earl; British naval officer who fought in American Revolution (1776-1778). JA made this remark to Lord Howe at the Staten Island Conference held September 11, 1776, to which JA, Benjamin Franklin, and Edward Rutledge had been sent by the Congress. Nothing came of the conference.

64. 88 battalions: The numerous resolutions recorded in the journal "contain the whole plan of an army of eighty-eight battalions, to be enlisted as soon as possible, to serve during the war" [III, 82n; CFA's editorial note] .

65. dash: John Langdon, 1741-1819; member of Continental Congress from New Hampshire (1775-76; 1786-87). Langdon enjoyed profitable business connections as long as Silas Deane was commissioner in Paris, so he regretted the decision of Congress to recall Deane and send JA in his place.

66. Ray de Chaumont: Donatien le Ray de C., who in 1778 donated his house at Passy to the American legation in Paris. He was influential and friendly toward the American Revolution and contributed supplies to American forces, but in his relationship with Silas Deane he encouraged private profiteering.

67. (1804): The year JA wrote his *Autobiography*, from which Pound has taken the lines referring to JA's visit to Lord Howe

and the affairs of Langdon, Deane, and Ray de Chaumont [III, 91-92] .

68. Capn Sam Tucker: Samuel T., 1747-1833, American naval officer; as captain of the *Franklin* and the *Hancock* he preyed on British shipping during the Revolution; he was commander of the frigate *Boston* which carried JA to his post as commissioner to France (1778).

69. W. Vernon: William V., 1719-1806, American merchant; in 1777 appointed chairman of the Navy Board of the Eastern Department.

70. J. Warren: James W., 1726-1808, Massachusetts political leader; paymaster general of Continental Army (1775-76); member of Navy Board (1776-1781); member of Massachusetts governor's council (1792-1794). His wife was Mercy Warren. He and Vernon signed the orders to Captain Tucker about the treatment of JA.

71. Navy Board: Navy Board of the Eastern Department, the American Continental Navy Board of Direction, established in Boston (1777) upon the recommendation of JA.

72. Sunday 15th: Date in February 1778 on which the *Boston* set sail. On the 19th Captain Tucker saw three large ships "bearing east, standing to the northward." He changed his course to see if they were chasing him. They were.

73. Smoke ... : JA's comment about "mal de mer."

74. in calm ... etcetera: Captain Tucker prepared to fight. JA notes: "[He] said his orders were to carry me to France, and to take any prizes that might fall in his way; he thought it his duty ... to avoid fighting, especially with an unequal force, if he could, but if he could not avoid an engagement, he would give them something that should make them remember him." The *Boston* lost sight of the enemy who did not seem "very ardent to overtake" the Americans. "But the wind increased to a hurricane" [III, 99]. The next 17 lines concern the effects of the hurricane. Pound interpolates the line "ane blasterend . . . ding" taken from the *Aeneid*, trans. Gavin Douglas.

75. Mr Johnnie: John Quincy Adams. JA took his eldest son, then 11, with him on his first journey to Europe in 1778, where he would act as his father's secretary, making copies of letters and duplicates of dispatches.

76. inexpressible . . . noise: These 11 lines are from JA's diary which contains a detailed criticism of the ship and its management. In fact, JA gave Captain Tucker a number of memos about how to run a ship and the captain followed them [III, 101-105].

77. What . . . army?: JA resolved that when he arrived "at any port in Europe" he would inquire first about the enemy: ". . . what is the state of the British nation? . . . what the state of finances and of stocks?" [III, 105-106].

78. So that . . . head: On Tuesday, March 9, Captain Tucker "spied a sail." He asked JA for permission to give chase "which was immediately granted." In his diary JA wrote: ". . . we soon came up with her; but as we had borne directly down upon her, she had not seen our broadside, and knew not our force. She was a letter of marque, with fourteen guns, eight nines, and six sixes. She fired upon us. . . . I happened to be upon the quarter deck . . . so that the ball went directly over my head. We, upon this, turned our broadside, which the instant she saw, she struck" [III, 108-109].

79. Tucker: CFA has a footnote about the story Captain Tucker told years later, a story that had doubtless "improved" with age. When he started to give chase to the enemy ship Tucker stipulated that JA would have to stay below in a safe place. "But no sooner had the battle commenced, than he was seen on deck, with a musket in his hands, fighting as a common marine." Ordered below again, JA still would not behave. When the captain's back was turned, he resumed firing until finally Tucker said:

"Why are you here, sir? I am commanded by the Continental Congress to carry you in safety to Europe, and I will do it" [III, 109n].

80. The Martha: English merchant ship, commanded by Captain McIntosh, which was captured (1778) by the *Boston*. It was loaded with a valuable cargo. Thus it was that the captain and four of his men were taken prisoners on the *Boston*, and the *Martha* was dispatched to Boston as a war prize with the consent of JA, who said in his diary: "The Captain is very much of a gentleman" [III, 109].

81. Oleron: Île d'Oléron, island in Bay of Biscay at mouth of Charente River in France; noted for its Laws of Oléron, a medieval code of maritime laws which forms the basis of modern maritime law. JA wrote of his landfall in Europe: "We have been becalmed all day in sight of Oléron" [*Diary*, March 29, 1778].

82. Bordeaux, at Blaye: Major port city on Gironde estuary; Blaye-et-Sainte-Luce is a village N of Bordeaux on the Gironde. JA wrote in his diary: "My first inquiry should be, who is Agent for the United States of America at Bordeaux, at Blaye, &c" [III, 116].

83. de lonh: P, "far-off." From a song by Jaufre Rudel [cf. *SR*, 42].

84. First dish . . . coops: These seven lines concern a dinner JA was invited to by the captain of a French ship in port bound for St. Domingue [III, 117].

85. the King: Louis XVI of France.

86. 4 sorts: Someone told JA that of "the first growths of wines in the Province of Guienne there are four sorts," and Pound lists them [III, 118].

87. fish and bean salad . . .: Source reads: ". . . we had fish and bread, and salad. . . ." JA was invited to dine with a Mr. McCreery "in the fashion of the country." After dinner they went to the opera [III, 118].

88. Trompette: Chateau near Bordeaux visited by JA on April 2, 1778.

89. Vauban: Sébastien Le Prestre, Marquis de V., 1633-1707, French military engineer; commissary general of fortifications (1678); marshal of France (1703).

90. Louis XV: [64:5].

91. Malesherbes: Chrétien Guillaume de Lamoignon de M., 1721-1794, French states-man and writer on politics and law; banished by Louis XV but recalled (1774) by Louis XVI; minister of the interior (1775-76). Here the premier-president of the Parlia-ment of Bordeaux has told JA that he sym-pathizes with all who suffer in the cause of liberty, since he himself had been banished because of his cooperation with Malesherbes in the reign of Louis XV [III, 119].

92. 'Les deux avares': A play by Fenouillot de Falbaire de Quingey (1770), which JA saw on April 2, 1778, while in Bordeaux.

93. Lights in the garden . . . : The people of Bordeaux gave a garden party to honor JA before his departure. It was "beautifully illuminated." The source reads: "God save the Congress, Liberty and Adams." The caps and curve are Pound's idea.

94. Their eagerness . . . : As JA passed through Châtellerault on his way to Paris, his carriage stopped for a change of horses and was immediately surrounded by young women selling knives and scissors [III, 121].

95. Rue Richelieu: Rue de Richelieu, street in Paris, runs past the Bibliothèque Nationale and the Palais Royal to the Louvre.

96. Hôtel de Valois: Hotel in Paris on the Rue de Richelieu where JA stayed upon his arrival in Paris.

97. Basse Cour: The house in Passy, form-erly the Hôtel de Valentinois, donated to the American ministers (1778) by Donatien le Ray de Chaumont. Benjamin Franklin lived there, and JA, aware of the reputation of Silas Deane, observed: "Although Mr.

Deane, in addition to these [apartments and furniture], had a house, furniture, and equipage, in Paris, I determined to put my country to no further expense on my account, but to take my lodgings under the same roof with Dr. Franklin, and to use no other equipage than his, if I could avoid it" [III, 123].

98. Mr Schweighauser: John Daniel S., U.S. commercial agent at Nantes. JA found the records and affairs of the commissioners charged with making military and other supplies in total disarray; there were few if any financial records. One of his first pro-jects was to bring order out of chaos and establish legitimate business records. Thus he wrote a series of letters to people who demanded money and put them off unless they could produce documents.

99. Lee: Arthur L., 1740-1792, American diplomat; appointed in 1776 by the Con-tinental Congress as one of the three com-missioners to negotiate a treaty with France; becoming suspicious of his associates, Benjamin Franklin and Silas Deane, Lee circulated charges against them. After the treaty was signed (1778) Deane was recalled; he charged in return that Lee did not have the confidence of the French foreign minis-ter. Lee was then recalled in 1779. Lee served in the Continental Congress (1781-1785), was a member of the Treasury Board (1784-1789), and opposed the adop-tion of the Constitution. But since JA and he agreed about settling accounts, Franklin joined in signing the letters.

100. J. Williams: Jonathan W., 1750-1815, American diplomat and army officer; lived abroad from 1776 to 1785 and acted at times as a purchasing agent for the colonies; superintendent of West Point (1805-1812). He was the grandnephew of Benjamin Franklin. This and the preceding reference reflect JA's concern that the financial records of the American commissioners, in some disarray as a result of the dealings of Silas Deane and, JA thought, the carelessness of Benjamin Franklin, be put in order as promptly as possible.

101. Mr Beaumarchais: [31:29].

102. Madame Helvetius: Anne Catherine H., 1719-1800, Countess of Ligniville d'Autricourt, wife of Claude Adrien Helvétius, French philospher.

103. Long Champ: Longchamp, racecourse in Bois de Boulogne, Paris, which JA visited on April 17, 1778. An annual parade of carriages took place there on Good Friday; the practice started because the theaters were closed for the week before Easter and fashionable people became "*si ennuyés* "so bored" that they cannot live" [III, 133].

104. descent: Pound's source reads "decent" [III, 136]. The word is used to describe the family of Mr. Ferdinand Grand, a Protestant from Switzerland who lived near JA at Passy and who, JA discovered, had "obtained the reputation and emolument of being the banker to the American ministers" [III, 136].

105. M. Condorcet: [31:37]. On April 20, 1778, JA dined at the home of the Duchesse d'Enville, whose guests included nobles, abbots, and M Condorcet. JA supposed his whiteness came from hard study.

106. Bancroft: Edward B., 1744-1821, American scientist and secret agent. During the American Revolution he served as a secret agent for the American commissioners in Paris and as a double agent for the British. In view of what is now known about Bancroft, JA's fear of spies in Paris proves to have been well founded [Van Doren, op. cit.].

107. the Lees: The brothers Arthur Lee, American diplomat, and William Lee (1739-1795), American merchant and diplomat. William Lee was appointed U.S. commercial agent in France (1777); negotiated a commercial treaty, never ratified, with Holland (1778); recalled by Congress (1779).

108. Voltaire: Assumed name of François Marie Arouet (1694-1778), French philoso-

pher. On April 27, 1778, JA attended a performance of Voltaire's *Alzire* and found himself seated near Voltaire.

109. Mme la Duchesse d'Agen: Henriette-Anne-Louise d'Aguesseau de Fresne, Duchesse d'Ayen, wife of Jean François Paul de Noailles. F, "Madame the Duchess d'Agen has five or six children contrary to the custom of the country." Source reads: "Mme la Duchesse d'Ayen a cinq ou six enfans, contre la coutume de ce pays çi" [III, 149].

110. des Noailles: Distinguished French family; head of the family during the time JA was in France was Philippe de Noailles, duc de Mouchy, 1715-1794, marshal of France; he was guillotined in 1794. The Marquis de Lafayette represented this family in the American Revolution, serving under General Washington. For faithful service to the Crown of France the Noailles family received "eighteen millions of livres [pounds, not louis d'or] annually from the crown" [III, 149].

111. The King's bed chamber: JA's first audience with Louis XVI of France, May 8, 1778, at Versailles.

112. Mr Deane: Silas D., 1737-1789, American diplomat and commercial representative in France in 1776 [cf. 39 above].

113. Many other qualities: JA's characterization of the French people: "There was a sort of morality. There was a great deal of humanity, and what appeared to me real benevolence. Even their politeness was benevolence. There was a great deal of charity and tenderness for the poor. There were many other qualities that I could not distinguish from virtues" [III, 171].

114. His Majesty: Louis XVI of France.

115. Offer to make 200 peers: Refers to a letter delivered anonymously to the American commissioners in Paris, interpreted as expressing sentiments of King George III of England, recommending that America be governed by a congress of American peers appointed by the king.

116. Mme du Barry: Marie Jeanne Bécu, 1743-1793, Comtesse Du Barry, mistress of Louis XV of France. On July 17, 1778, JA strolled to the house of Madame Du Barry but did not visit her because of the late hour.

117. Turgot: [31:35]. On November 26, 1778, after dining with the abbés Chalut and Arnous, JA returned to Passy to find Turgot, Condillac, and Mme. Helvétius present.

118. Condillac: Étienne Bonnot de C., 1715-1780, French philosopher.

119. Mme Helvetius: [102 above].

120. M. Genet: Edmé-Jacques Genêt, 1715-1781, head of Bureau of Correspondence of French Department of Foreign Affairs (1762). He was a close friend when JA was in France, and he supported American independence, editing, with help from Benjamin Franklin and, later, from JA, *Affaires de l'Angleterre et de l'Amerique* (1776-1779). His son, Edmond Charles Genêt (1763-1834), succeeded his father in the French foreign office; but when Edmond came to the U.S. as first minister of the French Republic (1793), calling himself "Citizen Genêt," he behaved so intemperately that the Washington administration demanded his recall to France.

121. Barbier de Séville: Play by Beaumarchais, first presented in 1775, which JA saw performed on April 14, 1779, in Nantes, where he had stopped on his way home.

122. Comédie: Theater in Nantes.

123. electrical eel: While at Nantes waiting to sail for home, JA enjoyed dinner talk: "At dinner, much conversation about the electrical eel, which gives a shock to a ring of persons, like the touch of a bottle or conductor. What is the name of this fish?" [III,199].

124. P. Jones: John Paul J., 1747-1792, naval officer serving America during the Revolution. JA met him at Nantes in May 1779. Between the line about Jones's voice

and the next canto line much happened. JA returned to the U.S. on the French frigate, the *Sensible*, arriving at Boston on August 2, 1779. On the 9th JA was chosen to represent Braintree at the convention called to frame a constitution for Massachusetts. After he served at the convention, he sailed again on the *Sensible* for Europe on November 13. The ship, leaking badly from damage in heavy weather, reached El Ferrol (near Corunna) in Galicia, Spain, on December 8 [III, 229, headnote; 229-231].

125. Visigoths: West Goths; founded kingdom in Spain, S France, and N Africa.

126. Justinian: J. I, 483-565, Byzantine emperor (527-565). His greatest accomplishment, codification of Roman law, called *Corpus Juris Civilis*, was done under his direction by Tribonian. This code and the "Laws of the Visigoths" were mentioned to JA by the French consul from Corunna, M Detournelles, who had come to El Ferrol to welcome JA and who extended to him and his party, including his sons John Quincy and Charles, many kindnesses during their stay in Corunna.

127. Galicia: Region and ancient kingdom in NW Spain.

128. Corunna: Seaport-commune of La Coruña Province in NW Spain from which JA began his overland journey to Paris on December 26, 1779. The canto lines from here to the middle of page 375 are JA's notes and reflections, recorded in his diary, on people, places, and things seen on this trip, which lasted ca. six weeks.

129. Chief Justice: President of the Sovereign Court of Galicia at Corunna whom JA visited on December 19.

130. la Belle Poule: French frigate anchored at Corunna; JA dined aboard on Christmas Eve [III, 240].

131. Galicia: JA's description of the house he stayed at in Castillano on December 27, early on his journey through N Spain.

132. O'Brien: Lewis O'B., an Irishman

whom JA met in Lugo, Spain, on December 30.

133. St James Campostella: St. James Compostela, church in Galicia where there is a shrine to St. James, a famous objective of pilgrims during the Middle Ages. JA gave an account of St. James in his diary entry for December 28 and wrote of meeting the Irishman O'Brien near the Lugo cathedral on the 30th, but he nowhere mentions Compostela. Pound added the word to complete the identification. Since the shrine was supposed to be the sepulcher of St. James, Pound may have visited it during the brief period he was acting as a tourist guide in Spain in 1906.

134. Frontenac: Prob. Frontignac, a French muscatel of the Pyrenees region.

135. Leon: Region in NW Spain comprising modern provinces of Léon, Salamanca, and Zamora. On New Year's Eve, 1779, JA wrote in his diary: "We are now on the highest ground of all, and within gun-shot of the line between Galice and Leon" [III, 245].

136. Valcaire: Valcarce, river in Léon Province, Spain, which JA described in his diary on January 1, 1780.

137. Astorga: Town in Léon Province, NW Spain, which JA reached on January 3, 1780.

138. Mauregato: Town near Astorga, Spain.

139. Hoy mismo ... tomaron: S, "Today have arrived at this square the knight / John Adams member / etc. / the Englishmen evacuating Rhode Island / the Americans took over" [III, 247].

140. Gazette de Madrid: While in Astorga JA was shown a copy of this newspaper containing the preceding passage.

141. Asturias: Mountainous region, NW Spain, described by JA in his diary on January 5.

142. Burgos: [3:16]. JA arrived here on January 11.

143. French consul: Detournelles, French consul at Corunna who took care of JA's party in December 1779.

144. Charent: Charente River, W France, which flows into the Bay of Biscay. JA noted that this river runs by the town of Angoulême, France, which his party passed by on February 4, 1780.

145. Vergennes: [41:45]. When JA arrived in Paris in February 1780, he carried with him two commissions from the Congress, one to negotiate a peace and the other to make a treaty of commerce with England. JA consulted Comte de Vergennes about making the commissions public, and Vergennes advised him to announce the peace commission but to keep the commerce commission secret. JA accepted the suggestion but refused to honor Vergennes's request that JA show him his instructions from Congress. JA believed that both commissions should be made known to the British and that Vergennes wanted to keep the U.S. "embroiled with England as much, and as long as possible," and to make the U.S. as dependent on France as possible. Only with the signing of the controversial Jay's Treaty with England (1794) was there to be normalization of trade with England, in JA's opinion. Vergennes's success in frustrating JA's efforts to be recognized in his full capacity as commissioner led JA to journey to Holland on his own initiative in the summer of 1780 in an effort to achieve an alliance there that would make the U.S. less dependent upon France. [III, 265].

146. John ... Baastun: Pound's comment about the effect of JA's success in extending US territorial rights to include the Atlantic fishing grounds.

147. Those who wish to investigate: JA thought that the members of the Continental Congress who had decided that American negotiation of a commerce treaty with England should be guided by the will of the French should be identified.

148. Amsterdam: [62:88]. On July 27,

1780, JA, with his sons John Quincy and Charles, set off for Amsterdam. At this time JA did not know that on June 20 Congress had commissioned him to seek a loan in the Netherlands.

149. rye, barley etc.: These five lines are from JA's account of what he saw while traveling to Brussels.

150. Italian style: On a visit to the cathedral in Brussels JA saw a picture in a tapestry "of a number of Jews stabbing the wafer, the *bon Dieu*, and blood gushing in streams from the bread. This insufferable piece of pious villany [sic] shocked me beyond measure; but thousands were before it, on their knees, adoring" [III, 268].

151. excellent character: Prince Charles, brother of the empress queen; uncle of the emperor and the queen of France. "He was extremely beloved by the people, and has left an excellent character. The Emperor did not like him, it is said" [III, 268].

152. Van der Capellen tot de Pol: [62:93]. In his diary [Jan. 14, 1781] JA noted Van der Capellen's view that those with English funds might try to protect their holdings by making a dishonorable peace.

153. Van Berckel: Engelbert Francois V. B., 1726-1796, pensioner of Amsterdam and friend of the American cause against England, took part in the first negotiations for a trade treaty between America and the Netherlands (1779).

154. Don Joas Tholomeno: D. J. Theolomico de Almeida, envoy extraordinary of Portugal at Paris Peace Conference (1782).

155. Mirabel: Comte Montagnini M., minister plenipotentiary of Victor Amadeus III, king of Sardinia, who asked JA why the British were reluctant to accept the fact of American independence [*Diary*, Sept. 14, 1782; III, 273].

156. aetat 46: JA was 46 years of age in 1782 when the treaties he had negotiated with the Dutch were prepared for signature.

157. Rheingrave: Rhinegrave de Salm, one of negotiators of Treaty of Paris (1783). JA dined with him September 14, 1782, at a formal dinner at court in Holland.

158. Colonel Bentinck: Berent Henrik B., 1753-1830, one of Dutch negotiators of Treaty of Paris. JA attended a formal dinner at court with him on September 14, 1782.

159. Prussian minister: Baron de Thulemeyer, minister from Prussia at the Paris Peace Conference (1783), whom JA met in Holland.

160. Verjaring ... Natie: Source reads "van" for "dan" and "op" for "of." D, from passage in *Rotterdamche Courant* copied by JA into his diary [Oct. 5, 1782]. The complete passage translates as follows: "It is remarkable that the States General have recognized the independence of the United States on exactly the 19th of April of this year, this day being the seventh anniversary of the battle at Lexington, and what makes the matter still more remarkable is that Mr. Adams' First Memorial, which has made such a deep impression on the Dutch nation, is dated 19 April 1781" [Butterfield, III, 14 and n. 2].

161. Deputies of Holland and Zeeland: Baron de Lynden de Blitterswyk and Baron Van den Santheuvel, who met JA at the State House for the signing of the treaty with the Dutch (Oct. 8, 1782). The source says "Zealand," largest of the Danish isles. Pound corrected the source to "Zeeland," a province in SW Netherlands.

162. firmness heaven has given you: Spoken by the French minister in Amsterdam, the Duke de la Vauguyon, to JA, upon learning that JA had been commissioned to go to Paris for peace negotiations with England [*Diary*, Oct. 1782]. Vauguyon, under instructions from Vergennes, had earlier tried to obstruct JA's mission in Holland.

163. Bruge: Bruges, capital of W Flanders, NW Belgium, once a great trading city.

164. Ostend: Port city of W Flanders Province, N Belgium.

165. vingt à . . . nourri: F, "twenty to twenty-five ships in the basin / . . . warehouses [or armories] of the city are filled / a man's day (is worth) 15 sous, / including food" [source reads "16 sous." Extract from the journal of Count Sarsfield for June 5, 1782; III, 283].

166. Count Sarsfield: Guy Claude, Comte de S., 1718-1789, French military officer and amateur philosopher who sought out JA's friendship during JA's stay in Holland.

167. Œuvre . . . de Vauguyon: F, "the work of the Duke of Vauguyon." Pound's source reads "ouvrage" [III, 285].

168. 16,000 times: JA's diary [Oct. 11, 1782] reads: "Spent most of the day in signing obligations for the United States. It is hard work to sign one's name sixteen hundred [sic] times after dinner" [III, 288-289].

169. Mr Vischer: Visscher, a pensioner of the Hague, with whom JA conversed on October 15, 1782.

170. the Stadtholder: William V, 1748-1806, Prince of Orange, stadtholder of the Netherlands (1751-1795).

171. le plus . . . une: F, "the biggest t . . . of this country / stubborn as a . . ." [III, 291]. [Butterfield, III, 28 n. 1, suggests the first phrase might read *le plus grand trouble* or *le plus grand tyran*].

172. Valenciennes: City in Nord department, N France, where JA, on his journey back to Paris for peace negotiations, was forced to stop (Oct. 23, 1782) because the axletree on his carriage had broken.

173. Mlle de Bourbon: Louise Adelaide de Bourbon-Conde, 1757-1824.

174. la mode: F, "fashion." Pound's source reads: ". . . to preserve . . . national influence over the *mode*" [III, 298]. JA is complaining that upon arrival in Paris one must "send for a tailor, peruke-maker, and shoemaker . . . neither clothes, wigs, nor shoes, made in any other place, will do."

175. des Petits Augustins: Rue des Petits Augustins, Paris; the Hôtel d'Orléans, where John Jay, the third peace negotiator (with JA and Benjamin Franklin), stopped, was on this street.

176. Franklin: In his diary [Oct. 27, 1782] JA speculated on what he would find in the conduct of his two fellow negotiators, Franklin and Jay. It was Jay whom JA quoted as saying, "I will make a good peace or no peace." ". . . he will make a good peace or none" [III, 300].

177. Gulf of St. Lawrence: Gulf off E coast of Canada.

178. Nova Scotia: [63:51].

179. Cape Sable: Cape Sable Island off S tip of Nova Scotia. This and the preceding two references appear in JA's draft of a fishing rights agreement presented to the British negotiators, Richard Oswald and Henry Strachey, on November 4, 1782.

180. Tartary: In conversation with Caleb Whitefoord, secretary to Richard Oswald, British negotiator, JA discussed the possibility that winds from Tartary might carry influenza to France. He went on to explain his view of the problems the U.S. would face in foreign policy. JA subsequently presented the same ideas to Mr. Oswald [III, 307-308].

181. FISHERIES . . . you have been: These 13 lines dwell on JA's anger and frustration with France whose policy was to pressure the U.S. to give up its right to the fisheries; to attain this goal French ministers had intrigued to keep JA from carrying out his commission to negotiate a treaty of commerce with England [III, 319-320]. Interspersed are other attitudes about the French, who JA finds have traits common with certain other men: ". . . such are the objects which men pursue,—titles, ribbons, stars, garters, crosses, keys, are the important springs that move the ambition of men in high life" [III, 326]. Speculating about the tensions between France and England over the fisheries, JA wrote in his diary: ". . . had England rather France should supply the markets of Lisbon and Cadiz with fish, and take the gold and silver, than we? France would never spend any of that money in London; we should spend it all very nearly" [III, 328-329]. Note that Pound changed the word "spend" in the source to "send" in the canto line. JA also recorded in his diary a conversation with Oswald [cf. 182 below]: " 'If I have not been mistaken in the policy of France, from my first observation of it to this hour, they have been as averse to other powers acknowledging our independence as you have been.' Mr. Jay joined me in the same declaration. 'God!' says he, 'I understand it now; there is a gentleman going to London this day,—I will go home and write upon the subject by him' " [III, 347]. Perhaps the words "and send it" are intended before the words "by him." The source shows that it was Jay and not Oswald who said "God . . ." etc.

182. Oswald: Richard Oswald, English statesman. In 1782 the Shelburne ministry authorized him to conduct the final peace negotiations.

183. To exempt fishermen: From an article proposed by Franklin for inclusion in the final draft of the peace treaty.

184. The King: Gustavus III of Sweden. JA, shown a miniature of the Swedish king on a snuffbox, made this observation of a likeness between John Hancock and the king.

185. Lady Lucan: Margaret Smyth Bingham, Countess of Lucan, d. 1814; famous for her paintings; celebrated by Horace Walpole. JA copied some of her verses on England's exploitation of Ireland in his diary [Dec. 25, 1782; III, 351].

186. Connecticut constitution: Connecticut Charter, granted (1662) to John Winthrop. JA in his diary gives neither the passages that were obscure to the Duc de la Rochefoucauld nor his explanation [III, 352].

187. Mr Eliot: Eliot is not mentioned in Pound's sources. It may be that the four lines in parentheses on this canto page are cut into the canto text and concern T. S. Eliot's visit to Pound while he was writing this canto. Eliot may have listened to Pound read Lady Lucan's verses on Ireland, made no comment, but got up and left, which may have seemed to Pound a "fairly English" gesture.

188. Mr Vaughn: Benjamin Vaughan, 1751-1835, British diplomat; a friend of Franklin's, he sided with the colonists during the Revolution and unofficially promoted conciliation in the Anglo-American negotiations of 1782. He settled in America in 1796. The reference here is to whether or not England should accept the principle of liberty of navigation claimed by the "confederated neutral powers" and the Dutch. JA had argued that England should accept and Vaughan agreed, though saying that England had to try to get some advantage by holding out [III, 353].

189. Billy Franklin: William Temple F., 1762-1823, grandson of Benjamin Franklin; served as secretary to his grandfather in Paris; published editions of Franklin's works (1816-1819). Reference is to a letter Benjamin Franklin wrote recommending his grandson to Congress as a possible future candidate for ministerial appointment [III, 355].

190. Mlle Bourbon: Elizabeth B.; JA's observation after his visit to Versailles on January 21, 1783, to pay his respects to Louis XVI.

191. Chatham: William Pitt, 1st Earl of C., 1708-1778, English statesman known as "the Elder Pitt" and later as the "Great Commoner." Here Mr. Oswald's secretary,

Mr. Whitefoord, has explained to JA how a policy of Chatham's had had a bad effect on England's ally, Sardinia [III, 359].

192. Sardegna: A reference to Victor Amadeus III.

193. congress has double XX'd me: JA's reference to instructions passed by Congress and sent to the commissioners in Paris saying that they were "ultimately to govern themselves by the advice and opinion of the French Ministry" in the peace negotiations. JA defied these instructions [III, 300n, 359].

194. M. Malesherbes: Chrétien Guillaume de Lamoignou de Malesherbes: "the famous first president of the Court of Aids, uncle of the Chevalier de la Luzerne, and son of the Chancelier de Lamoignon" [III, 360].

195. Luzerne: Anne César Chevalier de la L., 1741-1791, French diplomat; ambassador to America (1779-1783); played major role in Paris Peace Conference; ambassador to England (1788-1791).

196. tiers état: F, "third estate": the people, commons.

197. Passy: In the 18th century a village NW of Paris where the American delegation to France stayed; now a fashionable section of Paris.

198. S'il . . . savoir: F, "If a false knowledge reigns" [III, 362]. JA quotes from the *Mercure de France* (Feb. 1783): ". . . s'il y regne un faux savoir, pire que l'ignorance."

199. Livingston: [33:7]. Livingston, when secretary for foreign affairs, in a letter to Franklin dated January 7, 1782, set forth details to be followed in the peace negotiations. Franklin neglected to mention the letter to JA. Only by accident over a year later, after the negotiations were completed, did JA learn about the letter. JA often expressed frustration with Franklin's cavalier way of conducting affairs.

200. Englishman Duke: George Montagu,

1737-1788, 4th Duke of Manchester, English ambassador sent to France to treat for peace (1783).

201. Hartley: David H., 1732-1813, English diplomat who, with Benjamin Franklin, drafted and signed the peace treaty between the U.S. and Great Britain in 1783. In a struggle in Holland between the Republicans (who were fighting for the liberties of the people) and the stadtholder (who was trying to maintain and broaden the powers of the elite class), England and Prussia had taken the side of the stadtholder. JA told Hartley that they were wrong and that they ought to remain neutral, for if Holland "should be annexed to the Empire or to France, it would be fatal to Great Britain." JA said the kings of England and Prussia would do well to consider that, if they supported the stadtholder, "France and the Emperor would not assist the republicans, and thus throw all Europe into a flame" [III, 369].

202. Emperor: Frederick II of Prussia [32:38].

203. commerce: JA drafted a statement recommending to the Continental Congress that a trade treaty be negotiated between England and the U.S. [III, 374].

204. Gt Britain: JA wrote in his diary [May 22, 1783]: "It was observed last evening, that all the laws of Great Britain for the regulation of the plantation trade, were contrived solely for the benefit of Great Britain" [III, 374].

205. Dutch vessels: Pound's source reads "Danish vessels." Baron de Waltersdorf, chamberlain of the king of Denmark, told JA this as evidence of the potential growth of trade between Europe and the U.S. [III, 376].

206. Sardinian ambassador: This remark, made by Comte Montagnini Mirabel to JA at Versailles on June 17, 1783, emphasizes the illogicality of some commercial arrangements: furs from Hudson Bay end up in

Siberia, a short 150 leagues from where they started, but first they twice travel halfway around the world, to London and back. Thus the canto closes by calling attention to a major aspect of JA's role in the treaty negotiations: his bitter contest with the French ministry to speak directly for his country's interests in a commerce agreement along with his tireless insistence on an agreement that would bring reasonable and appropriate benefits to both England and the U.S. [III, 380].

CANTO LXVI

Sources

Charles Francis Adams, ed., *The Works of John Adams*, III; Frederick K. Sanders, *John Adams Speaking*, Orono, Maine, 1975, 265-301.

Background

Catherine Drinker Bowen, *John Adams and the American Revolution*, Boston, 1950; Peter Shaw, *The Character of John Adams*, Chapel Hill, N.C., 1974; Page Smith, *John Adams*, 2 vols., Garden City, N.Y., 1962; Marie (Goebel) Kimball, *Jefferson: The Scene of Europe, 1784 to 1789*, New York, 1950, chap. vii; L.H. Butterfield, ed., *Diary and Autobiography of John Adams*, III, Cambridge, Mass., 1961.

Exegeses

CE, *Ideas*, 43, 176-177; EH, *Approaches*, 14; CB-R, *ZBC*, 240.

Glossary

1. Could not ... seamen: In a conversation with the duc de la Vauguyon on June 18, 1783, JA continued to explore future trade relations between the U.S. and the countries of Europe. The duke's response here is to JA's question about whether the French will permit American ships to carry goods from French islands in the West Indies and the Atlantic to Europe [III, 381]. Source does not mention Spanish seamen.

2. (Bois de Boulogne): In September 1783 JA moved into Thomas Barclay's home at Auteuil, just outside Paris. Nearby was the Bois de Boulogne, a large park containing the Longchamp racetrack. From his bed-chamber at Auteuil JA could see the village of Issy and the chateau of Meudon, built by Louis XIV, surrounded by the Forêt de Meudon [III, 383].

3. Amiens: Manufacturing city in Somme department, N France, where JA dined on his journey to London with JQA in October 1783.

4. Abbeville: Commune in Somme department, N France, where JA and JQA stayed the night of October 21 on their journey to London.

5. Dover: On October 24 JA reached Dover and climbed up the cliffs, noting the nature of the soil. Once at the top he looked down and saw "the whole town and harbor of Dover" [III, 386].

6. Mr Johnson: Joshua J., 1742-1802, American merchant who settled in England before the Revolution. During the Revolution he lived for a time in Nantes where he undertook commissions for the Congress; he returned to London after the Revolution, where he served as the first U.S. consul (1790-1797). He was the father of Louisa Catherine, who married John Quincy Adams in 1797.

7. Gt Tower Hill: Joshua Johnson, after he returned from Nantes, took up residence in Cooper's Row, Great Tower Hill. JA used Johnson's residence as his mailing address during his visit to London in late 1783.

8. Messrs Willin(c)k(s): [62:107].

9. Hague: The Hague, Netherlands. In January 1784 JA made a perilous journey from London to Holland to save American credit by negotiating a second loan with the Dutch. He remained in the Netherlands through the summer of 1784 while Congress debated his future service in Europe. At length Congress took the side of JA's supporters rather than that of Benjamin Franklin and Thomas Jefferson, allowing him to negotiate treaties of amity and commerce with 23 foreign governments. JA's diary for June 22, 1784, concludes with the mention of treaties pre-viously negotiated with France (Feb. 6, 1778), Holland (Oct. 7, 1782), Great Britain (Sept. 3, 1783), and Sweden (ca. April 3, 1783).

10. Ambassador: A foreign ambassador at Versailles, upon learning that JA would be the first U.S. ambassador to England, asked him on May 3, 1785, if he was of English extraction. JA replied that since no member of his family had lived in England for 150 years, he had "not one drop of blood in my veins but what is American." The ambassador answered, "Ay, we have seen proof enough of that," an answer that flattered JA [III, 392].

11. Sends to Morocco: In a conversation with JA at Versailles on March 20, 1785, the Comte de Vergennes made this observation about France's trading policy with Morocco (III, 391]. Butterfield suggests that *glaces* should be *glasses* (looking glasses) [III, 175 n.2].

12. Lord Carmathen ... often: Words spoken to JA by the Duke of Dorset, British ambassador in Paris, on May 3, 1785, in a conversation about JA's new assignment as minister to the Court of St. James.

13. Lord Carmathen: Carmarthen Francis Osborne, 1751-1799, 5th Duke of Leeds, known until 1789 as Marquis of Carmarthen. As foreign secretary under Pitt (1783-1791), he introduced JA to King George III of England.

14. Mr Pitt: William, "the Younger Pitt," 1759-1806, English statesman; prime minister (1783-1801, 1804-1806).

15. Presq' isle: Presque Isle, once a military fort in N Maine controlled by the British in Canada. Source reads "Presqu' Isle."

16. Sandusky: Once a military fort on Sandusky Bay in N Ohio controlled by the British.

17. Detroit Michilimakinac: Two installations, one at Detroit and the other on the Straits of Mackinac in the far N of Michigan.

18. **St Joseph**: Military fort on the Great Lakes once controlled by the British.

19. **St Mary's**: Military fort on the Great Lakes. The names of these forts (Presq' isle ... St. Mary's) appear on a memorandum JA wrote in his diary on May 9 or 16, 1785. They were forts in American territory which the British continued to occupy in violation of the 1783 Treaty of Paris. The question of British occupation of the forts was not finally resolved until the signing of Jay's Treaty in 1794.

20. **daughter married**: On March 26, 1786, JA dined with Jonathan Shipley, bishop of Saint Asaph's, who was a friend of Benjamin Franklin's and of the colonial cause many years earlier. Mrs. Shipley made the remark about her daughter on this occasion.

21. **Mr Hamilton**: William H., 1745-1813, wealthy Pennsylvanian whose house near Philadelphia JA would later occupy when the federal government established itself at Philadelphia in 1790. JA presented him to the queen "at the drawing-room" on March 30, 1786 [III, 393].

22. **the Queen**: Charlotte Sophia, 1744-1818, wife of George III of England.

23. **Mr Jefferson**: In March 1786 Thomas Jefferson, who had succeeded Benjamin Franklin as minister to Versailles a year earlier, joined JA in London to conclude treaties of commerce with Portugal, Tripoli, and Great Britain. Early in April 1786, while in England, Jefferson joined JA on a tour of the famous estates and gardens on the Thames and its tributaries W of London.

24. **Woburn Farm**: Estate near Weybridge, Surrey, belonging at the time to Lord Peters, visited by JA and Jefferson on their second day out of London. Jefferson was later to incorporate certain characteristics of the gardens at Woburn Farm in his plans for Monticello.

25. **Stowe**: Estate belonging to the Marquis of Buckingham, in Buckinghamshire, whose gardens were widely known in Georgian England; JA and Jefferson visited Stowe on April 6, 1786.

26. **Stratford**: Stratford on Avon, Warwickshire, England, birthplace of William Shakespeare; visited by JA and Jefferson on April 6.

27. **Stourbridge**: Lord Lyttelton's seat at Hagley was near Stourbridge, Worcester; JA and Jefferson visited Hagley on April 8.

28. **Woodstock**: Municipal borough in Oxfordshire; Blenheim Palace, which JA and Jefferson visited on April 9, is near Woodstock.

29. **High Wycombe**: Municipal borough in Buckinghamshire, SE central England, visited by JA and Jefferson on their return journey to London.

30. **Grosvenor Sq.**: Fashionable square in London; residence of JA when he was in London as minister to the Court of St. James's.

31. **Pope**: On the first day of their tour JA and Jefferson visited Twickenham, Alexander Pope's famous residence and garden on the Thames.

32. **Thompson**: James Thomson, 1700-1748, Scottish poet, author of *The Seasons* (1726-1730).

33. **Shenstone**: William S., 1714-1763, English poet who developed Leasowes, one of the earliest landscape gardens in England; JA and Jefferson visited Leasowes in April 1786.

34. **Lexington**: [33:18].

35. **Child**: A descendant of Samuel Child, son of Sir Francis Child, 1642-1713, banker and lord mayor of London. The Child family seat at Osterly Park, Heston, Middlesex, was visited by JA and his family, accompanied by Jefferson, on April 20, 1786. The interior of the house was a famous example of the work of the brothers Adam.

36. **Dr. Grey**: Edward Whitaker G., botanist and keeper of natural history collections and

antiquities at the British Museum, which JA visited on April 24, 1786 [Butterfield, III, 191 n.1].

37. Buffon: Georges Louis Leclerc, Comte de B., 1707-1788, French naturalist.

38. Mr H.: Thomas Brand-Hollis, 1719-1804, English friend of JA's and a sympathizer with republican forms of government. He inherited the property of Thomas Hollis, benefactor of Harvard College, and added his benefactor's name to his own. JA and his family visited Brand-Hollis's country seat, the Hyde, in Essex, on July 24, 1786.

39. Palladio: [40:27].

40. July 18th: Pound's source reads "Quincy July 12." The year is 1796. Ten years have elapsed between this line and the preceding one. JA returned from Europe in 1788 and was elected vice-president for two terms with Washington. Although he was quite interested in the election in November 1788, most of his diary entries concern details of farm management at Quincy to which he had returned from Philadelphia in mid-May. Source reads: "mowed all the grass" [III, 416].

41. Stony Hill: Stony-field Hill, part of Stony Acres, JA's property in Braintree, Mass.

42. this day: July 13, 1796. This line, the preceding one, and the twelve that follow refer to the summer of 1796, before the election that was to bring JA the presidency and after the controversy in Congress concerning Jay's Treaty.

43. T.: Prob. Thomas Trask, one of JA's farmhands at Braintree.

44. Otis: Samuel Allyne O., 1740-1814, American statesman; member of Constitutional Convention; secretary of U.S. Senate (1789-1814). Otis dined with JA on July 16, 1796, and reported the maneuverings of both Federalists and Republicans to secure the successor to George Washington [III, 417].

45. Henry: Patrick H. He, with Jefferson and Aaron Burr, was interested in the coming election, all three jockeying for power and position [31:46].

46. leaves of white oaks: Pound's source reads "leaves only the white oaks" [III, 419].

47. To barley: JA's inspection of his farm on July 23, 1796.

48. Rhode Island: On August 10-11, 1796, David Howell from Rhode Island, former member of the Continental Congress, visited JA to discuss his commission to settle the boundary dispute between the U.S. and Canada called for by Jay's Treaty; while at Braintree he reported the latest gossip about the coming election.

49. Hamilton: [62:144]. David Howell told JA the "funding system" would make Rhode Islanders unanimous in choosing President Washington's successor. He also said that "they wanted Hamilton for Vice-President." JA adds: "I was wholly silent" [III, 423].

50. Wheretoward . . .: This and the following six lines come from the concluding pages of JA's *Dissertation on the Canon and the Feudal Law* (1765), in which he attacked the Stamp Act as a contemporary example of "feudal" oppression [III, 460-464].

51. Runing Mede: Runnymede, meadow on S bank of Thames in Surrey, S England, where King John signed the Magna Charta in 1215.

52. Prince of Orange: King William III, 1650-1702, king of England (1689-1702). JA refers to the Glorious Revolution of 1688 in which the Parliament deposed James II and made William of Orange king to protect the rights of the people from Stuart authoritarianism.

53. James Second: 1633-1701, king of Great Britain and Scotland (1685-1688); deposed in the Glorious Revolution.

54. Thos. Hollis: Thomas H., 1720-1774,

English student of political philosophy and an ardent supporter of republican principles. In 1765 he arranged for the publication of JA's *Dissertation on the Canon and the Feudal Law* in England, erroneously attributing the work to Jeremiah Gridley, as many citizens of Massachusetts had done on its first appearance. When he discovered the true author of the work, Hollis publicly corrected his error.

55. Ob Pecuniae Scars[c]itatem: L, "On account of the scarcity of money" [42:41]. In his "Braintree Instructions," written to explain the objections of the town of Braintree to the Stamp Act and printed in the *Boston Gazette* [Oct. 14, 1765], JA used an English form of this phrase: "considering the present scarcity of money" [III, 465]. Since England required that taxes be paid in specie [metal], one of the colonies' chief concerns was the effect on commerce, because in time they would have no money to do business with: " . . . for a short space of time would drain the country of its cash, strip multitudes of all their property, and reduce them to absolute beggary" [III, 465-466].

56. Stamp Act: [64:17].

57. yr / humanity . . . the subject: These 24 lines are all taken from JA's Clarendon letters; the Chinese ideogram is Pound's interpolation [cf. glosses below].

58. Earl [of] Clarendon: Pseudonym used by JA in a series of three letters sent to the *Boston Gazette* in January 1766 in answer to an article published in the *London Evening Post* [Aug. 20, 1765] and signed with the name Pym. Pym's essential argument was expressed in these words: " 'Let me inform my fellow-subjects in America, that a resolution of the British Parliament can at any time set aside all the charters that have ever been granted by our monarchs' " [III, 469].

59. Baastun Gazette: *Boston Gazette* [62: 57].

60. Jan 17th 1768: Pound's source reads "13 January, 1766" [III, 469 n. 1].

61. Danegeld: OE, annual tax paid by the Britons to the Danes; continued later as a land tax. In the first of his Clarendon letters, JA found the Stamp Act similar to the Danegeld in its effects.

62. what are powers: Anticipating that the local courts might not prosecute violations of the Stamp Act, Parliament had made the penalties " 'recoverable in any court of record or in any court of admiralty in the Colony, where the offence should be committed, or in any court of vice-admiralty, which might be appointed over all America, at the election of the informer or prosecutor' " [CFA quoting from *Minot's History of Massachusetts*, II, 167-168; III, 471 n. 1].

63. per pares . . . : L, "by peers and the law of the land." A phrase used by Sir Edward Coke which JA quoted to Pym, asking by what procedure and authority the admiralty courts would decide violations of the Stamp Act. Coke had used this phrase in speaking of an act of Parliament passed in the reign of Henry VII which stated "that justices of assize, as well as justices of peace, without any finding or presentment of twelve men, upon a bare information for the king, should have full power and authority to hear and determine, by their discretions, all offences against the form, ordinance, and effect of certain penal statutes" [III, 471]. Sir Richard Empson and Edmund Dudley, made justices under the act, committed many offenses against justice until the first year of Henry VIII's reign, when Parliament declared the act unconstitutional and void; Empson and Dudley, found guilty of treason, were executed.

64. petit: JA asked Pym whether, with the new powers enjoyed by the courts of admiralty, petit juries would be needed any longer to try the facts in any Stamp Act violations and thus to determine guilt or innocence [III, 471].

65. per legem terrae: L, "by the law of the land."

66. Institutes Digest Roman: Source does not have this title but reads: "the institutes, digests, and codes and novels of the Roman law" [III, 472].

67. Become ... just observation: JA's description to Pym of the colonists' reaction to the Stamp Act and to the nature of their liberties guaranteed by the English constitution.

68. ching ming: Chêng [M351]: "right"; Ming [M4524]: "name."

69. Jury answers ... : In the conclusion of his third letter to Pym, JA, as Clarendon, explained the meaning of trial by jury under English law: "But by the British Constitution, *ad quæstionem facti respondent juratores,*–the jurors answer to the question of fact. In this manner, the subject is guarded in the execution of the laws. The people choose a grand jury, to make inquiry and presentment of crimes. Twelve of these must agree in finding the bill. And the petit jury must try the same fact over again, and find the person guilty, before he can be punished. Innocence, therefore, is so well protected in this wise constitution, that no man can be punished till twenty-four of his neighbors have said upon oath that he is guilty. So it is also in the trial of causes between party and party. No man's property or liberty can be taken from him till twelve men in his neighborhood have said upon oath, that by laws of his own making it ought to be taken away, that is, that the facts are such as to fall within such laws" [III, 481].

70. pompous rituals ... as he please: These ten lines are taken from letters written by "Governor Winthrop to Governor Bradford" in January and February 1767 in response to Philanthropos (Jonathan Sewall) in a debate over (1) the value of the Puritan religion, which does not have "pompous rituals ... to terrify," and (2) the question of whether a ruler acting through chancery should decide the legality of elections, rather than the Commons. [III, 487].

71. Elizabeth: E. I, 1533-1603, queen of England (1558-1603). JA refers to an occasion when Queen Elizabeth tried to interfere in an election.

72. James First: 1566-1625, king of Great Britain and Scotland (1603-1625).

73. Goodwin: Sir Francis G., principal of the Goodwin case (1604) in which the House of Commons asserted its right to be the sole judge of the returns in elections of its members.

74. (London Chronicle): Not the London paper established in 1757; prob. refers to the parliamentary debates and court decisions during the reign of James I.

75. Stamp Act: This and the following 20 lines are taken from the "Boston Instructions" written by JA and adopted June 17, 1768, to protest the seizure of John Hancock's sloop *Liberty* and the impressment of American seamen in violation of a law (6 Anne chap. 37, sec. 9) dated February 14, 1707 [III, 501-504; cf. 64:56].

76. Braintree: Pound's source reads "Boston" [III, 501].

77. Anne: 1665-1714, queen of England (1702-1714).

78. Her Majesty: Queen Anne.

79. St Valentine's day: February 14.

80. Governor Hutchinson: In the spring of 1769, when a number of British troops were stationed in Boston, the main guard was assigned a house across from the courthouse door and, according to Governor Hutchinson, some small cannon outside the guardhouse "*happened* to point to the door of the court house" [III, 505]. But the implied intimidation provoked the Boston town meeting to call for instructions to protest the appearance of intimidation. JA drafted the "Boston Instructions" which were adopted May 15, 1769.

81. To the Hnbl ... recommended you: This 17-line passage is taken from JA's

"Boston Instructions" of May 15, 1769 [III, 505-510].

82. James Otis et al: Representatives of Boston in Massachusetts legislature, 1769.

83. 41st section: JA is concerned here with the jurisdiction of the courts of admiralty which he sees developing "by degrees into a system that is to overturn our constitution and to deprive us entirely of our best inheritance, the laws of the land." He adds later: " . . . in the forty-first section of the statute of the fourth [year] of George III. chap. XV. we find that 'all the forfeitures and penalties inflicted by this or any other act of parliament, relating to the trade . . . may be prosecuted, sued for, and recovered in any court of admiralty.' " Judgment was thus put into the hands of a single judge [III, 507-508].

84. Magna Charta: Not the original document now known as "The Charter of Runnymede" which the English barons forced King John to sign on June 15, 1215, at Runnymede, but a much later document Sir Edward Coke used as the basis of his work, *The Second Part of the Institutes of the Laws of England*. The later document, entitled *Magna Charta, Edita Anno Nono H. III*, is dated 1225, the ninth year of the reign of Henry III [107-109/756-774].

85. the 29th chapter: JA quotes the English translation of *Magna Charta* (1225) as given by Coke: "No freeman shall be taken or imprisoned, or disseised of his freehold or liberties or free customs or outlawed or exiled or any otherwise destroyed, nor will we pass upon him nor condemn him, but by lawful judgment of his peers or the law of the land" [III, 509]. The whole statute in *Magna Charta* has another sentence: "We will sell to no man, we will not deny or defer to any man either justice or right" [*Magna Charta*, cap. xxix; Coke's rendition, p. 45].

86. Lord Coke: [62:43]. As in his Clarendon letters to Pym the year before, JA in the "Boston Instructions" attacked the exten-

sion of the authority of the admiralty courts by quoting Edward Coke on *Magna Charta*.

87. Empson: Sir Richard E. [cf. 63 above], d. 1510; judge during the reign of Henry VII of England. Coke, in his commentary on cap. xxix of *Magna Charta*, used Empson and Dudley as examples of what can happen when judges condemn people on premises that are in defiance of the law of the land. In 11 Henry VII, Coke found an act of parliament which negated the guarantees of trial by a jury of one's peers given in *Magna Charta*. About that act, which was in force until Henry VII died, Coke said: "By colour of which act, shaking this fundamentall law, it is not credible what horrible oppressions, and exactions, to the undoing of infinite numbers of people, were committed by Sir Richard Empson knight, and Edm. Dudley." But in 1 Henry VIII, Parliament voided the act because it was against *Magna Charta*. Empson and Dudley were tried for treason, found guilty, and beheaded. Says Coke: " . . . the ill successe hereof, and the fearfull ends of these two oppressors, should deterre others from committing the like, and should admonish parliaments, that in stead of this ordinary, and pretious [precious] triall *per legem terrae*, they bring not in absolute, and partiall trialls by discretion" [*Magna Charta*, 51]. Pound's *direction* is doubtless an error for "discretion," which is found in his source [III, 509] as well as in JA's source, *Magna Charta* itself [cf. 63 above].

88. Dudley: Edmund D., ca. 1462-1510, a brilliant young man who, after studying at Oxford and Gray's Inn, was noticed by Henry VII and is said to have become a privy councillor when only 23. He and Empson assisted the king in controlling "the lawlessness of the barons" [*EB*] but in the process practiced extortion until they both amassed great wealth and became very unpopular. The two were tried for "constructive treason." In spite of Coke's interpretation, they were not found guilty on the legal issues of the charter, but on the quite different grounds of being *fiscales judices* or, in

Pound's terms, "hoggers of harvest, the curse of the people."

89. Natural tendency ...: The lines from here to the end of the canto concern the question as to whether or not judges should receive salary grants from the Crown. The first item concerns the decision of the Cambridge, Massachusetts, town meeting on December 21, 1772, to challenge the Crown grants. The meeting adopted a motion that the Cambridge representative to the legislature should protest the policy of paying Crown salary grants to judges without the consent of the citizens of Massachusetts.

90. Andrew Boardman: Town clerk of Cambridge in 1772.

91. Judges salaries: William Brattle argued that judges should be independent of both king and people by virtue of being appointed for life.

92. common lay: Pound's source reads "common law" [III, 518].

93. Wm/Brattle: William B., 1702-1776, brigadier general in Massachusetts militia. In 1773 JA and General Brattle engaged in a debate published in the Boston newspapers; their remarks were collected under the title, *The Independence of the Judiciary*. A loyalist, Brattle went to England during the Revolution.

94. It is the wish ...: From JA's essay in the *Boston Gazette* (Jan. 11, 1773).

95. Edward First: 1239-1307, king of England (1272-1307).

96. beneplacitu nostro: L, "in accordance with our [royal] good pleasure." Source reads "beneplacito" [III, 521].

97. Ad regis ...: L, "To endure at the king's command." This and the following 19 lines are taken from JA's essay in the *Boston Gazette* (Jan. 18, 1773).

98. Fortescue: Sir John F., ?1394-1476?, English jurist and one of England's first constitutional lawyers.

99. custos rotolorum: L, "keeper of the rolls." Source reads "rotulorum" [III, 527].

100. King: James I, 1566-1625. In November 1616, persuaded after a lengthy campaign by Francis Bacon, James dismissed Coke as lord chief justice of England.

101. timid jurors ... Crown: JA here quotes from Hume's *History of England*: "The people had entertained such violent prepossessions against the use which James [James II] here made of his prerogative, that he was obliged, before he brought on Hales's cause, to displace four of the judges" [III, 529].

102. James Second: 1633-1701, king of Great Britain and Scotland (1685-1688).

103. Hales: Sir Edward H., fl. 1686. Principal in a law case by which James II attempted to establish the Crown's dispensing power in regard to the Test Act; having failed to gain support for such power from Parliament, James tried to secure it by verdict of the judiciary (1686).

104. Jones: Sir Thomas J., d. 1692, English jurist, chief justice of Common Pleas, dismissed in 1686 by James II for refusing to rule in favor of the Crown's dispensing power in the Hales case. The king met the judges in secret to learn their opinions. He turned them all out saying that he'd have twelve judges of his own opinion. "... one of them, Jones, had the fortitude and integrity to tell the king to his face, that he might possibly make twelve judges, but *he would scarcely find twelve lawyers of his opinion*" [III, 530].

105. Charter: Charter of province of Massachusetts.

106. William III: King of England (1689-1702).

107. Edward IV: 1442-1483, king of England (1461-1470, 1471-1483).

108. Beauchamps: Richard de Beauchamp, ?1430-1481, bishop of Hereford and Salisbury, Chancellor of the Order of the Garter. JA quotes a letter patent granted by Edward IV: " 'We will and ordain that Richard Beauchampe, &c., should have it (that is, the office of the chancellor of the garter) for his life, and after his decease, that his successors should have it forever'; and 'it was resolved unanimously that this grant was void; for that a new office was erected, and it was not defined what jurisdiction or authority the officer should have; and, therefore, for the uncertainty, it was void' " [III, 538].

109. **Wales**: Part of the United Kingdom of Great Britain and Northern Ireland; made an English principality (1284); incorporated with England in reign of Henry VIII. The reference is to the conclusion of JA's *Boston Gazette* letter of January 25, 1773, in which JA quoted the statute of 27 Henry VIII chap. 24 to the effect that the king alone had the power to make judges, "by letters-patent [commissions], under the king's great seal," in all dominions of the realm [III, 539]. General Brattle had claimed that "by the charter and common law of England, there is no necessity of [the judges'] having any commission at all; a nomination and appointment recorded is enough" [III, 536]. But JA, quoting Matthew Bacon's *Abridgment*, argued that "all judges must derive their authority from the crown by some commission warranted by law," since a commission defined the limits of the judge's authority, something "a nomination and appointment" did not do.

CANTO LXVII

Sources

Charles Francis Adams, ed., *The Works of John Adams*, III, IV, V, VI; Frederick K. Sanders, *John Adams Speaking*, Orono, Maine, 1975, 302-355; Guido Cavalcanti, "Donna mi priegha," 5th ed., 1527.

Background

Hannah Arendt, *On Revolution*, New York, 1965; Zoltán Haraszti, *John Adams and the Prophets of Progress*, Cambridge, Mass., 1952; Clinton Rossiter, "The Legacy of John Adams," *Yale Review*, 46 (1957), 528-550; Peter Shaw, *The Character of John Adams*, Chapel Hill, N.C., 1974; Page Smith, *John Adams*, 2 vols., Garden City, N.Y., 1962; H. Blair, *An Introduction to Anglo-Saxon England*, Cambridge, 1970; L. H. Butterfield, ed., *Diary and Autobiography of John Adams*, II, Cambridge, Mass., 1961.

Exegeses

CE, *Ideas*, 43; Davis, *Vision*, 140-141.

Glossary

1. Whereof memory . . . his power: These 30 lines opening the canto continue JA's arguments for the independence of the judiciary in reply to General William Brattle's article in the *Massachusetts Gazette* (Jan. 4, 1773); the first 20 lines are taken from JA's essay in the *Boston Gazette* (Feb. 1, 1773) [III, 540-550].

2. Dome Book: Not the famous Domesday Book authorized by William the Conquerer, for the reference is to JA's description of the digest of laws collected by Edward the Confessor as "no more than a fresh promulgation of Alfred's code, or Dome Book, with such improvements as the experience of a century and a half had suggested." General Brattle had claimed [III, 518] that according to English common law judges had appointments for life, and JA undertook to refute this idea by examining what the term "common law" meant by tracing its roots back to Anglo-Saxon law.

3. Ina: 688-726, king of the West Saxons. He issued a code of laws which was later appended to a law code drawn up by King Alfred the Great.

4. Offa: 757-796, ruler of Mercia, one of the best and most powerful of the Anglo-Saxon kings. King Alfred the Great was familiar with the laws of Offa.

5. Aethelbert: Died A.D. 616; became king of Kent in 560, the first Christian English king. He issued, between 597 and 616, a code of laws based on Roman law, the "earliest surviving Anglo-Saxon document written in the vernacular" [cf. Blair, 329].

6. folcright: OE, *folcriht*, "the people's rights." They were expressed in the common law.

7. Gamaliel: Great teacher of Jewish law who died A.D. 88; the name is applied to any great teacher, especially of law.

8. Mr Read: George R., 1733-1798, American constitutional lawyer from Delaware.

Daniel Leonard, JA's opponent in the Novanglus correspondence, studied law with Read.

9. single dictum: Source reads "simple dictum" [III, 542].

10. arguendo: L, "in arguing or reasoning."

11. latterly': Source reads "lately" [III, 542]. JA quoted these words of General Brattle's to object to his tactic of claiming a point proven by past authorities without offering any proof himself.

12. Aula regum: L, "King's court." Source reads "aula regis" [III, 544], the single great court in Norman England. Near the end of the Norman period it was divided into four parts (High Court of Chancery, Queen's Bench, Exchequer, and Court of Common Pleas) in order to break the power and authority concentrated in the hands of the *summus justiciarius*, or chief justice, presiding officer of the great court.

13. summus justiciarius: L, "chief justice."

14. Capet: Hugh C., ?940-996, son of Hugh the Great; Duke of France (956-996); king of France (987-996); founder of Capetian line of French kings.

15. Regalia principis: L, "The rights royal of a prince." JA pointed out that "the creation and annihilation of judges was an important branch" of these rights [III, 545].

16. judiciary: Source reads "justiciary" (i.e., justice or judge). JA's point is that in those times the authority of the justice "ceased entirely in the king's presence" [III, 545].

17. cum delegans revocarit: L, "when one who sends a delegate calls him back" [cf. Bracton, *De Legibus* III, 10, where text reads: *Item cum delegans revocaverit jurisdictionem*; III, 546].

18. (Bracton): [63:40].

19. Ching: Chêng [M351]: "right."

20. (Brattle): [66:93].

21. Fortescue: [66:98].

22. Coke: [62:43].

23. Foster: Sir Michael F., 1689-1763, English jurist.

24. Hume: David H., 1711-1776, Scottish philosopher whose *History of Great Britain* JA used as a source for his arguments for the independence of the judiciary.

25. Rapin: Paul de R. de Thoyras, 1661-1725, French historian; author of *Histoire d'Angleterre* (8 vols., 1723) covering English history up to the accession of William and Mary.

26. Rushworth: John R., ?1612-1690, English historian; author of *Historical Collections* (8 vols., 1659-1701), covering the period 1618-1648.

27. de Burgh: Hubert de B., d. 1243, Earl of Kent; chief justice of England under Henry III (1216). JA mentioned him as an example of a chief justice who was said to have had an appointment for life; but knowing of no document to support the story, JA said it was without foundation.

28. Mr Shirley in 1754: This line begins a 109-line redaction of passages from JA's *Novanglus*, which first appeared as a series of articles in the *Boston Gazette*, starting in January 1775. The articles JA signed "Novanglus" were written in answer to articles by Daniel Leonard signed "Massachusettensis" and contained JA's view of the constitutional arguments justifying the patriot cause.

29. Mr Shirley: William S., 1694-1771, English lawyer and governor of Massachusetts colony (1741-1749, 1753-1756). In 1756 he was recalled to England to answer charges of financial mismanagement and poor military organization.

30. Dr. Franklin: JA wrote of Benjamin Franklin: "This sagacious gentleman, this eminent philosopher and distinguished pa-

triot, to his lasting honor, sent the Governor an answer in writing." Franklin wrote such things as these: "That the people always bear the burden best, when they have, or think they have, some *share* in the direction. That when public measures are generally distasteful to the people, the wheels of government must move more heavily.... That natives of America would be as likely to consult wisely and faithfully for the safety of their native country, as the governors sent from Britain, whose object is generally to make fortunes, and then return home" [IV, 19].

31. Shirley: [cf. 29 above]. JA is referring to the replacement of Governor Shirley by Thomas Pownall, a man friendly to the constitutional rights of the colonists; with Governor Pownall in office, the plan of Parliament to tax the colonies was not pursued. Pound added the word "skunk."

32. Pownall: Thomas P., 1722-1805, colonial governor of Massachusetts (1757-1760). An able governor, Thomas Pownall made enemies of the supporters of former Governor Shirley and of Thomas Hutchinson; faced with factional opposition in his province, according to JA, Pownall requested permission to return to England.

33. Bernard: [64:20, 26]. Sir Francis Bernard, governor of New Jersey, replaced Pownall as governor of Massachusetts in 1760.

34. and thus the total government: JA's description of the purpose of the revenue act, which was to have the Crown, rather than the citizens, pay salary grants to the governor, lieutenant governor, and judges so that both the executive and the judicial branches of the government would be independent of the people.

35. Novanglus: JA's pseudonym [cf. 28 above].

36. Mr. Grenville: [64:34]. While chancellor of the exchequer, Grenville was responsible for the Sugar Act (1764), the Stamp

Act (1765), and the Quartering Act (1765). The preposterous "improvement" he suggested was taxing the colonies and using the revenue to pay salaries to officials and to support the army in the colonies.

37. Obsta principiis: L, "Resist the beginnings." JA used this phrase to emphasize the necessity of firm protest at the first manifestations of oppression: "*Obsta principiis*, nip the shoots of arbitrary power in the bud, is the only maxim which can ever preserve the liberties of any people" [IV, 43].

38. the army: Said JA [as Novanglus]: "Besides, every farthing of expense which has been incurred on pretence of protecting ... America ... has been worse than thrown away.... Keeping an army in America has been nothing but a public nuisance."

39. Massachusetts: Source reads "Massachusettensis" (i.e., author of the articles JA answered in *Novanglus*) [IV, 57].

40. Irritat ... implet: L, "Annoys, soothes, and fills with false fears." Cf. Horace, *Epistles* II, i, 212, which JA quoted [IV, 99] to describe what Massachusettensis wanted to accomplish in writing his newspaper articles. Source has "Irritat, mulcet, falsis terroribus implet."

41. casus omissus: L, "omitted case." JA's argument was that nothing in English common law stated that colonies beyond the British Isles should be governed "by authority of parliament" [IV, 121].

42. Hen. VIIIth: Henry, 1491-1547, king of England (1509-1547). After he declared himself head of the English church, Henry assumed authority over Englishmen in whatever country and by act of Parliament invested in himself what had been the supremacy of the pope.

43. Cardinal Pole: Reginald P., 1500-1558, created cardinal by Pope Paul III in 1536; opposed the divorce and the religious reforms of Henry VIII.

44. Most fanatical: Source reads "most... fantastical" [IV, 125], the most fantastical idea being that "a king of England had a right to all the land his subjects could find, not possessed by any Christian state or prince, though possessed by heathen or infidel nations." But even if that were so, it would not, according to JA, mean that Parliament possessed authority "over the new countries conquered or discovered" [IV, 125].

45. right of contract: I.e., the king did have the right to grant charters to his subjects which would confer upon them the rights and liberties of Englishmen in colonies established under such charters. For this context the source reads: "... for an English king had no right to be absolute over Englishmen out of the realm, any more than in it" [IV, 126].

46. the oily writer: Pound's characterization of Massachusettensis in summarizing JA's repudiation of various of his claims.

47. Parliament: JA asserted that the citizens of Massachusetts wanted nothing new, but rather continuation of privileges enjoyed for 150 years, during which they had governed their own internal affairs and Parliament had governed their trade.

48. Wales: JA explained that Wales and the American colonies had analagous situations in that Wales was held by the Crown of England and so the English monarch had a right to homage from the Prince of Wales. "But yet Wales was not parcel of the realm or kingdom, nor bound by the laws of England" [IV, 133].

49. Edwardus ... dominium: L, "Edward by the Grace of God [King] of England, / Lord of Ireland, and Duke of Aquitaine (holding) the land of Wales together with its inhabitants / in possession of our private ownership." Source has "Dei" for "Deo," "Rex Angliæ" for "Angliae." Pound also leaves out a number of phrases and clauses found in the source and alters the word order [IV, 134].

50. now partly to divert ... Hibernia habet parliamentum: These 23 lines come from a long passage in *Novanglus* in which JA recounted how Ireland came to be under English dominion [IV, 151-165].

51. Becket: Thomas à B., 1117-1170, archbishop of Canterbury (1162-1170); murdered by agents of Henry II.

52. Adrian: A. IV, d. 1159, first and only English pope (1154-1159).

53. power of pence of Peter: Source reads "prospect of Peter's pence": an annual tax, originally one penny, levied on each householder in England by the papacy [IV, 152].

54. Henry's demand: Source reads "design" [IV, 152]; Henry II [6:17].

55. Eire: Ireland.

56. Macmorral: Dermot MacMurrough, ?1110-1171, king of Leinster, one of "five distinct sovereignties in Ireland." JA called him "a licentious scoundrel ... who had been driven from his kingdom ... by his own subjects" [IV, 152]. Source reads "Macmorrogh."

57. Rourke: Tiernan O'R., d. 1172, king of Breifne and ruler of part of Meath (1144). In 1152 his wife was carried off by Dermot MacMurrough. Henry II was able to use the greed of MacMurrough and O'Rourke to divide the Irish and make their subjugation easier. JA said that just as Henry II played different kings of Ireland against one another, so the government of England tried to play the colonies against one another, except that "the American colonies. . . have more sense than to be divided" [IV, 152]. Source has "Ororic."

58. our junto: Crown officers in Massachusetts, primarily Governor Bernard, Thomas Hutchinson, and the Oliver brothers.

59. Henry V: 1387-1422, king of England (1413-1422). JA quoted a statute of Henry V which stipulated that all Irishmen not belonging to certain categories ("graduates, sergeants") had to depart the realm of England [IV, 155].

60. "shall put in surety": This quotation comes from a statute of Henry VI which established specific conditions for any Irishmen entering England.

61. Poyning's law: Named for Sir Edward Poynings, 1459-1521, English soldier and diplomat. As governor of Ireland, he summoned the Drogheda Parliament (1494) which enacted Poynings' Law, providing that no bill could be introduced into the Irish Parliament unless it had first received the sanction of the English Privy Council and that all former laws of England would subsequently be binding in Ireland. JA's argument was that the American colonies had never agreed to or passed a "Poynings' law." Source has "Poyning."

62. Edgardus ... parliamentum: L, "Edgar, King of the English, / emperor and ruler of the isles of the ocean, I thank / almighty God who so enlarged and extended my kingdom beyond the kingdom of my fathers, / granted the good offices of divinity ... / Ireland has a parliament." JA here quoted Sir Edward Coke (*Reports*, 7, 22b) on the question of who first conquered Ireland for England. Coke had quoted the Latin of a charter made by Edgar, king of England (944-975), and then had acknowledged that the conquest of Ireland was customarily attributed to the later reign of Henry II [IV, 161]. Source reads "Edgarus" for "Edgardus," "gratias" for "gratium," "exaltavit" for "explicavit." Pound also omits words and phrases found in the source.

63. Sir J. Pilkington: Sir John P., fl. 1454. The case of Sir John Pilkington (32 Henry VI chap. 25) substantiated the fact that Ireland was a dominion separate and divided from England [Coke, *Reports*, 7, 22b].

64. majesty near the seventy: A reference to George II, 1683-1760, king of England (1727-1760). This and the following five lines come from the reaction of Lord Mansfield, as JA imagined it, as the reign of George II approached its end.

65. amiable successor: George III, who ascended the throne of England in 1760 at the age of 22.

66. militant spirit: Source reads "martial spirit" [IV, 167]. JA's characterization of Lord Mansfield's belief that, although the English would certainly defeat the French in the Seven Years War [French and Indian War in America], the English nation would be left with an immense debt. Thus the war should be brought to a close for "we have not the martial spirit and abilities of the great commoner" [the Elder Pitt].

67. How shall we manage it?: I.e., raise revenue to pay the war debt.

68. Lord Mansfield: William Murray, 1705-1793, 1st Earl of Mansfield; English jurist and parliamentary debater.

69. Hutchinson: [62:47]. As JA described it, the solution to the debt problem, according to Lord Mansfield and Thomas Hutchinson, lay in "annexing" North America to "the realm of England" [IV, 166].

70. regalia: L, *regalia principis*, "the rights royal of a prince" [cf. 15 above].

71. a little knowledge: Massachusettensis had written that Jersey and Guernsey "are no part of the realm of England, nor are they represented in parliament, but are subject to its authority" [IV, 169]; JA undertook to provide a better understanding of this subject.

72. Chester: City in NW England; also a palatine county, one that came under special jurisdiction of the prince. But Parliament passed laws preventing the citizens of Chester from committing crimes outside the county, or citizens outside from seeking legal refuge in the county. JA's point is that America could be included in no such acts of Parliament.

73. jure regalia: L, *jura regalia*, "royal rights."

74. 3 knights: Source reads "two knights." Earlier Chester "'had been excluded from

parliament, to have any knights and burgesses there' [i.e., representing it in Parliament].... For remedy whereof, two knights of the shire and two burgesses for the city are established" [IV, 172].

75. Durham: Palatine county in N England.

76. Queen's writ: Refers to 31 Elizabeth chap. 9.

77. 25 Charles II: JA used Chester and Durham as examples because, since they were counties palatine, their lords enjoyed "royal rights," although they did acknowledge the rights of the English king to his crown. The laws of Parliament and the judicial authority of the king did not extend into counties palatine, but when the two counties, previously exempt from Parliament's authority, asked permission to have representation in Parliament, it was quickly granted. "America, on the contrary, is not in the realm; never was subject to the authority of parliament by any principle of law; is so far from Great Britain that she never can be represented; yet, she is to be bound in all cases whatsoever!" [IV, 170-172]. 25 Charles II was the statute enabling Durham to send representatives to Parliament.

78. our oily opponent: Pound's characterization of Massachusettensis.

79. more zeal than knowing: JA on the claim of Massachusettensis that the terms of the first charter of Massachusetts made it a part of the British Empire and bound the original settlers to the laws of England.

80. Nation . . . into our charter: JA refers to the fact that at the time the first charter for settling Massachusetts was granted, the British Empire did not exist.

81. King: Charles I, 1600-1649, king of England (1625-1649); granted its first charter to colony of Massachusetts (March 4, 1629). Massachusettensis had claimed that the original charter had made the province subject to England's protection, but JA replied that no money had ever been provided to the first settlers for that purpose.

82. Style royal?: To the claim of Massachusettensis that the precedent for submission to Parliament was implicit in the "royal style" of the original charter, JA replied: "The style is this: 'Charles, by the grace of God, King of England, Scotland, France, and Ireland, Defender of the Faith,' &c. Now, in which capacity did he grant that charter; as King of France, or Ireland, or Scotland, or England? He governed England by one parliament, Scotland by another. Which parliament were we to be governed by?" [IV, 174].

83. homage, fealty: JA explains that in feudal language homage and fealty were due a lord in his natural person; one did not pay homage to "the body politic, the political capacity, which is not corporated, but only a frame in the mind, an idea" [IV, 176-177]. Since the king held lands in his natural person and not in his political capacity, Massachusettensis was wrong, according to JA, to declare that he was due the homage of political loyalty.

84. the king might have commanded: That the king did not command the original settlers of the province to return was tacit acknowledgment that they were out of his realm and therefore out of the legal jurisdiction of Parliament.

85. Lexington: The Novanglus papers are subtitled "A History of the Dispute with America, from its origin, in 1754, to the present time; written in 1774, by John Adams." They were collected and published together in 1819. CFA includes the whole edition in Volume IV of *WJA* along with a note that reads: "Hostilities at Lexington, between Great Britain and her colonies, commenced on the nineteenth of April, two days succeeding the publication of this last essay" [IV, 177].

86. Plan of Government: "The Plan," the first of three sections into which CFA divided JA's major writings dealing with the

form of American government; the other sections are titled "The Model" and "The Defence" [IV, 185-VI, 220].

87. Philadelphy: A letter JA sent from Philadelphia to Richard Henry Lee (Nov. 15, 1775) appears to be the earliest expression of JA's plan of government.

88. R. H. Lee: [65:53].

89. on sudden emergency: The imminent likelihood of independence from England would necessitate the creation of new governments for the colonies.

90. legislative, executive and judicial: JA's political philosophy had always centered on a division of powers that would encourage checks and balances in government, as was evident in his early letter to R. H. Lee.

91. Printer John Dunlap: 1747-1812, printer in Philadelphia who published the first edition of JA's *Thoughts on Government* (1776).

92. Mr Wythe: [65:43]. In January 1776 George Wythe had asked JA what plan he would recommend "in order to get out of the old government and into a new one" [IV, 191]. JA's answer was *Thoughts on Government*.

93. some forms . . . : This and the following 25 lines (except the Italian at the eighth line, which is Pound's interpolation) are all taken from *Thoughts on Government*.

94. Kung: K'ung [13:1]. JA used the more familiar form "Confucius" [IV, 193].

95. Zoroaster: Religious teacher of ancient Persia, fl. 5th century B.C. He founded Zoroastrianism, originally a kind of fertility religion which later developed a more complex cosmogony and eschatology, deriving from the struggle of the Zoroastrian supernatural spirits.

96. Mahomet: Mohammed, 570-632, Arabian prophet. JA says that these sages have agreed "that the happiness of man, as well as his dignity, consists in virtue" [IV, 193].

97. **in some principle**: Source reads "is some principle" [IV, 194].

98. **ma che si sente dicho**: I, "but that is felt, I say," from "Donna mi priegha" [36:1].

99. **Locke**: [50:9]. All those mentioned in this line preached the concept of government by law, not by men [IV, 194].

100. **Milton**: John M., 1608-1674, English poet.

101. **Nedham**: Marchamont N., 1620-1678, English political writer; author of *The Case of the Commonwealth of England Stated* (1650).

102. **Neville**: Henry N., 1620-1694, English political writer; author of *Discourses Concerning Government* (1698).

103. **Burnet**: Sir Thomas B., ?1694-1753, English judge and political writer.

104. **Hoadly**: Benjamin H., 1676-1761, bishop of Bangor and Hereford; author of religious and political treatises, among them *An Essay on the Origin of Civil Government.*

105. **of learning . . .** : JA's description of qualities needed by judges.

106. **Pat Henry**: [31:46]. The following 12 lines come from a letter Patrick Henry sent to JA from Williamsburg on May 20, 1776 [IV, 201-202].

107. **Declaration**: Patrick Henry's reference to a resolution approved by the Continental Congress on May 10, 1776, which recommended that the colonies adopt new governments of their own design to meet their needs in dealing with the current crisis. The preamble, written by JA, and adopted on May 15, called for the virtual abolition of all British authority in the colonies [Butterfield, II, 240-241 n. 2, gives details about this episode].

108. **Colonel Nelson**: Thomas N., 1738-1789, American Revolutionary patriot; colonel in 2d Regiment of Virginia; member of Continental Congress (1775-1777); signer of Declaration of Independence; governor of Virginia (1781).

109. **Paris**: Patrick Henry believed it very important that the colonies get their representatives to the French court ahead of the British and that they quickly make a public declaration of independence so that they could seek alliances in Europe.

110. **Bracton**: Source has "Braxton" [IV, 202]. Carter Braxton, Virginia delegate to the Continental Congress, had written a pamphlet in answer to JA's *Thoughts on Government* [cf. 86 above].

111. **Sam Adams**: Also S.A., four lines later [cf. 34:32].

112. **John Taylor**: 1753-1824, printer and political writer from Caroline County, Va. In his *Inquiry into Principles and Policy of the Government of the United States* (1814) he printed a letter JA had written to John Penn in 1776.

113. **John Penn**: ?1741-1788, American Revolutionary leader; member of Continental Congress from North Carolina (1775-1780) and signer of Declaration of Independence. JA wrote Penn in answer to a request from the North Carolina delegation that he, JA, suggest the form of government best suited to replace the administration of the Crown should that become necessary. The following six lines are taken from JA's letter to Penn. JA kept no copy, so the letter was not printed until 1814 [IV, 203].

114. **Jonathan Sergeant**: J. Dickinson S., 1746-1798, American lawyer; New Jersey delegate to First Continental Congress (1774). JA wrote him a letter similar to the one he wrote to Penn, "but no copy has been found" [IV, 209n].

115. **Fixed laws . . .** : These eight lines are from a resolution passed by the Massachusetts convention on September 3, 1779, which led to the drafting of a new constitution for Massachusetts.

116. **I was apprehensive**: In his draft of the

constitution of Massachusetts, JA had recommended, in section ii, the encouragement of literature, the sciences, and a natural history of the province, as well as such personal qualities as charity, honesty, and good humor.

117. Chawles Fwancis: Charles Francis Adams (1807-1886), editor of *WJA* (1850).

118. who have since been erected: The source reads "who have since been elevated" [IV, 261n]; the reference is to officials elected to the highest public offices.

119. and no public man: This and the following five lines come from CFA's preface to JA's *Defence of the Constitutions of Government of the United States of America, Against the Attack of M. Turgot, in His Letter to Dr. Price, Dated the Twenty-Second Day of March, 1778* [IV, 276-277]. In it CFA, noting the controversies provoked by the appearance of the work (1787-88), remarks that although by the time he is writing his preface (1850) government by democratic majority rule is so widely admired that no public official would risk criticizing its limitations, that was not true in the last decades of the 18th century when JA wrote about his theories of government and when the viability of the modern democratic republic remained unproven. JA had written *Defence* in response to Turgot's letter arguing the superiority of a unicameral assembly and also in response to the tax revolt in western Massachusetts known as Shay's Rebellion (1786). The three-volume work was a defense of state constitutions, not of the federal constitution, which did not exist at that time. Although JA was still in Europe when the Constitutional Convention of 1787 met, the first volume of *Defence* did influence the convention.

120. 'Either content . . . at large': Observing that theorizing about forms of government had gone out of fashion in the U.S., CFA speculated that the reason might be the awareness of dangers attendant upon think-

ing unpopular thoughts about democratic rule which might lead to ruined reputations; the reception of JA's *Defence* would be a case in point.

121. representatives of the people: This and the following 26 lines are taken from JA's preface to *Defence* [IV, 283-298]. Source reads "representations."

122. Thucydides: ?471-400, Greek historian. Refers to Thucydides' account of the consequences of unrestrained factionalism in Greece which, in JA's opinion, could have been prevented by a balance of powers in government.

123. Mr Hume: [cf. 24 above].

124. D. Siculus: Diodorus S., Greek historian of 1st century B.C.; author of *Biblioteca Historica* (40 vols.).

125. Ephesus: One of the principal Ionian cities on coast of Asia Manor.

126. Cyrenians: People of the ancient city of Cyrene in part of Africa known as Cyrenaica [modern Bardia in NE Libya].

127. Phaebidas: Phoebidas, Spartan commander who seized stronghold of Thebes in Boetia in 382 B.C. [IV, 286].

128. Philiasia: Phliasia, territory of Phlius, town in NE Peloponnesus.

129. Aegesta: Segesta, town on NW coast of Sicily [near modern Alcamo], said to have been founded by the Trojans; called Egesta or Aegesta by the Greeks. Of these brutalities (at Ephesus and Segesta) JA wrote: "Such were the fashionable outrages of unbalanced parties. In the name of human and divine benevolence, is such a system as this to be recommended to Americans, in this age of the world?" [IV, 287].

130. No interviews . . . this service: I.e., the service of designing the forms of American governments (state and federal).

131. Grosvenor Sq.: [66:30]. JA's residence at the time he wrote his preface (dated Jan. 1, 1787).

132. Vitruvius: Marcus V. Pollio, fl. 1st century B.C., Roman architect whose work served as one of the models for Renaissance architecture.

133. Palladio: [40:27]. Like architects called upon to design new buildings, who consult such masters as Vitruvius and Palladio, American patriots such as JA, called upon "to erect new systems of laws for their future government," consulted the wisest political philosophers on government [IV, 293].

134. the young gents of literature: Source has "younger gentlemen of letters" [IV, 294].

135. Tacitus: Publius Cornelius T., 55-120?, Roman historian. He praised the idea of a republic ruled by a governor, a senate, and a house of representatives, although he doubted the "practicability" or "duration" of such a division [IV, 294].

136. facilius . . . potest esse: L, "it is more easily praised than discovered / or not lasting / excellently blended in moderation . . . / is nevertheless brought about in unison . . . a state by agreement / where there is no justice, there can be no law." (For sources of these fragments see Tacitus, *Annales* IV, xxxiii, 20, where the test reads: . . . *laudari facilius quam evenire, vel si evenit, haud diaturna esse potest*; Cicero, *De Re Publica* II, xxiii, 41, where the text reads: *statu esse optimo . . . confusa modice*; Cicero, *De Re Publica* II, xlii, 69, and III, *Fragmenta*, where the text reads: *Ubi justitia vera non est, nec jus potest esse*, a quotation from St. Augustine, *De Civitate Dei* XIX, 21.) [IV, 294-296].

137. San Marino: Republic on Italian peninsula, cited by JA as an example of a government of "checks and limitations" which had lasted for "thirteen hundred years, while all the other states of Italy have several times changed masters and forms of government" [IV, 308, 304].

138. Dalmatia: [17:33].

139. their own rights: Source says "their own privileges" [IV, 345]; JA's comment on Geneva's history after the 16th century.

140. nobles . . . manufacturies: JA refers to Genoa where the nobles themselves were often prosperous merchants and thus not separated from a competing merchant class in a way that generated factionalism.

141. Venice: The 12 lines that follow deal with JA's account of Venetian history [IV, 347-356].

142. Anafeste: Paul Luc A., died A.D. 717, early tribune of Venice and first doge; reputed to have been a just magistrate.

143. 5 massacred . . . 5 abdications: JA's summary of fates of doges during one period of Venetian history. The doge was the chief magistrate of Venice.

144. before they thought . . . government: JA refers to Venetian government down to the 12th century.

145. cunning: "The aristocracy is always more sagacious than an assembly of the people. . . . It is always more cunning, too . . . " [IV, 354-355].

146. whereon nobles depend from: Source reads "dependent on" [IV, 355].

147. stadtholder: Chief of state in Holland; JA refers to the hereditary ruler of Holland.

148. Lolme: John Louis de L., 1740-1806, Swiss lawyer. Author of *The Constitution of England* (1771), said by JA to be "the best defence of the political balance of three powers that ever was written" [IV, 358].

149. Ukraine: JA quotes from the writings of King Stanislaus of Poland, who lamented the despair of the inhabitants of the Ukraine after their unsuccessful insurrection to assert their rights. JA's point is that a balance of powers in government would protect the people from such suppressions by king or nobles.

150. Neuchâtel: Swiss canton in Jura

Mountains. JA observes that the constitution of Neuchâtel divided the government into three branches, and that it was "the only constitution in which the citizens can truly be said to be in that happy condition of freedom and discipline, sovereignty and subordination, which the Greeks express so concisely by their ᾽αρχειν και ᾽αρχεσθαι" [IV, 377].

151. ᾽αρχειν και ᾽αρχεσθαι: H, "to rule and to be ruled." The words constitute a theme in Greek political thought, going back as far as Solon and reappearing in Aristotle's *Politics*: "Ruling and being ruled . . . not only belongs to the category of things necessary, but also to that of things expedient" (Barker's translation). Barker summarizes the chapter (I.v) thus: "There is a principle of rule and subordination in nature at large: it appears especially in the realm of animate creation. By virtue of that principle, the soul rules the body; and by virtue of it the master, who possesses the rational faculty of the soul, rules the slave, who possesses only bodily powers and the faculty of understanding the directions given by another's reason" [*Politics* 1277b, 15; III.iv].

152. Rhodes: [24:37]. JA believed that the constitution of ancient Rhodes was probably very similar to the constitution of Neuchâtel.

153. jura ordo . . . æquitas leges: L, "rights order . . . equity laws" [Livy, *Annals* III, 63]. In JA's opinion these are the characteristics of a government in which powers are divided and balanced. Source reads "æquatas" [IV, 377].

154. stadtholder: [cf. 147 above].

155. avoyer: F, chief magistrate of a free city or a canton in French Switzerland.

156. alcalde: S, "chief administrator."

157. capitaneo: I, an administrative official. In his "Recapitulation" at the end of Volume I, chapter 3 of *Defence*, JA observes that all republics in past history seem to have had some kind of chief magistrate, however different the titles given him in different countries.

158. Turgot: [31:35; 119 above]. JA's criticism of Turgot was that if Turgot had known of any examples of a successful country that did not have a chief officer, he would have revealed his knowledge to the world; but since he had not done so, there must be no such examples. Therefore, the Americans should not be censured for creating the office of "governor" for their states [IV, 379].

159. orders of officers: Source reads "orders of offices" [IV, 380]. In contrasting the American system with traditional European governments, JA observes: "In America, there are different orders of *offices*, but none of *men*. Out of office, all men are of the same species, and of one blood; there is neither a greater nor a lesser nobility" [IV, 380].

CANTO LXVIII

Sources

Charles Francis Adams, ed., *The Works of John Adams,* IV, V, VI, VII; Frederick K. Sanders, *John Adams Speaking*, Orono, Maine, 1975, 356-399.

Background

Peter Shaw, *The Character of John Adams*, Chapel Hill, N. C., 1974; Page Smith, *John Adams*, 2 vols., Garden City, N. Y., 1962; Samuel Flagg Bemis, *The Diplomacy of the American Revolutionn*, Bloomington, Indiana, 1957; L. H. Butterfield, ed., *Diary and Autobiography of John Adams*, II, Cambridge, Mass., 1961.

Exegeses

CE, *Ideas*, 43, 176, 177; Davis, *Vision*, 141-142; CB-R, *ZBC*, 121.

Glossary

1. Regis optimatium populique: L, "Of the king, of the aristocrats, of the people" [cf. Polybius, Fragments, VI, quoted by Jonathan Swift, *A Discourse of the Contests and Dissensions between the Nobles and Commons of Athens and Rome*; quoted in *WJA*, IV, 383]. The first 12 lines of this canto, which come from the chapter in JA's *Defence* [cf. 11 below] titled "Opinions of Philosophers," continue his major theme that the best form of government is one of divided powers with checks on one another.

2. Lycurgus: Spartan lawgiver, 9th century B.C.

3. Spartha: Sparta.

4. reges, seniores, et populus: L, "kings, elders, and people." Recognizing that people in each of these categories were subject to corruption, Lycurgus had proposed a government combining all three.

5. both greeks and italians: JA refers to "the most ancient and inherent principle" of limited and divided powers in government, recognized by both Greeks and Italians [IV, 384].

6. archons: Chief magistrates of Athens.

7. suffestes: L, *sufes* (*-fetis*): suffetes. A suffete was one of the two highest magistrates in Carthage. Source has "suffetes."

8. consuls: Joint magistrates of the Roman Republic. From JA's quotation of Jonathan Swift's remark about the similarities between Greek monarchies and Italian republics, that the Greek kings at Troy held a power comparable to that of the Athenian archons, the Carthaginian suffetes, and the Roman consuls.

9. Athenians . . . Achaians: Achaeans. Greek peoples that at one time or another tried to achieve a "universal monarchy" for Greece [IV, 387].

10. using the people . . . not in maintaining: JA quotes Swift's criticism of popular assemblies, that a people who think they rule are often manipulated into accepting a tyrant and that popular opinion can be more easily set to tearing down than to preserving what is valuable in government. [IV, 388]

11. Turgot: Anne Robert Jacques T., 1727-1781, wrote a letter that JA conceived to be an attack upon the U. S. system of government. JA's response, *A Defence of the Constitutions of Government of the United States of America, Against the Attack of M. Turgot, in His letter to Dr. Price, Dated the Twenty-Second Day of March, 1778*, appeared in three volumes in 1787, all of them included in *WJA* Volumes IV-VI. [This work is referred to elsewhere as

Defence, but the citations are to *WJA*, as here: IV, 405.]

12. How shall the plow: JA quotes Lord Bacon's observation that if the nobility grow too populous, commoners will tend to lose their independence and become little more than hired laborers, thus weakening the balance among monarch, aristocrats, and commoners [IV, 428]. Source has "plough."

13. Lycurgus: Reference to why Lycurgus wanted to balance the powers of three branches of government against one another [IV, 443].

14. Plato: After several pages of analysis of Plato's *Republic*, Book IV in particular, JA concludes with the lines Pound quotes and associates Plato's ten ideas with parts of Sir Thomas More's *Utopia* [IV, 461-463].

15. Sir Thos More: Sir Thomas M., 1478-1535, English statesman, humanist, and author of works on political philosophy which JA finds to be more than "Utopian."

16. Bedlam: Bethlehem Royal Hospital in London, where the insane were incarcerated.

17. Milton: Pound's summary of JA's criticism of Milton as a political philosopher. JA quotes a statement Milton made in *Ready and Easy Way to Establish a Free Commonwealth*: "I doubt not but all ingenuous and knowing men will easily agree with me, that a free commonwealth, without single person or house of lords, is by far the best government, if it can be had," but Milton goes on to elaborate this premise in such a way that JA concludes: "Can one read, without shuddering, this wild reverie of the divine, immortal Milton?" [IV, 464-465].

18. Lowered interest: Refers to Solon's policy, in ancient Greece, of reconciling the rich with the poor: " . . . this he accomplished by lowering the interest without annulling the debt, and by taking from the creditor the exorbitant powers over the person and family of the debtor" [IV,

477]—a principle of fiscal justice which Pound along with JA endorses.

19. in this transaction: Source reads "in this translation" [IV, 568], i.e., Pope's translation of the *Odyssey*.

20. Mr Pope: Alexander P., 1688-1744. Of Pope's translation of part of Alcinoüs's speech to Odysseus, "Twelve princes in our realm dominion share / O'er whom supreme imperial power I bear" [*Od.* VIII, 390-391], JA said: "Mr. Pope, indeed, in this translation, has given him the air of a sovereign; but there is nothing like it in the original. There, Alcinoüs, with all possible simplicity and modesty, only says,—'Twelve illustrious kings, or archons, rule over the people, and I myself am the thirteenth' " [IV, 568].

21. Tacitus: [67:135]. Source reads: "Through the whole of Tacitus and Homer, the three orders are visible both in Germany and Greece . . . [Troubles] arose entirely from the want of having the prerogatives and privileges of those orders defined, from the want of independence in each of them, and a balance between them" [IV, 578].

22. and mankind . . . Constitutions: At the end of Volume III of *Defence* (more than 800 pages later than preceding note), JA concludes that such a work will not be much encouraged because "mankind, in general, dare not as yet read or think upon CONSTITUTIONS" [VI, 217].

23. 'No man: I.e., no one who interpreted JA's *Discourses on Davila* (1790) as a pro-monarchy tract accepted his opinions on the dangers of the popular egalitarian dogmas of the French Revolution [VI, 227].

24. Davila: Enrico Caterino D., 1576-1631, author of *Istoria delle Guerre Civili di Francia* [*History of French Civil Wars*], 1630. While vice-president JA wrote *Discourses on Davila* (1790), partly in response to certain currents of thought stirred by the French Revolution and partly as a sequel to *Defence*, reminding his countrymen once again of the importance of a division of governmental powers for political stability. JA's defense of titles such as king and duke in this work led to attacks from Anti-Federalists who claimed that JA wanted to introduce hereditary offices into the U. S. government.

25. Be bubbled out . . . : Poss. refers to JA's quotation of Davila's description of the rights of princes in early French history [VI, 230].

26. Hume: [67:24]. JA's criticism (in *Defence*) of Hume for criticizing such writers as Locke, Sidney, and Hoadley for being inappropriately reputed to be the equals of the ancient philosophers.

27. Franks: Group of Germanic tribes. JA called it the "great misfortune" of the Franks that they never decided whether their national assembly or their king had sovereignty [VI, 228].

28. J.A.: John Adams began writing *Davila* in his first year as vice-president. In a footnote CFA cites JA's remark about reactions to the work. Of one reviewer he said: "The writer was 'a young man; a forward young man' " [VI, 229].

29. Pharamond: Legendary king of Salian Franks, ca. 5th century B.C. He supposedly published the Salic code, which included penal and civil laws.

30. Sala: River in the Netherlands, the modern Ijssel River, the N mouth of the Rhine. Sala, its ancient name, is applied to the inhabitants along its banks, the Salian Franks.

31. here . . . jargon: JA refers to the idea of a single central authority with the unresolved question of whether that authority lies in the States General or in the king, a dominant problem in French history.

32. Miseria . . . vagum: Source says "misera." L, "Slavery is a misery, where rights are undefined" [VI, 230n]. JA added this phrase in 1804 as a marginal comment on a passage in *Davila* about the calamities that had befallen the French because of their uncertainty over the claims of sovereignty in the different branches of government.

33. predilections: Source says "propensities" [VI, 232].

34. commended: Source says "considered" [VI, 232].

35. Mr Hillhouse: James A. H., 1754-1832, American lawyer, member of House of Representatives (1791-1808). In 1808 Hillhouse submitted to the Senate a pamphlet entitled "Propositions for Amending the Constitution of the United States." This and the following four lines are taken from JA's analysis of Hillhouse's propositions [VI, 525-550]. Hillhouse wrote that the U. S. Constitution had been modeled on that of England which, combining monarchy, aristocracy, and democracy, was an inappropriate model because the first two branches were hereditary. JA's answer was that a more accurate model was to be found in the colonial constitutions, in which offices were not hereditary.

36. Emissaries: Hillhouse had recommended annual elections for federal officials as a way to weaken the influence of party caucuses; JA replied that caucuses would continue in any event and that anyone seeking to influence policy, whether foreigner or American, would still do so if elections were held annually.

37. Commission to France: From a letter of Henry Laurens, president of Continental Congress, to JA, dated December 3, 1777, notifying JA of his appointment to replace Silas Deane [65:39] as commissioner to France [VII, 5].

38. Lafayette: In his letter to JA [cf. 37 above], Laurens mentioned a skirmish at Gloucester, N. J., in November 1777, in which Lafayette, leading a group of Morgan's Rifles, had bested a superior force of British and Hessians.

39. Morgan: Daniel M., 1736-1802, American Revolutionary soldier. He and his sharpshooters played a decisive role in the battles of Saratoga, New York, and Cowpens, South Carolina.

40. Henry Laurens: 1724-1792, American Revolutionary statesman from Charleston, South Carolina; member of Second Continental Congress and its president (1777-78). Sent to the Netherlands in 1780 as U.S. commissioner, he was captured en route by the British and imprisoned in the Tower of London; he was exchanged for Cornwallis in 1781. With Laurens was captured a copy of the proposed United States-Netherlands treaty, called the "Amsterdam treaty" by JA, which had been accepted by William Lee for the U.S. and by Jean de Neufville for the regency of Amsterdam in 1778 at Aix-la-Chapelle. The British used the discovery of this treaty as a pretext for war against the Netherlands [cf. Butterfield, II, 452-453 n. 1, for concise account].

41. Mons. le Comte de Broglie: Victor François, duc de B., 1718-1804, marshal of France (1759); minister of war (1789). Upon learning that JA had been appointed commissioner to France, Baron de Kalb [cf. 42 below] offered to provide JA letters of introduction to certain parties in France, including the duc de Broglie [VII, 9].

42. De Klab: Johann Kalb, 1721-1780, known as Baron de Kalb; German army officer commissioned major general in Continental Army (1777-1780); killed at battle of Camden, South Carolina.

43. Lafayette: Hearing that JA was going to France, Lafayette asked him to take a letter to friends reporting his experience in the "noble cause" of the fight for American independence [VII, 10-11].

44. novelty of the scene: From a letter JA wrote the Committee of Commerce of the Congress (May 24, 1778) reporting the disorder he found in American financial affairs when he reached France, its possible

cause, and what he planned to do to correct it.

45. some facilities: Source reads "same facilities" [VII, 23].

46. De Sartine: Antoine Raymond Jean Gualbet Gabriel de S., comte d'Aloy, 1729-1801, French statesman; minister of marine (1774-1780). On July 29, 1778, de Sartine wrote to the U.S. commissioners in France that the formal alliance with France signed in February 1778 should make it easier for American privateers to dispose of their prizes in French ports, and that, in reciprocation, he expected French privateers to receive similar opportunities in American ports [VII, 23].

47. B.Fr. A.Lee J.A. . . . : Benjamin Franklin, Arthur Lee, and John Adams to the comte de Vergennes. The preceding six lines come from a letter the U.S. commissioners wrote to Vergennes on August 28, 1778, requesting an additional 750,000-livre loan from the French government to allow the U.S. to pay interest due on paper money which had been borrowed in large quantities [VII, 25-27].

48. Vergennes: [45:45].

49. (Beaumarchais): [31:29]. Refers to a letter from the American commissioners to Beaumarchais dated September 10, 1778. The commissioners were trying to settle a dispute involving the French merchant ship *Theresa* as part of an effort to get American financial accounts in order. Beaumarchais claimed that the *Theresa* belonged to his firm, Roderique Hortalez & Co.

50. M. Monthieu: John Joseph de M., business partner of Beaumarchais also connected with Roderique Hortalez & Co. Monthieu arranged the sale and rental of armed vessels to America during the Revolution.

51. John Baptiste Lazarus: J.B.L. de Theveneau de Francy, commercial agent for Beaumarchais.

52. Roderique Hortalez: R.H. & Co., a

mock company set up secretly by Beau-marchais to sell military supplies to the American colonies during the Revolution. The reference here is to a letter from the Committee of Commerce of the Continental Congress to the American commissioners in France, who communicated it to Vergennes on September 10, 1778, stating that the Committee of Commerce had entered into a contract with the firm of Roderique Hortalez & Co. through agent Lazarus [cf. 51 above].

53. Ray de Chaumont: [65:66]. As part of his undertaking to straighten out American accounts in Europe, JA had inquired about rent due on the house at Passy where he and Franklin stayed. The preceding four lines come from Le Ray de Chaumont's letter to JA (Sept. 18, 1778), explaining that he refuses rent for this house as part of his support of the American struggle for inde-pendence [VII, 32-33].

54. Bersolle: Fl. 1778; Frenchman engaged in the repair of ships.

55. the Drake: English ship captured by John Paul Jones in 1778.

56. Jones's: John Paul J. [65:124].

57. supplies or slops: Source says "supplies of slops" [VII, 65]. The U.S. commis-sioners were saying that by act of Congress "the whole of all vessels of war taken by our frigates belong to the officers and men." Thus they, and not Congress, must pay for repairs.

58. the Ranger: Ship commanded by John Paul Jones in 1777-78.

59. the Chatham: This English ship, cap-tured by the *Ranger* during the American Revolution, created a special problem: "As the Lord Chatham belongs, half to the public and half to the captors, all necessary expenses on her account should be paid; a moiety out of the captors' half, and the other moiety out of the half which belongs to the United States" [VII, 65].

60. Schweighauser: [65:98]. The preceding ten lines come from a letter the American commissioners wrote to Schweighauser (Nov. 4, 1778) explaining which expenses of John Paul Jones should be paid with govern-ment funds and which expenses should come out of the bounty he and his men received from the prizes they captured.

61. de Sartine: [cf. 46 above]. The prece-ding six lines come from a letter the Amer-ican commissioners sent to de Sartine (Nov. 12, 1778) requesting that supplies for winter warfare be included in the cargo of French warships sailing to America [VII, 68-69].

62. It is certain ... wanted: From a letter JA wrote to Lafayette (Feb. 21, 1779) concerning the need of a loan to support the value of the paper currency issued by the Continental Congress [VII, 84].

63. Master Johnnie: Source reads "master Johnny": John Quincy Adams, mentioned in Franklin's letter of April 3, 1779, to JA. The letter exhibited the formal courtesies maintained by the two men despite their frequent disagreements about the conduct of the American mission in France [VII, 90].

64. Leghorn: Livorno, Italian seaport S of Pisa. In a letter of August 4, 1779, to John Jay, president of the Congress, JA pointed out that although the fortunes of Italy were in general decline, the U.S. after indepen-dence might find the privileges of the port of Leghorn useful if an American minister were accepted at the court of Vienna [VII, 109].

65. Huntington: Samuel H., 1731-1796, member of Continental Congress (1776-1783) and its president (1779-1781); signer of Declaration of Independence. Refers to Huntington's letter (Oct. 20, 1779) inform-ing JA that he had been appointed minister plenipotentiary to negotiate treaties of peace and commerce with Great Britain and telling him what his salary would be [VII, 119].

66. My Dear General: Salutation of JA's letter to Lafayette (Feb. 18, 1780) concern-ing England's propaganda and other activities, such as making "new contracts with other petty princes in Germany" [VII, 123].

67. Petersburg: JA told Lafayette that the English "claimed to have concluded a treaty with the Court of Petersburg, by which Russia is to furnish them with twelve ships of the line and twenty thousand men" [VII, 123].

68. (. . . and to Genet): JA sent a similar letter to Genêt [65:120] containing essentially the same information about British war propaganda intended to discourage other European powers from supporting the American war of independence [VII, 124-125].

69. 19th (next day): This and the following line come from Lafayette's reply to JA's letter in which he discounted the effectiveness of British rumors.

70. Mr Burke: [62:17, 71 below].

71. Mr Fox: Charles James F., 1749-1806, English statesman who sided with Burke against Lord North's policies toward the American colonies. This and the preceding line come from JA's letter of March 24, 1780, to President Huntington of the Congress, in which he mentioned a bill proposed by Edmund Burke doing away with the policies that had made British authority odious to the colonies, and Mr. Fox's charge that Thomas Hutchinson [62:47] had been, as JA put it, the "firebrand that lighted up all the fire between the two countries" [VII, 136].

72. Bolingbroke: Henry St. John, Viscount B., 1678-1751, English statesman and orator; author of *Idea of a Patriot King* (1749). The lines "the precise point . . . / prejudice" come from JA's letter to Genêt (April 29, 1780) recommending that Genêt print Bolingbroke's observation that the turning point in the shift of political power, like the point of the solstice, is often imperceptible and unrecognized.

73. Elbridge Gerry: [34:52]. The lines "For

the calling . . . / . . . by warrants" come from Gerry's letter to JA (May 5, 1780) reporting the steps Congress had taken to prop up the value of American currency [VII, 188-190].

74. $40 to 1 in specie: The rate of depreciation of American paper money adopted March 18, 1780, by resolution of Congress. Vergennes called JA's attention to this decision in a letter of June 21, 1780, protesting the loss such a policy would mean to the French. The 20 lines that follow deal with the depreciation controversy, the cause of a bitter quarrel between JA and Vergennes as well as between JA and Franklin. JA expected Franklin to support him in defending the depreciation policy; Vergennes wanted Franklin to back the French objections with the Congress. Franklin chose not to take sides, but in a letter to Congress declared that JA was an obstruction to the alliance with France. Vergennes attempted to have JA recalled; through the efforts of his agent in Philadelphia, the Chevalier de la Luzerne, Franklin did succeed in having JA's commerce commission withdrawn and JA's role in the peace negotiations diminished by having that commission enlarged to include (in addition to Franklin) Jefferson, Henry Laurens, and John Jay [cf. Shaw, chap. vi, for an account of this episode].

75. Chevalier de Luzerne: [65:195]. Vergennes, in his letter of June 21, 1780, to JA said that Luzerne had already received instructions to make strong objections to the Congress; in his reply (June 22, 1780) JA, suspecting that maneuvering had been going on behind his back, asked Vergennes whether the orders had been sent "so long ago as to have reached the hand of the Chevalier da la Luzerne" or had just recently been decided and sent [VII, 193].

76. Mazzei: Philip M., 1730-1816, Italian physician who came to Virginia in 1773. He strongly supported the American Revolution and served as an American agent in Italy (1779-1783). This and the three following lines come from a letter JA sent to Thomas

Jefferson (June 29, 1780) reporting a meeting with Mazzei.

77. Value . . . de Vergennes: Knowing he had a degree of sympathy from Franklin and from certain members of Congress for his objections to the depreciation policy, Vergennes sent JA a letter (June 30, 1780) chastising him for not recognizing the justice of the French objections. These seven lines are from that letter [VII, 213].

78. Rush: [65:56]. From a letter dated April 28, 1780, JA received from Rush, who reported on conditions at home.

79. If the french fleet: In a letter to Vergennes (July 13, 1780), JA detailed his analysis of the military situation and the role the French fleet could play. The context of the JA line suggests that "that coast" means the whole E coast of North America. Earlier in the same letter JA wrote: "The appearance of a French fleet upon our coasts has repeatedly compelled, and ever must compel, the English to call off from their cruises all their frigates and other ships, and to assemble them at New York for their security, and the defence of that place" [VII, 223].

80. Vergennes: On July 17, 1780, JA wrote Vergennes that he was unable to see any reasons for having had to conceal his authority to negotiate a commerce treaty with the British, as Vergennes had asked him to do in a letter of February 24, 1780.

81. Amsterdam: [62:88]. On July 23, 1780, JA wrote Huntington, president of the Congress, that he had informed Vergennes of his decision to go to Amsterdam [65:148].

82. Europe: JA remarked in a letter to Franklin (Aug. 17, 1780) that only when their countrymen demonstrate their ability to win the war by themselves can they expect European nations to extend them support.

83. to show U. S.: In another letter to Huntington (Sept. 5, 1780), JA wrote that because the Athenians and Romans had left eloquent records of their achievements, they had been models down through the centuries, convincing reasons why the U. S., in its literature, should want to leave posterity a worthy record of achievements.

84. Ching Ming: Chêng Ming, "Right name" [51:20].

85. Mr Bicker . . . Neufville: The advice, as JA recalled it in his *Letters to the Boston Patriot* (1809), of Henrick Bicker, 1722-1783, an Amsterdam merchant who in 1780 recommended to JA the best way to go about securing a loan from the Dutch.

86. Neufville: Jean de N. & Sons, Dutch banking house through which JA tried to arrange an American loan; his effort failed, although the firm did what it could to support JA's request.

87. provision . . . 3 million guilders: Terms of a loan to the U. S. as explained in a letter to JA (Sept. 29, 1780) [VII, 262].

88. I answered . . . to be known: From JA's explanation of how he came to write "Twenty-Six Letters upon Interesting Subjects respecting the Revolution of America," newspaper articles by which "just sentiments of American affairs began to spread, and prevail over the continual misrepresentations of English and Stadtholderian gazettes" [VII, 265-266].

89. Mr. Calkoen: [62:87].

90. wd / be burdensome . . . on the contrary: Comments from JA's "Twenty-Six Letters."

91. Charleston: City in South Carolina captured May 12, 1780, by Sir Henry Clinton and held by British forces until December 14, 1782.

92. when England . . . regular ministers: From a letter JA wrote to Franklin (Oct. 14, 1780) in which he mentioned the difficulties of securing a loan and the need for the U. S. to send ministers to all European courts in an effort to win recognition of U. S. independence.

93. Laurens: [cf. 40 above].

94. dont la fâcheuse . . . Congrès: F, "whose regrettable catastrophe makes me most unhappy . . . / a relative indicates to me that he is inclined to invest twenty thousand Dutch florins in it / Ven der Kemp can be very useful to the Congress" [VII, 317-318]. These lines come from a letter to JA from Joan Derk, Baron van der Capellen tot den Pol [62:93; 65:152], a leader of the Patriot party in the Netherlands friendly to the U. S.

95. King of Spain . . . (meaning placing one): These nine lines are taken from a letter Franklin wrote JA concerning another possibility for a loan to the U. S.

96. Monsieur Necker: Jacques N., 1732-1804, French statesman; minister of finance (1776-1781); director general of finance (1788-1790).

97. depuis qu'il . . . à la Tour: F, "since he . . . has been locked up in the Tower" [VII, 323]. In a letter to JA (Nov. 1, 1780), L. M. Dumas made this inquiry about the condition of Henry Laurens, held captive in England.

98. towYer of London: Tower of L., ancient fortress, prison, and royal residence.

99. America is willing: JA's observation to Henrick Bicker in a letter (Nov. 6, 1780) about conditions for a loan.

100. Mortier and Meerkemaer: Dutch brokers employed by banking house of Van Staphorst.

101. Mssrs Staphorst: [62:108].

102. Mr Blomberg: Banker in Amsterdam. This and the preceding line come from a letter Bicker sent to JA (Nov. 7, 1780). Blomberg's illness made it necessary for JA to deal with another broker.

103. Tenkate: The Messrs. Tenkate, Amsterdam brokers; this and the following line reflect Bicker's opinion.

104. Mr Van Vloten: Van Vlooten, Dutch broker, recommended by Bicker with some reservations in a letter to JA (Nov. 11, 1780) as another possible source for a loan.

105. H. Bicker: [cf. 85 above]. The preceding three lines come from Bicker's letter to JA (Nov. 11, 1780) [VII, 327-328].

106. but have never . . . J.A.: JA's comment on the failure of his efforts up to that time to secure a loan, written in a letter to Alexander Gillon of South Carolina, who was in Amsterdam to negotiate a loan for South Carolina and had submitted a request for money to JA [VII, 328].

107. Sir Jo. Yorke: Joseph Y., Baron Dover, 1724-1792, English diplomat; ambassador to The Hague (1751-1780). In a letter to Huntington, president of the Congress (Nov. 16, 1780), JA corrected an erroneous description of the government of the Netherlands presented by Sir Joseph Yorke in a memorial to the States General (Nov. 10, 1780), which contained British protests against the proposed "Amsterdam treaty" between the U.S. and the Dutch and demanded punishment of the regents who had supported it.

108. England: In a letter to Huntington (Nov. 17, 1780), JA explained that one difficulty hindering his efforts to secure a loan was the long-established habit the Dutch had of thinking of England as their natural ally and of France as their natural enemy. Taking advantage of their past relationship, George III was demanding that the Dutch repudiate the proposed Amsterdam treaty and punish the Amsterdam regents participating in its negotiation. When the Dutch did not submit to British demands, war broke out. In time JA succeeded in negotiating loans with the Dutch.

109. la persécution . . . d'Holland: F, "the persecution against M. Van Berckel / and his associates / . . . not to rush your departure / business . . . crisis . . . time could / object of the English beyond that of amusing the Republic of Holland" [VII, 334-336]. This passage comes from a letter Van der

Capellen sent JA (Nov. 28, 1780) in response to the controversy resulting from the British protest against the Amsterdam treaty. E. F. Van Berckel had been singled out for particular criticism because he had sponsored the treaty. Source reads "pourroit" for "pourrait."

110. loss of Charleston ... neutrality: JA's letter (Dec. 14, 1780) to Huntington contained these observations as to why the Dutch were not eager to provide political or monetary help to the U.S. [cf. 92 above].

111. tout crédit ... de faire face: F, "all credit whether of a people or an individual / ... of two things / the opinion as to the good faith / and as to the chances of his meeting." These lines come from a letter Van der Capellen sent to JA (Dec. 24, 1780)

reminding him of the conditions conducive to winning the support he was seeking [VII, 344].

112. Affaires ... upon 'change: Lines taken from JA's letter to Huntington (Dec. 25, 1780). Source reads "holydays" [VII, 346].

113. 'What they ... years later: Taken from *Letters to the Boston Patriot* (1809) in which JA again spoke of the need for checks and balances in governmental authority. Thus Pound returns to the theme that opened the canto: "There is nothing so instructive to aristocracy and democracy as the history of Holland ... nothing which ought so forcibly to admonish them to shake hands and mutually agree to choose an arbitrator between ..." [VII, 348n].

CANTO LXIX

Sources

Charles Francis Adams, ed., *The Works of John Adams,* VII, VIII; Frederick K. Sanders, *John Adams Speaking,* Orono, Maine, 1975, 400-427; Claude G. Bowers, *Jefferson and Hamilton,* New York, 1925; Dante, *Inferno,* passim.

Background

Broadus Mitchell, *Alexander Hamilton*, New York, 2 vols., 1957-1962; L. H. Butterfield, ed., *Diary and Autobiography of John Adams,* II, Cambridge, Mass. 1961; Samuel Flagg Bemis, *The Diplomacy of the American Revolution,* Bloomington, Indiana, 1957.

Exegeses

CE, *Ideas,* 43; Dekker, *Cantos,* 186; Davis, *Vision,* 142; WB, *Rose,* 46; CB-R, *ZBC,* 240.

Glossary

1. **Congress**: Still concerned with his problems in Amsterdam, JA wrote to the president of Congress that in the event that Holland aligned itself with France, Spain, and America, a permanent minister from Congress to Holland would be useful. He added: "In case the armed neutrality take it up, a minister authorized to represent the United States to all the neutral courts, might be of use" [VII, 348].

2. **Huntington**: Samuel H., 1731-1796, president of Continental Congress (1779-1781), sent JA a commission as minister plenipotentiary to the Low Countries.

3. **Madame . . . Schorn**: F, "Madame the widow of Henry Schorn." JA in a letter to Francis Dana revealed a secret address given him by the widow. The line in Dutch means: "up near the Agsterburg Wall in the Hoogstraat" [VII, 353].

4. **depreciation . . . only six**: These 18 lines summarize most of a letter from JA to Baron van der Capellen (Jan. 21, 1781) [62:93]. The letter of several pages includes: "England has spent sixty millions in this war. America six. Which people then are the ablest to pay? Yet England has credit, America not. Is this from reasoning or prejudice?" [VII, 357-360].

5. **a british minister**: A letter (March 17, 1781) from JA to Charles Dumas [cf. 21 below] asks a rhetorical question: "When will mankind cease to be the dupes of the insidious artifices of a British minister and stockjobber?" [VII, 379]. The minister referred to, not in source, is prob. Shelbourne [cf. 17 below].

6. **Vergennes**: French minister of foreign affairs [65:145]. JA, writing 28 years later (1809) to the *Boston Patriot* about a proposed congress of Vienna, protests that his many letters have been received in silence. He reports that he is happy because the plot of England to use such a congress to cheat the U.S. out of its liberty was defeated by his letters to Vergennes and with the help of two emperors, Alexander I of Russia and Joseph II of Austria. The congress, which did not take place, should not be confused with the Congress of Vienna of 1814-15.

7. **La Cour de Londres . . . Etats Unis**: F, "The Court of London will avoid as long as it can / the admission direct / or indirect of the independence of the United States." From letter of France to courts of Petersburg and Vienna about the proposed congress at Vienna [VII, 667]. Source has ". . . et aussi long-temps, qu'elle le pourra, l'aveu direct et indirect . . ."

8. **Cornwallis**: A return to the events of 1781. This line comes from JA's letter to the president of Congress saying that the defeat of Cornwallis has resulted in the "appearances of a growing interest" among Hollanders for "an alliance with France and America" [VII, 488].

9. **J'ai honte d'être Hollandais**: F, "I am ashamed of being Dutch." Said in letter to JA by Joan Derk, Baron van der Capellen, Dutch statesman and friend to America [62:93; 68:94], whose plan to lend 12,000 florins was circumvented. Source reads "Hollandois" [VII, 501].

10. **burgomasters**: To get a loan, JA went next to the "house of Haerlem" where he was met by the described people [VII, 505] who, he concluded in a letter to Franklin, were paid to refuse him [VII, 508-509].

11. **schepens**: D, "sheriffs."

12. **Friesland**: Province in N Netherlands to whose government JA made advances and by whom he was officially received.

13. **M. Berdsma**: Bergsma, fl. 1780, official of province of Friesland.

14. **Province House**: Official building of province of Friesland.

15. hanseatic: In another letter, JA said he had not been authorized to deal with the Hanseatic cities, but he believed it was in the nature of the situation that trade between them and America would flourish.

16. old gentleman: Henry Laurens [68: 40]. He was on parole from London for his health. JA talked with Laurens and reported to Franklin his opinions about the English government in 1782.

17. Shelbourne: Sir William Petty, 1737-1805, 2d Earl of Shelburne, 1st Marquis of Lansdowne; English statesman; secretary of state under Pitt (1766-1768) when he attempted conciliation of American colonies. But as first lord of the treasury and prime minister (1782-1783) Shelburne's attitude seemed ambiguous, although he eventually conceded American independence. Source has "Shelburne."

18. Fiseaux . . . etc.: Dutch banking houses and moneyed men. JA planned to obtain from them jointly a loan of 5 million. Source reads "Fizeaux" [VII, 575].

19. Le corps . . . Schiedam: F, "The businessmen of this city / wishing to add their acclamations to those of the whole nation / J. Nollet, Schiedam." From letter of Jacob Nolet to JA (April 19, 1782) expressing enthusiasm for the independence of the United States.

20. 'On m'a dit . . . de Rotterdam': F, "I have been told that these gentlemen of Schiedam / are giving this repast for a hundred people / and that there will be many people from Rotterdam." Source reads "donneront un repas" [VII, 576].

21. Dumas: From letter from Dumas to JA (April 30, 1782). Charles William Frederick D., Swiss man of letters employed by Franklin as an agent to promote American interests in Holland. He acted as secretary to JA while he was there and stayed in Holland as American chargé d'affaires after JA left.

22. remedium: L, "remedy." From letter of May 11, 1782. Pound dates it 1780 [VII, 583].

23. Willinck . . . : The bankers who made the loan of 5 million to JA.

24. piddling: JA in letter to Francis Dana (May 13, 1782). He added: "I shall be plagued with piddling politicians as long as I live" [VII, 584].

25. Van Vloten: Van Vlooten, Dutch broker who helped negotiate loan. From letter of JA to Willinck and other bankers [VII, 585].

26. The minister of the Emperor: Source says: "I come now to the most difficult task of all, the description of the foreign ministers. The minister of the Emperor is ninety years of age, and never appears at court, or anywhere else" [VII, 623]. The foreign minister and chancellor under Emperor Joseph II from 1753 to 1792 was Wenzel Anton, Fürst von Kaunitz, who was born in 1711. In 1782, therefore, he would have been only 71. JA's remark must have been based on rumor.

27. Oswald: Richard O., 1705-1784, English statesman. In 1782 he was authorized to make peace with the U.S. at the Paris peace negotiations. From letter of John Jay to JA (Sept. 28, 1782) [VII, 641-642].

28. statuum quorum: L, "of the condition of which."

29. (Lafayette): In a letter to Lafayette, JA tells how much money in loans he has got and says he hopes France will make up the rest that is needed [VII, 642].

30. J. A. to Jefferson: Source says this letter of October 7, 1782, is from JA to John Jay, not Jefferson [VII, 645].

31. France: In a letter to JA, Francis Dana analyzes France's efforts to convince Russia to sell to her during the war. Source reads "same from America" [VII, 650].

32. King's loans: JA wrote from Paris:

"There are great complaints of scarcity of money here, and what there is is shut up. The King's loans do not fill. The war has lasted so long, and money has been scattered with so much profusion, that it is now very scarce in France, Spain, and England, as well as Holland" [VII, 664].

33. Vergennes: JA believed that he and John Jay were deliberately given bad advice in protocol which, had they followed it, would have resulted in embarrassment to the U.S., and any European statesman would have known the advice was bad. Vergennes recommended that they deal with the English and Spaniards before they "were put upon the equal footing that our rank demanded." JA believed that if he and Jay "had yielded the punctilio of rank" they would have "sunk in the minds of the English, French, Spaniards, Dutch, and all the neutral powers." Since any European statesman would have known this, JA could only conclude that Vergennes meant to keep them down: ". . . to keep his hand under our chin to prevent us from drowning, but not to lift our heads out of the water?" [VIII, 4].

34. avoid . . . : JA is protesting that since 1775 he has advanced the principle that the U.S. should not become too dependent on any one European power [VIII, 35].

35. Nous sommes . . . la Société Bourgeoise: F, "Meanwhile we are delighted to see / that the states of the other provinces and consequently the / entire republic have, following the example of the States of Friesland / recognized . . . / (signed) the members of the Société Bourgeoise" [VIII, 56]. The sentence is completed by "the liberty and independence of America."

36. de Leeuwarde: Leeuwarden, commercial and industrial town, Friesland Province, N Netherlands.

37. W. Wopkins V. Cats: Officials of Friesland Province; members of the Société Bourgeoise established at Leeuwarden. Source has "Wopkens."

38. S. P. Q. Amst . . . juncta: L, "Senate and People of Amsterdam—in most fortunate union joined" [Vol. VIII of *WJA* has picture of the medal as a frontispiece].

39. factions etc.: In a letter to Robert Morris (May 21, 1783), JA says that many slanders and falsehoods are told him in the belief that he will relay them, and thus mislead, the Congress and the secretary of state. He adds: "I think it necessary, therefore, to employ a little discretion in such cases" [VIII, 59].

40. his Majesty: In his letter of May 27 JA says: "His Lordship then said, that . . . after the levee, I should be presented to his Majesty [Geo. III], in his closet, and there deliver my letter of credence" [VIII, 251-252].

41. To T. J / : JA asks Jefferson in letter of July 18, 1785: "Can it be a secret understanding between St. James's and Versailles? The design of ruining, if they can, our carrying trade, and annihilating all our navigation and seamen, is too apparent" [VIII, 279; the editor at top of page: *"The rest in Cipher, and kept secret"*].

42. St James: The Court of St. James's, London.

43. Act of navigation: JA in letter to John Jay (Aug. 8, 1785) opposes a law that would require all goods shipped to the U.S. to come in American ships navigated by American masters, with three-fourths of the seamen American [VIII, 297].

44. bubbles . . . : In a letter to Jay, JA says: "We have hitherto been the bubbles of our own philosophical and equitable liberality; and . . . both France and England have shown a constant disposition to take a selfish and partial advantage of us because of them." He hopes that "we shall be the dupes no longer than we must." Source dates this letter August 10, 1785 [VIII, 299].

45. Jay: John J., 1745-1829, American statesman who assisted in peace and trade negotiations with Great Britain.

46. Barbary: Barbary States, N Africa. JA wrote to Jefferson (Aug. 18, 1785): "He [the emissary from the Barbary States] should be instructed further, to make diligent inquiry concerning the productions of those countries which would answer in America, and those of the United States which might find a market in Barbary" [VIII, 301].

47. both governments: France and England. To Jefferson, JA says that, if these governments have been opening his mail, "much good may those contents do them. They both know they have deserved them. I hope they will convince them of their error, and induce them to adopt more liberal principles towards us" [VIII, 301].

48. Mr Pitt: William P. the Younger, 1759-1778 [66:14]. In a letter to Jay (Aug. 25, 1785), JA explains his explanation to Pitt, who had said the English got their interest on debts straight through wars. JA says that American lawyers believed that interest and principal, as well as all laws, were negated upon a declaration of war.

49. spermaceti: JA reporting to John Jay on a sales pitch he made (1785) to the British to persuade them to buy U.S. whale oil. He wrote that he had said (after the lines in the canto): ". . . we are all surprised that you prefer darkness, and consequent robberies, burglaries, and murders in your streets, to the receiving, as a remittance, our spermaceti oil. The lamps . . . in Downing Street . . . are dim by midnight, and extinguished by two o'clock; whereas our oil would burn bright till nine o'clock in the morning, and chase away, before the watchmen, all the villains, and save you the trouble and danger of introducing a new police into the city" [VIII, 308-309].

50. Portugal . . . better: JA protests the Methuen treaty which restricted trade. Port is a wine from Portugal [VIII, 324].

51. Lisbon: A sweet, light-colored wine produced in Estremadura and shipped from Lisbon, Portugal.

52. Madeira: Wine made on the island of Madeira; Malmsey, Sercial, and Bual are the best-known varieties.

53. His Lordship: Lord Carmarthen. JA wished there would be "nothing of greater difficulty and more danger between the two countries" [VIII, 325].

54. Holland: JA sent to John Jay an English translation of a contract for a new loan from Holland [letter of June 16, 1787; VIII, 441-442].

55. Lafayette: Letter to JA describes Lafayette's hopes for a French constitution. He says they will have the best, but one. "May *that one* . . . be forever the happy lot of the sons of America!" [VIII, 456].

56. T. Jefferson: JA says: "We agree . . . that the many should have a full, fair, and perfect representation. You are apprehensive of monarchy, I, of aristocracy" [VIII, 464].

57. In this matter of redeeming certificates . . . : This line and the remainder of the canto concern what is to Pound a major turning point in the economic direction of the nation. Pound's immediate source for the lines is Bowers, chapters iii and iv (pp. 43-91), which contains a discussion of the strategy and step-by-step maneuvering Hamilton employed to implement his elaborate plan for controlling the states and getting them into the power of the federal government: "With the startling effect of a magician at his tricks he created the machinery of his complicated department . . . outlined his plans for revenue immediately required, and sat down with joy to the preparation of his 'Report on the Public Credit,' which was to proclaim the public faith and establish the Nation's credit" [p. 43]. Part of Hamilton's plan was the so-called Assumption Bill, a mechanism by which the federal government would assume the debts of the states and redeem at full value certificates issued to pay soldiers and buy war materials—certificates that had sunk to a fraction of their face value. JA approved the plan as a necessary and honest measure to establish the credit of the nation. So did Madison at first. But it soon became known that Hamilton in secret meetings had leaked information to a number of friends and financial operators who were buying up the certificates at almost no cost in order to make a financial killing: "The greater part of the certificates were in the hands of the prosperous who had taken advantage of the necessities of the orignal holders—Revolutionary soldiers, small farmers, hard-pressed country merchants. The funding system would tax all the people to pay to the rich a hundred cents on the dollar for evidence of debts that had cost them fifteen or twenty. With the people taxed to pay the interest—it was proposed to perpetuate the debt. Thus, for generations . . . the Government would operate for the enrichment of the few already rich, and the masses would pay the piper" [p. 45].

58. in margine: L, "in the margin."

59. King . . . Sedgwick: Part of Hamilton's plan was a national bank, not conceived as part of the treasury but modeled upon the Bank of England. It was designed as a private institution from which the government as well as other banks, institutions, or individuals might borrow. In spite of a bitter fight which some say created the split between the Hamiltonians and the Jeffersonians and resulted in a two-party system, the first Bank of the United States was chartered in the summer of 1791. Bowers writes: "Then came the election of Bank directors in the fall, and indignation flamed when the prizes went to leaders in the Congress that had created the Bank—to Rufus King, Samuel Johnson of North Carolina, William Smith of South Carolina, Jeremiah Wadsworth of the 'fast sailing vessels,' John Laurance of New York, William Bingham of Philadelphia, Charles Carroll of Carrollton, George Cabot, Fisher Ames, and Thomas Willing, the partner of Robert Morris" [p. 90].

60. King: Rufus K., 1755-1827, American statesman, graduated Harvard, 1777; served in Revolution; practiced law in Massachusetts; delegate to Continental Congress (1784-1787); moved to New York and was elected to first U.S. Senate. A strong advocate of Federalist doctrines, he supported Hamilton's programs, defended Jay's Treaty, and was defeated at various times as a candidate for vice-president and president.

61. Sam Johnson: William Samuel J., 1727-1819, American jurist and educator; member of Continental Congress (1784-1787) and U.S. Senate (1789-1791); president of Columbia College (1787-1800).

62. Smith (W.): William Loughton S., ?1758-1812, American statesman; member of House of Representatives (1789-1797); minister to Portugal (1797-1801). He supported Hamilton's financial policies and was a heavy speculator in government paper.

63. Wadsworth (Jeremiah: J. W., 1743-1804, American soldier and politician; commissary general of Continental Army (1778-1779); member of House of Representatives from Connecticut (1789-1795). When he was assured the Assumption Bill would pass, he sent two fast-sailing vessels to the South to buy up certificates cheap. In the debate on the bill he responded to a speaker who said soldiers were being victimized: "Poor Soldiers! . . . I am tired of hearing about the poor soldiers" [Bowers, 55].

64. J. Lawrence: John Laurance, 1750-1810, Revolutionary soldier and statesman; member of House of Representatives (1789-1793); U.S. senator (1796-1800); active supporter of Hamilton's monetary policies.

65. Bingham: William B., 1752-1804, American politician from Philadelphia; founder of Bank of North America (1781); U.S. senator (1795-1801); elected director of first Bank of the United States.

66. Carrol of Carrolton: Charles Carroll of Carrollton, 1737-1832, Revolutionary leader from Maryland; member of Continental Congress (1776-1778); signer of

Declaration of Independence; member of U.S. Senate (1789-1792).

67. Hamilton: Alexander H., 1757-1804, American statesman, born in Nevis, West Indies, whence he came as a brilliant student to Columbia College in 1774. He wrote articles espousing the patriot cause so well that they were thought to be by John Jay [62:131]. As a captain of artillery in the war, he attracted the attention of Washington, who made him aide-de-camp and private secretary, in which offices he provided invaluable services. But in 1781 he left Washington's staff for more active field duty and performed brilliantly at Yorktown. Through marriage he connected himself with the old and powerful financial circles of New York, where he practiced law and became a member of the Continental Congress. Always the proponent of a strong federal authority, he was a delegate to the Annapolis Convention and to the federal Constitutional Convention. He helped get the Constitution ratified by a series of articles in *The Federalist Papers.* Washington made him the first secretary of the treasury, from which office he was able to promote his ideas for fiscal management of the young republic, which involved several premises: (1) the government should be run as a sound business venture; (2) the federal government should assume all debts of the states and pay them in full; (3) income to pay the debts should be derived from excise taxes, tariffs, and the like. Thus Hamilton [AH] tied the operation of government to the money interests. He himself founded the Bank of New York and knew the international banking and financial operations of Europe. Though Washington wanted to avoid political parties, AH's programs and his methods of getting them adopted resulted almost immediately in the formation of two political forces: the Federalists, led by AH and JA, and the Anti-Federalists who organized under the banner of Jefferson. Although AH never used his office to make money himself (on the contrary, he died without significant wealth), many of his followers did use secret information and the AH program to make huge fortunes. Since part of his program involved using the bank to lend the government money, a procedure that has kept the U.S. in debt for most of its history, Pound deems AH responsible for starting the country on the wrong road to eventual economic disaster; Pound's tone thus is that of an outraged moralist, and AH is the "pink-haired snot" and a traitor, and those who stood against him [Jefferson, Madison, and James Jackson] are the heroes.

68. Cabot: George C., 1752-1823, American businessman and politician; senator from Massachusetts (1791-1796).

69. Fisher Ames: 1758-1808, member of House of Representatives (1789-1797), where he was the eloquent defender of AH's financial program.

70. Thomas Willing: 1731-1821, American banker and statesman; member of Continental Congress (1775-1776); president of first Bank of the United States (1791-1807); supporter of Hamilton's financial policies; business partner of Robert Morris [cf. 71 below].

71. Robt Morris: Robert M., 1734-1806, American financier and statesman; member of Continental Congress (1776-1778); signer of Declaration of Independence; member of U.S. Senate (1789-1795). Morris was AH's chief legislative agent in the Senate [Bowers, 47]. During the debate on the Assumption Bill, "Sinister stories were finding their way into print" which involved Morris: if the bill was passed, "Robert Morris would benefit $18,000,000, Jeremiah Wadsworth [cf. 63 above] would profit $9,000,000" [Bowers, 50].

72. Sedgwick: Theodore S., 1746-1813, American jurist and statesman; member of Continental Congress (1785-1788), of House of Representatives (1789-1796, 1799-1801), and of Senate (1796-1799).

73. **natural burella**: I, "natural dungeon" [*Inf.* XXXIV, 98]. Implying that the followers of AH belong in the lowest depth of Hell.

74. **Arnold**: Benedict A., 1741-1801, American army officer and traitor, received rank of brigadier general in Continental Army. In 1779 he began correspondence with the British forces and in 1780, while he was commander of West Point, he arranged for the surrender of the fort to the British. The plot was discovered and Arnold fled to British protection.

75. **Bancroft**: Edward B., 1744-1821, b. Westfield, Mass., spy during the Revolution. While in London he became a friend of Ben Franklin's and began to serve as a secret agent, sending reports to the commissioners in France. But he was a double agent and reported movements of the Americans to the British. In 1778 he gave advance information about the Franco-American alliance to the British, thus clearly establishing himself as a traitor to the American cause.

76. **per l'argine sinistra dienno volta**: I, "by the bank to the left they wheeled around" [*Inf.* XXI, 136, "Per l'argine sinistro volta dienno"]. Dante is describing comic movements of devils guarding the grafters in the 5th ditch of the 8th circle of Hell. The tone of much of Bowers's account is one of hilarity; his first chapter is entitled "Days of Comedy." He wrote: "On the opening of the debate one champion of Assumption let the cat out of the bag with the statement that 'if the general Government has the payment of all the debts, it must of course have all the revenue, and if it possesses the whole revenue, it is equal, in other words, to the whole power.' 'Yes' cried the irrepressible Jackson [cf. 84 below] in stentorian tones, 'if it lulls the Shays of the North it will rouse the Sullivans of the South'—and the fight was on . . . . Very soon, Maclay [cf. 83 below], watching the proceedings in the House with ferret

eyes, thought he observed 'the rendezvousing of the crew of the Hamilton galley.' He found that 'all hands are piped to quarters'" [Bowers, 60-61]. In fact, opposition became heated and vocal enough to cause AH's supporters concern. They delayed a vote until Vining of Delaware could arrive. Wild rumor had it that AH was prepared to give him, says Bowers, "a thousand guineas for his vote. 'A thousand guineas,' snorted Maclay, . . .' they could get him for a tenth that sum'" [Bowers, 61].

77. **Mr Schuyler (Filippo)**: Philip John S., 1733-1804, American statesman; member of Senate (1789-1791); AH's father-in-law. By using the Italian form of his name, Pound links him with Filippo Argenti, famous denizen among the wrathful [*Inf.* VIII, 61]. Schuyler is one of those who became overwrought and nervous as the debate over assumption increased in violence. Says Bowers: "The debate was becoming bitter. The able, bitter-tongued Edanus Burke of South Carolina made a ferocious attack on Hamilton, and the lobbies, coffee-houses, streets, buzzed with talk of a duel. . . . King [cf. 60 above] 'looked like a boy who had been whipped.' And the hair on Schuyler, a heavy speculator and father-in-law of Hamilton, 'stood on end as if the Indians had fired at him'" [Bowers, 62].

78. **sifilides**: I, "ones with syphilis" [*Inf.* VIII, 51: *orribili dispregi!* "horrible diseases"; Pound probably supplies the word as an example].

79. **in their progeny**: The offspring of the latest generation of all those who in the beginning and for personal gain put the country on the wrong economic and financial basis. Pound's polemic tone comes from his conviction that even today they show no repentance.

80. **quindi . . . membruto**: I, "thus Cocytus, Cassius the big-membered" [amalgam of lines 52, 67, *Inf.* XXXIV, joining the lake of ice

at the pit of Hell with the Roman devoured in one of Satan's three mouths].

81. Mr Madison: James M., 1751-1836, 4th president of the U.S. (1809-1817). With JA, Washington, and others he opposed British colonial measures and helped generate the patriot cause. As a graduate of the College of New Jersey (now Princeton) he became an early expert in constitutional law. His knowledge increased with time and experience until he was deferred to by almost everybody as the single most authoritative and dispassionate interpreter of constitutional problems. In 1776 he helped to draft a constitution for Virginia and later served in the Continental Congress (1780-1783, 1787-1788). He saw the weakness of the Articles of Confederation and succeeded in having the federal Constitutional Convention convened in 1787. He was a contributor to *The Federalist Papers* and the chief hand in the actual drafting of the Constitution. He was also a strong advocate of the Bill of Rights. Although some consider him responsible for the conservative nature of the Constitution, he was opposed to the measures of AH and became a supporter of Thomas Jefferson. His loyalties became increasingly clear with his reactions to AH's specific bills in the first Congress.

82. not speculators: AH's "Report on the Public Credit" involved several pieces of legislation; one was the Assumption Bill and another was a funding measure that would provide the money to pay the debts assumed. Bowers says: "All men of honor sympathized with the purpose of discharging the debt. . . . Few at the moment found fault with the funding system, though some would have preferred a speedy liquidation through the sale of the public lands. Then—sudddenly—a low murmur of protest, followed by acrimonious attacks" [Bowers, 44-45]. Madison listened to the debate for a number of days without comment. Finally, deciding that justice was to be found on both sides, he offered a substitute measure which

included a formula for payment to original holders of the certificates rather than providing exorbitant profits to speculators. His last comment in the debate on his measure was that only when "he had parted with his self-respect 'could he admit that America ought to erect the monuments of her gratitude, not to those who saved her liberties, but to those who had enriched themselves on her funds.'" Several days later "Madison's plan was voted down. It was found long afterward that of the sixty-four members of the House, twenty-nine were security-holders" [Bowers, 56].

83. Maclay: William M., 1734-1804, American statesman; as a member of the Senate (1789-1791) he strongly opposed Hamilton's financial measures. Bowers wrote: "The astonishing thing is that the comparatively crude Maclay from the wilds of Pennsylvania and the leather-lunged James Jackson [cf. 84 below] from sparsely settled Georgia should have caught the full significance of it all [the Assumption Bill] before it dawned on Jefferson and Madison" [pp. 45-46]. As more and more congressmen got into the business of buying up certificates cheap, Maclay wrote: "I really fear the members of Congress are deeper in this business than any others" [p. 47].

84. Jim Jackson: James J., 1757-1806, American statesman, member of House of Representatives (1789-1791); governor of Georgia (1798-1801). Born in Devonshire, he came during boyhood to the Georgia frontier where he early became known for violence. Gallatin called him a "pugnacious animal." Said Mitchell: "He fought through the revolution . . . later held the rank of brigadier in the state militia pressing back the Indians. He liked single combat too, whether eye gouging or with pistols in his many duels; he killed the lieutenant governor in an 'interview' without seconds in 1780. . . . In politics he was irregularly Republican, but always violent" [Mitchell, II, 45-46].

85. Tom: Thomas Jefferson. Of Madison's

relationship with Jefferson, Bowers says: "Jefferson loved him as a son. . . . Through many years they constantly interchanged visits, corresponded regularly, and traveled together whenever possible." But after a page of comment on the closeness of the two men, Bowers adds: "But when Madison rose that cold February day to make his first attack on Hamilton's programme, he acted on his own volition and without consultation with the man who was to be his chief," meaning Tom Jefferson [Bowers, 53].

CANTO LXX

Sources

Charles Francis Adams, ed., *The Works of John Adams*, VIII, IX; Frederick K. Sanders, *John Adams Speaking*, Orono, Maine, 1975, 428-458; Guido Cavalcanti, "Donna mi priegha," 5th ed., 1527.

Background

L. H. Butterfield, ed., *Diary and Autobiography of John Adams*, II, Cambridge, Mass., 1961; Broadus Mitchell, *Alexander Hamilton*, New York, 1962; Catherine Drinker Bowen, *John Adams and the American Revolution*, Boston, 1950.

Exegeses

Sanders, "The French Theme of Canto 70," *Pai*, 2-3, 379-389; CE, *Ideas*, 43, 116, 176-177; Davis, *Vision*, 95, 143; DP, *Barb*, 7, 233; CB-R, *ZBC*, 240.

Glossary

1. **J.A.**: John Adams expressed this sentiment about being vice-president in a letter to John Trumbull (Jan. 23, 1971). He added: '. . . I wish myself again at the bar, old as I am" [IX, 573].

2. **Mr. Pinckney**: Charles C. P., 1746-1825, sent by Washington, near the end of his presidency, on a special peace mission to France (1796-97). Because the French refused to recognize his status, Pinckney was forced to go to Amsterdam, where members of the French government told him of Talleyrand's monetary requirements. The incident became the famous XYZ Affair [cf. 16 below]. In a memo

(dated April 14, 1797) to the secretary of state, JA, who had been president only a month, asked: "Whether the refusal to receive Mr. Pinckney, and the rude orders to quit Paris and the territory of the republic ... are bars to all further measures of negotiation" [VIII, 540].

3. Mr. Adams: A number of people seemed to be possessed with the idea of "leading" Mr. Adams. In a note CFA says "Fortunate would it have been for all the parties, if the idea of *leading* Mr. Adams had not been always uppermost in their minds!" VIII, 547n].

4. Blount: William B., 1749-1800, American political leader; U.S. senator from Tennessee (1796-97). Blount was expelled from the Senate on the charge of plotting to aid the British to get control of Spanish Florida and Louisiana. President Adams became suspicious of his money speculations abroad.

5. Gerry: Elbridge G., 1744-1814, American statesman, member of the XYZ mission to France [cf. 16 below]. In a letter (July 8, 1797) JA instructs Gerry to check into the general conduct of Americans abroad, including Blount. He adds: "... I fear these speculators have done this country no good.... Decorum must be observed. You will be surrounded with projectors and swindlers. You will not be deceived by them" [VIII, 548].

6. Marshall: John M., 1755-1835, American jurist who later became one of the great chief justices of the Supreme Court [32:29]. In 1797 he was one of the commissioners Adams sent to France in his efforts to prevent a war between that country and the U.S. JA wrote: "I sincerely wish peace and friendship with the French [frogs]; but, while they countenance none but enemies of our Constitution and administration ..., self-defence, as well as fidelity to the public, will compel me to have a care what appointments I make" [VIII, 549].

7. St Jago de Cuba: S, Santiago de Cuba, seaport and capital of Oriente Province in E Cuba. French privateers cast numbers of American sailors ashore on Cuba, a place where no trading ships stopped. To get off the island the sailors had to take service on privateers, on which they were mistreated. In response to this problem and others JA wrote: "[There] will be no relief to our commerce ... until our vessels arm in their own defence. This is my opinion" [Oct. 14, 1797; VIII, 553-554].

8. Secretary: Secretary of the treasury. A bill before the Congress (engineered by Hamilton behind the scenes) set that office up, "premeditatedly," to rival that of the president. JA wrote: "... and that policy will be pursued, if we are not on our guard, till we have a quintuple or a centuple executive directory, with all the Babylonish dialect which modern pedants most affect" [VIII, 555].

9. Vervennes: Charles Gravier, comte de Vergennes, French minister of foreign affairs [65:145]. In a letter to JA, Timothy Pickering [62:156], secretary of state, made a remark to which JA referred in a return letter to Pickering. CFA excerpted from Pickering's letter the passage involved and includes it in a footnote which has the sentence: "The friends of Vergennes ... do not like the facts laid to his charge. M. Marbois would have wished Colonel P. had not so deeply pressed that matter" [VIII, 556n]. The situation was extremely delicate. The note is of interest because it is one of JA's earliest official reactions as president to a problem that in the next four years grew to violent confrontation and increased the polarity between Congress and the public; it finally resulted in JA's defeat for a second term. The Hamilton-led forces were pro-British and increasingly called for war with France. The Jefferson forces were pro-French and antiwar. JA's efforts to ameliorate the differences, maintain the dignity of the new nation, and keep out of war satisfied extremists on neither side. As the situation developed, the extremist forces grew in numbers and in stridency.

10. Hamilton: As the clamor for war with France increased in the Hamilton-guided press, the possibility of such a war also increased; it therefore became JA's policy to "prepare for war and negotiate for peace." Although personally he was all for developing the navy, being certain that a war with France would be conducted mostly at sea, he finally nominated Washington to be "commander-in-chief of all the armies raised or to be raised in the United States." The question then was who should be second-in-command. Washington anguished over three people: Knox, Pinckney, and Hamilton. Hamilton's followers intrigued with Washington to get him appointed, but Washington couldn't decide. JA wanted no command for Hamilton. In a letter to James McHenry, secretary of war, he wrote (Aug. 29, 1798) that a procedure he outlined would result in Hamilton's being commissioned with the others but that Hamilton would not be in command. He added: "There has been too much intrigue in this business with General Washington and me" [VIII, 588].

11. McHenry: James M. [62:155]. Washington, late in his second term, had made McHenry secretary of war (1796). JA kept him on in his cabinet, but when he discovered that McHenry was serving Hamilton better than himself, he got rid of him.

12. We shd / have frigates: Sentiments of JA, who believed that merchant vessels should be armed and that the American merchant marine should be protected at sea.

13. expedient . . . Pickering: From a letter JA wrote from Quincy (Oct. 20, 1798), anticipating the opening of Congress. Some of the questions he raised are those of the canto lines [VIII, 609-610].

14. Pickering: Timothy P., 1745-1829; b. Salem, Mass.; graduated Harvard, 1763. He was active in the American cause both before and during the Revolution. He entered the colonial army as a colonel and rose to become adjutant general, member of the Board of War (1777), and quartermaster general (1780-1785). Pickering held other offices in which he so distinguished himself that Washington made him secretary of state in 1795. JA continued him in that office until his pro-Hamilton intriguing and his prowar stance became too blatant; JA finally dismissed him in 1800.

15. Talleyrand: [44:28]. Although Talleyrand supported the French Revolution, he was a firm believer in constitutional monarchy. After the fall of the monarchy he fled to England (1793); a year later he took refuge in the U.S., where he lived in poverty until the Directory was established in 1795. He then returned to France and in 1797 was made minister of foreign affairs and associated himself with the rising star of Napoleon. His involvement in the XYZ Affair (1797-98) [cf. 16 below] and his endorsement of Napoleon's plan to seize Egypt led to his resignation from office in July 1799. Later that year he was reappointed to the same office.

16. X, Y, Z: XYZ Affair, an incident in the diplomatic relations between America and France (1797-98). Members of the American commission to France, Charles Cotesworth Pinckney, John Marshall, and Elbridge Gerry, accused agents X, Y, and Z of suggesting that a bribe of £50,000 in the form of a loan to France would be welcomed by the Directory and particularly by Talleyrand. The uproar created by the incident in the United States aided those who wished to destroy Franco-American relations and to be more friendly toward England, the reverse of John Adams's foreign policy. The wave of frenzy was led by the Hamiltonian faction of the Federalists. Pinckney supposedly replied to the request for money: "Millions for defense, sir, but not one cent for tribute."

17. Mr. Gerry: [cf. 5 above].

18. Hague: The Hague, seat of government of the Netherlands, 30 miles SW of Amsterdam. Vans Murray dated his letter to JA from The Hague [cf. 19 below].

19. Vans M: William Vans Murray, 1760-1803, appointed in 1798 by JA as minister to The Hague to replace John Quincy Adams. Murray helped prepare the way for recognition of an American minister to France. The canto line, "peculators . . .," comes from a letter Murray wrote in cipher to JA. The second man in the moderate party told Murray in confidence that in certain circumstances "they meant to overturn the present men, whom he represented as peculators, and as men who exhausted every thing in enormous bribes, to arrange their internal affairs, and the first moment in their power to drive out the French" [VIII, 678]. The desire of the moderate party was to join with the U.S. against France and thus get out from under complete French domination.

20. Talleyrand: JA in a letter to Washington says he intended "to nominate Mr. Murray to be minister plenipotentiary to the French republic." He planned to do so on the strength of a letter from Talleyrand, who said that any such minister would be received with honor. JA adds: "As there may be some reserves for chicane, however, Murray is not to remove from his station at the Hague until . . ." He reflects, too: "There is not much sincerity in the cant about peace; those who snivel for it now, were hot for war against Britain a few months ago, and would be now, if they saw a chance. In elective governments, peace or war are alike embraced by parties, when they think they can employ either for electioneering purposes" [VIII, 624-626].

21. My appointment: The Murray appointment finally signaled to the Hamiltonian faction that their hopes for a war against France were doomed. In a letter to his attorney general, JA said his appointment of Murray "has shown to every observing and thinking man the real strength or weakness of the Constitution. . . . To me, it has laid open characters" [VIII, 629].

22. Tim Pickering: Beginning with the secret messages from Murray and special letters from Gerry, Adams began to gather information that Pickering as secretary of state had concealed from him in order to implement Hamilton's hopes for war with France. JA did not act hastily, but when the crisis with France had diminished he fired Pickering. The letter was formal and brief: "Sir,—Divers causes and considerations, essential to the administration of the government, in my judgment, requiring a change in the department of State, you are hereby discharged from any further service as Secretary of State/JOHN ADAMS/ *President of the United States*" [IX, 55].

23. John Marshall: [cf. 6 above]. JA directed the secretary of war "to execute the office of Secretary of State so far as to affix the seal of the United States to the inclosed commission to the present Secretary of State, John Marshall, of Virginia, to be Chief Justice of the United States, and to certify in your own name on the commission as executing the office of the Secretary of State *pro hâc vice*" [IX, 95-96].

24. pro hâc vice: L, "in return."

25. Hamilton's . . . : After the death of Washington (Dec. 14, 1799), Hamilton became angry because JA would not entrust to him the command of the army. That plus "the avowed disinclination of Mr. Adams further to pursue the war policy with France" [IX, 239], along with other more ancient animosities, led Hamilton to try to prevent JA's reelection. To this end he composed a pamphlet—"The public conduct and character of John Adams, Esquire, President of the United States"—and issued it surreptitiously so that as president JA could "take no notice of it without materially compromising the dignity of his position." But after his term expired on March 15, 1801, JA answered Hamilton's allegations: "Mr. Hamilton, in his pamphlet, speaking of Talleyrand's despatches, says, 'overtures so circuitous and informal . . . were a very inadequate basis for the institution of a new mission.' . . . Here again, Mr. Hamilton's total ignorance or oblivion of the practice of our own government, as well as the constant usage of other nations in diplomatic proceedings, appears in all its lustre" [IX, 273].

26. eternal neutrality: One of Hamilton's complaints concerned the way JA went about sending a new mission to France. AH implied that JA acted through unorthodox channels and without principle. JA later wrote: "The institution of an embassy to France, in 1779, was made upon principle, and in conformity to a system of foreign affairs, formed upon long deliberation . . . and supported in Congress,—that is, a system of eternal neutrality, if possible, in all the wars of Europe" [IX, 242]. The principle is significant as JA passed on his firm convictions about it to his son, JQA, who, as secretary of state under President Monroe, used it to counter widespread opposition in laying the foundation for the Monroe Doctrine [34:54].

27. Dec. 28th 1800: Date of a letter JA wrote after he was defeated for reelection: "Before this reaches you, the news will be familiar to you, that after the 3d of March I am to be a private citizen and your brother farmer. I shall leave the State with its coffers full, and the fair prospects of a peace with all the world smiling in its face" [IX, 577].

28. 73 for Jefferson: Hamilton based his efforts to have JA defeated in the election of 1800 on promoting Aaron Burr behind the scenes. His campaign split the vote between two Federalists, JA and Burr, and resulted in the election of Jefferson, who was anti-Federalist, anti-Burr, and anti-Hamilton. JA wrote ironically to Gerry: "How mighty a power is the spirit of party! How decisive and unanimous it is! Seventy-three for Mr. Jefferson and seventy-three for Mr. Burr" [IX, 577].

29. a few foreign . . . : In a letter to a friend (March 31, 1801), JA expressed concern about the nature of the electorate: "A group of foreign liars, encouraged by a few ambitious native gentlemen, have discomfited the education, the talents, the virtues, and the property of the country. The reason is, we have no Americans in America. The federalists have been no more Americans than the anties" [IX, 582].

30. formato loco: I, "formed space." The phrase occurs in "Donna mi priegha" as *formato locho* which, at 36/178, Pound translates as "forméd trace." In LE (187-188) he discusses the term in detail: "The 'formato locho' is the trait or locus marked out in the 'possible intelletto.' . . . I do not think the Egidio is sound in thinking the 'formato locho' is a single image. Determined locus or habitat would be nearer the mark." The memory image, from the same source, Pound translates at 36/177 as "where memory liveth." The line is not in *WJA*.

31. My compliments . . . Sirens: These four lines and the rest of the canto return to events in JA's life from 1773 to his first years as vice-president. The four lines are from a letter to James Warren (Dec. 22, 1773) which recommends in a spirit of jest a project to tell the story of the Boston Tea Party (Dec. 16, 1773) in mythological dress. JA was most elated about the "tea party" and wrote in this tone: "Make my compliments to Mrs. Warren, and tell her that I want a poetical genius to describe a late frolic among the sea-nymphs and goddesses" [IX, 335]. Hyson, Congo, and Bohea are kinds of tea.

32. Tories . . . : In a letter to J. Warren (April 9, 1774), JA estimates political attitudes: "The tories were never, since I was born, in such a state of humiliation as at this moment." He traces their affability to plain fear, but adds that "there is not spirit enough on either side to bring the question to a complete decision, and . . . we shall oscillate like a pendulum, and fluctuate like the ocean" [IX, 336-337].

33. slow starvation: JA's perception of a part of England's plan to subjugate Boston.

JA's own words are "slow torments and lingering degrees" [IX, 338].

34. conclave . . . statesmen: Some of JA's thoughts after he was selected as a delegate to the first Congress at Philadelphia. He wrote to J. Warren on June 25, 1774: I view the assembly, that is to be there, as I do the court of Aeropagus, the council of the Amphictyons, a conclave, a sanhedrim, a divan, I know not what. I suppose you sent me there to school. . . . It is to be a school of political prophets, I suppose, a nursery of American Statesmen" [IX, 338-339].

35. treasons . . . : In a letter (July 25, 1774) Joseph Hawley told JA he wanted Southern gentlemen to be deeply impressed by the fact that all acts of British legislation are "absolutely repugnant to liberty." For the future he expected "nothing but new treasons, new felonies, new misprisions, new præmunires and, not to say the Lord, the devil knows what" [IX, 345].

36. Virginia: A happy note on the cooperation of Virginia in reducing trade with Britain. By sowing wheat instead of tobacco, "so many of her planters have desisted from exporting the old crop, that the vessels cannot get freight. Their men are ready to march" [IX, 355].

37. never happy . . . : Source unknown, but the passage describes a character trait JA recognized in himself.

38. Quincy's knowledge: From letter to Josiah Quincy (July 29, 1775) in which JA said: "I have a great opinion of your knowledge and judgment . . . concerning the channels and islands in Boston harbor" [IX, 361].

39. 2 million: Sum that a committee of the whole house unanimously agreed should be issued in "bills of credit" [IX, 357].

40. old to bind . . . franchise: From a long speculation on majority and minority rights in government by the consent of the people: "Shall we say that every individual of the community, old and young, male and female, as well as rich and poor, must consent . . . to every act of legislation? . . . Whence arises the right of the men to govern the women, without their consent? Whence the right of the old to bind the young . . . ? But why exclude women?" And later in the same letter: ". . . power always follows property. . . . Nay, I believe we may advance one step farther, and affirm that the balance of power in a society, accompanies the balance of property in land" [IX, 375-376].

41. been months here . . . : Complaint in a letter of May 29, 1776, that JA had been required to neglect his health and forgo exercise [IX, 380].

42. Justinian . . . Taylor: In a letter to Jonathan Mason (Aug. 21, 1776), JA considers the "beauties" of the law. He includes Bracton in one list and then goes on to consider civil law: "You will find it so interspersed with history, oratory, law, politics, and war and commerce, that you will find advantages in it every day. Wood, Domat, Ayliffe, Taylor, ought to be read. But these should not suffice. You should go to the fountain-head, and drink deep of the Pierian spring. Justinian's Institutes, and all the commentators upon them that you can find, you ought to read" [IX, 433].

43. Justinian: [65:126].

44. Bracton: Henry de Bracton [63:40].

45. Domat: Jean D. [or Daumat], 1625-1696, French jurist; author of *Les Loix civiles dans leur ordre naturel*, "Civil Laws in Their Natural Order" (3 vols.; 1689-1694).

46. Ayliffe: John A., 1676-1732, English jurist and legal authority.

47. Taylor: John T., 1703-1766, English jurist and scholar; author of *Elements of Civil Law* (1755).

48. from 61: Source unidentified.

49. Aversion to paper . . . : From letter to Elbridge Gerry dated at Braintree (Dec. 6, 1777). The extreme inflation in the paper money issued by the colonies caused serious difficulties, and JA found "a general inclination among the people to barter" [IX, 469-470].

50. Rush: In a letter to Benjamin Rush (Feb. 8, 1778), JA expresses a sentiment he stated many times about a subject little understood: ". . . I mean money, is least understood of any. I fear the regulation of prices will produce ruin sooner than safety. It will starve the army and the country, or I am ignorant or every principle of commerce, coin, and society" [IX, 472].

51. English reports . . . devil knows that: These seven lines concern the kinds of lies the English were spreading all over Europe, "everyone of which," wrote JA, "I know to be false. They still, however, find stock-jobbers and other persons to believe them." The English were spreading the lies to create the impression that there were serious dissensions between the Americans and the French and among Americans themselves. The five lines in quotation marks are almost verbatim from the source [IX, 474].

52. 40,000 Russians: Source unidentified, but in a letter of February 18, 1780, JA mentioned British rumors about "20,000 Russians" ready for war [68:67].

53. solicitation: In a letter to E. Gerry (Nov. 4, 1779), JA wrote: "I am more solicitous about the means of procuring the salary you mention than the sum of it. I can make it do, if I can get it" [IX, 506].

54. quails, partridges . . . Europe: These 11 lines are from two different letters. One, to James Warren (June 17, 1782) at The Hague, contains a reminiscence about the country around Braintree: "I love every tree and every rock upon all those mountains. Roving among these, and the quails, partridges, squirrels, &c, that inhabit them, shall be the amusement of my declining years. God willing, I will not go to Vermont [where his wife had bought some land]. I must be within the scent of the sea" [IX, 512-513]. The lines in parentheses, the third of which

should be closed after the word "Europe," come from a letter to Jonathan Jackson, dated at Paris (Nov. 17, 1782), and are concerned with French policy: "In substance it has been this; in assistance afforded us in naval force and in money, to keep us from succumbing, and nothing more; . . . to prevent us from obtaining consideration in Europe" [IX, 515].

55. Holland: Letter from The Hague (Sept. 6, 1782) says: "One thing, thank God, is certain. I have planted the American standard at the Hague. . . . I shall look down upon the flagstaff with pleasure from the other world" [IX, 513].

56. populariser . . .: F, "popularize, depopularize." These three lines are from a letter written almost 15 years later (March 30, 1797), while JA was president. It confirms the same judgment about French policy he had made during his 1782 mission. Since Jefferson was pro-French and Washington was identified to some extent with the Hamiltonians, it was French policy to promote in the late 1790s the cause of Jefferson and to undermine the positions of the Federalists. In 1797 JA wrote about the French: "Their apparent respect and real contempt for all men and all nations but Frenchmen, are proverbial among themselves. They think it is in their power to give characters and destroy characters as they please, and they have no other rule but to give reputation to their tools, and to destroy the reputation of all who will not be their tools. Their efforts to '*populariser*' Jefferson, and to '*dépopulariser*' Washington, are all upon this principle" [VIII, 536].

57. our interest: These lines return to JA at The Hague. In a letter of April 12, 1783, he wrote: "French politics are now incessantly at work in England, and we may depend upon it they labor less for our good than their own. If our interests were the same with theirs, we might better trust them; yet not entirely, for they do not understand their own interests so well as we do ours" [IX, 518].

58. Dutch interest: Source reads: "I have hitherto paid the interest in Holland out of the principal." Letter to Arthur Lee (Sept. 6, 1785) [IX, 537].

59. Court as putrid: Source reads: "Perhaps you will say that the air of a Court is as putrid as that of Amsterdam. In a moral and political sense, perhaps"; but, he adds, "Politics are the divine science, after all" [IX, 512].

60. Sale of six million: This line occurs in a letter written five years after the preceding one by R. H. Lee to JA (Sept. 3, 1787). Lee says that the Congress had "lately contracted for the sale of six millions of acres, on the north-western side of Ohio, in the ceded territory, for lessening the domestic debt" [IX, 554].

61. the society . . . : Back in Braintree, JA reflects on what he missed in his years abroad: "I regret the loss of the book-shops, and the society of the few men of letters that I knew in London; in all other respects I am much better accommodated here. Shall I hope to hear from you as you have leisure? A letter left at the New England Coffee House will be brought me by some of our Boston captains." Pound adds the word "London" to make clear the place [IX, 558].

62. Hollis Brook: Earlier in the same letter [61 above], JA wrote to Thomas Brand-Hollis about the beautiful prospects from spots on his farm, but adds: "I wish . . . that Mr. Brand-Hollis would come and build a Hyde near us." Then JA lists a number of places he would rename Hollis, such as a mead and a hill, and continues: "There is a fine brook, through a meadow, by my house; shall I call it Hollis Brook?" [IX, 557]. "Hyde" means a park such as Hyde Park in London.

63. Hollis: Thomas Brand-Hollis [66:38].

64. After generous . . . : Source says: "After a generous contest for liberty, of twenty years' continuance, Americans forgot wherein liberty consisted" [letter of Aug. 18,

1789, which contains the following Latin quotation; IX, 560].

65. meminisse juvebit: L, "it will be pleasing to recall." Source reads "juvabit," [IX, 561].

66. seeks information: Source reads: "No man, I believe, has influence with the President [Washington]. He seeks information from all quarters, and judges more independently than any man I ever knew" [IX, 561].

67. fisheries . . . absence: In 1781 JA had been commissioned to act with Franklin, Jefferson, John Jay, and Henry Laurens to negotiate a peace treaty with Great Britain, a treaty finally confirmed in 1783. From this time on, as with all subsequent commercial treaties he was involved in, JA maintained the American rights to offshore fisheries, a concept he advanced in the face of strong European opposition and American indifference [71:51]. The source of the five lines reads: "The fisheries are so essential to the commerce and naval power of this nation, that it is astonishing that any one citizen should ever have been found indifferent about them. . . . But . . . when . . . more than one foreign nation would endeavor to deprive us of them, there were many Americans indifferent, and not a few even disposed to give them away. A knowledge of this was the first and strongest motive with me to embark for Europe a first and a second time. . . . The present of four boxes of fish has been received . . . and is in every point of view very acceptable to me" [from Braintree, Nov. 7, 1789; IX, 562-563].

68. Their constitution: Source reads: "The Constitution [of France] is but an experiment, and must and will be altered. I know it to be impossible that France should be long governed by it. If the sovereignty is to reside in one assembly, the king, princes of the blood, and principal quality, will govern it at their pleasure as long as they can agree; when they differ, they will go to war." JA added: "I thank you, Sir, for your kind compliment. As it has been the great aim of my life to be useful, if I had any reason to think I was so . . . it would make me happy. . . . It is incredible how small is the number, in any nation, of those who comprehend any system of constitution or administration, and those few it is wholly impossible to unite" [IX, 564].

69. Price: Richard P., 1723-1791, Welsh moral and political philosopher; author of *Observations on Civil Liberty and War with America* (1776), an attack on British policy during the Revolution. He was a friend of JA's and Franklin's.

70. Americans . . . balance: Source (letter to B. Rush, April 18, 1790] reads: "I own that awful experience has concurred with reading and reflection, to convince me that Americans are more rapidly disposed to corruption in elections that [sic] I thought they were fourteen years ago [thus, 1776, not 1774]. My friend Dr. Rush will excuse me, if I caution him against a fraudulent use of the words *monarchy* and *republic*. I am a mortal and irreconcilable enemy to monarchy. . . . I am for a balance between the legislative and executive powers [IX, 566].

71. Ideogram: Chung [M1504] : "the middle." Part of the title to one of the Stone classics, *Chung Yung*, which Pound translates as "The Unwobbling Pivot." "[It] contains,"

he said, "what is usually supposed not to exist, namely the Confucian metaphysics. It is divided into three parts: the axis; the process; and sincerity, the perfect word, or the precise word" [*CON*, 95]. The ideogram underlines Pound's conviction that JA was an American exemplum of Confucian ideals.

72. An aversion: Source reads: "I know not how it is, but mankind have an aversion to the study of the science of government. . . . To me, no romance is more entertaining" [letter of June 1, 1790; IX, 567].

73. Thames . . . : Line from letter to Thomas Brand-Hollis [66:38].

74. 73 . . . 73: [cf. 28 above].

75. Dum Spiro: L, "While I breathe"; *Dum Spiro Amo*: "While I breathe I love" [letter of June 1, 1790 to Brand-Hollis; IX, 569]. Pound added *Amo*.

76. nec lupo . . . : L, "nor entrust a lamb to a wolf," which JA tells Brand-Hollis (June 11, 1790) is his "fundamental maxim of government" [IX, 571].

78. rational theory: Source, which concerns JA's reflections on government, reads: "But . . . the feelings of mankind are so much against any rational theory, that I find my labor has all been in vain" [IX, 573].

CANTO LXXI

Sources

Charles Francis Adams, ed., *The Works of John Adams*, IX, X; Frederick K. Sanders, *John Adams Speaking*, 459-506, Orono, Maine, 1975.

Background

L. H. Butterfield, ed., *Diary and Autobiography of John Adams*, II, Cambridge, Mass., 1961; Saul Padover, *The Complete Jefferson*, New York, 1943; Broadus Mitchell, *Alexander Hamilton*, New York, 1962.

Exegeses

LL, *Motive*, 96, 114; CE, *Ideas*, 43; Dekker, *Cantos*, 139; DD, *Sculptor*, 163; Davis, *Vision*, 87, 143, 148-149; DP, *Barb*, 233; WB, *Rose*, 123-124; HK, *Era*, 319.

Glossary

1. St. Paul: Most of Canto 71 is taken from letters written between 1804 and 1819 at Quincy, where JA had retired after his defeat for reelection in 1800. The first three lines are from a letter (March 3, 1804) to F. A. Vanderkemp, who inquired about a manuscript he had sent to an academy JA belonged to. In his reply JA wrote: "A German ambassador once told me, 'he could not bear St. Paul, he was so severe against fornication.' On the same principle these philosophers cannot bear a God, because he is just" [IX, 588].

2. Dismissed . . . parties: Source [JA to Vanderkemp, Feb. 5, 1805] reads: "At the close of the 18th century, I was dismissed, to the joy of both parties, to a retirement in which I was never more to see any thing but my plough between me and the grave" [IX, 589-590].

3. curse the day: Source [JA to B. Rush, May 1, 1807] reads: "Now, Sir, to be serious, I do not curse the day when I engaged in public affairs" [IX, 593].

4. Now in . . . constitution: These nine lines are from a letter to Rush [May 21, 1807] which contains JA's lengthy reminiscence about the idea of the Revolution being in the minds of the people before it was in the minds of the leaders. In 1774 JA, on circuit court, stopped at a tavern in Shrewsbury and overheard the conversation which Pound summarizes by key phrases. Source has "half a dozen, or half a score . . . yeomen" [IX, 597].

5. build frigates: JA had urged that the U.S. build "fast-sailing frigates" from pre-Revolutionary days on, particularly at times when American shipping was being attacked

at sea [70:7]. In 1808 [letter of Dec. 26] he was still at it: "In the mean time apply all our resources to build frigates, some in every principal seaport. . . . I never was fond of the plan of building line of battle ships. Our policy is not to fight squadrons at sea, but to have fast-sailing frigates to scour the seas and make impression on the enemy's commerce; . . . I conclude with acknowledging that we have received greater injuries from England than from France, abominable as both have been" [IX 607-608].

6. I am for fighting: Source reads: "If either of the belligerent powers [England or France] forces us all into a war, I am for fighting that power, whichever it may be" [March 13, 1809; IX, 615].

7. swindling banks: Source [letter of Feb. 16, 1809] reads: "Our medium is depreciated by the multitude of swindling banks, which have emitted bank bills to an immense amount beyond the deposits of gold and silver in their vaults, by which means the price of labor and land and merchandise and produce is doubled, tripled, and quadrupled. . . . Every dollar of a bank bill that is issued beyond the quantity of gold and silver in the vaults, represents nothing, and is therefore a cheat upon somebody" [IX, 610].

8. Cape Breton . . . 89-'09: These ten lines are based on an impassioned reminiscence by JA [letter of March 11, 1809] which reads in part: "From my earliest infancy I had listened with eagerness to his [my father's] conversation with his friends during the whole expedition to Cape Breton, in 1745, and I had received very grievous impressions of the injustice and ingratitude of Great Britain towards New England in that whole transaction, as well as many others before and after it, during the years 1754, 1755, 1756, and 1757. The conduct of Generals Shirley, Braddock, Abercrombie, Webb, and above all Lord Loudon . . . gave me . . . a disgust of the British government. . . . In 1758 and 1759, Mr. Pitt coming into power, sent Wolfe, and Amherst, whom I saw with his army, . . . and these conquered Cape Breton and Quebec. I then rejoiced that I was an Englishman. . . . But, alas! how short was my triumph in British wisdom and justice! In February, 1761, I heard the argument . . . upon writs of assistance, and there saw that Britain was determined to let nothing divert me from my fidelity to my country." [By the Peace of Utrecht (1713) the French lost Nova Scotia and Newfoundland but retained Cape Breton and were allowed to fortify the island. In 1745 a volunteer force from New England led by Sir William Pepperell captured Cape Breton with the aid of the British fleet under Commodore Warren. JA, ten years old at the time, was excited by stories of the campaign.] At this time [32:1] JA was being consulted about the history of the Revolution. In this letter he is answering 20 specific questions asked by Skelton Jones about his life and career. Jones's seventh question was when and why JA had retired from public affairs. JA's answer: "The 4th of March, 1801 [date of Jeffersons's inauguration]. The causes of my retirement are to be found in the writings of Freneau [he lists eight more causes] and many others, but more specifically in the circular letters of members of Congress from the southern and middle States. Without a complete collection of all these libels, no faithful history of the last twenty years can ever be written, nor any adequate account given of the causes of my retirement from public life" [IX, 611-612]. Pound added "89-'09".

9. Shirley: William S., 1694-1771 [67:29]. Shirley started the issuing of Writs of Assistance in Boston in 1761; they were supposed to aid in the search for smuggled goods, but

they caused discontent without being very effective [63:66].

10. Braddock: Edward B., 1695-1775, commander in chief of British forces in America (1754).

11. Abercrombie: Sir Robert A., 1740-1827, British general in the French and Indian Wars and in the American Revolution.

12. Webb: Daniel W., English soldier who commanded the British forces in America until succeeded by Abercrombie after 1756.

13. Lord Loudon: John Campbell, 4th Earl of Loudoun, 1705-1782, commander of British forces in the French and Indian Wars. He distressed the people of Boston by quartering his troops on them.

14. Pitt: William P. [64:33]. JA was happy because the Elder Pitt opposed the Stamp Act.

15. Wolf: James Wolfe, 1727-1759, British major general who commanded the expedition against Montcalm at Quebec.

16. Amherst: Lord Jeffrey A., 1717-1797, English general who commanded the British force that captured Cape Breton from the French (1758); took Ticonderoga (1759); and was made commander in chief of British forces in America (1759).

17. totis viribus: L, "with all my strength." Source [letter of March 13, 1809] reads: "I am *totis viribus* against any division of the Union, by the North River, or by Delaware River, or by the Potomac, or any other river, or by any chain of mountains. I am for maintaining the independence of the nation at all events" [IX, 615].

18. Independence . . . : In the source [letter of April 20, 1809] JA speaks of his lifelong fight for independence from both Britain and France. He adds: "The federal papers for the last year or two, assisted by English hirelings, have been employed in varnishing over the conduct of Great Britain . . . till they appear to have obtained a temporary majority in New England. I greatly respect the public opinion of New England, when it is truly informed. In the present instance, with infinite grief I fear it is not" [IX, 621].

19. Vergennes: [70:9] Source reads: "... the Comte de Vergennes, once said to me, 'Mr. Adams, the newspapers govern the world!' ... Let me ask you ... if the world is governed by ungovernable newspapers, whether it does not follow ... that the world is ungovernable" [letter of June 19, 1809; IX, 622].

20. Took Matlock ... : Source [same as 19 above] reads: "A Convention in Pennsylvania had adopted a government in one representative assembly, and Dr. Franklin was the President of that Convention. The Doctor, when he went to France in 1776, carried with him the printed copy of that Constitution, and it was immediately propagated through France that this was the plan of government of Mr. Franklin. In truth it was not Franklin, but Timothy Matlack, James Cannon, Thomas Young, and Thomas Paine, who were the authors of it. Mr. Turgot, the Duke de la Rochefocauld, Mr. Condorcet, and many others, became enamored with the Constitution of Mr. Franklin. And in my opinion, the two last owed their final and fatal catastrophe to this blind love." JA does not mention Beaumarchais [IX, 622-623].

21. Matlock: Timothy Matlack, d. 1829; assistant secretary to Continental Congress (1775); member of Pennsylvania Constitutional convention (1776) and of committee that drafted the instrument.

22. James Cannon: Member of committee to draft the constitution of Pennsylvania (1776).

23. Thomas Young: ?1731-1777, American Revolutionary patriot and physician; member of Pennsylvania Constitutional Convention (1776) and of committee that drafted the instrument.

24. Thomas Paine: [31:17].

25. Beaumarchais: [31:29; 32:10].

26. Condorcet: [31:37].

27. English Constitution: Source [same as 19 above] reads: "I have represented the British Constitution as the most perfect model that has as yet been discovered ... for the government of the great nations of Europe. It is a masterpiece. ... Our own Constitutions I have represented as the best for us in our peculiar situation, and while we preserve ourselves independent and unallied to any of the great powers of Europe. An alliance with either France or England would, in my humble opinion, put an end to our fine system of liberty" [IX, 622].

28. Their inexperience: Source [same as 19 above] concerns Turgot, Rochefoucauld, and Condorcet, whom JA knew during his 1780 mission to France. JA wrote: "They were as amiable, as learned, and as honest men as any in France. But such was their inexperience in all that relates to free government, so superficial their reading in the science of government, and so obstinate their confidence in their own great characters for science and literature, that I should trust the most ignorant of our honest town meeting orators to make a Constitution sooner than any or all of them" [IX, 624].

29. Merchants wd/ say: JA is answering a question asked by a friend concerning the best means by which the "military and commercial spirit" might be made most helpful to a free nation. He wrote: "Nine tenths of our nation would say the militia, the other tenth a standing army. The merchants would all say, 'let commerce alone—merchants do as they please;' others would say, 'protect trade with a navy'" [IX, 625].

30. without Louisiana ... intentions: These five lines express JA's ideas about the Louisiana Purchase and the congressional interpretation of the Constitution which justified the purchase. The source [JA to

Josiah Quincy, Feb. 9, 1811] is adequately summarized by Pound [IX, 631].

31. oligarchy: Source [JA to Josiah Quincy, Feb. 18, 1811] concerns Americans who are jealous of European nobility: "This jealousy is often actuated by the purest spirit of patriotism, . . . but . . . it never has ceased to encroach, until it has made the executive a mere head of wood, and drawn all the power and resources of the nation into the insatiable gulf, the irresistible vortex, of an aristocracy or an oligarchy" [IX, 634].

32. church-going . . . Hamilton: These three lines come from a letter to B. Rush [Aug. 28, 1811] which emphasizes JA's belief that "religion and virtue are the only foundations" of any government. But JA did not feel free to say much about his belief: ". . . if I should inculcate this doctrine in my will, I should be charged with hypocrisy . . . and for being a church-going animal." He adds: "If I should inculcate 'fidelity to the marriage bed,' it would be said that it proceeded from resentment to General Hamilton, and a malicious desire to hold up to posterity his libertinism" [IX, 636-637].

33. forgot . . . himself: These three lines are a footnote JA added to the letter [32 above] three days later [Aug. 31]: "I had forgot the story of the four English girls whom General Pinckney was employed to hire in England, two for me and two for himself" [IX, 637].

34. The number . . . year: These six lines [source as in 32] are from a lengthy disquisition on JA's lifelong and zealous but losing fight against the public's use of alcohol: "Fifty-three years ago I was fired with a zeal . . . against ardent spirits, the multiplication of taverns . . . dram-shops, and tippling houses. Grieved to the heart . . . I applied to the Court of Sessions . . . [and] reduced the number of licensed houses." But JA was called a "hypocrite" and a "demagogue." "The number of licensed houses was soon reinstated; drams, grog, and sotting were not diminished, and remain to this day as deplorable as ever. You may as well preach to the Indians against rum as to our people. Little Turtle petitioned me to prohibit rum to be sold to his nation, for a very good reason; because he said I had lost three thousand of my Indian children in his nation in one year by it" [IX, 637-638].

35. Funds . . . crazy: These nine lines express convictions of JA which Pound responded to strongly, frequently quoting them as well as similar passages: "Funds and banks I never approved, or was satisfied with our funding system; it was founded in no consistent principle; it was contrived to enrich particular individuals at the public expense. Our whole banking system I ever abhorred, I continue to abhor, and shall die abhorring. But I am not an enemy to funding systems. They are absolutely and indispensably necessary in the present state of the world. An attempt to annihilate or prevent them would be as romantic an adventure as any in Don Quixote or in Oberon. A national bank of deposit I believe to be wise, just, prudent, economical, and necessary. But every bank of discount, every bank by which interest is to be paid or profit of any kind made by the deponent, is downright corruption. It is taxing the public for the benefit and profit of individuals; it is worse than old tenor, continental currency, or any other paper money. Now, Sir, if I should talk in this strain, after I am dead, you know the people of America would pronounce that I had died mad" [source same as 32 above].

36. Wigwams . . . left there: These six lines continue JA's pleasurable memories of local Indians. Source [JA to TJ, June 28, 1812] says: "There was a numerous family in this town, whose wigwam was within a mile of this house. This family were frequently at my father's house, and I, in my boyish rambles, used to call at their wigwam, where I never failed to be treated with whortleberries, blackberries, strawberries, or apples, plums, peaches, &, for they had planted a variety of fruit trees about them; but the girls went out to service and the boys to sea, till not a soul is left" [X, 20].

37. and so . . . England: These three lines are from a letter [Nov. 25, 1812] concerned with party forces which paralyze the nation: "When I was exerting every nerve to vindicate the honor, and demand a redress of the wrongs of the nation against the tyranny of France, the arm of the nation was palsied by one party. Now Mr. Madison is acting the same part . . . against Great Britain, the arm of the nation is palsied by the opposite party. And so it will always be while we feel like colonists, dependent for protection on France or England" [X, 23].

38. With wood . . . please: The two lines are from an anecdote JA tells to show the amazement of Europeans that America never used its vast natural resources to become a first-rate sea power. Source [letter of Jan. 5, 1813] tells the story of a conversation JA had in 1779 with an admiral, "or, as the French call him, *Général* or *Chef d'Escadre,*" who said, "Your Congress will soon become one of the great maritime powers." JA replies that it will not be soon. The admiral wanted to know why not: "No nation has such nurseries for seaman so near it. You have the best timber for the hulks of ships, and best masts and spars . . . [he lists much more]. What is wanting?" To JA's response, "The will . . . may be wanting and nothing else," the admiral continued: "We have a maxim among us mariners, that with wood, hemp, and iron, a nation may do what it pleases" [X, 26].

39. Taxes laid . . . : Source [letter of March 28, 1813] gives JA's frank opinion about the War of 1812: "The taxes must be laid, and the war supported" [X, 36].

40. Histories . . . : Source [letter to TJ, July 9, 1813] concerns the difficulties of making improvements or preserving historical truth under any form of government: "I say,

parties and factions will not suffer improvements to be made. As soon as one man hints at an improvement, his rival opposes it. No sooner has one party discovered or invented any amelioration of the condition of man . . . than the opposite party belies it, misconstrues it, misrepresents it, ridicules it, insults it, and persecutes it. Records are destroyed. Histories are annihilated or interpolated or prohibited; sometimes by Popes, sometimes by Emperors, sometimes by aristocratical, and sometimes by democratical assemblies, and sometimes by mobs" [X, 50].

41. our 'pure . . . : Source [letter to TJ, Sept. 2, 1813] asks Jefferson's opinion about JA's translation from Greek of a poem by Theognis and wonders whether anyone else had ever caught the idea better: "Tell me, also, whether poet, orator, historian, or philosopher, can paint the picture of every city, county, or State, in our pure, uncorrupted, unadulterated, uncontaminated federal republic . . . in more precise lines or colors?" [X, 64].

42. Sir Wm. Keith: Sir William K., 1680-1749. British colonial governor of Pennsylvania and Delaware (1714-1726). Source [Thomas McKean to JA, Sept. 28, 1813] contains memories about ways the British devised for raising revenues in America, one of which was to appoint congresses: "In 1739, Sir William Keith, a Scotch gentleman, who had been a lieutenant-governor of Pennsylvania, proposed such an assembly to the ministry. He also proposed the extension of the British stamp-duties to the colonies. He was then, I believe, in the Fleet prison. The hints he gave were embraced, the first in 1754, the second in 1764. It has been long a matter of surprise to me, that no gentleman of talents and character has undertaken to write a history of the former British colonies . . . at least from 1756 to 1806, a period of fifty very important years. . . . On reflection, I cannot refer to a single instance of . . . friendship of Great Britain towards this country during the period you mention" [X, 74-75].

43. Thos. McKean: Thomas M., 1734-1814, member of Continental Congress (1774-1783) and its president in 1781; signer of Declaration of Independence; governor of Pennsylvania (1799-1808).

44. (1600-1813): JA had written to McKean [Aug. 31, 1813] asking for information McKean supplied [cf. 42 above]. In his letter JA said: "Were I a man of fortune, I would offer a gold medal to the man who should produce the most instances of the friendship of Great Britain toward this country from 1600 to 1813" [X, 62].

45. THEMIS CONDITOR: H, "Themis." L, "the founder." Source [JA to TJ, Oct. 4, 1813] has Θέμιϛ [another name for Hera or Juno] but Pound adds the Latin. JA wrote: "Θέμιϛ was the goddess of honesty, justice, decency, and right. . . . She presided over all oracles, deliberations, and councils. She commanded all mortals to pray to Jupiter for all lawful benefits and blessings. Now, is not this (so far forth) the essence of Christian devotion?" [X, 75].

46. In the Congress . . . third: These five lines are from two sources [JA to TJ, Nov. 12, 1813; JA to James Lloyd, Jan. 1815]. The first says: "In the Congress of 1774, there was not one member, except Patrick Henry, who appeared to me sensible of the precipice . . . on which he stood, and had candor and courage enough to acknowledge it. America is in total ignorance, or under infinite deception, concerning that assembly; . . . one third tories, another whigs, and the rest mongrels" [X, 78-79]. And the second source, on divisions of the people, says: " . . . I should say that full one third were averse to the revolution. . . . An opposite third conceived a hatred of the English, and gave themselves up to an enthusiastic gratitude to France. The middle third . . . yeomanry, the soundest part of the nation . . . were rather lukewarm both to England and France" [X, 110].

47. Persons . . . cease: Source [T. McKean to JA, Nov. 15, 1813] reads: "The Society in London 'for propagating the gospel in foreign parts,' . . . foresaw, that if America became an independent state or nation, their salaries [i.e., of the society's ministers in the colonies] would necessarily cease. It was their interest . . . to oppose the revolution, and they did oppose it, though with as much secrecy as practicable" [X, 81].

48. Laws of Charondas . . . fury: These five lines continue JA's polemic against the destructiveness of party spirit. Source [JA to TJ, Dec. 25, 1813] suggests some of JA's Christmas Day reading at the age of 78: "Zaleucus, the legislator of Locris, and Charondas of Sybaris, were disciples of Pythagoras, and both celebrated to immortality for the wisdom of their laws, five hundred years before Christ. Why are those laws lost? I say, the spirit of party has destroyed them; civil, political, and ecclesiastical bigotry. Despotical, monarchical, aristocratical, and democratical fury, have all been employed in this work of destruction of every thing that could give us true light, and a clear insight of antiquity. For every one of these parties, when possessed of power, or when they have been undermost, and struggling to get uppermost, has been equally prone to every species of fraud and violence and usurpation" [X, 84-85].

49. adopted by Moses: JA is here quoting from Priestley an idea, with which he does not concur, about the Fall of man and the Mosaic law: ". . . this history [in Genesis] is either an allegory, or founded on uncertain tradition, . . . a hypothesis to account for the origin of evil, adopted by Moses, which, by no means, accounts for the facts." JA says, a few lines later: "I shall never be a disciple of Priestley." At another place in this letter to TJ, which was written at intervals [Feb.-March 1814], JA says: "There is a work which I wish I possessed. It has never crossed the Atlantic . . . Acta Sanctorum, in forty-seven volumes in folio" [X, 93].

50. Acta Sanctorum: L, "Acts of the Saints." Source continues to speculate on this book and adds: "What would I give to possess, in one immense map, . . . all the legends, true, doubtful, and false?" He lists several legends he would like to know the truth about and concludes with these: ". . . whether the face of Jesus Christ was painted on the handkerchief of St. Veronique; and whether the prepuce of the Savior of the world, which was shown in the church at Antwerp, could be proved to be genuine" [X, 94].

51. many a kept . . . ocean: These seven lines concern the nature of heroism, the fisheries, and naval power. Source [JA to Richard Rush, May 30, 1814] starts with listing heroes such as Alexander, Caesar, "and millions of others" who come to bad ends: "Read the history of our missionary societies. Is there not the same enthusiasm, the same heroism? I scarcely dare to say what I know, that many a kept mistress has dared for her lover as great hazards and sufferings." The letter later turns to the Tories, who say such things as "Mr. Adams saved the fisheries once I hope his son will save them a second time. We have no confidence in Gallatin, Clay, Russell, or even Bayard; we believe they would all sacrifice the fisheries for Canada or even for peace." But JA was not one to be taken in by Tory ploys and give them ammunition which they could use to interfere with the delicate negotiations his son JQA and the others named were engaged in at the time in London. He said his invariable answer was that "you deceive yourself with imaginary fears. You know that the men Bayard, Russell, Clay and even Gallatin would cede the fee simple of the United States, as soon as they would the fisheries." He goes on to comment on the idea that America should command the Great Lakes: "The lakes, the lakes, the lakes! shocking, indeed, that we have not the command of the lakes! But I could convince you that it is still more shocking that we have not the command of the ocean, or at least an independent power upon the ocean" [X, 97-98].

52. Clay, Gallatin, Russell: [34:47; 34:21; 31:40].

53. J. Bull: Source [JA to Mrs. Mercy Warren, July 15, 1814] reads: "France is humbled and Napoleon is banished; but the tyrant, the tyrant of tyrants is not fallen. John Bull still paws, and bellows terrible menaces and defiances" [X, 100].

54. I wish France: Source [JA to TJ, July 16, 1814] says: "He [Bonaparte] could no longer roar or struggle, growl or paw, he could only gasp his grin of death; I wish that France may not still regret him" [X, 102].

55. our treaty: Source [JA to President Madison, Nov. 28, 1814] is specific about the War of 1812: "All I can say is, that I would continue this war forever, rather than surrender one acre of our territory, one iota of the fisheries, as established by the third article of the treaty of 1783, or one sailor impressed from any merchant ship" [X, 106].

56. No part . . . navy: Source [letter written sometime in Jan. 1815] dwells upon JA's attempts while president to build up the navy, to build ships, to purchase navy yards, to select officers: "And what was the effect? No part of my administration was so unpopular, not only in the western, the southern, and middle States, but in all New England, and, strange to tell, even in Marblehead." Later in same letter JA defended his missions to France as "the most disinterested and meritorious actions" of his life: "I reflect upon them with so much satisfaction, that I desire no other inscription over my gravestone than: 'Here lies John Adams, who took upon himself the responsibility of the peace with France in the year 1800'" [X, 111,113].

57. No printer . . . Sanctorum: Source of these five lines, a letter to James [not L.] Lloyd [Feb. 11, 1815], expresses great frustration about parties and churches reading only their own newspapers, circulars, ets., and condemning anyone else's writings as heresy. Thus any party reads only "its own libels." JA goes on: "With us, the press is under a virtual imprimatur, to such a degree, that I do not believe I could get these letters to you printed in a newspaper in Boston." JA continues to describe the continuous spate of circular letters from members of Congress to their constituents, filled with lies, many of them against JA, which began in 1789 and continued to 1801. These letters "swelled, raged, foamed in all the fury of a tempest at sea against me. A collection of those circular letters would make many volumes, and contain more lies . . . than the *Acta Sanctorum*" [cf. 49, 50 above; X, 117-119].

58. Mihites: Unknown term. Perhaps a mistranscription of L, *Milites,* for soldiers, or poss. a play on L, *mihi,* thus "egoists"; or perhaps a garbled version of a nickname for the Irish, such as *Mickies.*

59. they believed . . . : Source [JA to J. Lloyd, Feb. 14, 1815] reads: . . . the English, Scotch, and Irish Presbyterians [plus four other sects] with Dr. Preistley at their head . . . had been carried away with the French revolution, and firmly believed that Bonaparte was the instrument of Providence to destroy the Pope and introduce the millennium. . . . Mr. Jefferson knew them all. These parties had all been making their court to him for fifteen years" [X, 120].

60. My answer . . . delegates): Source of these five lines [JA to J. Lloyd, Feb. 17, 1815] concerns Hamilton's intrigue to prevent JA's reelection in 1800. While AH was in New England trying to get voters there to "sacrifice Adams," JA, about the same time, on a walk in Philadelphia, met Colonel Joseph Lyman of Springfield who, seeing the president, crossed the street to tell him he had some news. JA said he hoped his news was good. Lyman said: "Hamilton has divided the federalists, and proposed to them to give you the go-by and bring in

Pinckney. By this step he has divided the federalists and given great offence to the honestest part of them. I am glad of it, for it will be the ruin of his faction." JA saw in the plot also the ruin of his own faction, which led to his defeat. So he said: "Colonel Lyman, it will be, as you say, the ruin of his faction; but it will also be the ruin of honester men than any of them." During the intrigue, a list of mediocre men Hamilton was promoting as candidates in New York was brought to Aaron Burr by a friend: "Burr . . . read it over, with great gravity folded it up, put it in his pocket; and, without uttering another word said 'Now I have him all hollow.'" Burr went about making a list of his own and getting Hamilton's men defeated, but Burr's men elected electors who went unanimously for Jefferson "though New York in all antecedent elections voted unanimously for Adams" [X, 124-125].

61. Walcott: Oliver Wolcott [62:157], JA's secretary of the treasury. In seeking loans to support the army, Wolcott maintained that proposals should be announced for 8 percent interest. JA in "consultation after consultation," insisted that 8 percent was too much and that the money could be had for 6 percent. JA finally lost patience and gave in [X, 129-130].

62. South Americans: In the source [JA to J. Lloyd, March 26, 1815], JA expressed his amazement that Pitt and the British cabinet could believe that South America could be revolutionized: "Did they believe the South Americans capable of a free government, or a combination of free federative republics?" [X, 141].

63. lucid interval: Source [JA to Lloyd, March 29, 1815] says: "Very fortunately for me and for this nation, the French Directory had a lucid interval [70:19-21] and gave me a fair opportunity to institute that mission to France" [X, 147].

64. No people: Source [JA to J. Lloyd,

March 30, 1815] expresses an old, growing, and frustrating conviction of JA's: "The truth is, there is not one people of Europe that knows or cares any thing about constitutions. There is not one nation in Europe that understands or is capable of understanding any constitution whatever. . . . If there is a colorable exception, it is England" [X, 149-150].

65. God forbid . . . : And in a letter to Lloyd the next day [March 31] JA wrote about another primary concern: "God forbid that American naval power should ever be such a scourge to the human race as that of Great Britain has been!" And in the same paragraph, speaking of his "most earnest, sedulous, and . . . expensive exertions to preserve peace with the Indians" all the time he was president, he concludes: "I had the inexpressible satisfaction of complete success. Not a hatchet was lifted in my time" [X, 153].

66. Nor has . . . Mississippi: In the source of these five lines [JA to R. Rush, April 5, 1815], JA restates his adamant convictions about the fisheries controversy: "Neither nature nor art has partitioned the sea into empires, kingdoms, republics, or states. There are no dukedoms, earldoms, baronies, or knight's fees, no freeholds, pleasure grounds, ornamented or unornamented farms, gardens, parks, groves . . . as there are upon land. . . . We have a stronger and clearer right to all these fisheries . . . than any Britons or Europeans ever had or could have." The Treaty of Ghent, the document agreed upon between the U.S. and Great Britain in ending the War of 1812, resolved few differences and left many questions unanswered. But JQA stuck to his father's guns and agreed only to British rights of navigation on the Mississippi in return for concessions to the U.S. on the fisheries. The treaty, finally ratified on February 17, 1815, did not end controversy in the U.S. So JA kept up his clamor to most people he wrote to: "Former treaties not formally repeated in a new treaty, are presumed to be received and acknowledged. The fisheries are therefore ours, and the navigation of the Mississippi theirs, that is the British, as much as ever" [X, 160-161].

67. Money or no money: Source [JA to T. McKean, July 6, 1815] says, as a third point among six proven by the Madison administration: "That money or no money, government or no government, Great Britain can never conquer this country or any considerable part of it" [X, 168].

68. They will print . . . unopened: Source [JA to TJ, Aug. 24, 1815] says: "That our correspondence has been observed, is no wonder. . . . No printer has asked me for copies, but it is no surprise that you have been requested. These gentry will print whatever will sell; and our correspondence is thought such an oddity by both parties, that they imagine an edition would soon go off, and yield them profits. There has, however, been no tampering with your letters to me. They have all arrived in good order" [X, 173].

69. Price: Richard P., Welsh friend of JA's [70:69]. A book JA received, *Memoirs of the Life of Dr. Price,* by William Morgan, is the source of the four lines [JA to TJ, Nov. 13, 1815]. JA quotes some things Morgan said concerning Dr. Price's disappointment that his [Price's] views about the success of and his hopes for the French Revolution were not embraced by Adams. In his letter JA quotes from Morgan: "'In a long letter . . . he [JA] expresses himself in terms of contempt in regard to the French revolution; and after asking . . . what good was to be expected from a nation of atheists, he concludes with foretelling the destruction of a million of human beings, as the probable consequence of it. These harsh censures and gloomy predictions were particularly ungrateful to Dr. Price.'" After the quotation JA says he does not know what to think of one who 25 years later finds private correspondence and produces it before the world. He adds: "Mr. Morgan has been more discreet and complaisant to you than to me. He has mentioned respectfully your letters from Paris to Dr. Price, but has given us none of them. As I would give more for those letters than for all the rest of the book, I am more angry with him" [X, 175-176].

70. speeches . . . Spain: Source [T. McKean to JA, Nov. 20, 1815] contains thoughts that show JA's gloomy predictions 25 years earlier to Dr. Price [cf. 69 above] to have been correct: "I do not recollect any *formal* speeches . . . to have been made in the revolutionary Congress . . . We had no time to hear . . . speeches . . . ; action was the order of the day." And later: "What changes in Europe have occurred . . . ! Louis XVIII, is again on the throne of France; the great Napoleon at the bottom of the wheel, never to rise more, a prisoner for life. The French nation miserable; Spain has reëstablished the tribunal of the Inquisition" [X, 177-178].

71. black, white . . . : Source [JA to T. McKean, Nov. 26, 1815] says: "General Wilkinson may have written the military history of the war that followed the Revolution; that was an effect of it, and was supported by the American citizens in defence of it against an invasion of it by the government of Great Britain and Ireland, and all her allies, black, white, and pied; but this will by no means be a history of the American Revolution" [X, 180].

72. fleet to protect: In a long letter to Dr. J. Morse [Jan. 1, 1816] JA reviews the growing spirit behind the Revolution and focuses on events of the mid-1760s. After "a new act of tyrannical taxation rekindled all the fires of opposition and resistance on this side the water," the colonies rebelled so strongly that the British ministry "thought it necessary to send a fleet and army to protect Temple, Hallowell, Paxton, Birch, and Robinson, their adherents and followers" [X, 199].

73. Paxton: Charles P. [64:110]. British customs commissioner.

74. Birch, Temple: Minor English agents operating in Boston in 1766.

75. Otis: James O. [34:33]. Lawyer and Revolutionary leader who opposed the Stamp Act and organized the Stamp Congress in 1765.

76. Poor soldiers: Source [same as 72 above] summarizes attitudes toward British soldiers, whose officers "put themselves and their men upon the compassionate list. 'The poor soldiers were innocent. They knew not why they were sent here'" [X,199].

77. North called 'em: [62:20]. In the source [as in 72 above] JA outlines growing discontent which climaxed in the Boston Massacre (March 5, 1771) and celebrates Samuel Adams for his "caution, his discretion, his ingenuity" [and four more such attributes], which received applause from both parties and had a good result: "The troops were ordered to the Castle, and Lord North called them from this time 'Sam Adams's two regiments'" [X, 200].

78. Hutchinson: Thomas H., chief justice and later royal governor of Massachusetts [62:47]. JA comments on Hutchinson's style of dress: "I pass over that scenery, which he introduced, so showy and so shallow, so theatrical and so ecclesiastical, of scarlet and sable robes . . . and enormous tie wigs, more resembling fleeces of painted meriono wool than any thing natural to man" [X, 233].

79. State Trials: [64:63].

80. At State House . . . Paddock: Of the crisis in Boston after massacre [62:26-38], source [JA to W. Tudor, April 15, 1817] says: "The whole militia of the city" was called up. And "I had the honor to be summoned, in my turn, and attended at the State House with my musket and bayonet, my broadsword and cartridge-box, under the command of the famous Paddock." Now nearing 82, JA looks back to his early exploits with more and more relish [X, 251].

81. Paddock: Adino P., Boston coachmaker and captain of militia, was called up for the "civilian night watch" after the Boston Massacre on March 5, 1770.

82. Jesuits . . . : Source [JA to TJ, April 19, 1817] concerns JA's denial of total human depravity: "The most abandoned scoundrel that ever existed, never yet wholly extinguished his conscience, and, while conscience remains, there is some religion. Popes, Jesuists [sic], and Sorbonnists, and Inquisitors, have some conscience and some religion. So had Marius and Sylla" [X, 254].

83. Sylla: Lucius Cornelius Sulla, 138-78 B.C., Roman general who served with Marius in Africa, led a bloody sack of Athens, made himself dictator of Rome in 82 B.C., and began a systematic butchery of his enemies. His name and that of Marius became synonymous with cruelty.

84. Marius: Caius M., ca. 155-86 B.C., Roman general, tribune, and praetor. He became a rival of Sulla, lost, and fled Rome. But, allied with the consul Cinna, he returned home and butchered his opponents.

85. Hancock: John H. [64:56]. Source of next eight lines [JA to W. Tudor, June 1, 1817] is a paean to Hancock: "If he had vanity and caprice, so had I. And if his vanity and caprice made sometimes sputter, . . . mine . . . had often a similar effect upon him. . . . His uncle, the most opulent merchant in Boston, . . . adopted him, . . . educated him at Harvard college, and then took him into his store. And what a school was this! Four large ships constantly plying between Boston and London. . . . This was in 1755. He became an example to all the young men of the town. . . . His uncle sent him to London, from whence . . . he returned to his store . . . unaltered in manners or deportment, and pursued his employments with the same punctuality and assiduity, till the death of his uncle, who left him his business. . . . No alteration appeared in Mr. Hancock either from his travels in England, or from his accession to the fortune of his uncle. . . . Your honored father told

me, at that time, that not less than a thousand families were . . . dependent on [him]." JA one day met Sam Adams on a walk. They came upon Hancock's house, whereupon Sam said that the town had done a wise thing that day. To JA's question as to what the wise thing was, Sam replied that the town had that day "chosen Mr. Hancock into the legislature of the province" [X, 259-260].

86. Joseph Hawley: [64:49]. Although Hawley was one of the first to urge a declaration of independence, no source includes him with the others. Source [JA to W. Tudor, June 5, 1817] says about the most important men in starting the Revolution: "James Otis, Samuel Adams, and John Hancock were the three most essential characters; and Great Britain knew it, though America does not" [X, 263].

87. Jay: John J. [62:131].

88. Magis . . . fabulis: L, "more suitable to poetic myths." From the preface to Livy's histories: *Ab Urbe Condita* ["From the Founding of the City"], Book I (Loeb, p. 4). The phrase is taken from this sentence: "Quae ante conditam condendamve urbem poeticis magis decora fabulis quam incorruptis rerum gestarum monumemtis traduntur, ea nec adfirmare nec refellere in animo est." [Loeb trans.: "Such traditions as belong to the time before the city was founded, or rather was presently to be founded, and are rather adorned with poetic legends than based upon trustworthy historical proofs, I purpose neither to affirm nor to refute."] JA used parts of the Livy sentence in his letter to W. Tudor [see 86 above].

89. Otis: Source of lines here from two letters that deal with the education, talents, and skills of Otis, who wrote Latin and Greek prosodies: ". . . I asked his daughter whether she had found that work [on Greek prosody] among her father's manuscripts. She answered . . . that she 'had not a line from her father's pen; that he had spent much time, and taken great pains, to collect together all his letters and other papers, and, in one of his unhappy moments, committed them all to the flames'" [X, 265].

90. may be . . . neutrality: Source or significance of these two lines is unknown; perhaps the "swat on the pow" refers to the beating by the "coffee house bandits" [cf. 91 below]. If Otis survived the beating for a time before his death, he may have burned his papers during that period.

91. the greek prosody: JA borrowed Otis's work on Greek prosody. Source of six lines [JA to H. Niles, Jan. 14, 1818] says: "When I returned it, I begged him to print it. He said there were no Greek types in the country, or, if there were, there was no printer who knew how to use them." In the same letter JA continues to amass facts to show that Otis was a great patriot: "Mr. Otis resigned his commission from the crown, as Advocate-General, an office very lucrative at that time, and a sure road to the highest favors of government in America, and engaged in the cause of his country without fee or reward." And later, in consequence of this act, which both JA and Pound saw as patriotic, "Otis was basely assassinated in a coffee-house, in the night, by a well-dressed banditti, with a commissioner of the customs at their head" [X, 275-278].

92. Otis . . . writs: Writs of Assistance [cf. 9 above].

93. JA . . . judiciary: Against the judicial system of the Crown as it was developing in Boston.

94. Defended Preston: Captain Preston, the British officer whom JA defended [62:37].

95. Fisheries . . . 1800: List of some of the greatest ideas and accomplishments of JA [65:20].

96. Gold . . . lumber: Expression of one of JA's and Pound's profound conceptions concerning the nature of money. Source [JA to J. Taylor, March 12, 1819] says: "Silver and gold are but commodities, as much as wheat and lumber." JA then refers

to a work by Count Destutt de Tracy which TJ had translated from the French and sent to him: "His chapter 'of money' contains the sentiments that I have entertained all my lifetime. . . . 'It is to be desired, that coins had never borne other names than those of their weight, and that the arbitrary denominations . . . had never been used'" [X, 375-376].

97. Keep out of Europe: JA's Lifelong refrain about keeping America neutral and not getting entangled in the affairs of any one nation or group of nations [18, 27 above].

98. Charlie Mordecai: Unknown person and unknown source. The *Index* suggests that the name might refer to Karl Marx. But since most of the remaining lines in this canto derive from statutes of William III which refer to acts of Parliament in "the reign of the late King Charles II" and "in the 22nd and 23rd years of his said late Majesties reign" [X, 339], I am satisfied to believe that "Charlie Mordecai" means "Charles, the dead," or, closer to the Latin root, "Charles of the teeth."

99. Not free 'em . . . 1818: These 17 lines show JA's outrage at British laws deliberately intended to subjugate people, particularly seamen, women, and Negroes. Source [JA to W. Tudor, Aug. 6, 1818] says: "Mr. Otis had reasoned like a philosopher upon the navigation acts, and all the tyrannical acts of Charles II.; but when he came to the revenue laws, the orator blazed out." JA goes on to say that, while it may be tedious to read those old statutes; "yet it behoves our young and old yeomen, mechanics and laborers, philosophers, politicians, legislators, and merchants to read them. However tedious and painful it may be for you to read, or me to transcribe any part of these dull statutes, we must endure the task, or we shall never understand the American Revolution." These lines must be either an ironic suggestion or a come-on, for the statutes, which are full of blood, are anything but dull. JA then transcribes the preamble to one statute which has as its intent no less than the enslavement of "all the colonies in Europe, Asia, and America, and, indeed, all nations, to the omnipotence of the British Parliament and its royal navy! . . . Recollect and listen to the preamble of this statute, of the 7th and 8th of William III, Chapter 22d." JA then goes on to show the effect of such statutes on British colonial landowners: "Will you be so good, Sir, as to pause a moment on this preamble? To what will you liken it? Does it resemble a great, rich, powerful West India planter, Alderman Beckford, for example, preparing and calculating and writing instructions for his overseers?" JA quotes such instructions: "You are to have no regard to the health, strength, comfort, natural affections, or moral feelings, or intellectual endowments of my negroes. You are only to consider what subsistence [not "substance"] to allow them, and what labor to exact [not "extract"] of them will subserve my interest. According to the most accurate calculation I can make, the proportion of subsistence and labor, which will work them up, in six years upon an average, is the most profitable to the planter. And this allowance, surely, is very humane; for we estimate here the lives of our coal-heavers upon an average at only two years, and our fifty thousand girls of the town at three years at most. And our soldiers and seamen no matter what." After exploding this (dull?) bombshell, JA has a question for his correspondent: "Is there, Mr. Tudor, in this preamble, or in any statute of Great Britain . . . the smallest consideration of the health, the comfort, the happiness, the wealth, the growth, the population, the agriculture, the manufactures, the

commerce, the fisheries of the American people?" The question was rhetorical, but JA gives an answer and a warning: "All these things are to be sacrificed to British wealth, British commerce, British domination, and the British navy, as the great engine and instrument to accomplish all" [X, 338-340] .

100. Hobhouse: John Cam H. [33:33]. Pound is implying that many of Hobhouse's liberal ideas about the emancipation of people from all kinds of slavery can be found in JA, as shown in the letters he wrote in 1818. In 1842 (24 years later), Hobhouse was fighting for child labor laws in England.

101. Ignorance . . . circulation: An Adams concept to which Pound often referred was the first item in his "Introductory Textbook" on economics. JA wrote: "All the perplexities, confusion, and distress in America arise, not from defects in their constitution or confederation, not from want of honour and virtue, so much as from downright ignorance of the nature of coin, credit, and circulation" [*SP, 159*] .

102. κύδιστ' . . . κυβερνῶν: H, "Most honored of the immortals, worshipped under many names, all powerful forever, Zeus, founder of the natural order, who rules over all things by law." Pound has rearranged the opening two lines of Cleanthes' *Hymn to Zeus* [*OBGV*, no. 483] to suit his own metrical fancy. He gives his own free rendition of the lines as a note to the table of contents for Cantos LII-LXXI (p. 256): "Glorious, deathless of many names, Zeus aye ruling all things, founder of the inborn qualities of nature, by laws piloting all things."

Select Bibliography

Baumann, Walter. *The Rose in the Steel Dust: An Examination of the Cantos of Ezra Pound.* Bern: Francke Verlag, 1967; Coral Gables: University of Miami Press, 1970.

Brooke-Rose, Christine. *A ZBC of Ezra Pound.* Berkeley and Los Angeles: University of California Press, 1971; London: Faber & Faber, 1971.

Bush, Ronald. *The Genesis of Ezra Pound's Cantos.* Princeton: Princeton University Press, 1977.

Cornell, Julien. *The Trial of Ezra Pound: A Documented Account of the Treason Case by the Defendant's Lawyer.* New York: John Day, 1966.

Davie, Donald. *Ezra Pound.* New York: Viking, 1975.

———. *Ezra Pound, Poet as Sculptor.* New York: Oxford University Press, 1964; London: Routledge, 1965.

Davis, Earle. *Vision Fugitive: Ezra Pound and Economics.* Lawrence: University of Kansas Press, 1968.

Dekker, George. *Sailing after Knowledge: The Cantos of Ezra Pound, a Critical Appraisal.* London: Routledge, 1963; New York: Barnes & Noble, 1963.

Dembo, Lawrence Sanford. *The Confucian Odes of Ezra Pound: A Critical Appraisal.* Berkeley and Los Angeles: University of California Press, 1963; London: Faber & Faber, 1963.

Edwards, John Hamilton, and William V. Vasse. *Annotated Index to the Cantos of Ezra Pound: Cantos I-LXXXIV.* With the assistance of John J. Espey and Frederic Peachy. Berkeley and Los Angeles: University of California Press, 1957; 2d ptg. (with additions and corrections), 1959.

Emery, Clark. *Ideas into Action: A Study of Pound's Cantos.* Coral Gables: University of Miami Press, 1958.

Espey, John J. *Ezra Pound's Mauberley: A Study in Composition.* Berkeley and Los Angeles: University of California Press, 1955; London: Faber & Faber, 1955.

Fraser, G. S. *Ezra Pound.* Edinburgh and London: Oliver & Boyd, 1960; New York: Grove Press, 1961.

Goodwin, K. L. *The Influence of Ezra Pound.* London: Oxford University Press, 1966.

Grover, Philip, ed. *Ezra Pound: The London Years, 1908-1920.* New York: AMS, 1978.

Hesse, Eva, ed. *New Approaches to Ezra Pound.* Berkeley and Los Angeles: University of California Press, 1969; London: Faber & Faber, 1969.

Hutchins, Patricia. *Ezra Pound's Kensington: An Exploration, 1885-1913.* London: Faber & Faber, 1965.

Jackson, Thomas H. *The Early Poetry of Ezra Pound.* Cambridge: Harvard University Press, 1969.

Kenner, Hugh. *The Poetry of Ezra Pound.* New York: New Directions, 1951; London: Faber & Faber, 1951.

———. *The Pound Era.* Berkeley, Los Angeles, and London: University of California Press, 1971; London: Faber & Faber, 1971.

Leary, Lewis, ed. *Motive and Method in the Cantos of Ezra Pound.* New York: Columbia University Press, 1954.

Makin, Peter. *Provence and Pound*. Berkeley, Los Angeles, and London: University of California Press, 1979.

Mayo, Robert, ed. *The Analyst*. A serial mimeographed newsletter containing source studies by different editors and writers. Evanston: Northwestern University, 1953-1971.

Mullins, Eustace Clarence. *This Difficult Individual, Ezra Pound*. New York: Fleet Publishing Corp., 1961.

de Nagy, N. Christoph. *Ezra Pound's Poetics and Literary Tradition: The Critical Decade*. Bern: Francke Verlag, 1966.

———. *The Poetry of Ezra Pound: The Pre-Imagist Stage*. Bern: Francke Verlag, 1960.

Norman, Charles. *The Case of Ezra Pound*. New York: Macmillan, 1960.

———. *Ezra Pound: A Biography*. Rev. version of earlier ed. London: Macdonald, 1969.

O'Connor, William Van, and Edward Stone. *A Casebook on Ezra Pound*. New York: Crowell, 1959.

Pearlman, Daniel S. *The Barb of Time*. New York and London: Oxford University Press, 1969.

Rachewiltz, Mary de. *Discretions*. Boston and London, 1971.

Rosenthal, M. L. *A Primer of Ezra Pound*. New York: Macmillan, 1960.

Russell, Peter, ed. *Ezra Pound: A Collection of Essays to Be Presented to Ezra Pound on his 65th Birthday*. London: Peter Nevill, 1950; New York: New Directions, 1950 (with title *An Examination of Ezra Pound: A Collection of Essays*).

Ruthven, K. K. *A Guide to Ezra Pound's "Personæ" (1926)*. Berkeley and Los Angeles: University of California Press, 1969.

Schafer, R. Murray, ed. *Ezra Pound and Music: The Complete Criticism*. New York: New Directions, 1978.

Schneidau, Herbert N. *Ezra Pound: The Image and the Real*. Baton Rouge: Louisiana State University Press, 1969.

Sieburth, Richard. *Instigations: Ezra Pound and Remy de Gourmont*. Cambridge: Harvard University Press, 1978.

Stock, Noel. *The Life of Ezra Pound*. New York: Random House, 1970.

———. *Poet in Exile: Ezra Pound*. Manchester: Manchester University Press, 1964; New York: Barnes & Noble, 1964.

———. *Reading the Cantos: A Study of Meaning in Ezra Pound*. New York: Random House, 1966.

Sullivan, J. P., ed. *Ezra Pound: A Critical Anthology*. Middlesex, England: Penguin Books, 1970.

———. *Ezra Pound and Sextus Propertius: A Study in Creative Translation*. Austin: University of Texas Press, 1964; London: Faber & Faber, 1964.

Sutton, Walter, ed. *Ezra Pound: A Collection of Critical Essays*. Eaglewood Cliffs, N. J.: Prentice-Hall, 1963.

Watts, Harold H. *Ezra Pound and the Cantos*. Chicago: Henry Regnery, 1952.

Wilhelm, James J. *Dante and Pound: The Epic of Judgement*. Orono: University of Maine Press, 1975.

———. *The Later Cantos of Ezra Pound*. New York: Walker, 1977.

Yeats, W. B. *A Packet for Ezra Pound*. Dublin: Cuala Press, 1929.